DATE DUE

GOVERNORS STATE UNIVERSITY
LIBRARY

DEMCO

The Art of the Critic

The Art of the Critic
Literary Theory and Criticism from the Greeks to the Present

Volume 1
Classical and Medieval

EDITED WITH AN INTRODUCTION BY
HAROLD BLOOM
Sterling Professor of the Humanities, Yale University

1985
CHELSEA HOUSE PUBLISHERS
NEW YORK

Editorial Staff: Joy Johannessen, Kevin Pask, James Uebbing

Copyright © 1985 by Chelsea House Publishers, a division of Chelsea House Educational Communications, Inc. Introduction copyright © 1985 by Harold Bloom

All rights reserved. No part of this publication may be reproduced or transmitted, in any form or by any means, without the written permission of the publisher.

Printed and bound in the United States of America

Library of Congress Cataloging in Publication Data
Main entry under title:

The Art of the critic.

    Contents: v. 1. Classical and medieval—.
    1. Criticism—Collected works. 2. Literature—
Philosophy—Collected works. I. Bloom, Harold.
PN86.A77   1984   809   84-15547
ISBN 0-87754-493-X (set)
    0-87754-494-8 (vol. 1)

Chelsea House Publishers
Harold Steinberg, Chairman & Publisher
Susan Lusk, Vice President
A Division of Chelsea House Educational Communications, Inc.
133 Christopher Street, New York, NY 10014

Contents

Introduction · vii ·
Gorgias of Leontini · 3 ·
    From *A Defence of Helen* · 5 ·
Aristophanes · 7 ·
    The Frogs · 9 ·
Plato · 79 ·
    From *Phaedrus* · 81 ·
    Ion · 86 ·
    From *Republic* · 97 ·
    From *Laws* · 136 ·
Aristotle · 145 ·
    Poetics · 149 ·
    From *Rhetoric* · 179 ·
Demetrius · 211 ·
    From *On Style* · 213 ·
Cicero · 221 ·
    From *De Inventione* · 223 ·
    From *De Oratore* · 231 ·
    From *Orator* · 256 ·
Horace · 263 ·
    Ars Poetica · 265 ·
Dionysius of Halicarnassus · 277 ·
    From *On Literary Composition* · 279 ·
Quintilian · 285 ·
    From *Institutio Oratoria* · 287 ·
Longinus · 323 ·
    On the Sublime · 325 ·
Plutarch · 361 ·
    From *Moralia* · 363 ·
Hermogenes · 399 ·
    From *On Types* · 401 ·
Plotinus · 417 ·
    From *The Enneads* · 419 ·
Euanthius and Donatus · 425 ·
    On Drama (Euanthius) · 427 ·
    On Comedy (Donatus) · 431 ·

St. Augustine · 435 ·
    From *On Christian Doctrine* · 437 ·
Proclus · 467 ·
    The Nature of Poetic Art · 469 ·
Fulgentius · 479 ·
    On Vergil · 481 ·
Dante · 493 ·
    From *De Vulgari Eloquentia* · 497 ·
    From *Letter to Can Grande della Scala* · 531 ·
Bibliography · 535 ·

Index and Glossary are contained in Volume 11

Line references are only included in those selections for which a standard set of such references exists (e.g., Plato's *Republic*).

Classical Literary Criticism: Mimesis and the Sublime

Harold Bloom

1

A CONTEMPORARY STUDENT of literature, and of literary interpretation, knows that the Greeks invented literary theory and criticism. But if the modern critic is compared to any ancient forerunner, considerable bafflement can afflict the student. D. A. Russell, the author of a valuable recent study, *Criticism in Antiquity*, remarks that we are trapped in a paradox when we read ancient criticism.

> It is the recorded critical judgements that are puzzling. We find them often inadequate and unsatisfactory, if we compare them with our own responses to the same texts. But at the same time we cannot help reasoning that the Greeks and Romans must after all know what is best, since the language and the culture were their own.

This paradox testifies to our great distance from the ancients, a distance that prolonged study never quite overcomes. What we call "classicism," whether as a literary tradition, a critical stance, or a scholarly profession, is a particular interpretation of ancient Greek culture—an interpretation frequently called into question by Friedrich Nietzsche, classical philologist, genealogist of morals, and the crucial philosopher of the modern art of interpretation. Nietzsche never ceased to speculate upon the Greeks, and his restless later insights help illuminate not just our estrangement from and puzzlement at Greek aesthetic judgements but the ancients' progressive estrangement from and puzzlement at themselves.

> Gradually everything genuinely Hellenic is made responsible for the state of decay (and Plato is just as ungrateful to Pericles, Homer, tragedy, rhetoric, as the prophets were to David and Saul). The decline of Greece is understood as an objection to the foundations of Hellenic culture: basic error of philosophers—. Conclusion: the Greek world perishes. Cause: Homer, myth, the ancient morality, etc. [*The Will to Power*, Bk. 2, no. 427, trans. W. Kaufmann]

Implicit here as elsewhere in Nietzsche is his vision of Greek culture as essentially agonistic, as contrasted to Hebraic culture, with its central piety of honoring one's father and one's mother. Nietzsche probably owed his sense of Greek agon to his colleague and good acquaintance Jakob Burckhardt, but in his development of the insight Nietzsche surpassed Burckhardt by centering upon the enormous struggle between Plato and Homer (or Socrates and Homer) for the mind of Athens. What Nietzsche found wanting in the classical philologists of his day seems still lacking in many of the more recent scholars: a keen sense that the Greek spirit unfolded itself only in fighting, only in the contest for the foremost place, whether in civic matters, in poetry, or in cognitive achievement. So, Nietzsche praises Goethe for taking possession of the ancient world "always with a competitive soul." Our failure to compete with the ancients comes from our weakness, since we are not Goethe (or Nietzsche), and yet is it a weakness that we know more about the Greeks than Goethe and Nietzsche did? Is this knowledge purchased by the loss of power?

In some sense, all ancient literary criticism stems from the Platonic agon with Homer, and can be regarded therefore as a critique of Homer, whose poems formed the educational texts upon which all of Greece founded what Rome later called "culture," in itself not a Greek idea, strictly considered. The *Iliad* in particular is the fundamental classical text, analogous in status and function to what we now call Genesis, Exodus and Numbers in the Hebrew Bible. Ancient Greek and Hebrew literature share very little, but they possess in common the fact of an overwhelming precursor—the author or final author of the *Iliad,* named Homer by Greek tradition, and the writer called J or the Yahwist by modern biblical criticism. The *Iliad* and the oldest narrative strand in the Hebrew Bible constitute the texts of authority, the stories that augment and dominate societies. This analogue between Homer and the Yahwist is a very limited one, as no greater human and moral contrast exists, in literature, than that between Achilles and Jacob, between the heroic slayer of Hector and the superbly canny wrestler who fights a nameless one among the Elohim until the new name, Israel, is awarded as a blessing. The author of the *Iliad* and the teller of the tales of Jacob are as irreconcilable as the traditions they fostered. There is no mode of cognition available in the Western world that is not ultimately Greek, yet the morality of the West remains in some sense Christian, and Christianity, in its orgins, was a Jewish heresy. The greatness of Western literature has something to do with this enormous split in Western consciousness, this endless sense that the mind goes one way, while the spirit moves in a contrary direction.

Western literary speculation, however, had only Greek antecedents until St. Augustine began to formulate a Christian rhetoric. I suspect that this is our central difficulty in understanding classical literary theory and criticism, which oddly seems more difficult to us than does ancient epic, tragedy, and lyric. Plato's banishment of the poets, Aristotle's subtle notions of *mimesis,* or "imitation," and the broodings of "Longinus" on the Sublime seem further away from Dr. Samuel Johnson and William Hazlitt than Homer seems from Milton, or Aeschylus from Shakespeare. An ode by Pindar and an ode by Wordsworth are majestic leagues apart, yet such distance appears to shrink when compared to the light-years that separate Horace and Kenneth Burke on the art of poetry, or Aristotle and Walter Benjamin on tragedy. There is a "dumbfoundering abyss" between ancient and modern criticism, a void that compels us to posit a similar gap between ancient poetry and the criticism it provoked. Nothing would seem odder than to search for ancient Hebrew literary criticism and theory. Yet it may be more curious than we know to quest for the origins of Western literary thought in Plato and Aristotle. Partly this is because the actual origin of aesthetic criticism was not in philosophy but in poetry itself, the ferocious poetry of farce and extravagant satire written by Aristophanes in his astonishing comedies.

I rely here upon Bruno Snell's *The Discovery of the Mind: The Greek Origins of European Thought,* which may be the most profound account of Greek thought processes since Burckhardt and Nietzsche. Snell portrays a Homer whose standard of judgement is "quantity, not intensity," and who does not yet know ambivalence, but whose mind, however archaic, is not just "a battleground of arbitrary forces and uncanny powers," because of the coherence bestowed by the Olympian mythology. That coherence, profoundly altered, is preserved in the tragedies of Aeschylus, who centers upon the will and the decision of individuals yet continues to honor the Olympians, though his Zeus is far more abstract and withdrawn than the Zeus of Homer. Euripides, under the shadow of Aeschylus, swerves away into a rationalistic and realistic art, in which the Olympian mythology has ceased to be something possible to be believed, however abstracted. Aesthetic criticism, in our sense, begins with the violent reaction of Aristophanes to this Euripidean modernism. Snell locates the essence of literary criticism by isolating what Aristophanes could not abide in Euripides (and in Socrates).

> ... the fundamental purpose or the chief function of the poets [is] that they make men better. This version of the idea is coined by Aristophanes: the poets were teachers—Orpheus of the mysteries and rites, Musaeus of medicine and oracles, Hesiod of agriculture, the divine Homer of honor and glory—and for adults they still play the same role as the schoolmaster does for the children. Even today Aristophanes is the key witness of those who hold that education is the basic concern of the arts, and of all culture in general. Plato makes this moral precept his own; his appointment of Socrates to be the judge of what is good would no doubt have startled Aristophanes. Against this philosophical axiom Plato, in the *Gorgias,* sets the empirical finding that tragedy merely appeals to the pleasure of the senses (*hedone*); with that he opens the doors to endless discussions which via Horace continue well into the eighteenth century: the debate whether the proper task of poetry is *prodesse* or *delectare,* to profit or to please.

Snell's crucial insight here is that Plato (like Aristotle after him) overlooks the antithetical origin of a specifically aesthetic criticism, in the strong preference expressed by Aristophanes for Aeschylus over the "decadent" Euripides. The satirist's preference for an ideal, religious, moral art was turned upside down by the long line of aesthetes from the Alexandrian Callimachus to Oscar Wilde. It is a Wildean irony, and not an Aristophanic one, that the stance of aesthetic criticism, the vision of Walter Pater, was invented by Aristophanes as a villain's position, as the attitude towards poetic language of Aristophanes' outrageous "Euripides" of *The Frogs*. This paradox is so peculiar, indeed so dialectical, that one wonders if so subtle a consciousness as Aristophanes' did not somehow anticipate it.

Snell, who sides with Euripides, makes a complex judgement against Aristophanes, seeing him as one who studied the nostalgias and so was a kind of first Last Romantic.

> The humanization of myth which runs its course from Aeschylus to the late Euripides proves to us that the inherited myth is increasingly rejected as unnatural. The questions of the day are no longer solved by reference to the distant personages of a half-divine world, to their exceptional situations and quarrels which are on the whole foreign to the natural problems of human life. Socrates who progresses, or returns, to the domain of natural man, documents his speculations with examples from ordinary human affairs. With the tools of natural reasoning and common sense he proceeds to answer any questions that may arise. As a result, of course, the questions themselves are tinged with a philosophical shade. "We know the good, but we do not perform it," says the Phaedra of Euripides. Socrates seeks to fortify this knowledge of the good, and to have men yield to its authority. He takes thinking seriously because it is the unique and natural gift of man, and because it adds new strength to the feeble resources of the individual.
>
> It is, of course, difficult to see how this theoretical interest in the good could have sustained the creation of tragedies or any other poetry. Attic tragedy breathed its last with Euripides, and Socrates bears the blame for its death. But at the same time he brought about the birth of something new: Attic philosophy. The judgement of Aristophanes is correct, but let us not be mistaken about him. He is a romantic reactionary who refuses to give up what is already best, and, instead of welcoming the new, mourns the passing of the old.

This is persuasive, yet Snell himself brings to the side of Aristophanes the formidable critical tradition that goes from August Wilhelm Schlegel, in 1800, through Nietzsche's *The Birth of Tragedy,* a tradition that makes Socrates and Euripides responsible for the death of ancient tragedy, which is to say, for the death of myth and mythmaking. What Snell ultimately establishes is a double heritage that literary criticism owes to Aristophanes. Criticism rises from the defense of myth against rationalism, and criticism becomes truly aesthetic or perceptive when it reverses a moral stance in the name of the idiosyncratic, as Callimachus and those who came after him have reversed Aristophanes.

2

Plato's attitude towards Aristophanes must have been complex, partly because of the unfair and pragmatically destructive portrait of Socrates in *The Clouds;* in any case the Socratic irony pervades the answering portrait of Aristophanes in the *Symposium.* Yet there is a common element of moral criticism in the attitudes towards poetry of Aristophanes and Plato. The difference is that Plato appears to reject even Aeschylus—indeed, even Homer—in his fierce attack upon poetry as imitation twice removed from reality. We ought never to underestimate the vehemence and seriousness of Plato's polemic. There is a formidable Platonic irony, perhaps apart from the Socratic irony, but there seems nothing ironic about Plato's absolute rejection of the great tradition of Greek poetry from Homer to Euripides. Morality and truth, Plato stubbornly insists, demand that poetry be cast out of the educational process. At all but the very origin of Western literary theory, we are confronted by a theorist who urges us to choose him over Homer as a guide to right thinking and right action.

The severity of Plato's judgements could hardly be surpassed. Poetry is an illness, a cognitive laming, and an immoral stimulant, akin to fame, power, money. Nothing could be further from this Platonic view than Shelley's equally fierce idealization of poetry in his supposedly Platonic *Defence of Poetry:* "Poetry, and the principle of self, of which money is the visible incarnation, are the God and Mammon of this world." We are at home with Shelley's formulation, and we simply do not know what to make of Plato's, when he says of poetry, "We have to protect our city of the soul against her." Such a rhetoric of defense emphasizes the power and beauty of Homer, yet emphasizes even more strongly that such beauty is destructive, such power immoral. The *Iliad,* Hesiod, Aeschylus, are cast out with a fervor and moral intensity worthy of the prophet Elijah's expulsion of Baal and his idols.

What are we to do with this overwhelming rejection of epic and tragedy? The leading scholars of Plato give us very mixed guidance, perhaps out of reluctance to see their philosopher as rejecting his only true rivals in Greek culture. Paul Friedlander asserts that Plato's polemic was not so much intended against Homer and Aeschylus, but rather against Euripides and, in some sense, even against the earlier Plato himself, since he had begun with the desire to be a tragic poet.

> Plato wages his struggle against Homer as the founder of all imitative art, although Plato himself is praised, in the most significant Greek work of aesthetic criticism (*De Sublimate,* ch. 13) as the "most Homeric of all authors." And this judgement seems justified; for do not the Platonic dialogues contain a stream of artistic presentation, that is, of "Homeric" elements, far beyond anything created by earlier forms of mimetic art: Socrates taking a walk with Phaidros, Socrates at the banquet, in the gymnasium, in prison? Thus the struggle with mimesis is, after all and primarily, also a struggle of the philosopher against the poet, and therefore a form of watchfulness constantly exercised against himself and others. Again and again Plato's written work is mimesis; but it struggles against being nothing but mimesis.

This defense is hardly persuasive, since it understates Plato's condemnation of Homer and the tragedians, though it engagingly reminds us that Plato paradoxically is an aesthetic as well as a cognitive alternative to Homer. What

Friedlander partly evades is that Plato's polemic urges upon us a *spiritual* preference for the cognitive over the mimetic or aesthetic. G. M. A. Grube still more evasively asserts that Plato casts out "not all poets indeed . . . but such as are given to excessive impersonation, for these are dangerous." I find it difficult not to be more persuaded by Eric Havelock's *Preface to Plato*, which insists that Plato was "committed to a passionate warfare upon the poetic experience as such," a warfare founded on Plato's attempt to revise Greek education. This revision would have substituted the "supreme music" of Socratic philosophy for Homer's encyclopaedic texts. Havelock centers his argument on the "technological" functions of Homeric epic in Greek culture: poetry as preserved communication, and the performance of poetry as the dissemination of the social encyclopaedia that held Greece together as a single culture. The strongest effect of Havelock's emphasis is to tell us that the Greeks, and Plato in particular, simply did not mean by "poetry" what nevertheless they created and bequeathed to us.

> Plato writes as though he had never heard of aesthetics, or even of art. Instead he insists on discussing the poets as though their job was to supply metrical encyclopaedias. The poet is a source on the one hand of essential information and on the other of essential moral training. Historically speaking, his claims even extend to giving technical instruction. It is as though Plato expected poetry to perform all those functions which we relegate on the one hand to religious instruction or moral training and on the other to classroom texts, to histories and handbooks, to encyclopaedias and reference manuals. This is a way of looking at poetry which in effect refuses to discuss it as poetry in our sense at all. It refuses to allow that it may be an art with its own rules rather than a source of information and a system of indoctrination.

The limitation of Havelock's insight comes not so much in his reading of Plato as in his reading of Homer. Is the *Iliad* really a vision of a unified culture? Could it have served as a manual of traditional behavior, a handbook giving knowledge of heroes? After all, its hero is not Hector but Achilles, who is hardly a model for indoctrination. Achilles will not go forth to battle, despite societal codes, until he views the naked corpse of his companion, Patroklos—which is not quite a paradigm for "essential moral training" in traditional Greek culture. Perhaps again it is Nietzsche who gives essential guidance here, correcting Havelock by restoring the image of agon to its full intensity.

> The agonistic element is also the danger in every development; it overstimulates the creative impulse. . . .
> The greatest fact remains always the preconsciously panhellenic HOMER. All good things derive from him; yet at the same time he remained the mightiest obstacle of all. He made everyone else superficial, and this is why the really serious spirits struggled against him. But to no avail. Homer always won. [Trans. W. Arrowsmith]

Nietzsche's understanding of the agonistic culture of Greece remains unsurpassed. It also remains relatively unrecognized by contemporary classi-

INTRODUCTION

cists and literary theorists. A posthumously published fragment, "Homer's Contest" of 1872, may be his most powerful statement of the agon, and is in my judgement the best explanation for Plato's repudiation of mimetic art.

> The greater and more sublime a Greek is, the brighter the flame of ambition that flares out of him, consuming everybody who runs on the same course. Aristotle once made a list of such hostile contests in the grand manner; the most striking of all the examples is that even a dead man can still spur a live one to consuming jealousy. That is how Aristotle describes the relationship of Xenophanes of Colophon to Homer. We do not understand the full strength of Xenophanes' attack on the national hero of poetry, unless—as again later with Plato—we see that at its root lay an overwhelming craving to assume the place of the overthrown poet and to inherit his fame....
>
> ... That is the core of the Hellenic notion of the contest: it abominates the rule of one and fears its dangers; it desires, as a *protection* against the genius, another genius.
>
> Every talent must unfold itself in fighting: that is the command of the Hellenic popular pedagogy, whereas modern educators dread nothing more than the unleashing of so-called ambition.... And just as the youths were educated through contests, their educators were also engaged in contests with each other. The great musical masters, Pindar and Simonides, stood side by side, mistrustful and jealous; in the spirit of contest, the sophist, the advanced teacher of antiquity, meets another sophist; even the most universal type of instruction, through the drama, was meted out to the people only in the form of a tremendous wrestling among the great musical and dramatic artists. How wonderful! "Even the artist hates the artist." Whereas modern man fears nothing in an artist more than the emotion of any personal fight, the Greek knows the artist *only as engaged in a personal fight*. Precisely where modern man senses the weakness of a work of art, the Hellene seeks the source of its greatest strength. What, for example, is of special artistic significance in Plato's dialogues is for the most part the result of a contest with the art of the orators, the sophists, and the dramatists of his time, invented for the purpose of enabling him to say in the end: "Look, I too can do what my great rivals can do; indeed, I can do it better than they. No Protagoras has invented myths as beautiful as mine; no dramatist such a vivid and captivating whole as my *Symposium;* no orator has written orations like those in my *Gorgias*—and now I repudiate all this entirely and condemn all imitative art. Only the contest made me a poet, a sophist, an orator..." [*The Portable Nietzsche*, trans. W. Kaufmann]

Nietzsche's power as an interpreter confirms the most valid aspect of Havelock's critique of such Platonic scholars as Friedlander and Grube: it is indeed Homer who is being rejected, and it is as an educator that he is most vehemently denied. The agon is for the mind of Athens, and so for the spiritual authority of all Greece. Yet Homer lived (probably) at least three hundred and fifty years before Plato, and Homer has the authority of originality, the strength of the beginning. Hannah Arendt observes that in ancient Greece "to begin" meant also to lead and to rule and so to be truly free. In his last work, the *Laws*, Plato remarked, "The beginning is like a god which as long as it dwells among men saves all things" (725). In some sense, Plato's contest with Homer is for the prize of usurping the foremost place, and thus becoming that beginning.

In what way, then, can Plato be considered a literary theorist? Possibly only as Freud, rather despite himself, must be considered the foremost modern literary theorist, for Plato and Freud are universal theorists, and their maps of the spirit necessarily map literature also. Plato, however, is more precisely the great theorist of *paideia*, the Greek word that the scholar Werner Jaeger expounded in three remarkable volumes of commentary. *Paideia*, according to Jaeger, at once signifies civilization, culture, tradition, literature, and education. The clearest moral accusation that Plato levels against Homer as educator is when he questions whether Homer should be called a "leader of *paideia*" of the stature of Pythagoras or, by implication, Socrates. That questioning seems to me literary theorizing at its most profound, because it compels us to weigh poetry against shamanism and against dialectic, or more generally against religion and against philosophy.

3

Most academic literary criticism rightly finds its ultimate ancestor in Aristotle, who in a formal sense is certainly a literary theorist, unlike Aristophanes or even Plato. A major modern theorist, W. K. Wimsatt, definitively observed that Aristotle answered his teacher Plato's rejection of poetry as inadequate imitation by putting forward a theory of poetry as *structure*. Wimsatt saw an essentially empirical purpose in Aristotle, correcting the "rational severity" of Plato by "looking at poetry in its own perspective as a thing having its own peculiar character." If Wimsatt was correct, then Aristotle is the valid paradigm for all Western literary criticism, which "must be rational and aim at definitions, whether it can or cannot quite achieve them. But what is left over and above definition . . . is still an objective quality of poems, knowable if indefinable, and distinguishable from that other realm, the dark realm of mystery and inspiration—which is the poet's alone." Thus Wimsatt exalted Aristotle as the standard for a *cognitive* criticism, as against the *affective* criticism with which Wimsatt associated the tradition that began with *On the Sublime*.

Wimsatt was hardly unique in his high estimate of Aristotle's *Poetics*, which enjoys all but universal esteem in our time. Yet the treatise had almost no reputation among the Greeks and the Romans, and first achieved fame in the Renaissance. It remains a puzzling book, marked strongly by its agon with Plato, and perhaps its modern and indeed contemporary influence upon literary theory and criticism is not altogether a fortunate one. This is (to me) the refreshing stance taken up in a recent book, *The Reach of Criticism*, by Paul Fry:

> Aristotle's formulation not only averts the attention of criticism from much that is valuable in literature but also hinders a just estimate of what remains. . . .
>
> There is no passage opened in the *Poetics* from the temporal medium of representation to the ideal space of mythmaking which Aristotle calls the *psuche,* or soul, of tragedy. He distinguishes among the objects, the manner, and the medium of imitation but he does not explain how the only palpable dimension of art, the medium, can incorporate an object in any manner. . . .
>
> I have been trying to make good the assertion that Aristotle's formalism is tenuous and fragile yet rigid: brittle, in short. I have also suggested that it is "intellectual" and far closer to the formalism of the master he is trying to refute than is commonly recognized. His bias in favor of structure considered as the soul of a thing undermines the rational dichotomy between form and matter that he is normally said to maintain. Either the form is intuitive and everything material is extraneous to it, including performance and even the lexical basis of reading, or else the form is embodied within material, and the material in its turn is either wholly somatic or wholly semiotic, with no implicit principle of intentionality. . . .

On this reading, which I find persuasive, Aristotle becomes a formalist version of Plato rather than a defender of poetry against Plato. Plato's deep distrust of the affective element in the performance of poetry is essentially repeated in Aristotle's notion of the catharsis or purging of fear and pity in auditors, since a moral distrust of strong emotions is shared by both philosophers. Aristotle too sees Homer as a liar, or at least as a seducer, teaching other poets the art of lying. If poetry, for Plato, was an inadequate copy of a copy, it is at least a kind of estrangement from reality for Aristotle, almost indeed a defense, as Paul Fry remarks. Such a judgement has its own authentic power, whether in Aristotle or in Freud, but we ought to be clear that Aristotle, not unlike Freud, prefers his version of the reality principle to any imaginative vision whatsoever.

Wimsatt's reverence for Aristotle is a celebration of the mimetic or "realistic" that makes possible a metaphoric theory of poetry "which does justice to the world of things and real values and keeps our criticism from being merely idealistic." This formulation in turn depends upon a praise of metaphor as the poetic trope proper; as Wimsatt says, "Let us observe that metaphor combines the element of necessity or universality (the prime poetic quality which Aristotle noted) with that other element of concreteness or specificity which was implicit in Aristotle's requirement of the mimetic object." This is Wimsatt at his most Johnsonian, and is worthy of Johnson; it is admirable criticism, morally and cognitively precise and powerful. But hidden in it, as in Aristotle and Johnson, is an extracritical belief that can be termed a belief in metaphor as substitute for or sublimation of the whole range of human drives. Nietzsche taught us to realize that the prestige of metaphor and the prestige of sublimation tend to rise and fall together as any culture goes through its various phases. Aristotle's "realistic" defense of mimesis, against Plato, still relies upon a Platonic valorization of the necessity for sublimation. Such a stance defends culture against its own discontents but cannot hope to choose Homer over Plato, if indeed such a choice finally requires to be made.

4

Criticism, which found three separate beginnings in Aristophanes, Plato, and Aristotle, emerges fully as an art only with the writer whom tradition has chosen to call "Longinus." We know that the work usually called "Longinus on the Sublime" was composed no later than the third century of the Common Era, but it had no influence until the sixteenth century, when the first modern edition appeared. Boileau translated it into French in 1674, and from then until the High Romantic period of the early nineteenth century, no other work of ancient criticism had anything like its intellectual effect and its literary popularity. Indeed the European literary period that goes from the last quarter of the seventeenth century all through the eighteenth century and on into the first quarter of the nineteenth might well be called "the Age of the Sublime," for the Sublime may be the category that most unites the Enlightenment and Romanticism. But what then was and is "the Sublime"?

To Alexander Pope, Longinus was "himself the great sublime he draws," a judgement confirmed by the historian Gibbon and by many after him. Emerson spoke of "the reader's Sublime," another emphasis upon the Sublime not so much as an affective as opposed to a cognitive phenomenon, but rather as an experience in which cognitive limits appear to be surpassed. Strictly speaking, the Sublime, or *hypsos,* of the treatise's title should be translated as "greatness" or "the height or heights" or even "great writing" or, as I would say, "strong poetry." The English word "sublime," however inappropriate for *hypsos,* is now traditional, and can even be rendered useful if approached properly, under the guidance of Cohn and Miles in their remarkable article "The Sublime: In Alchemy, Aesthetics and Psychoanalysis" (*Modern Philology*, February 1977).

> ...the modern meanings of *sublime* developed... from its more spiritual and metaphysical sense, as used in the seventeenth century. From the alchemical meanings of purification and from the idea, again from alchemy, of elevation, came religious and secular meanings of purity and loftiness....
>
> Beyond the religious uses of the word and the general seventeenth century meaning of the lofty and the purified, we find in this period the first relation between *sublime* and the art of rhetoric: the expression of lofty ideas in an elevated manner. The *OED* cites the first rhetorical use of the word in 1586, the point at which *sublime* enters the realm of aesthetics in English. By the eighteenth century the uses of *sublime* in aesthetics revealed the same confusion that the theological applications had shown in the seventeenth. While the *sublime* resided first in the

style in which elevated ideas were expressed, it eventually came to mean the elevated ideas themselves. This shift accomplished, it was not difficult to find the source of such loftiness not only in art but in nature. The most important alteration of meaning, however, occurs when the *sublime* is used by English critics in the Longinian sense to describe not the eternal cause of a particular aesthetic state in the beholder, but that state itself; the sublime has moved from the object to the subject.

That shift in meaning indeed is Longinian, but in a complex sense that seeks to overcome what Wallace Stevens termed "the dumbfoundering abyss" between subject and object. *Contra* Wimsatt, who consistently condemns Longinus for critical subjectivity, it can be affirmed of Longinus that he inaugurates the true agon of criticism with philosophy, of poetry with Plato and even with Aristotle. Aristotle, like all his descendants down to Wimsatt, wishes to convince himself that a poem possesses a structure intrinsic to it. Longinus knows better; he had the implicit realization, still shocking to many scholars, that the true poem is the reader's mind, or as Emerson once remarked, that the student had to take herself or himself for text and then had to regard all received texts as commentaries upon the self. I do not find it useful, though, to regard Longinus (or Emerson) as an antiformalist or affectivist; more simply I would say that Longinus was the very first *experiential* critic, the first critic to bring forward his own pathos or personality. There is after all no truth of the poem apart from the actual experience of reading it, and the reader's Sublime is therefore the only pragmatic Sublime, the only literary difference that can make a difference.

Longinus rightly begins by insisting that *hypsos* is an attribute only of the very greatest writers, whether of poetry or prose. Paul Fry, certainly his most sympathetic contemporary champion, finds this emphasis upon greatness the one weakness of Longinus, because "it authorizes the Superman at certain moments." Yes, but the Longinian (or Nietzschean) Superman is precisely the person without a superego, or rather that aesthetic aspect of a person that can escape the sadistic sway of the superego. Freud's "above-I," or superego, demands that the ego surrender its aggressivity, and then goes on tormenting the hapless ego even more for every sacrifice of aggressivity. But Longinus, like the Greek poets, knows only the agon, which is the aesthetic transformation of aggressivity. His call to greatness truly is a denial of the superego, and so does call us to what Blake later was to term Intellectual Warfare. The dismissal of the superego is at one with the dismissal of pity and fear, affects that structure reading for Aristotle but that Longinus rightly dismisses as being antithetical to sublimity or aesthetic greatness, the proper transport or ecstasy of reading.

Homer, rather than Plato, is the hero of *On the Sublime*, the Homer of the *Iliad*, which Longinus praises as being always on the heights of the bard's power. Homer's noble mind echoes in the *Iliad*, and reading the poem, Longinus comes to be filled with joy and pride, until he believes he has created what he has heard, which is precisely what Plato most deprecated. But this may be the point where Longinus manifests the first "modern" sort of critical anxiety of influence, in regard to Plato. Aristotle's anxiety about Plato, like that of Euripides towards Aeschylus, is authentic enough, but neither relationship seems as central as the shadowing effect of Plato upon Longinus or, say, that of Dante upon Petrarch in another time. As Paul Fry accurately notes, Longinus has a far less impoverished view of literary allusion than most scholars now enjoy. Allusion, Longinus says, causes a lustre to bloom upon our words, as our minds are troped or colored by the power of our precursors' language. Fry observes that Longinus "cannot praise his literary ancestor Plato without some word of qualification," because the great style and the agonistic concepts of Plato pervade *On the Sublime*.

Is psychic ambivalence then not the center of the Longinian Sublime, and perhaps of every Romantic theory of criticism following it? The contemporary rhetorical school headed by Jacques Derrida and the late Paul de Man would argue otherwise, an argument that has been elaborated by Neil Hertz in the subtlest essay yet published upon Longinus. Hertz associates Longinus with the modern critic Walter Benjamin and deconstructs the method of both critics as

> . . . the more or less violent fragmentation of literary bodies into "quotations," in the interests of building up a discourse of one's own, a discourse which, in its turn, directs attention to passages that come to serve as emblems of the critic's most acute, least nostalgic sense of what he is about.

To Hertz, this figurative movement of disintegration and subsequent reconstitution is essentially a rhetorical problematic masking itself as psychic ambivalence or as cultural history. But the ambivalence towards Plato in Longinus seems clear, and is grounded in literary inheritance rather than in literary language alone. Longinus understood implicitly what Nietzsche taught us to know explicitly, which is the agonistic nature of the literary experience, and so of all literary interpretation also. To achieve the reader's Sublime is to gain power over a text through interpretation, and to know greatness the reader needs to confront greatness. Longinus prophesied all the great personalist critics, even the neoclassical Dr. Samuel Johnson, even the Christian Romantic Coleridge, but more particularly Longinus fathered the Oedipal line of critics that includes Hazlitt, Carlyle, Ruskin, Emerson, Pater, Oscar Wilde, and Kenneth Burke, as well as certain contemporary figures who emphasize Nietzschean and Freudian approaches to interpretation. It is from Longinus that we continue to learn a vision in which the Sublime and the agonistic merge into one.

5

Plato's moral legacy to the subsequent history of criticism cannot be understood without reference to what W. K. Wimsatt named "the Neoplatonic conclusion" to classical literary theory. Six and a half centuries intervened between Plato and Plotinus, and perhaps they provided enough critical distance to make

INTRODUCTION

plausible so extraordinary a departure from Plato that yet continued to assert its essential Platonism. Here is Plotinus actually contraverting Plato on mimesis, while relying wholly upon Plato's vision of the Ideas as a final reality.

> Still the arts are not to be slighted on the ground that they create by imitation of natural objects; for, to begin with, these natural objects are themselves imitations; then, we must recognize that they give no bare reproduction of the thing seen but go back to the Ideas from which nature derives, and, furthermore, that much of their work is all their own; they are molders of beauty and add where nature is lacking. Thus Pheidas wrought the Zeus upon no model among things of sense but by apprehending what form Zeus must take if he chose to become manifest to sight. [*Ennead* 5. 8. 1]

It remained for the later Neoplatonists to confront this extraordinary reversal of Plato, but they chose to evade the stance of Plotinus in favor of a remarkable interpretation of the relation of Plato to Homer. For a theorist like Proclus, there had to be a way of reconciling Plato and Homer, and this way surprisingly turned out to be an insistence that Plato was the disciple of Homer: in myth, in style, and even in argument. Here is Proclus boldly seeking to reconcile the irreconcilable:

> ... If Plato correctly set out to refute Homer and show that he is out of harmony with the truth concerning reality, how is it still possible to include this poet among those who possess true knowledge, true knowledge moreover, of doctrines concerning the divine peoples and eternal beings? But if, on the other hand, these and other matters as well have been deemed worthy by Homer of a suitable treatment, how can we still allow that Plato is acting intelligently and with irrefutable knowledge? ... Plato himself is self-contradictory in what he says about Homer. For how can there be any agreement between the "divine poet" of the *Phaedo* (95a) and the poet of the *Republic* (10. 597e), who is shown to be at three removes from the truth?

Proclus sets himself the quest of resolving this dilemma so that

> ... both Homer and Plato may be revealed to us as contemplating the divine world with understanding and knowledge, to be teaching, both of them, the same doctrines about identical matters, to have proceeded from one God and to be participating in the same chain of being, both of them expounders of the same truth concerning reality.

James A. Coulter, in his crucial monograph *The Literary Microcosm*, is deeply sympathetic to Proclus but argues that the Neoplatonic defense of Plato "radically misinterpreted the substance of Plato's qualifications" in his attack on Homer. What Proclus sees as qualified assertions are not, after all, asserted qualifications; they remain profound moral objections to the civic and psychological consequences of listening to Homer read aloud. Coulter emphasizes the opportunities for interpretation left open by Plato's complex ironies and by the ambiguities of Plato's style, and the ambivalences of the Platonic stance towards poetry.

> ... it is not surprising that Proclus should have been able to "rescue" Homer. Exploiting Plato's remarks about the "divine" and "inspired" Homer, as well as his failure explicitly to deny the existence of allegorical meanings, Proclus read back into Homer's text the metaphysical universe of late Neoplatonism and, in the process, endowed with an abundant reality that ill-defined and only negatively implied species of poetry which for Plato belonged to the category of the non-mimetic.

It is true that Socrates, in *Republic* 10, rejects poetry that is *imitation*, but nowhere does Plato discourse explicitly as to what the nature of a nonmimetic or visionary poetry might be. Still, it was the tradition of Plotinus and Proclus that made possible the long development of Christian Neoplatonism, with its emphasis upon the moral redemptiveness of visionary and allegorical poetry. The greatest of neoclassical poets, Alexander Pope, writing in 1715, may be permitted the last word in this Introduction to a comprehensive collection of classical and medieval literary theory and criticism.

> A strict Verisimilitude ... is not requir'd in the Descriptions of this visionary and allegorical kind of Poetry, which admits of every wild Object that Fancy may present in a Dream, and where it is Sufficient if the moral meaning atone for the Improbability.

The Art of the Critic

Gorgias of Leontini
c. 483–c. 376 B.C.

In fifth-century Athenian society Sophists assumed the role of itinerant professionals teaching the various arts of living. Gorgias of Leontini concentrated on the teaching of rhetoric. Though his work survives only in fragments, his analysis of the forms of rhetoric and the power of speech makes him an important figure in the development of literary criticism. His ornate style and antithetical symmetries made a huge impression on Athens when he arrived there as ambassador from his hometown in 427 B.C. Subsequently he traveled throughout Greece and attracted many students, of whom the most famous was Isocrates. His writings, such as A Defence of Helen *and* A Defence of Palamedes, *served as* technai, *manuals of rhetorical instruction.*

The general effect of the Sophists in Greece was to speed the development of intellectual scepticism. Gorgias himself is credited by the ancients with the thesis that "nothing exists, and if anything did we could not know about it." This proposition, however seriously it was advanced, distinguishes Gorgias from Parmenides and Plato, who both posit a single changeless truth. In the Platonic dialogue named for him, Gorgias is rebuked by Socrates for his view that rhetoric is the queen of all the arts. The position attributed to Gorgias anticipates Nietzsche in asserting that in the absence of a single changeless truth, only rhetorical prowess and linguistic convention establish what is true and what is false.

In A Defence of Helen, *a fictionalized courtroom defense of Helen of Troy, Gorgias remarks upon the tremendous power of speech* (logos) *to shape the mind. "The effect of speech," he writes, "bears the same relation to the constitution of the mind as the prescribing of drugs does to the nature of the body." He was apparently quite successful in his own prescriptions, living, so the authorities assure us, to at least the age of one hundred and five.*

The selection from A Defence of Helen *(lines 8–14), translated by D. A. Russell, is reprinted by permission of Oxford University Press from D. A. Russell and M. Winterbottom, eds.,* Ancient Literary Criticism: The Principal Texts in New Translations *(Oxford, 1972). © 1972 by Oxford University Press.*

FROM
A Defence of Helen

If it was speech that persuaded her and deceived her soul, it is not difficult to make her defence and get the charge dismissed.

Thus:

Speech is a great prince. With tiny body and (? strength) unseen, he performs marvellous works. He can make fear cease, take away pain, instil joy, increase pity. I will explain how; the audience [i.e., the imaginary jury which has to be persuaded of the validity of the defence] must feel convinced of this. I hold all poetry to be speech with metre, and that is how I use the word. Those who hear poetry feel the shudders of fear, the tears of pity, the longings of grief. Through the words, the soul experiences its own reaction to successes and misfortunes in the affairs and persons of others.

Let me shift my ground. Inspired charms which use speech are summoners of pleasure and banishers of pain. The force of the charm meets the conviction of the mind and bewitches, persuades, and changes it by sorcery. Of sorcery and magic, two arts have been discovered, to mislead the mind and deceive the judgement.

Think how many people, by inventing false words, have deceived, and do every day deceive, many minds on many matters! If everyone had memory of all the past, knowledge of the present, and foresight of the future, speech would not be (? like this). But as it is, we have no facility in remembering the past or viewing the present or divining the future; so that on most subjects most people summon opinion to be the mind's adviser. But opinion is treacherous and unstable, and involves her employers in treacherous and unstable successes . . . [*corrupt sentence omitted*].

For speech the persuader forces the persuaded mind to agree with what is said and approve what is done. The persuader therefore does wrong because he compels, and the persuaded, because she is compelled by speech, deserves no abuse.

The alliance of speech and persuasion shapes the mind as it wishes. We can see this in various ways. First, in the talk of the scientists, who rob us of one opinion to give us another, and make the incredible and unseen apparent to the eyes of opinion. Secondly, in the debates which events force upon men, wherein a single speech pleases and persuades a multitude, by the skill of its writing, not the sincerity of its utterance. Thirdly, in the contentions of philosophers, where is displayed a rapidity of intellect that makes it easy to change the conviction with which an opinion is held.

The effect of speech bears the same relation to the constitution of the mind as the prescribing of drugs does to the nature of the body. For just as various drugs expel various humours from the body, some ending disease and some ending life, so some speeches give pain, some pleasure, some fear, some confidence, while others again poison and bewitch the mind with a malevolent persuasiveness.

Aristophanes
c. 450–c. 385 B.C.

Aristophanes was the leading poet of the Old Attic Comedy in Greece. We have very little information about his life other than what comes from the internal evidence of his work. An Athenian citizen and a pacifist, he composed the bulk of his plays during the Peloponnesian War (431–404). Throughout his artistic career, he remained an essentially conservative playwright, concerned with the preservation of the older Athenian values.

In all, Aristophanes may have written and produced as many as forty-three plays, of which we possess today only eleven. Among the most famous are The Clouds *(423), which lampoons Socrates as a Sophistic teacher of rhetoric, and* Lysistrata *(411), in which the women of the Greek states force the men to make peace by withholding their sexual favors.*

The Frogs, translated and with Introductory Note and footnotes by Dudley Fitts, is reprinted by permission of Harcourt Brace Jovanovich, Inc., from Aristophanes: Four Comedies *(New York, 1957). © 1957 by Harcourt Brace Jovanovich, Inc.*

THE FROGS

TRANSLATOR'S NOTE

Frogs was produced at the Lenaian Festival of 405 B.C., in the twenty-sixth year of the Peloponnesian War, only a few months before the final surrender of Athens to Sparta at the battle of Aigospotamoi. The competing comedies were the *Muses* of Phrynichos and the *Kleophôn* of Plato *Comicus*. Aristophanes took first prize, and his play was so well received that there was an augmented repeat performance. It has been a favourite ever since, though largely (like *Gulliver's Travels,* which it resembles) for the wrong reasons.

The plot of the comedy is simple, though somewhat inconsistent. Euripides had died in 406, to be followed almost immediately by Sophoklês. The future of drama seemed unpromising, at best; so Dionysos, the god presiding over the theatre, resolved to go down into Hadês, release Euripides, and bring him back to Athens. *Frogs* is the account of his experiences on this infernal errand. Disguised as Heraklês, who had made his own descent into Hell, and accompanied by Xanthias, a kind of Sancho Panza, Dionysos gets his directions from Heraklês, obligingly works his passage across the Styx in Charon's ferry, and arrives at his destination on the great Feast of Demêter and Persephonê, just in time to encounter the Initiates on their way to the celebration of the annual Mysteries at Eleusis. After a series of ribald mishaps he finds himself appointed judge—who could be a better choice?—of a poetry contest. It seems that Euripides, in his usual pushing way, has managed to seize the Chair of Poetry from Aischylos, who has been Laureate ever since his death in 456. The populace is happy enough with the usurpal, but a few strong-minded ghosts insist that Euripides should at least be tested by fair competition; and since Sophoklês ("he's happy anywhere") refuses to intervene unless Aischylos is defeated, the two poets contend publicly before Pluto's palace. Aischylos wins, and as a reward he is permitted to return with Dionysos *in luminis oras*.

Such a plot has obvious, not to say vulgar, attractions, and they are played for all they are worth. There is a dismaying encounter with the archetype of all insolent doorkeepers; there is a slapstick scene in which the god and his companion are belaboured by loutish underlings; there are indelicate physical and mental situations in which no man, let alone a god, should be expected to involve himself; and there is, of course, the unseen boisterous chorus of Frogs which Yale-cheers Dionysos across the Styx. The material for the *agôn*, however, is at first sight less attractive. Euripides and Aischylos attack each other's work by anatomizing or parodying the poetry itself. If appreciation of this method made considerable demands upon the literary background of the ordinary Athenian playgoer—and some commentators have thought the demands so excessive that Aristophanes must have provided his subsequent audience with a libretto—it throws an even heavier burden upon us, especially since most of the plays cited are lost. It must be confessed, too, that Aristophanes knows a good joke when he gets hold of one, and has no intention of letting it go until he has extracted the last possible laugh. In spite of such disadvantages, what might have been the duller part of the play is actually its passionate core: the philosophical criticism implicit in the poetry contest itself. And it is here that the inconsistency is evident. At the beginning of the play Dionysos goes in quest of Euripides because he is a fashionable, decadent, effeminate god who has been captivated by a fashionable, decadent, "modernist" dramatist. There is no question of serious purpose. But in the end he decides that Aischylos, not Euripides, must be returned to Athens, because the salvation of the state depends upon restoring the manly conservative principles for which the elder poet stands. What has happened is not unusual in comic satire: the initial raillery has become serious.

When we compare *Frogs* with the earlier war plays—*Peace*, for example, or *Lysistrata*—we are struck by an apparent difference of emphasis. The War itself is handled less overtly. Of course there are the usual attacks upon reckless demagogues and bone-headed commanders, the usual jokes about slaves liberated because of military service and honest citizens persecuted for dissident opinions; but the War was the whole thing in *Lysistrata*, when there was still some hope of a reasonable peace, whereas in *Frogs* the references are intermittent, almost muted, as though the poet were trying to escape from actuality into a Hadês of dream. It is easy enough to read the play as a yielding, to see its theme in the grim last words of the *parábasis:* "If we win, there will be praise for us. If we lose, we shall have the consolation of losing handsomely and to the applause of wise men." But such a reading, I think, is superficial. Aristophanes had never imagined that the War could be won by either side. Wars were as futile in his day as they are in ours. Even the gay *Lysistrata*—though it is not so gay as it looks—showed that the spirit of unconditional surrender could be as harmful to Athens as to Sparta; and in *Frogs,* with conditions incomparably worse, with collapse only a matter of months away, the poet is surer than ever that his point is sound. His play, therefore, is almost an I-told-you-so tract; with the difference that he now regards the War, desperate as it is, as only another symptom of the disease of his time. What we call pragmatism or materialism is the element that he deplores in the new teaching of the Sophists, the modernism of his age.

What an age! we are accustomed to say. But Aristophanes would not agree. It is undeniable that the greatest comic genius of antiquity, surely as mordant a satirist as the world has ever known, was a reactionary of reactionaries. There is nothing of the modernist in Aristophanes. Even what looks like "advanced' blasphemy to us—his scandalous treatment of Dionysos, for instance—is demonstrably and firmly traditional. Living early in the very period of Athenian development that seems to us so exciting in retrospect—the brilliant innovations in art, in rhetoric, in philosophical speculation, in science—he found it only hateful, a prelude to the abyss. He would have agreed with the dimmest of Sokratês' judges that Sokratês was in truth a demented iconoclast, a perverter of young minds. Consequently he seized upon Euripides as symbolizing in literature all that was dangerous in the new radical theories. If we are really to understand *Frogs*, we must apprehend the deeper animus beneath the comic surface. We must see that the attack upon the Sophists in general, and upon Euripides in particular, is something more than a splenetic crotchet, a slap at a fashionable dramatist. *Frogs* is a moral and political polemic disguised as literary criticism. The laughter is enormous, of course, and we respond with laughter; but the poem transcends topicality and fun, and may even have a meaning for our own day. . . .

. . . translation from any language means sacrifice and compromise. Especially when one is dealing with the dead: slavish fidelity is stupid, and not even fidelity; and the attempt to "modernize" generally beats itself insensible. All the translator can hope for, working within his own limitations, is to extract what is viable for him, put it into as credible a shape as he can command and communicate to someone else an idea, however spectral, of the original. The dream of any poet is *Volito vivos per ora virum*. The translator has a duty to the shades.

PERSONS REPRESENTED:

XANTHIAS
DIONYSOS
HERAKLES
A CORPSE
CHARON
CHORUS OF FROGS*
CHORUS OF INITIATES
AIAKOS
MAIDSERVANT TO PERSEPHONE
AN ELDERLY BARMAID
A YOUNG WAITRESS
SERVANT TO PLUTO
AISCHYLOS
EURIPIDES
PLUTO

*This is an accessory Chorus, heard offstage, unseen.

SCENE: *After the Prologue, the scene shifts from before the house of* HERAKLES *(presumably in Athens) to the hither shore of the Infernal Lake; thence to the other shore. From the* Párodos *on, we are in deepest Hell, before* PLUTO's *palace.*

The supernumeraries include four undertaker's assistants, women in the train of the CHORUS OF INITIATES, three Skythian constables, and a decaying prostitute.

PROLOGUE

[*A street before the house of* HERAKLES. *Enter the god* DIONYSOS, *wearing a saffron gown partly covered by a lion skin, carrying a huge club; and his slave* XANTHIAS, *bent double under an enormous amount of luggage, riding on an ass.*

XANTHIAS:
Well, Master, we seem to be here. I suppose you want me to entertain the audience with one of my jokes?
DIONYSOS:
By all means. Anything but the one that goes "Stop, you're killing me!" I couldn't stand that again.
XANTHIAS:
Something funnier, maybe?
DIONYSOS:
                Yes; but not "That's what *she* said."
XANTHIAS:
You're fussy today.
DIONYSOS:
                Oh, come on! Whatever you like, except—
XANTHIAS:
       Except?
DIONYSOS:
             Don't shrug that knapsack back and forth and say, "Ouch! Out from under!"
XANTHIAS:
             But if I *don't* get out from under pretty damned soon, there'll be a disaster in the rear.
DIONYSOS:
I swear, you make me sick.
XANTHIAS:
              Then what was the point of loading me down with this trash, if I can't behave like those low-comedy porters of Phrynichos,[1] not to mention Messrs Lykis and Ameípsias?
DIONYSOS:
Forget them. Any comedy of theirs ages a man by a good ten years.
XANTHIAS:
                Maybe; but my back won't hold up much longer.

DIONYSOS:
                    Who ever heard
such insolence! Here I am, Dionysos, son of
Juice,[2] hobbling along, wearing myself out; and you
with a first-class donkey, the gift of my own hands,
to save you the trouble of carrying the load!
XANTHIAS:
You mean I'm not carrying it?
DIONYSOS:
                    No; the donkey is.
XANTHIAS:
If you say so. But it's strange.
DIONYSOS:
                    What's strange?
XANTHIAS:
                        This nothing
that seems to weigh so much.
DIONYSOS:
                    That's the donkey's business.
XANTHIAS:
No, by God, it's mine!
DIONYSOS:
                    You're supported, not supporting.
XANTHIAS:
My shoulder's insupportable!
DIONYSOS:
                    Well, if my donkey's no help to you,
pick him up and carry him for a while.
XANTHIAS:
                        If only I were
a Navy veteran![3]
DIONYSOS:
            Why?
XANTHIAS:
                    Why, then I could answer you
man to man, not like a damnèd slave.
DIONYSOS:
Get down, you imbecile! We've arrived.
                        [XANTHIAS *dismounts*.
Hey, you, doorkeeper!
                Porter!
                    Open up!
            [*The voice of* HERAKLES *is heard, within.*
HERAKLES:
In Hell's name, what's out there? Sounds like a centaur
kicking the door in.

[*Enter* HERAKLES
For God's sake, what have we here?
[*Aside, to* XANTHIAS

DIONYSOS:
　Boy.
XANTHIAS:
　　　　Yes?
DIONYSOS:
　　　　　　　You've observed?
XANTHIAS:
　　　　　　　　　　　Observed what?
DIONYSOS:
　　　　　　　　　　　　　　Damn it, observed
　the way I scared him!
XANTHIAS:
　　　　　　　　Who's crazy now?
HERAKLES:
　　　　　　　　　　　　I swear by Demêter,
　I can't help laughing, rude as it is.—Forgive me.
DIONYSOS:
　Take courage, man, and draw near. We need your help.
HERAKLES:
　This lion skin! this saffron gown!⁴ bedroom slippers and
　a new shillelagh! What in the world are you?
　Somehow I don't get the point.
DIONYSOS:
　　　　　　　　　　　　　Give ear:
　I was under Admiral Kleisthenês—
HERAKLES:
　　　　　　　　　　　　Must have been fun.
DIONYSOS:
　　　　　　　　　　　　　　　　We sent
　twelve or thirteen to the bottom.
HERAKLES:
　　　　　　　　　　Between you?
DIONYSOS:
　　　　　　　　　　　　　　　　　Yes.
XANTHIAS:
　Wake up, the dream's over.
DIONYSOS:
　　　　　　　　　　No, let me tell you:
　I was reclining in the poop, perusing
　a play by Euripides—the *Andrómeda*, I remember—
　when suddenly my breast was wrenched with a wild desire.
HERAKLES:
　A big one?

DIONYSOS:
>Gigantic.

HERAKLES:
>For a woman?

DIONYSOS:
>Certainly not!

HERAKLES:
Of course not. A boy, then?

DIONYSOS:
>Brother, you're insulting.

HERAKLES:
Good God. You mean you wanted a full-grown man?

DIONYSOS:
Come, really, Heraklês!

HERAKLES:
>Well, the only thing left
would seem to be Kleisthenês.

DIONYSOS:
>Brother, don't make fun of me.
This passion of mine is tearing me to pieces.

HERAKLES:
Divulge, Brother, divulge.

DIONYSOS:
>No, I can't; at least, not directly;
but maybe a hint—
Tell me, O Heraklês:
hast ever been seized by a craving for pea soup?

HERAKLES:
Over and over again.

DIONYSOS:
>"Spake not my tongue plainly,"
or must I elaborate?

HERAKLES:
>I see pea soup
in my mind's eye.

DIONYSOS:
>Just such a longing consumeth me now
for Euripides.

HERAKLES:
>For Euripides? But he's dead!

DIONYSOS:
No merely human force shall hinder me
from seeking him out.

HERAKLES:
>You mean you'd go down to Hell?

DIONYSOS:
   Deeper, if need be.
HERAKLES:
               But why?
DIONYSOS:
                       My heart is fixed
   on that mighty poet. As he himself has written:
      Many men no more are.
      Those that are, no good are.[5]
HERAKLES:
   How about Iophôn?
DIONYSOS:
               The only good poet left alive.
   and sometimes I have my doubts about *him*.
HERAKLES:
                       Well; but Sophoklês?
   If you must drag a literary man back from the grave,
   why not him? He's worth a dozen Euripideses.
DIONYSOS:
   Not until I'm sure that Iophôn can stand
   on his own feet, without help from Sophoklês. Besides,
   Euripides knows all the tricks. He'll find a way
   to get out of Hell. But Sophoklês—
   why, he's contented anywhere!
HERAKLES:
               And Agathôn?
DIONYSOS:
   Departed. Much regretted by his friends.
HERAKLES:
   I didn't know. Departed whither?
DIONYSOS:
               Thither,
   to the Banquet o' th' Blest.
HERAKLES:
           You don't say. How about Xenoklês?
DIONYSOS:
   To hell with Xenoklês.
HERAKLES:
           Pythángelos, then?
XANTHIAS: [*Aside*
               I wish to God
   someone would mention Xanthias. My aching back!
HERAKLES:
   In fact, there must be thousands of pretty scribblers
   who can outrun your Euripides by miles
   when it comes to tragic jabber.

DIONYSOS:
                                    Scrannel pipes,
I tell you; chirping birdlets; the death of Art.
One tragedy, and they're spent
without giving Melpomenê so much as a *frisson*.
I don't care where you look,
you won't find a poet today who is really
generative.
HERAKLES:
               Generative?
DIONYSOS:
                              Yes, generative. I mean
a poet who can sing of "the skyey sky of Zeus,"
or "fleet-fitting Time," or "when last
your eye I eyed," or (best of all, in my judgment)
"Sworn hath my tongue; my soul stands yet unpledged."[6]
HERAKLES:
You really like that sort of thing?
DIONYSOS:
                                Mad about it.
HERAKLES:
But it's trash, and you know it.
DIONYSOS:
                              "O thou rash intruder,
creep not into my mind";[7] you've one of your own.
HERAKLES:
Have you no critical sense?
DIONYSOS:
                              I'll accept
kitchen criticism from you; no other kind.
XANTHIAS: [*Aside*
And still not a word about *me*!
DIONYSOS:
                              But now, to business.
I'm on my way to Hell in your uniform,
and of course I turn to you for information.
What was it like down there when you stole the Dog?
The natives? The hospitality? The general tone of the place?
The sights? The shops?
Whorehouses, taverns, restaurants, the hotels
with the fewest bedbugs?
XANTHIAS: [*Aside*
                         Still not a word!
HERAKLES:
                                              You're raving.
Do you really have the courage to go to Hell?

DIONYSOS:
    Are you deaf? Tell me the best route (not too hot,
    yet not too cold) to the Houses of the Dead.
HERAKLES:
    The best route, hey? Take a rope and hang yourself.
DIONYSOS:
    No. Delicate throat.
HERAKLES:
                       How about hemlock?
DIONYSOS:
    No. Feet get cold, legs swell up.
HERAKLES:
    I'll tell you the quickest way.
DIONYSOS:
                       Good. I hate walking.
HERAKLES:
    Go out to Potterville—
DIONYSOS:
                       Yes?
HERAKLES:
                       Climb the tallest tower—
DIONYSOS:
    Yes?
HERAKLES:
    And wait for the start of the torch-race.
    When the fans shout "Throw down the torch!,"
    then you just throw yourself—
DIONYSOS:
                       Where?
HERAKLES:
                       Down.
DIONYSOS:
                       Oh.
    But that might scramble my brains.
                       No, give me
    a better route than that.
HERAKLES:
                       You're hard to please.
DIONYSOS:
    Tell me how *you* got there.
HERAKLES:
                       That was a long, long trip.
    Well, first you come to an enormous dismal lake—
DIONYSOS:
    How do you get across?

THE FROGS

HERAKLES:
                    There's an old man
who runs a little ferry. Two pennies round trip.
DIONYSOS:
Dear me. Even Hell's gone commercial.
HERAKLES:
                             It was Theseus
started the custom.   Well, after you get over,
you'll meet mobs of snakes and all kinds of disgusting beasts.
DIONYSOS:
You can't scare *me*! I've been seeing them all my life.
HERAKLES:
Then a great swamp with an almighty stink.
Here they throw criminals: pathics who cheat their boys
of pay for the pleasure they've had; stingy hosts;
men who maul their mothers or flatten their fathers;
perjured persons—
DIONYSOS:
                 And don't forget to add
the publishers of Morismos, and those fools
who admire the lyric spasms of Kinêsias.
HERAKLES:
And then a grove with lovely light and the sound
of soft flutes everywhere, and happy crowds
of men and women, and laughter, and applause.
DIONYSOS:
Who are these men and women?
HERAKLES:
                      The Initiates.[8]
XANTHIAS: [*Aside*
And I am the Initiated Ass! No, I've had enough.
HERAKLES:
These will tell you whatever you need to know.
They live quite near the road, at Pluto's gates.
—Good-bye, Brother, and good luck!
DIONYSOS:
                            The same to you.
                             [*Exit* HERAKLES
Xanthias, pick up the baggage.
XANTHIAS:
                      Before I've laid it down?
DIONYSOS:
And make it quick!
XANTHIAS:
                  No! Please! Hire someone who's going there!

DIONYSOS:
  What if I can't find someone?
XANTHIAS:
                        Then I suppose
  I'll have to go.
DIONYSOS:
                  Fair enough.
                        —But here comes a dead man.
  [Enter, R, four undertaker's assistants carrying a
  corpse on an elaborate litter
  —My dear sir,
              you, I mean, the Late Lamented,
  Mr Corpse: will you carry my luggage with you to Hell?
CORPSE:
  How heavy?
DIONYSOS:
              Look at it.
CORPSE:
                        Hm. Let's say two drachmai.
DIONYSOS:
  Too much.
CORPSE:
            On your way, men!
DIONYSOS:
                        Wait a minute!
  I'm sure we can strike a bargain.
CORPSE:
                        I said two drachmai.
DIONYSOS:
  Nine obols?
CORPSE:
            Not on your death!
                        —Go on, men.
                  [Exeunt bearers, L, with CORPSE
XANTHIAS:
  That cadaver's too clever. To hell with him.
                                    Master,
  I'm with you!
DIONYSOS:
              My noble Xanthias.
        [XANTHIAS retrieves the baggage and remounts his
        donkey; exeunt, L.

SCENE I

[*The shore of a great lake separating our world from the world below.* CHARON *is discovered standing in a dilapidated skiff. Enter* DIONYSOS *and* XANTHIAS.

DIONYSOS:
What's that?
XANTHIAS:
           That? A lake.
DIONYSOS:
                    By God, the very one
he told us about!
XANTHIAS:
           Yes. And there's the boat.
DIONYSOS:
So it is, by Poseidon!
XANTHIAS:
               And there's old Charôn himself!
DIONYSOS:
Greetings, Charôn!
XANTHIAS:
            Greetings, Charôn!
BOTH:
                       GREETINGS, CHARON!

[CHARON *raises a large megaphone and addresses them.*

CHARON:
Who are you, coming from the world of woe and care?
Who are you, coming to Lethê? to the Mare's Nest?
to the Land of Dogdays? to Perdition Plaza? to
Hell in all its glory?
DIONYSOS:
            Me.
CHARON:
               All aboard, then.
And hurry up: we're running behind schedule.
DIONYSOS:
Does this ship really touch at those ports?
CHARON:
                     With *you* aboard, yes.
Come, be quick!
DIONYSOS:
          This way, Xanthias.

CHARON:
                              No slaves on my boat!
   Unless, of course, he's a Navy veteran.
XANTHIAS:
                    No.
   God knows I tried, but they wouldn't take me. Bad eyes.
CHARON:
   Walk around the lake, then.
XANTHIAS:
                         Where do I meet you?
CHARON:
   At old Arid's tavern by the Desiccated Rock.
DIONYSOS:
                              Got it?
XANTHIAS:
   I've got it, all right.
                    —Must've met a black cat this morning!
         [*Exit* XANTHIAS; DIONYSOS *struggles into the boat.*
CHARON:
   Sit down. There's your oar.
                    —All aboard! Anyone else coming?
                         [DIONYSOS *sits down on an oar.*
   What in hell do you think you're doing?
DIONYSOS:
                         Just what you told me:
   I'm sitting on my oar.
CHARON:
                    You gastric hyperbole!
   Sit there, on the bench!
DIONYSOS:
              All right.
CHARON:
                         Flex your biceps,
   stick out your hands
DIONYSOS:
              All right.
CHARON:
                    And row, man, row!
DIONYSOS:
   Me? Row? Unshipbroken, unoceanized, unoared?
   How can I row?
CHARON:
              Easiest thing in the world. Just try,
   and you'll have the most marvelous music to help you on.
DIONYSOS:
   What music?

THE FROGS

CHARON:
        Frogswans. A grade-A troupe.
DIONYSOS:
                I'm ready.
Give me the stroke.
CHARON:
        O opóp! O opóp!
        [The skiff leaves the shore, wobbling.

KOMMOS: CHORAL EPISODE

[The ACCESSORY CHORUS *of* FROGS *is heard, offstage.*

FROGS:
        Brekekekéx koáx koáx
        Brekekekéx koáx koáx!
We are the swamp-children
            Greeny and tiny,
Fluting our voices
        As all in time we
    Sing our koáx koáx
    Koáx koáx koáx
For Dionysos
      Nysa-born
On the Winey Festival
          When the throng
Lurches in through his temple gate,
Every man as drunk as a hake.
        Brekekekéx koáx koáx
        Brekekekéx koáx koáx!
DIONYSOS:
My arse is sore, koáx koáx.
FROGS:
        Brekekekéx koáx koáx.
DIONYSOS:
And you don't give a damn, koáx.
FROGS:
        Brekekekéx koáx koáx.
DIONYSOS:
Go jump in the lake, koáx koáx!
Let's have a different tune, koáx!
FROGS:
Different? What a
           Meddlesome fool!

    Pan and the Muses
                     Love us, our whole
        Koáx koáx koáx
        Koáx koáx koáx
    Draws down Apollo
                     Golden-lyred:
    Ours are the marsh-reeds
                     God-inspired
    That sing to his heavenly fingering
    Their music with our own mingling
        Brekekekéx koáx koáx.

DIONYSOS:
  My hands are ablaze, my bottom's a wreck!
  In a minute or two you'll hear it speak.

FROGS:
        Brekekekéx koáx koáx!

DIONYSOS:
  Silence, you lily-pad lyrists, koáx!

FROGS:
  No, we must sing. The
    Sunshine will bring the
      Glint to the pools,
        The shimmer of reeds,
  And when Zeus descends
    In rain on our heads
      We'll leap with our friends
      And pipe from our souls
        Brekekekéx koáx koáx!

DIONYSOS:
        Brekekekéx koáx koáx!
  Come, that's enough!

FROGS:
                We've hardly begun!

DIONYSOS:
  I suppose you think that rowing is fun?
    [*A furious increase in volume and tempo to the end
    of the chorus*

FROGS:
        Brekekekéx koáx koáx!

DIONYSOS:
        Brekekekéx koáx koáx!
  I wish you'd die!

FROGS:
            We'll swell up and cry
    Brekekekéx koáx koáx!
    Brekekekéx koáx koáx!

DIONYSOS:
>Brekekekéx koáx koáx!

I can beat you at that koáx koáx!

FROGS:
The devil you can, koáx koáx!

DIONYSOS:
I will, by God, if it takes all day!
>*Brekekekéx koáx koáx!*

Go and koáx yourselves away!
>KOAX KOAX *KOAX!*
>>[*He breaks wind hugely; the* FROGS *are silent.*

There! That settles your damned koáx!
>[*The boat has reached the opposite shore.*

SCENE II

>[*The shore of Hell; in the background, an expanse of weary grey land; the air is faintly brown.*

CHARON:
Easy all. Oars in. Step right out and pay
at the gate.

DIONYSOS:
>Here's your money.
>>[*Exit* CHARON
>—Xanthias!

Xanthias! Where in hell is Xanthias?

XANTHIAS [*offstage*]:
>Coming, coming!

DIONYSOS:
Late, as usual.
>[*Enter* XANTHIAS, R

XANTHIAS:
>Welcome to the underworld, Chief!

DIONYSOS:
What's in that direction?

XANTHIAS:
>Murk and mud.

DIONYSOS:
Did you see those damned souls he told us about?

XANTHIAS:
Didn't you?

DIONYSOS:
Yes, by Poseidon! And I still do.

[*Points to the audience*
—Well, what's next?

XANTHIAS:
I think we ought to get out of here. This is the place
where that awful menagerie is, the one
Heraklês mentioned.

DIONYSOS:
Oh, *him*. He was just blustering,
trying to scare me off, because he knows
I'm unbeatable in battle. "Breathes there the man
with soul so drunk"[9] as Heraklês? Unlikely.
Oh for a beast, a monstrous beast,
to justify my valiant coming hither!

[XANTHIAS *feigns acute terror.*

XANTHIAS:
Did you hear that noise?

DIONYSOS:
No. Where? Where?

XANTHIAS:
Over there, in back of you.

DIONYSOS:
You get in back of me!

XANTHIAS:
Now it's in front of us.

DIONYSOS:
Come on, stand in front!

XANTHIAS:
Almighty Zeus, what a monster!

DIONYSOS:
What is it like?

XANTHIAS:
Horrible. Keeps changing its shape, too. First it's an ox,
then it's a mule, and now
it's the prettiest girl.

DIONYSOS:
Girl? Where? Lead me to her!

XANTHIAS:
Now she's turned into a mastiff.

DIONYSOS:
It's the Empûsa!

XANTHIAS:
A face like a bonfire!

DIONYSOS:
Legs of brass?

XANTHIAS:
Yes, one of them.
The other one's donkey-manure.[10]

THE FROGS

DIONYSOS:
                              Where can I hide?
XANTHIAS:
   Me, too.
DIONYSOS [*to the audience*]:
   Is there a doctor in the house?[11]
XANTHIAS:
   Lord Heraklês, we're done for!
DIONYSOS:
                           Name not that hateful name.
XANTHIAS:
   "Lord Dionysos," then.
DIONYSOS:
                  Nor that.
XANTHIAS:
                           It's all right, Master.
DIONYSOS:
   What do you mean?
XANTHIAS:
                  As Hegélochos would say,
   "After the storm I see the clam again."[12]
   The Empûsa's pushed off.
DIONYSOS:
                           Swear it by Zeus.
XANTHIAS:
   I swear it.
DIONYSOS:
          Swear it again.
XANTHIAS:
                  I
swear it.
DIONYSOS:
       Again.
XANTHIAS:
              I swear it.
DIONYSOS:
                     I went all white
   when I saw the Empûsa.
XANTHIAS:
                     Yes; and part of your robe
   went all brown.
DIONYSOS:
              Alas, what god is to blame
   for this dreadful visitation?
XANTHIAS:
                     Might it not be
   "the skyey sky of Zeus," or "fleet-flitting Time?"

[A *sound of flutes, off* R

DIONYSOS: Hark!

XANTHIAS: What?

DIONYSOS: Can't you hear them?

XANTHIAS: What?

DIONYSOS: The flutes.

XANTHIAS: Yes; and the wind blows the scent of crackling torches.
They are celebrating the Mysteries.

DIONYSOS: Then let's be quiet, and hide over there and watch.

[*The* CHORUS OF INITIATES *is heard offstage*, R.

CHORUS:
Iacchos! O Iacchos!
Iacchos! O Iacchos!

XANTHIAS:
The Initiates, Master, the ones
he told us about. That is their holy ground
where they sing of you, as they do in the Agora.

DIONYSOS:
I think so, too; but until we're sure of it
let's lie low and listen.

CHORUS:
O Iacchos! [STROPHE
God of many hymns!
Come to this meadow of delight
Come
Dancing with laurel
The bright
Flowers circling the holy hair that streams
Gold in the golden air
Whirl our choirs
In the maze of the Graces
Iô!
As the quick feet go.

XANTHIAS:
O Persephoneia! Lady! Demêter's daughter!
What a heavenly smell of pork![13]

THE FROGS   29

DIONYSOS:
                              Oh, do be quiet!
A sniff of sausage, and you can't control yourself.

CHORUS:
   Up the torches   [ANTISTROPHE
                  Let them flare again
   Radiant god
              Pure star of our night
     The glade's aflame:
                    and care, and age—how light-
   ly borne in the Bacchants' train!
         Lead us, bright glancer
                           Whirl our choirs
           In the maze of the Graces
                              Iô!
     As the quick feet go.

PÁRODOS[14]

[The scene has changed to the innermost part of Hell, before the palace of PLUTO. *Enter, R, the* CHORUS OF INITIATES: *twenty-four men vested in white, crowned, carrying torches. They are accompanied by a throng of women who dance to the choral passages, although they take no part in the singing. The* KORYPHAIOS *assumes the rôle of the Hierophant, or President of the Mysteries.*

KORYPHAIOS:
  Silence, O ye profane! Make way for our mystical Chorus,
    Ye to the Muses unknown * yé unvers'd in their dance!
  Leave us, all ye unskill'd in the art of mighty Kratínos,
    Lovers of ancient jokes * friends of the easy laugh!
  Let the bad man depart, fomenter of civic subversion,
    Venal commander in war * traitor on land or sea,
  Public servant for sale, chéap déaler in contraband oarlocks,
    Sails and caulking pitch, * dallier with the foe,
  Cyclic chorister dropping his filth at the shrinelets of Hékat',
    Orator hating the poet, * grudging him his poor pay.
  Let them be gone, I say, and I say it again, and a third time.
    Yield to the holy choir! * Brothers, begin the song!

CHORUS:
>Oh sacred dance in the sacred fields, [STROPHE 1
>   Oh mystery of laughter!
>We sing the praise of Her who shields
>   Her City from disaster:

>Athêna goddess, swift to save   [ANTISTROPHE 1
>   In times of mortal treason,
>Queen of our joy this side the grave,
>   Our hope in every season.

KORYPHAIOS:
  Now let us raise a hymn to Demêter, Queen of the deep
    fields,
  Goddess of waving wheat * crowned with the harvest-gold.

CHORUS:
>Demêter, Mistress of our mysteries,   [STROPHE 2
>   Be with us today.
>Satire and laughter-barbed sobrieties
>   Make up our play:

>   [ANTISTROPHE 2
>When the last scene is done, the final wry
>   Verse has been said,
>Grant me to wear the victor's wreath on my
>   Ecstatic head!

KORYPHAIOS:
  Sing the adorable god who leads us all in our dancing,
    Sing Dionysos the fair, * draw him to us in song.

CHORUS [*three solo voices with choral responsory*]:
A:
  Iacchos, festal Musician, come down to us now:
  The journey is long to the Goddess; we're dying to go.
       Dionysos, lead me.
B:
  Our costumes are tatters and worse, to cut the expense.
  Anything for a laugh; it won't matter a century hence.
       Dionysos, lead me.
C:
  I just glimpsed the prettiest girl in this part of the town,
  And a pink little nipple popped through a rip in her gown!
       Dionysos, lead me.

DIONYSOS:
  I'd like to play with that pink little nipple.
XANTHIAS:
                                            Me, too!

THE FROGS

KORYPHAIOS:
    For Archedémos let us drop
      A small but lyric tear.
    No voter yet; but that won't stop
      His antics, never fear!
        Demagogue, prig, fop, and liar:
        Hell scarify him with its fire!

CHORUS:
    They say that Kleisthenês, in tears
      On his Sebinos' tomb,
    Is pulling out his nether hairs
      And prophesying doom.
        Pederast, pig, effeminate:
        From such as him God save the State!

KORYPHAIOS:
    I've heard the ever-valiant son
      Of Hippobine the Mighty
    Routs hosts of women one by one,
      No armour but his nighty—
        But that is made of lion skin:
        The girls look once, and then give in.

DIONYSOS: [*Politely, to the* CHORUS
    Can any of you gentlemen
      Direct me to the place
    That Pluto holds his revels in?
      I long to see his face.
        We're strangers here, my slave and I:
        We just came in on the last ferr-y.

KORYPHAIOS:
    Stranger, rejoice! Your journey's at
      An end. You see that gate?
    Enter to grow in wisdom. That
      Is all I care to state.
        All men who come from earth a-helling
        Are welcome in that aústere dwelling.

DIONYSOS:
    Pick up the bags, then, Xanthias.
XANTHIAS:
      That's all I needed, Master!
    A Korinthian baggomania's[15]
      Consuming you, by Kastor!
        If Korinth really is "God's City,"
        Xanthias is—well, no self-pity!

[DIONYSOS *and* XANTHIAS *approach* PLUTO'S *gate.*
KORYPHAIOS:
Let us dance.
Dance to Demêter with flowers, to the goddess of flowers
  undying!
Jewel her meadow with song! * Meanwhile, I will depart,
Torch in hand, with these maidens (themselves the kindlers
  of torches)
To a secluded spot. * Béar úp! I'm sure *I* shall!
[*Exit* KORYPHAIOS *with the company of women*
CHORUS:
Ah the sweet dance   [STROPHE 3
            the graced
Rose-ritual
          in places
Secret
     fair:
         O blest
Plain of all

Souls' desire!   [ANTISTROPHE 3
          O Fire
Hélios:
      good men
Hail thee
         find in thee
                  kindliest
Goodness to all!

SCENE III

[DIONYSOS *stands timidly at* PLUTO'S *gate; suddenly he turns back.*

DIONYSOS:
Xanthias, how does one knock at the door of Hell?
We mustn't violate local etiquette.
XANTHIAS:
Go ahead and knock. Remember, you're Heraklês!
                          [DIONYSOS *knocks.*
DIONYSOS:
Anyone home?
AIAKOS [*within*]:
            Who wants to know?

DIONYSOS:
                              Heraklês the Remorseless.
          [AIAKOS *bursts from the house.*
AIAKOS:
  O wretched, rash, intruding, hateful cheat!
  Rogue of rogues, all rogues excelling! Dog-
  napper—
          and that behind my back!
                              Never mind:
  This time I've got you!
          Ay, and gloomhearted Styx[16]
  and the bloodthrobbing jetty of Acheron and
  the ranging ghastly dogs of Kokytos await you!
  Echidna shall rip you with her hundred mouths!
  Tartessan eels shall gnaw your lungs away!
  Teithrasian Gorgons shall chew your liver and lights!
  Just you wait here: I'll be back with them in a minute.
              [*He re-enters the house, slams the door.*
DIONYSOS:
  Xanthias.
XANTHIAS:
          What's the matter?
DIONYSOS:
                      I seem to have soiled myself.
  "Invoke the god."[17]
XANTHIAS:
              Nonsense. Pull yourself together.
  What if someone should see you?
DIONYSOS:
                      I am dying, Xanthias, dying.
  Bring me a sponge and apply it to my heart.
XANTHIAS:
  Here you are. Apply it yourself.
              [DIONYSOS *takes the sponge and washes himself.*
                      Merciful God,
  Is *that* where your heart is?
DIONYSOS:
                      Yes, it seems to have sunk.
XANTHIAS:
  You colossal coward, disgrace of gods and men!
DIONYSOS:
  Who calls me coward? Did I not ask for a sponge?
  A weaker man would never have dared.
XANTHIAS:
                              How so?

DIONYSOS:
He'd have lain there, radiating. But *I* faced the matter,
and now I'm as good as new.
XANTHIAS:
                    Poseidon, what a man!
DIONYSOS:
Exactly.—But you,
weren't you appalled by that dreadful speech of his?
XANTHIAS:
Me? Not at all.
DIONYSOS:
            I congratulate you.
                            —Here,
since you're so heroic, take my lion skin
and my club. I'll carry the baggage.
XANTHIAS:
                        I hear and I obey.
Give me your uniform, quick. Here's mine, and the luggage.
                        [*After the exchange:*
You behold a new kind of god, a Xanthioheraklês.
Do *I* look like a coward?
DIONYSOS:
                    You look like hell to me!
[*He picks up the baggage and they start to leave,*
XANTHIAS *leading the way.*

SCENE IV

[*The door suddenly opens.* DIONYSOS *cringes in terror behind* XANTHIAS. *Enter from the house a pretty* MAID-SERVANT *to Persephonê.*

MAID:
Welcome, dearest Heraklês!
So nice to have you back again! Her Majesty
no sooner heard you were here than she baked a mountain of
        bread
with her own hands, put three or four pots of peas
on the fire, roasted an immense ox, and made
I don't know how many hundreds of little cookies and cakes.
Come in, do!
XANTHIAS:
            You're very kind, but I'm not hungry.

MAID:
    Mercy, but you *must* be!
                        I forgot to mention
that there's chicken, too, and wine, and the darlingest
    dessert.
XANTHIAS:
    Thank you, but no.
MAID:
               You're *always* teasing!
                            Well, what about
a flute-girl (a real artist) and two or three
ballerinas?
XANTHIAS:
        Did you say ballerinas?
MAID:
                          Lovely girls, too,
all perfumed and plucked, not one of them over fifteen.
Come in:
the fish is broiled to a turn, and they're setting the table.
XANTHIAS:
    That's different! Tell the girls I'm on my way.
                                [*Exit* MAID
Slave, pick up the luggage and follow me.
DIONYSOS:
    Stop right there! I let you play Heraklês
for the fun of it. Did you think I was serious?
Xanthias, don't be a fool. Pick up the baggage.
XANTHIAS:
    You mean you didn't mean what you meant?
DIONYSOS:
                                  I mean
that I'm the master here. Take off that lion skin.
XANTHIAS:
    Witness, O gods from whom no secrets are hid,
how the man treats me!
DIONYSOS:
                 Idiot, thou art the man!
How can a deathbound slave be Alkmenê's son?[18]
XANTHIAS:
    Oh, I suppose so. Here you are.
                      [*They exchange costumes*.
                      But the day will come
when you'll need my help. By God, just wait till then!
CHORUS:
        The prudent man, it seems to me,   [STROPHE
           Who knocks about in boats

>   Is careful, when he goes to sea,
>   To set his sail
>   Before the gale:
>   If he succeeds, he floats.
>   Extreme inflexibility
>   Is bad for you, is bad for me.

DIONYSOS:
>   To think of Xanthias asprawl
>   On an expensive couch
>   Tumbling a dancing-girl, while all
>   The time I stand
>   With busy hand
>   Watching the frolic! Ouch!
>   This kind of speculati-on
>   Is profitless, and scarcely fun.

[*Enter*, R, *an* ELDERLY BARMAID *accompanied by* PLATHANE, *a young waitress.*]

BARMAID:
Pláthánê, Pláthánê,[19] there he is! Remember him?
It's the very same tramp that broke into our place one day
and ate up sixteen loaves of the best bread.

PLATHANE:
                                                    By God, so it is.
The very same!

XANTHIAS: [*Aside*
This is going to be hard on somebody.

BARMAID:
And twenty roasts or so.

XANTHIAS: [*Aside*
Somebody's in for it!

BARMAID:
And the dear knows how many pounds of garlic.

DIONYSOS: Madam,
you're mad. Do you know what you're saying?

BARMAID:
                                                     You!
D'you think I don't know you, never mind them fancy
    clothes?
—And I forgot the marinated smelts!

PLATHANE:
                                       Yes, and the cheese.
He swallows it whole, rind, basket, and all, and when I give
    him the bill,
he belches at me.

XANTHIAS: [*Aside*
        That's what he always does.
PLATHANE:
    And he hauls out his sword, like he's crazy-like—
BARMAID:
    Yes, dearie, you poor thing!
PLATHANE:
            And scares us to death and chases us upstairs,
    and then he walks off with the table-cloth.
XANTHIAS: [*Aside*
            Of course.
PLATHANE:
    We ought to do *some*thing!
BARMAID:
            Go get Lawyer Kleôn.
XANTHIAS: [*Aside*
    Or Hypérbolos, if you can find him.
BARMAID:
                We'll settle *his* hash!
    —Yes, Guts, how I wish I had a stone
    to smash in them teeth of yours that chewed up my food!
XANTHIAS: [*Aside*
    I could go for that.
PLATHANE:
            I'd like to take a sickle
    and rip up that gullet of his that's swallowed my tripe!
    But I'll get Kleôn.
    He'll have him up before the judge today,
    or else there's no justice.
                [*Exeunt women*, R
DIONYSOS:
    Xanthias.
XANTHIAS:
        Yes?
DIONYSOS:
            Xanthias, I swear
    that I love you beyond all men living or dead.
XANTHIAS:
    Hey, none of that! I'm through being Heraklês.
DIONYSOS:
    Oh please, please, Xanthy!
XANTHIAS:
                As you said yourself,
    how can a deathbound slave be Alkmenê's son?
DIONYSOS:
    I know, I know. You're angry, and I don't blame you.

Hit me, if you want to.
                    But this time, Xanthias,
if I try to take back the lion skin, may I be
cast out root and branch with my wife and children—
and you can toss in old blear-eyed Archedémos.
XANTHIAS:
All right. If you really mean that, I'll play along.
                    [They exchange rôles.

CHORUS:
    Nice work! You have the clothes again, [ANTISTROPHE
    And now *you're* Heraklês.
Swagger and strut, and strut again:
        For if you fail
        To make men quail,
He'll beat you to your knees.
    Permit me to recite the adage:
    "The coward always bears the baggage."

XANTHIAS:
    Friends, you have harped my fear aright:
    He'll cheat me if he can.
But I'll be fierce, and growl, and bite,
        And goggle so
        That all will know
I'm a catastrophic man.
    Be with me now, propitious Fate!
    I hear a knocking at the gate.

    [The door opens. Enter AIAKOS *carrying a horse-
    whip, accompanied by three Skythian constables.*

AIAKOS:
Arrest that dog-thief and be quick about it.
His time has come!
DIONYSOS: *[Aside*
                    Somebody's in for it.
XANTHIAS:
                              Go to hell!
One step more, and you get a taste of my club!
AIAKOS:
Tut. Resisting an officer!
                    —Ditylas, Skeblyas,
and you, Pardokas:[20] come here and get him.
          [The constables disarm XANTHIAS *and bind him.*
There. Now he'll get the kind of treatment
a dog-rustler deserves.

THE FROGS

DIONYSOS: [*Aside*
A horrid fate!

XANTHIAS:
I hope to die if I was ever here before,
or if I stole so much as a hair of your dog!
But I'll be generous:
suppose you torture that lousy slave of mine.
If he proves me guilty, I don't care what you do to me.

AIAKOS:
Well... What kind of torture do you suggest?

XANTHIAS:
Oh, the rack, or hang him by the thumbs, or stretch him
on the ladder, or flay him, or pour vinegar up his nose,
or pile stones upon him—it's all one to me.

AIAKOS:
Excellent, excellent! But suppose I damage him
permanently? You won't bring suit, I hope?

XANTHIAS:
Certainly not. I make no conditions at all.

AIAKOS:
Better do it here, so that you can watch what he says.
—Here you, put down the baggage. And swear to tell
the truth and nothing but the truth.

DIONYSOS:
One moment.
You can not torture me. I am a god.

AIAKOS:
What say?

DIONYSOS:
I said that I
am Dionysos, son of Zeus Almighty.
That person is my slave.

AIAKOS [*to* XANTHIAS]:
Did you hear that?

XANTHIAS:
Yes. Incredible blasphemy.
But whip him!
If he's a god, he'll never feel a thing.

DIONYSOS [*to* XANTHIAS]:
You say *you're* a god. Why don't you get whipped too?

XANTHIAS:
That's reasonable.
—All right, whip us both; and the one
who cries *Uncle!*, or shows the least sign of feeling pain—
that one's no god.

AIAKOS:
> Good. You understand justice.
—All right: strip, both of you.
XANTHIAS:
> The procedure?
AIAKOS:
Simple. First I hit one, then the other.
XANTHIAS:
Brilliant!
AIAKOS: [*He lashes* XANTHIAS' *buttocks.*
> Take that!
XANTHIAS:
> Well, why don't you begin?
AIAKOS:
I did!
XANTHIAS:
> Ridiculous.
AIAKOS: [*Lashes* DIONYSOS
> Then let's try the other.
DIONYSOS:
Come on; haven't got all day!
AIAKOS:
> You didn't feel that?
DIONYSOS:
Never a feel.
AIAKOS:
> Strange. Back to the first one.
>> [*Lashes* XANTHIAS
XANTHIAS:
Oh my God!
AIAKOS:
> Felt it, hey?
XANTHIAS:
> Not at all. I was thinking
of the Festival of Heraklês Diomeios.
AIAKOS:
> Hm.
The religious type.
> Well, let's have a go at the other one.
>> [*Lashes* DIONYSOS
DIONYSOS:
Oooh! Oooh!
AIAKOS:
> What's the matter?
DIONYSOS:
> Look at the gorgeous cavalry![21]

AIAKOS:
   Then why the tears?
DIONYSOS:
                        Some onions popped into my mind.
AIAKOS:
   And you don't give a damn for the whipping?
DIONYSOS:
                                          Not a damn.
AIAKOS:
   What's going on here?
                              [Lashes XANTHIAS
XANTHIAS:
                    Oh, please! please!
AIAKOS:
                                     "Please" what?
XANTHIAS:
   Got a thorn in my heel. Please pull it out for me.
AIAKOS:
   Funny, aren't you?
                    —Well, it's your turn again.
                              [Lashes DIONYSOS
DIONYSOS:
   Oh Apollo!
           "Regent of Delos and of Delphoi."
XANTHIAS:
   He felt that, all right. Just listen to him!
DIONYSOS:
                                    Not a bit.
   I was merely reciting a verse from Hippónax.[22]
XANTHIAS:
   You're not getting anywhere. Hit him in the groin.
AIAKOS:
   You're right, I'm not getting anywhere. Turn around!
                              [Lashes XANTHIAS' *belly*
XANTHIAS:
   Poseidon!
AIAKOS:
          Aha! At last!
XANTHIAS:
                 "Thou holding sway
   o'er th' Aigaian cliffs and the winedark wave!"[23]
AIAKOS:
   No, by Demêter, it's beyond me! I can't tell
   which one of you is the god.
                           Come in: I'll ask Persephoneia
   and the King to decide. After all, they're gods themselves.

XANTHIAS:
A good idea; but I wish you'd thought of it sooner.
[*Exeunt into the house*

PARÁBASIS

[*The* CHORUS *turns and faces the audience, the* KORYPHAIOS *standing apart from the group.*

CHORUS:
        Descend, O Muse: strike with divine fire   [ODE
        Our mystic choir.
Grant us the grace of song, that we
        Harmoniously
  May charm this audience,
  Ten thousand men of sense
Whose hearts are angry when they see
Kleophôn on his Thracian tree—[25]
        That twittering split-tongued swallow
        Whose hollow
  Trillings tell
  Of Philomel
"So rudely forced."
        (As well he may:
  For if the jurymen should vote
  Acquittal, we would cut his throat.)

KORYPHAIOS:
                                  [EPIRRHEMA
There is no function more noble than that of the god-touched Chorus
  Teaching the City in song. * Hear what we have in our hearts!
First, we pray for an end to unequal justice in Athens.
  Phrynichos with his tricks,[26] * desperate wrestling-holds,
May have tripped some of us up. If he has, we beg you forget it.
  Must we reject our own? * Do we not need each man?
Shall we, because of one battle, make slaves the peers of Plataians[27]
  (No, I approve your decree. * Then, for once, you were wise.)
And debase these neighbours of ours whose fathers and grandfathers, fighting

Oúr fight in oúr ships, * saved the City from shame?
Should they not have, as the dark comes down, storms
    bursting about us,
  Rights that are common to all? * Is there no Greek faith
    left?
Pride and revenge are human; but pride can be death, and
    revenge is
  Joy in the act, but pain * when the cleared brain reflects.

CHORUS:
      "If aught of skill in augury   [ANTODE
          Dwelleth in me,"[28]
    I say that tiny Kleigenês,
        That foe of peace,
     That drunken latrine-sweeper,
     That monkey-gaited creeper,
  Smells coming trouble—yes, and worse.
  (I'm always decorous in verse.)
      Else why does he every night,
          When he's tight,
  Insist
  On a club in his fist?
  It's plain enough:
         as he's weaving home,
    He fears some citizen may take it
    Into his head to strip him naked.

KORYPHAIOS:
                                  [ANTEPIRRHEMA
Yet there are sensible men and good in Athêna's City,
  True as an ancient coin, * gold against modern brass.
Everyone knows the gold, here in Greece and the outlandish
    nations:
  How often we toss it aside, * stretch out our hands for
    what's new!
So with our dealings with men: When we find one worthy of
    honour,
  Old Athenian stock, * brave for his country, wise.
Skilled in the arts, a scholar, an athlete, a soldier, a poet—
  What do we do with *him*? * Drive him away from our sight!
No, we prefer the brass: the connivers, the bland politicians,
  Faddists from overseas, * parvenus, plausible scamps,
Slippery scum that the City would once have disdained to
    consider
  Even as scapegoats fit * for the expiatory rites.
Ah, we are mad, we are mad! And we may go down in our
    madness,

Or God may restore our sense. * Victory? It may be.
But if we fall, let us fall so that children to come will remember
Sane men meeting their fate, * not a surd grunt in the dark!

SCENE V

[*Enter from the house* XANTHIAS *and a* SERVANT TO PLUTO. XANTHIAS *has resumed his own clothing.*

SERVANT:
A great man, your master, by God the Saviour, yes,
a very great man!
XANTHIAS:
      Well, yes, I suppose so.
First prize for guzzling and nuzzling, at any rate.
SERVANT:
Do not belittle those accomplishments.
I liked the way
he finally proved you were lying, and then didn't try
the Outraged Employer routine.
XANTHIAS:
        He didn't dare to.
SERVANT:
By God! As one servant to another,
that's the way I like to hear a servant talk.
XANTHIAS:
You do?
SERVANT:
   Yes. I like to get off by myself
and think up horrible things about my master.
XANTHIAS:
Well, well! And when he beats you?
SERVANT:
        Grist to my mill.
XANTHIAS:
My, my! And if he catches you spying on him?
SERVANT:
        Man, it's heaven!
XANTHIAS:
O God of Kinship!
    You listen to the family secrets?

SERVANT:
  I do.
XANTHIAS:
    And spread them around?
SERVANT:
          Yes. There's nothing like it,
  except maybe a good strong emission.
XANTHIAS:
            O Phoibos Appollo!
  Come, let me kiss that hand.
      [*They embrace; loud cries from within.*
            What's that?
SERVANT:
  Aischylos and Euripides, I imagine.
XANTHIAS:
            Oh?
SERVANT:
  It's a damned nuisance. Hell's foundations quiver.
XANTHIAS:
  Since when?
SERVANT:
        We've a custom here, you see,
  that when a great artist or scientist arrives
  and can prove that he's better than any of his rivals,
  we invite him to lunch in the Prytaneion
  right next to Pluto.
XANTHIAS:
          I begin to see.
SERVANT:
  Of course, if an even greater man comes along,
  the first has to yield his place.
XANTHIAS:
            But how does this
  touch Aischylos?
SERVANT:
        Why, as the greatest of poets,
  he was on the Tragedy Foundation.
XANTHIAS:
            And now who's on it?
SERVANT:
  Euripides, I'm sorry to say. When he died and came down
      here,
  he began giving public readings from his plays
  before our audience of pickpockets, barratrists,
  adulterers, parricides—the general run of Hell.
  His metrical writhings and convolutions pleased them,

so they gave him the crown; and poor Aischylos
had to resign the Chair.
XANTHIAS:
                        There was no protest?
SERVANT:
Yes, from a certain faction.
They insisted that we should hold a poetry contest
to determine which artist really deserved the Chair.
XANTHIAS: [*Indicating audience*
You mean this assembly of jailbirds?
SERVANT:
                                  I do indeed.
Their howling smote the stars.
XANTHIAS:
No one supported Aischylos?
SERVANT:
                            Respectable men
                           [*Indicating audience*
are few in this place.
                   Just take a look at that crowd!
XANTHIAS:
Well, what has Pluto decided?
SERVANT:
                           Oh, we'll have the contest.
The two of them will recite—and then, the judgement.
XANTHIAS:
Do you mean to tell me
that Sophoklês hasn't announced *his* candidacy?
SERVANT:
No. *That* one's a gentleman! When he arrived here
he kissed Aischylos and took him by the hand.
He could have had part of the Chair, too, for Aischylos
    offered
to share it with him. But no; as Kleidemidês puts it,
"He sitteth i' th' reserve."
                             That is to say,
if Aischylos gets the verdict, he'll be content;
but if Euripides wins,
by God, we'll have Sophoklês in there on his own.
XANTHIAS:
When do they start?
SERVANT:
                   Any minute now. Just where you're standing
the frenzy of poetic strife will rage,
and Thespis will be weighed.

XANTHIAS:
                    What do you mean?
Can tragedies be weighed?
SERVANT:
                    Of course they can.
More than that: there'll be compasses and rulers
and T-squares—
XANTHIAS:
                    What for? Are you building a brick wall?
SERVANT:
Also wedges, and instruments to calculate
diameters.
            Euripides has sworn
that he'll dissect each drama verse by verse.
XANTHIAS:
Aischylos isn't taking this lightly?
SERVANT:
                    If you could see him!
He's glaring like a bull.
XANTHIAS:
                    Who's to be judge?
SERVANT:
Ah, that was the question! Real critics are scarce in this
        place.
And besides,
Aischylos never did get along with Athens.
XANTHIAS:
I suppose he disliked the criminal majority.
SERVANT:
Yes; and he always held that art was wasted there.
At any rate,
they finally agreed on your master Dionysos.[29]
He *does* know his poetry, after all.
                    —But look!
They're coming. Let's go in. This is no place
for us servants when our masters are about.
Come, Xanthias.
        [*They enter the house; the* KORYPHAIOS *indulges in
        an Aischylean tirade.*]
KORYPHAIOS:
The rage! The cardiac tumult! Psychic disasters!
The fury of the thunder-kissing bard when he perceives
his piddling opponent picking his dentures with dactyls!
Regard his orbs, how they roll: one this way, one the other!
Ah the logotomy! Verb breasting adverb, the cristate nouns
plunging 'gainst pavid pronouns. Let the bull stylistic

(husband of cows) rise up and whirl his whiskers!
Ah the lambent raiding of verse, the (my God!) tripsis
of boant anapaests leaping in lucent line
against the skiaphagous luculent ululant
phalanges of the foe!
                      Yet must we bear in mind
the hepatic ingenium of the adversary, whose
herpetic tongue knows too well how to rive
the hyaline dynamis of our archarchitect!

The rest is silence.

SCENE VI [AGON: α]

[*Enter from the house* DIONYSOS, AISCHYLOS, EURIPIDES

EURIPIDES:
  No, Dionysos, I will not give up the Chair.
  I'm better than he in every branch of the art.
DIONYSOS:
  Say something, Aischylos. You heard the man.
EURIPIDES:
  He's going into one of his Portentous Silences.
  It's a favourite trick of his to impress the audience.
DIONYSOS:
  Euripides, please don't *talk* so much!
EURIPIDES:
                              I know him,
  and I know those noble-savage heroes of his with their
  raving tongues:
                no restraint, no decent respect
  for language, but a flood of chaotic bombast
  spewed out of that doorless cave he calls a mouth!
AISCHYLOS:
  "And is it thou, scion of the vegetable garden,"[30]
  rag-picker, old-clothes-man, confector of
  beggars, incarnate cliché? You'll get no comfort here!
DIONYSOS:
  Enough, Aischylos.
  "Do not o'erheat, raging, thy raging heart."[31]
AISCHYLOS:
  Not till I have shown how this Master of the Limp[32]
  has fooled all Athens with his casts of cripples.

THE FROGS

DIONYSOS:
   A lamb, a lamb, a black lamb, slaves! Bring it quickly!
   The sky is full of thunder!
AISCHYLOS:
                           And as for his Kretan
   arias,[33] his idiotic filthy
   bridal-scenes (miasma of art)—
DIONYSOS:
                        My dear Aischylos,
   remember your blood-pressure.
                                [*To* EURIPIDES
               And you, friend, keep back.
   Do you know what a really terrible man this is?
   He's perfectly capable of knocking you on the head
   with a word that would alkalize your *Alkestis*.[34]
                                    —Come,
   let's be calm. It's a shocking thing when poets
   shriek at each other like fishwives over a sale.
EURIPIDES:
   I merely ask for judgement.
   Let him attack or defend, I don't care which.
   Let him examine my dialogue, my lyric
   passages—the core of Tragedy—; let him investigate
   my *Peleus*, my *Aiolos*, my *Meleágros*, and, above all,
   my *Telephos*.
DIONYSOS:
   Well, Aischylos, will you begin?
AISCHYLOS:
                      If you say.
                                —And yet,
   this contest is bound to be one-sided.
DIONYSOS:
                        One-sided?
AISCHYLOS:
   My poems are still on earth in the mouths of men.
   All of his are with him here in Hell. However,
   let us proceed.
DIONYSOS:
                 Bring me fire, slaves, and incense.
   Before this mighty argument, I must pray
   for guidance to a right verdict.
                        Friends,
   invoke the Muses in song.
        [*Burning incense is brought, which* DIONYSOS
        places upon the altar while the CHORUS *sings.*

CHORUS:
    O Nine
        O virgin daughters of Zeus
    Chaste lovers of the delicate craft of words
              Breathe now
    On these unparalleled antagonists!
        Grant one a new thunder of poetry
            Grant the other
    Increase of the subtle sweet sleights of language
           As they advance
        Toward this great duel of Art.

DIONYSOS:
Pray to the gods, both of you, before we begin.
AISCHYLOS:
Demêter! Goddess! Matrix of my mind!
Grant me wisdom in these Mysteries!
                        [*Censes the altar*
DIONYSOS:
Now it is your turn, Euripides.
EURIPIDES:
                  Very kind of you,
but my gods are different.
DIONYSOS:
                You have gods of your own,
made in your image, after your likeness?
EURIPIDES:
                         Yes.
DIONYSOS:
Then pray to your special gods.
EURIPIDES:
                  O succulent Aither!
O nimble Loquacity! Quivering quick Nose!
Be with me now in this Confabulation!
CHORUS:
                        [STROPHE
Breathes the man with soul so benumbed by Lethê
That he burns not when he regards these champions
Stripped for word-play in the arena óf our
   Elegant contest?
One will strike with subtlety, one with fury.
Who will win? Rise up, O my soul, and stretch thine
Ears! The strife is mortal, the triumph doubtful—
                        [*A gong-stroke*
   There goes the bell now!

SCENE VII [AGON: β]

[DIONYSOS *seats himself on an elaborate stool,* C, *facing the audience.* AISCHYLOS *and* EURIPIDES *have plain stools at opposite sides of the stage, where they sit facing each other.*

DIONYSOS:
 Let's not waste time, gentlemen. What we want is elegance:
 no pointless decoration, no second-hand imagery.
                                         [EURIPIDES *rises.*
EURIPIDES:
 For myself and my poetry
 I shall not speak at the moment. What I propose to do
 is to show how this charlatan, this gaudy boaster,
 has taken advantage of a trusting public
 brought up on the plays of Phrynichos.
                                —This is his method:
 He brings on a single actor, veiled—a Niobê, maybe,
 or an Achilleus, it makes no difference—, and has him sit
 in a chair. And then the audience is treated
 to a long Aischylean Silence.
DIONYSOS:
                     Yes, I remember.
EURIPIDES:
 And then his Chorus enters:
 strophê, antistrophê; strophê, antistrophê: four stanzas
 on the same subject. Then silence. Meanwhile the actor
    sleeps.
DIONYSOS:
 I like that. Too much chatter on the stage these days.
EURIPIDES:
 That's because you're so easily taken in.
DIONYSOS:
                           I suppose I am.
 But how does he manage it?
EURIPIDES:
                    Simply by mystification.
 There you are in the audience waiting for Niobê
 to get something off her mind, and she never does.
 So the drama drams.
DIONYSOS [*to* AISCHYLOS]:
                   Why are you making
 those hideous faces?

EURIPIDES:
                             He knows that I see through him.
As I was saying: After a long period of this,
about half way through the piece, the actors wake up
and begin to shout. I will say this for his diction:
it's ravine-like, hairy, mad-bull-like, crustacean,
battering, craggy, shattering,—and it makes no sense.
AISCHYLOS:
  I object!
DIONYSOS:
             Sit down.
EURIPIDES:
                         Not a man in the house
can tell what it's all about.
DIONYSOS [*to* AISCHYLOS]:
                             Stop gnashing your teeth.
EURIPIDES:
  Something about Skamándrosses and entrenchments,
  dragons in brass rampant on rutilant shields—
  language to fry a man's brain!
DIONYSOS:
                             Right, by God!
"I spent a sleepless night in my naked bed"[35]
trying to figure out what, of all possible fowls,
that "flavescent horse-cock"[36] of his might be.
AISCHYLOS:
  A figure-head for a ship, you abysmal rustic!
DIONYSOS:
  I took it for Eryxis.
EURIPIDES:
                         Besides, what good is a cock
  in tragedy?
AISCHYLOS:
                 Damn you, what can *you* show us?
EURIPIDES:
                                                Well,
  I may not be so clever as you when it comes to
  horse-cocks and goat-elks and the other weird beasts
  you've plagiarized from the Persian; but just the same,
  I have done what I could.
                             I inherited tragedy
  from you—a flabby legacy, all puffed out
  with dropsical big words and inane bluster—,
  and I went to work.
  I cut away the bloat; I injected tickling phrases
  here and there; I prescribed gentle exercise

and a white-beet diet with a cup of gossip-juice
before each meal, and filtered book-dust. Then
I fed it softboiled monodies—
DIONYSOS [aside]:
                                 With a dash
of Kephisophôn.
EURIPIDES:
                      This was no haphazard treatment,
no grabbing in the dark at bottles on the shelf.
Everything was planned. And at the very outset
I'd describe the source of my plot.
DIONYSOS [aside]:
                                  That was better
than describing your own source, I swear by God it was!
EURIPIDES:
From the first line of the Prologue
to the end of the play there was never an Aischylean
Vacuum: everyone spoke—women, slaves,
kings, virgins, hags—
AISCHYLOS:
                       They certainly did,
and you ought to have been hanged for it.
EURIPIDES:
                                    No, by Apollo!
It was the true democratic Art.
DIONYSOS [aside, to EURIPIDES]:
                                 Forget it, friend.
That's not the best way in the world to plead your case.
EURIPIDES:
I taught people how to speak—
AISCHYLOS:
                           You did, you did,
and I wish you had burst your guts first!
EURIPIDES:
                                    I taught them
the planes and angles of language. Taught them Semantics:
that is to say,
how to think straight, see straight, plan straight, cheat
    straight,
debate straight, arrange straight, hate straight, and be
    straight
in any emergency.
AISCHYLOS:
                    No doubt about that!

EURIPIDES:
                                           And what's more,
   I brought real life to the stage, men and women
   just like those out there in the audience.
   This was really audacious, since the cheapest
   critic could understand me and complain.
   I never tried to numb them with narcotic adverbs
   or scare them to death with Kyknosses and Memnons
   charging about in cars drawn by bell-bedizened
   bullocks!
             —Influence? Consider the Aischylean school,
   and then the Euripidean. He has his Phormisios
   and that Megainetos person they call Snake Eyes—
   the virile clique: horns and lances
   and horrible howls and skin-corroding laughter.
   But who are my followers?
   Kleitophôn and Beau Theramenês.
DIONYSOS:
   Theramenês? He's a canny bird! He's a
   caution, *he* is! Say a friend of his
   gets into some sort of trouble, and Theramenês is there:
   just you watch how gracefully he'll leave,
   with never a word to anyone!
EURIPIDES:
        And thus I teach the crowd to say:
                  "From day to day
                     In every way
            I'm clearly growing better."
        My verses bring them new insight:
                  Night after night
                  They think aright
        On things that really matter.
DIONYSOS:
        Yes. When a householder comes home
                  Drunk as an owl,
                  He's learned to howl:
        "Hey, where the hell's the grub?"
        Blest be Euripides's name!
                  Before you came,
                  He'd have hidden his shame
        In a bedroom at his club.

CHORUS:
                                        [ANTISTROPHE
   "You have heard thé prater, Achilleus."[37] Answer!
   But confine your answer: the storm's upon you.

THE FROGS

> Shall your ship gó down in this verbal tempest?
>> Not by a long shot!
>
> Set your sail ánd scoot for a placid harbour.
> You, the first Greek poet t' explore these waters:
> Shall this chartless charlatan win the combat?
>> Tell it to Thespis!

DIONYSOS:
Aischylos has the floor.
AISCHYLOS:
       Wrangling of this kind
sickens me; my cup
runneth over. Still, I must reply to this verse-jockey.
Euripides, tell me:
what do you consider the chief duty of a poet?
EURIPIDES:
To speak truth for the improvement of the City.
AISCHYLOS:
And if you yourself have not done this; if your poems
have poisoned our citizens, made rascals of good men:
what do you deserve?
       [EURIPIDES *is scornfully silent*.
DIONYSOS:
     Death. But that is not a proper question.
AISCHYLOS:
He laughs at my legacy of tragic verse.
Let him. But can he find in any of my plays
a shirker of public duty, a clown, a pavement
cavalier, a slippery shifter, an intriguer?
He can not.
My men are truly men. They breathe crests and helms
actinic, the cuirasse-clatter, the sonant
whack of spear on spear.
EURIPIDES:
       Gentlemen,
beware the hardware!
DIONYSOS:
       Tell me, Aischylos:
what play are you talking about?
        —And please *don't* be so noisy!
AISCHYLOS:
A play aërated by Arês.
DIONYSOS:
      The title?
AISCHYLOS:
Seven Against Thebes. If you ask my opinion,

one of my best. Every man in the audience
went out and enlisted.
DIONYSOS:
                              Oh? So you taught the Thebans
greater manliness in war?—Sounds subversive to me.
AISCHYLOS:
You might have learned something from it yourself
if you'd been inclined that way.
                              —Then I staged my *Persians,*
where I prove that a man's whole life must be given up
to conquering what adversary soever.
That play had a record run.
DIONYSOS:
                              I still remember
the joy I felt when Dareios' ghost
rose up, and the Chorus all clapped their hands
and shouted "Eeee-YOW!"
AISCHYLOS:
                              These are the only themes
worthy of poetry, these high themes. Think: from the first
it has been the poets who have served men best.
Orpheus: he taught us to understand the Mysteries
and to hate murder; Musaios: the arts of healing
and divination; Hesiod: sowing and reaping;
and godlike Homer in his deathless chant:
did he not teach us the glory of bearing arms,
the black joy of battle?
DIONYSOS:
                              If he did, Pantaklês missed it.
Just the other day I saw him leading a troop
in the Panathenaia: he'd forgotten to screw the crest
into his helmet, and was dangling it in his hand.
AISCHYLOS:
Remember rather the true men Homer has taught,
men like our hero Lamachos.
                              —From these poems
I took my Patroklosses and my lionhearted
Teukrosses as examples for every man
when the trumpet sings to arms. But you will find
never a Sthenoboia in my plays,
nor a nasty Phaidra: I would not dirty my stage
with a love-drooling woman.
EURIPIDES:
                              No; Aphroditê and you
never had much in common.

AISCHYLOS:
                              I thank God for it.
But you and your Modernists are haunted by her:
you see her everywhere, in every possible shape.
As a matter of fact, you personally have suffered from her.
DIONYSOS: [*To* EURIPIDES
By God, that's true enough!
The very things that you showed other men's wives doing
your own wife did to you.
EURIPIDES:
                        Aischylos, you fraud,
how have my Sthenoboias hurt the City?
AISCHLYOS:
By corrupting the decent wives of decent men.
Those Bellerophons of yours have led them
to death by hemlock out of the shame you've taught them.
EURIPIDES:
I suppose you'll say *I* invented the myth of Phaidra?
AISCHYLOS:
Not at all.
But the poet's duty is to conceal the filth,
not drag it onto the stage. We have schoolmasters
for little boys; we have poets for grown men.
Let our concern be only with what's good.
EURIPIDES:
And when you howl your Lykabettos-language,
your Parnês-periods—, is that what you call teaching?
Is that your "good"? Why not speak like a man?
AISCHYLOS:
Fool!
High thoughts must have high language. As the dress
of our actor demigods is nobler than our own,
so must their speech be nobler. I have adorned
the theatre; you have debased it.
EURIPIDES:
                              Tell me how.
AISCHYLOS:
First of all, you dress your kings in tatters
to squeeze tears out of the audience.
EURIPIDES:
                              What if I do?
AISCHYLOS:
It's a bad precedent. There's not a rich man in Athens
who will outfit a galley these days. All the millionaires
say they're too poor, and walk about in rags.

DIONYSOS:
    Yes, by Demêter! And all the time they're wearing
    the finest cloth underneath; and when they're done
    cheating us, they head for the most expensive markets.
AISCHYLOS:
    Also, you have taught bragging and silly gossip.
    The gymnasiums have shut down because the boys
    are scraping their buttocks thin on library benches,
    learning your verses. Even the common sailors
    are drunk with your clever talk, and dare answer back
    to their officers. Why, in my time
    all they did was chew hardtack and sing "Yo-ho-ho!"
DIONYSOS:
    Yes, and poop in the face of the oarsman beneath,
    and daub the next man with dirt, and steal from the shops
    when they got shore leave. Nowadays their brawn
    is all in their tongues; they never flex their muscles.
AISCHYLOS:
        What evil has Euripides
          Not brought upon the stage?
    He gives us leering pimperies,
    Obstetric scenes in sacristies,
    Incestuous adulteries,
        "The denial of the Age."
                He's filling the City
                with second-rate wit. He
        Founds a school of writing apes,
        Thumbs his nose, and off he trapes.
DIONYSOS:
        The good oldfashioned manly ways
          Are lost, thanks to his art.
    Just watch a modern relay-race:
    Fat fancy fellows without grace,
    Limp in the legs and green in the face,
        Outrun before the start!
            The customers grumble,
            But only a rumble
        Mutters in the sagging bowels.
        Quick, boy: water and clean towels!

CHORUS:
        Ah the sweet rage of logomachy,   [STROPHE
          The fury of the word,
    When trope meets trope's hostility
        With syntax for a sword!
    The screams of zeugma! Howls of tmesis!

> Moans of apocopé ripped to pieces!
> > Curses of syzygy!
> What wonder that this warfare teases
> > Gods from the sky!
>
> If, subtle combatants, you fear   [ANTISTROPHE
> > Our audience may not un-
> derstand the wiles you'll practise here
> Before the battle's won:
> Take heart; the Newer Education
> Has brought enlightenment to the nation:
> > We're an erudite folk:
> Each member of this congregation
> > Has read a book.

SCENE VIII [AGON: γ]

EURIPIDES:
I should like to begin with his prologues.
   —I hope to show,
Gentlemen, that this "accomplished wash-out"
was a bungler from the beginning.
DIONYSOS:
   Which prologue do you want?
EURIPIDES:
A lot. But first let's listen to the *Orestês*.
DIONYSOS:
Silence, everyone!—Begin reading, Aischylos.
AISCHYLOS:
O Hermês, Angel of the nether world,[38]
Guardian of fathers, help me in my need!
I come again, returning to this land.
DIONYSOS:
Anything wrong with that?
EURIPIDES:
   A dozen things.
DIONYSOS:
But there are only three verses!
EURIPIDES:
   With twenty mistakes
in each.
AISCHYLOS:
   You see? the man's mad.

EURIPIDES:
                         It makes no difference to me.
AISCHYLOS:
   Show me a single mistake!
EURIPIDES:
                              Recite it again.
AISCHYLOS:
   O Hermês, Angel of the nether world,
   Guardian of fathers—
EURIPIDES:
                    Stop!—Orestês is speaking
   at his dead father's tomb?
AISCHYLOS:
                         He is.
EURIPIDES:
                              Does he mean
   that this Patron Saint of fathers merely looked on
   when Agamemnon died at a woman's hands,
   "murther'd in secret shame"?
AISCHYLOS:
                              Not at all. He invokes
   Hermês as "Angel of the nether world,"
   the Helper, in darkness working the will
   of his father.
EURIPIDES:
            Worse and worse: for if his father
   makes him work underground—
DIONYSOS:
                         That would seem to imply
   that Zeus is a grave-robber.
AISCHYLOS:
                    I consider that joke in bad taste.
DIONYSOS:
   Give us the rest.—Euripides, watch for mistakes.
AISCHYLOS:
               —*help me in my need!*
   I come again, returning to this land.
EURIPIDES:
   Brilliant Aischylos! He says the same thing twice.
DIONYSOS:
   Twice?
EURIPIDES:
            Twice. Just look at his words. He says
   I come again and *returning to this land*.
   What's the difference between "coming again" and "re-
         turning"?

DIONYSOS:
  By God, you are right! It's as if I should say,
  "lend me a wash-pot or a pot to wash in."
AISCHYLOS:
  Not the same thing at all, you impossible chatterer!
  It's a beautiful verse.
DIONYSOS:
                    It is, is it? Show me why.
AISCHYLOS:
  "To come again" to his country is said of the man
  who has travelled and now comes home to his father's fields.
  Not so the fugitive: he both "comes back" and "returns."
DIONYSOS:
  A palpable hit, by Apollo!—Euripides?
EURIPIDES:
  I will not allow that Orestês "returned": he came
  like a smuggler, stealing past the border guards.
DIONYSOS:
  An excellent answer, by Hermês!
                           Though I must confess
   that I don't understand it.
EURIPIDES:
                    Shall we have some more?
DIONYSOS:
  Yes, Aischylos, finish the passage.
AISCHYLOS:
  Prostrate on this paternal mound, I beg
  My father's ghost to hear me and give ear.
EURIPIDES:
  There he goes again: *hear me* and *give ear*.
AISCHYLOS:
  Blasphemer! Orestês is calling upon the dead!
  Even our three-fold *Hail!*[39] is not enough.
DIONYSOS:
  Tell us how *you* write prologues, Euripides.
EURIPIDES:
  I will. And if you find me chasing my own tail
  in repetitions or padding my lines with garbage,
  spit in my eye!
DIONYSOS:
                 Your prologues have always enchanted me.
EURIPIDES:
  Once was Oidipûs a fortunate man—[40]
AISCHYLOS:
  Stop! Even in the womb he was most wretched.
  The Oracle sang that he would kill his father
  before he was born.

DIONYSOS:
                    A precocious embryo!
AISCHYLOS:
  How can you call him fortunate?
EURIPIDES:
                                    Let me finish.
  But later became the unhappiest of mortals.
AISCHYLOS:
  Wrong again! He was unhappy all his life.
  Examine the evidence. The very day he was born
  he was put in a jug[41] and left out in the mountain snow
  to die, so that he might not murder his father.
  Later he travelled to Korinth on his swollen feet;
  and later, though still young,
  he married a hag who turned out to be his mother,
  and then he poked out his eyes. A fortunate man!
DIONYSOS:
  At least he never went into politics.
EURIPIDES:
  Talk as you will, you can't talk away my prologues!
AISCHYLOS:
  I certainly won't dissect them phrase by phrase;
  but with God's help I think I can do for them
  with a little oil.
EURIPIDES:
                    You said oil?
AISCHYLOS:
                                    Just a drop or two.
  This poetry of yours is such predictable stuff
  that a man can tag it with almost anything:
  a pinch of cobweb, an oil-jar, a sack. I'll show you.
EURIPIDES:
  You really think so?
AISCHYLOS:
                    I do.
DIONYSOS:
                                    Come on: begin.
EURIPIDES:
  Aigyptos—so the rumour runs i' th' world—
  Sailing the broad sea, landing at Argos with
  His fifty stalwart sons—[42]
AISCHYLOS:
                                    Ran out of oil.
DIONYSOS:
  Ran out of oil?—Watch out, Euripides!
  Let's have a different prologue.

EURIPIDES:
Dionysos, dressed in fawn skin, he who leads
The choric revels upon high Parnassos,
Waving his holy thyrsos—[43]
AISCHYLOS:
        Ran out of oil.

DIONYSOS:
 Is that so!
EURIPIDES:
     Never mind. I have a prologue here
that's oil-proof. Let's see what he can do to this:
No man is truly happy in all things.
Say one was nobly born: today he's bankrupt;
Another, of humble parents—[44]
AISCHYLOS:
        Ran out of oil.

DIONYSOS:
 Euripides.
EURIPIDES:
    Dionysos?
DIONYSOS:
       Reef your sail.
We're in for an oil storm.
EURIPIDES:
        Do you think I care?
I'll drown him in his own oil, by Demêter!
DIONYSOS:
           Good.
Another prologue, then. But mind what you say!
EURIPIDES:
Kadmos, Agênor's son, departing from
The citadel of Sidon—[45]
AISCHYLOS:
      Ran out of oil.

DIONYSOS:
 Euripides, you'd better buy up that oil of his
before it stickies all your favourite prologues.
EURIPIDES:
 Never! I've all sorts of prologues left
that he can't touch. For example:
Pelops, Tantalos' son, on his way to Pisa,
Drawn by swift coursers a-gallop—[46]
AISCHYLOS:
        Ran out of oil.

DIONYSOS:
 You see? There he is again with his old oil-jar.

—Come, Aischylos, let the son of Tantalos have it:
you can buy a better one anywhere for a penny.
EURIPIDES:
No so fast! I haven't given up yet.
Oineus, reaping in the fields—
AISCHYLOS:

        Ran out of oil.

EURIPIDES:
Let me finish. Let me finish.
*Oineus, reaping in the fields the season's foison,
Sacrificed to the gods but—*[47]
AISCHYLOS:

        Ran out of oil.

DIONYSOS:
While he was sacrificing? Where was the leak?
EURIPIDES:
Let me try once more.
Zeus, as Truth itself asserts—[48]
DIONYSOS:

        That's enough!
Can't you hear him saying that Zeus ran out of oil?
An unorthodox thought!
    —That oil of his
dirties your verse like the droppings from your eyes.
For God's sake, take up his choruses!
EURIPIDES:

        I will.
I'll prove that he's incompentent as a lyrist
and given to vacant iterati-on.

CHORUS:
   What cán he do? What cán he say?
    How cán he hope to damn
   The finest lyrics of our day?
    Am I confused? I am.

SCENE IX [AGON: δ]

EURIPIDES:
"The finest lyrics," eh? All right: I'll prove
that these marvelous songs of his
are nothing more than the tune the old cow died to.
What's more, I'll compress them all into one example.

THE FROGS   65

DIONYSOS:
   And I'll keep score with these pebbles.

EURIPIDES: [Singing to flute accompaniment
         Achilleus, Laird o' Phthia,[49]
      Hear'st not the onset
                    of the wife-
      dehonestizing, childimpaling foe?
                                      Oh,
      Praise to Hermês, inaugurator of swamp life!
      Hear'st not the onset?

DIONYSOS:
                    Here go
      two pebbles against you, Aischylos.
                                      —Proceed.

EURIPIDES:
         Son of Atreus, glory o' th' Achaians!
         Thou World Federation incarnate! Bend thine ear:
         Hear'st not the onset?

DIONYSOS:
      Another onset. Really, Aischylos!

EURIPIDES:
         Be auspicious, O ye tongues of mortal dust!
                    The honeybear girls
            Expand the fane of Artemis.
                                Hear'st not the onset!
                    The greathearted
            Heroes are gone! The glory is departed!
         Hear'st not the onset?

DIONYSOS:
      Merciful God, these onsets!
      My knees ache, and a drowsy numbness pains
      my pants, as though I needed a hot bath.
EURIPIDES:
      Wait till you've heard another number of his,
      composed for voice and harp.
DIONYSOS:
                          If I must, I must.
      but no more onsets!

EURIPIDES:
      Alas! Can it be that the doublethroned power of Hellas[50]
            phlattothrattophlattothrát
      Has yielded unto the Sphinx, that deathwhiffing bitch?

>   phlattothrattophlattothrát
> *With hand and lance arm'd, the bombinating squallbird*
>   phlattothrattophlattothrát
> *Cedes to the heav'nengender'd dogs*
>   phlattothrattophlattothrát
>   *The adherents of Aias-Aiantos!*
>   phlattothrát!

DIONYSOS: [*To* AISCHYLOS
 What's all this phlatting and thratting? A battle-cry
 from Marathon, maybe? or something you picked up at sea?

AISCHYLOS:
 I found beauty, and made it more beautiful. You cannot say
 that I worked in the Muses' fields with Phrynichos.[51]
 But this man, like a sad little whore,
 took anything from anyone: a catch from Meletos,
 a flute-turn from Karia, snatches here and there
 of dirges and dances.
                    Bring me my lyre!
 Yet why should I waste my lyre upon this buffoon?
 No. Let me have a castanet girl.
                         Approach,
 Euripidean Muse: embellish thy master's music!
     [*Enter a decaying prostitute, nude; she accompanies the following aria on a pair of large castanets.*

DIONYSOS:
 That Muse never came from Lesbos,[52] Aischylos.

AISCHYLOS:
>   *Halcyons, halcyons,*[53]
>   *Chirruping gossipers on the spume of the wave,*
>   *Ye roscid-wing'd!*
>   *And spi-spi-spiders,*
>   *Tangle-angle-angle-angling*
>   *With threadlittle feet your ingle-dainty webs,*
>   *As the dolphin darts*
>   *Sheer from the surge,*
>   *presaging*
>   *Safe passage to harbour!*
>   *Vineshoots, lacy*
>   *Voles o' the vine!*
>   *Kiss me, darling, I'm*
>   *Coming!*
 You recognize the manner, do you not?

DIONYSOS:
 I do.

THE FROGS

AISCHYLOS:
  And this man dares to laugh at me!
This man, whose poetry apes the twelve positions
of Kyrenê in her bed!
     —Well, that was a lyric example.
Now for a Euripidean monody.
   [*Castanets and flute; the* CHORUS *mimes the following monody:*

Night
  and dreaming dreamless O
   Son of sightless Night[54]
 from
  whát dreaming dream'd
  into my spiritless spirit,
     Sable ghost,
   There is no
 speculation in those eyes:
     Claws acute!
    Beaut-
  y hurts me.
    Virgins:
Siphon the wellsprings off and heat the water!
O friends, friends,
    purloinèd hath been my rooster
      By Glykê.
  Let me wash away this dream.
     Oreads,
 Take her! Seize her, Susan!
    Who's an
Idler here? Not I!
    Worra-worra-working,
  Over a hot loom,
Sp-sp-sp-spinning
   dreamwoofs, dreamwarplets:
And off he wing'd, winging the wind with his wings,
  And left me idle in tears. I know not what they mean.
 O Kretans, offspring of Ida,
Bring your arrows (and bows) and invest my residence!
  And thou, young Artemis, Diktynna: have the
   sense
    To scout thy dogs
    Across the bogs!
      O Hekatê
Daughter of Zeus, ambidextrous flare-flarer,
   Light me to Gly-Gly-Glykê's.
I propose to search her premises, and will do so.

DIONYSOS:
That's enough of the lyric style.
AISCHYLOS:
You are right.
The one thing left is to weigh my verse against his
in the scales. That will decide.
DIONYSOS:
Whatever you say.
[*To the* SERVANTS
Go, one of you, and bring us the cheese-scales:
they're the only thing for weighing poetry.
CHORUS:
I admire the ingenuity   [STROPHE
    Of the artistic mind.
It would not have occurred to me
    That problems of this kind
        Could really be
        So easily
Resolved. If my own brother
        Had told me so,
        I'd have said: "No,
My dear Charles, you're another!"

SCENE X [AGON: ε]

[*A large pair of scales is placed on a block before* DIONYSOS.

DIONYSOS:
Take your places by the scales.
AISCHYLOS *and* EURIPIDES:
All ready!
DIONYSOS:
Each of you hold one of the pans and recite a line,
and don't let go until I say "Cuckoo!"
AISCHYLOS *and* EURIPIDES:
All right.
DIONYSOS:
Begin. Speak your verses into the pans.
EURIPIDES:
I would that the good ship Argo had never sailed![55]
AISCHYLOS:
O stream of Spercheios, where the cattle roam![56]

THE FROGS

DIONYSOS:
  Cuckoo! Let go!
            [*They release the pans;* AISCHYLOS' *drops.*
    Aischylos wins that bout.
EURIPIDES:
  But why?
DIONYSOS:
                Why? He tossed in a whole river,
  like merchants who soak their wool to make it heavier.
  Your line was winged; it flew away.
AISCHYLOS:
                                Try again!
DIONYSOS:
  Hands on the scales!
AISCHYLOS *and* EURIPIDES:
                  We're ready.
DIONYSOS:
                          Begin, Euripides.
EURIPIDES:
  Skill in speech is Persuasion's inner shrine.[57]
AISCHYLOS:
  Death is the sole god who cannot be bought.[58]
DIONYSOS:
  Cuckoo!
            [AISCHYLOS' *pan drops.*
EURIPIDES:
        I don't understand. What happened that time?
DIONYSOS:
  He threw in Death, the heaviest of evils.
EURIPIDES:
  I threw in Persuasion, and made an adorable verse.
DIONYSOS:
  Persuasion's a tricky, bodiless affair.
  Come, look through your plays:
  You must find something solid.
EURIPIDES:
                      Solid? But where?
DIONYSOS:
  Try this:
  Dicing Achilleus rolled a two and a four.[59]
  Take it from there: it's the last chance you'll have.
EURIPIDES:
  In his right hand a cudgel loaded with iron.[60]
AISCHYLOS:
  Chariot upon chariot, corpse upon corpse.[61]

DIONYSOS:
  Beaten again!
EURIPIDES:
           But why?
DIONYSOS:
              In a single line
  he had two chariots and a pair of corpses.
  A hundred Egyptians couldn't lift that verse!
AISCHYLOS:
  That's enough! Let him climb into his scale
  with his wife, his children, Kephisophôn, and all his plays.
  I'll outweigh the whole caboodle with two lines!
       [*The palace door opens. Enter* PLUTO, *crowned, sceptred, escorted by interestingly infernal attendants.*
DIONYSOS:
  Your Majesty *must* help me! How can I be their judge?
  I can't bear the thought of either of them hating me!
  Euripides is *so* sophisticated,
  and Aischylos so rewarding!
PLUTO:
              Then you've wasted your trip.
DIONYSOS:
  And if I give a verdict?
PLUTO:
              Take whichever one wins
  back to earth with you.
DIONYSOS:
              Oh dear. Well, if I must!
       [*He turns to* AISCHYLOS *and* EURIPIDES.
  Now listen carefully to what I'm going to say.
  —I came down here to find a poet. Why?
  To restore the splendour of Dramatic Art
  to the City. And so,
  whichever of you can be of more service to Athens,
  he shall go back with me to the world above
  Tell me, then:
  What is your opinion of Alkibiadês?
  Our unhappy citizens
  "love him, abhor him, and would have him back."
  Tell me what you think.
                    [*A pause*
EURIPIDES:
              I hate a citizen
  slow to aid the State, quick to undermine it,
  server only of self at the public peril.

DIONYSOS:
   Excellent, by Poseidon!
                              —Now, Aischylos?
AISCHYLOS:
   The lion's whelp should not be brought up in the City;
   but if it has been, the people must learn to live with it.
DIONYSOS:
   I *can* not decide! One of them is deep;
   the other, profound.
                              —Another question:
   What is the surest way to rescue Athens?
EURIPIDES:
   I know, and I will tell you.
DIONYSOS:
                              Let me hear it.
EURIPIDES:
   When we put our trust in what is untrustworthy
   and distrust what we should put our trust in—
DIONYSOS:
                                          I don't understand.
   Speak less gnomically, and more clearly.
EURIPIDES:
   If we reject the leaders we follow today
   and follow those whom we reject, we can be saved.
DIONYSOS:
   Aischylos?
AISCHYLOS:
                Who *are* the current leaders?
   Honest men?
DIONYSOS:
                Absurd! Athens always discards them.
AISCHYLOS:
   She prefers bad men?
DIONYSOS:
                        Not really; but they're forced upon her.
AISCHYLOS:
   I see no hope for a State
   that cannot make up its mind between silk and hemp.
DIONYSOS:
   Think of some way, if you hope to see sunlight again!
AISCHYLOS:
   I will tell you as we journey, not in this place.
DIONYSOS:
   No. Let the City have your advice from Hell.
AISCHYLOS:
   Let Athens remember:

The Enemy's land is Athens',[62] and Athens' land
is the Enemy's. The only safety lies in our ships.
DIONYSOS:
Yes... But the dicasts gobble up everything!
PLUTO:
The judgement, come!
DIONYSOS:
        Judgement is yours by right;
but "him I choose o'er whom my heart doth yearn."[63]
EURIPIDES:
Remember, you swore by the gods you would take me back!
DIONYSOS:
"Sworn hath my tongue...";[64] but I choose Aischylos.
EURIPIDES:
Liar and slave! What have you done?
DIONYSOS:
What have I done? Chosen Aischylos. Why not?
EURIPIDES:
You can look me in the eye after this betrayal?
DIONYSOS:
It's no betrayal unless our audience thinks so.[65]
EURIPIDES:
And you will leave me here among the dead?
DIONYSOS:
"Which of us can say that life's not death's twin brother,"[66]
or that breathing's not eating, or that going to bed's not a
 sheep?
       [*Exit* EURIPIDES *indignantly*, L
PLUTO:
And now, Dionysos, you must come into my house.
DIONYSOS [*terrified*]:
           What for?
PLUTO:
For a feast before you leave.
DIONYSOS:
      Oh.
     —Here I come!
  [*All but the* CHORUS *enter the palace.*

CHORUS:
          [ANTISTROPHE 1
  Thrice blessèd is the man who's found
   The true Philosophy!
  Take Aischylos: he's upward bound
   To Earth's felicity.
     His sapience
     And prescience

Restore him to the sunlight.
> His own shall greet
> Him on the street
With loud cries of "You've done right!"

How different is Sokratês　　　　　[ANTISTROPHE 2
　And his sophistic school
Of Tragic Art. There, if you please,
　The smart twist is the rule.
> The Sisters Nine,
> The craft divine,
Languish in clever phrases,
> While tasteless lips
> Pollute with quips
Our placid public places.

ÉXODOS

[*Enter from the house* PLUTO, DIONYSOS, AISCHYLOS

PLUTO:
And so, Aischylos, fare well!
Go back and save our City with your wise art.
Restore our men—there are many!—to their senses.

Here are three gifts for you to distribute in Athens:
this knife for Kleophôn, this halter for
Myrmex and Nikomachos, and this poison
for Archenomos. They'll know how to use them,
and I hope to greet them here soon. If not, they'll feel
the hot brand; yes, and I'll bind the three of them up
with Admiral Adeimantos, old Whitefeather's son,
and fry them on the hottest plates of Hell.

AISCHYLOS:
I will see that it's done.
　　　　　　　　　—Let Sophoklês have my Chair
until I come again, if I ever do.
I name him second among the serious poets.
But as for that quack Euripides,
let him never again hold the Tragic Foundation,
not even if he's elected in spite of himself.

PLUTO:
O ye Initiate: lift high your holy torches
and lead this mighty poet on his way,
singing his music to him as he ascends.

CHORUS:
O spirits of the world below!
　　The poet moves up to the world of light:
May he heal the sick State, fight
The ignoble cowardly inward foe,
　　And bring us peace.
　　　　　　　　　Let Kleophôn and his friends[67]
Disrupt their own lands for their selfish ends!

NOTES

Σ = Scholiast

1. A comic poet, rival of Aristophanes.
2. Dionysos calls himself "son of the Jug" instead of the expected "son of Zeus."
3. The slaves who served at the great naval victory of Arginusai (406) were given their freedom.
4. Dionysos' costume, like his language, is a bizarre combination of the heroic and the effeminate.
5. Parodied from the lost *Oineus* of Euripides.
6. A verse from the *Hippolytos* of Euripides.
7. "From the *Andromachê* [of Euripides]," says Σ; but it is not. Possibly from the lost *Andrómeda*, which has just been mentioned by Dionysos.
8. Participants in the Eleusinian Mysteries, which were celebrated once a year in honour of Demêter and Persephonê. Heraklês himself was admitted to the Minor Mysteries before undertaking his journey to Hadês.
9. The Greek parodies a verse from the lost *Philoktetês* of Euripides [Σ].
10. A beautiful but puzzling statement. In *Elektra* Sophoklês says that the Furies advance with strides of brass, and that is reason enough for attributing a brass leg to the Empûsa. Lucian reports a never-never land where the women have asses' legs. The "manure" may be a fanciful addition on Xanthias' part or a covert reference to his master's present condition.
11. In the original, Dionysos turns to his own priest, who would be sitting officially in the front row of the audience, and begs him to intervene.
12. The story is that the actor Hegelochos muffed a line in the *Orestês* of Euripides: instead of "After the storm I see once more the calm," he proclaimed—by a slip of the tongue almost imperceptible in Greek—"After the storm I see once more the polecat." ⟨note abridged⟩
13. Σ says that pigs were sacrificed to Demêter and Dionysos.
14. The *párodos* is the entrance of the Chorus into the dance-enclosure (*orchêstra*). We have already heard off stage the chanting of the accessory chorus of Frogs and a preliminary strophe and antistrophe by the Chorus itself. Now the Initiates enter, gowned for the infernal counterpart of their solemn annual procession to the earthly Eleusis. As in the *parábasis* (p. 42), to which this may be considered a detached prelude, the poet addresses the audience directly through his Chorus.
15. According to their jealous neighbours, the inhabitants of Korinth could never forget that they lived in "God's City." Xanthias thinks Dionysos has a comparable obsession with baggage.

16. *Verba tragica,* as Fielding would say. The whole passage is a glorious parody of the Inflated Manner.

17. Ritual phrase in making libation.

18. Both Heraklês and Dionysos were sons of Zeus by mortal mothers. This reference to the human parent rather than to the divine is pleasantly illogical.

19. Plathanê and her unnamed friend are *pandokeútriai*—that is to say, "hostesses" in a public place of refreshment. Since they are of low (though not servile) condition, their interests are represented by professional patrons—in Hadês the demagogues Kleôn and Hyperbolos.

20. "Names of barbarian archers" [Σ]. The police force of Athens was composed largely of Skythian bowmen.

21. Obviously an attempt to twist "Oooh! Oooh!" into a cry of delight; but the remark is inane, even for Dionysos, and I join the commentators in failing to understand it.

22. Dionysos' "Oh Apollo!" is a cordial yelp of pain, and he tries to save the situation by tacking on a fragment of poetry. According to Σ, the verse is by Ananios, not Hipponax. Is Aristophanes confused? or Dionysos? or Σ?

23. From *Laokoön,* a lost play by Sophoklês.

24. *Parábasis* is the technical term for the interlude when the poet suspends the action of his play and addresses the audience through the Chorus. It is a moment of great topical interest, though not always of great art; and like all topicalities—the joking of the Porter in *Macbeth,* for instance—it can be heavy going for readers who have lost the key. In this *parábasis* Aristophanes is concerned with the deteriorating War and the resultant political recriminations and retaliations in Athens. He urges tolerance in the face of the common danger and expresses hope for a victorious peace, but there is a sense of catastrophe throughout and the ending of the address is particularly ominous.

25. Kleophôn's mother, at least, came from Thrace; consequently Aristophanes ridicules him as a barbarian, "split-tongued," and associates him with the horrible Tereus-Philomela-Prognê legend. At the time of *Frogs* Kleophôn was indeed in danger, and a year later he was convicted on charges involving his citizenship and put to death. But the reasons for Aristophanes' animosity are deeper. The demagogue had come to power in 410 after a series of convulsive governmental changes and had re-established some of the abuses of the discredited old régime. He was, moreover, immovably opposed to the repeated peace overtures of Sparta—overtures which Aristophanes perhaps regarded as offering a practical and honourable solution to a desperate problem.

26. This Phrynichos was a public official who had been involved in an unsuccessful attempt to restore the oligarchy of the Four Hundred. Later, because of his ambiguous attitude towards Sparta, he was formally disgraced and informally assassinated (410).

27. Plataia had been an ally of Athens since the Persian Wars and in 421 the Plataians were granted honorary Athenian citizenship. In 406 the Athenian slaves who fought at Arginusai were freed. Aristophanes approves of the emancipation but finds it hard that slaves should be better treated than many citizens in disfavour only for adherence to the wrong political party.

28. Parody of a verse by Iôn of Chios [Σ].

29. As god of the theatre Dionysos is a logical choice for umpire.

30. Parody of a verse from an unknown lost play by Euripides. According to his enemies, Euripides' mother conducted a vegetable-&-herb shop.

31. Another parody of Euripides; the source is lost.

32. Aristophanes repeatedly condemns Euripides for bringing deformed or down-at-the-heels characters onto the stage.

33. These monodies accompanied by dancing mimes were not the invention of Euripides, but he seems to have used them to excess.

34. Not a translation, but a pass at a comparable effect. The Greek says "knock your *Telephos* out of your head," the title of a (lost) tragedy being substituted for the expected word "brains."

35. Parody of a passage in the *Hippolytos* of Euripides.

36. This strange device was a ship's figurehead in the (lost) *Myrmidons* of Aischylos.

37. Σ says that this was the first line of Aischylos' *Myrmidons*.

38. The opening of Aischylos' *Choephoroi*. The lines owe their survival to this citation by Aristophanes.

39. As part of the funeral ritual, the name of the dead was called out three times.

40. Opening of the *Antigonê* of Euripides [Σ].

41. This jug (*óstrakon*) will surprise readers of Sophoklês. It seems to be a bit of Athenian local colour: thus, in *Thesmophoriazûsai* Aristophanes had a midwife carrying a baby in an earthen pot.

42. From an unknown play, probably by Euripides. Σ and the later commentators are at a loss.

43. Beginning of the *Hypsipylê* of Euripides, now lost. The third line ends: "with the Delphic virgins."

44. Beginning of the lost *Sthenoboia* of Euripides [Σ]. The third line ends: "tills the rich plain."

45. "Opening of the second *Phrixos* of Euripides. The rest of the [second] line: 'came to the Theban plain.'" [Σ]

46. Beginning of the *Iphigeneia in Tauris* of Euripides. "The rest of the [second] line is: 'married Oinomaos' lass.'" [Σ]

47. From the prologue to Euripides' lost *Meleagros*. The original conclusion: "no off'ring made / to Artemis" [Σ]. Aristotle in an absent moment attributed the passage to Sophoklês.

48. Beginning of the lost *Sage Melanippê* of Euripides [Σ]. The verse is complete.

49. Euripides composes an absurd "chorus" of verses parodied from here and there in Aischylos and punctuated by a ridiculous question.

50. Another kind of burlesque. This time the Aischylean lines are interrupted by the nonsense refrain "phlattothrattophlattothrát!" which Dionysos affects to mistake for a battle slogan.

51. Tragic poet; a "sweet melodist," according to Σ. Except for fragments his work is lost, but Aischylos seems to have been indebted to him for certain ideas in *Persians* and speaks of him with reserve.

52. Sappho and her girls may have been maligned, as recent scholarship contends, but the Lesbian lie is old enough to have created a perverse verb in Greek that accounts for the under-meaning here.

53. Another choral parody, this time in the manner of Euripides. The outlandish "new" diction is burlesqued, and the reduplicated syllables constitute an attack upon Euripides' melodic innovations.

54. This burlesque of the "Kretan arias" mentioned on p. 49 is an almost hysterically elaborated affair, as though Aristophanes had decided to expose in one song all the hateful Euripidean tricks. The "plot," if any exists, seems to concern a woman who has fallen asleep at her loom and waked to discover that a neighbour, Glykê, has stolen a cock.

55. First line of the *Medea* of Euripides.

56. "From the [lost] *Philoktetês* of Aischylos." [Σ]

57. "From the *Antigonê* of Euripides." [Σ]

58. "From the [lost] *Niobê* of Aischylos." [Σ]

59. From an unknown play, probably by Euripides.

60. From Euripides' *Meleagros*.

61. "From the [lost] *Glaukos* of Aischylos." [Σ]

62. This advice, as Σ notes, is taken from Periklês. Dionysos retorts that it is all very well to talk about naval expansion, but the officials are bankrupting the treasury.

63. Possibly from Euripides.

64. See note 6.

65. The sentiment is parodied from the lost *Aiolos* of Euripides: "What's disgrace, if our friends do not think it so?"

66. "From the *Polyïdos* of Euripides." [Σ] Van Leeuwen observes that the next line is absurd. He is right.

67. See note 25.

Plato

c. 429–347 B.C.

Plato lived in the twilight of the High Classical period, when the political consensus of Periclean Athens was beginning to crumble. His family was distinguished, and his youth was occupied with various poetic attempts. He aspired at one point to be a statesman but soon grew disillusioned and concluded that there would be no hope for the polis (*the Greek city-state*) until the philosophers became rulers or the rulers philosophers.

At the age of about twenty, Plato gave up both poetry and politics after coming into the philosophic orbit of Socrates, an experience that seems to have entirely transformed his life. For the next several years he studied with Socrates. Plato's own relatives led the oligarchic revolution of 404, though it is unclear what role he himself played. By 399 the democracy had been restored, and its leaders convicted Socrates, who had been influential among young aristocrats, of corrupting the youth of Athens. He was put to death the same year.

After Socrates' execution, Plato left Athens for Megara, where he studied at the school of Euclid. He then traveled throughout the Mediterranean, meeting the Italian Pythagoreans in Sicily, and possibly studying the mathematical and historical lore of the priests of Egypt. On his return to Athens around 386, his friends bought him a suburban olive grove named after the local hero Academus, and Plato devoted most of the next forty years to teaching there. The Academy became the center of Greek intellectual activity during his lifetime.

Plato made one further attempt to enter the political arena in order to realize the ideal of the philosopher-king. In 367 his old friend Dion of Syracuse invited him to Sicily to transform the new king, Dionysius II, into the model Platonic ruler. The effort, however, ended in failure when Dionysius became jealous of the friendship between Plato and Dion.

Plato is uniformly suspicious of the poetic arts, constantly setting them in opposition to the philosophic virtues of rationality. In the Republic *he is concerned to eliminate from the education of the young the "lies" that the poets, particularly Homer, tell about the gods. By presenting the foibles of the gods, says Plato, the poets undermine the morality of the young.

A more fundamental criticism, in the Platonic system, is that *poetry in its essence represents a turning away from truth. Truth, in the Platonic dialogues, inheres in the Ideal Forms. These Ideas are somehow detached from the sensual world, where the objects that we perceive constitute copies of that higher world. Plato locates artistic representations even further away from the Ideas, making them copies of copies. This denigration of art relies upon the claim that art is always mimetic, that it always imitates something else.*

Plato's system favors unity over multiplicity and the supersensuous world over the sensuous, since knowledge for Plato is always knowledge of the One, which is the Idea. In the Phaedrus, *for instance, Socrates expresses a preference for the spoken word over the written, primarily because it is more difficult to preserve a single meaning for the written word once the author is absent. The philosopher, says Plato, concentrates on unity, while the poet and the audience become lost in a multiplicity of mere images. This opposition allows Plato to separate art and philosophy radically. Philosophy is unity, self-knowledge, the supersensual, while art is multiplicity, ecstasy, the sensual. Art, then, represents a barrier to reason, and as such it is one of the greatest dangers to a state governed by reason. Thus when Plato discusses the composition of the state in the* Republic, *he severely delimits the function of the artist. It is true that the more "realistic" state proposed in the* Laws *foresees a positive role for poetry, but even here judges strictly regulate the circulation of poetry.*

Plato's Ion *is an important text for the subsequent development of literary criticism. In conversation with Ion, a rhapsode (professional reciter of poetry), Socrates seems to denigrate him, and by extension all poetry, as irrational. However, the dialogue is sufficiently ambiguous that the later Neoplatonists were able to reinterpret it as a defense of the "inspired" nature of poetry.*

The selections from Plato, translated by Benjamin Jowett, are reprinted by permission of Oxford University Press from The Dialogues of Plato, *trans. Benjamin Jowett, 4th ed. (Oxford, 1953). The footnotes, unless otherwise indicated, are reprinted by permission of the publisher from Alex Preminger et al., eds.,* Classical and Medieval Literary Criticism: Translations and Interpretations *(New York: Frederick Ungar Publishing Co., 1974).*

FROM
Phaedrus

SOCRATES. I dare say that you are thoroughly at home in the views of Tisias. Now we have one more thing to ask him. Does he not define probability to be that which the many think?

PHAEDRUS. Certainly, he does.

SOC. I believe that he has a clever and ingenious case of this sort: He supposes a feeble and valiant man to have assaulted a strong and cowardly one, and to have robbed him of his coat or of something or other; he is brought into court, and then Tisias says that both parties should tell lies: the coward should say that he was assaulted by more men than one; the other should prove that they were alone, and should argue thus: "How could a weak man like me have assaulted a strong man like him?" The complainant will not like to confess his own cowardice, and will therefore invent some other lie which his adversary will thus gain an opportunity of refuting. And there are other devices of the same kind which have a place in the system. Am I not right, Phaedrus?

PHAEDR. Certainly.

SOC. Bless me, what a wonderfully mysterious art is this which Tisias or some other gentleman, in whatever name or country he rejoices, has discovered. Shall we say a word to him or not?

PHAEDR. What shall we say to him?

SOC. Let us tell him that, before he appeared, you and I were saying that the probability of which he speaks was engendered in the minds of the many by the likeness of the truth, and we had just been affirming that he who knew the truth would always know best how to discover the resemblances of the truth. If he has anything else to say about the art of speaking we should like to hear him; but if not, we are satisfied with the view recently expressed, that unless a man estimates the various characters of his hearers and is able to divide all things into classes and to comprehend every one under single ideas, he will never be a skillful rhetorician even within the limits of human power. And this skill he will not attain without a great deal of trouble, which a good man ought to undergo, not for the sake of speaking and acting before men, but in order that he may be able to say what is acceptable to God and always to act acceptably to Him as far as in him lies; for there is a saying of wiser men than ourselves, that a man of sense should not try to please his fellow servants (at least this should not be his first object) but his good and noble masters; (274) and therefore, Tisias, if the way is long and circuitous, marvel not at this, for, where the end is great, there we may take the longer road, but not for lesser ends such as yours. However, our argument says that even these are best secured as the consequence of higher aims.

PHAEDR. I think, Socrates, that this is admirable, if only practicable.

SOC. But provided one's aim is honorable, so is any ill success which may ensue.

PHAEDR. True.

SOC. Enough appears to have been said by us of a true and false art of speaking.

PHAEDR. Certainly.

SOC. But there is something yet to be said of propriety and impropriety of writing.

PHAEDR. Yes.

SOC. Do you know how you can speak or act about rhetoric in a manner which will be acceptable to God?

PHAEDR. No, indeed, Do you?

SOC. I have heard a tradition of the ancients, whether true or not they only know; although if we had found the truth ourselves, do you think that we should care much about the opinions of men?

PHAEDR. Your question needs no answer; but simply tell me what you say that you have heard.

SOC. At the Egyptian city of Naucratis there was a famous old god whose name was Theuth; the bird which is called the Ibis is sacred to him, and he was the inventor of many arts, such as arithmetic and calculation and geometry and astronomy as well as draughts and dice, but his great discovery was the use of letters. Now in those days [the god] Thamus was the king of the whole country of Egypt; and he dwelt in that great city of Upper Egypt which the Hellenes call Egyptian Thebes, and the god himself is called by them Ammon. To him came Theuth and showed his inventions, desiring that the other Egyptians might be allowed to have the benefit of them; he enumerated them, and Thamus inquired about their several uses, and praised some of them and censured others, as he approved or disapproved of them. It would take a long time to repeat all that Thamus said to Theuth in praise or blame of the various arts. But when they came to letters, Theuth said: O king, here is a study which will make the Egyptians wiser and give them better memories; it is a specific both for the memory and for the wit. Thamus replied: O most ingenious Theuth, the parent or inventor of an art is not always the best judge of the utility or inutility of his own inventions to the users of them. (275) And in this instance, you who are the father of letters, from a paternal love of your own children have been led to attribute to them a quality which they cannot have; for this discovery of yours will create forgetfulness in the learners' souls, because they will not use their memories; they will trust to the external written characters and not remember of themselves. And so the specific which you have discovered is an aid not to memory, but to reminiscence. As for wisdom, it is the reputation, not the reality, that you have to offer to those who learn from you; they will have heard many things and yet received no teaching; they will appear to be omniscient and will generally know nothing; they will be tiresome company, having acquired not wisdom, but the show of wisdom.

PHAEDR. Yes, Socrates, you can easily invent tales of Egypt, or of any other country.

SOC. There was a tradition in the temple of Dodona [a sanctuary and oracular shrine of Zeus, located in the mountains of Epirus] that oaks first gave prophetic utterances. The men of old, far simpler than you sophisticated young men, deemed that if they heard the truth even from "oak or rock," it was enough; whereas you seem to consider not whether a thing is or is not true, but who the speaker is and from what country the tale comes.

PHAEDR. I acknowledge the justice of your rebuke; and I think that the Theban is right in his view about letters.

SOC. He would be a very simple person, and quite a stranger to the oracles of Thamus or Ammon, who should suppose that he had left his "Art" in writings or who should accept such an inheritance in the hope that the written word would give anything intelligible or certain; or who deemed that writing could be any more than a reminder to one who already knows the subject.

PHAEDR. That is most true.

SOC. I cannot help feeling, Phaedrus, that writing has one grave fault in common with painting; for the creations of the painter have the attitude of life, and yet if you ask them a question they preserve a solemn silence. And the same may be said of books. You would imagine that they had intelligence, but if you require any explanation of something that has been said, they preserve one unvarying meaning. And when they have been once written down they are tumbled about anywhere, all alike, among those who understand them and among strangers, and do not know to whom they should or should not reply: and, if they are maltreated or abused, they have no parent to protect them; for the book cannot protect or defend itself.

PHAEDR. That again is most true.

SOC. Is there not another kind of word or speech far better than this, and having far greater power—a son of the same family, but lawfully begotten?

PHAEDR. Whom do you mean, and what is his origin?

SOC. I mean an intelligent word graven in the soul of the learner, which can defend itself, and knows with whom to speak and with whom to be silent.

PHAEDR. You mean the living word of knowledge which has a soul, and of which the written word is properly no more than an image?

SOC. Yes, of course that is what I mean. And now may I be allowed to ask you a question?: Would a husbandman, who is a man of sense, take seeds which he values and which he wishes to bear fruit, and in sober seriousness plant them during the heat of summer, in some garden of Adonis, that he may rejoice when he sees them in eight days appearing in beauty? At least he would do so, if at all, only for the sake of amusement and for show. But when he is in earnest he employs his art of husbandry and sows in fitting soil, and is satisfied if in eight months the seeds which he has sown arrive at perfection?

PHAEDR. Yes, Socrates, that will be his way when he is in earnest; he might act otherwise for the reasons which you give.

SOC. And can we suppose that he who knows the just and good and honorable has less understanding than the husbandman about his own seeds?

PHAEDR. Certainly not.

SOC. Then he will not seriously incline to "write" his thoughts "in water" with pen and ink, sowing words which can neither speak for themselves nor teach the truth adequately to others.

PHAEDR. No, that is not likely.

SOC. No, that is not likely—in the garden of letters he will sow and plant, but only for the sake of recreation and amusement; he will write them down as memorials to be treasured against the forgetfulness of old age, by himself, or by any other man who is treading the same path. He will rejoice in beholding their tender growth; and while others are refreshing their souls with banqueting and the like, this will be the pastime in which his days are spent.

PHAEDR. A pastime, Socrates, as noble as the other is ignoble, the pastime of a man who can be amused by serious talk and can discourse merrily about justice and the like.

SOC. True, Phaedrus. But nobler far is the serious pursuit of the dialectician, who, finding a congenial soul, by the help of science sows and plants therein words which are able to defend themselves and him who planted them, (277) and are not unfruitful, but have in them a seed which others brought up in different soils render immortal, making the possessors of it happy to the utmost extent of human happiness.

PHAEDR. Far nobler, certainly.

SOC. And now at last, Phaedrus, having agreed upon this, we may decide the original question.

PHAEDR. What question was that?

SOC. I mean those problems, in trying to solve which we have made our way hither; we wished to examine the censure passed on Lysias for his professional speech-writing, and to distinguish the speech composed with art from that which is composed without art. And I think that we have now pretty well distinguished the artistic from its opposite.

PHAEDR. Yes, I thought so, but I wish that you would repeat what was said.

SOC. Until a man knows the truth of the several particulars of which he is writing or speaking, and is able to define them as they are, and having defined them again to divide them until they can be no longer divided; and until in like manner he is able to discern the nature of the soul, and discover the different modes of discourse which are adapted to different natures, and to arrange and dispose them in such a way that the simple form of speech may be addressed to the simpler nature, and the complex form, with many variations of key, to the more complex nature—until he has accomplished all this, he will be unable to handle arguments according to rules of art, as far as their nature allows them to be subjected to art, either for the purpose of teaching or persuading;—such is the view which is implied in the whole preceding argument.

PHAEDR. Yes, that was our view, certainly.

SOC. Secondly, as to the censure which was passed on the speaking or writing of discourses, and when they might be rightly or wrongly censured—did not our previous arguments show—?

PHAEDR. Show what?

SOC. That whether Lysias or any other writer that ever was or will be, whether private man or statesman, proposes laws and so becomes the author of a political treatise, fancying that there is any great certainty and clearness in his performance, the fact of his so writing is only a disgrace to him, whatever men may say. For not to know the nature of justice and injustice, and good and evil, and not to be able to distinguish the dream from the reality, cannot in truth be otherwise than disgraceful to him, even though he have the applause of the whole world.

PHAEDR. Certainly.

SOC. But he who thinks that in the written word, whatever its subject, there is necessarily much which is not serious, and that no discourse worthy of study has ever yet been written in poetry or prose, and that spoken ones are no better if, like the recitation of rhapsodes, they are delivered for the sake of persuasion, and not with any view to criticism or instruction; (278) and who thinks that even the best of writings are but a memorandum for those who know, and that only in principles of justice and goodness and nobility taught and communicated orally for the sake of instruction and graven in the soul, which is the true way of writing, is there clearness and perfection and seriousness, and that such principles should be deemed a man's own and his legitimate offspring;—being, in the first place, the word which he finds in his own bosom; secondly, the brethren and descendants and relations of his idea which have been duly implanted by him in the souls of others;—and who cares for them and no others—this is the right sort of man; and you and I, Phaedrus, would pray that we may become like him.

PHAEDR. This is most assuredly my desire and prayer.

SOC. And now the play is played out; and of rhetoric enough. Go and tell Lysias that to the fountain and school of the Nymphs we went down, and were bidden by them to convey a message to him and to other composers of speeches—to Homer and other writers of poems, whether set to music or not; and to Solon and others who have composed writings in the form of political discourses which they would term laws—to all of them we are to say that if their compositions are based on knowledge of the truth, and they can defend or prove them, when they are put to the test, by spoken arguments, which leave their writings poor in comparison of them, then they are to be called, not only poets, orators, legislators, but are worthy of a higher name, befitting the serious pursuit of their life.

PHAEDR. What name would you assign to them?

SOC. Wise, I may not call them; for that is a great name which belongs to God alone,—lovers of wisdom or philosophers is their modest and befitting title.

PHAEDR. Very suitable.

SOC. And he who cannot rise above his own compilations and compositions, which he has been long patching and piecing, adding some and taking away some, may be justly called poet or speech-maker or law-maker.

Ion

530 SOCRATES. Welcome, Ion. Are you from your native city of Ephesus?

ION. No, Socrates; but from Epidaurus, where I attended the festival of Aesculapius.

SOC. Indeed! Do the Epidaurians have a contest of rhapsodes[1] in his honor?

ION. O yes; and of other kinds of music.

SOC. And were you one of the competitors—and did you succeed?

ION. I—we—obtained the first prize of all, Socrates.

SOC. Well done; now we must win another victory, at the Panathenaea.[2]

ION. It shall be so, please heaven.

SOC. I have often envied the profession of a rhapsode, Ion; for it is a part of your art to wear fine clothes and to look as beautiful as you can, while at the same time you are obliged to be continually in the company of many good poets, and especially of Homer, who is the best and most divine of them, and to understand his mind, and not merely learn his words by rote; all this is a thing greatly to be envied. I am sure that no man can become a good rhapsode who does not understand the meaning of the poet. For the rhapsode ought to interpret the mind of the poet to his hearers, but how can he interpret him well unless he knows what he means? All this is much to be envied, I repeat.

ION. Very true, Socrates; interpretation has certainly been the most laborious part of my art; and I believe myself able to speak about Homer better than any man; and that neither Metrodorus of Lampsacus, nor Stesimbrotus of Thasos, nor Glaucon, nor anyone else who ever was, had as good ideas about Homer as I have, or as many.

SOC. I am glad to hear you say so, Ion; I see that you will not refuse to acquaint me with them.

ION. Certainly, Socrates; and you really ought to hear how exquisitely I display the beauties of Homer. I think that the Homeridae should give me a golden crown.[3]

SOC. I shall take an opportunity of hearing your embellishments of him at some other time. (531) But just now I should like to ask you a question: Does your art extend to Hesiod and Archilochus, or to Homer only?

ION. To Homer only; he is in himself quite enough.

SOC. Are there any things about which Homer and Hesiod agree?

ION. Yes; in my opinion there are a good many.

SOC. And can you interpret what Homer says about these matters better than what Hesiod says?

ION. I can interpret them equally well, Socrates, where they agree.

SOC. But what about matters in which they do not agree? For example, about divination of which both Homer and Hesiod have something to say—

ION. Very true.

SOC. Would you or a good prophet be a better interpreter of what these two poets say about divination, not only when they agree, but when they disagree?

ION. A prophet.

SOC. And if you were a prophet, and could interpret them where they agree, would you not know how to interpret them also where they disagree?

ION. Clearly.

SOC. But how did you come to have this skill about Homer only, and not about Hesiod or the other poets? Does not Homer speak of the same themes which all other poets handle? Is not war his great argument? And does he not speak of human society and of intercourse of men, good and bad, skilled and unskilled, and of the gods conversing with one another and with mankind, and about what happens in heaven and in the world below, and the generations of gods and heroes? Are not these the themes of which Homer sings?

ION. Very true, Socrates.

SOC. And do not the other poets sing of the same?

ION. Yes, Socrates; but not in the same way as Homer.

SOC. What, in a worse way?

ION. Yes, in a far worse.

SOC. And Homer in a better way?

ION. He is incomparably better.

SOC. And yet surely, my dear friend Ion, where many people are discussing numbers, and one speaks better than the rest, there is somebody who can judge which of them is the good speaker?

ION. Yes.

SOC. And he who judges of the good will be the same as he who judges of the bad speakers?

ION. The same.

SOC. One who knows the science of arithmetic?

ION. Yes.

SOC. Or again, if many persons are discussing the wholesomeness of food, and one speaks better than the rest, will he who recognizes the better speaker be a different person from him who recognizes the worse, or the same?

ION. Clearly the same.

SOC. And who is he, and what is his name?

ION. The physician.

SOC. And speaking generally, in all discussions in which the subject is the same and many men are speaking, will not he who knows the good know the bad speaker also? (532) For obviously if he does not know the bad, neither will he know the good, when the same topic is being discussed.

ION. True.

SOC. We find, in fact, that the same person is skillful in both?

ION. Yes.

SOC. And you say that Homer and the other poets, such as Hesiod and Archilochus, speak of the same things, although not in the same way; but the one speaks well and the other not so well?

ION. Yes; and I am right in saying so.

SOC. And if you know the good speaker, you ought also to know the inferior speakers to be inferior?

ION. It would seem so.

soc. Then, my dear friend, can I be mistaken in saying that Ion is equally skilled in Homer and in other poets, since he himself acknowledges that the same person will be a good judge of all those who speak of the same things; and that almost all poets do speak of the same things?

ION. Why then, Socrates, do I lose attention and have absolutely no ideas of the least value and practically fall asleep when anyone speaks of any other poet; but when Homer is mentioned, I wake up at once and am all attention and have plenty to say?

soc. The reason, my friend, is not hard to guess. No one can fail to see that you speak of Homer without any art or knowledge. If you were able to speak of him by rules of art, you would have been able to speak of all other poets; for poetry is a whole.

ION. Yes.

soc. And when anyone acquires any other art as a whole, the same may be said of them. Would you like me to explain my meaning, Ion?

ION. Yes, indeed, Socrates; I very much wish that you would: for I love to hear you wise men talk.

soc. O that we were wise, Ion, and that you could truly call us so; but you rhapsodes and actors, and the poets whose verses you sing, are wise; whereas I am a common man, who only speak the truth. For consider what a very commonplace and trivial thing is this which I have said—a thing which any man might say: that when a man has acquired a knowledge of a whole art, the inquiry into good and bad is one and the same. Let us consider this matter; is not the art of painting a whole?

ION. Yes.

soc. And there are and have been many painters good and bad?

ION. Yes.

soc. And did you ever know anyone who was skillful in pointing out the excellences and defects of Polygnotus the son of Aglaophon, but incapable of criticizing other painters; (533) and when the work of any other painter was produced, went to sleep and was at a loss, and had no ideas; but when he had to give his opinion about Polygnotus, or whoever the painter might be, and about him only, woke up and was attentive and had plenty to say?

ION. No indeed, I have never known such a person.

soc. Or take sculpture—did you ever know of anyone who was skillful in expounding the merits of Daedalus the son of Metion, or of Epeius the son of Panopeus, or of Theodorus the Samian, or of any individual sculptor; but when the works of sculptors in general were produced, was at a loss and went to sleep and had nothing to say?

ION. No indeed; no more than the other.

soc. And if I am not mistaken, you never met with anyone among flute-players or harp-players or singers to the harp or rhapsodes who was able to discourse of Olympus or Thamyras or Orpheus, or Phemius the rhapsode of Ithaca, but was at a loss when he came to speak of Ion of Ephesus, and had no notion of his merits or defects?

ION. I cannot deny what you say, Socrates. Nevertheless I am conscious in my own self, and the world agrees with me, that I do speak better and have more to say about Homer than any other man; but I do not speak equally well about others. After all, there must be some reason for this; what is it?

soc. I see the reason, Ion; and I will proceed to explain to you what I imagine it to be. The gift which you possess of speaking excellently about Homer is not an art, but, as I was just saying, an inspiration; there is a divinity moving you, like that contained in the stone which Euripides calls a magnet, but which is commonly known as the stone of Heraclea. This stone not only attracts iron rings, but also imparts to them a similar power of attracting other rings; and sometimes you may see a number of pieces of iron and rings suspended from one another so as to form quite a long chain: and all of them derive their power of suspension from the original stone. In like manner the Muse first of all inspires men herself; and from these inspired persons a chain of other persons is suspended, who take the inspiration. For all good poets, epic as well as lyric, compose their beautiful poems not by art, but because they are inspired and possessed. (534) And as the Corybantian revelers[4] when they dance are not in their right mind, so the lyric poets are not in their right mind when they are composing their beautiful strains: but when falling under the power of music and meter they are inspired and possessed; like Bacchic maidens who draw milk and honey from the rivers when they are under the influence of Dionysus but not when they are in their right mind. And the soul of the lyric poet does the same, as they themselves say; for they tell us that they bring songs from honeyed fountains, culling them out of the gardens and dells of the Muses; they, like the bees, winging their way from flower to flower. And this is true. For the poet is a light and winged and holy thing, and there is no invention in him until he has been inspired and is out of his senses, and reason is no longer in him: no man, while he retains that faculty, has the oracular gift of poetry.

Many are the noble words in which poets speak concerning the actions of men; but like yourself when speaking about Homer, they do not speak of them by any rules of art: they are simply inspired to utter that to which the Muse impels them, and that only; and when inspired, one of them will make dithyrambs,[5] another hymns of praise, another choral strains, another epic or iambic verses, but not one of them is of any account in the other kinds. For not by art does the poet sing, but by power divine; had he learned by rules of art, he would have known how to speak not of one theme only, but of all; and therefore God takes away reason from poets, and uses them as his ministers, as he also uses the pronouncers of oracles and holy prophets, in order that we who hear them may know them to be speaking not of themselves, who utter these priceless words while bereft of reason, but that God himself is the speaker, and that through them he is addressing us. And Tynnichus the Chalcidian affords a striking instance of what I am saying: he wrote no poem that anyone would care to remember but the famous paean[6] which is in everyone's mouth, one of the finest lyric poems ever written, simply an invention of the Muses, as he himself says. For in this way God would seem to demonstrate to us and not to allow us to doubt that these beautiful poems are not human, nor the work of man, but divine and the work of God; and that the poets are only the interpreters of the gods by whom they are severally possessed. (535) Was not this the lesson which God intended to teach when by the mouth of the worst of poets he sang the best of songs? Am I not right, Ion?

ION. Yes, indeed, Socrates, I feel that you are; for your words touch my soul, and I am persuaded that in these works the good poets, under divine inspiration, interpret to us the voice of the gods.

SOC. And you rhapsodists are the interpreters of the poets?

ION. There again you are right.

SOC. Then you are the interpreters of interpreters?

ION. Precisely.

SOC. I wish you would frankly tell me, Ion, what I am going to ask of you: When you produce the greatest effect upon the audience in the recitation of some striking passage, such as the apparition of Odysseus leaping forth on the floor, recognized by the suitors and shaking out his arrows at his feet, or the description of Achilles springing upon Hector, or the sorrows of Andromache, Hecuba, or Priam—are you in your right mind? Are you not carried out of yourself, and does not your soul in an ecstasy seem to be among the persons or places of which you are speaking, whether they are in Ithaca or in Troy or whatever may be the scene of the poem?

ION. That proof strikes home to me, Socrates. For I must frankly confess that at the tale of pity my eyes are filled with tears, and when I speak of horrors, my hair stands on end and my heart throbs.

SOC. Well, Ion, and what are we to say of a man who at a sacrifice or festival, when he is dressed in an embroidered robe, and has golden crowns upon his head, of which nobody has robbed him, appears weeping or panic-stricken in the presence of more than twenty thousand friendly faces, when there is no one despoiling or wronging him—is he in his right mind or is he not?

ION. No indeed, Socrates, I must say that, strictly speaking, he is not in his right mind.

SOC. And are you aware that you produce similar effects on most of the spectators?

ION. Only too well; for I look down upon them from the stage, and behold the various emotions of pity, wonder, sternness, stamped upon their countenances when I am speaking: and I am obliged to give my very best attention to them; for if I make them cry I myself shall laugh, and if I make them laugh I myself shall cry, when the time of payment arrives.

SOC. Do you know that the spectator is the last of the rings which, as I am saying, receive the power of the original magnet from one another? The rhapsode like yourself and the actor are intermediate links, and the poet himself is the first of them. (536) Through all these God sways the souls of men in any direction which He pleases, causing each link to communicate the power to the next. Thus there is a vast chain of dancers and masters and undermasters of choruses, who are suspended, as if from the stone, at the side of the rings which hang down from the Muse. And every poet has some Muse from whom he is suspended, and by whom he is said to be possessed, which is nearly the same thing; for he is taken hold of. And from these first rings, which are the poets, depend others, some deriving their inspiration from Orpheus, others from Musaeus; but the greater number are possessed and held by Homer. Of whom, Ion, you are one, and are possessed by Homer; and when anyone repeats the words of another poet you go to sleep, and know not what to say; but when anyone recites a strain of Homer you wake up in a moment, and your soul leaps within you, and you have plenty to say; for not by art or knowledge about Homer do you say what you say, but by divine inspiration and by possession; just as the Corybantian revelers too have a quick perception of that strain only which is appropriated to the god by whom they are possessed, and have plenty of dances and words for that, but take no heed of any other. And you, Ion, when the name of Homer is mentioned have plenty to say, and have nothing to say of others. You ask, "Why is this?" The answer is that your skill in the praise of Homer comes not from art but from divine inspiration.

ION. That is good, Socrates; and yet I doubt whether you will ever have eloquence enough to persuade me that I praise Homer only when I am mad and possessed; and if you could hear me speak of him I am sure you would never think this to be the case.

SOC. I should like very much to hear you, but not until you have answered a question which I have to ask. On what part of Homer do you speak well?—not surely about every part?

ION. There is no part, Socrates, about which I do not speak well: of that I can assure you.

SOC. Surely not about things in Homer of which you have no knowledge?

ION. And what is there in Homer of which I have no knowledge?

SOC. Why, does not Homer speak in many passages about arts? For example, about driving; if I can only remember the lines I will repeat them.

ION. I remember, and will repeat them.

SOC. Tell me then, what Nestor says to Antilochus, his son, where he bids him be careful of the turn at the horse-race in honor of Patroclus.

ION. "Bend gently," he says, "in the polished chariot to the left of them, and urge the horse on the right hand with whip and voice; and slacken the rein. And when you are at the goal, let the left horse draw near, so that the nave of the well-wrought wheel may appear to graze the extremity; but have a care not to touch the stone."[7]

SOC. Enough. Now, Ion, will the charioteer or the physician be the better judge of the propriety of these lines?

ION. The charioteer, clearly.

SOC. And will the reason be that this is his art, or will there be any other reason?

ION. No, that will be the reason.

SOC. And every art is appointed by God to have knowledge of a certain work; for that which we know by the art of the pilot we shall not succeed in knowing also by the art of medicine?

ION. Certainly not.

SOC. Nor shall we know by the art of the carpenter that which we know by the art of medicine?

ION. Certainly not.

SOC. And this is true of all the arts—that which we know with one art we shall not know with the other? But let me ask a prior question: You admit that there are differences of arts?

ION. Yes.

SOC. You would argue, as I should, that if there are two kinds of knowledge, dealing with different things, these can be called different arts?

ION. Yes.

SOC. Yes, surely; for if the object of knowledge were the same, there would be no meaning in saying that the arts were different—since they both gave the same knowledge. For example, I know that here are five fingers, and you know the same. And if I were to ask whether I and you became acquainted with this fact by the help of the same art of arithmetic, you would acknowledge that we did?

ION. Yes.

SOC. Tell me, then, what I was intending to ask you—whether in your opinion this holds universally? If two arts are the same, must not they necessarily have the same objects? And if one differs from another, must it not be because the object is different?

ION. That is my opinion, Socrates.

SOC. Then he who has no knowledge of a particular art will have no right judgment of the precepts and practice of that art?

ION. Very true.

SOC. Then which will be the better judge of the lines which you were reciting from Homer, you or the charioteer?

ION. The charioteer.

SOC. Why, yes, because you are a rhapsode and not a charioteer.

ION. Yes.

SOC. And the art of the rhapsode is different from that of the charioteer?

ION. Yes.

SOC. And if a different knowledge, then a knowledge of different matters?

ION. True.

SOC. You know the passage in which Hecamede, the concubine of Nestor, is described as giving to the wounded Machaon a posset, as he says, "made with Pramnian wine; and she grated cheese of goat's milk with a grater of bronze, and at his side placed an onion which gives a relish to drink."[8] Now would you say that the art of the rhapsode or the art of medicine was better able to judge of the propriety of these lines?

ION. The art of medicine.

SOC. And when Homer says, "And she descended into the deep like a leaden plummet, which, set in the horn of ox that ranges the fields, rushes along carrying death among the ravenous fishes,"[9] will the art of the fisherman or of the rhapsode be better able to judge what these lines mean, and whether they are accurate or not?

ION. Clearly, Socrates, the art of the fisherman.

SOC. Come now, suppose that you were to say to me: "Since you, Socrates, are able to assign different passages in Homer to their corresponding arts, I wish that you would tell me what are the passages of which the excellence ought to be judged by the prophet and prophetic art"; and you will see how readily and truly I shall answer you. For there are many such passages, particularly in the Odyssey; as, for example, the passage in which Theoclymenus the prophet of the house of Melampus says to the suitors:

> (539) Wretched men! what is happening to you? Your heads and your faces and your limbs underneath are shrouded in night; and the voice of lamentation bursts forth, and your cheeks are wet with tears. And the vestibule is full, and the court is full, of ghosts descending into the darkness of Erebus, and the sun has perished out of heaven, and an evil mist is spread abroad.[10]

And there are many such passages in the Iliad also; as for example in the description of the battle near the rampart, where he says:

> As they were eager to pass the ditch, there came to them an omen: a soaring eagle, skirting the people on his left, bore a huge blood-red dragon in his talons, still living and panting; nor had he yet resigned the strife, for he bent back and smote the bird which carried him on the breast by the neck, and he in pain let him fall from him to the ground into the midst of the multitude. And the eagle, with a cry, was borne afar on the wings of the wind.[11]

These are the sort of things which I should say that the prophet ought to consider and determine.

ION. And you are quite right, Socrates, in saying so.

SOC. Yes, Ion, and you are right also. And as I have selected from the Iliad and Odyssey for you passages which describe the office of the prophet and the physician and the fisherman, do you, who know Homer so much better than I do, Ion, select for me passages which relate to the rhapsode and the rhapsode's art, and which the rhapsode ought to examine and judge of better than other men.

ION. All passages, I should say, Socrates.

SOC. Not all, Ion, surely. Have you already forgotten what you were saying? A rhapsode ought to have a better memory.

ION. Why, what am I forgetting?

SOC. Do you not remember that you declared the art of the rhapsode to be different from the art of the charioteer?

ION. Yes, I remember.

SOC. And you admitted that being different they would know different objects?

ION. Yes.

SOC. Then upon your own showing the rhapsode, and the art of the rhapsode, will not know everything?

ION. I should exclude such things as you mention, Socrates.

soc. You mean to say that you would exclude pretty much the subjects of the other arts. As he does not know all of them, which of them will he know?

ion. He will know what a man and what a woman ought to say, and what a freeman and what a slave ought to say, and what a ruler and what a subject.

soc. Do you mean that a rhapsode will know better than the pilot what the ruler of a sea-tossed vessel ought to say?

ion. No; the pilot will know best.

soc. Or will the rhapsode know better than the physician what the ruler of a sick man ought to say?

ion. Again, no.

soc. But he will know what a slave ought to say?

ion. Yes.

soc. Suppose the slave to be a cowherd; the rhapsode will know better than the cowherd what he ought to say in order to soothe infuriated cows?

ion. No, he will not.

soc. But he will know what a spinning-woman ought to say about the working of wool?

ion. No.

soc. At any rate he will know what a general ought to say when exhorting his soldiers?

ion. Yes, that is the sort of thing which the rhapsode will be sure to know.

soc. What! Is the art of the rhapsode the art of the general?

ion. I am sure that I should know what a general ought to say.

soc. Why, yes, Ion, because you may possibly have the knowledge of a general as well as that of a rhapsode; and you might also have a knowledge of horsemanship as well as of the lyre, and then you would know when horses were well or ill managed. But suppose I were to ask you: By the help of which art, Ion, do you know whether horses are well managed, by your skill as a horseman or as a performer on the lyre—what would you answer?

ion. I should reply, by my skill as a horseman.

soc. And if you judged of performers on the lyre, you would admit that you judged of them as a performer on the lyre, and not as a horseman?

ion. Yes.

soc. And in judging of the general's art, do you judge as a general, or as a good rhapsode?

ion. To me there appears to be no difference between them.

soc. What do you mean? Do you mean to say that the art of the rhapsode and of the general is the same?

ion. Yes, one and the same.

soc. Then he who is a good rhapsode is also a good general?

ion. Certainly, Socrates.

soc. And he who is a good general is also a good rhapsode?

ion. No; I do not agree to that.

soc. But you do agree that he who is a good rhapsode is also a good general.

ion. Certainly.

soc. And you are the best of Hellenic rhapsodes?

ION. Far the best, Socrates.

SOC. And are you also the best general, Ion?

ION. To be sure, Socrates; and Homer was my master.

SOC. But then, Ion, why in the name of goodness do you, who are the best of generals as well as the best of rhapsodes in all Hellas, go about reciting rhapsodies when you might be a general? Do you think that the Hellenes are in grave need of a rhapsode with his golden crown, and have no need at all of a general?

ION. Why, Socrates, the reason is that my countrymen, the Ephesians, are the servants and soldiers of Athens, and do not need a general; and that you and Sparta are not likely to appoint me, for you think that you have enough generals of your own.

SOC. My good Ion, did you never hear of Apollodorus of Cyzicus?

ION. Who may he be?

SOC. One who, though a foreigner, has often been chosen their general by the Athenians: and there is Phanosthenes of Andros, and Heraclides of Clazomenae, whom they have also appointed to the command of their armies and to other offices, although aliens, after they had shown their merit. And will they not choose Ion the Ephesian to be their general, and honor him, if they deem him qualified? Were not the Ephesians originally Athenians, and Ephesus is no mean city? But, indeed, Ion, if you are correct in saying that by art and knowledge you are able to praise Homer, you do not deal fairly with me, and after all your professions of knowing many glorious things about Homer, and promises that you would exhibit them, you only deceive me, and so far from exhibiting the art of which you are a master, will not, even after my repeated entreaties, explain to me the nature of it. You literally assume as many forms as Proteus, twisting and turning up and down, until at last you slip away from me in the disguise of a general, in order that you may escape exhibiting your Homeric lore. (542) And if you have art, then, as I was saying, in falsifying your promise that you would exhibit Homer, you are not dealing fairly with me. But if, as I believe, you have no art, but speak all these beautiful words about Homer unconsciously under his inspiring influence, then I acquit you of dishonesty, and shall only say that you are inspired. Which do you prefer to be thought, dishonest or inspired?

ION. There is a great difference, Socrates, between the two alternatives; and inspiration is by far the nobler.

SOC. Then, Ion, I shall assume the nobler alternative; and attribute to you in your praises of Homer inspiration, and not art.

NOTES

1. Professional reciters of poetry.
2. Greek festival celebrated annually at Athens.
3. Or, "I think I have well deserved the golden crown given me by the Homeridae."—JOWETT'S EDITORS. The latter were reciters of Homer's poetry and claimed to be his descendants.
4. Mythical attendants of the nature goddess Cybele, who engaged in orgiastic ritual dances.
5. Originally, choral hymns that were sung to Dionysus. Developed into a formal art form by Arion of Corinth (ca. 600 B.C.) and introduced into Athens by Lasus of Hermione, dithyrambic poetry became one of the competitive subjects at the Greek festivals. In Plato's time it was the most important type of lyric poetry.
6. Originally, a choral song in honor of Apollo or his sister Artemis.
7. *Il.* 23. 335.
8. *Il.* 11. 639–40.
9. *Il.* 24. 80.
10. *Od.* 20. 351.
11. *Il.* 12. 200.

REPUBLIC

FROM

Book III

Persons of the Dialogue
Socrates   Adeimantus   Glaucon

Then as far as the gods are concerned, I ⟨Socrates⟩ said, such tales are to be told, and such others are not to be told to our disciples from their youth upwards, if we mean them to honor the gods and their parents, and to value friendship with one another.

Yes; and I think that our principles are right, he ⟨Adeimantus⟩ said.

But if they are to be courageous, must they not learn other lessons besides these, and lessons of such a kind as will take away the fear of death? Can any man be courageous who has the fear of death in him?

Certainly not, he said.

And can he be fearless of death, or will he choose death in battle rather than defeat and slavery, who believes the world below to be real and terrible?

Impossible.

Then we must assume a control over the narrators of this class of tales as well as over the others, and beg them not simply to revile, but rather to commend the world below, intimating to them that their descriptions are untrue, and will do harm to our future warriors.

That will be our duty, he said.

Then, I said, we shall have to obliterate many obnoxious passages, beginning with the verses, "I would rather be a serf on the land of a poor and portionless man than rule over all the dead who have come to nought."[1] We must also expunge the verse, which tells us how Pluto feared: "Lest the mansions grim and squalid which the gods abhor should be seen both of mortals and immortals."[2] And again: "O heavens! verily in the house of Hades there is soul and ghostly form, but no mind at all in them!"[3] Again of Tiresias: "[To him even after death did Persephone grant mind] that he alone should be wise; but the other souls are flitting shades."[4] Again: "The soul flying from the limbs had gone to Hades, lamenting her fate, leaving manhood and youth."[5] Again: "And the soul, with shrilling cry, passed like smoke beneath the earth."[6] (387) And, "As bats in hollow of mystic cavern, whenever any of them has dropped out of the string and falls from the rock, fly shrilling and cling to one another, so did they with shrilling cry hold together as they moved."[7] And we must beg Homer and the other poets not to be angry if we strike out these and similar passages, not because they are unpoetical, or unattractive to the popular ear, but because the greater the poetical charm of them, the less are they meet[8] for the ears of boys and men who are meant to be free, and who should fear slavery more than death.

Undoubtedly.

Also we shall have to reject all the terrible and appalling names which describe the world below—Cocytus and Styx, ghosts under the earth, and sapless shades, and any similar words of which the very mention causes a shudder to pass through the inmost soul[4] of him who hears them. I do not say that these horrible stories may not have a use of some kind; but there is a danger that our guardians may be rendered too excitable and effeminate by them.

There is a real danger, he said.

Then we must have no more of them.

True.

Our poets must sing in another and a nobler strain.

Clearly.

And shall we proceed to get rid of the weepings and wailings of famous men?

They will go with the rest.

But shall we be right in getting rid of them? Reflect: our principle is that the good man will not consider death terrible to any other good man who is his comrade.

Yes; that is our principle.

And therefore he will not sorrow for his departed friend as though he had suffered anything terrible?

He will not.

Another thing which we should say of him is that he is the most sufficient for himself and his own happiness, and therefore is least in need of other men.

True, he said.

And for this reason the loss of a son or brother, or any deprivation of fortune, is to him of all men least terrible.

Assuredly.

And therefore he will be least likely to lament, and will bear with the greatest equanimity any misfortune of this sort which may befall him.

Yes, he will feel such a misfortune far less than another.

Then we shall be right in getting rid of the lamentations of famous men, and making them over to women (and not even to women who are good for anything), (388) or to men of a baser sort, that those who are being educated by us to be the defenders of their country may scorn to do the like.

That will be very right.

Then we will once more entreat Homer and the other poets not to depict Achilles,[9] who is the son of a goddess, first lying on his side, then on his back, and then on his face; then starting up and sailing[10] in a frenzy along the shores of the barren sea; now taking the sooty ashes in both his hands and pouring them over his head, or weeping and wailing[11] in the various modes which Homer has delineated. Nor should he describe Priam the kinsman of the gods as praying and beseeching, "rolling in the dirt, calling each man loudly by his name."[12] Still more earnestly will we beg of him at all events not to introduce the gods lamenting and saying, "Alas! my misery! Alas! that I bore the bravest to my sorrow."[13] But if he must introduce the gods, at any rate let him not dare so completely to misrepresent the greatest of the gods, as to make him say: "O heavens! with my eyes verily I behold a dear friend of mine chased round and round the city, and my heart is sorrowful."[14] Or again: "Woe is me that I am fated to have Sarpedon, dearest of men to me, subdued at the hands of Patroclus the son of Menoetius."[15] For if, my dear Adeimantus, our young men seriously listen to such unworthy representations of the gods, instead of laughing at them as they ought, hardly will any of them deem that he himself, being but a man, can be dishonored by similar actions; neither will he rebuke any inclination which may arise in his mind to say and do the like. And instead of having any shame or endurance, he will be always whining and lamenting on slight occasions.

Yes, he said, that is most true.

Yes, I replied; but that surely is what ought not to be, as the argument has just proved to us; and by that proof we must abide until it is disproved by a better.

It ought not to be.

Neither ought our guardians to be given to laughter. For a fit of laughter which has been indulged to excess almost always demands a violent reaction.

So I believe.

Then persons of worth, even if only mortal men, must not be represented as overcome by laughter, and still less must such a representation of the gods be allowed.

Still less of the gods, as you say, he replied.

Then we shall not suffer such an expression to be used about the gods as that of Homer when he describes how "inextinguishable laughter arose among the blessed gods, when they saw Hephaestus bustling about the mansion."[16] On your views, we must not admit them.

On my views, if you like to father them on me; that we must not admit them is certain.

Again, truth should be highly valued; if we were right in saying that falsehood is useless to the gods, and useful only as a medicine to men, then the use of such medicines should be restricted to physicians; private individuals have no business with them.

Clearly not, he said.

Then if anyone at all is to have the privilege of lying, the rulers of the state should be the persons; and they, in their dealings either with enemies or with their own citizens, may be allowed to lie for the public good. But nobody else should meddle with anything of the kind; and although the rulers have this privilege, for a private man to lie to them in return is to be deemed a more heinous fault than for the patient or the pupil of a gymnasium not to speak the truth about his own bodily illnesses to the physician or to the trainer, or for a sailor not to tell the captain what is happening about the ship and the rest of the crew, and how things are going with himself or his fellow sailors.

Most true, he said.

If, then, the ruler catches in a lie anybody beside himself in the state, "any of the craftsmen, whether he be priest or physician or carpenter,"[17] he will punish him for introducing a practice which is equally subversive and destructive of ship or state.

Most certainly, he said, if our talk about the state is ever translated into action.[18]

In the next place our youth must be temperate?

Certainly.

Are not the chief elements of temperance, speaking generally, obedience to commanders and command of oneself in the pleasures of eating and drinking, and of sexual relations?

True.

Then we shall approve such language as that of Diomede in Homer, "Friend, sit still and obey my word,"[19] and the verses which follow, "The Greeks marched breathing prowess,[20] . . . in silent awe of their leaders,"[21] and other sentiments of the same kind.

We shall.

What of this line, "O heavy with wine, who hast the eyes of a dog and the heart of a stag,"[22] and of the words which follow? (390) Would you say that these, or any similar impertinences which private individuals are supposed to address to their rulers, whether in verse or prose, are well or ill spoken?

They are ill spoken.

They may very possibly afford some amusement, but they do not conduce to temperance. And therefore they are likely to do harm to our young men—you would agree with me there?

Yes.

And then, again, to make the wisest of men say that nothing in his opinion is more glorious than "When the tables are full of bread and meat, and the cup-bearer carries round wine which he draws from the bowl and pours into the cups";[23] is it fit or conducive to self-control for a young man to hear such words? Or the verse "The saddest of fates is to die and meet destiny from hunger"?[24] What would you say again to the tale of Zeus, who, while other gods and men were asleep and he the only person awake, lay devising plans, but forgot them all in a moment through his lust, and was so completly overcome at the sight of Hera that he would not even go into the hut, but wanted to lie with her on the ground, declaring that he had never been in such a state of rapture before, even when they first used to meet one another "without the knowledge of their parents";[25] or that other tale of how Hephaestus, because of similar goings-on, cast a chain around Ares and Aphrodite?[26]

Indeed, he said, I am strongly of opinion that they ought not to hear that sort of thing.

But any instances of endurance of various ills by famous men which are recounted or represented in drama, these they ought to see and hear; as, for example, what is said in the verses, "He smote his breast and thus reproached his heart,/Endure, my heart; far worse hast thou endured!"[27]

Certainly, he said.

In the next place, we must not let them be receivers of bribes or lovers of money.

Certainly not.

Neither must we sing to them of "gifts persuading gods, and persuading reverend kings."[28] Neither is Phoenix, the tutor of Achilles, to be approved or deemed to have given his pupil good counsel when he told him that if the Greeks offered him gifts he should assist them;[29] but that without a gift he should not lay aside his anger. Neither will we believe or acknowledge Achilles himself to have been such a lover of money that he took Agamemnon's gifts, or that when he had received payment he restored the dead body of Hector, but that without payment he was unwilling to do so.[30]

Undoubtedly, he said, these are not sentiments which can be approved.

Loving Homer as I do,[31] I hardly like to say that to attribute these feelings to Achilles, or to accept such a narrative from others, is downright impiety. As little can I believe the narrative of his insolence to Apollo, where he says, "Thou hast wronged me, O far-darter, most abominable of deities. Verily I would be even with thee, if I had only the power";[32] or his insubordination to the river-god,[33] on whose divinity he is ready to lay hands; or his offering to the dead Patroclus of his own hair,[34] which had been previously dedicated to the other river-god Spercheius, and that he actually performed this vow; or that he dragged Hector round the tomb of Patroclus,[35] and slaughtered the captives at the pyre;[36] all this we shall declare to be untrue, and shall not allow our citizens to be persuaded that he, the wise Cheiron's pupil, the son of a goddess and of Peleus who was the most modest of men and third in descent from Zeus, was so confused within as to be affected with two seemingly inconsistent diseases, meanness, not untainted by avarice, and overweening contempt of gods and men.

You are quite right, he replied.

And let us equally refuse to believe, or allow to be repeated, the tale of Theseus son of Poseidon, and Peirithous son of Zeus, going forth as they did to perpetrate a horrid rape; or of any other hero or son of a god daring to do such impious and dreadful things as they falsely ascribe to them in our day: and let us further compel the poets to declare either that these acts were not done by them, or that they were not the sons of gods—both in the same breath they shall not be permitted to affirm. We will not have them trying to persuade our youth that the gods are the authors of evil, and that heroes are no better than men—sentiments which, as we were saying, are neither pious nor true, for we have already proved that evil cannot come from the gods.

Assuredly not.

And further they are likely to have a bad effect on those who hear them; for everybody will begin to excuse his own vices when he is convinced that similar wickednesses are always being perpetrated by "the kindred of the gods, near descendants of Zeus, who worship him their ancestor at his altar, aloft in air on the peak of Ida," and who have "the blood of deities yet flowing in their veins."[37] And therefore let us put an end to such tales, lest they engender laxity of morals among the young. (392)

By all means, he replied.

But now that we are determining what classes of tales are or are not to be told, let us see whether any have been omitted by us. The manner in which gods and demigods and heroes and the world below should be treated has been already laid down.

Very true.

And it remains for us to decide what to say about men?

Clearly so.

But we are not in a condition to answer this question at present, my friend.

Why not?

Because, if I am not mistaken, we shall have to say that, about men, poets and story-tellers are guilty of making the gravest misstatements when they tell us that wicked men are often happy and the good miserable; and that injustice is profitable when undetected, but that justice is a man's own loss and another's gain—these things we shall forbid them to utter, and command them to sing and describe the opposite.

To be sure we shall, he replied.

But if you admit that I am right in this, then I shall maintain that you have implied the principle for which we have been all along contending.

I grant the truth of your inference.

That such things are or are not to be said about men is a question which we cannot determine until we have discovered what justice is, and how naturally advantageous to the possessor, whether he seem to be just or not.

Most true, he said.

Enough of the subjects of poetry: let us now speak of the style; and when this has been considered, both matter and manner will have been completely treated.

I do not understand what you mean, said Adeimantus.

Then I must make you understand; and perhaps I may be more intelligible if I put the matter in this way. You are aware, I suppose, that all mythology and poetry is a narration of events, either past, present, or to come?

Certainly, he replied.

And narration may be either simple narration, or imitation, or a union of the two?

That again, he said, I do not quite understand.

I fear that I must be an absurdly vague teacher. Like a bad speaker, therefore, I will not take the whole of the subject, but will break a piece off in illustration of my meaning. You know the first lines of the Iliad, in which the poet says that Chryses prayed Agamemnon to release his daughter, and that Agamemnon flew into a passion with him; whereupon Chryses, failing of his object, invoked the anger of the god against the Achaeans. (393) Now as far as these lines, "And he prayed all the Greeks, but especially the two sons of Atreus, the chiefs of the people,"[38] the poet is speaking in his own person; he never even tries to distract us by assuming another character. But in what follows he takes the person of Chryses, and then he does all that he can to make us believe that the speaker is not Homer, but the aged priest himself. And in this double form he has cast the entire narrative of the events which occurred at Troy and in Ithaca and throughout the Odyssey.

Yes.

And a narrative it remains both in the speeches which the poet recites from time to time and in the intermediate passages?

Quite true.

But when the poet speaks in the person of another, may we not say that he assimilates his style to that of the person who, as he informs you, is going to speak?

Certainly we may.

And this assimilation of himself to another, either by the use of voice or gesture, is the imitation of the person whose character he assumes?

Of course.

Then in this case the narrative of the poet, whether Homer or another, may be said to proceed by way of imitation?

Very true.

Or, if the poet were at no time to disguise himself, then again the imitation would be dropped, and his poetry become simple narration. However, in order that you may not have to repeat that you do not understand, I will show how the change might be effected. If Homer had said, "The priest came, having his daughter's ransom in his hands, supplicating the Achaeans, and above all the kings"; and then if, instead of speaking in the person of Chryses, he had continued in his own person, the words would have been, not imitation, but simple narration. The passage would have run as follows (I am no poet, and therefore I drop the meter), "The priest came and prayed the gods on behalf of the Greeks that they might capture Troy and return safely home, but begged that they would give him back his daughter, and take the ransom which he brought, and respect the god. Thus he spoke, and the other Greeks revered the priest and assented. But Agamemnon was wroth, and bade him depart and not come again, lest the staff and chaplets[39] of the god should be of no avail to him, and told him that before his daughter should be released, she should grow old with him in Argos. And then he told him to go away and not to provoke him, if he intended to get home unscathed. (394) And the old man went away in fear and silence, and, when he had left the camp, he called upon Apollo by his many names, reminding him of everything which he had done pleasing to him, whether in building his temples or in offering sacrifice, and praying that his good deeds might be returned to him and that the Achaeans might expiate his tears by the arrows of the god,"—and so on. In this way the whole becomes simple narrative.

I understand, he said.

And you must realize that an opposite case occurs, when the poet's comments are omitted and the passages of dialogue only are left.

That also, he said, I understand; you mean, for example, as in tragedy.

You have conceived my meaning perfectly; and I think I can now make clear what you failed to apprehend before, that some poetry and mythology are wholly imitative (and, as you say, I mean tragedy and comedy); there is likewise the opposite style, in which the poet is the only speaker—of this the dithyramb affords the best example; and the combination of both is found in epic, and in several other styles of poetry. Do I take you with me?

Yes, he said; I see now what you meant.

I will ask you to remember also what I began by saying, that we had done with the subject and might proceed to the style.

Yes, I remember.

In saying this, I intended to imply that we must come to an understanding about the mimetic art—whether the poets, in narrating their stories, are to be allowed by us to imitate, and if so, whether in whole or in part, and if the latter, in what parts; or should all imitation be prohibited?

You mean, I suspect, to ask whether tragedy and comedy shall be admitted into our state?

Perhaps, I said; but there may be more than this in question: I really do not know as yet, but whither the argument may blow, thither we go.

And go we will, he said.

Then, Adeimantus, let me ask you to consider whether our guardians should or should not be fond of imitation; or rather, has not this question been decided by the rule already laid down that one man can only do one thing well, and not many; and that one who grasps at many will altogether fail of gaining much reputation in any?

Certainly.

And this is equally true of imitation; no one man can imitate many things as well as he would imitate a single one?

He cannot.

Then the same person will hardly be able to play a serious part in life, and at the same time to be an imitator and imitate many other parts as well; for even when two species of imitation are nearly allied, the same persons cannot succeed in both, as for example, the writers of tragedy and comedy—did you not just now call them imitations?

Yes, I did; and you are right in thinking that the same persons cannot succeed in both.

Any more than they can be rhapsodists and actors at once?

True.

Neither do comic and tragic writers employ the same actors; yet all these things are imitations.

They are so.

And human nature, Adeimantus, appears to have been coined into yet smaller pieces, and to be as incapable of imitating many things well, as of performing well the actions of which the imitations are copies.

Quite true, he replied.

If then we adhere to our original notion and bear in mind that our guardians, released from every other business, are to dedicate themselves wholly to the maintenance of the freedom of the state, making this their craft and engaging in no work which does not bear on this end, then they ought not to practice or even imitate anything else; if they imitate at all, they should imitate from youth upward only those characters which are suitable to their profession—the courageous, temperate, holy, free, and the like; but they should not depict or be skillful at imitating any kind of illiberality or baseness, lest the fruit of imitation should be reality. Did you never observe how imitations, beginning in early youth and continuing far into life, at length grow into habits and become a second nature, affecting body, voice, and mind?

Yes, certainly, he said.

Then, I said, we will not allow those for whom we profess a care and of whom we say that they ought to be good men, to imitate a woman, whether young or old, quarrelling with her husband, or striving and vaunting against the gods in conceit of her happiness, or when she is in affliction, or sorrow, or weeping; and certainly not one who is in sickness, love, or labor.

Very right, he said.

Neither must they represent slaves, male or female, peforming the offices of slaves?

They must not.

And surely not bad men, whether cowards or any others, who do the reverse of what we have just been prescribing, who scold or mock or revile one another in drink or out of drink, (396) or who in any other manner sin against themselves and their neighbors in word or deed, as the manner of such is. Neither should they be trained to imitate the action or speech of madmen; they must be able to recognize madness and vice in man or woman, but none of these things is to be practiced or imitated.

Very true, he replied.

Neither may they imitate smiths or other artificers, or oarsmen, or boatswains, or the like?

How can they, he said, when they are not allowed to apply their minds to the callings of any of these?

Nor may they imitate the neighing of horses, the bellowing of bulls, the murmur of rivers and roll of the ocean, thunder, and all that sort of thing?

Nay, he said, if madness be forbidden, neither may they copy the behavior of madmen.

You mean, I said, if I understand you aright, that there is one sort of narrative style which is likely to be employed by an upright and good man when he has anything to say, and another sort, very unlike it, which will be preferred by a man of an opposite character and education.

And which are these two sorts? he asked.

As for the man of orderly life, I answered, when the time comes to describe some saying or action of another good man,—I think he will be willing to personate him, and will not be ashamed of this sort of imitation: he will be most ready to play the part of the good man when he is acting firmly and wisely; less often and in a less degree when he is overtaken by illness or love or drink, or has met with any other disaster. But when he comes to a character which is unworthy of him, he will not seriously assume the likeness of his inferior, and will do so, if at all, for a moment only when he is performing some good action; at other times he will be ashamed, both because he is not trained in imitation of such characters, and because he disdains to fashion and frame himself after the baser models; he feels the employment of such an art, unless in jest, to be beneath him.

So I should expect, he replied.

Then he will adopt a mode of narration such as we have illustrated out of Homer, that is to say, his style will be both imitative and narrative; but there will be, in a long story, only a small proportion of the former. Do you agree?

Certainly, he said; that is the model which such a speaker must necessarily take. (397)

But there is another sort of character who will narrate anything, and, the worse he is, the more unscrupulous he will be; nothing will be too bad for him: and he will be ready to imitate anything, in right good earnest, and before a large company. As I was just now saying, he will attempt to represent the roll of thunder, the noise of wind and hail, or the creaking of wheels, and pulleys, and the various sounds of flutes, pipes, trumpets, and all sorts of instruments: he will bark like a dog, bleat like a sheep, or crow like a cock; his entire art will consist in imitation of voice and gesture, or will be but slightly blended with narration.

That, he said, will be his mode of speaking.

These, then, are the two kinds of style I had in mind.

Yes.

And you would agree with me in saying that one of them is simple and has but slight changes; and that if an author expresses this style in fitting harmony and rhythm, he will find himself, if he does his work well, keeping pretty much within the limits of a single harmony (for the changes are not great), and in like manner he will make a similar choice of rhythm?

That is quite true, he said.

Whereas the other requires all sorts of harmonies and all sorts of rhythms if the music and the style are to correspond, because the style has all sorts of changes.

That is also perfectly true, he replied.

And do not the two styles, or the mixture of the two, comprehend all poetry and every form of expression in words? No one can say anything except in one or other of them or in both together.

They include all, he said.

And shall we receive into our state all the three styles, or one only of the two unmixed styles? Or would you include the mixed?

I should prefer only to admit the pure imitator of virtue.

Yes, I said, Adeimantus; and yet the mixed style is also charming: and indeed the opposite style to that chosen by you is by far the most popular with children and their attendants, and with the masses.

I do not deny it.

But I suppose you would argue that such a style is unsuitable to our state, in which human nature is not twofold or manifold, for one man plays one part only?

Yes; quite unsuitable.

And this is the reason why in our state, and in our state only, we shall find a shoemaker to be a shoemaker and not a pilot also, and a husbandman to be a husbandman and not a dicast[40] also, and a soldier a soldier and not a trader also, and the same throughout?

True, he said.

And therefore when any one of these pantomimic gentlemen, who are so clever that they can imitate anything, comes to us and makes a proposal to exhibit himself and his poetry, we will fall down and worship him as a sacred, marvellous and delightful being; but we must also inform him that in our state such as he are not permitted to exist; the law will not allow them. And so when we have anointed him with myrrh, and set a garland of wool upon his head, we shall send him away to another city. For we mean to employ for our souls' health the rougher and severer poet or storyteller, who will imitate the style of the virtuous only, and will follow those models which we prescribed at first when we began the education of our soldiers.

We certainly will, he said, if we have the power.

Then now, my friend, I said, that part of music or literary education which relates to the story of myth may be considered to be finished; for the matter and manner have both been discussed.

I think so too, he said.

Next in order will follow melody and song.

That is obvious.

Everyone now would be able to discover what we ought to say about them, if we are to be consistent with ourselves.

I fear, said Glaucon, laughing, that the word "everyone" hardly includes me, for I cannot at the moment say what they should be, though I have a suspicion.

At any rate you are aware that a song or ode has three parts—the words, the melody, and the rhythm.

Yes, he said; so much as that I know.

And as for the words, there will surely be no difference between words which are and which are not set to music; both will conform to the same laws, and these have been already determined by us?

Yes.

And the melody and rhythm will be in conformity with the words?

Certainly.

We were saying, when we spoke of the subject-matter, that we had no need of lamentation and strains of sorrow?

True.

And which are the harmonies expressive of sorrow? You are musical, and can tell me.

The harmonies which you mean are the mixed or tenor Lydian, and the full-toned or bass Lydian, and such-like.

These then, I said, must be banished; even to women who have a character to maintain they are of no use, and much less to men.

Certainly.

In the next place, drunkenness and softness and indolence are utterly unbecoming the character of our guardians.

Utterly unbecoming.

And which are the soft and convivial harmonies?

The Ionian, he replied, and some of the Lydian which are termed "relaxed."

Well, and are these of any use for warlike men?

Quite the reverse, he replied; and if so the Dorian and the Phrygian are the only ones which you have left.

I answered: Of the harmonies I know nothing, but would have you leave me one which can render the note or accent which a brave man utters in warlike action and in stern resolve; and when his cause is failing, and he is going to wounds or death or is overtaken by disaster in some other form, at every such crisis he meets the blows of fortune with firm step and a determination to endure; and an opposite kind for times of peace and freedom of action, when there is no pressure of necessity, and he is seeking to persuade God by prayer, or man by instruction and admonition, or when on the other hand he is expressing his willingness to yield to the persuasion of entreaty or admonition of others. And when in this manner he has attained his end, I would have the music show him not carried away by his success, but acting moderately and wisely in all circumstances, and acquiescing in the event. These two harmonies I ask you to leave; the strain of necessity and the strain of freedom, the strain of the unfortunate and the strain of the fortunate, the strain of courage, and the strain of temperance; these, I say, leave.

And these, he replied, are the Dorian and Phrygian harmonies of which I was just now speaking.

Then, I said, if these and these only are to be used in our songs and melodies, we shall not want multiplicity of strings or a panharmonic scale?

I suppose not.

Then we shall not maintain the artificers of lyres with three corners and complex scales, or the makers of any other many-stringed, curiously harmonized instruments?

Certainly not.

But what do you say to flute-makers and flute-players? Would you admit them into our state when you reflect that in this composite use of harmony the flute is worse than any stringed instrument; even the panharmonic music is only an imitation of the flute?

Clearly not.

There remain then only the lyre and the harp for use in the city, and the shepherds in the country may have some kind of pipe.

That is surely the conclusion to be drawn from the argument.

The preferring of Apollo and his instruments to Marsyas and his instruments is not at all strange, I said.

Not at all, he replied.

And so, by the dog of Egypt, we have been unconsciously purging the state, which not long ago we termed luxurious.

And we have done wisely, he replied.

Then let us now finish the purgation, I said. Next in order to harmonies, rhythms will naturally follow, and they should be subject to the same rules, for we ought not to seek out complex systems of meter, and a variety of feet, but rather to discover what rhythms are the expressions of a courageous and harmonious life; (400) and when we have found them, we shall adapt the foot and the melody to words having a like spirit, not the words to the foot and melody. To say what these rhythms are will be your duty—you must teach me them, as you have already taught me the harmonies.

But, indeed, he replied, I cannot tell you. I know from observation that there are some three principles of rhythm out of which metrical systems are framed, just as in sounds there are four notes[41] out of which all the harmonies are composed. But of what sort of lives they are severally the imitations I am unable to say.

Then, I said, we must take Damon into our counsels; and he will tell us what rhythms are expressive of meanness, or insolence, or fury, or other unworthiness, and what are to be reserved for the expression of opposite feelings. And I think that I have an indistinct recollection of his mentioning a complex Cretic rhythm; also a dactylic or heroic, and he arranged them in some manner which I do not quite understand, making the rhythms equal in the rise and fall of the foot, long and short alternating; and, unless I am mistaken, he spoke of an iambic as well as of a trochaic rhythm, and assigned to them short and long quantities.[42] Also in some cases he appeared to praise or censure the movement of the foot quite as much as the rhythm; or perhaps a combination of the two; for I am not certain what he meant. These matters, however, as I was saying, had better be referred to Damon himself, for the analysis of the subject would be difficult, you know?

Rather so, I should say.

But it does not require much analysis to see that grace or the absence of grace accompanies good or bad rhythm.

None at all.

And also that good and bad rhythm naturally assimilate to a good and bad style; and that harmony and discord in like manner follow style; for our principle is that rhythm and harmony are regulated by the words, and not the words by them.

Just so, he said, they should follow the words.

And will not the words and the character of the style depend on the temper of the soul?

Yes.

And everything else on the style?

Yes.

Then beauty of style and harmony and grace and good rhythm depend on simplicity—I mean the true simplicity of a rightly and nobly ordered mind and character, not that other simplicity which is only a euphemism for folly?

Very true, he replied.

And if our youth are to do their work in life, must they not make these graces and harmonies their perpetual aim?

They must.

And surely the art of the painter and every other creative and constructive art are full of them—weaving, embroidery, architecture, and every kind of manufacture; also nature, animal and vegetable—in all of them there is grace or the absence of grace. And ugliness and discord and inharmonious motion are nearly allied to ill words and ill nature, as grace and harmony are the twin sisters of goodness and self-restraint and bear their likeness.

That is quite true, he said.

But shall our superintendence go no further, and are the poets only to be required by us to express the image of the good in their works, on pain, if they do anything else, of expulsion from our state? Or is the same control to be extended to other artists, and are they also to be prohibited from exhibiting the opposite forms of vice and intemperance and meanness and deformity in sculpture and building and the other creative arts; and is he who cannot conform to this rule of ours to be prevented from practicing his art in our state, lest the taste of our citizens be corrupted by him? We would not have our guardians grow up amid images of moral deformity, as in some noxious pasture, and there browse and feed upon many a baneful herb and flower day by day, little by little, until they silently gather a festering mass of corruption in their own soul. Let us rather search for artists who are gifted to discern the true nature of the beautiful and graceful; then will our youth dwell in a land of health, amid fair sights and sounds, and receive the good in everything; and beauty, the effluence of fair works, shall flow into the eye and ear, like a health-giving breeze from a purer region, and insensibly draw the soul from earliest years into likeness and sympathy with the beauty of reason.

There can be no nobler training than that, he replied.

And therefore, I said, Glaucon, musical training is a more potent instrument than any other, because rhythm and harmony find their way into the inward places of the soul, on which they mightily fasten, imparting grace, and making the soul of him who is rightly educated graceful, or of him who is ill-educated ungraceful; and also because he who has received this true education of the inner being will most shrewdly perceive omissions or faults in art and nature, (402) and with a true taste, while he praises and rejoices over and receives into his soul the good, and becomes noble and good, he will justly blame and hate the bad, now in the days of his youth, even before he is able to know the reason why; and when reason comes he will recognize and salute the friend with whom his education has made him long familiar.

Yes, he said, I quite agree with you in thinking that it is for such reasons that they should be trained in music.

Just as in learning to read, I said, we were satisfied when we knew the letters of the alphabet, few as they are, in all their recurring combinations; not slighting them as unimportant whether they occupy a space large or small, but everywhere eager to make them out, because we knew we should not be perfect in the art of reading until we could do so:

True—

And as we recognize the reflection of letters in water, or in a mirror, only when we know the letters themselves, the same art and study giving us the knowledge of both:

Exactly—

Even so, as I maintain, neither we nor the guardians, whom we say that we have to educate, can ever become musical until we and they know the essential forms of temperance, courage, liberality, magnanimity, and their kindred, as well as the contrary forms, in all their combinations, and can recognize them and their images wherever they are found, not slighting them either in small things or great, but believing them all to be within the sphere of one art and study.

Most assuredly.

And when nobility of soul is observed in harmonious union with beauty of form, and both are cast from the same mold, that will be the fairest of sights to him who has an eye to see it?

The fairest indeed.

And the fairest is also the loveliest?

That may be assumed.

And it is with human beings who most display such harmony that a musical man will be most in love; but he will not love any who do not possess it.

That is true, he replied, if the deficiency be in the soul; but if there be any bodily defect he will be patient of it, and may even approve it.

Book X

Persons of the Dialogue
Socrates   Glaucon

Of the many excellences which I ⟨Socrates⟩ perceive in the order of our state, there is none which upon reflection pleases me better than the rule about poetry.

To what do you refer?

To our refusal to admit the imitative kind of poetry, for it certainly ought not to be received; as I see far more clearly now that the parts of the soul have been distinguished.

What do you mean?

Speaking in confidence, for you will not denounce me to the tragedians and the rest of the imitative tribe, all poetical imitations are ruinous to the understanding of the hearers, unless as an antidote they possess the knowledge of the true nature of the originals.

Explain the purport of your remark.

Well, I will tell you, although I have always from my earliest youth had an awe and love of Homer which even now makes the words falter on my lips, for he seems to be the great captain and teacher of the whole of that noble tragic company[1]; but a man is not to be reverenced more than the truth, and therefore I will speak out.

Very good, he said.

Listen to me then, or rather, answer me.

Put your question.

Can you give me a general definition of imitation? for I really do not myself understand what it professes to be.

A likely thing, then, that I should know.

There would be nothing strange in that, for the duller eye may often see a thing sooner than the keener.

Very true, he said; but in your presence, even if I had any faint notion, I could not muster courage to utter it. Will you inquire yourself?

Well then, shall we begin the inquiry at this point, following our usual method: Whenever a number of individuals have a common name, we assume that there is one corresponding idea or form[2]—do you understand me?

I do.

Let us take, for our present purpose, any instance of such a group; there are beds and tables in the world—many of each, are there not?

Yes.

But there are only two ideas or forms of such furniture—one the idea of a bed, the other of a table.

True.

And the maker of either of them makes a bed or he makes a table for our use, in accordance with the idea—that is our way of speaking in this and similar instances—but no artificer makes the idea itself: how could he?

Impossible.

And there is another artificer—I should like to know what you would say of him.

Who is he?

One who is the maker of all the works of all other workmen.

What an extraordinary man!

Wait a little, and there will be more reason for your saying so. For this is the craftsman who is able to make not only furniture of every kind, but all that grows out of the earth, and all living creatures, himself included; and besides these he can make earth and sky and the gods, and all the things which are in heaven or in the realm of Hades under the earth.

He must be a wizard and no mistake.

Oh! you are incredulous, are you? Do you mean that there is no such maker or creator, or that in one sense there might be a maker of all these things but in another not? Do you see that there is a way in which you could make them all yourself?

And what way is this? he asked.

An easy way enough; or rather, there are many ways in which the feat might be quickly and easily accomplished, none quicker than that of turning a mirror round and round—you would soon enough make the sun and the heavens, and the earth and yourself, and other animals and plants, and furniture and all the other things of which we were just now speaking, in the mirror.

Yes, he said, but they would be appearances only.

Very good, I said, you are coming to the point now. And the painter too is, as I conceive, just such another—a creator of appearances, is he not?

Of course.

But then I suppose you will say that what he creates is untrue. And yet there is a sense in which the painter also creates a bed? Is there not?

Yes, he said, but here again, an appearance only.

And what of the maker of the bed? Were you not saying that he too makes, not the idea which according to our view is the real object denoted by the word bed, but only a particular bed?

Yes, I did.

Then if he does not make a real object he cannot make what *is*, but only some semblance of existence; and if any one were to say that the work of the maker of the bed, or of any other workman, has real existence, he could hardly be supposed to be speaking the truth.

Not, at least, he replied, in the view of those who make a business of these discussions.

No wonder, then, that his work too is an indistinct expression of truth.

No wonder.

Suppose now that by the light of the examples just offered we inquire who this imitator is?

If you please.

Well then, here we find three beds: one existing in nature, which is made by God, as I think that we may say—for no one else can be the maker?

No one, I think.

There is another which is the work of the carpenter?

Yes.

And the work of the painter is a third?

Yes.

Beds, then, are of three kinds, and there are three artists who superintend them: God, the maker of the bed, and the painter?

Yes, there are three of them.

God, whether from choice or from necessity, made one bed in nature and one only; two or more such beds neither ever have been nor ever will be made by God.

Why is that?

Because even if He had made but two, a third would still appear behind them of which they again both possessed the form, and that would be the real bed and not the two others.

Very true, he said.

God knew this, I suppose, and He desired to be the real maker of a real bed, not a kind of maker of a kind of bed, and therefore He created a bed which is essentially and by nature one only.

So it seems.

Shall we, then, speak of Him as the natural author or maker of the bed?

Yes, he replied; inasmuch as by the natural process of creation He is the author of this and of all other things.

And what shall we say of the carpenter—is not he also the maker of a bed?

Yes.

But would you call the painter an artificer and maker?

Certainly not.

Yet if he is not the maker, what is he in relation to the bed?

I think, he said, that we may fairly designate him as the imitator of that which the others make.

Good, I said; then you call him whose product is third in the descent from nature, an imitator?

Certainly, he said.

And so if the tragic poet is an imitator, he too is thrice removed from the king and from the truth; and so are all other imitators.

That appears to be so.

Then about the imitator we are agreed. And what about the painter? Do you think he tries to imitate in each case that which originally exists in nature, or only the creations of artificers?

The latter.

As they are or as they appear? You have still to determine this.

What do you mean?

I mean to ask whether a bed really becomes different when it is seen from different points of view, obliquely or directly or from any other point of view? Or does it simply appear different, without being really so? And the same of all things.

Yes, he said, the difference is only apparent.

Now let me ask you another question: Which is the art of painting designed to be—an imitation of things as they are, or as they appear—of appearance or of reality?

Of appearance, he said.

Then the imitator is a long way off the truth, and can reproduce all things because he lightly touches on a small part of them, and that part an image. For example: A painter will paint a cobbler, carpenter, or any other artisan, though he knows nothing of their arts; and, if he is a good painter, he may deceive children or simple persons when he shows them his picture of a carpenter from a distance, and they will fancy that they are looking at a real carpenter.

Certainly.

And surely, my friend, this is how we should regard all such claims: whenever anyone informs us that he has found a man who knows all the arts, and all things else that anybody knows, and every single thing with a higher degree of accuracy than any other man—whoever tells us this, I think that we can only retort that he is a simple creature who seems to have been deceived by some wizard or imitator whom he met, and whom he thought all-knowing, because he himself was unable to analyse the nature of knowledge and ignorance and imitation.

Most true.

And next, I said, we have to consider tragedy and its leader, Homer; for we hear some persons saying that these poets know all the arts; and all things human; where virtue and vice are concerned, and indeed all divine things too; because the good poet cannot compose well unless he knows his subject, and he who has not this knowledge can never be a poet. We ought to consider whether here also there may not be a similar illusion. Perhaps they may have come across imitators and been deceived by them; they may not have remembered when they saw their works that these were thrice removed from the truth, (599) and could easily be made without any knowledge of the truth, because they are appearances only and not realities? Or, after all, they may be in the right, and good poets do really know the things about which they seem to the many to speak so well?

The question, he said, should by all means be considered.

Now do you suppose that if a person were able to make the original as well as the image, he would seriously devote himself to the image-making branch? Would he allow imitation to be the ruling principle of his life, as if he had nothing higher in him?

I should say not.

But the real artist, who had real knowledge of those things which he chose also to imitate, would be interested in realities and not in imitations; and would desire to leave as memorials of himself works many and fair; and, instead of being the author of encomiums, he would prefer to be the theme of them.

Yes, he said, that would be to him a source of much greater honor and profit.

Now let us refrain, I said, from calling Homer or any other poet to account regarding those arts to which his poems incidentally refer: we will not ask them, in case any poet has been a doctor and not a mere imitator of medical parlance, to show what patients have been restored to health by a poet, ancient or modern, as they were by Asclepius; or what disciples in medicine a poet has left behind him, like the Asclepiads. Nor shall we press the same question upon them about the other arts. But we have a right to know respecting warfare, strategy, the administration of states and the education of man, which are the chiefest and noblest subjects of his poems, and we may fairly ask him about them. "Friend Homer," then we say to him, "if you are only in the second remove from truth in what you say of virtue, and not in the third—not an image maker, that is, by our definition, an imitator—and if you are able to discern what pursuits make men better or worse in private or public life, tell us what state was ever better governed by your help? The good order of Lacedaemon is due to Lycurgus, and many other cities great and small have been similarly benefited by others; but who says that you have been a good legislator to them and have done them any good? Italy and Sicily boast of Charondas, and there is Solon who is renowned among us; but what city has anything to say about you?" Is there any city which he might name?

I think not, said Glaucon; not even the Homerids themselves pretend that he was a legislator.

Well, but is there any war on record which was carried on successfully owing to his leadership or counsel?

There is not.

Or is there anything comparable to those clever improvements in the arts, or in other operations, which are said to have been due to men of practical genius such as Thales the Milesian or Anacharsis the Scythian?

There is absolutely nothing of the kind.

But, if Homer never did any public service, was he privately a guide or teacher of any? Had he in his lifetime friends who loved to associate with him, and who handed down to posterity an Homeric way of life, such as was established by Pythagoras who was especially beloved for this reason and whose followers are to this day conspicuous among others by what they term the Pythagorean way of life?

Nothing of the kind is recorded of him. For surely, Socrates, Creophylus, the companion of Homer, that child of flesh, whose name always makes us laugh, might be more justly ridiculed for his want of breeding, if what is said is true, that Homer was greatly neglected by him in his own day when he was alive?

Yes, I replied, that is the tradition. But can you imagine, Glaucon, that if Homer had really been able to educate and improve mankind—if he had been capable of knowledge and not been a mere imitator—can you imagine, I say, that he would not have attracted many followers, and been honored and loved by them? Protagoras of Abdera, and Prodicus of Ceos, and a host of others, have only to whisper to their contemporaries: "You will never be able to manage either your own house or your own state until you appoint us to be your ministers of education"—and this ingenious device of theirs has such an effect in making men love them that their companions all but carry them about on their shoulders. And is it conceivable that the contemporaries of Homer, or again of Hesiod, would have allowed either of them to go about as rhapsodists, if they had really been able to help mankind forward in virtue? Would they not have been as unwilling to part with them as with gold, and have compelled them to stay at home with them? Or, if the master would not stay, then the disciples would have followed him about everywhere, until they had got education enough?

Yes, Socrates, that, I think, is quite true.

Then must we not infer that all these poetical individuals, beginning with Homer, are only imitators, who copy images of virtue and the other themes of their poetry, but have no contact with the truth? (601) The poet is like a painter who, as we have already observed, will make a likeness of a cobbler though he understands nothing of cobbling; and his picture is good enough for those who know no more than he does, and judge only by colors and figures.

Quite so.

In like manner the poet with his words and phrases[3] may be said to lay on the colors of the several arts, himself understanding their nature only enough to imitate them; and the other people, who are as ignorant as he is, and judge only from his words, imagine that if he speaks of cobbling, or of military tactics, or of anything else, in meter and harmony and rhythm, he speaks very well—such is the sweet influence which melody and rhythm by nature have. For I am sure that you know what a poor appearance the works of poets make when stripped of the colors which art puts upon them, and recited in simple prose. You have seen some examples?

Yes, he said.

They are like faces which were never really beautiful, but only blooming, seen when the bloom of youth has passed away from them?

Exactly.

Come now, and observe this point: The imitator or maker of the image knows nothing, we have said, of true existence; he knows appearances only. Am I not right?

Yes.

Then let us have a clear understanding, and not be satisfied with half an explanation.

Proceed.

Of the painter we say that he will paint reins, and he will paint a bit?

Yes.

And the worker in leather and brass will make them?

Certainly.

But does the painter know the right form of the bit and reins? Nay, hardly even the workers in brass and leather who make them; only the horseman who knows how to use them—he knows their right form.

Most true.

And may we not say the same of all things?

What?

That there are three arts which are concerned with all things: one which uses, another which makes, a third which imitates them?

Yes.

And the excellence and beauty and rightness of every structure, animate or inanimate, and of every action of man, is relative solely to the use for which nature or the artist has intended them.

True.

Then beyond doubt it is the user who has the greatest experience of them, and he must report to the maker the good or bad qualities which develop themselves in use; for example, the flute-player will tell the flute-maker which of his flutes is satisfactory to the performer; he will tell him how he ought to make them, and the other will attend to his instructions?

Of course.

So the one pronounces with knowledge about the goodness and badness of flutes, while the other, confiding in him, will make them accordingly?

True.

The instrument is the same, but about the excellence or badness of it the maker will possess a correct belief, since he associates with one who knows, and is compelled to hear what he has to say; (602) whereas the user will have knowledge?

True.

But will the imitator have either? Will he know from use whether or no that which he paints is correct or beautiful? Or will he have right opinion from being compelled to associate with another who knows and gives him instructions about what he should paint?

Neither.

Then an imitator will no more have true opinion that he will have knowledge about the goodness or badness of his models?

I suppose not.

The imitative poet will be in a brilliant state of intelligence about the theme of his poetry?

Nay, very much the reverse.

And still he will go on imitating without knowing what makes a thing good or bad, and may be expected therefore to imitate only that which appears to be good to the ignorant multitude?

Just so.

Thus far then we are pretty well agreed that the imitator has no knowledge worth mentioning of what he imitates. Imitation is only a kind of play or sport, and the tragic poets, whether they write in iambic or in heroic verse,[4] are imitators in the highest degree?

Very true.

And now tell me, I conjure you—this imitation is concerned with an object which is thrice removed from the truth?

Certainly.

And what kind of faculty in man is that to which imitation makes its special appeal?

What do you mean?

I will explain: The same body does not appear equal to our sight when seen near and when seen at a distance?

True.

And the same objects appear straight when looked at out of the water, and crooked when in the water; and the concave becomes convex, owing to the illusion about colors to which the sight is liable. Thus every sort of confusion is revealed within us; and this is that weakness of the human mind on which the art of painting in light and shadow, the art of conjuring, and many other ingenious devices impose, having an effect upon us like magic.

True.

And the arts of measuring and numbering and weighing come to the rescue of the human understanding—there is the beauty of them—with the result that the apparent greater or less, or more or heavier, no longer have the mastery over us, but give way before the power of calculation and measuring and weighing?

Most true.

And this, surely, must be the work of the calculating and rational principle in the soul?

To be sure.

And often when this principle measures and certifies that some things are equal, or that some are greater or less than others, it is, at the same time, contradicted by the appearance which the objects present?

True.

But did we not say that such a contradiction is impossible—the same faculty cannot have contrary opinions at the same time about the same thing?

We did; and rightly.

Then that part of the soul which has an opinion contrary to measure can hardly be the same with that which has an opinion in accordance with measure?

True.

And the part of the soul which trusts to measure and calculation is likely to be the better one?

Certainly.

And therefore that which is opposed to this is probably an inferior principle in our nature?

No doubt.

This was the conclusion at which I was seeking to arrive when I said that painting or drawing, and imitation in general, are engaged upon productions which are far removed from truth, and are also the companions and friends and associates of a principle within us which is equally removed from reason, and that they have no true or healthy aim.

Exactly.

The imitative art is an inferior who from intercourse with an inferior has inferior offspring.

Very true.

And is this confined to the sight only, or does it extend to the hearing also, relating in fact to what we term poetry?

Probably the same would be true of poetry.

Do not rely, I said, on a probability derived from the analogy of painting; but let us once more go directly to that faculty of the mind with which imitative poetry has converse, and see whether it is good or bad.

By all means.

We may state the question thus: Imitation imitates the actions of men, whether voluntary or involuntary, on which, as they imagine, a good or bad result has ensued, and they rejoice or sorrow accordingly. Is there anything more?

No, there is nothing else.

But in all this variety of circumstances is the man at unity with himself—or rather, as in the instance of sight there was confusion and opposition in his opinions about the same things, so here also is there not strife and inconsistency in his life? Though I need hardly raise the question again, for I remember that all this has been already admitted; and the soul has been acknowledged by us to be full of these and ten thousand similar oppositions occurring at the same moment?

And we were right, he said.

Yes, I said, thus far we were right; but there was an omission which must now be supplied.

What was the omission?

Were we not saying that a good man, who has the misfortune to lose his son or anything else which is most dear to him, will bear the loss with more equanimity than another?

Yes, indeed.

But will he have no sorrow, or shall we say that although he cannot help sorrowing, he will moderate his sorrow?

The latter, he said, is the truer statement.

Tell me: will he be more likely to struggle and hold out against his sorrow when he is seen by his equals, or when he is alone in a deserted place?

The fact of being seen will make a great difference, he said.

When he is by himself he will not mind saying many things which he would be ashamed of anyone hearing, and also doing many things which he would not care to be seen doing?

Ture.

And doubtless it is the law and reason in him which bids him resist; while it is the affliction itself which is urging him to indulge his sorrow?

True.

But when a man is drawn in two opposite directions, to and from the same object, this, as we affirm, necessarily implies two distinct principles in him?

Certainly.

One of them is ready to follow the guidance of the law?

How do you mean?

The law would say that to be patient under calamity is best, and that we should not give way to impatience, as the good and evil in such things are not clear, and nothing is gained by impatience; also, because no human thing is of serious importance, and grief stands in the way of that which at the moment is most required.

What is most required? he asked.

That we should take counsel about what has happened, and when the dice have been thrown, according to their fall, order our affairs in the way which reason deems best; not, like children who have had a fall, keeping hold of the part struck and wasting time in setting up a howl, but always accustoming the soul forthwith to apply a remedy, raising up that which is sickly and fallen, banishing the cry of sorrow by the healing art.

Yes, he said, that is the true way of meeting the attacks of fortune.

Well then, I said, the higher principle is ready to follow this suggestion of reason?

Clearly.

But the other principle, which inclines us to recollection of our troubles and to lamentation, and can never have enough of them, we may call irrational, useless, and cowardly?

Indeed, we may.

Now does not the principle which is thus inclined to complaint, furnish a great variety of materials for imitation? Whereas the wise and calm temperament, being always nearly equable, is not easy to imitate or to appreciate when imitated, especially at a public festival when a promiscuous crowd is assembled in a theatre. For the feeling represented is one to which they are strangers.

Certainly.

Then the imitative poet who aims at being popular is not by nature made, nor is his art intended, to please or to affect the rational principle in the soul; but he will appeal rather to the lachrymose and fitful temper, which is easily imitated?

Clearly.

And now we may fairly take him and place him by the side of the painter, for he is like him in two ways: first, inasmuch as his creations have an inferior degree of truth—in this, I say, he is like him; and he is also like him in being the associate of an inferior part of the soul; and this is enough to show that we shall be right in refusing to admit him into a state which is to be well ordered, because he awakens and nourishes this part of the soul, and by strengthening it impairs the reason. As in a city when the evil are permited to wield power and the finer men are put out of the way, so in the soul of each man, as we shall maintain, the imitative poet implants an evil constitution, for he indulges the irrational nature which has no discernment of greater and less, but thinks the same thing at one time great and at another small—he is an imitator of images and is very far removed from the truth.

Exactly.

But we have not yet brought forward the heaviest count in our accusation—the power which poetry has of harming even the good (and there are very few who are not harmed), is surely an awful thing?

Yes, certainly, if the effect is what you say.

Hear and judge: The best of us, as I conceive, when we listen to a passage of Homer or one of the tragedians, in which he represents some hero who is drawling out his sorrows in a long oration, or singing, and smiting his breast—the best of us, you know, delight in giving way to sympathy, and are in raptures at the excellence of the poet who stirs our feelings most.

Yes, of course I know.

But when any sorrow of our own happens to us, then you may observe that we pride ourselves on the opposite quality—we would fain be quiet and patient; this is considered the manly part, and the other which delighted us in the recitation is now deemed to be the part of a woman.

Very true, he said.

Now can we be right in praising and admiring another who is doing that which any one of us would abominate and be ashamed of in his own person?

No, he said, that is certainly not reasonable.

Nay, I said, quite reasonable from one point of view.

What point of view?

If you consider, I said, that when in misfortune we feel a natural hunger and desire to relieve our sorrow by weeping and lamentation, and that this very feeling which is starved and suppressed in our own calamities is satisfied and delighted by the poets—the better nature in each of us, not having been sufficiently trained by reason or habit, allows the sympathetic element to break loose because the sorrow is another's; and the spectator fancies that there can be no disgrace to himself in praising and pitying anyone who while professing to be a brave man, gives way to untimely lamentation; he thinks that the pleasure is a gain, and is far from wishing to lose it by rejection of the whole poem. Few persons ever reflect, as I should imagine, that the contagion must pass from others to themselves. For the pity which has been nourished and strengthened in the misfortunes of others is with difficulty repressed in our own.

How very true!

And does not the same hold also of the ridiculous? There are jests which you would be ashamed to make yourself, and yet on the comic stage, or indeed in private, when you hear them, you are greatly amused by them, and are not at all disgusted at their unseemliness—the case of pity is repeated—there is a principle in human nature which is disposed to raise a laugh, and this, which you once restrained by reason because you were afraid of being thought a buffoon, is now let out again; and having stimulated the risible faculty at the theater, you are betrayed unconsciously to yourself into playing the comic poet at home.

Quite true, he said.

And the same may be said of lust and anger and all the other affections, of desire and pain and pleasure, which are held to be inseparable from every action—in all of them poetry has a like effect; it feeds and waters the passions instead of drying them up; she lets them rule, although they ought to be controlled if mankind are ever to increase in happiness and virtue.

I cannot deny it.

Therefore, Glaucon, I said, whenever you meet with any of the eulogists of Homer declaring that he has been the educator of Hellas, and that he is profitable for education and for the ordering of human things, and that you should take him up again and again and get to know him and regulate your whole life according to him, we may love and honor those who say these things—they are excellent people, as far as their lights extend; (607) and we are ready to acknowledge that Homer is the greatest of poets and first of tragedy writers; but we must remain firm in our conviction that hymns to the gods and praises of famous men are the only poetry which ought to be admitted into our state. For if you go beyond this and allow the honeyed Muse to enter, either in epic or lyric verse, not law and the reason of mankind, which by common consent have ever been deemed best,[5] but pleasure and pain will be the rulers in our state.

That is most true, he said.

And now since we have reverted to the subject of poetry, let this our defense serve to show the reasonableness of our former judgment in sending away out of our state an art having the tendencies which we have described; for reason constrained us. But that she may not impute to us any harshness or want of politeness, let us tell her that there is an ancient quarrel between philosophy and poetry; of which there are many proofs, such as the saying of "the yelping hound howling at her lord," or of one "mighty in the vain talk of fools," and "the mob of sages circumventing Zeus," and the "subtle thinkers who are beggars after all";[6] and there are innumerable other signs of ancient enmity between them. Notwithstanding this, let us assure the poetry which aims at pleasure, and the art of imitation, that if she will only prove her title to exist in a well-ordered state we shall be delighted to receive her—we are very conscious of her charms; but it would not be right on that account to betray the truth. I dare say, Glaucon, that you are as much charmed by her as I am, especially when she appears in Homer?

Yes, indeed, I am greatly charmed.

Shall I propose, then, that she be allowed to return from exile, but upon this condition only—that she make a defense of herself in some lyrical or other meter?

Certainly.

And we may further grant to those of her defenders who are lovers of poetry and yet not poets the permission to speak in prose on her behalf: let them show not only that she is pleasant but also useful to states and to human life, and we will listen in a kindly spirit; for we shall surely be the gainers if this can be proved, that there is a use in poetry as well as a delight?

Certainly, he said, we shall be the gainers.

If her defense fails, then, my dear friend, like other persons who are enamored of something, but put a restraint upon themselves when they think their desires are opposed to their interests, so too must we after the manner of lovers give her up, though not without a struggle. We too are inspired by that love of such poetry which the education of noble states has implanted in us, (608) and therefore we shall be glad if she appears at her best and truest; but so long as she is unable to make good her defense, this argument of ours shall be a charm to us, which we will repeat to ourselves while we listen to her strains; that we may not fall away into the childish love of her which captivates the many. At all events we are well aware that poetry,[7] such as we have described, is not to be regarded seriously as attaining to the truth; and he who listens to her, fearing for the safety of the city which is within him, should be on his guard against her seductions and make our words his law.

Yes, he said, I quite agree with you.

Yes, I said, my dear Glaucon, for great is the issue at stake, greater than appears, whether a man is to be good or bad. And what will any one be profited if under the influence of honor or money or power, aye, or under the excitement of poetry, he neglect justice and virtue?

Yes, he said; I have been convinced by the argument, as I believe that anyone else whould have been.

And yet we have not described the greatest prizes and rewards which await virtue.

What, are there any greater still? If there are, they must be of an inconceivable greatness.

Why, I said, what was ever great in a short time? The whole period from childhood to age is surely but a little thing in comparison with eternity?

Say rather "nothing," he replied.

And should an immortal being be anxious for this little time rather than for the whole?

For the whole, certainly. But why do you ask?

Are you not aware, I said, that the soul of man is immortal and imperishable?

He looked at me in astonishment, and said: No, by heaven: And are you really prepared to maintain this?

Yes, I said, I ought to be, and you too—there is no difficulty in proving it.

I see a great difficulty; but I should like to hear you state this argument of which you make so light.

Listen then.

I am attending.

There is a thing which you call good and another which you call evil?

Yes, he replied.

Would you agree with me in thinking that the corrupting and destroying element is the evil, and the saving and improving element the good?

True.

And you admit that everything has a good and also an evil; (609) as ophthalmia is the evil of the eyes and disease of the whole body; as blight is of corn, and rot of timber, or rust of copper and iron: in everything, or in almost everything, there is an inherent evil and disease?

Yes, he said.

And any of these evils, when it attacks a thing, first makes it rotten and at last wholly dissolves and destroys it?

True.

The vice and evil which is inherent in each is the destruction of each; or if this does not destroy them there is nothing else that will; for good certainly will never destroy anything, nor, again, will that which is neither good nor evil.

Certainly not.

If, then, we find any nature which has indeed some inherent corruption, but of a kind whereby it cannot be dissolved or destroyed, we may be certain that of such a nature there is no destruction?

That may be assumed.

Well, I said, and is there no evil which corrupts the soul?

Yes, he said, there are all the evils which we were just now passing in review: unrighteousness, intemperance, cowardice, ignorance.

But does any of these dissolve and destroy her? And here do not let us fall into the error of supposing that the unjust and foolish man, when he is detected, perishes through his own injustice, which is an evil of the soul. You should represent it rather in this way: The evil of the body is a disease which dissolves and wastes it, till it is no longer a body at all; and all the things of which we were just now speaking come to annihilation through their own corruption attaching to them and inhering in them and so destroying them. Is not this true?

Yes.

Consider the soul in like manner. Does injustice, or vice in some other form, waste and consume her? Do they by attaching to the soul and inhering in her at last bring her to death, and so separate her from the body?

Certainly not.

And yet, I said, it is unreasonable to suppose that anything can perish under a disease proper to another thing, which could not be destroyed by a corruption of its own?

It is, he replied.

Consider, I said, Glaucon, that even the badness of food, whether staleness, decomposition, or any other bad quality, when confined to the actual food, is not supposed to destroy the body; although, if the badness of food causes the body to become corrupt in its own fashion, then we should say that the body has been destroyed by a corruption of itself, which is disease, brought on by this; (610) but that the body, being one thing, can be destroyed by the badness of food, which is another, unless it has implanted the corruption peculiar to the body—this we shall absolutely deny?

Very true.

On the same principle, then, unless some bodily evil can produce in the soul an evil of the soul, we must not suppose that the soul, which is one thing, can be dissolved, in the absence of its own disease, by an evil which belongs to another?

Yes, he said, there is reason in that.

Either, then, let us refute this conclusion, or, while it remains unrefuted, let us never say that fever, or any other disease, or the knife put to the throat, or even the cutting up of the whole body into the minutest pieces, can destroy the soul, until she herself is proved to become more unholy or unrighteous in consequence of these things being done to the body; but that the soul or anything else can be free from its special evil and yet be destroyed because a foreign evil is found in something else, is not to be affirmed by any man.

And surely, he replied, no one will ever prove that the souls of dying men become more unjust in consequence of death.

But if someone, lest he be obliged to admit the immortality of the soul, boldly goes out to meet our argument, and says that the dying do really become more evil and unrighteous, then, if the speaker is right, I suppose that injustice, like disease, must be assumed to be fatal to the unjust, and that those who take this disorder die by the natural inherent power of destruction which evil has, and which kills them sooner or later, but in quite another way from that in which, at present, the wicked receive death at the hands of others as the penalty of their deeds?

Nay, he said, in that case injustice, if fatal to the unjust, will not be so very terrible to him, for he will thus be delivered from evil. But I rather suspect the opposite will prove to be the truth, and that injustice which, if it have the power, will murder others, gives the murderer greater vitality—aye, and keeps him well awake too; so far removed is her dwelling-place from being a house of death.

True, I said; if the inherent natural vice or evil of the soul has not the force to kill or destroy her, hardly will that which is appointed to be the destruction of some other body destroy a soul, or anything else except that of which it was appointed to be the destruction.

Yes, that can hardly be.

But the soul which cannot be destroyed by any evil, whether its own or that of something else, must exist for ever, and if existing for ever, must be immortal?

Certainly.

Let that be our conclusion, I said; and, if it is a true conclusion, you will observe that the souls must always be the same, for if none be destroyed they will not diminish in number. Neither will they increase, for the increase of the immortal natures must, as you know, come from something mortal, and all things would thus end in immortality.

Very true.

But this we cannot believe—reason will not allow us—any more than we can believe the soul, in her truest nature, to be a thing full of variety and internal difference and dissimilarity.

What do you mean? he said.

It is not easy, I said, for that thing to be immortal which is a compound of many elements not perfectly adapted to each other, as the soul has appeared to us to be.

Certainly not.

Her immortality is demonstrated by the previous argument, and there are many other proofs; but to see her as she really is, not, as we now behold her, marred by association with the body and other miseries, you must contemplate her with the eye of reason, in her original purity; and then her greater beauty will be revealed, and the forms of justice and injustice and all the things which we have described will be more vividly discerned. Thus far, we have spoken the truth concerning her as she appears at present, but we have seen her only in a condition which may be compared to that of the sea-god Glaucus, whose original nature could hardly be discerned by those who saw him because his natural members were either broken off or crushed and damaged by the waves in all sorts of ways, and incrustations had grown over them of seaweed and shells and stones, so that he was more like some monster than to his own natural form. And the soul which we behold is in a similar condition, disfigured by ten thousand ills. But not there, Glaucon, not there must we look.

Where then?

At her love of wisdom. Let us see whom she affects, and what society and converse she seeks in virtue of her near kindred with the immortal and eternal and divine; also how different she would become if wholly following this superior principle, and borne by a divine impulse out of the ocean in which she now is, and disengaged from the stones and shells and things of earth and rock which in wild variety spring up around her because she feeds upon earth, (612) and is overgrown by the good things of this life as they are termed: then you would see her as she is, and know whether she have one shape only or many, or what her nature and state may be. Of her affections and of the forms which she takes in this present life I think that we have now given a very fair description.

True, he replied.

And thus, I said, we have disproved the charges brought against justice without introducing the rewards and glories, which, as you were saying, are to be found ascribed to her in Homer and Hesiod; but justice in her own nature has been shown to be best for the soul in her own nature. Let a man do what is just, whether he have the ring of Gyges or not, and even if in addition to the ring of Gyges he put on the helmet of Hades.

Very true.

And now, Glaucon, there will be no harm in further enumerating how many and how great are the rewards which justice and the other virtues procure to the soul from gods and men, both in life and after death.

Certainly not, he said.

Will you repay me, then, what you borrowed in the argument?

What did I borrow?

The assumption that the just man should appear unjust and the unjust just: for you were of opinion[8] that even if the true state of the case could not possibly escape the eyes of gods and men, still this admission ought to be made for the sake of the argument, in order that pure justice might be weighed against pure injustice. Do you remember?

The injustice would be mine if I had forgotten.

Then, as the cause is decided, I demand on behalf of justice that we should admit the estimation in which she is held by gods and men to be what it really is; since she has been shown to confer the blessings which come from reality, and not to deceive those who truly possess her, let what has been taken from her be given back, that so she may win the palm of appearance which is hers also, and which she gives to her own.

The demand, he said, is just.

In the first place, I said—and this is the first thing which you will have to give back—the nature both of the just and unjust is truly known to the gods.

Granted.

And if they are both known to them, one must be the friend and the other the enemy of the gods, as we admitted from the beginning?

True.

And the friend of the gods may be supposed to receive in its best form whatever the gods bestow, excepting only such evil as may have been the necessary consequence of former sins?

Certainly.

Then this must be our notion of the just man, that even when he is in poverty or sickness, or any other seeming misfortune, these things will bring him finally to some good end, either in life, or perhaps in death; for the gods surely will not neglect anyone whose earnest desire is to become just and by the pursuit of virtue to be like God, as far as man can attain the divine likeness?

Yes, he said; if he is like God he will surely not be neglected by Him.

And of the unjust must not the opposite be supposed?

Certainly.

Such, then, are the palms of victory which the gods give the just?

That, at least, is my conviction.

And what do they receive of men? Look at things as they really are, and you will see that the clever unjust are in the case of runners, who run well from the starting-place to the goal but not back again from the goal: they go off at a great pace, but in the end only look foolish, slinking away with their ears draggling on their shoulders, and without a crown; but the true runner comes to the finish and receives the prize and is crowned. And this is the way with the just; they endure to the end of every action and association, and of life itself, and so win a good report and carry off the prizes which men have to bestow.

True.

Will you then allow me to repeat of the just the blessings which you were attributing to the fortunate unjust? I shall say of them that as they grow older they become rulers in their own city if they care to be; they marry whom they like and give in marriage to whom they will; all that you said of the others I now say of these. And, on the other hand, of the unjust I say that the greater number, even though they escape in their youth, are found out at last and look foolish at the end of their course, and when they come to be old and miserable are flouted alike by stranger and citizen; they are beaten, and then come those things unfit for ears polite, as you truly term them; they will be racked and have their eyes burned out, as you were saying. And you may suppose that I have repeated the remainder of your tale of horrors. I ask once more, will you allow all this?

Certainly, he said, for what you say is true.

These, then, are the prizes and rewards and gifts which are bestowed upon the just by gods and men in this present life, in addition to the other good things which justice of herself provides.

Yes, he said; and they are fair and lasting.

And yet, I said, all these are as nothing either in number or greatness in comparison with those other recompenses which await both just and unjust after death. And you ought to hear them, and then both just and unjust will have received from us a full payment of the debt which the argument owes to them.

Speak, he said; there are few things which I would more gladly hear.

Well, I said, I will tell you a tale; not one of the tales which Odysseus tells[9] to the hero Alcinous, yet this too is a tale of a hero, Er the son of Armenius, a Pamphylian by birth. He was slain in battle, and ten days afterwards, when the bodies of the dead were taken up already in a state of corruption, his body was found unaffected by decay, and carried away home to be buried. And on the twelfth day, as he was lying on the funeral pile, he returned to life and told them what he had seen in the other world. He said that when his soul left the body it went on a journey with a great company, and that they came to a mysterious place at which there were two openings in the earth; they were near together, and over against them were two other openings in the heaven above. In the intermediate space there were judges seated, who commanded the just, after they had given judgment on them and had bound their sentences in front of them, to ascend by the way up through the heaven on the right hand; and in like manner the unjust were bidden by them to descend by the lower way on the left hand; these also bore tokens of all their deeds, but fastened on their backs. He drew near, and they told him that he was to be the messenger who would carry the report of the other world to men, and they bade him hear and see all that was to be heard and seen in that place. Then he beheld and saw on one side the souls departing at either opening of heaven and earth when sentence had been given on them; and at the two other openings other souls, some ascending out of the earth dusty and worn with travel, some descending out of heaven clean and bright. And arriving ever and anon they seemed to have come from a long journey, and they went forth with gladness into the meadow, where they encamped as at a festival; and those who knew one another embraced and conversed, the souls which came from earth curiously inquiring about the things above, and the souls which came from heaven about the things beneath.

And they told one another of what had happened by the way, (615) those from below weeping and sorrowing at the remembrance of the things which they had endured and seen in their journey beneath the earth (now the journey lasted a thousand years), while those from above were describing heavenly delights and visions of inconceivable beauty. The full story, Glaucon, would take too long to tell; but the sum was this: He said that for every wrong which they had done and every person whom they had injured they had suffered tenfold; or once in a hundred years—such being reckoned to be the length of man's life, and the penalty being thus paid ten times in a thousand years. If, for example, there were any who had been the cause of many deaths by the betrayal of cities or armies, or had cast many into slavery, or been accessory to any other ill treatment, for all their offences, and on behalf of each man wronged, they were afflicted with tenfold pain, and the rewards of beneficence and justice and holiness were in the same proportion. I need hardly repeat what he said concerning young children dying almost as soon as they were born. Of piety and impiety to gods and parents, and of murder, there were retributions other and greater far which he described. He mentioned that he was present when one of the spirits asked another, "Where is Ardiaeus the Great?" (Now this Ardiaeus lived a thousand years before the time of Er: he had been the tyrant of some city of Pamphylia and had murdered his aged father and his elder brother, and was said to have committed many other abominable crimes.) The answer of the other spirit was: "He comes not hither and will never come. And this," said he, "was one of the dreadful sights which we ourselves witnessed. We were at the mouth of the cavern, and, having completed all our experiences, were about to reascend, when of a sudden, we saw Ardiaeus and several others, most of whom were tyrants; but there were also some private individuals who had been great criminals: they were just, as they fancied, about to return into the upper world, but the mouth, instead of admitting them, gave a roar, whenever any of these whose wickedness was incurable or who had not been sufficiently punished tried to ascend; and then wild men of fiery aspect, who were standing by and heard the sound, seized and carried them[10] off; (616) but Ardiaeus and others they bound head and foot and hand, and threw them down, and flayed them with scourges, and dragged them along the road outside the entrance, carding them on thorns like wool, and declaring to the passers-by what were their crimes, and that they were being taken away to be cast into Tartarus." And of all the many terrors of every kind which they had endured, he said that there was none like the terror which each of them felt at that moment, lest they should hear the voice; and when there was silence, one by one they ascended with exceeding joy. These, said Er, were the penalties and retributions, and there were blessings as great.

Now when each band which was in the meadow had tarried seven days, on the eighth they were obliged to proceed on their journey, and, on the fourth day after, he said that they came to a place where they could see from above a line of light, straight as a column, extending right through the whole heaven and through the earth, in color resembling the rainbow, only brighter and purer; another day's journey brought them to the place, and there, in the midst of the light, they saw the ends of the chains of heaven let down from above: for this light is the belt of heaven, and holds together the circumference of the universe, like the under-girders of a trireme.[11] From these ends is extended the spindle of Necessity, on which all the revolutions turn. The shaft and hook of this spindle are made of adamant, and the whorl is made partly of steel and also partly of other materials. The nature of the whorl is as follows; it is, in outward shape, like the whorl used on earth; and his description of it implied that there is one large hollow whorl which is quite scooped out, and into this is fitted another lesser one, and another, and another, and four others, making eight in all, like vessels which fit into one another; the whorls show their circular edges on the upper side, and on their lower side all together form one continuous whorl. This is pierced by the shaft which is driven home through the centre of the eighth. The first and outermost whorl has the rim broadest, and the seven inner whorls are narrower, in the following proportions—the sixth is next to the first in size, the fourth next to the sixth; then comes the eighth; the seventh is fifth, the fifth is sixth, the third is seventh, last and eighth comes the second. The largest [or fixed stars] is spangled, and the seventh [or sun] is brightest; (617) the eighth [or moon] colored by the reflected light of the seventh; the second and fifth [Saturn and Mercury] are in color like one another, and yellower than the preceding; the third [Venus] has the whitest light; the fourth [Mars] is reddish; the sixth [Jupiter] is in whiteness second. Now the whole spindle has the same motion; but, as the whole revolves in one direction, the seven inner circles move slowly in the other, and of these the swiftest is the eighth; next in swiftness are the seventh, sixth, and fifth, which move together; third in swiftness appeared to move, because of this contrary motion, the fourth; the third appeared fourth and the second fifth. The spindle turns on the knees of Necessity; and on the upper surface of each circle stands a siren, who goes round with them, chanting a single tone or note. The eight together form one harmony; and round about, at equal intervals, there is another band, three in number, each sitting upon her throne: these are the Fates, daughters of Necessity, who are clothed in white robes and have chaplets upon their heads, Lachesis and Clotho and Atropos, who accompany with their voices the harmony of the sirens—Lachesis singing of the past, Clotho of the present, Atropos of the future; Clotho from time to time assisting with a touch of her right hand the revolution of the outer circle of the whorl or spindle, and Atropos with her left hand touching and guiding the inner ones, and Lachesis laying hold of either in turn, first with one hand and then with the other.

When Er and the spirits arrived, their duty was to go at once to Lachesis; but first of all there came a prophet who arranged them in order; then he took from the knees of Lachesis lots and samples of lives, and having mounted a high pulpit, spoke as follows: "Hear the word of Lachesis, the daughter of Necessity. Mortal souls, behold a new cycle of life and mortality. Your genius will not be allotted to you, but you will choose your genius; and let him who draws the first lot have the first choice, and the life which he chooses shall be his destiny. Virtue is free, and as a man honors or dishonors her he will have more or less of her; the responsibility is with the chooser—God is not responsible." When the

Interpreter had thus spoken he scattered lots indifferently among them all, and each of them took up the lot which fell near him, (618) all but Er himself (he was not allowed), and each as he took his lot perceived the number which he had obtained. Then the Interpreter placed on the ground before them the patterns of lives; and there were many more lives than the souls present, and they were of all sorts. There were lives of every animal and of man in every condition. And there were tyrannies among them, some lasting out the tyrant's life, others which broke off in the middle and came to an end in poverty and exile and beggary; and there were lives of famous men, some who were famous for their form and beauty as well as for their strength and success in games, or, again, for their birth and the qualities of their ancestors; and some who were the reverse of famous for the opposite qualities. And of women likewise. The disposition of the soul was not, however, included in them, because the soul, when choosing a new life, must of necessity become different. But there was every other quality, and they all mingled with one another, and also with elements of wealth and poverty, and disease and health; and there were also states intermediate in these respects.

And here, my dear Glaucon, is the supreme peril of our human state; and therefore each one of us must take the utmost care to forsake every other kind of knowledge and seek and study one thing only, if peradventure he may be able to discover someone who will make him able to discern between a good and an evil life, and so to choose always and everywhere the better life as he has opportunity. He should consider the bearing of all these things which have been mentioned severally and collectively upon the excellence of a life; he should know what the effect of beauty is, for good or evil, when combined with poverty or wealth in this or that kind of soul, and what are the good and evil consequences of noble and humble birth, of private and public station, of strength and weakness, of cleverness and dullness, and of all the natural and acquired gifts of the soul, and the operation of them when blended with one another; he will then look at the nature of the soul, and from the consideration of all these qualities he will be able to determine which is the better and which is the worse; and so he will choose, giving the name of evil to the life which will tend to make his soul more unjust, and good to the life which will make his soul more just; all else he will disregard. For we have seen and know that this is the best choice both in life and after death. (619) A man must take with him into the world below an adamantine faith in truth and right, that there too he may be undazzled by the desire of wealth or the other allurements of evil, lest he be drawn into tyrannies and similar activities, and do irremediable wrongs to others and suffer yet worse himself; but may know how to choose a life moderate in these respects and avoid the extremes on either side, as far as possible, not only in this life but in all that which is to come. For this way brings men to their greatest happiness.

And according to the report of the messenger from the other world this was what the prophet said at the time: "Even for the last comer, if he chooses wisely and will live diligently, there is appointed a happy and not undesirable existence. Let not him who chooses first be careless, and let not the last despair."

And when he had spoken, he who had the first choice came forward and in a moment chose the greatest tyranny; his mind having been darkened by folly and sensuality, he had not made any thorough inspection before he chose, and did not perceive that he was fated, among other evils, to devour his own children. But when he had time to examine the lot and saw what was in it, he began to beat his breast and lament over his choice, forgetting the proclamation of the prophet; for, instead of throwing the blame of his misfortune on himself, he accused chance and the gods, and everything rather than himself. Now he was one of those who came from heaven, and in a former life had dwelt in a well-ordered state, virtuous from habit only, and without philosophy. And for the most part it was true of others who were caught in this way, that the greater number of them came from heaven and therefore they had never been schooled by trial, whereas the pilgrims who came from earth having themselves suffered and seen others suffer were not in a hurry to choose. And owing to this inexperience of theirs, and also to the accident of the lot, the majority of the souls exchanged a good destiny for an evil or an evil for a good. For if a man had always on his arrival in this world dedicated himself from the first to sound philosophy, and had been moderately fortunate in the number of the lot, he might, as the messenger reported, be happy here, and also his journey to another life and return to this, instead of being rough and underground, would be smooth and heavenly. Most curious, he said, was the spectacle—sad and laughable and strange; for the choice of the souls was in most cases based on their experience of a previous life. (620) There he saw the soul which had once been Orpheus choosing the life of a swan out of enmity to the race of women, hating to be born of a woman because they had been his murderers; he beheld also the soul of Thamyras choosing the life of a nightingale; birds, on the other hand, like the swan and other musicians, wanting to be men. The soul which obtained the twentieth lot chose the life of a lion, and this was the soul of Ajax the son of Telamon, who would not be a man, remembering the injustice which was done him in the judgment about the arms. The next was Agamemnon, who took the life of an eagle, because, like Ajax, he hated human nature by reason of his sufferings. About the middle came the lot of Atalanta; she, seeing the great fame of an athlete, was unable to resist the temptation: and after her there followed the soul of Epeus the son of Panopeus passing into the nature of a woman skilled in some craft; and far away among the last who chose, the soul of the jester Thersites was putting on the form of a monkey. There came also the soul of Odysseus having yet to make a choice, and his lot happened to be the last of them all. Now the recollection of former toils had disenchanted him of ambition, and he went about for a considerable time in search of the life of a private man who had no cares; he had some difficulty in finding this, which was lying about and had been neglected by everybody else; and when he saw it, he said that he would have done the same had his lot been first instead of last, and gladly chose it. And not only did men pass into animals, but I must also mention that there were animals tame and wild who changed into one another and into corresponding human natures—the righteous into the gentle and the unrighteous into the savage, in all sorts of combinations.

All the souls had now chosen their lives, and they went in the order of their choice to Lachesis, who sent with them the genius whom they had severally chosen, to be the guardian of their lives and and the fulfiller of the choice: this genius led the souls first to Clotho, and drew them within the revolution of the spindle impelled by her hand, thus ratifying the destiny of each; and then, when they were fastened to this, carried them to Atropos, who spun the threads and made them irreversible, (621) whence without turning round they passed beneath the throne of Necessity; and when they had all passed, they marched on to the plain of Forgetfulness, in intolerable scorching heat, for the plain was a barren waste destitute of trees and verdure; and then towards evening they encamped by the river of Unmindfulness, whose water no vessel can hold; of this they were all obliged to drink a certain quantity, and those who were not saved by wisdom drank more than was necessary; and each one as he drank forgot all things. Now after they had gone to rest, about the middle of the night there was a thunderstorm and earthquake, and then in an instant they were driven upwards in all manner of ways to their birth, like stars shooting. He himself was hindered from drinking the water. But in what manner or by what means he returned to the body he could now say; only in the morning, awaking suddenly, he found himself lying on the pyre.

And thus, Glaucon, the tale has been saved and has not perished, and will save us if we are obedient to the word spoken; and we shall pass safely over the river of Forgetfulness and our soul will not be defiled. Wherefore my counsel is that we hold fast ever to the heavenly way and follow after justice and virtue always, considering that the soul is immortal and able to endure every sort of good and every sort of evil. Thus shall we live dear to one another and to the gods, both while remaining here and when, like conquerors in the games who go round to gather gifts, we receive our reward. And it shall be well with us both in this life and in the pilgrimage of a thousand years which we have been describing.

NOTES

Book III

1. Spoken by the ghost of Achilles, *Od*. 11. 489.
2. *Il*. 20. 64.
3. Said by Achilles when he tries, in vain, to embrace the ghost of Patroclus, *Il*. 23. 103.
4. *Od*. 10. 495.
5. *Il*. 16. 856.
6. *Il*. 23. 100.
7. *Od*. 24. 6 (refers to the souls of the slain suitors of Penelope).
8. Appropriate.
9. Mourning his friend Patroclus, *Il*. 24. 10.

10. Perhaps in a metaphorical sense, "reeling." Plato has slightly altered the text of Homer.—JOWETT'S EDITORS.
11. *Il.* 18. 23.
12. When he saw Achilles mistreating the body of his son Hector, *Il.* 22. 414.
13. The speaker is Thetis, the mother of Achilles, *Il.* 18. 54.
14. Zeus when he saw Hector pursued by Achilles, *Il.* 22. 168.
15. *Il.* 16. 433.
16. *Il.* 1. 599.
17. *Od.* 17. 383ff.
18. Or, "if his words are accompanied by actions."—B.J.
19. *Il.* 4. 412.
20. *Il.* 3. 3.
21. *Il.* 4. 431.
22. Spoken by Achilles to his king Agamemnon, *Il.* 1. 225.
23. Odysseus is the speaker, *Od.* 9. 8.
24. *Od.* 12. 342.
25. *Il.* 14. 294ff.
26. *Od.* 8. 266.
27. Odysseus is speaking, *Od.* 20. 17.
28. Quoted by Suidas (a historical and literary encyclopedia compiled about 1,000 A.D.) as ascribed to Hesiod.
29. *Il.* 9. 515.
30. *Il.* 24. 175.
31. Cf. *Rep.* 10. 595.
32. *Il.* 22. 15ff.
33. *Il.* 21. 130, 223ff.
34. *Il.* 23. 151.
35. *Il.* 22. 395.
36. *Il.* 23. 175.
37. From the *Niobe* of Aeschylus.
38. Agamemnon and Menelaus, *Il.* 1. 15.
39. A wreath or garland worn on the head.
40. Juror.
41. I.e. the four notes of the tetrachord.—B.J.
42. Socrates expresses himself carelessly in accordance with his assumed ignorance of the details of the subject. In the first part of the sentence he appears to be speaking of paeonic rhythms, which are in the ratio of 3/2; in the second part, of dactylic and anapaestic rhythms, which are in the ratio of 1/1; in the last clause, of iambic and trochaic rhythms, which are in the ratio of 1/2 or 2/1.—B.J. ⟨See n. 46, p. 206.⟩

Book X

1. Stories taken from epic poetry often served as the plots of Greek tragedies. Thus Homer was considered the first tragic poet.
2. Or (probably better), "we have been accustomed to assume that there is one single idea corresponding to each group of particulars; and to these we give the same name (as we give the idea)."—JOWETT'S EDITORS, note abridged.
3. Or, "with his nouns and verbs."—B.J.
4. Dactylic hexameter.

5. Or, "law and the principle which the community in every case has pronounced to be the best,"—JOWETT'S EDITORS.

6. Reading and sense uncertain. The origin of all these quotations is unknown.—JOWETT'S EDITORS.

7. I.e. imitative poetry. The word imitation, in the recent argument, had not the same sense as in Book III; but it has always been implied that there might be poetry which is not imitative.—JOWETT'S EDITORS.

8. Text doubtful. Perhaps "you demanded . . . this admission should be made."—JOWETT'S EDITORS.

9. *Od.* 11–12.

10. I.e. those who were not incurable, but had further punishment to endure.—JOWETT'S EDITORS.

11. War galley; the earliest kind of a Greek warship.

Laws

FROM

Book VII

ATHENIAN STRANGER. Let us then affirm the paradox that strains of music are our laws (*nomoi*), and this latter being the name which the ancients gave to lyric songs, they probably would not have very much objected to our proposed application of the word. (800) Some one, either asleep or awake, must have had a dreamy suspicion of their nature. And let our decree be as follows: No one in singing or dancing shall offend against public and consecrated models, and the general fashion among the youth, any more than he would offend against any other law. And he who observes this law shall be blameless; but he who is disobedient, as I was saying, shall be punished by the guardians of the laws, and by the priests and priestesses. Suppose that we imagine this to be our law.

CLEINIAS. Very good.

ATH. Can anyone who makes such laws escape ridicule? Let us see. I think that our only safety will be in first framing certain models for composers. One of these models shall be as follows: if a sacrifice has been offered, and the victims burnt according to law—if, I say, anyone who may be a son or brother, standing by another at the altar and over the victims, horribly blasphemes, will not his words inspire despondency and evil omens and forebodings in the mind of his father and of his other kinsmen?

CLE. Of course.

ATH. And this is just what takes place in almost all our cities. A magistrate offers a public sacrifice, and there come in not one but many choruses, who take up a position a little way from the altar, and from time to time pour forth all sorts of horrible blasphemies on the sacred rites, exciting the souls of the audience with words and rhythms and melodies most sorrowful to hear; and he who at the moment when the city has offered sacrifice makes the citizens weep most, carries away the palm of victory. Now, ought we not to forbid such strains as these? And if ever our citizens must hear such lamentations, then on some unblest and inauspicious day let there be choruses of foreign and hired minstrels, like those hirelings who accompany the departed at funerals with barbarous Carian chants. That is the sort of thing which will be appropriate if we have such strains at all; and let the apparel of the singers of the funeral dirge be, not circlets and ornaments of gold, but the reverse. Enough of all this. I will simply ask once more whether we shall lay down as one of our principles of song——

CLE. What?

ATH. That we should avoid every word of evil omen; let that kind of song which is of good omen be heard everywhere and always in our state. I need hardly ask again, but shall assume that you agree with me.

CLE. By all means; that law is approved by the suffrages of us all.

ATH. But what shall be our next musical law or type? Ought not prayers to be offered up to the gods when we sacrifice?

CLE. Certainly.

ATH. And our third law, if I am not mistaken, will be to the effect that our poets, understanding prayers to be requests which we make to the gods, will take especial heed that they do not by mistake ask for evil instead of good. To make such a prayer would surely be too ridiculous.

CLE. Very true.

ATH. Were we not a little while ago quite convinced that no silver or golden Plutus should dwell in our state?[1]

CLE. To be sure.

ATH. And what has it been the object of our argument to show? Did we not imply that the poets are not always quite capable of knowing what is good or evil? And if one of them utters a mistaken prayer in song or words, he will make our citizens pray for the opposite of what we ordain in matters of the highest import; than which, as I was saying, there can be few greater mistakes. Shall we then propose as one of our laws and models relating to the Muses——

CLE. What? Will you explain the law more precisely?

ATH. Shall we make a law that the poet shall compose nothing contrary to the ideas of the lawful, or just, or beautiful, or good, which are allowed in the state? Nor shall he be permitted to communicate his compositions to any private individuals, until he shall have shown them to the appointed judges and the guardians of the law, and they are satisfied with them. As to the persons whom we appoint to be our legislators about music[2] and as to the director of education,[3] these have been already indicated. Once more then, as I have asked more than once, shall this be our third law, and type, and model—what do you say?

CLE. Let it be so, by all means.

ATH. Then it will be proper to have hymns and praises of the gods,[4] intermingled with prayers; and after the gods prayers and praises should be offered in like manner to demigods and heroes, suitable to their several characters.

CLE. Certainly.

ATH. In the next place there will be no objection to a law, that citizens who are departed and have done good and energetic deeds, either with their souls or with their bodies, and have been obedient to the laws, should receive eulogies; this will be very fitting.

CLE. Quite true. (802)

ATH. But to honor with hymns and panegyrics those who are still alive is not safe; a man should run his course, and make a fair ending, and then we will praise him; and let praise be given equally to women as well as men who have been distinguished in virtue. The order of songs and dances shall be as follows: There are many ancient musical compositions and dances which are excellent, and from these it is fair to select what is proper and suitable to the newly-founded city; and they shall choose judges of not less than fifty years of age, who shall make the selection, and any of the old poems which they deem sufficient they shall include; any that are deficient or altogether unsuitable, they shall either utterly throw aside, or examine and amend, taking into their counsel poets and musicians, and making use of their potential genius; but explaining to them the wishes of the legislator in order that they may regulate dancing, music, and all choral strains, according to the mind of the judges; and not allowing them to indulge, except in some few matters, their individual pleasures and fancies. Now the irregular strain of music is always made ten thousand times better by attaining to law and order, and rejecting the honeyed Muse[5]— not however that we mean wholly to exclude pleasure, which is the characteristic of all music. And if a man be brought up from childhood to the age of discretion and maturity in the use of the orderly and severe music, when he hears the opposite he detests it, and calls it illiberal; but if trained in the sweet and vulgar music, he deems the severer kind cold and displeasing. So that, as I was saying before, while he who hears them gains no more pleasure from the one than from the other, the one has the advantage of making those who are trained in it better men, whereas the other makes them worse.

CLE. Very true.

ATH. Again, we must distinguish and determine on some general principle what songs are suitable to women, and what to men, and must assign to them their proper melodies and rhythms. It is shocking for a whole harmony to be inharmonical, or for a rhythm to be unrhythmical, and this will happen when the melody is inappropriate to them. And therefore the legislator must assign to these also their forms. Now both sexes have melodies and rhythms which of necessity belong to them; and those of women are clearly enough indicated by their natural difference. The grand, and that which tends to courage, may be fairly called manly; (803) but that which inclines to moderation and temperance, may be declared both in law and in ordinary speech to be the more womanly quality. This, then, will be the general order of them.

Let us now speak of the manner of teaching and imparting them, and the persons to whom, and the time when, they are severally to be imparted. As the shipwright first lays down the lines of the keel, and thus, as it were, draws the ship in outline, so do I seek to distinguish the patterns of life, and lay down their keels according to the nature of different men's souls; seeking truly to consider by what means, and in what ways, we may go through the voyage of life best. Now human affairs are hardly worth considering in earnest, and yet we must be in earnest about them—a sad necessity constrains us. And having got thus far, there will be a fitness in our completing the matter, if we can only find some suitable method of doing so. But what do I mean? Someone may ask this very question, and quite rightly, too.

CLE. Certainly.

ATH. I say that about serious matters a man should be serious, and about a matter which is not serious he should not be serious; and that God is the natural and worthy object of our most serious and blessed endeavors, for man, as I said before,[6] is made to be the plaything of God, and this, truly considered, is the best of him; wherefore also every man and woman should walk seriously, and pass life in the noblest of pastimes, and be of another mind from what they are at present.

CLE. In what respect?

ATH. At present they think that their serious pursuits should be for the sake of their sports, for they deem war a serious pursuit, which must be managed well for the sake of peace; but the truth is, that there neither is, nor has been, nor ever will be, either amusement or instruction in any degree worth speaking of in war, which is nevertheless deemed by us to be the most serious of our pursuits. And therefore, as we say, every one of us should live the life of peace as long and as well as he can.[7] And what is the right way of living? Are we to live in sports always? If so, in what kind of sports? We ought to live sacrificing, and singing, and dancing, and then a man will be able to propitiate the gods, and to defend himself against his enemies and conquer them in battle. The type of song or dance by which he will propitiate them has been described, and the paths along which he is to proceed have been cut for him. (804) He will go forward in the spirit of the poet: "Telemachus, some things thou wilt thyself find in thy heart, but other things God will suggest; for I deem that thou wast not born or brought up without the will of the gods."[8] And this ought to be the view of our alumni; they ought to think that what has been said is enough for them, and that any other things their genius and god will suggest to them—he will tell them to whom, and when, and to what gods severally they are to sacrifice and perform dances, and how they may propitiate the deities, and live according to the appointment of nature; being for the most part puppets, but having some little share of reality.

· · · · · ·

ATH. That is quite true; and you mean to imply that the road which we are taking may be disagreeable to some but is agreeable to as many others, or if not to as many, at any rate to persons not inferior to the others, and in company with them you bid me, at whatever risk, to proceed along the path of legislation which has opened out of our present discourse, and to be of good cheer, and not to faint.

CLE. Certainly.

ATH. And I do not faint; I say, indeed, that we have a great many poets writing in hexameter, trimeter, and all sorts of measures—some who are serious, others who aim only at raising a laugh—and all mankind declare that the youth who are rightly educated should be brought up in them and saturated with them; some insist that they should be constantly hearing them read aloud, and always learning them, so as to get by heart entire poets; (811) while others select choice passages and long speeches, and make compendiums of them, saying that these ought to be committed to memory, if a man is to be made good and wise by experience and learning of many things. And you want me now to tell them plainly in what they are right and in what they are wrong.

CLE. Yes, I do.

ATH. But how can I in one word rightly comprehend all of them? I am of opinion, and if I am not mistaken, there is a general agreement, that every one of these poets has said many things well and many things the reverse of well; and if this be true, then I do affirm that much learning is dangerous to youth.

CLE. How would you advise the guardian of the law to act?

ATH. In what respect?

CLE. I mean to what pattern should he look as his guide in permitting the young to learn some things and forbidding them to learn others. Do not shrink from answering.

ATH. My good Cleinias, I rather think that I am fortunate.

CLE. How so?

ATH. I think that I am not wholly in want of a pattern, for when I consider the words which we have spoken from early dawn until now, and which, as I believe, have been inspired by heaven, they appear to me to be quite like a poem. When I reflected upon all these words of ours, I naturally felt pleasure, for of all the discourses which I have ever learnt or heard, either in poetry or prose, this seemed to me to be the justest, and most suitable for young men to hear; I cannot imagine any better pattern than this which the guardian of the law who is also the director of education can have. He cannot do better than advise the teachers to teach the young these words and any which are of a like nature, if he should happen to find them, either in poetry or prose, or if he come across unwritten discourses akin to ours, he should certainly preserve them, and commit them to writing. And, first of all, he shall constrain the teachers themselves to learn and approve them, and any of them who will not, shall not be employed by him, but those whom he finds agreeing in his judgment, he shall make use of and shall commit to them the instruction and education of youth. (812) And here and on this wise let my fanciful tale about letters and teachers of letters come to an end.

· · · · · ·

ATH. Enough of wrestling; we will now proceed to speak of other movements of the body. Such motion may be in general called dancing, and is of two kinds: one of nobler figures, imitating the honorable, the other of the more ignoble figures, imitating the mean; and of both these there are two further subdivisions. Of the serious, one kind is of those engaged in war and vehement action, and is the exercise of a noble person and a manly heart; the other exhibits a temperate soul in the enjoyment of prosperity and modest pleasures, and may be truly called and is the dance of peace. (815) The warrior dance is different from the peaceful one, and may be rightly termed pyrrhic[9]; this imitates the modes of avoiding blows and missiles by dropping or giving way, or springing aside, or rising up or falling down; also the opposite postures which are those of action, as, for example, the imitation of archery and the hurling of javelins, and of all sorts of blows. And when the imitation is of brave bodies and souls, and the action is direct and muscular, giving for the most part a straight movement to the limbs of the body—that, I say, is the true sort; but the opposite is not right. In the dance of peace what we have to consider is whether a man bears himself naturally and gracefully, and after the manner of men who duly conform to the law. But before proceeding I must distinguish the dancing about which there is any doubt, from that about which there is no doubt. Which is the doubtful kind, and how are the two to be distinguished? There are dances of the Bacchic sort, both those in which, as they say, they imitate drunken men, and which are named after the nymphs, and Pan, and Silenuses, and satyrs; and also those in which purifications are made or mysteries celebrated—all this sort of dancing cannot be rightly defined as having either a peaceful or a warlike character, or indeed as having any meaning whatever, and may, I think, be most truly described as distinct from the warlike dance, and distinct from the peaceful, and not suited for a city at all. There let it lie; and so leaving it to lie, we will proceed to the dances of war and peace, for with these we are undoubtedly concerned. Now the unwarlike muse, which honors in dance the gods and the sons of the gods, is entirely associated with the consciousness of prosperity; this class may be subdivided into two lesser classes, of which one is expressive of an escape from some labor or danger into good, and has greater pleasures, the other expressive of preservation and increase of former good, in which the pleasure is less exciting—in all these cases, every man when the pleasure is greater, moves his body more, and less when the pleasure is less; and, again, if he be more orderly and has learned courage from discipline he moves less, (816) but if he be a coward, and has no training or self-control, he makes greater and more violent movements, and in general when he is speaking or singing he is not altogether able to keep his body still; and so out of the imitation of words in gestures the whole art of dancing has arisen. And in these various kinds of imitation one man moves in an orderly, another in a disorderly manner; and as the ancients may be observed to have given many names which are according to nature and deserving of praise, so there is an excellent one which they have given to the dances of men who in their times of prosperity are moderate in their pleasures—the giver of names, whoever he was, assigned to them a very true, and poetical, and rational name, when he called them Emmeleiai, or dances of order, thus establishing two kinds of dances of the nobler sort, the dance of war which he called the pyrrhic, and the dance of peace which he called Emmeleia,[10] or the dance of order; giving to each their appropriate and becoming name. These things the legislator should indicate in general outline, and the guardian of the law should inquire into them and search them out, combining dancing with music, and assigning to the several sacrificial feasts that which is suitable to them; and when he has consecrated all of them in due order, he shall for the future change nothing, whether of dance or song. Thenceforward the city and the citizens shall continue to have the same pleasures, themselves being as far as possible alike, and shall live well and happily.

I have described the dances which are appropriate to noble bodies and generous souls. But it is necessary also to consider and know uncomely persons and thoughts, and those which are intended to produce laughter in comedy, and have a comic character in respect of style, song, and dance, and of the imitations which these afford. For serious things cannot be understood without laughable things, nor opposites at all without opposites, if a man is really to have intelligence of either; but he cannot carry out both in action, if he is to have any degree of virtue. And for this very reason he should learn them both, in order that he may not in ignorance do or say anything which is ridiculous and out of place—he should command slaves and hired strangers to imitate such things, but he should never take any serious interest in them himself, nor should any freeman or freewoman be discovered taking pains to learn them; and there should always be some element of novelty in the imitation. Let these then be laid down, both in law and in our discourse, as the regulations of laughable amusements which are generally called comedy. (817) And, if any of the serious poets, as they are termed, who write tragedy, come to us and say: "O strangers, may we go to your city and country or may we not, and shall we bring with us our poetry—what is your will about these matters?" How shall we answer the divine men? I think that our answer should be as follows:[11] Best of strangers, we will say to them, we also according to our ability are tragic poets, and our tragedy is the best and noblest; for our whole state is an imitation of the best and noblest life, which we affirm to be indeed the very truth of tragedy. You are poets and we are poets, both makers of the same strains, rivals and antagonists in the noblest of dramas, which true law can alone perfect, as our hope is. Do not then suppose that we shall all in a moment allow you to erect your stage in the agora,[12] or introduce the fair voices of your actors, speaking above our own, and permit you to harangue our women and children, and the common people, about our institutions, in language other than our own, and very often the opposite of our own. For a state would be mad which gave you this license, until the magistrates had determined whether your poetry might be recited, and was fit for publication or not. Wherefore, O ye sons and scions of the softer Muses, first of all show your songs to the magistrates, and let them compare them with our own, and if they are the same or better we will give you a chorus; but if not, then, my friends, we cannot. Let these, then, be the customs ordained by law about all dances and the teaching of them, and let matters relating to slaves be separated from those relating to masters, if you do not object.

NOTES

1. *Laws* 5. 741e.
2. *Laws* 6. 764c.
3. *Laws* 6. 765d.
4. Cf. *Rep.* 10. 607a.
5. Or, . . . "even though the pleasure of music is not counted."—JOWETT'S EDITORS.
6. *Laws* 1. 644D.e.

7. *Laws* 1. 628.
8. *Od.* 3. 26ff.
9. The shortest metrical foot in classical verse, consisting of two short syllables (⌣⌣).
10. The solemn dance of the chorus in Greek tragedy.
11. Cf. *Rep.* 3. 398a and 10. 607a.
12. Public square in which the popular political assembly met.

Aristotle

384–322 B.C.

Aristotle was born in the Greek colony of Stagirus in Macedonia. His father was the physician and friend of Amyntas III (sometimes called Amyntas II) of Macedonia, father of Philip II and grandfather of Alexander the Great. Aristotle inherited his father's interest in the natural sciences and shared the characterisitc Ionian fascination with direct scientific observation and natural change. This fundamental concern clearly distinguished him from his teacher Plato, who focused his philosophic inquiry on the changeless realm of Being.

Aristotle entered Plato's Academy at age seventeen and remained one of his most devoted students until Plato's death in 347 B.C. Diogenes Laertius reports that when Plato read the Academy his treatise on the soul, Aristotle "was the only person who sat it out, while all the rest rose up and went away." The relationship between the two men is of enormous interest, but very little, alas, is known about it. Philosophically Aristotle achieved a substantial revision of Platonism by working his own empiricism into Plato's metaphysical foundation. Aristotle was drawn to the classification process of the natural sciences as strongly as Plato was to mathematics and metaphysics. It is probable that his thinking began to develop along original lines even in his early days at the Academy.

After Plato's death, Aristotle left Athens and spent several years in Asia Minor, first in Assos and then in Mytilene, directing philosophical centers patterned on the Academy. During this time he wrote part of his Politics and turned increasingly to the study of biology.

In 343–42 Philip II of Macedonia invited Aristotle to his court at Pella to tutor his son Alexander. Aristotle composed for Alexander two works on politics and seems to have developed the young man's interest in the subject, though the precise effect of his teaching on the future Alexander the Great is a matter of speculation. Around 339, after some three years as Alexander's tutor, Aristotle returned to his family home in Stagirus.

In 335 Aristotle went back to Athens and opened his own academy, the Lyceum. He and his followers became known as the Peripatetic school because Aristotle often lectured in the peripatos, a covered walkway common in Greek buildings. The Lyceum came to assume an *importance as great as Plato's Academy. Aristotle organized a library and a museum in order to illustrate his lectures, and under his supervision scholars initiated a tremendous variety of researches. According to some sources, Alexander the Great himself directed the hunters and fishermen of his empire to send specimens and scientific observations to the school.*

After the death of Alexander in 323, Athens experienced a wave of anti-Macedonian sentiment. A natural target because of his ties with Macedonia, Aristotle was charged with impiety, and he retired to Chalcis, reportedly to save the Athenians from "sinning twice against philosophy" (a reference to the execution of Socrates). He died at Chalcis the next year.

Aristotle's works on literary theory, notably his Poetics, *were the first to examine the formal structure of the literary work. As such, they are the precursors of much subsequent literary scholarship, including much of the contemporary work in the field. Aristotle takes Plato as a point of departure, but he significantly revises Plato's negative appraisal of poetry. Like Plato, Aristotle holds that* mimesis *(imitation) is necessary to art, but for Aristotle* mimesis *has a much more positive function. He claims, for instance, that tragedy imitates people who are "better than the present population" and that the poet is more "philosophical" than the historian because he is more concerned with generalities than with individual facts. Thus, Aristotelian* mimesis *connotes something very different from Plato's definition, in which art copies only the particular, itself a copy of a higher Ideal Form. Aristotle emphasizes that art can illuminate human existence; its goal is the essentially intellectual one of presenting insights into human action. Aristotle indicates in the* Poetics *that he considers tragedy the highest form of* mimesis.

Aristotle's formal analysis of tragedy (the missing second book of the Poetics *was supposed to concern comedy) introduces many important terms into critical discourse.* Cartharsis *is a key concept in Aristotle even though he mentions it only briefly in the* Poetics. *By* catharsis *he seems to mean some combination of emotional purgation and intellectual clarification provided by the action of a tragedy. Although Aristotle never discusses the moral impact of the drama (which itself distinguishes him from most classical critics), he seems to imply that it is part of the dramatic structure rather than a result of the imitation of moral action. Such an implication suggests that his conception of the nature of a work of art is more complex than Plato's. The* Poetics *intimates that the work of art resembles a living organism and has meanings analogous to organic meanings. Art, then, performs two functions: it both imitates reality and conforms to its own inner logic.*

Plot (mythos) is for Aristotle the "soul" of the living organism. His Poetics *consists primarily of a taxonomy of tragedy in which he isolates the elements of the play. Aristotle stresses* hamartia, *the "tragic flaw" that dwells in the protagonist of the tragedy. This complements his insistence that the tragic character must be* spoudaios, *or "noble." That is, the hero's downfall must be sufficiently tragic to arouse pity in the audience. Aristotle defines, for the first time, elements of the plot such as reversal (a radical change of fortune), recognition (a change from ignorance to knowledge), complication, and resolution.*

The Poetics *was not an extremely influential text until the Renaissance, when it was rediscovered as the authoritative work for neoclassical criticism, a position it has maintained down to the present. It may be said that all Western formalist criticism is in direct descent from Aristotle, just as all expressive and Romantic criticism derives from Longinus.*

Formalist criticism has always been intimately allied with rhetorical criticism, an alliance essentially formed by the tradition's belated absorption of Aristotle's Poetics *into its already intense utilization of Aristotle's* Rhetoric. *The dominant rhetorical tradition, though Sophist in its roots, nevertheless took on a Platonic coloring largely because Aristotle codified and transmitted the Sophistic heritage. There is an irony in this; Socrates honed his dialectic in an agon with the Sophists, but his disciple Plato's student, Aristotle, won the ultimate, rather dry triumph of philosophy over the orators by giving a philosophic idea of order to rhetoric.*

The text of the Poetics *that has come down to us (itself not the original Greek text) is most probably a series of lecture notes, either Aristotle's own or one of his student's. It is terse to the point of obscurity in places, and editors are divided as to its interpretation. The translation reprinted here is by Ingram Bywater, with the exception of the translations from Greek verse by Lane Cooper on pages 167–68 and pages 172–73, reprinted by permission of the publisher from Lane Cooper,* Aristotle on the Art of Poetry: An Amplified Version with Supplementary Illustrations *(Ithaca, N.Y.: Cornell University Press, 1962). The bracketed footnotes are reprinted by permission of the publisher from Friedrich Solmsen, ed.,* The Rhetoric and the Poetics of Aristotle *(New York: Random House, 1954). The selection from Aristotle's* Rhetoric, *translated by M. E. Hubbard, is reprinted by permission of Oxford University Press from D. A. Russell and M. Winterbottom, eds.,* Ancient Literary Criticism: The Principal Texts in New Translations *(Oxford, 1972). © 1972 by Oxford University Press.*

POETICS

PRELIMINARY DISCOURSE ON TRAGEDY, EPIC POETRY, AND COMEDY, AS THE CHIEF FORMS OF IMITATIVE POETRY

Our subject being Poetry, I propose to speak not only of the art in general but also of its species and their respective capacities; of the structure of plot required for a good poem; of the number and nature of the constituent parts of a poem; and likewise of any other matters in the same line of inquiry. Let us follow the natural order and begin with the primary facts.

Epic poetry and Tragedy, as also Comedy, Dithyrambic poetry, and most flute-playing and lyre-playing, are all, viewed as a whole, modes of imitation. But at the same time they differ from one another in three ways, either by a difference of kind in their means, or by differences in the objects, or in the manner of their imitations.

The Poetic Arts Distinguished (1) by the Means They Use

Just as colour and form are used as means by some, who (whether by art or constant practice) imitate and portray many things by their aid, and the voice is used by others; so also in the above-mentioned group of arts, the means with them as a whole are rhythm, language, and harmony—used, however, either singly or in certain combinations. A combination of harmony and rhythm alone is the means in flute-playing and lyre-playing, and any other arts there may be of the same description, e.g. imitative piping. Rhythm alone, without harmony, is the means in the dancer's imitations; for even he, by the rhythms of his attitudes, may represent men's characters, as well as what they do and suffer. There is further an art which imitates by language alone, without harmony, in prose or in verse, and if in verse, either in some one or in a plurality of metres. This form of imitation is to this day without a name. We have no common name for a mime of Sophron or Xenarchus and a Socratic Conversation;[1] and we should still be without one even if the imitation in the two instances were in trimeters or elegiacs or some other kind of verse—though it is the way with people to tack on "poet" to the name of a metre, and talk of elegiac-poets and epic-poets, thinking that they call them poets not by reason of the imitative nature of their work, but indiscriminately by reason of the metre they write in. Even if a theory of medicine or physical philosophy be put forth in a metrical form, it is usual to describe the writer in this way; Homer and Empedocles, however, have really nothing in common apart from their metre;[2] so that, if the one is to be called a poet, the other should be termed a physicist rather than a poet. We should be in the same position also, if the imitation in these instances were in all the metres, like the *Centaur* (a rhapsody in a medley of all metres) of Chaeremon;[3] and Chaeremon one has to recognize as a poet. So much, then, as to these arts. There are, lastly, certain other arts, which combine all the means enumerated, rhythm, melody, and verse, e.g. Dithyrambic and Nomic poetry, Tragedy and Comedy; with this difference, however, that the three kinds of means are in some of them all employed together, and in others brought in separately, one after the other. These elements of difference in the above arts I term the means of their imitation.

The Poetic Arts Distinguished
(2) by Their Objects

1448a   The objects the imitator represents are actions, with agents who are necessarily either good men or bad—the diversities of human character being nearly always derivative from this primary distinction, since the line between virtue and vice is one dividing the whole of mankind. It follows, therefore, that the agents represented must be either above our own level of goodness, or beneath it, or just such as we are; in the same way as, with the painters, the personages of Polygnotus[4] are better than we are, those of Pauson[5] worse, and those of Dionysius[6] just like ourselves. It is clear that each of the above-mentioned arts will admit of these differences, and that it will become a separate art by representing objects with this point of difference. Even in dancing, flute-playing, and lyre-playing such diversities are possible; and they are also possible in the nameless art that uses language, prose or verse without harmony, as its means; Homer's personages, for instance, are better than we are; Cleophon's[7] are on our own level; and those of Hegemon[8] of Thasos, the first writer of parodies, and Nicochares,[9] the author of the *Diliad*, are beneath it. The same is true of the Dithyramb and the Nome: the personages may be presented in them with the difference exemplified in the . . . of . . . and Argas,[10] and in the Cyclopses of Timotheus and Philoxenus.[11] This difference it is that distinguishes Tragedy and Comedy also; the one would make its personages worse, and the other better, than the men of the present day.

The Poetic Arts Distinguished
(3) by the Manner of Their Imitations

A third difference in these arts is in the manner in which each kind of object is represented. Given both the same means and the same kind of object for imitation one may either (1) speak at one moment in narrative and at another in an assumed character, as Homer does; or (2) one may remain the same throughout, without any such change; or (3) the imitators may represent the whole story dramatically, as though they were actually doing the things described.

As we said at the beginning, therefore, the differences in the imitation of these arts come under three heads, their means, their objects, and their manner.

So that as an imitator Sophocles will be on one side akin to Homer, both portraying good men; and on another to Aristophanes, since both present their personages as acting and doing. This in fact, according to some, is the reason for plays being termed dramas, because in a play the personages act the story. Hence too both Tragedy and Comedy are claimed by the Dorians as their discoveries; Comedy by the Megarians—by those in Greece as having arisen when Megara became a democracy, and by the Sicilian Megarians on the ground that the poet Epicharmus[12] was of their country, and a good deal earlier then Chionides and Magnes;[13] even Tragedy also is claimed by certain of the Peloponnesian Doreans. In support of this claim they point to the words "comedy" and "drama." Their word for the outlying hamlets, they say, is *comae*, whereas Athenians call them *demes*—thus assuming that comedians got the name not from their *comoe* or revels, but from their strolling from hamlet to hamlet, lack of appreciation keeping them out of the city. Their word also for "to act," they say, is *dran*, whereas Athenians use *prattein*.

1448b

So much, then, as to the number and nature of the points of difference in the imitation of these arts.

Origin and Development of Poetry and Its Kinds

It is clear that the general origin of poetry was due to two causes, each of them part of human nature. Imitation is natural to man from childhood, one of his advantages over the lower animals being this, that he is the most imitative creature in the world, and learns at first by imitation. And it is also natural for all to delight in works of imitation. The truth of this second point is shown by experience: though the objects themselves may be painful to see, we delight to view the most realistic representations of them in art, the forms for example of the lowest animals and of dead bodies. The explanation is to be found in a further fact: to be learning something is the greatest of pleasures not only to the philosopher but also to the rest of mankind, however small their capacity for it; the reason of the delight in seeing the picture is that one is at the same time learning—gathering the meaning of things, e.g. that the man there is so-and-so; for if one has not seen the thing before, one's pleasure will not be in the picture as an imitation of it, but will be due to the execution or colouring or some similar cause. Imitation, then, being natural to us—as also the sense of harmony and rhythm, the metres being obviously species of rhythms—it was through their original aptitude, and by a series of improvements for the most part gradual on their first efforts, that they created poetry out of their improvisations.

Poetry, however, soon broke up into two kinds according to the differences of character in the individual poets; for the graver among them would represent noble actions, and those of noble personages; and the meaner sort the actions of the ignoble. The latter class produced invectives at first, just as others did hymns and panegyrics. We know of no such poem by any of the pre-Homeric poets, though there were probably many such writers among them; instances, however, may be found from Homer downwards, e.g. his *Margites*,[14] and the similar poems of others. In this poetry of invective its natural fitness brought an iambic metre into use; hence our present term "iambic," because it was the metre of their "iambs" or invectives against one another. The result was that the old poets became some of them writers of heroic and others of iambic verse. Homer's position, however, is peculiar: just as he was in the serious style the poet of poets, standing alone not only through the literary excellence, but also through the dramatic character of his imitations, so too he was the first to outline for us the general forms of Comedy by producing not a dramatic invective, but a dramatic picture of the Ridiculous; his *Margites* in fact stands in the same relation to our comedies as the *Iliad* and *Odyssey* to our tragedies. As soon, however, as Tragedy and Comedy appeared in the field, those naturally drawn to the one line of poetry became writers of comedies instead of iambs, and those naturally drawn to the other, writers of tragedies instead of epics, because these new modes of art were grander and of more esteem than the old.

1449a

If it be asked whether Tragedy is now all that it need be in its formative elements, to consider that, and decide it theoretically and in relation to the theatres, is a matter for another inquiry.

It certainly began in improvisations—as did also Comedy; the one originating with the authors of the Dithyramb, the other with those of the phallic songs, which still survive as institutions in many of our cities. And its advance after that was little by little, through their improving on whatever they had before them at each stage. It was in fact only after a long series of changes that the movement of Tragedy stopped on its attaining to its natural form. (1) The number of actors was first increased to two by Aeschylus, who curtailed the business of the Chorus, and made the dialogue, or spoken portion, take the leading part in the play. (2) A third actor and scenery were due to Sophocles. (3) Tragedy acquired also its magnitude. Discarding short stories and a ludicrous diction, through its passing out of its satyric stage, it assumed, though only at a late point in its progress, a tone of dignity; and its metre changed then from trochaic to iambic. The reason for their original use of the trochaic tetrameter was that their poetry was satyric and more connected with dancing than it now is. As soon, however, as a spoken part came in, nature herself found the appropriate metre. The iambic, we know, is the most speakable of metres, as is shown by the fact that we very often fall into it in conversation, whereas we rarely talk hexameters, and only when we depart from the speaking tone of voice. (4) Another change was a plurality of episodes or acts. As for the remaining matters, the superadded embellishments and the account of their introduction, these must be taken as said, as it would probably be a long piece of work to go through the details.

Comedy and Epic Poetry

As for Comedy, it is (as has been observed[15]) an imitation of men worse than the average; worse, however, not as regards any and every sort of fault, but only as regards one particular kind, the Ridiculous, which is a species of the Ugly. The Ridiculous may be defined as a mistake or deformity not productive of pain or harm to others; the mask, for instance, that excites laughter, is something ugly and distorted without causing pain.

Though the successive changes in Tragedy and their authors are not unknown, we cannot say the same of Comedy; its early stages passed unnoticed, because it was not as yet taken up in a serious way. It was only at a late point in its progress that a chorus of comedians was officially granted by the archon;[16] they used to be mere volunteers. It had also already certain definite forms at the time when the record of those termed comic poets begins. Who it was who supplied it with masks, or prologues, or a plurality of actors and the like, has remained unknown. The invented Fable, or Plot, however, orginated in Sicily, with Epicharmus and Phormis;[17] of Athenian poets Crates[18] was the first to drop the Comedy of invective and frame stories of a general and non-personal nature, in other words, Fables or Plots.

1449b

Epic poetry, then, has been seen to agree with Tragedy to this extent, that of being an imitation of serious subjects in a grand kind of verse. It differs from it, however, (1) in that it is in one kind of verse and in narrative form; and (2) in its length—which is due to its action having no fixed limit of time, whereas Tragedy endeavours to keep as far as possible within a single circuit of the sun, or something near that. This, I say, is another point of difference between them, though at first the practice in this respect was just the same in tragedies as in epic poems. They differ also (3) in their constituents, some being common to both and others peculiar to Tragedy—hence a judge of good and bad in Tragedy is a judge of that in epic poetry also. All the parts of an epic are included in Tragedy; but those of Tragedy are not all of them to be found in the Epic.

DEFINITION OF A TRAGEDY, AND THE RULES FOR ITS CONSTRUCTION

Definition, and Analysis into Qualitative Parts

Reserving hexameter poetry and Comedy for consideration hereafter,[19] let us proceed now to the discussion of Tragedy; before doing so, however, we must gather up the definition resulting from what has been said. A tragedy, then, is the imitation of an action that is serious and also, as having magnitude, complete in itself; in language with pleasurable accessories, each kind brought in separately in the parts of the work; in a dramatic, not in a narrative form; with incidents arousing pity and fear, wherewith to accomplish its catharsis of such emotions. Here by "language with pleasurable accessories" I mean that with rhythm and harmony or song superadded; and by "the kinds separately" I mean that some portions are worked out with verse only, and others in turn with song.

As they act the stories, it follows that in the first place the Spectacle (or stage-appearance of the actors) must be some part of the whole; and in the second Melody and Diction, these two being the means of their imitation. Here by "Diction" I mean merely this, the composition of the verses; and by "Melody," what is too completely understood to require explanation. But further: the subject represented also is an action; and the action involves agents, who must necessarily have their distinctive qualities both of character and thought, since it is from these that we ascribe certain qualities to their actions. There are in the natural order of things, therefore, two causes, Thought and Character, of their actions, and consequently of their success or failure in their lives. Now the action (that which was done) is represented in the play by the Fable or Plot. The Fable, in our present sense of the term, is simply this, the combination of the incidents, or things done in the story; whereas Character is what makes us ascribe certain moral qualities to the agents; and Thought is shown in all they say when proving a particular point or, it may be, enunciating a general truth. There are six parts consequently of every tragedy, as a whole (that is) of such or such quality, viz. a Fable or Plot, Characters, Diction, Thought, Spectacle, and Melody; two of them arising from the means, one from the manner, and three from the objects of the dramatic imitation; and there is nothing else besides these six. Of these, its formative elements, then, not a few of the dramatists have made due use, as every play, one may say, admits of Spectacle, Character, Fable, Diction, Melody, and Thought.

The most important of the six is the combination of the incidents of the story. Tragedy is essentially an imitation not of persons but of action and life, of happiness and misery. All human happiness or misery takes the form of action; the end for which we live is a certain kind of activity, not a quality. Character gives us qualities, but it is in our actions—what we do—that we are happy or the reverse. In a play accordingly they do not act in order to portray the Characters; they include the Characters for the sake of the action. So that it is the action in it, i.e. its Fable or Plot, that is the end and purpose of the tragedy; and the end is everywhere the chief thing. Besides this, a tragedy is impossible without action, but there may be one without Character. The tragedies of most of the moderns are characterless—a defect common among poets of all kinds, and with its counterpart in painting in Zeuxis[20] as compared with Polygnotus; for whereas the latter is strong in character, the work of Zeuxis is devoid of it. And again: one may string together a series of characteristic speeches of the utmost finish as regards Diction and Thought, and yet fail to produce the true tragic effect; but one will have much better success with a tragedy which, however inferior in these respects, has a Plot, a combination of incidents, in it. And again: the most powerful elements of attraction in Tragedy, the Peripeties and Discoveries, are parts of the Plot. A further proof is in the fact that beginners succeed earlier with the Diction and Characters than with the construction of a story; and the same may be said of nearly all the early dramatists. We maintain, therefore, that the first essential, the life and soul, so to speak, of Tragedy is the Plot; and that the Characters come second—compare the parallel in painting, where the most beautiful colours laid on without order will not give one the same pleasure as a simple black-and-white sketch of a portrait. We maintain that Tragedy is primarily an imitation of action, and that it is mainly for the sake of the action that it imitates the personal agents. Third comes the element of Thought, i.e. the power of saying whatever can be said, or what is appropriate to the occasion. This is what, in the speeches in Tragedy, falls under the arts of Politics and Rhetoric; for the older poets make their personages discourse like statesmen, and the moderns like rhetoricians. One must not confuse it with Character.

Character in a play is that which reveals the moral purpose of the agents, i.e. the sort of thing they seek or avoid, where that is not obvious—hence there is no room for Character in a speech on a purely indifferent subject. Thought, on the other hand, is shown in all they say when proving or disproving some particular point, or enunciating some universal proposition. Fourth among the literary elements is the Diction of the personages, i.e., as before explained,[21] the expression of their thoughts in words, which is practically the same thing with verse as with prose. As for the two remaining parts, the Melody is the greatest of the pleasurable accessories of Tragedy. The Spectacle, though an attraction, is the least artistic of all the parts, and has least to do with the art of poetry. The tragic effect is quite possible without a public performance and actors; and besides, the getting-up of the Spectacle is more a matter for the costumier than the poet.

The Plot

Arrangement and length of the play. Having thus distinguished the parts, let us now consider the proper construction of the Fable or Plot, as that is at once the first and the most important thing in Tragedy. We have laid it down that a tragedy is an imitation of an action that is complete in itself, as a whole of some magnitude; for a whole may be of no magnitude to speak of. Now a whole is that which has beginning, middle, and end. A beginning is that which is not itself necessarily after anything else, and which has naturally something else after it; an end is that which is naturally after something itself, either as its necessary or usual consequent, and with nothing else after it; and a middle, that which is by nature after one thing and has also another after it. A well-constructed Plot, therefore, cannot either begin or end at any point one likes; beginning and end in it must be of the forms just described. Again: to be beautiful, a living creature, and every whole made up of parts, must not only present a certain order in its arrangement of parts, but also be of a certain definite magnitude. Beauty is a matter of size and order, and therefore impossible either (1) in a very minute creature, since our perception becomes indistinct as it approaches instantaneity; or (2) in a creature of vast size—one, say, 1,000 miles long—as in that case, instead of the object being seen all at once, the unity and wholeness of it is lost to the beholder. Just in the same way, then, as a beautiful whole made up of parts, or a beautiful living creature, must be of some size, but a size to be taken in by the eye, so a story or Plot must be of some length, but of a length to be taken in by the memory. As for the limit of its length, so far as that is relative to public performance and spectators, it does not fall within the theory of poetry. If they had to perform a hundred tragedies, they would be timed by water-clocks, as they are said to have been at one period. The limit, however, set by the actual nature of the thing is this: the longer the story, consistently with its being comprehensible as a whole, the finer it is by reason of its magnitude. As a rough general formula, "a length which allows of the hero passing by a series of probable or necessary stages from misfortune to happiness, or from happiness to misfortune," may suffice as a limit for the magnitude of the story.

Unity of action. The Unity of a Plot does not consist, as some suppose, in its having one man as its subject. An infinity of things befall that one man, some of which it is impossible to reduce to unity; and in like manner there are many actions of one man which cannot be made to form one action. One sees, therefore, the mistake of all the poets who have written a *Heracleid*, a *Theseid*, or similar poems; they suppose that, because Heracles was one man, the story also of Heracles must be one story. Homer, however, evidently understood this point quite well, whether by art or instinct, just in the same way as he excels the rest in every other respect. In writing an *Odyssey*, he did not make the poem cover all that ever befell his hero—it befell him, for instance, to get wounded on Parnassus and also to feign madness at the time of the call to arms, but the two incidents had no necessary or probable connexion with one another—instead of doing that, he took as the subject of the *Odyssey*, as also of the *Iliad*, an action with a Unity of the kind we are describing. The truth is that, just as in the other imitative arts one imitation is always of one thing, so in poetry the story, as an imitation of action, must represent one action, a complete whole, with its several incidents so closely connected that the transposal or withdrawal of any one of them will disjoin and dislocate the whole. For that which makes no perceptible difference by its presence or absence is no real part of the whole.

The probable and the universal. From what we have said it will be seen that the poet's function is to describe, not the thing that has happened, but a kind of thing that might happen, i.e. what is possible as being probable or necessary. The distinction between historian and poet is not in the one writing prose and the other verse—you might put the work of Herodotus into verse, and it would still be a species of history; it consists really in this, that the one describes the thing that has been, and the other a kind of thing that might be. Hence poetry is something more philosophic and of graver import than history, since its statements are of the nature rather of universals, whereas those of history are singulars. By a universal statement I mean one as to what such or such a kind of man will probably or necessarily say or do—which is the aim of poetry, though it affixes proper names to the characters; by a singular statement, one as to what, say, Alcibiades did or had done to him. In Comedy this has become clear by this time; it is only when their plot is already made up of probable incidents that they give it a basis of proper names, choosing for the purpose any names that may occur to them, instead of writing like the old iambic poets about particular persons. In Tragedy, however, they still adhere to the historic names; and for this reason: what convinces is the possible; now whereas we are not yet sure as to the possibility of that which has not happened, that which has happened is manifestly possible, else it would not have come to pass. Nevertheless even in Tragedy there are some plays with but one or two known names in them, the rest being inventions; and there are some without a single known name, e.g. Agathon's *Antheus*,[22] in which both incidents and names are of the poet's invention; and it is no less delightful on that account. So that one must not aim at a rigid adherence to the traditional stories on which tragedies are based. It would be absurd, in fact, to do so, as even the known stories are only known to a few, though they are a delight none the less to all.

It is evident from the above that the poet must be more the poet of his stories or Plots than of his verses, inasmuch as he is a poet by virtue of the imitative element in his work, and it is actions that he imitates. And if he should come to take a subject from actual history, he is none the less a poet for that; since some historic occurrences may very well be in the probable and possible order of things; and it is in that aspect of them that he is their poet.

Of simple Plots and actions the episodic are the worst. I call a Plot episodic when there is neither probability nor necessity in the sequence of its episodes. Actions of this sort bad poets construct through their own fault, and good ones on account of the players. His work being for public performance, a good poet often stretches out a Plot beyond its capabilities, and is thus obliged to twist the sequence of incident.

Tragedy, however, is an imitation not only of a complete action, but also of incidents arousing pity and fear. Such incidents have the very greatest effect on the mind when they occur unexpectedly and at the same time in consequence of one another; there is more of the marvellous in them then than if they happened of themselves or by mere chance. Even matters of chance seem most marvellous if there is an appearance of design as it were in them; as for instance the statue of Mitys at Argos[23] killed the author of Mitys' death by falling down on him when a looker-on at a public spectacle; for incidents like that we think to be not without a meaning. A Plot, therefore, of this sort is necessarily finer than others.

Simple and complex plots. Plots are either simple or complex since the actions they represent are naturally of this twofold description. The action, proceeding in the way defined, as one continuous whole, I call simple, when the change in the hero's fortunes takes place without Peripety or Discovery; and complex, when it involves one or the other, or both. These should each of them arise out of the structure of the Plot itself, so as to be the consequence, necessary or probable, of the antecedents. There is a great difference between a thing happening *propter hoc* and *post hoc*.

Peripety, discovery, and suffering. A Peripety is the change of the kind described from one state of things within the play to its opposite, and that too in the way we are saying, in the probable or necessary sequence of events; as it is for instance in *Oedipus:* here the opposite state of things is produced by the Messenger, who, coming to gladden Oedipus and to remove his fears as to his mother, reveals the secret of his birth.[24] And in *Lynceus:*[25] just as he is being led off for execution, with Danaus at his side to put him to death, the incidents preceding this bring it about that he is saved and Danaus put to death. A Discovery is, as the very word implies, a change from ignorance to knowledge, and thus to either love or hate, in the personages marked for good or evil fortune. The finest form of Discovery is one attended by Peripeties, like that which goes with the Discovery in *Oedipus*. There are no doubt other forms of it; what we have said may happen in a way in reference to inanimate things, even things of a very casual kind; and it is also possible to discover whether some one has done or not done something. But the form most directly connected with the Plot and the action of the piece is the first-mentioned. This, with a Peripety, will arouse either pity or fear—actions of that nature being what Tragedy is assumed to represent; and it will also serve to bring about the happy or unhappy ending. The Discovery, then, being of persons, it may be that of one party only to the other, the latter being already known; or both the parties may have to discover themselves. Iphigenia, for instance, was discovered to Orestes by sending the letter;[26] and another Discovery was required to reveal him to Iphigenia.

Two parts of the Plot, then, Peripety and Discovery, are on matters of this sort. A third part is Suffering; which we may define as an action of a destructive or painful nature, such as murders on the stage, tortures, woundings, and the like. The other two have been already explained.

The Quantitative Parts of a Tragedy

The parts of Tragedy to be treated as formative elements in the whole were mentioned in a previous Chapter.[27] From the point of view, however, of its quantity, i.e. the separate sections into which it is divided, a tragedy has the following parts: Prologue, Episode, Exode, and a choral portion, distinguished into Parode and Stasimon; these two are common to all tragedies, whereas songs from the stage and *Commoe* are only found in some. The Prologue is all that precedes the Parode of the chorus; an Episode all that comes in between two whole choral songs; the Exode all that follows after the last choral song. In the choral portion the Parode is the whole first statement of the chorus; a Stasimon, a song of the chorus without anapaests or trochees; a *Commos*, a lamentation sung by chorus and actor in concert. The parts of Tragedy to be used as formative elements in the whole we have already mentioned; the above are its parts from the point of view of its quantity, or the separate sections into which it is divided.

The Emotional Effect of Tragedy

The tragic hero. The next points after what we have said above will be these: (1) What is the poet to aim at, and what is he to avoid, in constructing his Plots? and (2) What are the conditions on which the tragic effect depends?

We assume that, for the finest form of Tragedy, the Plot must be not simple but complex; and further, that it must imitate actions arousing fear and pity, since that is the distinctive function of this kind of imitation. It follows, therefore, that there are three forms of Plot to be avoided. (1) A good man must not be seen passing from happiness to misery, or (2) a bad man from misery to happiness. The first situation is not fear-inspiring or piteous, but simply odious to us. The second is the most untragic that can be; it has no one of the requisites of Tragedy; it does not appeal either to the human feeling in us, or to our pity, or to our fears. Nor, on the other hand, should (3) an extremely bad man be seen falling from happiness into misery. Such a story may arouse the human feeling in us, but it will not move us to either pity or fear; pity is occasioned by undeserved misfortune, and fear by that of one like ourselves; so that there will be nothing either piteous or fear-inspiring in the situation. There remains, then, the intermediate kind of personage, a man not preeminently virtuous and just, whose misfortune, however, is brought upon him not by vice and depravity but by some error of judgement, of the number of those in the enjoyment of great reputation and prosperity; e.g. Oedipus, Thyestes, and the men of note of similar families. The perfect Plot, accordingly, must have a single, and not (as some tell us) a double issue; the change in the hero's fortunes must be not from misery to happiness, but on the contrary from happiness to misery; and the cause of it must lie not in any depravity, but in some great error in his part; the man himself being either such as we have described, or better, not worse, than that. Fact also confirms our theory. Though the poets began by accepting any tragic story that came to hand, in these days the finest tragedies are always on the story of some few houses, on that of Alcmeon, Oedipus, Orestes, Meleager, Thyestes, Telephus, or any others that may have been involved, as either agents or sufferers, in some deed of horror. The theoretically best tragedy, then, has a Plot of this description. The critics, therefore, are wrong who blame Euripides for taking this line in his tragedies, and giving many of them an unhappy ending. It is, as we have said, the right line to take. The best proof is this: on the stage, and in the public performances, such plays, properly worked out, are seen to be the most truly tragic; and Euripides, even if his execution be faulty in every other point, is seen to be nevertheless the most tragic certainly of the dramatists. After this comes the construction of Plot which some rank first, one with a double story (like the *Odyssey*) and an opposite issue for the good and the bad personages. It is ranked as first only through the weakness of the audiences; the poets merely follow their public, writing as its wishes dictate. But the pleasure here is not that of Tragedy. It belongs rather to Comedy, where the bitterest enemies in the piece (e.g. Orestes and Aegisthus) walk off good friends at the end, with no slaying of any one by any one.

The tragic deed. The tragic fear and pity may be aroused by the Spectacle; but they may also be aroused by the very structure and incidents of the play—which is the better way and shows the better poet. The Plot in fact should be so framed that even without seeing the things take place, he who simply hears the account of them shall be filled with horror and pity at the incidents; which is just the effect that the mere recital of the story in *Oedipus* would have on one. To produce this same effect by means of the Spectacle is less artistic, and requires extraneous aid. Those, however, who make use of the Spectacle to put before us that which is merely monstrous and not productive of fear, are wholly out of touch with Tragedy; not every kind of pleasure should be required of a tragedy, but only its own proper pleasure.

1453b

The tragic pleasure is that of pity and fear, and the poet has to produce it by a work of imitation; it is clear, therefore, that the causes should be included in the incidents of his story. Let us see, then, what kinds of incident strike one as horrible, or rather as piteous. In a deed of this description the parties must necessarily be either friends, or enemies, or indifferent to one another. Now when enemy does it on enemy, there is nothing to move us to pity either in his doing or in his meditating the deed, except so far as the actual pain of the sufferer is concerned; and the same is true when the parties are indifferent to one another. Whenever the tragic deed, however, is done within the family—

when murder or the like is done or meditated by brother on brother, by son on father, by mother on son, or son on mother—these are the situations the poet should seek after. The traditional stories, accordingly, must be kept as they are, e.g. the murder of Clytaemnestra by Orestes and of Eriphyle by Alcmeon. At the same time even with these there is something left to the poet himself; it is for him to devise the right way of treating them. Let us explain more clearly what we mean by "the right way." The deed of horror may be done by the doer knowingly and consciously, as in the old poets, and in Medea's murder of her children in Euripides.[28] Or he may do it, but in ignorance of his relationship, and discover that afterwards, as does the Oedipus in Sophocles. Here the deed is outside the play; but it may be within it, like the act of the Alcméon in Astydamas,[29] or that of the Telegonus[30] in *Ulysses Wounded*. A third possibility is for one meditating some deadly injury to another, in ignorance of his relationship, to make the discovery in time to draw back. These exhaust the possibilities, since the deed must necessarily be either done or not done, and either knowingly or unknowingly.

The worst situation is when the personage is with full knowledge on the point of doing the deed, and leaves it undone. It is odious and also (through the absence of suffering) untragic; hence it is that no one is made to act thus except in some few instances, e.g. Haemon and Creon in *Antigone*.[31] Next after this comes the actual perpetration of the deed meditated. A better situation than that, however, is for the deed to be done in ignorance, and the relationship discovered afterwards, since there is nothing odious in it, and the Discovery will serve to astound us. But the best of all is the last; what we have in *Cresphontes*,[32] for example, where Merope, on the point of slaying her son, recognizes him in time; in *Iphigenia*, where sister and brother are in a like position; and in *Helle*,[33] where the son recognizes his mother, when on the point of giving her up to her enemy.

This will explain why our tragedies are restricted (as we said just now)[34] to such a small number of families. It was accident rather than art that led the poets in quest of subjects to embody this kind of incident in their Plots. They are still obliged, accordingly, to have recourse to the families in which such horrors have occurred.

On the construction of the Plot, and the kind of Plot required for Tragedy, enough has now been said.

Rules for the Character of Tragic Personages

In the Characters there are four points to aim at. First and foremost, that they shall be good. There will be an element of character in the play, if (as has been observed)[35] what a personage says or does reveals a certain moral purpose; and a good element of character, if the purpose so revealed is good. Such goodness is possible in every type of personage, even in a woman or a slave, though the one is perhaps an inferior, and the other a wholly worthless being. The second point is to make them appropriate. The Character before us may be, say, manly; but it is not appropriate in a female Character to be manly, or clever. The third is to make them like the reality, which is not the same as their being good and appropriate, in our sense of the term. The fourth is to make them consistent and the same throughout; even if inconsistency be part of the man before one for imitation as presenting that form of character, he should still be consistently inconsistent. We have an instance of baseness of character, not required for the story, in the Menelaus in *Orestes*;[36] of the incongruous and unbefitting in the lamentation of Ulysses in *Scylla*,[37] and in the (clever) speech of Melanippe;[38] and of inconsistency in *Iphigenia at Aulis*,[39] where Iphigenia the suppliant is utterly unlike the later Iphigenia. The right thing, however, is in the Characters just as in the incidents of the play to endeavour always after the necessary or the probable; so that whenever such-and-such a personage says or does such-and-such a thing, it shall be the necessary or probable outcome of his character; and whenever this incident follows on that, it shall be either the necessary or the probable consequence of it. From this one sees (to digress for a moment) that the Dénouement also should arise out of the plot itself, and not depend on a stage-artifice, as in *Medea*,[40] or in the story of the (arrested) departure of the Greeks in the *Iliad*.[41] The artifice must be reserved for matters outside the play—for past events beyond human knowledge, or events yet to come, which require to be foretold or announced; since it is the privilege of the gods to know everything. There should be nothing improbable among the actual incidents. If it be unavoidable, however, it should be outside the tragedy, like the improbability in the *Oedipus* of Sophocles. But to return to the Characters. As Tragedy is an imitation of personages better than the ordinary man, we in our way should follow the example of good portrait-painters, who reproduce the distinctive features of a man, and at the same time, without losing the likeness, make him handsomer than he is. The poet in like manner, in portraying men quick or slow to anger, or with similar infirmities of character, must know how to represent them as such, and at the same time as good men, as Agathon and Homer have represented Achilles.

1454b

All these rules one must keep in mind throughout, and, further, those also for such points of stage-effect as directly depend on the art of the poet, since in these too one may often make mistakes. Enough, however, has been said on the subject in one of our published writings.[42]

Appendix to Discussion of Plot

The various forms of discovery. Discovery in general has been explained already.[43] As for the species of Discovery, the first to be noted is (1) the least artistic form of it, of which the poets make most use through mere lack of invention, Discovery by signs or marks. Of these signs some are congenital, like the "lance-head which the Earth-born have on them,"[44] or "stars," such as Carcinus[45] brings in his *Thyestes;* others acquired after birth—these latter being either marks on the body, e.g. scars, or external tokens, like necklaces, or (to take another sort of instance) the ark in the Discovery in *Tyro*.[46] Even these, however, admit of two uses, a better and a worse; the scar of Ulysses is an instance; the Discovery of him through it is made in one way by the nurse[47] and in another by the swineherds.[48] A Discovery using signs as a means of assurance is less artistic, as indeed are all such as imply reflection; whereas one bringing them in all of a sudden, as in the *Bath-story*,[49] is of a better order. Next after these are (2) Discoveries made directly by the poet; which are inartistic for that very reason; e.g. Orestes' Discoveries of himself in *Iphigenia*; whereas his sister reveals who she is by the letter,[50] Orestes is made to say himself what the poet rather than the story demands.[51] This, therefore, is not far removed from the first-mentioned fault, since he might have presented certain tokens as well. Another instance is the "shuttle's voice" in the *Tereus* of Sophocles. (3) A third species is Discovery through memory, from a man's consciousness being awakened by something seen. Thus in *The Cyprioe* of Dicaeogenes,[52] the sight of the picture makes the man burst into tears; and in the *Tale of Alcinous*,[53] hearing the harper Ulysses is reminded of the past and weeps; the Discovery of them being the result. (4) A fourth kind is Discovery through reasoning; e.g. in *The Choephoroe*;[54] "One like me is here; there is no one like me but Orestes; he, therefore, must be here." Or that which Polyidus the Sophist[55] suggested for *Iphigenia*; since it was natural for Orestes to reflect: "My sister was sacrificed and I am to be sacrificed like her." Or that in the *Tydeus* of Theodectes:[56] "I came to find a son, and am to die myself." Or that in *The Phinidae*:[57] on seeing the place the women inferred their fate, that they were to die there, since they had also been exposed there. (5) There is, too, a composite Discovery arising from bad reasoning on the side of the other party. An instance of it is in *Ulysses the false Messenger*: he said he should know the bow—which he had not seen; but to suppose from that that he would know it again (as though he had once seen it) was bad reasoning. (6) The best of all Discoveries, however, is that arising from the incidents themselves, when the great surprise comes about through a probable incident, like that in the *Oedipus* of Sophocles; and also in *Iphigenia*;[58] for it was not improbable that she should wish to have a letter taken home. These last are the only Discoveries independent of the artifice of signs and necklaces. Next after them come Discoveries through reasoning.

Additional rules for the construction of a play. At the time when he is constructing his Plots, and engaged on the Diction in which they are worked out, the poet should remember (1) to put the actual scenes as far as possible before his eyes. In this way, seeing everything with the vividness of an eye-witness as it were, he will devise what is appropriate, and be least likely to overlook incongruities. This is shown by what was censured in Carcinus, the return of Amphiaraus from the sanctuary; it would have passed unnoticed, if it had not been actually seen by the audience; but on the stage his play failed, the incongruity of the incident offending the spectators. (2) As far as may be, too, the poet should even act his story with the very gestures of his personages. Given the same natural qualifications, he who feels the emotions to be described will be the most convincing; distress and anger, for instance, are portrayed most truthfully by one who is feeling them at the moment. Hence it is that poetry demands a man with a special gift for it, or else one with a touch of madness in him; the former can easily assume the required mood, and the latter may be actually beside himself with emotion. (3) His story, again, whether already made or of his own making, he should first simplify and reduce to a universal form, before proceeding to lengthen it out by the insertion of episodes. The following will show how the universal element in *Iphigenia,* for instance, may be viewed: A certain maiden having been offered in sacrifice, and spirited away from her sacrificers into another land, where the custom was to sacrifice all strangers to the Goddess, she was made there the priestess of this rite. Long after that the brother of the priestess happened to come; the fact, however, of the oracle having for a certain reason bidden him go thither, and his object in going, are outside the Plot of the play. On his coming he was arrested, and about to be sacrificed, when he revealed who he was—either as Euripides puts it, or (as suggested by Polyidus) by the not improbable exclamation, "So I too am doomed to be sacrificed, as my sister was"; and the disclosure led to his salvation. This done, the next thing, after the proper names have been fixed as a basis for the story, is to work in episodes or accessory incidents. One must mind, however, that the episodes are appropriate, like the fit of madness[59] in Orestes, which led to his arrest, and the purifying[60] which brought about his salvation. In plays, then, the episodes are short; in epic poetry they serve to lengthen out the poem. The argument of the *Odyssey* is not a long one. A certain man has been abroad many years; Poseidon is ever on the watch for him, and he is all alone. Matters at home too have come to this, that his substance is being wasted and his son's death plotted by suitors to his wife. Then he arrives there himself after his grievous sufferings; reveals himself, and falls on his enemies; and the end is his salvation and their death. This being all that is proper to the *Odyssey,* everything else in it is episode.

(4) There is a further point to be borne in mind. Every tragedy is in part Complication and in part Dénouement; the incidents before the opening scene, and often certain also of those within the play, forming the Complication; and the rest the Dénouement. By Complication I mean all from the beginning of the story to the point just before the change in the hero's fortunes; by Dénouement, all from the beginning of the change to the end. In the *Lynceus* of Theodectes, for instance, the Complication includes, together with the presupposed incidents, the seizure of the child and that in turn of the parents; and the Dénouement all from the indictment for the murder to the end. Now it is right, when one speaks of a tragedy as the same or not the same as another, to do so on the ground before all else of their Plot, i.e. as having the same or not the same Complication and Dénouement. Yet there are many dramatists who, after a good Complication, fail in the Dénouement. But it is necessary for both points of construction to be always duly mastered.[61] (5) There are four distinct species of Tragedy—that being the number of the constituents also that have been mentioned:[62] first, the complex Tragedy, which is all Peripety and Discovery; second, the Tragedy of suffering, e.g. the *Ajaxes* and *Ixions*;[63] third, the tragedy of character, e.g. *The Phthiotides* and *Peleus*.[64] The fourth constituent is that of "Spectacle," exemplified in *The Phorcides,* in *Prometheus,*[65] and in all plays with the scene laid in the nether world. The poet's aim, then, should be to combine every element of interest, if possible, or else the more important and the major part of them. This is now especially necessary owing to the unfair criticism to which the poet is subjected in these days. Just because there have been poets before him strong in the several species of tragedy, the critics now

1456a

1455b

1456a

expect the one man to surpass that which was the strong point of each one of his predecessors. (6) One should also remember what has been said more than once,[66] and not write a tragedy of an epic body of incident (i.e. one with a plurality of stories in it), by attempting to dramatize, for instance, the entire story of the *Iliad*. In the epic owing to its scale every part is treated at proper length; with a drama, however, on the same story the result is very disappointing. This is shown by the fact that all who have dramatized the fall of Ilium in its entirety, and not part by part, like Euripides, or the whole of the Niobe story, instead of a portion, like Aeschylus, either fail utterly or have but ill success on the stage; for that and that alone was enough to ruin even a play by Agathon. Yet in their Peripeties, as also in their simple plots, the poets I mean show wonderful skill in aiming at the kind of effect they desire—a tragic situation that arouses the human feeling in one, like the clever villain (e.g. Sisyphus) deceived, or the brave wrongdoer worsted. This is probable, however, only in Agathon's[67] sense, when he speaks of the probability of even improbabilities coming to pass. (7) The Chorus too should be regarded as one of the actors; it should be an integral part of the whole, and take a share in the action—that which it has in Sophocles, rather than in Euripides. With the later poets, however, the songs in a play of theirs have no more to do with the Plot of that than any other tragedy. Hence it is that they are now singing intercalary pieces, a practice first introduced by Agathon. And yet what real difference is there between singing such intercalary pieces, and attempting to fit in a speech, or even a whole act, from one play into another?

The Thought of the Tragic Personages

The Plot and Characters having been discussed, it remains to consider the Diction and Thought. As for the thought, we may assume what is said of it in our *Art of Rhetoric*,[68] as it belongs more properly to that department of inquiry. The Thought of the personages is shown in everything to be effected by their language—in every effort to prove or disprove, to arouse emotion (pity, fear, anger, and the like), or to maximize or minimize things. It is clear, also, that their mental procedure must be on the same lines in their actions likewise, whenever they wish them to arouse pity or horror, or to have a look of importance or probability. The only difference is that with the act the impression has to be made without explanation; whereas with the spoken word it has to be produced by the speaker, and result from his language. What, indeed, would be the good of the speaker, if things appeared in the required light even apart from anything he says?

As regards the Diction, one subject for inquiry under this head is the turns given to the language when spoken; e.g. the difference between command and prayer, simple statement and threat, question and answer, and so forth. The theory of such matters, however, belongs to Elocution and the professors of that art. Whether the poet knows these things or not, his art as a poet is never seriously criticized on that account. What fault can one see in Homer's "Sing of the wrath, Goddess"?—which Protagoras[69] has criticized as being a command where a prayer was meant, since to bid one do or not do, he tells us, is a command. Let us pass over this, then, as appertaining to another art, and not to that of poetry.

The Diction of Tragedy

The ultimate constituents of language. The Diction viewed as a whole is made up of the following parts: the Letter (or ultimate element), the Syllable, the Conjunction, the Article, the Noun, the Verb, the Case, and the Speech. (1) The Letter is an indivisible sound of a particular kind, one that may become a factor in an intelligible sound. Indivisible sounds are uttered by the brutes also, but no one of these is a Letter in our sense of the term. These elementary sounds are either vowels, semi-vowels, or mutes. A vowel is a Letter having an audible sound without the addition of another Letter. A semi-vowel, one having an audible sound by the addition of another Letter; e.g. S and R. A mute, one having no sound at all by itself, but becoming audible by an addition, that of one of the Letters which have a sound of some sort of their own; e.g. G and D. The Letters differ in various ways: as produced by different conformations or in different regions of the mouth; as aspirated, not aspirated, or sometimes one and sometimes the other; as long, short, or of variable quantity; and further as having an acute, grave, or intermediate accent. The details of these matters we must leave to the metricians. (2) A Syllable is a non-significant composite sound, made up of a mute and a Letter having a sound (a vowel or semivowel); for GR, without an A, is just as much a Syllable as GRA, with an A. The various forms of the Syllable also belong to the theory of metre. (3) A Conjunction is (*a*) a non-significant sound which, when one significant sound is formable out of several, neither hinders nor aids the union, and which, if the Speech thus formed stands by itself (apart from other Speeches), must not be inserted at the beginning of it; e.g. *men, dē, toi, de.* Or (*b*) a non-significant sound capable of combining two or more significant sounds into one; e.g. *amphi, peri,* &c. (4) An Article is a non-significant sound marking the beginning, end, or dividing-point of a Speech, its natural place being either at the extremities or in the middle. (5) A Noun or name is a composite significant sound not involving the idea of time, with parts which have no significance by themselves in it. It is to be remembered that in a compound we do not think of the parts as having a significance also by themselves; in the name "Theodorus," for instance, the *dōron* means nothing to us. (6) A Verb is a composite significant sound involving the idea of time, with parts which (just as in the Noun) have no significance by themselves in it. Whereas the word "man" or "white" does not imply *when*, "walks" and "has walked" involve in addition to the idea of walking that of time present or time past. (7) A Case of a Noun or Verb is when the word means "of" or "to" a thing, and so forth, or for one or many (e.g. "man" and "men"); or it may consist merely in the mode of utterance, e.g. in question, command, &c. "Walked?" and "Walk!" are Cases of the verb "to walk" of this last kind. (8) A Speech is a composite significant sound, some of the parts of which have a certain significance by themselves. It may be observed that a Speech is not always made up of

1457a

Noun and Verb; it may be without a Verb, like the definition of man; but it will always have some part with a certain significance by itself. In the Speech "Cleon walks," "Cleon" is an instance of such a part. A Speech is said to be one in two ways, either as signifying one thing, or as a union of several Speeches made into one by conjunction. Thus the *Iliad* is one Speech by conjunction of several; and the definition of man is one through its signifying one thing.

The different kinds of terms. Nouns are of two kinds, either (1) simple, i.e. made up of non-significant parts, like the word *gē*, or (2) double; in the latter case the word may be made up either of a significant and a non-significant part (a distinction which disappears in the compound), or of two significant parts. It is possible also to have triple, quadruple, or higher compounds, like most of our amplified names; e.g. "Hermocaïcoxanthus" and the like.

Whatever its structure, a Noun must always be either (1) the ordinary word for the thing, or (2) a strange word, or (3) a metaphor, or (4) an ornamental word, or (5) a coined word, or (6) a word lengthened out, or (7) curtailed, or (8) altered in form. By the ordinary word I mean that in general use in a country; and by a strange word, one in use elsewhere. So that the same word may obviously be at once strange and ordinary, though not in reference to the same people; *sigunon*, for instance, is an ordinary word in Cyprus, and a strange word with us. Metaphor consists in giving the thing a name that belongs to something else; the transference being either from genus to species, or from species to genus, or from species to species, or on grounds of analogy. That from genus to species is exemplified in "Here stands my ship";[70] for lying at anchor is the "standing" of a particular kind of thing. That from species to genus in "Truly ten thousand good deeds has Ulysses wrought,"[71] where "ten thousand," which is a particular large number, is put in place of the generic "a large number." That from species to species in "Drawing the life with the bronze," and in "Severing with the enduring bronze";[72] where the poet uses "draw" in the sense of "sever" and "sever" in that of "draw," both words meaning to "take away" something. That from analogy is possible whenever there are four terms so related that the second (B) is to the first (A), as the fourth (D) to the third (C); for one may then metaphorically put D in lieu of B, and B in lieu of D. Now and then, too, they qualify the metaphor by adding on to it that to which the word it supplants is relative. Thus a cup (B) is in relation to Dionysus (A) what a shield (D) is to Ares (C). The cup accordingly will be metaphorically described as the "shield of *Dionysus*" (D + A), and the shield as the "cup of *Ares*"[73] (B + C). Or to take another instance: As old age (D) is to life (C), so is evening (B) to day (A). One will accordingly describe evening (B) as the "old age *of the day*" (D + A)—or by the Empedoclean equivalent; and old age (D) as the "evening" or "sunset *of life*" (B + C). It may be that some of the terms thus related have no special name of their own, but for all that they will be metaphorically described in just the same way. Thus to cast forth seed-corn is called "sowing"; but to cast forth its flame, as said of the sun, has no special name. This nameless act (B), however, stands in just the same relation to its object, sunlight (A), as sowing (D) to the seed-corn (C). Hence the expression in the poet, "sowing around a god-created *flame*"[74] (D + A). There is also another form of qualified metaphor. Having given the thing the alien name, one may by a negative addition deny of it one of the attributes naturally associated with its new name. An instance of this would be to call the shield not the "cup *of Ares,*" as in the former case, but a "cup *that holds no wine....*" A coined word is a name which, being quite unknown among a people, is given by the poet himself; e.g. (for there are some words that seem to be of this origin) *ernuges* for horns, and *arētēr* for priest. A word is said to be lengthened out, when it has a short vowel made long, or an extra syllable inserted; e.g. *poleōs* for *poleōs*, *Pēlēiadeō* for *Pēleidou*. It is said to be curtailed, when it has lost a part; e.g. *kri, dō,* and *ops* in *mia ginetai amphoterōn ops.*[75] It is an altered word, when part is left as it was and part is of the poet's making; e.g. *dexiteron* for *dexion*, in *dexiteron kata mazon.*[76]

1458a

The Nouns themselves (to whatever class they may belong) are either masculines, feminines, or intermediates (neuter). All ending in N, R, S, or in the two compounds of this last, PS and X, are masculines. All ending in the invariable long vowels, Ē and Ō, and in A among the vowels that may be long, are feminines. So that there is an equal number of masculine and feminine terminations, as PS and X are the same as S, and need not be counted. There is no Noun, however, ending in a mute or in either of the two short vowels, E and O. Only three (*meli, kommi, peperi*) end in I, and five in Y. The intermediates, or neuters, end in the variable vowels or in N, R, S.

The characteristics of the language of poetry. The perfection of Diction is for it to be at once clear and not mean. The clearest indeed is that made up of the ordinary words for things, but it is mean, as is shown by the poetry of Cleophon[77] and Sthenelus.[78] On the other hand the Diction becomes distinguished and non-prosaic by the use of unfamiliar terms, i.e. strange words, metaphors, lengthened forms, and everything that deviates from the ordinary modes of speech.—But a whole statement in such terms will be either a riddle or a barbarism, a riddle, if made up of metaphors, a barbarism, if made up of strange words. The very nature indeed of a riddle is this, to describe a fact in an impossible combination of words (which cannot be done with the real names for things, but can be with their metaphorical substitutes); e.g. "I saw a man glue brass on another with fire,"[79] and the like. The corresponding use of strange words results in a barbarism.—A certain admixture, accordingly, of unfamiliar terms is necessary. These, the strange word, the metaphor, the ornamental equivalent, etc., will save the language from seeming mean and prosaic, while the ordinary words in it will secure the requisite clearness. What helps most, however, to render the Diction at once clear and non-prosaic is the use of the lengthened, curtailed, and altered forms of words. Their deviation from the ordinary words will, by making the language unlike that in general use, give it a non-prosaic appearance; and their having much in common with the words in general use will give it the quality of clearness. It is not right, then, to condemn these modes of speech, and ridicule the poet for using them, as some have done; e.g. the elder Euclid,[80] who said it was easy to make poetry if one were to be allowed to lengthen the words in the statement itself as much as one likes—a procedure he caricatured by reading "I saw Epichares a-walking Marathonwards," and *ouk an g' eramenos ton ekeinou elleboron*[81] as verses. A too

1458b

apparent use of these licenses has certainly a ludicrous effect, but they are not alone in that; the rule of moderation applies to all the constituents of the poetic vocabulary; even with metaphors, strange words, and the rest, the effect will be the same, if one uses them improperly and with a view to provoking laughter. The proper use of them is a very different thing. To realize the difference one should take an epic verse and see how it reads when the normal words are introduced. The same should be done too with the strange word, the metaphor, and the rest; for one has only to put the ordinary words in their place to see the truth of what we are saying. The same iambic, for instance, is found in Aeschylus and Euripides, and as it stands in the former it is a poor line; whereas Euripides, by the change of a single word, the substitution of a strange for what is by usage the ordinary word, has made it seem a fine one. Aeschylus having said in his *Philoctetes*:

> The cancer that is eating the flesh of my foot.[82]

Euripides has merely altered the "is eating" here into "feasts on."[83] Or suppose

> Lo, now a dwarf, a man of no worth and a weakling[84]

to be altered, by the substitution of the ordinary words, into

> See, now, a small man, feeble, and unprepossessing.[85]

Or the line

> And placed for him an unseemly settle and a meagre table[86]

into

> And brought him a sorry chair and a small table.[87]

Or "the sea-beach bellows" into "the beach is roaring."[88] Add to this that Ariphrades[89] used to ridicule the tragedians for introducing expressions unknown in the language of common life, "from the house away" (for "away from the house"), "of thee" (for "yours"), "Achilles about" (for "about Achilles"),[90] and the like. The mere fact of their not being in ordinary speech gives the Diction a non-prosaic character; but Ariphrades was unaware of that. It is a great thing, indeed, to make a proper use of the poetical forms, as also of compounds and strange words. But the greatest thing by far is to be a master of metaphor. It is the one thing that cannot be learnt from others; and it is also a sign of genius, since a good metaphor implies an intuitive perception of the similarity in dissimilars.

Of the kinds of words we have enumerated it may be observed that compunds are most in place in the dithyramb, strange words in heroic, and metaphors in iambic poetry. Heroic poetry, indeed, may avail itself of them all. But in iambic verse, which models itself as far as possible on the spoken language, only those kinds of words are in place which are allowable also in an oration, i.e. the ordinary word, the metaphor, and the ornamental equivalent.

Let this, then, suffice as an account of Tragedy, the art imitating by means of action on the stage.

RULES FOR THE CONSTRUCTION OF AN EPIC

Unity of Action

As for the poetry which merely narrates, or imitates by means of versified language (without action, it is evident that it has several points in common with Tragedy.

The construction of its stories should clearly be like that in a drama; they should be based on a single action, one that is a complete whole in itself, with a beginning, middle, and end, so as to enable the work to produce its own proper pleasure with all the organic unity of a living creature. Nor should one suppose that there is anything like them in our usual histories. A history has to deal not with one action, but with one period and all that happened in that to one or more persons, however disconnected the several events may have been. Just as two events may take place at the same time, e.g. the sea-fight off Salamis and the battle with the Carthaginians in Sicily, without converging to the same end, so too of two consecutive events one may sometimes come after the other with no one end as their common issue. Nevertheless most of our epic poets, one may say, ignore the distinction.

Herein, then, to repeat what we have said before,[91] we have a further proof of Homer's marvellous superiority to the rest. He did not attempt to deal even with the Trojan war in its entirety, though it was a whole with a definite beginning and end—through a feeling apparently that it was too long a story to be taken in in one view, or if not that, too complicated from the variety of incident in it. As it is, he has singled out one section of the whole; many of the other incidents, however, he brings in as episodes, using the Catalogue of the Ships, for instance, and other episodes to relieve the uniformity of his narrative. As for the other epic poets, they treat of one man, or one period; or else of an action which, although one, has a multiplicity of parts in it. This last is what the authors of the *Cypria*[92] and *Little Iliad*[92] have done. And the result is that whereas the *Iliad* or *Odyssey* supplies materials for only one, or at most two tragedies, the *Cypria* does that for several and the *Little Iliad* for more than eight: for an *Adjudgment of Arms*, a *Philoctetes*, a *Neoptolemus*, a *Eurypylus*, a *Ulysses as Beggar*, a *Laconian Women*, a *Fall of Ilium*, and a *Departure of the Fleet*; as also a *Simon*, and a *Women of Troy*.

Epic Poetry and Tragedy

Besides this, Epic poetry must divide into the same species as Tragedy; it must be either simple or complex, a story of character or one of suffering. Its parts, too, with the exception of Song and Spectacle, must be the same, as it requires Peripeties, Discoveries, and scenes of suffering just like Tragedy. Lastly, the Thought and Diction in it must be good in their way. All these elements appear in Homer first; and he has made due use of them. His two poems are each examples of construction, the *Iliad* simple and a story of suffering, the *Odyssey* complex (there is Discovery throughout it) and a story of character. And they are more than this, since in Diction and Thought too they surpass all other poems.

There is, however, a difference in the Epic as compared with Tragedy, (1) in its length, and (2) in its metre. (1) As to its length, the limit already suggested[93] will suffice: it must be possible for the beginning and end of the work to be taken in in one view—a condition which will be fulfilled if the poem be shorter than the old epics, and about as long as the series of tragedies offered for one hearing. For the extension of its length epic poetry has a special advantage, of which it makes large use. In a play one cannot represent an action with a number of parts going on simultaneously; one is limited to the part on the stage and connected with the actors. Whereas in epic poetry the narrative form makes it possible for one to describe a number of simultaneous incidents; and these, if germane to the subject, increase the body of the poem. This then is a gain to the Epic, tending to give it grandeur, and also variety of interest and room for episodes of diverse kinds. Uniformity of incident by the satiety it soon creates is apt to ruin tragedies on the stage. (2) As for its metre, the heroic has been assigned it from experience; were any one to attempt a narrative poem in some one, or in several, of the other metres, the incongruity of the thing would be apparent. The heroic in fact is the gravest and weightiest of metres—which is what makes it more tolerant than the rest of strange words and metaphors, that also being a point in which the narrative form of poetry goes beyond all others. The iambic and trochaic, on the other hand, are metres of movement, the one representing that of life and action, the other that of the dance. Still more unnatural would it appear, if one were to write an epic in a medley of metres, as Chaeremon did.[94] Hence it is that no one has ever written a long story in any but heroic verse; nature herself, as we have said,[95] teaches us to select the metre appropriate to such a story.

Homer, admirable as he is in every other respect, is especially so in this, that he alone among epic poets is not unaware of the part to be played by the poet himself in the poem. The poet should say very little *in propria persona,* as he is no imitator when doing that. Whereas the other poets are perpetually coming forward in person, and say but little, and that only here and there, as imitators, Homer after a brief preface brings in forthwith a man, a woman, or some other Character—no one of them characterless, but each with distinctive characteristics.

The marvellous is certainly required in Tragedy. The Epic, however, affords more opening for the improbable, the chief factor in the marvellous, because in it the agents are not visibly before one. The scene of the pursuit of Hector would be ridiculous on the stage—the Greeks halting instead of pursuing him, and Achilles shaking his head to stop them;[96] but in the poem the absurdity is overlooked. The marvellous, however, is a cause of pleasure, as is shown by the fact that we all tell a story with additions, in the belief that we are doing our hearers a pleasure.

Homer more than any other has taught the rest of us the art of framing lies in the right way. I mean the use of paralogism. Whenever, if A is or happens, a consequent, B, is or happens, men's notion is that, if the B is, the A also is—but that is a false conclusion. Accordingly, if A is untrue, but there is something else, B, that on the assumption of its truth follows as its consequent, the right thing then is to add on the B. Just because we know the truth of the consequent, we are in our own minds led on to the erroneous inference of the truth of the antecedent. Here is an instance, from the *Bath-story* in the *Odyssey*.[97]

A likely impossibility is always preferable to an unconvincing possibility. The story should never be made up of improbable incidents; there should be nothing of the sort in it. If, however, such incidents are unavoidable, they should be outside the piece, like the hero's ignorance in *Oedipus* of the circumstances of Laius' death; not within it, like the report of the Pythian games in *Electra*,[98] or the man's having come to Mysia from Tegea without uttering a word on the way in *The Mysians*.[99] So that it is ridiculous to say that one's Plot would have been spoilt without them, since it is fundamentally wrong to make up such Plots. If the poet has taken such a Plot, however, and one sees that he might have put it in a more probable form, he is guilty of absurdity as well as a fault of art. Even in the *Odyssey* the improbabilities in the setting-ashore of Ulysses[100] would be clearly intolerable in the hands of an inferior poet. As it is, the poet conceals them, his other excellences veiling their absurdity. Elaborate Diction, however, is required only in places where there is no action, and no Character or Thought to be revealed. Where there is Character or Thought, on the other hand, an over-ornate Diction tends to obscure them.

POTENTIAL OBJECTIONS TO AN EPIC OR TRAGEDY

As regards Problems and their Solutions, one may see the number and nature of the assumptions on which they proceed by viewing the matter in the following way. (1) The poet being an imitator just like the painter or other maker of likenesses, he must necessarily in all instances represent things in one or other of three aspects, either as they were or are, or as they are said or thought to be or to have been, or as they ought to be. (2) All this he does in language, with an admixture, it may be, of strange words and metaphors, as also of the various modified forms of words, since the use of these is conceded in poetry. (3) It is to be remembered, too, that there is not the same kind of correctness in poetry as in politics, or indeed any other art. There is, however, within the limits of poetry itself a possibility of two kinds of error, the one directly, the other only accidentally connected with the art. If the poet meant to describe the thing correctly, and failed through lack of power of expression, his art itself is at fault. But if it was through his having meant to describe it in some incorrect way (e.g. to make the horse in movement have both right legs thrown forward) that the technical error (one in a matter of, say, medicine or some other special science), or impossibilities of whatever kind they may be, have got into his description, his error in that case is not in the essentials of the poetic art. These, therefore, must be the premisses of the Solutions in answer to the criticisms involved in the Problems.

As to the criticisms relating to the poet's art itself. Any impossibilities there may be in his descriptions of things are faults. But from another point of view they are justifiable, if they serve the end of poetry itself—if (to assume what we have said of that end)[101] they make the effect of either that very portion of the work or some other portion more astounding. The Pursuit of Hector is an instance in point. If, however, the poetic end might have been as well or better attained without sacrifice of technical correctness in such matters, the impossibility is not to be justified, since the description should be, if it can, entirely free from error. One may ask, too, whether the error is in a matter directly or only accidentally connected with the poetic art; since it is a lesser error in an artist not to know, for instance, that the hind has no horns, than to produce an unrecognizable picture of one.

If the poet's description be criticized as not true to fact, one may urge perhaps that the object ought to be as described—an answer like that of Sophocles, who said that he drew men as they ought to be, and Euripides as they were. If the description, however, be neither true nor of the thing as it ought to be, the answer must be then, that it is in accordance with opinion. The tales about gods, for instance, may be as wrong as Xenophanes thinks,[102] neither true nor the better thing to say; but they are certainly in accordance with opinion. Of other statements in poetry one may perhaps say, not that they are better than the truth, but that the fact was so at the time; e.g. the description of the arms: "their spears stood upright, butt-end upon the ground";[103] for that was the usual way of fixing them then, as it is still with the Illyrians. As for the question whether something said or done in a poem is morally right or not, in dealing with that one should consider not only the intrinsic quality of the actual word or deed, but also the person who says or does it, the person to whom he says or does it, the time, the means, and the motive of the agent—whether he does it to attain a greater good, or to avoid a greater evil.

Other criticisms one must meet by considering the language of the poet: (1) by the assumption of a strange word in a passage like *oureas men prōton*,[104] where by *oureas* Homer may perhaps mean not mules but sentinels. And in saying of Dolon, "He was ill-favored of figure,"[105] his meaning may perhaps be, not that Dolon's body was deformed, but that his face was ugly, as *eueidēs* is the Cretan word for handsome-faced. So, too, *zōroteron de keraie*[106] may mean not "mix the wine stronger," as though for topers, but "mix it quicker." (2) Other expressions in Homer may be explained as metaphorical; e.g. in "Now *all* gods and men were sleeping through the night,"[107] as compared with what he tells us at the same time, "And whenever he looked at the Trojan plain he marvelled at the sound of flutes and pipes,"[108] the word *hapantes*, "all," is metaphorically put for "many," since "all" is a species of "many." So also his "and she alone hath no part"[109] is metaphorical, the best known standing "alone." (3) A change, as Hippias of Thasos[110] suggested, in the mode of reading a word will solve the difficulty in "we grant him to obtain his prayer,"[111] and in "the wood of which is rotted with rain."[112] (4) Other difficulties may be solved by another punctuation; e.g. in Empedocles, "Suddenly things became mortal that before had learnt to be immortal and things unmixed before mixed."[113] Or (5) by the assumption of an equivocal term, as in "Of the night full two watches are spent,"[114] where "full" is equivocal. Or (6) by an appeal to the custom of language. Wine-and-water we call "wine"; and it is on the same principle that Homer speaks of a "greave of new-wrought tin."[115] A worker in iron we call a "brazier"; and it is on the same principle that Ganymede is described as the "*wine-server*" of Zeus,[116] though the gods do not drink wine. This latter, however, may be an instance of metaphor. But whenever also a word seems to imply some contradiction, it is necessary to reflect how many ways there may be of understanding it in the passage in question; e.g. in Homer's "There stuck the spear of bronze"[117] one should consider the possible senses of "was stopped there"—whether by taking it in this sense or in that one will best avoid the fault of which Glaucon[118] speaks: "They start with some improbable presumption; and having so decreed it themselves, proceed to draw inferences, and censure the poet as though he had actually said whatever they happen to believe, if his statement conflicts with their own notion of things." This is how Homer's silence about Icarius has been treated. Starting with the notion of his having been a Lacedaemonian, the critics think it strange for Telemachus not to have met him when he went to Lacedaemon. Whereas the fact may have been as the Cephallenians say, that the wife of Ulysses was of a Cephallenian family, and that her father's name was Icadius, not Icarius. So that it is probably a mistake of the critics that has given rise to the Problem.

Speaking generally, one has to justify (1) the Impossible by reference to the requirements of poetry, or to the better, or to opinion. For the purposes of poetry a convincing impossibility is preferable to an unconvincing possibility; and if men such as Zeuxis depicted the impossible, the answer is that it is better they should be like that, as the artist ought to improve on his model. (2) The Improbable one has to justify either by showing it to be in accordance with opinion, or by urging that at times it is not improbable; for there is a probability of things happening also against probability. (3) The contradictions found in the poet's language one should first test as one does an opponent's confutation in a dialectical argument, so as to see whether he means the same thing, in the same relation, and in the same sense, before admitting that he has contradicted either something he has said himself or what a man of sound sense assumes as true. But there is no possible apology for improbability of Plot or depravity of character, when they are not necessary and no use is made of them, like the improbability in the appearance of Aegeus in *Medea* and the baseness of Menelaus in *Orestes*.

The objections, then, of critics start with faults of five kinds; the allegation is always that something is either (1) impossible, (2) improbable, (3) corrupting, (4) contradictory, or (5) against technical correctness. The answers to these objections must be sought under one or other of the above-mentioned heads, which are twelve in number.

THE ARTISTIC SUPERIORITY OF TRAGEDY TO EPIC POETRY

The question may be raised whether the epic or the tragic is the higher form of imitation. It may be argued that, if the less vulgar is the higher, and the less vulgar is always that which addresses the better public, an art addressing any and every one is of a very vulgar order. It is a belief that their public cannot see the meaning, unless they add something themselves, that causes the perpetual movements of the performers—bad flute-players, for instance, rolling about, if quoit-throwing is to be represented, and pulling at the conductor, if Scylla is the subject of the piece. Tragedy, then, is said to be an art of this order—to be in fact just what the later actors were in the eyes of their predecessors; for Mynniscus used to call Callippides[119] "the ape," because he thought he so overacted his parts; and a similar view was taken of Pindarus also. All Tragedy, however, is said to stand to the Epic as the newer to the older school of actors. The one, accordingly, is said to address a cultivated audience, which does not need the accompaniment of gesture; the other, an uncultivated one. If, therefore, Tragedy is a vulgar art, it must clearly be lower than the Epic.

The answer to this is twofold. In the first place, one may urge (1) that the censure does not touch the art of the dramatic poet, but only that of his interpreter; for it is quite possible to overdo the gesturing even in an epic recital, as did Sosistratus, and in a singing contest, as did Mnasitheus of Opus.[120] (2) That one should not condemn all movement, unless one means to condemn even the dance, but only that of ignoble people—which is the point of the criticism passed on Callippides and in the present day on others, that their women are not like gentlewomen. (3) That Tragedy may produce its effect even without movement or action in just the same way as Epic poetry; for from the mere reading of a play its quality may be seen. So that, if it be superior in all other respects, this element of inferiority is no necessary part of it.

In the second place, one must remember (1) that Tragedy has everything that the Epic has (even the epic metre being admissible), together with a not inconsiderable addition in the shape of the Music (a very real factor in the pleasure of the drama) and the Spectacle. (2) That its reality of presentation is felt in the play as read, as well as in the play as acted. (3) That the tragic imitation requires less space for the attainment of its end; which is a great advantage, since the more concentrated effect is more pleasurable than one with a large admixture of time to dilute it—consider the *Oedipus* of Sophocles, for instance, and the effect of expanding it into the number of lines of the *Iliad*. (4) That there is less unity in the imitation of the epic poets, as is proved by the fact that any one work of theirs supplies matter for several tragedies; the result being that, if they take what is really a single story, it seems curt when briefly told, and thin and waterish when on the scale of length usual with their verse. In saying that there is less unity in an epic, I mean an epic made up of a plurality of actions, in the same way as the *Iliad* and *Odyssey* have many such parts, each one of them in itself of some magnitude; yet the structure of the two Homeric poems is as perfect as can be, and the action in them is as nearly as possible one action. If, then, Tragedy is superior in these respects, and also, besides these, in its poetic effect (since the two forms of poetry should give us, not any or every pleasure, but the very special kind we have mentioned, it is clear that, as attaining the poetic effect better than the Epic, it will be the higher form of art.

So much for Tragedy and Epic poetry—for these two arts in general and their species; the number and nature of their consituent parts; the causes of success and failure in them; the Objections of the critics, and the Solutions in answer to them.

NOTES

1. [Sophron and his son Xenarchus wrote brief prose dialogues on rural and city life, called "mimes." Sophron was much admired by Plato, who, in writing his "Socratic Conversations," the dialogues, was thought to have been influenced by Sophron's technique.]

2. [Empedocles of Agrigentum, the physical philosopher, used hexameters, the metre of the epics, for his philosophical poems.]

3. [Tragedian of the 4th cent.]

4. [Polygnotus of Thasus, the great painter, active between 475–445 B.C.]

5. [A painter of the time of Aristophanes, who makes fun of him.]

6. [Dionysius of Colophon, a contemporary of Polygnotus, was admired for his realistic portraits.]

7. [Cleophon may be the tragedian, more likely an epic poet of the same name, cp. *Rhet.* 1408a15.]

8. [Hegemon of Thasus, active in late 5th cent.; the passage must mean that he invented the genre.]

9. [It is not likely that the comedian is meant here; the poem is lost.]

10. [Argas is a tempting conjecture. If it is correct Aristotle here is speaking of the well-known cytharoede and poet of the 4th cent.]

11. [Timotheus of Milet and Philoxenus of Citera, poets of the 5th and 4th centuries. Of their poems "Cyclops" fragments are left.]

12. [Sicilian writer of comedies of the 6th or 5th cent.]

13. [Chionides and Magnes, Attic writers of comedy of the 5th cent.]

14. [This burlesque poem was generally attributed to Homer until long after Aristotle's time.]

15. 1448a17; 1448b37.

16. [A competition of comedies was admitted to the Great Dionysians in 486 B.C., to the Lenaeans in 440 B.C.]

17. [Sicilian writer of comedies, younger contemporary of Epicharmus.]

18. [Athenian writer of comedies of the middle 5th cent.]

19. For hexameter poetry cf. 1459a16ff.; comedy was treated of in the lost Second book.

20. [Zeuxis of Heraclea, distinguished painter of the late 5th and early 4th cent. For Polygnotus cp. 1448a6.]

21. 1449b34.
22. [Agathon, tragedian of late 5th–early 4th cent. The name of this lost tragedy has given rise to many speculations.]
23. [Nothing definite known of the man or the event.]
24. Soph. *O.T.* 911–1085.
25. By Theodectes.
26. Eurip. *Iph. Taur.* 727 ff.
27. 1449b20 ff.
28. *Med.* 1236.
29. [A much produced tragedian, contemporary of Aristotle.]
30. [Telegonus, the son of Odysseus and Circe, sets out to find his father and without recognizing him wounds him fatally. This post-Homeric theme was the subject of a tragedy of Sophocles, which may be the play Aristotle here has in mind.]
31. 1231.
32. By Euripides.
33. Authorship unknown.
34. 1453a19.
35. 1450b8.
36. [Euripides.]
37. A dithyramb by Timotheus.
38. Euripides.
39. 1211ff., 1368ff.
40. 1317.
41. 2. 155.
42. In the lost dialogue *On Poets*.
43. 1452a29.
44. Authorship unknown.
45. [Tragedian of the 5th cent.]
46. [By Sophocles.]
47. Hom. *Od.* 14. 386–475.
48. *Od.* 21. 205–25.
49. *Od.* 19. 392.
50. *Iph. Taur.* 727ff.
51. *Iph. Taur.* 800ff.
52. [Writer of dithyrambs and tragedies, late 5th and early 4th cent.]
53. *Od.* 8. 521ff. (cf. 8. 83ff.).
54. 168–234.
55. [Noted writer of dithyrambs of late 5th and early 4th cent.]
56. [The tragedian and rhetorician, a friend of Aristotle.]
57. [Timotheus composed a dithyrambus "The Phinidae."]
58. *Iph. Taur.* 582.
59. *Iph. Taur.* 281ff.
60. *Iph. Taur.* 1163ff.
61. [Not everybody would accept the transposition in the text which the translator makes here.]
62. This does not agree with anything actually said before.
63. [Tragedies of the type of the *Ajax* of Sophocles and of the *Ixion* of Euripides.]
64. [Tragedies of the type of these plays of Sophocles.]
65. [Both are plays of Aeschylus.]
66. A loose reference to 1449b12; 1466b15.
67. [Tragedian of the late 5th cent.]

68. Cf. especially *Rhet.* 1356a1. [However, Aristotle probably is thinking of his doctrine of proofs and emotions as set forth in the greater part of Books I and II of the *Rhetoric.*]

69. [Famous sophist of the 5th cent.]

70. *Od.* 1. 185, 24. 308.

71. Hom. *Il.* 2. 272.

72. [Fragm. of Empedocles' *Purifications.*]

73. [Fragm. of Timotheus.]

74. Authorship unknown.

75. [Fragm. of Empedocles.]

76. *Il.* 5. 393.

77. [An Athenian writer of tragedies, cp. *Rhet.* 1408a15.]

78. [Probably the tragic poet of the late 5th cent.]

79. [A riddle famous already at the time of Aristotle and often quoted later.]

80. [Athenian wit and collector of books, famous for his brilliant remarks.]

81. [*Epicharēn eidon Marathōnade badizonta.* The text (of the other phrase) is corrupt.]

82. [*phagedaina hē mou sarkas esthiei podos.* The play is lost and so is the play of Euripides mentioned next.]

83. [Euripides replaces *esthiei* by *thoinatai.*]

84. [*nun de m' eōn oligos te kai outidanos kai aeikēs. Od.* 9. 515.]

85. [*nun de m' eōn mikros te kai asthenikos kai aeidēs.*]

86. [*diphron aeikelion katatheis oligēn te trapezan. Od.* 20. 259.]

87. [*diphron mochthēron katatheis mikran te trapezan.*]

88. [*ēiones booōsin (Il.* 17. 265) into *ēiones krazousin.*]

89. [His identity is not known to us.]

90. [*dōmatōn apo* (for *apo dōmatōn*), *sethen* (for *egō de nin*), *Achilleōs peri* (for *peri Achilleōs*).]

91. 1451a23ff.

92. Authorship unknown. [Epics belonging to the early epic cycle and dealing with events before and after those included in Homer's *Iliad.*]

93. 1451a3.

94. *Centaur,* cf. 1447b21.

95. 1449a24.

96. *Il.* 22. 205.

97. 19. 164–260.

98. Soph. *El.* 660ff.

99. Probably by Aeschylus.

100. 13. 116ff.

101. 1452a4, 1454a4, 1455a17, 1460a11.

102. [Xenophanes of Colophon, traditionally associated with the Eleatic school of philosophy.]

103. *Il.* 10. 152.

104. *Il.* 1. 50.

105. [*hos rh' ē toi eidos men eēn kakos. Il.* 10. 11–13.]

106. ["Mix the drink livelier." *Il.* 9. 202.]

107. [*alloi men rha theoi to kai aneres eudon (hapantes) pannuchioi. Il.* 2. 1, 10. 1.]

108. [*he tio hot' es pedion to Trōikon athrēseien, aulōn suriggōn (te homadon). Il.* 10. 11–13.]

109. [*oiē d' ammoros* (sc. the Bear alone has no part in the bath of the Ocean). *Il.* 18. 489, *Od.* 5. 275.]

110. [A grammarian mentioned only here.]

111. [*didomen de hoi*. The Greek for "we grant him to obtain his prayer" may also be construed as meaning "grant him . . ." (The reference is to *Il.* 2. 15 where however our manuscripts have an entirely different text.)]

112. [*to men hou kataputhetai ombrō*. *Il.* 23. 327 (the alternative interpretation would be "the wood is not rotted.").]

113. [*aipsa de thnēt' ephuonto, ta prin mathon athanata zōra te prin kekrēto*. (Fragm. of Empedocles; the ambiguity lies in the construction of the last four words).]

114. [*parōchēken de pleō nux*. *Il.* 10. 251 (*pleō* corresponds to "full").]

115. [*knēmis neoteuktou kassiteroio*. *Il.* 21. 592.]

116. *Il.* 20. 234.

117. [*tē rh' escheto chalkeon egchos*. *Il.* 20. 267.]

118. [Probably the same Glaucon whom Plato (*Ion* 530d) mentions as an authority on the explanation of Homer.]

119. [Mynniscus of Chalcis, an actor; Callippides, a much admired writer of tragedies of the late 5th cent.]

120. [Both rhapsodes are mentioned only here.]

RHETORIC

Book III

PREFACE TO THE DISCUSSION OF VERBAL EXPRESSION AND ARRANGEMENT

There are three things that need to be treated in discussing speaking, the sources of convincing arguments, their verbal expression, and the proper arrangement of the parts of the speech.[1] I have dealt with convincing arguments, stating the number of their sources (three), and what they are, and why there are no others (the reason is that in all cases people feel conviction either because they are affected in some particular way themselves, or because they suppose the speaker to have some particular character, or because they are offered demonstrative proof); I have also dealt with the proper sources of rhetorical inferences (*enthumēmata*), some of which are specific and some commonplaces. The next subject to be discussed is expression. This is necessary because it is not enough to know what to say; one must also say it in the right way, and this does a good deal towards giving a speech its particular character.

The first subject that people investigated was naturally what came naturally first, the sources of convincingness in what is being talked about; next came how to express and arrange them; there is a third which is powerfully effective but has not yet been seriously treated, the subject of delivery. Even in relation to tragic acting and to epic recitation it was a long time before it came to the fore, as the poets themselves acted their own tragedies at first. Now clearly there is something of this kind in the study of oratory as well as in the study of poetry, where it has been treated by Glaucon of Teos among others. This study is about the proper use of the voice (loud, soft, and moderate, to express individual emotions), the proper use of accents (acute, grave, and circumflex), and the rhythms appropriate to different things. These are the three subjects they investigate, loudness, harmony, and rhythm. Generally speaking it is actors good at delivery who win prizes in the dramatic contests, and nowadays the actors have more influence there than the poets; the same is true of political contests, because of the low character of the citizens.[2] But, as I said, there is no treatise on the subject (naturally enough, as even the study of verbal expression made a late appearance) and it[3] is thought vulgar, and rightly so. Still, as the whole study of rhetoric is directed towards producing belief,[4] we should attend to it on the assumption that it is necessary even if not strictly proper. Of course the proper thing is not to bother about anything in speaking except the avoidance of giving either pain or pleasure; for the proper thing is to use no weapons other than the actual facts, so that everything except demonstrative proof is superfluous. Nevertheless, it is, as I said, very effective because of the low character of the auditor.

Now the study of verbal expression has some minimal necessity in all forms of instruction, as it makes some difference to clarity of exposition whether one says a thing in this way or that, though not all that much difference, since all this is mere presentation and directed at the hearer; that is why nobody tries to teach geometry in a rhetorical fashion. Now whenever you find successful expression it will have the same effect as delivery; there has been a little systematic discussion of it, for example by Thrasymachus in his *Eleoi*.[5] And whereas delivery is a matter of natural endowment rather than of technique, the study of verbal expression is a technical one. So people who are powerful in this field also win prizes, just like the speakers who rely on delivery; for the written speeches are more efficacious because of their expression than because of their thought.[6]

VERBAL EXPRESSION[7]

The Origins and Nature of Prose Style

Now the first originators [of style] were naturally the poets, as words[8] are imitative of things and the voice is the most imitative of all our organs (hence the development of the various arts of epic recitation, acting, and others). Since the poets, because what they said was naïve, were held to have earned their repute by the way they said it, [prose] style was at first poetical, for instance, that of Gorgias; and even today the majority of the uneducated think such speakers the best. This is wrong, the style of oratory being different from that of poetry, as the facts show; for the tragedians no longer use it in the same way either, and just as they changed from the trochaic tetrameter to the iambic trimeter because this is of all metres the one most like prose, they have also given up words unfamiliar in ordinary usage, which were used for decorative effect by the earlier tragedians and are still used by hexameter poets. So it is absurd to imitate the poets, when they themselves no longer follow the former style. Clearly then we need not concern ourselves in detail with every aspect of style, but only with what belongs to the sort of style we mean; the other has been discussed in the *Poetics*.

So much for that inquiry. Now let us define the excellence of prose style as being clear (for as speech indicates something, it will not do its job if it does not make that thing clear) and neither mean nor too elevated for its purpose, but appropriate;[9] for a poetical style is perhaps not mean, but it is not appropriate to prose. Now among nouns and verbs those that produce clarity are the standard ones (*kuria*), whereas the others described in the *Poetics*[10] make the style decorated and not mean; departure from the ordinary makes it look more dignified, as men have the same reaction to style as they do when comparing strangers with fellow citizens. That is why one should make one's style something out of the ordinary; men feel wonder at what is not to hand, and what rouses wonder gives pleasure. Now in verse many things produce this effect and in verse they are suitable, because the subject-matter and the persons involved are more out of the ordinary, but prose has much more restricted resources, as its theme is less grand. (Even in poetry it would be inappropriate to put fine language into the mouth of a slave or a boy or to use it of trivial subjects; even there propriety demands a lowering as well as a heightening of tone.) That is why one should not produce this effect obviously, but should give the impression that one is speaking naturally, not artificially. Naturalness is convincing, artificiality the reverse; people think they are being got at and take offence, as they do at blended wines. One should aim at the effect attained by Theodorus' voice in comparison with other actors'; his seems to belong to the character, theirs to be imposed on it.[11] Artifice is successfully concealed when one carefully chooses words from ordinary speech and puts them together; this Euripides does and he was the first to show how.[12]

The Resources of Prose Style

Their nature and proper use. The components of a speech are nouns and verbs, and the nouns are classifiable in the way investigated in the *Poetics*. Of the classes there mentioned, there are very few times or places where it is right to use dialect words, compounds, and neologisms (I shall say where later, and the reason has already been given: they involve too great a departure from the appropriate); the only ones that are really useful for prose are standard proper words and metaphor. This is shown by the fact that they are the only ones everybody uses; everyone talks in metaphor and standard proper words, so that clearly if one does this well, the result will be out of the ordinary and yet not obvious, and it will be clear. And this is what we said was excellence in oratorical style.[13]

The definition of each of these, the enumeration of the species of metaphor, and the statement that the latter is most effective both in poetry and in prose, is to be found, as I said, in the *Poetics*; one should take all the more pains with metaphors in prose, because it has fewer resources than verse. It is metaphor more than anything that provides clarity, pleasure, and the unusual; moreover one cannot learn metaphor from anyone else. One's use of both epithets[14] and of metaphors should be appropriate. This is secured by using the right analogy; otherwise it will seem inappropriate, as opposites show up most when juxtaposed. Instead, one should consider, given that a scarlet cloak suits a youth, what suits an old man (it is not the same dress), and if one wants to make something look finer, one should derive one's metaphor from what is best in the same genus, and if one intends blame, from the worse. For instance, since opposites belong to the same genus, to say that a beggar is praying or that someone praying is begging, both being varieties of requesting, is doing what I describe. Another instance is Iphicrates' calling Callias a mendicant priest instead of a torch-carrier, to which Callias rejoined that Iphicrates could not have been initiated, as otherwise he would have called him a torch-carrier, not a mendicant priest (both offices are religious, but one is honourable, and other disreputable). Similarly someone called actors Dionysus' hangers-on, while they refer to themselves as artists (both of these are metaphors, one derogatory, the

1405a

other the reverse), and pirates nowadays call themselves "providers." That is why one can say that a wrongdoer errs and the man in error does wrong, and use both "takes" and "plunders" of a thief. But Telephus' phrase in Euripides,

> lord of the oar, landing in Mysia,

is inappropriate because "lord" is too grand for the subject; so the artifice is not concealed. There is also a fault in the syllables, if they do not express an agreeable sound; for instance, Dionysius Chalcus in his elegies calls poetry "Calliope's scream" because both are vocal sounds, but the metaphor is a bad one because of the non-significant sounds.[16]

Moreover metaphors should not be far-fetched; instead one should derive them from things of the same genus or species so as to give to things that have no name one that will be obviously akin as soon as it is said, as in the celebrated riddle

1405b
> I saw a man weld bronze on a man with fire;

what is happening has no name, but both are a sort of application, and so he used "welding" of the application of the cup.[17] Generally indeed one can derive good metaphors from good riddles, as metaphors do pose riddles, so that the metaphor [borrowed from a riddle] is clearly successful.

The sources from which one derives metaphors should also be beautiful. Beauty of words depends partly, as Licymnius says, on their sounds or on the object signified, and so does ugliness. There is also a third possibility, which answers a sophistic argument: it is not the case that, as Bryson says, nobody uses indecent words since the meaning is the same whether you say this or that; this is false, because one word is more standard than another and more like the object and more akin, by virtue of putting the thing spoken of before one's eyes. Moreover the thing is not regarded in the same light when one indicates it by this word rather than that, so that in this respect too one must take one word to be more beautiful or uglier than the other; both of them signify the beautiful or ugly thing, but not *qua* beautiful or ugly, or if they do, they express the beauty or ugliness in greater or less degree. One must then derive metaphors from sources that are beautiful either because of their sound or because of what they can signify or because of the appeal to the eyes or some other sense. It makes a difference whether one says "rosy-fingered dawn" in preference to "scarlet-fingered" or, worse still, "red-fingered."

Similarly in the case of epithets,[18] the qualities attributed can be derived from a bad or ugly source, like "matricide," or from a nobler one, like "father's avenger";[19] so too Simonides, when offered a small fee by the victor in the mule-race, refused to write a poem on the ground that he felt distaste at writing for mules, but when given an acceptable fee, wrote

> Hail, daughters of the tempest-footed mares,

though they were of course the asses' daughters too. One can also use diminutives [for the same purpose]; a diminutive is what diminishes both evil and good, as, for instance, in Aristophanes' jests in the *Babylonians*, where he uses diminutive forms for "gold-piece," "cloak," "abuse," and "disease." One should be careful and keep an eye on the right proportion in both [epithets and diminutives].

Misuse of stylistic resources. Bathetic lapses[21] are found in four stylistic features:

(i) The first is in the use of compounds, like Lycophron's "many-countenanced heaven of high-peaked earth" and "narrow-pathed shore," or Gorgias' "beggarly-muse-flatterers false-swearing against one true-swearing," or Alcidamas' "his soul swelling with wrath, fire-coloured his visage" and his saying he had thought their zeal would be "achievement-bringing," and making persuasion in speeches "achievement-bringing," and the sea's foundation "indigo-coloured"; all these appear poetical because of the compounding.

(ii) The second reason for failure is the use of dialect words...[22]

(iii) A third is in the use of epithets that are too long, unseasonable, or over-frequent; though it is appropriate in poetry to talk of "white milk," some things of this kind are inappropriate in prose, while others, if used to satiety, convict the work of being manifestly poetry. For though one should use the latter kind because they transform the usual and make the style out of the ordinary, one should aim at a mean since the result can be much worse than speaking haphazard; the latter misses excellence, but the former can incur failure. That is why Alcidamas' works fall flat; for he uses his epithets not as a seasoning but as the main dish, since they are so frequent, grandiose, and obtrusive. For example, he says not "sweat" but "damp sweat," not "to the Isthmia" but "to the gathering at the Isthmia," not "laws" but "laws that are kings of cities," not "at a run" but "with his soul's impulse arace," and "taking over" not "learning's shrine" but "nature's shrine of learning," and "his soul's anxiety glowering," and "artificer" not "of favour" but "of a whole people's favour," and "dispenser of the hearers' pleasure," and not "with branches" but "with the branches of the wood he concealed...," and "he clothed" not "his body" but "his body's shame," and "the desire of his soul counter-imitative" (this is compound as well as an epithet, so that the result is a piece of poetry), and "the excess of depravity so beyond all bounds." So by speaking in poetical style such people produce ridiculous and bathetic results because of the lack of propriety, while their garrulousness makes for lack of clarity; for whenever a speaker piles more on someone who already understands, he destroys the clarity of his expression by obscuring it. In ordinary life people use compounds when the thing referred to has no name and the compounding is easy, as in *chronotribein*, "passing time"; but if this is done much, the result is altogether poetical. That is why the compounded style is most useful to dithyrambic poets, as they make a great deal of din, dialect words to hexameter poets, as the epic is grand and domineering, and metaphor to iambic poets (it is metaphor that they use nowadays, as I said before).[23]

(iv) A fourth kind of failure is in metaphor. Metaphors, too, can be inappropriate, some because they are ludicrous (comic poets also use metaphors), some because they are too grand and tragic; they are also unclear if far-fetched, like Gorgias' "affairs pale and bloodless," "you sowed this in baseness and reaped it in misery" (this is too poetical). The same is true of Alcidamas' calling philosophy "an outpost to assail the law" and the *Odyssey* "a fair mirror of human life" and "not employing any such toy in his poetry"; all these are unconvincing for the reasons given. But Gorgias' remark to the swallow when she flew overhead and dropped on him is in fine tragic style; he said "Shame, Philomela!" It was no disgrace to a bird to do it, but it would be shocking if a girl did. There is elegance in his reproaching her by calling her what she was, not what she is.

Eikones.[24] The *eikōn*[25] is also a metaphor, as there is only a slight difference; for when he says "Like a lion he leapt upon him" it is an *eikōn*, while "A lion, he leapt upon him" is a metaphor (because both are brave he[26] metaphorically called Achilles a lion). The *eikōn* can be used in prose, but only rarely, as it is poetical. They should be derived from the same sources as metaphors, since they are really metaphors, apart from the difference mentioned.

An example of an *eikōn* is Androtion's remark against Idrieus, "He is like unchained curs; they rush at people and bite, and Idrieus grew tyrannical once freed from his chains." There is also Theodamas' comparison of Archidamus to a Euxenus ignorant of geometry, which is analogical, as Euxenus will be an Archidamus with knowledge of geometry. So too in Plato's *Republic* the comparison of those who strip the dead with curs that bite the stone but do not touch the thrower, and of the people in a democracy with a sturdy but rather deaf ship's captain, and of the poets' verses with those who have the bloom of youth without beauty; for when the boys have lost their bloom or the verses are broken up, they no longer look the same.[27] And Pericles' saying of the Samians "They are like children, who wail as they take the sop," and of the Boeotians "They are like holm-oaks; just as the oaks are cut down by themselves, the Boeotians are ruined by intestine wars."[28] And Demosthenes' saying of the people that they were like sea-sick passengers.[29] And Democrates' comparison of politicians with nurses who swallow the sop they chew, and smear the baby with the spittle.[30] And Antisthenes' comparison of the thin Cephisodotus with frankincense, because he gave pleasure by wasting away. One can produce all these either as *eikones* or as metaphors; so any such comparisons that have won favour when stated as metaphors will clearly be [possible] *eikones* as well, and *eikones* [possible] metaphors if used without the reason being given. One should always give the analogical metaphor reciprocity, so that it is applicable to either of the things of the same genus; for instance, if the cup is Dionysus' shield, it is also appropriate for the shield to be called Ares' cup.[31]

So much for the elements of which a speech is composed.

The Essential Characteristics and Virtues of Prose Style

Correctness. The first requirement of style is speaking pure Greek. This consists in five things:

(i) The first is in the use of particles, giving them in sequence in their natural order, in the way some of them require; for instance, "Now . . ." and

"Now I . . ." require "but . . ." and "but he . . ."[32] One should duly produce the second while the first is still in mind, and not append it at too great a distance, nor put another particle before the one needed, as this is very rarely suitable. "Now I, when he had spoken (for Cleon, came with both demands and entreaties), set off with them as company." Here many particles are interpolated before the "but he . . ." demanded by the "Now I . . ."; if there is a long interval before the "set off," the result is unclear.[33] One element, then, is the correct use of particles.

(ii) The second is the use of particular terms and not inclusive ones.

(iii) The third is the use of unambiguous terms, unless of course one intends the opposite effect, as people do when they have nothing to say, but pretend they have; such persons do use ambiguous expressions in verse, Empedocles, for example. This long circumlocution imposes on the hearers, who are affected in the same way as the majority are by fortune-tellers; when they speak ambiguously, people nod solemn assent ("Croesus by crossing the Halys will destroy a great empire"). And because it involves less error fortune-tellers use generic descriptions of what is being discussed; one would be more likely to succeed in playing "odd and even" if one said "Odd" or "Even" and not how many the other player had, and similarly with saying an event will occur rather than when it will occur; that is why oracle-mongers never define the when. All these are akin to one another, so that, unless for some such purpose, one should avoid them.

(iv) The fourth is the correct use of Protagoras' classification of nouns into masculine, feminine, and things; these must also properly and duly correspond.

(v) The fifth is the correct use of number.[34]

Clarity. Generally speaking, a written work should be easy to read aloud[35] and to deliver, which is really the same thing. This is impaired by a superfluity of particles or in works not easy to punctuate, like those of Heraclitus. Punctuating Heraclitus is hard work because it is not clear whether something is to be taken with what precedes or what follows, as, for example, at the beginning of his treatise, where he says, "This truth which is constant ever misunderstood by men" and it is not clear to which phrase one should attach the "ever." Another thing that produces solecism is not giving the due accompaniment, I mean if you link [to two terms] one that does not suit both; for instance, "seeing" is not appropriate to both sound and colour, while "perceiving" is. It is also unclear if you do not make a full statement beforehand when you mean to interpolate many things in between, like saying "I intended after a discussion with him about this and that and in these terms to set out," rather than "I intended to set out after a discussion with him," and then "This and that took place and in these terms."[36]

Pomp.[37] Pomp of style is aided by the following means:

(i) The use of a definition instead of a word, saying, for instance, not "circle" but "the surface with a circumference equidistant from its centre'; concision results from the opposite, using a word instead of a definition.

(ii) When something is ugly or lacking in propriety, then if the ugliness is in the definition one should use the word, if in the word use the definition.

(iii) Representing things by metaphor and epithets, while taking care to avoid the poetical.

(iv) Using the plural for the singular, as the poets do; for even when there is only one harbour they still say "to the Achaean harbours" and "Here are the many-leaved folds of the tablet."[38]

(v) Not combining [two words with one article], but giving each its own . . .[39]; for concision one should do the opposite.

(vi) Using particle linkings; for concision one should not use particles, but not write asyndetically either. Examples are "having gone and had a discussion," "having gone I had a discussion."[40]

(vii) One can also use Antimachus' trick of describing a thing by qualities it does not have (so he says of Teumessus "There is a little windless hill") ; this gives limitless possibilities of amplification. One can also use this "It does not have so and so" of things good and bad, in whichever direction it is serviceable; this is the source of the poetical phrases like "stringless" or "lyreless music." The poets give things such privative epithets, a practice that finds favour when used in analogical metaphors, saying, for instance, that the trumpet gives forth a lyreless music.

Propriety. There are three conditions for propriety: that the style be capable of expressing emotion and of expressing character, and that it be proportioned to its subject-matter. Proportion consists in not talking in an off-hand way about subjects that require pomp nor in a grand style about trivial subjects, and in not attaching a decorative epithet to a trivial word; otherwise the result seems a piece of comedy as in Cleophon, whose expression in some cases was very much in the style of "Lady fig."

By "capable of expressing emotion," I mean that if an outrage is being described the style should be that of an angry man, if impious and shameful acts, that of a person feeling disgust and reluctant even to describe them, if praiseworthy, that one should speak admiringly, if pitiable, miserably and so on. A fact is made more credible by the style that belongs to it; for our mind assumes that a man is speaking with genuine feeling and falsely infers that the feeling is roused by the events described, so that people think the facts are what the speaker says, even if they are not. Moreover the hearer always feels in sympathy with the person who expresses emotion, even if he says nothing of substance; that is why many speakers try to stun the audience with din.

One can express character too by this indication by signs, when the suitable indication goes with the relevant class and disposition. By "class" here I mean, for example, determination by age or sex or nationality, while I confine "disposition" to those that make us say that in his life a man has such and such a character; of course not every disposition helps to characterize a life. Well then, if a speaker uses the words adapted to his disposition he will express his character; a rustic and an educated man would not use the same terms or in the same way.

The hearers are also affected by the trick that the speech-writers use *ad nauseam*, "Who does not know?" and "Everyone knows." The hearer assents in shame, so that he can share this universal knowledge.

Seasonable and unseasonable use is something common to all the kinds. The cure for every excess is the one constantly used, of reproaching oneself; this is thought to be all right, since the speaker is aware of what he is doing. Moreover one should not use all the elements of a proportion at once, as the hearer is less aware of what is happening if one does not; I mean, for example, if the words are harsh, you should not also employ a voice and a facial expression to suit, as otherwise it is obvious what is going on in each case. But if one is one thing and one another, this secures the same effect without being obvious. So if one says soft things in a harsh tone and harsh ones softly, it is convincing.[41]

Compound words and plurality of epithets and terms out of the ordinary best suit the speaker who is expressing emotion; one forgives an angry man for saying that an evil is "heaven-high" or "monstrous,"[42] and also a speaker who already has a grip on his audience and has filled them with high excitement[43] by encomium or invective or anger or love, as Isocrates too does in the *Panegyricus* at the end . . .[44] People do voice such expressions when excited, so that an audience in the same state will obviously find them acceptable. That is why I said they suit poetry, as it involves such high excitement. One should use them therefore either in the circumstances described or ironically, as Gorgias did or as in the *Phaedrus*.[45]

Prose Rhythm

The form of expression should be neither metrical nor unrhythmical. The former is unconvincing because it seems artificial, and it is also distracting because it makes one attend to the similarity and wonder when it will recur, just as children anticipate the answer to the herald's cry "Whom does the freedman choose as his patron?" with "Cleon." On the other hand, the unrhythmical is indefinite, whereas the form should be defined, though not metrically, because the indefinite gives not pleasure and is hard to recognize. In every case it is number that gives definition, and number in the context of verbal expression is rhythm, of which verses (*metra*) are sections. That is why a speech should have rhythm, though not metre, as that would make it a piece of poetry. The rhythm moreover should not be too precise, and this is achieved by restricting its use.

Of the various rhythms the dactylic is grand but lacks the conversational tone, while the iambic is the rhythm of ordinary speech (which is why in conversation people utter more iambic trimeters than any other metre), whereas one needs grandeur and an effect higher than usual. The trochaic is too appropriate to the comic dance, as one can see from the tetrameter, which is a bustling rhythm. So we are left with the paean, which people have used from the time of Thrasymachus, though they were not able to describe it. The paean is a third rhythm, related to those mentioned, as it has the ratio of 3:2, while of the others the dactylic is 1:1, the iambic and trochaic 2:1; 1½: 1 is related to these and is the ratio of the paean.[46] So the others should be left alone for the reasons given and also because they have fixed verse forms,[47] while the paean should be accepted, as it is the only one of the rhythms mentioned that has no fixed verse form and is therefore least obvious. Now at the moment people use the same form of paean both at the beginning of a sentence and at the end, but the end should be different from the beginning. There are two kinds of paean that are opposites, and one of them is suitable at the beginning, where people do in fact use it; this is the one with its first syllable long and the other three short.[48] The reverse form is that which starts with three shorts and ends with a long.[48] This makes a suitable end, as a short ending, being incomplete, makes the rhythm look maimed. Instead one should cut the sentence off with a long and make the ending clear not with the scribe's help, using a punctuation mark, but by means of the rhythm.[49]

So much for the subject of the necessity to prose of agreeable rhythm, and what rhythms are agreeable and how they are constructed.

The Loose and the Periodic Styles

The style will inevitably be either strung together (*eiromenē*) and made one by connection, like the preludes in dithyrambs, or neatly ended like the antistrophes of the ancient choral lyrists. The strung-together style is the ancient one[50] (it was universally practised formerly, but rarely nowadays); by "strung-together" I mean that the sentence has no end prescribed by its own structure, unless the thing being talked of is finished with. It is disagreeable because of its lack of definition, as everyone wants to have the end in view. That is why runners only pant hard and relax when they pass the goal; they do not flag earlier because they can see the end in front of them. Such, then, is the strung-together style.

By "neatly-ended" I mean the periodic style. By "period" I mean an expression that has a beginning and end determined by its own structure and a length that can be seen as a whole. This gives pleasure and is easy to grasp. It gives pleasure because it is the opposite of the indefinite and because the hearer constantly thinks that he has got hold of something and that something has been made definite for him, whereas not being able to foresee or finish something off is disagreeable; it is easy to grasp because it is easily remembered, the reason for this being that the periodic style involves number, which is of all things the easiest to remember. That is why everyone can remember verses better than pell-mell phrases; verses have number to measure them. The period should also be completed along with the thought and not cut up like Sophocles' lines[51]—

This land is Calydon. Of Pelops' isle . . .

Such a division can lead one to suppose what is contrary to fact, in this case, for example, that Calydon is in the Peloponnese.

The period is of two kinds, that composed of *cōla* and the simple one. By "that composed of *cōla*" I mean the one that is completely finished off and has its parts distinct and can be uttered without exhausting the breath, not with a stop at an arbitrary point as in the period cited, but as a whole (by "*cōlon*" I mean one of the two parts of the period), while by "simple" I mean that which has only one *cōlon*. Both the *cōla* and the periods should be neither curtailed nor over-long.

Shortness makes the hearer often stumble; it is inevitable, when he is still making for a distant point and for the limit that he defines for himself and then is pulled into reverse because the *cōlon* or period comes to an end, that he should as it were stumble because of the check. Excessive length on the other hand makes him feel left behind, just as those who only turn when they have passed the limit leave behind the people they are walking with; similarly periods that are too long become a speech in themselves and are like a dithyrambic prelude. The result is like what Democritus of Chios mocked at in Melanippides, who composed preludes instead of antistrophic works:

> In working woe to another a man works woe to himself;
> and a long trailing prelude is worst for the poet's self.[52]

One can say the same of periods with over-long *cōla*. Those where the *cōla* are too short are not periods at all; and consequently they send the hearer flying headlong.

The expression composed of *cōla* has two species, the divided and the antithetical; an example of a divided one is "I have often marvelled at the men by whom assemblies are constituted and athletic games instituted"; while the antithetical is that in which in the pair of clauses either opposite answers opposite or one word serves as a bridge between the opposites. Examples are: "They benefited both those who stayed at home and those who went out; for the latter they acquired more than they had at home, for the former they left their possessions at home adequate" (staying at home is opposed to going out, more to adequate); "so that both those who needed money and those who wanted enjoyment" (enjoyment is opposed to acquisition). And again: "It often happens in these affairs that the sensible fail and the senseless succeed," "Then and there they were deemed worthy of the prize of valour, and not long after they acquired the empire of the sea," "to sail over the land, to march over the sea, by bridging the Hellespont and channelling through Athos," "and though by nature they are citizens, by law they are deprived of citizenship," "some of them wretchedly perished, some were disgracefully saved," "and as private citizens to use barbarians as slaves, but as a state allow many of their allies to be enslaved [to barbarians]," "either to have in life or to leave at death."[53] And what someone said in court against Pitholaus and Lycophron: "while at home they sold you, and when they came to you they bought you." All these produce the effect described. Such a form of expression gives pleasure because opposites are easiest to recognize (and even easier when put beside each other), and because it is like a piece of reasoning; for refutation involves bringing together opposite conclusions.[54]

[There follows a short section, mainly made up of examples, on *parisosis* (equal *cōla*) and similar figures: we resume where the next topic begins.]

Wit[55]

Now that we have got clear descriptions of all this, the next thing to discuss is the source of witty expressions that are well thought of. Though producing them is a task for the person of natural talent or practised skill, showing how to is a proper subject for this inquiry. So let us say what they are and list them, taking this as our starting-point: anybody naturally enjoys understanding something easily, and as words signify something those that produce understanding in us give most pleasure. Now as we are unfamiliar with dialect words and know standard terms already, it is metaphor that most produces this effect; for when he[56] calls old age stubble, he makes us understand and realize something via their generic similarity, as both are past their prime. The poets' *eikones*[57] also produce the same effect, and therefore, when successful, give an impression of wit. The *eikōn*, as I said before, is a metaphor with a difference in the way of setting it out; that is why it gives less pleasure, because it is more long-winded, and it does not say that this is that, so that our soul does not even inquire whether it is. So necessarily wit will be found in expressions and inferences that produce immediate understanding. That is why people think nothing of superficial inferences (those, I mean, that are obvious to anybody and are found without investigation), nor of those that we do not understand when they are expressed, but admire those whose force we realize the moment they are uttered, even though we had no notion of them before, or those where the understanding lags only a little behind; this produces a sort of sudden realization which is absent in the other two cases. Well then, so far as the sense is concerned, people think well of the sort of inferences described. In the expression of them a similar effect is produced by the form of the statement, if it is put antithetically, as in "and they thought a peace all others shared a war directed against their own interests"[58] (war is opposed to peace), and also by the individual words if they involve metaphor, and a metaphor neither far-fetched, as that makes it hard to see the two things together, nor superficial, as that leaves us unaffected. The expression should also bring things before our eyes,[59] as we should see them as happening rather than likely to happen. So one should aim at these three things, antithesis, metaphor, [an impression of] activity.

Of the four kinds of metaphor[60] the most highly thought of is the analogical. So Pericles said that the young men lost in the war had vanished from the city as if one were to take the spring from the year. Leptines said of the Spartans, that they would not let Greece lose one of her two eyes. Cephisodotus, when Chares was eager to pass his audit[61] about the Olynthian war, complained that he was choking the people to suffocation in trying to pass his audit. And when urging the Athenians to take provisions and proceed to Euboea, he said they should march to Miltiades' decree.[62] Iphicrates, when the Athenians made a truce with Epidaurus and the coastal area, complained that they had filched the travel-rations of the war. Pitholaus called the state-trireme the people's cudgel, and Sestos the corn-booth of the Piraeus. Pericles urged them to remove Aegina, the eyesore of the Piraeus. Moerocles said he was no worse than a prominent citizen he named, as the latter played the scoundrel at 33 per cent, while he himself was content with 10. And Anaxandrides' line about daughters being past the time for marriage:

> My girls are in arrears for marriage now.

And Polyeuctus' phrase of a paralytic called Speusippus, that he could not keep quiet though ill luck had locked him in a pillory of disease. And Cephisodotus called the warships gaily painted millstones, and the Cynic[63] said the cookshops were the mess-halls of Athens.[64] And Aesion that they had poured the city down the drain of Sicily; this is both metaphorical and vivid. And "so that all Greece cried out" is also a kind of metaphor and vivid. And as Cephisodotus urged them to beware of meeting in too many mobs.[65] And Isocrates of those who rushed together for the festivals. And as in the *Funeral Speech*,[66] that it was right that at the tomb of those who died at Salamis Greece should cut her hair in mourning, as her freedom was buried with their valour; if he had just said it was right to weep because their valour was buried with them, that would be a metaphor and vivid, but "her freedom with their valour" involves a sort of antithesis. And in Iphicrates' phrase "The path of my words lies through the midst of Chares' deeds" there is an analogical metaphor, and the "through the midst" is vivid. And saying one is inviting dangers to help out dangers is vivid and a metaphor. And Lycoleon on Chabrias, "not even feeling awe at the symbol of his supplication, the bronze statue"; that was a metaphor at the moment, though not for ever, but it is always vivid; for it is when he is in danger that the statue supplicates, the "inanimate animated," the memorial of the city's achievements.[67] And "practising poor-spiritedness with all his might";[68] "practising" implies trying to increase something. And "the god kindled intelligence as a light in the soul"; both make things clear. "We do not put a truce to wars, but merely adjourn them";[69] both involve the future, adjournment and a peace of this kind. And saying that a treaty is a much finer trophy than those set up in war, because the latter are for trivial achievements and a single success, while the former celebrates success in the whole war;[70] here both are signs of victory. And "cities pay a heavy reckoning to men's censure"; "reckoning" is a punishment imposed by law.

So much for the fact that witty expressions are derived from analogical metaphor and from vivid presentation. The next thing to discuss is the meaning of "vivid presentation," and what one does to secure this effect. Well then, I say it is produced by all expressions that signify activity; for example, to say that a good man is "four-square"[71] is a metaphor, both being perfect, but does not signify activity. But "with the prime of his manhood in bloom"[72] is [an expression of] activity, and so is "but you, like a free-ranging creature," and in "and then the Greeks darting on"[73] the "darting on" is both expressive of activity and a metaphor, as it indicates speed. And Homer's frequent practice of attributing life to inanimate things via metaphor. In all such cases the expression finds favour because it produces [the impression of] activity, for example, "once more the unmanageable boulder rolled down to the plain"[74] and "the arrow flew"[75] and "eager to hit its mark"[76] and "they stuck in the ground longing for their fill of flesh"[77] and "the spear rushed through his breast, quivering with eagerness."[78] In all these cases they seem to be active because animate, as "being insolent" and "quivering with eagerness" and the rest are [expressions of] activity.[79] He has attached them to the objects via analogical metaphor, since the boulder is to Sisyphus as the insolent man is to the object of his insolence. He does the same with inanimate things in the *eikones* that find favour, "arched, foam-crested, some first, then others after them";[80] he makes them all moving and living, and activity is a species of motion.

One should, as I said before, derive metaphors from things that are akin and not obvious, just as in philosophy it is the keen-witted man who can see the similarity in things remote from each other, like Archytas' saying that an arbitrator was the same as an altar, as both were the refuge of the ill-used. Or if one were to say that an anchor and a crane-sling are the same, as they are the same something but differ in that one goes down, and the other goes up. And "levelling" used of political societies is the same concept applied to very different objects, namely, equality to surface and to power.

Most witty expressions depend not only on metaphor but on rousing a false expectation, as that makes it more obvious that one has learnt something because of the contrariety, and our soul seems to say "How true, and I missed it!" And witty apophthegms are derived from not meaning what one says, like Stesichorus' "The cicadas will sing to themselves from the ground."[81] And good riddles give pleasure for the same reason that they involve both realization and metaphor. And so does saying something strange, to use Theodorus' phrase; this happens when the phrase is unexpected and, in his words, "not in line with our previous opinion," but is instead like the parodic turns in jokes (the same effect is produced by puns, as they also cheat expectation) and in verse lines, as they too do not run in the way the hearer assumed ("he went on his way and beneath his feet were chilblains," when the hearer expected "sandals"). Such a turn should be obvious the moment it is uttered.

[We omit a section on puns and the like, again mainly composed of examples, some of which are unintelligible.]

1412b These expressions are all of the same kind; but the more succinctly and antithetically they are expressed, the better thought of they are. The reason is that we understand better because of the antithesis and faster because of the brevity. It should always have as well correct expression of its personal application, if what is said is to be both true and free of superficiality;[82] an expression can have one of these qualities[83] without the other, like "One should die without doing wrong," "The deserving man should marry the deserving woman." But there is no wit unless both qualities are present, "It is right to die when it is not right for one to die."[84] The more of the qualities described an expression has the wittier it will appear, I mean, if the terms are metaphorical and the metaphor is of a particular kind and there is antithesis and *parisōsis*, and an expression of activity.

As I said above, the *eikones* that are well thought of are also metaphors in a way, as they always involve two terms, like analogical metaphors; for instance, *1413a* to use our ordinary example, "the shield is Ares' cup" and "the bow is a lyre without strings." When they speak in this way the expression is not simple, like calling the bow a lyre or the shield a cup. And they produce *eikones* in the same way, for instance likening a flute-player to an ape, a short-sighted man to a lamp with water dripping on it, because both blink. Excellence in them demands metaphor; one can produce an *eikōn* comparing the shield to Ares' cup and ruins to the rags of a house,[85] and Niceratus can be called "a Philoctetes bitten by Pratys," as in Thrasymachus' *eikōn* when he saw Niceratus after his defeat by Pratys in the citharoedic contest, still dishevelled and unwashed. Such comparisons earn poets the most hisses when they fail and the most applause when they succeed, I mean, when they make them correspond:

> His legs are curly like parsley-leaves.[86]

> Like Philammon at close quarters with the punch-ball.[87]

All such expressions are *eikones*. And I have said often already that *eikones* are metaphors.

Proverbs are also metaphors, of the species to species kind.[88] For instance, if a man calls in another expecting to benefit and is then hurt, he says "Like the Carpathian with the rabbit,"[89] as each of them has suffered the fate described. Well then, the sources of witty expression and the reasons why they are sources have been just about dealt with. Hyperboles of the kind that are well thought of are also metaphors, for instance, of the man with the black eye, "You would have thought he was a basket of mulberries"; the black eye *is* red, but the expression is very extreme. The "Just like such and such" is really a hyperbole with a different form of expression: "like Philammon at close quarters with the punch-ball," "You would have thought he was Philammon fighting with the punch-ball," "His legs are curly like parsley-leaves," "You would have thought his legs not legs but parsley, they were so curly." Hyperboles are juvenile, as they indicate vehemence. That is why they are most used by people in a temper: "Not if he were to give me gifts as many as the sand and dust. I shall not marry the daughter of Agamemnon, Atreus' son, not if she vies in beauty with golden Aphrodite and in handiwork with Athena."[90] That is why such expression is inappropriate in the mouth of an older man.

1413b

The Various Kinds of Style

One must not forget that different styles are suitable for different kinds of discourse. The styles of written composition and extemporary debate are not the same, and [within the latter] the style of political debate is different from that of the law-courts. One needs to know both; capability in debate is knowing how to express oneself in Greek, and the other means you are not compelled to be silent if you want to impart your ideas to the rest of the world, a fate suffered by those who do not know how to produce written compositions. The written style is the most finished, the style of debate that most capable of being delivered (the latter has two species, one expressive of character, the other of emotion); that is why actors eagerly seek for plays in this style and poets for such actors, while the poets who can be read are continually in our hands, like Chaeremon (he is as finished as a writer of speeches) and Licymnius among the dithyrambic poets. When the two sorts are put side by side the speeches of the writers seem too constrained in actual delivery, while those of the extemporary speakers, which were admirable when delivered, seem unprofessional when one takes them up to read. The reason is that it[91] is suitable in real debate; this is also why, when delivery is removed, the features adapted for delivery seem inane because they are not producing their proper effect, things, for instance, like asyndeta and frequent repetitions of the same idea, which are rightly disapproved of in the written style but not in that of debate, and are in fact used by the orators, as such a style is adapted for delivery. In repeating the same idea one should use variation, since this paves the way for the form of delivery, as in "He is the one who robbed you, he is the one who cheated you, he the one who finally attempted to betray you," or as the actor Philemon did in Anaxandrides' *Old Men's Madness*,[92] whenever he said "Rhadamanthys and Palamedes," and the "I" in the prologue of the *Devotees*;[93] if one does not deliver such things expressively, one would be like a man who had swallowed a poker. The same is true of asyndeta, "I came, I approached him, I besought him"; one needs to deliver this expressively and not give it a uniform vehemence and a uniform expression of character as if one were saying only one thing. There is moreover a special feature of asyndeta, that many things are taken to be said in the time it would take to say one, since connection makes a unity out of plurality, so that its removal obviously turns a unit into a plurality. It therefore gives an effect of magnification:[94] "I came, I spoke to him, I besought him" (this seems a lot of things), "he contemned everything I said."[95] This is what Homer aims to do with his

> Nireus from Syme . . .
> Nireus son of Aglaia . . .
> Nireus the most beautiful . . .[96]

If one says a lot about a thing, one must speak of it more than once; so if one speaks of it more than once, one is taken to be saying a lot about it. So Homer here has magnified Nireus, though mentioning him only once, because we make the false inference, and has made us remember him though he says nothing at all about him later in the poem.

The style adapted to public assemblies is throughout like outline painting, since the more numerous the crowd, the further the individuals stand away from the picture. That is why in both cases exact finish is superfluous and indeed produces an inferior impression. The style of the law-courts is more finished, and most of all the style that depends on a single judge, as it least admits the arts of the speaker; it is easier here to keep in one view what is relevant to the case and what not, and as there is no public debate, the judgement is unimpeded. That is why the same speakers do not find favour in all three kinds; instead, whenever delivery is most in point, finish is least required. And this is the case where we need a voice and most of all where we need a loud voice.

Well then, the style of epideictic speeches is best adapted to writing, as its function is to be read, and next to it comes the style of the courts. It is superfluous to go in for further distinctions about style and say, for instance, that it should give pleasure and be magnificent. Why that rather than temperate or liberal or endowed with any other moral virtue? The qualities described above will obviously make it give pleasure, if excellence of style has been rightly defined. What else is the point of its being clear and not mean but appropriate? If one is garrulous one is not clear, and nor is one if one is over-concise, so that the mean between these is obviously suitable. The things described will make it give pleasure if they are well-blended, the usual and the out-of-the-ordinary, and rhythm, and the convincingness produced by propriety. So much for style, both the general discussion common to all kinds and the particular description of each.

ARRANGEMENT

The Essential Parts of a Speech: Arguments Against the Current Over-Elaborate Terminology

The remaining subject is arrangement. There are two [real] parts of a speech: one must necessarily state what one is talking about, and then prove it. That is why it is impossible to make the statement and not proceed to proof, or to prove one's case without making the preliminary statement, since anyone producing proofs is trying to prove something, and anyone who makes a preliminary statement makes it with a view to proving it. These two parts are the preliminary setting-out and the argument, analogous to the division [in dialectic] between stating the problem and giving a demonstrative proof. The current method of division is ludicrous [for several reasons]:

(i) Narration belongs only to speeches in the courts, while epideictic and political oratory cannot possibly admit a narration of the kind they describe, nor yet the arguments directed against one's rival litigant.

(ii) Demonstrative arguments cannot admit a peroration.[97]

(iii) The proem and the comparison of opposite positions and the review occur in political oratory only where there is an opposing speech (for that matter, accusation and defence also occur there, but not in so far as it is political advice).

(iv) Moreover the peroration does not belong even to forensic oratory as a whole, for instance, if the speech is short and the subject easily remembered; for its effect is to remove the [impression made by] length.

So the necessary sections are the setting-forth and the argument. These are the parts that characterize a speech, while the maximum is proem, setting-forth, argument, peroration; arguments against the other litigant are part of the argument, while comparison of opposite positions is an amplification of the arguments for one's case, so that it too is part of the argument, as the person who does it is trying to prove something. But this is not true of the proem or the peroration, as that serves instead as a reminder. If one goes in for divisions of the fashionable kind, as in Theodorus and his school, one will get narrative as one thing and supplementary narrative as another, and preliminary narrative and refutation and supplementary refutation.[98] But one should state a species and use a differentia when assigning names; otherwise the result is inane chatter of the kind Licymnius produces in his treatise, using words like "on-wafting" and "off-wandering" and "branches."

1414b

The Proem

Well then, a proem is the beginning of a speech, corresponding to the prologue in poetry and the prelude in flute-playing; all these are beginnings and pave the way for what is to come.

The proem in epideictic oratory. The flute-prelude is like the proem of epideictic speeches. Flautists play their best piece first and then link it to the theme, and one should write in the same way in epideictic speeches, saying straight away whatever one likes and then entering on the theme and linking it up. This is in fact what they all do; an example is the proem of Isocrates' *Helen*, where the eristics[99] have nothing to do with Helen. It is suitable for the speaker even to go off on an alien topic and for the speech not to seem all of one kind. The opening words of epideictic proems concern praise or blame, as in Gorgias' *Olympic,* "There are many reasons, fellow Greeks, for admiring . . ." (he goes on to praise the organizers of the festal assemblies, whereas Isocrates[100] blames them for honouring only physical excellence and not establishing any prize for the intelligent); or they can start with advice (for example, that one should honour the good, which is why the speaker is praising Aristides, or one should honour those who are neither highly reputed nor base, but are good without being noticed, like Priam's son Paris, who is giving the advice);[101] they can also take their start from forensic proems, that is, be directed to conciliating the hearer, if the speech is about something surprising or difficult or trite, so as to win pardon as in Choerilus'

> Now that all is assigned.[102]

Well then, the proems of epideictic speeches start from the topics mentioned, praise, blame, suasion, dissuasion, and appeal to the hearer; the opening themes may be either alien from or akin to the speech.

The proem in forensic oratory. As for the proem of the forensic speech, one should take it to have the same point as prologues in plays and proems in epics. The proems of dithyrambs are like those of epideictic speeches ("Because of you and your gifts or should I call them spoils?"), whereas in prologues and in epic there is an indication of what is to be said, so that the hearers can know beforehand what the work is about and the mind not be kept in suspense, since what is undefined makes the attention wander. So the speaker who as it were puts the beginning in the hearer's hand makes him hold fast and follow what is said. That is why we have

> Sing of the wrath, goddess . . .[103]
>
> Tell me of the man, Muse . . .[104]
>
> Tell me another story, how from the Asian land there came to Europe a great war . . .[105]

And the tragedians similarly tell what the play is about, if not at once as Euripides does, still somewhere in the prologue, like Sophocles' "My father was Polybus";[106] the same is true of comedy. So the most necessary and the characteristic function of the proem is telling what the speech is aiming at (which is why one need not use a proem if that is clear and the subject a small one).

The other general heads that they use [in proems] are "remedies" and common to other parts of the speech. Remedies of this kind take their starting-point from the speaker, the hearer, the subject-matter, or the adversary. In the case of oneself and the adversary it is a matter of doing away with prejudice or creating it. The method is not similar: if one is defending oneself one answers the prejudice first, while if one is accusing another one attacks him in the peroration, for the obvious reason that in defence, if one is going to put oneself across, one must get rid of obstacles and therefore deal first with prejudice, whereas in rousing prejudice one should do it in the peroration, so that the audience remembers it better. Remedies directed at the hearer start from making him well-disposed or angry, and sometimes attentive or the reverse; it is not always useful to make him attentive, which is why many speakers try to divert him to laughter. So far as his being disposed to learn goes, everything produces that result if one wants it, including giving an impression of virtue, since people do pay special attention to the virtuous. The things people attend to are important ones, and ones that concern them or surprise them or give them pleasure; that is why one should try to produce the notion that one's speech deals with matters of this kind, while if one wants them inattentive, one should suggest that the matter is trivial, of no interest to them, and painful. One should be aware that all such things are alien to the speech proper, as they are directed at a low-class hearer who listens to what does not concern the real subject-matter; if he is of a different kind one does not need a proem, except to state the subject in a summary form, so that the body can have a head. Moreover securing the audience's attention is something common to all parts of the speech, if it is required at all; there is nowhere they are less likely to relax than at the beginning, so that it is ridiculous to put it at the beginning, that is, at the point where everybody listens most attentively anyway. Instead, whenever the right moment comes, one should say, "And listen carefully to what I say; it concerns you just as much as me," and "I shall tell you something more dreadful and more surprising than you have ever heard." This is the same as what Prodicus said, that whenever his audience showed signs of nodding off, he threw in a bit of the fifty-drachmae course. It is obviously directed at the hearer not *qua* hearer [of the speech proper], since everyone uses the proem when they are trying to rouse prejudice or remove alarm ("Lord, I shall not tell you that with haste..."[107] and "Why this proem?")[108] Similarly with those who have or think they have a bad case; they think it better to spend their speech on any subject rather than the facts of the case. That is why slaves do not answer the question asked but beat about the bush and produce a long proem. The sources of conciliating goodwill have already been stated,[109] and everything else of the same kind. "Let the Phaeacians befriend me and pity me when I come to them" is a good saying; so one should aim at these two things.

In epideictic speeches one should make the hearer feel that he too is being praised, either himself or his family or his pursuits or something or other; there is truth in Socrates' remark in the *Epitaphios*[110] that it is not hard to praise Athenians among Athenians, though it is among Spartans.

The proem in political oratory. The proems of political oratory are derived from those of forensic oratory. Of its own nature it needs the proem hardly at all, since the audience knows what the speech is about and the facts require no proem unless because of oneself and opposing speakers, or if the audience assumes the matter to be of greater or less importance than you want it to, so that one has to rouse or dilute prejudice or heighten or diminish the importance of the subject. These are the reasons for needing a proem, or else for decorative effect, since it appears off-hand not to have one. An example is Gorgias' encomium on the Eleans; that begins without any prelude or preliminary sparring with "Elis, blessed city."

Prejudice.[111] On the question of prejudice, one subject is the means of doing away with a damaging assumption (it makes no difference whether someone has voiced it or not, so that this is a general description). Another topic is how to deal with the things one contests, by denying either that they are the case or that they are injurious or injurious to him, or saying that they are not so important as he says, or not a wrong or not a substantial one, or not disgraceful or not a substantial disgrace. These are the sort of things that are contested, as by Iphicrates against Nausicrates; he admitted that he had done what his opponent said and that he had inflicted injury, but denied inflicting wrong. Or when one has done wrong one can try to compensate for it, by saying that if it was an injury it was nevertheless noble, if painful, yet beneficial or something else of the kind. Another topic is that it was done in error or by ill chance or under constraint; so Sophocles said that he was trembling not, as his adversary said, so as to be thought old, but because he could not help it; it was not of intent that he was eighty. One can also compensate by stating the expected result, that he meant to do no injury but something else, and did not do what he is accused of, as the injury was incidental ("It would be fair to hate me if I had intended this result of my action"). Another topic arises if the accuser himself or someone connected with him has been involved in the same charge, either now or formerly. Another, if others are involved in it who are agreed to be innocent, for example, "If X is an adulterer because he dresses neatly, so must Y be." Another, if someone else or the accuser himself has roused unfair prejudice against others, or if, without such an attack, others were exposed to the same suspicion as you are now, and were later shown to be innocent. Another from retorting the attack on one's accuser, and saying that it would be absurd to trust his words when his character is distrusted. Another, if there has been a previous decision, as in Euripides' reply to Hygiaenon in the exchange case, when he accused him of impiety for saying

> My tongue has sworn, my mind remains unsworn;[112]

he retorted that it was not fair of Hygiaenon to bring judgements from the Dionysiac contest into court, as he had given account of his words there, or would do so if Hygiaenon wanted to accuse him. Another from the accusation of arousing prejudice, with the arguments that it is monstrous, that it introduces judgements about irrelevant matters, that it does not show confidence in the facts. Both accuser and defender can use the topic of tokens, as in the *Teucer*[113] Odysseus argues that Teucer was related to Priam, whose sister Hesione was, Teucer that his father Telamon was hostile to Priam and that he himself had not denounced the spies. Another is open to the attacker, praising the trivial at great length and blaming a substantial fault concisely, or setting forth many good qualities in his opponent and blaming just one, the one being that which really furthers the charge; such topics are the most skilful and most unfair, as they try to damage the good qualities by mixing them up with the bad. Another topic common to both accuser and defender is that of motive, as the same act can be done for different reasons; the accuser should disparage the act by taking the worse motive, while the defender should take the better, saying, for example, that Diomede chose Odysseus because he was the bravest, whereas the accuser says that this was not the reason but that he was the only Greek whose rivalry Diomede did not fear, taking him to be a coward. So much for unfair prejudice.

The Narrative

The narrative in epideictic oratory. Narration in epideictic speeches should be not consecutive but divided. The reason is that one has to report the achievements on which the speech is based, since the speech is a composite unity, part of which does not involve technical skill, as the speaker is in no way responsible for the achievements, and part of which does, that is, showing that something is the case, if it is hard to believe, or that it has some particular quality or importance, or doing all these at once. One's narration should sometimes be broken up, as displaying things consecutively is hard on the memory; the achievements that show his courage are different from those that show his wisdom or justice. And this sort of speech is less complicated, whereas a differently constructed one is elaborate and not plain enough. One should merely remind people of well-known achievements; that is why people need no narration if you mean, for instance, to praise Achilles, as everyone knows his achievements, and one should just use them; but one does need a narration in praising Critias, as not many know about him . . .[114]

The narrative in forensic oratory. . . . As things are they absurdly say that the narration should be swift. In fact, there is point here too in what the man said to the baker when he asked whether he should knead the dough hard or soft, "Why, can't you do it just right?" One should not make one's narration long-winded, any more than one's proem or the statement of one's arguments; there too excellence does not consist in speed or concision but in a due length, that is, in saying enough to explain the facts, or to make the hearer take it that the act, the damage, the injury did happen and was as important as you wish to convey, while the opponent needs to do the opposite. Along with the narration one should tell everything that helps to give an impression of one's own merits (for example, "I tried to restrain him, by reiterating what was fair, from leaving his children in the lurch") or of your opponent's demerits ("And he answered that wherever he was himself, he could get other children," as Herodotus says the mutinous Egyptians replied). One should also add what gives pleasure to the jury. In defence the narration is less extensive, as one's retort is that it did not happen or was not a damage or not an injury or not so important, so that one need not waste time on what is agreed, unless something contributes to the desired aim, for example, if you admit the deed but claim it was not an injury. One should also tell of things as past, unless they tend to rouse pity or indignation when represented as actually going on; examples are the story told to Alcinous, which is retold to Penelope in sixty lines, and Phayllus' treatment of the epic cycle, and the prologue to the *Oeneus*.[115]

The narrative should be expressive of character, and will be so if we know what produces this effect. One thing is what reveals moral purpose; the character is of some particular kind because the purpose is of a particular kind, and the purpose is of a particular kind because of the end one aims at. That is why mathematical treatises do not express character, as they do not indicate moral purpose, not having any particular motive, whereas the Socratic dialogues do, as this is the sort of subject they are talking about. Other things indicative of character are the concomitants of different sorts of character, like for instance, "He went on walking as he spoke," an act that shows insolence and boorishness of character. And not giving the impression of speaking from the intellect as people do nowadays, but from moral purpose ("I wanted it, and indeed had purposed it; but even if I gained nothing by it, it was better"; this shows both a prudent and a good man, as a prudent man pursues advantage and a good man what is honourable). And if the thing is hard to believe one should add the reason, as Sophocles does; an example is Antigone's saying that she cared more for her brother than for husband and children, as she could have more children if she lost them, "But with my mother and father in Hades no other brother could be born for me."[116] If you cannot give a reason, you should say you know what you are saying is hard to believe, but that is just how you naturally are, since people disbelieve that men willingly do anything except what is to their advantage. Part of your narrative should also employ such elements of emotional significance as the natural and known concomitants of an emotion and particular characteristics of yourself or your adversary ("He went off, giving me a scowl," and what Aeschines said about Cratylus, "furiously hissing and waving his arms"); such things are convincing because they are known tokens of the unknown. One can derive many such indications from Homer, "So he spoke, and the old woman threw her hands over her face";[117] people beginning to weep do cover their eyes. And introduce yourself at once as having a certain character so that the audience can contemplate you as such, and do the same with your adversary, but without being obvious. It is easy to do, as you can see from people who tell us stories, who give us an impression even of people we know nothing about. There are many places where narration is in point, and sometimes it is not in point at the beginning.

The narrative in political oratory. In political oratory narration has very little place, as no one uses narration of the future; but if there is narration, it should tell what has happened, so that people can deliberate better about the future for being reminded of the past, or by way of rousing prejudice or praising merit; but in this the speaker is not doing the job of giving political advice. If it is hard to believe, one should both promise and state the explanation at once and set it out with any details they want, as for instance Carcinus' Jocasta in the *Oedipus* keeps making promises when questioned by the man who is looking for her son, and like Sophocles' Haemon.[118]

The Arguments

Arguing a positive case.[119] One's arguments should be demonstrative, and the demonstration should bear on the point at issue, of which there are four kinds; for instance, if one disputes the actual occurrence of the event, one should direct one's demonstration to deciding this, if its being a damage, to this, and similarly to showing that it is not so important or not an injury, in the same way as if the occurrence of the event were in question. One should be aware that it is only in this last case that one or other of the contestants must necessarily be a scoundrel, since ignorance cannot be responsible for the dispute as it might be if they disputed about whether or not it was an injury; so one must spend time in this case, but need not in the others. In epideictic speeches one's method of amplification should usually be stating that things are honourable and beneficial, as the facts should be taken on trust; there are a few occasions when one offers demonstrative proof of them, when they are hard to believe or someone else is supposed responsible for them. In political oratory one might dispute that something will be the case, or grant that it will be the case if they do what one's opponent recommends and argue that it will be injurious or not useful or not so important.

One should also keep an eye out for any lies that do not concern the fact in dispute, as they are indications that he is lying in other things as well. Examples belong more to political oratory, inferences to forensic, as the former concerns the future and so necessarily cites examples from the past, while the latter deals with things that are or are not the case, where there is more possibility of demonstrative proof and necessary statements, as past statements are necessarily true. One should not state one's inferences one after another but mix them up [with other things]; otherwise they damage each other, as there is also a quantitative limit ("My friend, since you have said as much as a sensible man would"; "as much" he says, not "what"). And one should not look for inferences about everything; otherwise you will end up like some philosophers, who arrive at conclusions better known and more convincing than the premisses they start from. And when you try to produce an impression of emotion do not employ an inference (it will either expel the emotion or itself be stated to no purpose, as simultaneous movements operate against each other and either destroy or weaken each other's effect). Similarly, when the statement is expressive of character one should not look for an inference at the same time, as demonstrative proof does not imply character or moral purpose. Instead one should use general reflections both in the narrative and in the argument, as they do express character ("And I gave it, though I well knew one should not be over-trusting") and can also be used for emotional effect ("And I do not regret it, despite the injury done me; he has the profit, but I have the advantage of acting rightly").

Political oratory is more difficult than forensic, reasonably enough, since it concerns the future and forensic oratory the past, which is already known even to prophets, as Epimenides the Cretan said (he did not produce divination about the future, but only about things past but lost in obscurity). Another reason is that the law provides the first premiss in forensic argument, and given the starting-point it is easier to find a demonstrative proof. Moreover, political oratory does not offer many chances of wasting time, in talking, for example, against one's adversary or about oneself or producing emotional effects; indeed it offers less than any other kind, unless it departs from its proper nature. So if one is short of matter one should do what the speakers at Athens do and also Isocrates; in giving political advice he produces an accusation, of the Spartans, for instance, in the *Panegyricus*,[120] of Chares in the speech *On the Alliance*.[121] In epideictic oratory one should divide the speech into acts by laudations as Isocrates does; he is perpetually introducing some person or other. And what Gorgias said, that he was never at a loss for something to say, comes to the same; if his subject is Achilles, he praises his father, his grandfather, his divine great-grandfather, and also courage, which produces such and such effects or is a quality of such and such a kind.

When one has demonstrative arguments one should display one's character as well as produce arguments, while if you have no inferences to produce, you should just express character; and indeed it is more suitable to a good man to give an impression of virtue than produce a speech exactly argued.

Of inferences those that refute find more favour than those that prove something, because those that produce refutation more clearly show syllogistic reasoning, since opposites are better recognized when set beside each other.

Refutation. The refutation of one's adversary is not a separate element; to refute some of his case by producing a contrary proposition, some by reasoning, is part of the argument. Both in political and in forensic oratory one should, if one is the opening speaker, state one's own arguments first, and later meet the opponent's arguments by refutation, i.e. by pulling them to pieces before he produces them. If the opposition is very diversified, you should begin with the opponent's case, as Callistratus did in the Messenian assembly; he stated his own case only after destroying beforehand the arguments they were going to use. If one speaks second, one should deal first with the opponent's case, refuting it and producing counter-reasonings, most especially if it has found favour; the mind refuses a welcome to a man against whom prejudice has been created, and similarly to an argument, if the opponent is thought to have spoken well. So one should make room in the hearer for the speech that is to come, and this you will do if you destroy the arguments against you; that is why one should try to make one's own case convincing only after combating all or the most important or the most favourably received or the most easily refuted on the other side ("First I shall speak in the goddesses' defence; I think that Hera . . .";[122] with these words she attacked first the silliest opposing argument).

So much for arguments.

Character.[123] So far as character goes, it is invidious, long-winded, or open to contradiction to say some things about oneself, and abusive or boorish to say some things about other people; one should therefore ascribe them to another speaker, as Isocrates does in the *Philip*[124] and the *Antidosis*,[125] and as Archilochus[126] does in invective, where he makes the father speak of his daughter in the lampoon beginning "Nothing is unexpected, nothing one would take one's oath will not happen," and introduces the carpenter Charon in that beginning "Not Gyges' wealth for me." Similarly Sophocles' Haemon defends Antigone against his father by citing other speakers.[127]

One should also occasionally change the form of one's inferences and express them as general maxims, for example, "Men of sense should make peace when they are successful, as that would bring them the greatest gains" (in the form of an inference this would be "If one should make peace when the peace would be most useful and bring most gain, one should make it when one is successful").

Interrogation. As for interrogation, the most advantageous occasion for its use is when your opponent has stated one [of two contradictory propositions], so that with one further question an absurdity will result. For instance, when Pericles questioned Lampon about initiation into the rites of Demeter and Lampon said it was impossible for the uninitiated to be told, Pericles asked if he knew them himself, and when he said yes, continued "And how, when you are not initiated?" The second best is when one premiss of an inference is obvious and it is clear that he will grant the other if questioned; one should ask him about the one premiss and not proceed to a question about the obvious one, but simply state the conclusion. An example is Socrates' question when Meletus denied that he recognized gods but said that he spoke of a *daimonion*; he asked whether the *daimones* were either children of gods or something divine, and when he said "Yes," went on, "Well, is there anyone who thinks there are children of gods but no gods?"[128] A third case is where one means to show that one's opponent is saying something self-contradictory or paradoxical. A fourth where he can resolve the difficulty only by a sophistic answer; if he gives such a reply, like "It is and it isn't," "Sometimes yes, sometimes no," or "In some ways yes, in some ways no," the audience shout him down and think he is at a loss. Otherwise do not attempt it, as if he resists you will be thought to have been defeated, since one cannot ask many questions because of the feebleness of the audience. That is why one should try to make one's inferences, too, as compact as possible.

1419a

In answering, you should meet ambiguous questions with a developed distinction, not a concise one, and deal with supposed contradictions by producing the solution straight away in your reply, before he asks the next question and proceeds to the conclusion, as it is quite easy in some cases to foresee what he will say. Both this and the forms of solution are clear to us from the *Topics*. And when he draws the conclusion, if he puts it in the form of a question, one should give the explanation, as Sophocles did when Pisander asked if he, like the other *probouloi*, had assented to the establishment of the Four Hundred. "Yes," he said. "Well then, did you think this wrong?" "Yes." "So you committed this wrong act?" "Yes, as there was no better one possible," Or like the Spartan being examined on his ephorate and asked if he thought the condemnation of his colleagues had been fair: "Yes," he replied. "Did you concur in their actions?" "Yes." "Then would it not be fair to condemn you too?" "Certainly not," he said. "They did it for bribes, I because I thought it best." That is why one should not ask another question after stating the conclusion nor put the conclusion itself in the form of a question, unless there is a tremendous surplus of truth on your side.

Jokes. So far as jokes go, they are thought to have some use in actual debate, and Gorgias rightly said that one should ruin one's opponent's seriousness with laughter and his laughter with seriousness. Jokes are to be found classified in the *Poetics*,[129] some of them suitable for a gentleman, some not, so that one can choose what suits one. Irony is more gentlemanly than buffoonery, as the ironical man makes a jest for his own amusement, the buffoon for another's.

The Epilogue

The epilogue is composed of four elements: they are making the hearer well-disposed towards oneself and the contrary towards one's opponent, amplification and belittling, rousing emotion in the hearer, recapitulating. It is natural that one should first prove one's own truth and one's opponent's falsehood, and then go on to praise, blame, and hammer the point home. [In the first of the four] one should aim at one of two things, being thought good by this jury or being thought good without qualification (and also at making your opponent seem bad to them or bad without qualification). The sources from which one can produce this impression have been stated, that is, the topics basic to producing an impression of goodness or badness. The next thing, when the proof is over, is naturally amplification or belittling, since the facts must be admitted before one can assign a particular importance to them, just as bodily growth is growth from what was there before. The sources of amplification and belittling have also been stated previously. After this, when it is clear what the facts are and how important, is the time to produce emotion in the hearer. These emotions are pity, indignation, anger, hatred, envy, emulation, quarrelsomeness. The sources of these have also been previously described, so that the remaining subject is the recapitulation. The suitable place for this is not the proem, as usually but wrongly recommended (we are urged to be repetitive there so as to make the hearer receptive). Well now, in the proem one should state the subject, so as to make the hearer aware what his decision is about, and in the epilogue the various proofs of it, in a summary way. The starting-point is that one has performed what one promised, and so one must say what and why. This is sometimes based on a comparison with your adversary. One can compare what both have said on the same subject, either directly ("But he said this about that, while I said this other thing and for the following reasons"), or ironically ("He said this, I that" and "What would he have done if he had proved this rather than that?"), or in question form ("Well then, what has been proved?" or "What has *he* proved?"). Either then one can do it this way via comparison or in the natural order as it was said, recapitulating one's own argument and in turn, if one likes, stating separately what one's opponent said. As the ending of the speech an asyndeton is suitable, something to finish off the speech, not make another one: "I have said my say, you have heard it all, it is in your hands, give your judgements."

NOTES

1. Standard rhetorical theory added two others, memory and delivery. Aristotle says nothing of memory and confines to the preface of this book the brief remarks he has to make on delivery.
2. This is a conjecture; the manuscripts have "of the political institutions."
3. The reference in the rest of this paragraph is to delivery, not verbal expression.
4. That is, not knowledge.
5. Presumably a work on the production of pathetic effects.
6. The paragraph is rather incoherent, and bears some signs of incomplete revision; it seems, for instance, to have two starting-points ("Now the study..." and "Now whenever..."). Cope's note, which has misled translators, suggests that the subject of the second sentence is "oratorical delivery" and that the word here translated "delivery" means "acting"; but this interpretation imports even more confusion into the paragraph.
7. The word *lexis* is the active abstract noun derived from *legein* "to speak." In the following discussion it is sometimes translated "verbal expression" or just "expression," sometimes "style," and occasionally "the way they said them" or some such phrase.
8. The word used is *onomata* "names," which in its stricter use means "nouns and adjectives."
9. Contrast the excellence of poetic style "to be at once clear and not mean" (p. 167).
10. Cf. pp. 166ff.
11. Cf. Proust on the acting of Berma: "I could not even, as I could with her companions, distinguish in her diction and in her playing intelligent intonations, beautiful gestures. I listened to her as though I were reading *Phèdre,* or as though Phaedra herself had at that moment uttered the words that I was hearing, without its appearing that Berma's talent had added anything at all to them."
12. Cf. "Longinus," p. 351.
13. After this the manuscripts add: "The sophist can use homonyms, as these are his instruments in cheating, the poet synonyms, I mean words both standard and synonymous, like *poreuesthai* and *badizein*; both these are standard and synonymous with each other" (they mean "go"). This sentence is pointless in the context, laboured and tiresome in expression, and introduces a different classification from the one in the *Poetics.* It is tempting to regard it as an interpolation.
14. Cf. n. 18.
15. Fr. 705.
16. The text is corrupt and the drift of the second criticism uncertain.
17. The reference is to medical "cupping."
18. Epithets are "accessory expressions"; the word covers genitival and other qualifications as well as adjectives.
19. The examples are from Eur. *Orestes* 1587–8.

20. The point is clearer in Greek, where the standard term for mules is "half-asses."

21. *Psuchra.* "Bathos" is not an ancient critical term, but belongs to the English eighteenth century (cf. "Longinus", pp. 326f.). The concept however is very like that which the Greeks expressed by *psuchros* and the Romans by "frigidus" and which is often translated "frigid" (cf. Demetrius, p. 214). The term is used of things that "fall flat," "do not come off," like bad jokes or, as here, unsuccessful attempts at elevation.

22. Aristotle gives several examples of the use in prose of words belonging to high poetry. Cf. the discussion in the *Poetics,* pp. 167f.

23. Cf. p. 168.

24. One would expect this section to come earlier, as part of the discussion of the resources of prose, not to follow the treatment of their misuse.

25. Conventionally rendered "simile," which suits the initial description well enough. But the statement that the *eikōn* is a possible metaphor if used without the reason for the comparison being stated suggests a more elaborate form, which appears in many of the examples, "X is like Y; for Y is A and so is X." But cf. M. H. McCall, *Ancient Rhetorical Theories of Simile and Comparison* (Harvard, 1969), pp. 32ff.

26. Hom. *Il.* 22. 164.

27. Plato *Rep.* 469d, 488a, 601b; Aristotle has misremembered the second example.

28. The comparison involves an ironical twist, as the first statement is like our "They are real heart-of-oak," and the *eikōn* therefore seems laudatory at first, and then turns out not to be.

29. If the Demosthenes referred to is the orator, this is Aristotle's only reference to him.

30. Nurses chewed the baby's food to soften it.

31. Cf. p. 166.

32. The Greek *men . . . de*: the commonest particles to indicate an adversative relationship between two statements.

33. If the text is right, Aristotle himself has not succeeded in making it clear whether he approves or disapproves of the example he has constructed. Perhaps he wrote: "Here *not* many . . . ; but if . . ."

34. Aristotle gives examples of the last two classes, which there is no point in translating into an uninflected language.

35. The first person of whom we are told explicitly that he read without sound is St. Ambrose (Aug. *Conf.* 6. 3).

36. The "and then" is normally taken to be part of the example.

37. *Onkos.*

38. Eur. *Iph. Taur.* 727.

39. Aristotle gives a simple example of a common idiom.

40. It is far from clear what these are examples of.

41. So the manuscripts: but interpretation is difficult. Thurot conjectured "convincing," but the advice still seems quaint.

42. The Greek word is one of the dialect terms censured on p. 183.

43. This idea is expressed by the verb *enthousiazein*, which in earlier writers is used of divinely inspired excitement, as in the *Ion,* pp. 89ff. In Aristotle the word has no such religious overtones and seems quite conventional.

44. Aristotle misquotes some elevated phrases.

45. 231d, 241e.

46. In measuring the quantity of syllables, a long syllable is taken to be equivalent to two shorts; thus the long of the dactylic or anapaestic foot ($-\cup\cup$, $\cup\cup-$) exactly balances the two shorts, that is, they are in a 1:1 ratio, while the iambic and trochaic ($\cup-$, $-\cup$) have a 1:2 or 2:1 ratio. The long of the paean ($-\cup\cup\cup$, $\cup\cup\cup-$) is 2 to its 3 short syllables,

which gives a ratio midway between the 1:1 of the dactyl and the 2:1 of the iambic and trochaic.

47. i.e. they are organized in trimeters, tetrameters, hexameters, and so on.

48. We omit Aristotle's examples.

49. Whether or not for Aristotle's mathematical reason, ancient prose did increasingly take as its basic rhythmical unit the cretic ($-\smile-$), of which the paeans are resolved forms. There is not however much sign that writers took to heart the advice to begin with a first paean and end with a fourth, though there is again an increasing dislike for a short syllable ending.

50. The manuscripts add "This is the setting-forth of the inquiries of Herodotus of Thurii," a misquotation of the opening phrase of Herodotus, which disrupts the sentence and is not even an example of the "strung-together" style, though that is frequent in Herodotus.

51. Actually Euripides (fr. 515). The next line may be rendered: "The adverse shore confronts its fertile plains." But the two lines could also be translated: "This land is Calydon in Pelops' isle, / With fertile plains upon the adverse shore."

52. A parody of Hesiod, *Works and Days* 265f.

53. The examples in this sentence are all quotations or misquotations from Isocrates' *Panegyricus*.

54. Or, "refutation involves inferring opposite conclusions." Aristotle seems to be referring to the form of refutation in which a respondent can be shown that his premises are in conflict by deriving from them directly contradictory conclusions, rather than a situation where one speaker says A and the other arrives at the conclusion not-A.

55. *asteia*, in Latin *urbane dicta*. "Wit" is unfortunately devalued in modern English; it is used here in the hope that its older usage will carry over. The concept that Aristotle is deploying is very like "wit" in the two aspects that Dr. Johnson suggests in the *Life of Cowley*: "If by a more noble and more adequate conception that be considered as wit which is at once natural and new, that which, though not obvious, is, upon its first production, acknowledged to be just; if it be that which he that never found it wonders how he missed . . . But wit, abstracted from its effects upon the hearer, may be more rigorously and philosophically considered as a kind of *discordia concors*; a combination of dissimilar images, or discovery of occult resemblances in things apparently unlike."

56. Hom. *Od.* 14. 214; cf. n. 26.

57. Cf. pp. 183ff.

58. Isocrates, *Philippus* 73.

59. The phrase "before our eyes" develops some curious syntactic usages later in the book and will sometimes be translated "vividness" or "vivid presentation."

60. Cf. p. 166.

61. Athenian magistrates had to submit an account of their tenure of office and persuade the people to accept it.

62. As at the time of Marathon. One should perhaps accept Victorius's conjecture "to proceed to Euboea and get their provisions there."

63. Diogenes.

64. Mess-halls were a Spartan institution.

65. Used instead of "assemblies."

66. Ps.-Lys. 2. 60; in fact, and more plausibly, the reference is to the Athenian dead at Aegospotami, not at Salamis.

67. The statue, of a hoplite with spear protruded and his shield resting on the left knee, commemorated an exploit of Chabrias' in 378 B.C. It is not clear how much of the last clause is a quotation from Lycoleon, nor what precisely Aristotle is saying.

68. Isocrates, *Panegyricus* 151.

69. Ibid. 172.
70. Ibid. 180.
71. Simonides, fr. 542. 3.
72. Isocrates, *Philippus* 10; the next example is from *Philippus* 127.
73. Eur. *Iph. Aul.* 80.
74. *Od.* 11. 598.
75. *Il.* 13. 587.
76. *Il.* 4. 126.
77. *Il.* 11. 574.
78. *Il.* 15. 542.
79. One may contrast with Aristotle's praise the condemnation of Ruskin in his essay on the Pathetic Fallacy (*Modern Painters* iii, pt. 4, § 6): "Now we are in the habit of considering this fallacy as eminently a character of poetical description, and the temper of mind in which we allow it as one eminently poetical, because passionate. But, I believe, if we look well into the matter, that we shall find the greatest poets do not often admit this kind of falseness—that it is only the second order of poets who much delight in it"; (§ 11) "it is one of the signs of the highest power in a writer to check all such habits of thought, and to keep his eyes fixed firmly on the *pure fact*, out of which if any feeling comes to him or his reader, he knows it must be a true one."
80. *Il.* 13. 799.
81. Aristotle's manuscripts almost all offer the reflexive, which gives the threat two points, that the trees will be cut down and the people massacred; the scholiast and Demetrius (p. 213) have "will sing to them" (or "will sing to you"). Aristotle cites the saying also in Book 2 (1395a2) with no pronoun at all.
82. The text here is uncertain.
83. i.e. truth and freedom from superficiality.
84. In the section omitted Aristotle cited a line of Anaxandrides, "It is fine to die before doing what rightly merits death," which he said was equivalent to the formulation given here.
85. The opposite comparison of rags to "ruins of clothes" occurs in *trag. adesp.* 7, Eur. *Tro.* 1025.
86. *Com. adesp.* 208.
87. *Com. adesp.* 207.
88. Cf. p. 96.
89. "Like the Australians and the rabbit" would make the same point nowadays.
90. *Il.* 9. 385ff. At this point the manuscripts add: "Its use is very frequent in Attic orators."
91. If the text is right the "it" must be something like "such a style."
92. *Com.* 2. 138f.K.
93. Also by Anaxandrides, ibid. 140.
94. *Auxēsis*.
95. The text is uncertain.
96. *Il.* 2. 671ff.
97. Interpretation uncertain.
98. Cf. Plato *Phaedr.* 266d–267a.
99. Isocrates begins with an attack on "eristic" logicians.
100. *Panegyricus* 1f.
101. If this interpretation is right, this defence of Paris, which Aristotle also mentions several times in Book 2, was put into his own mouth, and is the earliest known example of a form of declamation that later became common.

102. An epic poet who wrote on the Persian wars and used this phrase to excuse the novelty; for this sentiment, cf. Virg. *Georg.* 3. 4.
103. *Il.* 1. 1.
104. *Od.* 1. 1.
105. Choerilus.
106. It is not easy to believe that Aristotle so far forgot the *Oedipus Tyrannus* as to attribute line 774 to the prologue. Ross conjectures "if not at once as Euripides does in the prologue, still somewhere or other . . . "; but this will hardly do in a context talking of prologues.
107. The watchman's opening words in Soph. *Ant.* 223.
108. *Iph. Taur.* 1162.
109. In Book 2.
110. Plato, *Menexenus* 235d.
111. This development, prompted by the mention of prejudice in the discussion of the proem in forensic oratory, is not altogether tidily worked in.
112. *Hippolytus* 608.
113. Of Sophocles.
114. Several sentences have been lost at this point.
115. These seem to be cited as summary narratives of past events, suitable models for cases that do not demand a more elaborate and impasssioned account.
116. *Antigone* 909ff.
117. *Od.* 19. 361.
118. The point of this reference is quite obscure.
119. The main lines of this section are fairly clear, but it seems to degenerate into a rag-bag of assorted notes at the end.
120. §§ 110ff.
121. *De Pace* 27.
122. Eur. *Troades* 969f.
123. This and the following two sections are appendices to the discussion of argument.
124. 4ff., 23.
125. 141ff.
126. Frs. 74 and 22 Diehl.
127. *Antigone* 688ff.
128. Plato, *Apology* 27d.
129. In the lost second book.

Demetrius

*T*he actual author of On Style *is unknown. The treatise was once widely attributed to the Athenian orator and statesman Demetrius of Phalerum (c. 345–283 B.C.), but its internal evidence, chronology, and style suggest a later date. In its present form,* On Style *cannot be earlier than 275 B.C. and may have been written as late as the first century B.C. Whatever its precise date, most scholars agree that it is the only surviving critical analysis of style between Aristotle and the early Roman writers. Its Hellenistic or early Roman author is clearly familiar with the methods of Aristotle's Peripatetic school and seems sympathetic to that approach.*

On Style *is something of a handbook of classic Greek notions of literary style, though the word "style" is perhaps misleading. For the ancients "style" was much more objectively definable than our present, rather broad concept. In general the Greeks distinguished three principal styles: the grand, the elegant, and the plain. Demetrius adds a fourth, the forceful, and analyzes each according to diction, word arrangement, and subject matter. The typology elaborated in* On Style *exerted considerable influence on later writers such as Cicero.*

The selection from On Style, *translated by G. M. A. Grube, is reprinted by permission of University of Toronto Press from G. M. A. Grube, ed.,* A Greek Critic: Demetrius on Style *(Toronto, 1961). The footnotes have been omitted.*

FROM
On Style

There are four simple types of style: the plain, the grand, the elegant, and the forceful. The rest are combinations of these, but not all combinations are possible: the elegant can be combined with both the plain and the grand, and so can the forceful; the grand alone does not mix with the plain; these two face one another as opposite extremes. That is why some critics recognize only these last two as styles, and the other two as intermediate. They class the elegant rather with the plain, because the elegant is somewhat slight and subtle; while the forceful, which has weight and dignity, is classed with the grand.

Such a theory is absurd. With the exception of the two opposite extremes mentioned (the plain and the grand), we find combinations of all these types in the Homeric epic, in the works of Plato, Xenophon, Herodotus, and many other writers who display a frequent mixture of grandeur, forcefulness, and charm, so that the number of types is such as we have indicated, and the manner of expression appropriate to each will be seen in what follows. . . .

THE FORCEFUL OR INTENSE STYLE

As for forcefulness, it follows from what has been said that it, too, shows itself in the same three ways as the previous styles. Certain things are forceful in themselves so that those who speak about them are thought to be forceful even when they do not speak forcefully. When Theopompus, for example, describes the Piraeus with its flute-girls and brothels, and the male flute-players as singing and dancing, he uses words which have an intensity of their own; although his style is feeble, it is considered forceful.

As regards word-arrangement, forcefulness follows if, firstly, short phrases take the place of clauses. Length dissolves vehemence, and a more forceful effect is attained where much is said in a few words. An example of this is the warning of the Spartans to Philip: "Dionysius [is] in Corinth." If they had amplified this and said: "Dionysius has lost his throne and is now a beggarly schoolteacher in Corinth," this would have been a statement of fact rather than a taunt.

The Spartans were always naturally inclined to brevity of speech. Brevity is more forceful and commanding, while it is more appropriate to speak at length in requests and supplications.

Symbola (tokens) also have force, because they resemble brevity of speech. From a little that is said one must understand a great deal, just as in the case of tokens. In this way "The grasshoppers will sing to you from the ground" is more forceful for being spoken by allegoria than if he had simply said: "Your trees shall be cut down."

The periods should be securely knotted at the end, for the periodic structure which brings us round to an end is forceful, while a looser structure is simpler and a sign of simpler character. All early writers used this simpler style, for the ancients were simple men.

And so, in the forceful style, we should avoid the old-fashioned in character and rhythm, but rather resort to the forcefulness now in fashion. The rhythm should make the sentence come to a definite stop, as in the first sentence of Demosthenes' speech against Leptines which clings to the rhythm I mentioned.

Violence contributes to forcefulness in word-arrangement, for harsh sounds are often forceful, like rough roads. We have an example in the same passage of Demosthenes.

We should avoid antitheses and balanced clauses in the periods. They make for weight but not for forcefulness, and frequently result in frigidity instead of force, as in Theopompus' attack on the friends of Philip where the antithesis destroys the intensity. The excessive elaboration, or rather the poor technique, attracts the attention of the reader who is quite untouched by anger.

The subject itself will often compel us to adopt a compact and forceful word-arrangement, as in this passage of Demosthenes: "If any one of them had been convicted, you would not have proposed this bill; and, if you are now convicted, no one else will make such a proposal." The subject itself and the steps in the argument clearly demanded a word-arrangement that grows out of them; no one could easily have constructed the sentence differently, not even if he did violence to the subject-matter. For in adopting a certain sentence-structure we are often carried along by the subject like people running downhill.

It also contributes to forcefulness to put the most forceful expression at the end as Antisthenes did. Its force will be blunted in the middle of other words. For if anyone changes the order of the words, though he says the same thing, he will not be thought to do so.

The kind of antithesis which I condemned in Theopompus is inappropriate even in Demosthenes, where he says: "You were the temple-servant, I was the initiate; you were the teacher, I the pupil; you were a minor actor, I was a spectator; you were hissed, I hissed." The exact correspondence of parallel clauses is poor art; it is more like a jest than an expression of anger.

When being forceful, it is appropriate to use periods continuously, although this is not suitable in other styles. For if one period follows another the effect will be as of metre following metre, and a forceful metre at that, like choliambs.

These continuous periods should at the same time be short, that is, periods of two clauses, for the effect of periods consisting of many clauses is beautiful rather than forceful.

Brevity is so useful in this style that it is often even more forceful *not* to say something, as when Demosthenes says: "Now I might remark—but I myself certainly do not wish to say anything offensive, and my accuser has the advantage in slandering me."

And, by the gods, even obscurity is frequently forceful. For what is implied is more forceful, whereas what is explained is thought common-place.

Sometimes discordant sounds (kakophōnia) are forceful, especially if the subject matter demands it, as in Homer's line: "The Trojans shivered when they saw the writhing snake." This could have been said more euphoniously while preserving the metre, but then neither the poet nor the snake would have seemed as forceful.

From this example we can deduce similar examples: instead of *panta an hegrapsen* we might write *hegrapsen an* and *paregeneto ouchi* for *ou paregeneto*.

Sometimes forcefulness may be attained by ending with a connective like *de* or *te*. We are taught to avoid such endings but they are often useful, as in "he gave him no praise although he deserved it, he insulted him though"; or like "Schoinos and Skolon too . . . ," but in the Homeric lines the connectives at the end give an impression of grandeur.

A sentence like the following (with repetition of the connective *te*) will sometimes be forceful too. For pleasant smoothness is characteristic of the elegant, not of the forceful manner, and these (two) styles seem most opposed to one another.

Forcefulness of a kind often results from an admixture of playfulness, as in comedy and all works written in the Cynic manner. So Crates says:

"There is a land of Pēra (= wallet) in the midst of the wine-dark ocean."

Another example is Diogenes' announcement at Olympia. After the race in armour he ran forward and proclaimed himself Olympian victor over all men in personal worth and beauty. The words excite both laughter and wonder, and have a gentle hidden sting in them.

Still another example is what Diogenes said to the beautiful youth. In wrestling with him Diogenes had an erection, and when the boy got scared and leapt away "Don't worry," said the philosopher, "I'm not your equal there." The surface meaning is funny, but the hidden significance has a certain forcefulness. And this is true of all Cynic discourse as a whole. To put it briefly: it is like a dog that fawns and bites at the same time.

Orators too will sometimes use this sort of pointed jest as they have done in the past. As Lysias said to the old woman's lover that "her teeth were easier to count than her fingers." These words put the old woman in a most forceful and ridiculous light. And so with Homer's "I shall eat Nobody last."

Forceful Figures

We shall now discuss how forcefulness can arise from use of figures. First, from figures of thought; for example that which is called *paraleipsis*: "I make no mention of Olynthus, Methone, Apollonia, and the thirty-two cities in Thrace." With these words the orator has said all he wanted to say, and he says he will not mention them in order to give the impression that he has even more dreadful things to say.

Aposiōpēsis, which was mentioned before, has the same character; it also makes for forcefulness.

The figure of thought called *prosōpopoiia* can also be used with forceful effect: "Consider that it is your forefathers who are reproaching you and saying such things to you, or Greece, or your own city in the form of a woman...."

Or as in Plato's Funeral Speech: "Children, that your fathers were brave men...." He does not speak in his own person but in that of their fathers. To bring them in as *dramatis personae* makes the passage much more real and forceful; indeed it becomes a dramatic presentation.

The different figures and forms of thought may be used as stated. We have said this much by way of examples. As for figures of speech, a varied choice of them will make the style more forceful.

There is anadiplōsis: "Thebes, Thebes, our neighbouring city, has been snatched from the middle of Greece." The repeated word gives forcefulness.

Then there is that called anaphora, as in: "You call him against yourself as a witness, you call him against the laws as a witness, you call him against the people as a witness." This is a triple figure. It is, as already stated, an epanaphora, because the same words are repeated at the beginning of each clause; it is an asyndeton because there are no connectives; it is an homoioteleuton because every clause ends with the same words. The forcefulness is due to the combination of all three figures. If one said: "You call him as a witness against yourself, the laws, and the people," the figures would disappear, and so would the force of the passage.

We should realize, however, that lack of connectives, more than anything else, produces forcefulness: "He walks through the market, puffing out his cheeks, raising his eyebrows, keeping in step with Pythocles." If you join these clauses by connectives, the effect is much gentler.

The figure called *klimax* should also be used, as Demosthenes uses it in: "I did not say these things and then refuse to move a proposal; I did not move a proposal and fail to go as an envoy; I did not go as an envoy and fail to persuade the Thebans." This passage is like a man climbing higher and higher. If you were to put it like this: "After my speech, and after moving a proposal I went as an envoy, and persuaded the Thebans," he would be narrating facts, but saying nothing forceful.

In general, figures of speech give the speaker an opportunity for histrionic delivery in debate, that is for forcefulness, and this is especially true when connectives are omitted. So much for figures of both kinds.

Forceful Diction

The diction should in every respect be the same as in the grand style, except that it is not used with the same end in view, and metaphors too contribute to forcefulness; for example: "Python, that bold torrent of oratory rushing upon you...."

Similes too can be used, as by Demosthenes where he says: "This decree made the danger which then threatened the city pass away like a cloud."

Long comparisons, however, are unsuited to forcible passages because of their length: "As a noble inexperienced hound leaps at a boar recklessly...." There is beauty and precision in this image, but forcefulness requires a vehement brevity, like men aiming blows in a close fight.

The use of a compound word can also be forceful; and common usage forms many forceful compounds. Many such can be found in the speeches of the orators.

One should try to use words appropriate to the subject. If an action is violent and wicked, we say a man perpetrated it, or, according to the nature of the deed, that he committed, performed, or executed it.

A sudden rise in emotional tension is not only impressive but forceful, as where Demosthenes says: "It is not necessary to keep your hands in the folds of your cloak when you are speaking, Aeschines, but you should keep them there when on an embassy."

And again in the passage: "When he was appropriating Euboea. . ." the *epanastasis* does not aim at grandeur but at forcefulness. And this happens when, in the middle of what we are saying, we are emotionally aroused and denounce somebody. The first example was a denunciation of Aeschines, here of Philip.

It is also forceful to ask your audience questions without giving the answer. "When Philip was appropriating Euboea, and made it a base against Attica, was he doing wrong, was he breaking the peace, or was he not?" He embarrasses his audience, and seems to prove them wrong, and they have no answer. But if one changes this to read: "Philip did wrong and broke the peace," it is like a piece of obvious information and does not put them in the wrong.

The figure called *epimonē*, dwelling on a point longer than is required to state the facts, may also contribute to forcefulness. Here is an example from Demosthenes: "A dread disease, men of Athens, has fallen upon Greece. . . ." Put differently, it would not have been forceful.

Euphemism, as it is called, can also be forceful, when bad things are given fair names, and impiety is made to sound pious. The Athenian who proposed that the golden Victories should be melted down, and the gold used for war purposes, did not say bluntly: "Let us melt down the Victories to prosecute the war." That would have sounded like a bad omen and an insult to the goddesses. He put it more euphemistically: "We shall have the Victories to help us with the war." Put in this way it did not sound like destroying the Victories, but seeking their help.

There are, too, the forceful expressions of Demades. These are of a peculiar and strange kind; their force results from three things: expressive words, a kind of allēgoria, and hyperbole.

When he said, for example, "Alexander is not dead or the whole world would smell his corpse," the use of "smell" instead of "be aware of" is a hyperbole and at the same time has an element of allēgoria, while to say that the whole earth would be aware of it pointedly expresses Alexander's power. The phrase is startling as a combination of these three figures at the same time. What is startling is always forceful, for it inspires fear.

Here is another example of the same kind: "This decree was not drafted by me; the war itself drafted it, with Alexander's sword as its pen." And again: "The power of Macedon, with Alexander gone, is like a blinded Cyclops."

On another occasion he said: "Our city, no longer the warrior of Salamis, but a slippered old dame greedily gulping her gruel." The old woman implies weakness and exhaustion, and he expresses this feeble state hyperbolically; "gulping her gruel" also means that the city was spending its war resources on public feasts and banquets.

This must suffice about Demades' forcefulness; its use involves a certain risk, and it is hard to imitate; it has a poetic flavour, if indeed veiled meanings, hyperboles, and expressive words are poetical, but the poetic is here mixed with the comic.

Innuendo

What we call innuendo is employed by the speakers of our own day in a ridiculous manner, with a vulgar expressiveness which may be said to make the meaning obvious, but it is a true figure if used for two purposes: good taste and discretion.

To preserve appearances, as when Plato wants to censure Aristippus and Cleombrotus for living daintily in Aegina while Socrates was for many days imprisoned in Athens, and for not crossing the straits to their friend and teacher, although the distance was less than twenty-five miles. He does not blame them explicitly, for that would have been mere abuse, but he expresses his feelings tactfully as follows: Phaedo is asked who was with Socrates and enumerates those present. Then he is asked whether Aristippus and Cleombrotus were there too and he says: "No, for they were in Aegina." The point of all that precedes is made clear by the words "they were in Aegina." And the result is much more forceful in that the facts themselves, rather than the speaker, seem to point to the enormity of their conduct. Although it was presumably quite safe for Plato to attack Aristippus and his friends, yet he prefers to do so by innuendo.

Frequently, however, when we are speaking to a dictator or some other violent individual and we want to censure him, we are of necessity driven to do so by innuendo. So when Craterus of Macedon was insolently receiving Greek envoys while lying on a high golden couch and clad in royal purple, Demetrius of Phalerum censured him by using this figure: "We too received these envoys at one time, and Craterus there was among them." For by pointing to him with the word "there" (*touton*) all the insolence of Craterus is pointed to and censured by using the figure.

The same kind of device is seen in what Plato said to Dionysius when the latter was telling lies and going back on a promise he had made. "It was not I, Plato, who made any agreement with you, but, by the gods, you did so yourself." These words prove Dionysius a liar, and the form of speech has both dignity and discretion.

Men often speak equivocally. If one wishes to speak like that, and also one's censure not to sound like censure, then what Aeschines said about Telauges is a model to follow. Almost his whole account of the man leaves one puzzled as to whether he is expressing admiration for him or satirizing him. This kind of writing is ambiguous; although it is not irony, yet there are indications of irony.

Innuendo may also be used in another way, like this: men and women in positions of power dislike any reference to their faults. When we are advising them on a course of action, therefore, we shall not speak frankly. We should either blame others who have acted in a similar way; we may, for example, condemn the despotic severity of Phalaris when talking to Dionysius; or again we shall praise others, be it Gelon or Hiero, who have acted in the opposite way and say they were like fathers or teachers to their Sicilian subjects. As he hears these things, Dionysius is being admonished, but he is not being censured; moreover he will envy the praise bestowed on Gelon, and he will want to deserve such praise himself.

There are many such occasions in the company of despotic rulers. Philip, for example, had only one good eye, and any reference to a Cyclops angered him, indeed any reference to eyes. Hermias, ruler of Atarneus, though in other ways gentle, found it difficult to endure any reference to knives or surgical operations, because he was a eunuch. I mention these things to draw attention to the proper way to speak to princes, and that it very much requires the circumspect manner of speech which is called innuendo.

Moreover, great and powerful popular assemblies frequently need to be addressed in the same manner as despots, as did the people of Athens when they were masters of Greece and nurtured such flatterers as Cleon and Cleophon. Flattery is ugly, but censure is dangerous; that manner is best which lies between the two, namely innuendo.

And sometimes we shall praise even the wrongdoer, not for what he did wrong, but for what he did right. You will tell a bad-tempered man that you heard him praised for the gentleness he displayed yesterday when so and so was in the wrong and that he is an example to his fellow-citizens. For everybody likes to be a model to himself, and wants to be praised more and more, indeed to be praised continually.

Different Modes of Speech

Just as from the same wax one man will make a dog, another an ox, a third a horse, so the same subject-matter can be expressed in the pointed and accusatory manner of Aristippus: "Men leave property to their children, but they do not leave along with it the knowledge of how to use the legacy," and this is the Aristippean manner; or it can be put as a suggestion, as Xenophon mostly does: "One should not leave only property to one's children, but also the knowledge of how to use it."

Then there is the peculiar manner called Socratic, which seems to have been emulated especially by Aeschines and Plato. Here the above advice becomes a question, something like this: "Well, my boy, how much money did your father leave you? Quite a lot, more than you can easily account for?—Quite a lot, Socrates—Then surely he also left you the knowledge of how to use it?" The boy is in difficulties before he realizes it; he is made aware of his ignorance, and set on the path of education. All these different manners are suitably in character, and certainly not the proverbial Scythian manner of speech.

This type of writing was very successful at the time it was first discovered; people were struck by its vivid imitation of actual conversation and its high-minded exhortations.

So much for the various forms of expression into which a subject can be moulded, and for innuendos.

Forcible Arrangement

Smoothness in the arrangement of words, as especially affected by the school of Isocrates, who avoid all hiatus, is not very suitable in the forceful style. A hiatus often increases forcefulness, its avoidance deprives the passage of force, for the echoing sound of the clashing vowels contributes to its forcefulness.

Indeed what is unpremeditated and spontaneous itself makes a more forceful impression, especially when we show our anger at a wrong we have suffered. The care which a smooth and melodious arrangement betrays belongs not to the expression of anger but to jest or display.

Just as we mentioned that the figure of omitted connectives contributes to forcefulness, so does an altogether loose word-arrangement. A proof of this is found in Hipponax. When he wants to attack his enemies he breaks his rhythm, makes it halting instead of straightforward, less rhythmical, and this suits the forcefulness of his attack. Rhythm which is smooth to the ear is more appropriate to eulogy than to censure. So much for hiatus.

The Vice of Coarseness

There is, as we would expect, a faulty style neighbouring on the forceful, and this we call the coarse. There is coarseness of subject-matter where an author openly speaks of things ugly and unmentionable, as when the man who was accusing Timandra of prostitution filled the courtroom with descriptions of her basin, her instruments, her rush-mat, and many other such unseemly details.

The arrangement of words appears coarse when it is jerky; also when the clauses are quite unconnected, like fragments of speech. Continuous long periods, too, which make a reader pant for breath not only surfeit but repel him.

The choice of words can make disagreeable even subjects which are pleasing in themselves, as when Clitarchus says of a kind of bee: "it feeds on the countryside, and rushes into hollow oaks." You would think he was talking about a wild bull or the Erymanthian boar instead of a bee. The passage is both coarse and frigid, and indeed these two faults are close neighbours.

Cicero

106–43 B.C.

Marcus Tullius Cicero was the first Roman to make a major contribution to literary criticism, primarily in works on the orator's art (like his contemporaries, he considered oratory the highest form of literature). These works served as the standard for composition throughout the rest of Roman history.

Cicero lived during the transformation of Rome from a republic into an empire and became a victim of that transformation. His father, a profoundly cultured man, raised his sons in Rome in order to provide them with a proper education. As a boy, Cicero listened to the great orators of the day and studied with a Stoic tutor, Diodotus. Beginning in 79 B.C., he spent two years studying in Athens and Rhodes. In his mid-twenties Cicero began to appear in the senatorial courts, and in 75 B.C. he was appointed to the post of quaestor, which was the preliminary step for men pursuing public careers. By age thirty-six, he had established himself as one of the leaders of the Roman bar.

At the height of his power Cicero was drawn into a great rivalry with Catiline, who was pursuing a demagogic path to power. In 63 he defeated Catiline for the consulship, the supreme civil and military position in the Roman republic, and he later thwarted Catiline's conspiracy to overthrow the government. When the triumvirate of Pompey, Caesar, and Crassus came to power, Cicero retired from public life, resumed his practice at the bar, and began to devote himself to writing.

In the civil wars that followed, Cicero, after much hesitation, supported Pompey against Caesar. When Caesar gained control of Rome in 48, Cicero became reconciled to his rule but remained in the background of public affairs, continuing to write. He did not participate in Caesar's murder and violently opposed his successor, Antony, whom he denounced in his famous Philippics. Antony's ally Octavian had Cicero executed in 43 B.C.

Cicero's first love was politics. He turned to writing only when barred from public affairs, and even his theoretical works are concerned with the relationship between rhetoric and the res publica. He believed that the study of rhetoric should not be relegated to an academic consideration of the technical details of the art, arguing for a broader conception of rhetorical education that included history and philosophy. He inherited from Plato, either directly or indirectly, a concern for the philosophical education of the aspiring leader, and so feared the abuse of rhetorical skills in the hands of the depraved. Cicero's insistence on a marriage of rhetoric and philosophy created the basis for Rome's classical humanism. He achieved the union of the rhetorical studies of his own day with the philosophical concerns of Plato and Aristotle.

Cicero's earliest rhetorical treatise, De Inventione ("On Invention"), is a highly technical analysis of the structure of a speech. It was dismissed by the mature Cicero as the work of a "youthful schoolboy," but unlike his later writings, it survived and was influential in the Middle Ages. De Oratore ("On the Orator," 55 B.C.), Cicero's most detailed theoretical and practical discussion of the rhetorical arts, is cast in the form of a fictional conversation set in 91 B.C. The principal characters are Crassus and Antonius, both leading Roman orators, and their younger colleagues Sulpicius and Cotta. The Caesar who discourses on wit in Book II is not Julius Caesar but the Roman politician C. Julius Caesar Strabo Vopiscus.

In Orator (46 B.C.), his last rhetorical work, Cicero drew upon a lifetime of experience and reflection to expound his conception of the ideal orator in a letter to his friend Marcus Junius Brutus. He also addressed the growing controversy surrounding the "Attic" and "Asiatic" styles in oratory. Many speakers of the period consciously rejected the fullness of style represented by Cicero himself, desiring instead to return to the plain, "Attic" style of the Greek orators Lysias and Hyperides. In both Orator and another work, Brutus, Cicero defended his style, reasoning that the effective speaker must utilize aspects of both styles. The irony is, of course, that Cicero came to represent for later writers, especially Quintilian, the " classic" style of Latin oratory to which their own age should aspire.

The selections from De Inventione and Orator, translated by H. M. Hubbell, and from De Oratore, translated by E. W. Sutton and H. Rackham, are reprinted by permission of Harvard University Press and the Loeb Classical Library.

DE INVENTIONE

FROM

Book I

Then, after all these points about the case have been discovered, the separate divisions of the whole case must be considered. For it does not follow that everything which is to be said first must be studied first; for the reason that, if you wish the first part of the speech to have a close agreement and connexion with the main statement of the case, you must derive it from the matters which are to be discussed afterward. Therefore when the point for decision and the arguments which must be devised for the purpose of reaching a decision have been diligently discovered by the rules of art, and studied with careful thought, then, and not till then, the other parts of the oration are to be arranged in proper order. These seem to me to be just six in number: exordium, narrative, partition, confirmation, refutation, peroration.

Now since the exordium has to come first, we shall likewise give first the rule for a systematic treatment of the exordium. An exordium is a passage which brings the mind of the auditor into a proper condition to receive the rest of the speech. This will be accomplished if he becomes well-disposed, attentive, and receptive. Therefore one who wishes his speech to have a good exordium must make a careful study beforehand of the kind of case which he has to present. There are five kinds of cases: honourable, difficult, mean, ambiguous, obscure. An honourable case is one which wins favour in the mind of the auditor at once without any speech of ours: the difficult is one which has alienated the sympathy of those who are about to listen to the speech. The mean is one which the auditor makes light of and thinks unworthy of serious attention; the ambiguous is one in which the point for decision is doubtful, or the case is partly honourable and partly discreditable so that it engenders both goodwill and ill-will; the obscure case is one in which either the auditors are slow of wit, or the case involves matters which are rather difficult to grasp. Hence, since the kinds of cases are so diverse, it is necessary to construct the exordium on a different plan in each kind of case. The exordium is, then, divided into two species, *introduction* and *insinuation*. An introduction is an address which directly and in plain language makes the auditor well-disposed, receptive, and attentive. Insinuation is an address which by dissimulation and indirection unobtrusively steals into the mind of the auditor.

In the difficult case, if the auditors are not completely hostile, it will be permissible to try to win their good-will by an introduction; if they are violently opposed it will be necessary to have recourse to the insinuation. For if amity and good-will are sought from auditors who are in a rage, not only is the desired result not obtained, but their hatred is increased and fanned into a flame. In the mean case, on the other hand, it is necessary to make the audience attentive in order to remove their disdain. If an ambiguous case has a doubtful point for the judge's decision, the exordium must begin with a discussion of this very point. But if the case is partly honourable and partly discreditable, it will be proper to try to win good-will so that the case may seem to be transferred to the honourable class. When, however, the case is really in the honourable class, it will be possible either to pass over the introduction or, if it is convenient, we shall begin with the narrative or with a law or some very strong argument which supports our plea: if, on the contrary, it is desirable to use the introduction, we must use the topics designed to produce good-will, that the advantage which already exists may be increased. . . .

25 This is about all that it seemed necessary to say concerning the introduction and the insinuation separately: now it seems desirable to state some brief rules which will apply to both alike.

The *exordium* ought to be sententious to a marked degree and of a high seriousness, and, to put it generally, should contain everything which contributes to dignity, because the best thing to do is that which especially commends the speaker to his audience. It should contain very little brilliance, vivacity, or finish of style, because these give rise to a suspicion of preparation and excessive ingenuity. As a result of this most of all the speech loses conviction and the speaker, authority.

26 The following are surely the most obvious faults of *exordia*, which are by all means to be avoided: it should not be general, common, interchangeable, tedious, unconnected, out of place, or contrary to the fundamental principles. A *general* exordium is one which can be tacked to many cases, so as to seem to suit them all. A *common* exordium is one equally applicable to both sides of the case. The *interchangeable* can with slight changes be used by the opponent in a speech on the other side. The *tedious* exordium is one which is spun out beyond all need with a superabundance of words or ideas. The *unconnected* is one which is not derived from the circumstances of the case nor closely knit with the rest of the speech, as a limb to a body. It is *out of place* if it produces a result different from what the nature of the case requires: for example, if it makes the audience receptive when the case calls for good-will, or uses an introduction when the situation demands an insinuation. It is contrary to fundamental principles when it achieves none of the purposes for which rules are given about exordia, that is, when it renders the audience neither well-disposed, nor attentive, nor receptive, or produces the opposite result; and nothing surely can be worse than that. This is enough to say about the exordium.

27 The *narrative* is an exposition of events that have occurred or are supposed to have occurred. There are three kinds: one which contains just the case and the whole reason for the dispute; a second in which a digression is made beyond the strict limits of the case for the purpose of attacking somebody, or of making a comparison, or of amusing the audience in a way not incongruous with the business in hand, or for amplification. The third kind is wholly unconnected

with public issues, which is recited or written solely for amusement but at the same time provides valuable training. It is subdivided into two classes: one concerned with events, the other principally with persons. That which consists of an exposition of events has three forms: *fabula, historia, argumentum*. *Fabula* is the term applied to a narrative in which the events are not true and have no verisimilitude, for example:

> Huge winged dragons yoked to a car.

Historia is an account of actual occurrences remote from the recollection of our own age, as:

> War on men of Carthage Appius decreed.

Argumentum is a fictitious narrative which nevertheless could have occurred. An example may be quoted from Terence:

> For after he had left the school of youth.

But the form of narrative which is concerned with persons is of such a sort that in it can be seen not only events but also the conversation and mental attitude of the characters. For example: "He comes to me perpetually, crying, 'What are you about, Micio? Why are you bringing the boy to ruin on our hands? Why this licence? Why these drinking parties? Why do you pile him up the guineas for such a life and let him spend so much at the tailor's? It's extremely silly of you.' He himself is extremely hard, past right and sense." This form of narrative should possess great vivacity, resulting from fluctuations of fortune, contrast of characters, severity, gentleness, hope, fear, suspicion, desire, dissimulation, delusion, pity, sudden change of fortune, unexpected disaster, sudden pleasure, a happy ending to the story. But these embellishments will be drawn from what will be said later about the rules of style. . . .

The narrative will be plausible if it seems to embody characteristics which are accustomed to appear in real life; if the proper qualities of the character are maintained, if reasons for their actions are plain, if there seems to have been ability to do the deed, if it can be shown that the time was opportune, the space sufficient and the place suitable for the events about to be narrated; if the story fits in with the nature of the actors in it, the habits of ordinary people and the beliefs of the audience. Verisimilitude can be secured by following these principles.

In addition to observing these precepts, one must also be on guard not to insert a narrative when it will be a hindrance or of no advantage, and also not to have it out of place or in a manner other than that which the case requires. A narrative can be a hindrance when a presentation of the events alone and by themselves gives great offence, which it will be necessary to mitigate in arguing and pleading the case. When this situation arises, it will be necessary to distribute the narrative piecemeal throughout the speech and to add an explanation directly after each section so that the remedy may heal the wound and the defence may immediately lessen the animosity. A narrative is of no advantage when the facts have been explained by the opponents and it is of no importance to us to tell the story again or in a different way. The narrative is also useless when the audience has grasped the facts so thoroughly that it is of no advantage to us to instruct them in a different fashion. In such a case one must dispense with narrative altogether. The narrative is out of place when it is not set in that part of the speech which the situation demands; this topic we shall take up when we discuss arrangement, for it affects the arrangement. The narrative is not presented in the manner required by the case when a point which helps the opponent is explained clearly and elegantly, or a point which helps the speaker is presented obscurely and carelessly. Therefore, to avoid this fault, the speaker must bend everything to the advantage of his case, by passing over all things that make against it which can be passed over, by touching lightly on what must be mentioned, and by telling his own side of the story carefully and clearly.

Sufficient has, I think, been said about narrative; let us now pass to the *partition*.

31   In an argument a partition correctly made renders the whole speech clear and perspicuous. It takes two forms, both of which greatly contribute to clarifying the case and determining the nature of the controversy. One form shows in what we agree with our opponents and what is left in dispute; as a result of this some definite problem is set for the auditor on which he ought to have his attention fixed. In the second form the matters which we intend to discuss are briefly set forth in a methodical way. This leads the auditor to hold definite points in his mind, and to understand that when these have been discussed the oration will be over.

Now I think I ought to present briefly the method of using each form of partition. A partition which shows what is agreed upon, and what is not, should turn the subject of agreement to the advantage of the speaker's case, in the following manner: "I agree with my opponents that the mother was killed by her son." In the same way on the other side of the case, "It is agreed that Agamemnon was killed by Clytemnestra." For here each speaker stated what was agreed upon, yet was mindful of the advantage of his own side of the case. Secondly, what is in controversy should be set forth in explaining the point for the judge's decision, how this is discovered has been stated above.

32   The form of partition which contains a methodical statement of topics to be discussed ought to have the following qualities: brevity, completeness, conciseness. Brevity is secured when no word is used unless necessary. It is useful in this place because the attention of the auditor should be attracted by the facts and topics of the case, and not by extraneous embellishments of style. Completeness is the quality by which we embrace in the partition all forms of argument which apply to the case, and about which we ought to speak, taking care that no useful argument be omitted or be introduced late as an addition to the plan of the speech, for this is faulty and unseemly in the highest degree. Conciseness in the partition is secured if only *genera* of things are given and they are not confused and mixed with their *species*. To explain: a *genus* is a class that embraces several *species*, as *animal*. A *species* is that which is a part of a *genus*, as *horse*. But often the same thing is a genus in relation to one thing and a species in relation to another. For example, man is a species of animal, but a genus of which Thebans or Trojans are species. . . .

Now that the rules for partition have been stated, it is necessary to remind the orator that throughout the speech he should bear in mind to complete the sections in order one after another as they have been planned in the partition, and that after all have been dispatched he should bring the speech to a close so that nothing be introduced after the conclusion. The old man in the Andria of Terence makes a brief and neat partition of what he wishes his freedman to know: "In this way you will learn my son's manner of life, my plan, and what I wish you to do in the matter." And his narrative follows the plan laid down in the partition: first, his son's manner of life,

> For after he had left the school of youth . . .

then his plan:

> And now I am anxious . . .

then what he wishes Sosia to do, which was the last point in the partition, is stated last:

> Now your task is . . .

Just as he turned his attention first to each point as it arose, and after dispatching them all stopped speaking, so I favour turning our attention to each topic and when all have been dispatched, winding up the speech.

Now it seems desirable to give in turn the rules about *confirmation* as is demanded by the regular order of the speech. Confirmation or proof is the part of the oration which by marshalling arguments lends credit, authority, and support to our case. For this section of the speech there are definite rules which will be divided among the different kinds of cases. But I think that it will not be inconvenient to set forth in the beginning, without any attempt at order or arrangement, a kind of raw material for general use from which all arguments are drawn, and then later to present the way in which each kind of case should be supported by all the forms of argumentation derived from this general store.

All propositions are supported in argument by attributes of persons or of actions. We hold the following to be the attributes of persons: name, nature, manner of life, fortune, habit, feeling, interests, purposes, achievements, accidents, speeches made . . . .

All argumentation drawn from these topics which we have mentioned will have to be either probable or irrefutable. For, to define it briefly, an argument seems to be a device of some sort to demonstrate with probability or prove irrefutably.

Those things are proved irrefutably which cannot happen or be proved otherwise than as stated; for example, "If she has borne a child, she has lain with a man." This style of argument which is used for rigorous proof, generally in speaking takes the form of a dilemma, or of an enumeration or of a simple inference. A dilemma is a form of argument in which you are refuted, whichever alternative you grant, after this fashion: "If he is a scoundrel, why are you intimate with him? If he is an honest man, why accuse him?" Enumeration is a form of argument in which several possibilities are stated, and when all but one have been disproved, this one is irrefutably demonstrated; the following is an example: "He must have been killed by the defendant either because of his enmity to him, or through fear or hope or to gratify a friend; if none of these statements is true, he cannot have been killed by the defendant. For a crime cannot be committed without a motive. If there was no enmity, and no fear, and no hope of any advantages from his death and his death was of no interest to any friend of the defendant, it therefore follows that the defendant did not kill him." A simple inference arises from a necessary consequence, as follows: "If you say that I did this at that time, but at that particular time I was overseas, it follows that I not only did not do what you say, but that I was not even in a position to do it." And it will be necessary to keep a sharp watch that this kind of argument cannot be refuted in any way, so that the proof may not contain in itself only a form of argument and a mere appearance of a necessary conclusion, but rather that the argument may rest on rigorous reasoning.

46 That is probable which for the most part usually comes to pass, or which is a part of the ordinary beliefs of mankind, or which contains in itself some resemblance to these qualities, whether such resemblance be true or false. In the class of things which for the most part usually come to pass are probabilities of this sort: "If she is his mother, she loves him." "If he is avaricious, he disregards his oath." Under the head of ordinary beliefs or opinions come probabilities of this sort: "Punishment awaits the wicked in the next world." "Philosophers are atheists." Resemblance is seen mostly in contraries, in analogies, and in those things which fall under the same principle. In contraries, as follows: "For if it is right for me to pardon those who have wronged me unintentionally, I ought not to be grateful to those who have assisted me

47 because they could not help it." In analogies, thus: "For as a place without a harbour cannot be safe for ships, so a mind without integrity cannot be relied on by friends." In the case of those things which fall under the same principle, probability is considered after this fashion: "For if it is not disgraceful for the Rhodians to farm out their customs-duties, neither is it disgraceful for Hermocreon to take the contract." Arguments of this kind are sometimes rigorous—for example: "Since there is a scar, there has been a wound"—sometimes they are only plausible, for instance: "If there was much dust on his shoes, he must have been on a journey...."

89 On the other hand, the very nature of the argumentation may be shown to be faulty for the following reasons: if there is any defect in the argumentation itself or if it is not adapted to prove what we purpose to prove. To be specific, there will be a defect in the argument itself if it is wholly false, general, common, trifling, far-fetched, a bad definition, controvertible, self-evident, disputable, discreditable, offensive, "contrary," inconsistent, or adverse....

97 Hermagoras puts the digression next, and then finally the peroration. In this digression he thinks a passage should be introduced unconnected with the case and the actual point to be decided; it might contain praise of oneself or abuse of the opponent, or lead to some other case which may supply confirmation or refutation not by argument but by adding emphasis by means of some amplification. If anyone thinks this is a proper division of a speech, he may follow Hermagoras' rule. For some of the rules for amplification and praise and

vituperation have already been given, and the rest will be given in the proper place. But we do not think that this should be listed among the regular parts of the speech, because we disapprove of digressing from the main subject except in case of "commonplaces"; and this topic is to be discussed later. Moreover, I am of the opinion that praise and vituperation should not be made a separate part, but should be closely interwoven with the argumentation itself. Now we shall discuss the peroration.

The peroration is the end and conclusion of the whole speech; it has three parts, the summing-up, the *indignatio* or exciting of indignation or ill-will against the opponent, and the *conquestio* or the arousing of pity and sympathy. *98*

The summing-up is a passage in which matters that have been discussed in different places here and there throughout the speech are brought together in one place and arranged so as to be seen at a glance in order to refresh the memory of the audience. If this is always treated in the same manner, it will be perfectly evident to everyone that it is being handled according to some rule or system. But if it is managed in different ways it will be possible to avoid both this suspicion and the boredom which comes from repetition. Therefore it will be proper at times to sum up in the manner which the majority of speakers employ, because it is easy, *i.e.* to touch on each single point and so to run briefly over all the arguments. At times, however, it is well to take the harder course and state the topics which you have set out in the partition and promised to discuss, and to recall to mind the lines of reasoning by which you have proved each point, in this fashion: "We have demonstrated this, we have made this plain." At times one may inquire of the audience what they might rightly wish to have proved to them. Thus the auditor will refresh his memory and think that there is nothing more that he ought to desire. . . .

The *indignatio* is a passage which results in arousing great hatred against some person, or violent offence at some action. In discussing this topic we wish it to be understood at the beginning that *indignatio* is used in connexion with all the topics which we laid out when giving rules for confirmation. In other words, all the attributes of persons and things can give occasion for any use of amplification that may be desired, or any method of arousing enmity. . . . *100*

Conquestio (lament or complaint) is a passage seeking to arouse the pity of the audience. In this the first necessity is to make the auditor's spirit gentle and merciful that he may be more easily moved by the *conquestio*. This ought to be done by the use of "commonplaces" which set forth the power of fortune over all men and the weakness of the human race. When such a passage is delivered gravely and sententiously, the spirit of man is greatly abased and prepared for pity, for in viewing the misfortune of another he will contemplate his own weakness. After that the first topic with which to evoke pity is that by which it is shown what prosperity they once enjoyed and from what evils they now suffer. The second employs a division according to time, and shows in what troubles they have been, still are, and are destined to be. The third, in which each separate phase of misfortune is deplored; for example, in lamenting the death of a son, one might mention the delight that his father took in his childhood, his love, his hope for the boy's future, the comfort he derived from him, the careful *106*

107

training, and whatever in a similar case can be said in bewailing any misfortune. The fourth, in which one recounts shameful, mean, and ignoble acts and what they have suffered or are likely to suffer that is unworthy of their age, race, former fortune, position or preferment. The fifth, in which all misfortunes are presented to view one by one, so that the auditor may seem to see them, and may be moved to pity by the actual occurrence, as if he were present, and not by words alone. The sixth, in which it is shown that one is in distress contrary to all expectation, and when he looked forward to receiving some benefit, he not only did not gain it, but fell into the greatest distress. The seventh, in which we turn to the audience and ask them when they look at us to think of their children or parents or some one who ought to be dear to them. The eighth, in which something is said to have happened which ought not, or that something did not happen which ought to have happened: for example, "I was not present, I did not see him, I did not hear his last words, I did not catch his last breath."

DE ORATORE

FROM

Book I

On the Nature and Functions of Rhetoric

In that place, as Cotta was fond of relating, Crassus introduced a conversation on the pursuit of oratory, with a view to relieving all minds from the discourse of the day before. He began by saying that Sulpicius and Cotta seemed not to need exhortation from him but rather commendation, seeing that thus early they had acquired such skill as not merely to be ranked above their equals in age, but to be comparable with their elders. "Moreover," he continued, "there is to my mind no more excellent thing than the power, by means of oratory, to get a hold on assemblies of men, win their good will, direct their inclinations wherever the speaker wishes, or divert them from whatever he wishes. In every free nation, and most of all in communities which have attained the enjoyment of peace and tranquility, this one art has always flourished above the rest and ever reigned supreme. For what is so marvellous as that, out of the innumerable company of mankind, a single being should arise, who either alone or with a few others can make effective a faculty bestowed by nature upon every man? Or what so pleasing to the understanding and the ear as a speech adorned and polished with wise reflections and dignified language? Or what achievement so mighty and glorious as that the impulses of the crowd, the consciences of the judges, the austerity of the Senate, should suffer transformation through the eloquence of one man? What function again is so kingly, so worthy of the free, so generous, as to bring help to the suppliant, to raise up those that are cast down, to bestow security, to set free from peril, to maintain men in their civil rights? What too is so indispensable as to have always in your grasp weapons wherewith you can defend yourself, or challenge the wicked man, or when provoked take your revenge?

"Nay more (not to have you for ever contemplating public affairs, the bench, the platform, and the Senate-house), what in hours of ease can be a pleasanter thing or one more characteristic of culture, than discourse that is graceful and nowhere uninstructed? For the one point in which we have our very greatest advantage over the brute creation is that we hold converse one with another, and can reproduce our thought in word. Who therefore would not rightly admire this faculty, and deem it his duty to exert himself to the utmost in this field, that by so doing he may surpass men themselves in that particular respect wherein chiefly men are superior to animals? To come, however, at length to the highest achievements of eloquence, what other power could have been strong enough either to gather scattered humanity into one place, or to lead it out of its brutish existence in the wilderness up to our present condition of civilization as men and as citizens, or, after the establishment of social communities, to give shape to laws, tribunals, and civic rights? And not to pursue any further instances—wellnigh countless as they are—I will conclude the whole matter in a few words, for my assertion is this: that the wise control of the complete orator is that which chiefly upholds not only his own dignity, but the safety of countless individuals and of the entire State. Go forward therefore, my young friends, in your present course, and bend your energies to that study which engages you, that so it may be in your power to become a glory to yourselves, a source of service to your friends, and profitable members of the Republic."

Thereupon Scaevola observed, in his courteous way, "On his other points I am in agreement with Crassus (that I may not disparage the art or the renown of my father-in-law Gaius Laelius, or of my son-in-law here), but the two following, Crassus, I am afraid I cannot grant you: first your statement that the orators were they who in the beginning established social communities, and who not seldom have preserved the same intact, secondly your pronouncement that, even if we take no account of the forum, of popular assemblies, of the courts of justice, or of the Senate-house, the orator is still complete over the whole range of speech and culture. For who is going to grant you, that in shutting themselves up in walled cities, human beings, who had been scattered originally over mountain and forest, were not so much convinced by the reasoning of the wise as snared by the speeches of the eloquent, or again that the other beneficial arrangements involved in the establishment or the preservation of States were not shaped by the wise and valiant but by men of eloquence and fine diction? Or do you perhaps think that it was by eloquence, and not rather by good counsel and singular wisdom, that the great Romulus gathered together his shepherds and refugees, or brought about marriages with the Sabines, or curbed the might of the neighbouring tribes? Is there a trace of eloquence to be discerned in Numa Pompilius? Is there a trace in Servius Tullius? Or in the other kings who have contributed so much that is excellent to the building-up of the State? Then even after the kings had been driven forth (and we note that such expulsion had itself been accomplished by the mind of Lucius Brutus and not by his tongue), do we not see how all that followed was full of planning and empty of talking? For my part, indeed, should I care to use examples from our own and other communites, I could cite more instances of damage done, than of aid given to the cause of the State by men of first-rate eloquence, but putting all else aside, of all men to whom I have listened except you two, Crassus, it seems to me that the most eloquent were Tiberius and Gaius Sempronius, whose father, a man of discretion and character, but no speaker whatever, was many a time and most particularly when Censor the salvation of the commonwealth. Yet it was not any studied flow of speech, but a nod and a word of his that transferred the freedmen into the city tribes; and had he not done so, we should long ago have lost the constitution which, as it is, we preserve only with difficulty. His sons, on the other hand, who were accomplished speakers and equipped for oratory with every advantage of nature or training, after they had taken over a State that was flourishing exceedingly because of their father's counsels and their ancestors' military achievements, wrecked the commonwealth by the use of this eloquence to which, according to you, civil communities still look for their chief guidance.

"What of our ancient ordinances and the customs of our forefathers? What of augury, over which you and I, Crassus, preside, greatly to the welfare of the Republic? What of our religious rites and ceremonies? What of those rules of private law, which have long made their home in our family, though we have no reputation for eloquence? Were these things contrived or investigated or in any way taken in hand by the tribe of orators? Indeed I remember that Servius Galba, a man who spoke as a god, and Marcus Aemilius Porcina and Gaius Carbo himself, whom you crushed in your early manhood, were all of them ignorant of the statutes, all at a complete loss among the institutions of our ancestors, all uninstructed in the law of the Romans; and except yourself, Crassus, who rather from your own love of study, than because to do so was any peculiar duty of the eloquent, have learned the Roman system from our family, this generation of ours is unversed in law to a degree that sometimes makes one blush.

"But as for the claim you made at the close of your speech, and made as though in your own right—that whatever the topic under discussion, the orator could deal with it in complete fullness—this, had we not been here in your own domain, I would not have borne with, and I should be at the head of a multitude who would either fight you by injunction, or summon you to make joint seizure by rule of court, for so wantonly making forcible entry upon other people's possessions.

"For, to begin with, all the disciples of Pythagoras and Democritus would bring statutory process against you, and the rest of the physicists would assert their claims in court, elegant and impressive speakers with whom you could not strive and save your stake. Besides this, schools of philosophers, back to great Socrates their fountain-head, would beset you: they would demonstrate that you have learned nothing concerning the good in life, or of the evil, nothing as to the emotions of the mind or of human conduct, nothing of the true theory of living, that you have made no research at all and are wholly without understanding respecting these things; and after this general assault upon you each sect would launch its particular action against you in detail. The Academy would be at your heels, compelling you to deny in terms your own allegation, whatever it might have been. Then our own friends the Stoics would hold you entangled in the toils of their wranglings and questionings. The Peripatetics again would prove that it is to them that men should resort for even those very aids and trappings of eloquence which you deem to be the special aids of orators, and would show you that on these subjects of yours Aristotle and Theophrastus wrote not only better but also much more than all the teachers of rhetoric put together. I say nothing of the mathematicians, men of letters or devotees of the Muses, with whose arts this rhetorical faculty of yours is not in the remotest degree allied. And so, Crassus, I do not think you should make professions so extensive and so numerous. What you are able to guarantee is a thing great enough, namely, that in the courts whatever case you present should appear to be the better and more plausible, that in assemblies and in the Senate your oratory should have most weight in carrying the vote, and lastly, that to the intelligent you should seem to speak eloquently and to the ignorant truthfully as well. If you can achieve anything more than this, therein you will seem to me not an orator but a Crassus, who is making use of some talent that is peculiarly his own and not common to orators in general."

45   Then Crassus replied, "I know very well, Scaevola, that these views of yours are often put forward and discussed among the Greeks. For I listened to their most eminent men, on my arrival in Athens as a quaestor from Macedonia, at a time when the Academy was at its best, as was then asserted, with Charmadas, Clitomachus and Aeschines to uphold it. There was also Metrodorus, who, together with the others, had been a really diligent disciple of the illustrious Carneades himself, a speaker who, for spirited and copious oratory, surpassed, it was said, all other men. Mnesarchus too was in his prime, a pupil of your great
46 Panaetius, and Diodorus, who studied under Critolaus the Peripatetic. There were many others besides, of distinguished fame as philosophers, by all of whom, with one voice as it were, I perceived that the orator was driven from the helm of State, shut out from all learning and knowledge of more important things, and thrust down and locked up exclusively in law-courts and petty little
47 assemblies, as if in a pounding-mill. But I was neither in agreement with these men, nor with the author and originator of such discussions, who spoke with far more weight and eloquence than all of them—I mean Plato—whose *Gorgias* I read with close attention under Charmadas during those days at Athens, and what impressed me most deeply about Plato in that book was, that it was when making fun of orators that he himself seemed to me to be the consummate orator. In fact controversy about a word has long tormented those Greeklings,
48 fonder as they are of argument than of truth. For, if anyone lays it down that an orator is a man whose sole power is that of speaking copiously before the Praetor or at a trial, or in the public assembly or the Senate-house, none the less even to an orator thus limited such critic must grant and allow a number of attributes, inasmuch as without extensive handling of all public business, without a mastery of ordinances, customs and general law, without a knowledge of human nature and character, he cannot engage, with the requisite cleverness and skill, even in these restricted activities. But to a man who has learned these things, without which no one can properly ensure even those primary essentials of advocacy, can there by anything lacking that belongs to the knowledge of the highest matters? If, on the other hand, you would narrow the idea of oratory to nothing but the speaking in ordered fashion, gracefully and copiously, how, I ask, could your orator attain even so much, if he were to lack that knowledge whereof you people deny him the possession? For excellence in speaking cannot be made manifest unless the speaker fully comprehends the matter he speaks
49 about. It follows that, if the famous natural philosopher Democritus spoke with elegance, as he is reported and appears to me to have spoken, those notable subjects of his discourse belonged to the natural philosopher, but his actual elegance of diction must be put down to the orator. And if Plato spoke with the

voice of a god of things very far away from political debate, as I allow that he did, if again Aristotle and Theophrastus and Carneades, on the themes which they treated, were eloquent and displayed charm of style and literary form, then, granting that the topics of their discourse may be found in certain other fields of research, yet their actual style is the peculiar product of this pursuit which we are now discussing and investigating, and of no other. For we see that sundry authorities dealt with these same subjects in spiritless and feeble fashion, Chrysippus for instance, reputed as he is to have been the most acute of disputants, and not to have failed to meet the requirements of philosophy just because he had not acquired this gift of eloquence from an alien art.

"What then is the difference, or by what means will you discriminate between the rich and copious diction of those speakers whom I have mentioned, and the feebleness of such as do not adopt this variety and elegance of language? The sole distinction will surely be that the good speakers bring, as their peculiar possession, a style that is harmonious, graceful, and marked by a certain artistry and polish. Yet this style, if the underlying subject-matter be not comprehended and mastered by the speaker, must inevitably be of no account or even become the sport of universal derision. For what so effectually proclaims the madman as the hollow thundering of words—be they never so choice and resplendent—which have no thought or knowledge behind them? Therefore whatever the theme, from whatever art or whatever branch of knowledge it be taken, the orator, just as if he had got up the case for a client, will state it better and more gracefully than the actual discoverer and the specialist. For if anyone is going to affirm that there are certain ideas and subjects which specially belong to orators, and certain matters whereof the knowledge is railed-off behind the barriers of the Courts, while I will admit that these oratorical activities of ours are exercised within this area with less intermission than elsewhere, nevertheless among these very topics there are points in abundance which even the so-called professors of rhetoric neither teach nor understand. Who indeed does not know that the orator's virtue is preeminently manifested either in rousing men's hearts to anger, hatred, or indignation, or in recalling them from these same passions to mildness and mercy? Wherefore the speaker will not be able to achieve what he wants by his words, unless he has gained profound insight into the characters of men, and the whole range of human nature, and those motives whereby our souls are spurred on or turned back. And all this is considered to be the special province of philosophers, nor will the orator, if he take my advice, resist their claim; but when he has granted their knowledge of these things, since they have devoted all their labour to that alone, still he will assert his own claim to the oratorical treatment of them, which without that knowledge of theirs is nothing at all. For this is the essential concern of the orator, as I have often said before,—a style that is dignified and graceful and in conformity with the general modes of thought and judgement.

"And while I acknowledge that Aristotle and Theophrastus have written about all these things, yet consider, Scaevola, whether it is not wholly in my favour, that, whereas I do not borrow from them the things that they share with the orator, they on their part grant that their discussions on these subjects are the orator's own, and accordingly they entitle and designate all their other treatises by some name taken from their distinctive art, but these particular books as dealing with Rhetoric. And indeed when, while a man is speaking—as often happens—such commonplaces have cropped up as demand some mention of the immortal gods, of dutifulness, harmony, or friendship, of the rights shared by citizens, by men in general, and by nations, of fair-dealing moderation or greatness of soul, or virtue of any and every kind, all the academies and schools of philosophy will, I do believe, raise the cry that all these matters are their exclusive province, and in no way whatever the concern of the orator. But when I have allowed that they may debate these subjects in their holes and corners, to pass an idle hour, it is to the orator none the less that I shall entrust and assign the task of developing with complete charm and cogency the same themes which they discuss in a sort of thin and bloodless style. These points I used to argue at Athens with the philosophers in person, under pressure from our friend Marcus Marcellus, who is now Aedile of the Chair, and assuredly, if he were not at this moment producing the Games, would be taking part in our present colloquy; indeed even in those days of his early youth his devotion to these studies was marvellous.

"But now as regards the institution of laws, as regards war and peace, allies and public dues, and the legal rights assigned to classes of citizens according to variations of rank and age, let the Greeks say, if they please, that Lycurgus and Solon (although I hold that they should be rated as eloquent) were better informed than Hyperides or Demosthenes, who were really accomplished and highly polished orators; or let our own folk prefer in this regard the Ten Commissioners—who wrote out the Twelve Tables and were necessarily men of practical wisdom—to Servius Galba and your father-in-law Gaius Laelius, whose outstanding renown for eloquence is established. For never will I say that there are not certain arts belonging exclusively to those who have employed all their energies in the mastery and exercise thereof, but my assertion will be that the complete and finished orator is he who on any matter whatever can speak with fullness and variety.

"Indeed in handling those causes which everybody acknowledges to be within the exclusive sphere of oratory, there is not seldom something to be brought forth and employed, not from practice in public speaking—the only thing you allow the orator—but from some more abstruse branch of knowledge. I ask, for instance, whether an advocate can either assail or defend a commander-in-chief without experience of the art of war, or sometimes too without knowledge of the various regions of land or sea? Whether he can address the popular assembly in favour of the passing or rejection of legislative proposals, or the Senate concerning any of the departments of State administration, if he lack consummate knowledge—practical as well as theoretical—of political science? Whether a speech can be directed to inflaming or even repressing feeling and passion—a faculty of the first importance to the orator—unless the speaker has made a most careful search into all those theories respecting the natural characters and the habits of conduct of mankind, which are unfolded by the philosophers?

"And I rather think I shall come short of convincing you on my next point—at all events I will not hesitate to speak my mind: your natural science itself, your mathematics, and other studies which just now you reckoned as belonging peculiarly to the rest of the arts, do indeed pertain to the knowledge of their professors, yet if anyone should wish by speaking to put these same arts in their full light, it is to oratorical skill that he must run for help. If, again, it is established that Philo, that master-builder who constructed an arsenal for the Athenians, described the plan of his work very eloquently to the people, his eloquence must be ascribed not to his architectural, but rather to his oratorical ability. So too, if Marcus Antonius here had had to speak on behalf of Hermodorus upon the construction of dockyards, having got up his case from his client, he would then have discoursed gracefully and copiously of an art to which he was not a stranger. Asclepiades also, he with whom we have been familiar both as physician and as friend, at the time when he was surpassing the rest of his profession in eloquence, was exhibiting, in such graceful speaking, the skill of an orator, not that of a physician. In fact that favourite assertion of Socrates—that every man was eloquent enough upon a subject that he knew—has in it some plausibility but no truth: it is nearer the truth to say that neither can anyone be eloquent upon a subject that is unknown to him, nor, if he knows it perfectly and yet does not know how to shape and polish his style, can he speak fluently even upon that which he does know.

"Accordingly, should anyone wish to define in a comprehensive manner the complete and special meaning of the word, he will be an orator, in my opinion worthy of so dignified a title, who, whatever the topic that crops up to be unfolded in discourse, will speak thereon with knowledge, method, charm and retentive memory, combining with these qualifications a certain distinction of bearing. If however someone considers my expression 'whatever the topic' to be altogether too extensive, he may clip and prune it to his individual taste, but to this much I shall hold fast—though the orator be ignorant of what is to be found in all the other arts and branches of study, and know only what is dealt with in debate and the practice of public-speaking; none the less, if he should have to discourse even on these other subjects, then after learning the technicalities of each from those who know the same, the orator will speak about them far better than even the men who are masters of these arts. For example, should our friend Sulpicius here have to speak upon the art of war, he will inquire of our relative Gaius Marius, and when he has received his teachings, will deliver himself in such fashion as to seem even to Gaius Marius to be almost better informed on the subject than Gaius Marius himself; while if his topic is to be the law of private rights, he will consult yourself and, notwithstanding your consummate learning and skill in these very things which you have taught him, he will surpass you in the art of exposition. If again some matter should confront him wherein he must speak of human nature, human vices or the passions, of moderation or self-control, of sorrow or death, then perhaps if he thinks fit—although an orator must have knowledge of such things—he will have taken counsel with Sextus Pompeius, a man accomplished in moral science; so much he will assuredly achieve, that whatever his subject and whoever his

68 instructor, on that subject he will express himself far more gracefully than his master himself. Nevertheless, if he will listen to me, since philosophy is divided into three branches, which respectively deal with the mysteries of nature, with the subtleties of dialectic, and with human life and conduct, let us quit claim to the first two, by way of concession to our indolence, but unless we keep our hold on the third, which has ever been the orator's province, we shall leave the orator
69 no sphere wherein to attain greatness. For which reason this division of philosophy, concerned with human life and manners, must all of it be mastered by the orator; as for the other matters, even though he has not studied them, he will still be able, whenever the necessity arises, to beautify them by his eloquence, if only they are brought to his notice and described to him.

"Indeed if it is agreed in learned circles that a man who knew no astronomy—Aratus to wit—has sung of the heavenly spaces and the stars in verse of consummate finish and excellence, and that another who was a complete stranger to country life, Nicander of Colophon, has written with distinction on rural affairs, using something of a poet's skill and not that of a farmer, what reason is there why an orator should not discourse most eloquently concerning those subjects which he has conned for a specific argument and
70 occasion? The truth is that the poet is a very near kinsman of the orator, rather more heavily fettered as regards rhythm, but with ampler freedom in his choice of words, while in the use of many sorts of ornament he is his ally and almost his counterpart; in one respect at all events something like identity exists, since he sets no boundaries or limits to his claims, such as would prevent him from
71 ranging whither he will with the same freedom and licence as the other. For with regard to your remark, Scaevola, that, had you not been in my domain, you would not have endured my assertion that the orator must be accomplished in every kind of discourse and in every department of culture, I should certainly never have made that assertion, did I consider myself to be the man I am
72 endeavouring to portray. But, as was often said by Gaius Lucilius—who was not altogether pleased with you, and for that very reason less intimate with myself than he wished, but for all that an instructed critic and thorough gentlemen of the city—my opinion is this, that no one should be numbered with the orators who is not accomplished in all those arts that befit the well-bred; for though we do not actually parade these in our discourse, it is none the less made clear to demonstration whether we are strangers to them or have learned to know them.
73 Just as ball-players do not in their game itself employ the characteristic dexterity of the gymnasium, and yet their very movements show whether they have had such training or know nothing of that art; and, just as, in the case of those who are portraying anything, even though at the moment they are making no use of the painter's art, there is none the less no difficulty in seeing whether or not they know how to paint; even so is it with these same speeches in the Courts, the popular assembly and the Senate-house—granting that the other arts may not be specially brought into play, still it is made easily discernible whether the speaker has merely floundered about in this declamatory business or whether, before approaching his task of oratory, he has been trained in all the liberal arts."
74 At this point Scaevola smilingly declared: "Crassus, I will strive with you no

longer. For, in this very speech you have made against me, you have by some trick so managed matters as both to grant me what I said did not belong to the orator, and then somehow or another to wrest away these things again and hand them over to the orator as his absolute property. And as regards these subjects, when on my arrival in Rhodes as praetor I discussed with Apolonius, that supreme master of this science of rhetoric, the things that I had learned from Panaetius, he as usual jeered at philosophy and expressed contempt for it and talked at large in a vein more graceful than serious; whereas your argument has been of such a kind that you not only refrained from despising any of the arts or sciences, but described them all as the attendants and handmaids of oratory. And for my own part, if ever any one man should have mastered all of them, and that same man should have united with them this added power of perfectly graceful expression, I cannot deny that he would be a remarkable kind of man and worthy of admiration; but if such a one there should be, or indeed ever has been, or really ever could be, assuredly you would be that one man, who both in my opinion and in that of everyone else, have left all other orators—if they will pardon my saying so—almost without glory. But if you yourself, while lacking nothing of the knowledge that has to do with law-court speaking and politics, have nevertheless not mastered the further learning which you associate with the orator, let us see whether you may not be attributing to him more than the real facts of the case allow."

Here Crassus interposed: "Remember that I have not been speaking of my own skill, but of that of an orator. For what have men like myself either learned or had any chance of knowing, who entered upon practice before ever we reached the study of theory, whom our professional activities in public speaking, in the pursuit of office, in politics, and about the affairs of our friends, wore out ere we could form any conception of the importance of these other matters? But if you find such excellence in me who, if perhaps—as you hold—I have not been completely wanting in ability, have assuredly been wanting in learning and leisure and (to tell the truth) in the requisite enthusiasms for instruction as well, what think you would be the quality and stature of an orator in whom all that I have not attained should be combined with ability such as my own or greater?"

Thereupon Antonius observed: "Crassus, to my mind you establish your case, and I do not doubt that, if a man has grasped the principles and nature of every subject and of every art, he will in consequence be far better equipped as a speaker. But in the first place such knowledge is hard to win, especially in the life we lead, and amid the engagements that are ours, and then again there is the danger of our being led away from our traditional practice of speaking in a style acceptable to the commonalty and suited to advocacy. For it seems to me that the eloquence of these men, to whom you referred just now, is of an entirely different kind, albeit they speak gracefully and cogently, either upon natural philosophy or upon the affairs of mankind: theirs is a polished and flowery sort of diction, redolent rather of the training-school and its suppling-oil than of our political hurly-burly and of the Bar. For—when I think of it—although it was late in life and only lightly that I came into touch with Greek literature, still, when on my journey to Cilicia as proconsul I reached Athens, I tarried there for several days by reason of the difficulty in putting to sea: at any rate, as I had about me daily the most learned men, pretty nearly the same as those whom you have lately mentioned, a rumour having somehow spread among them that I, just like yourself, was usually engaged in the more important causes, every one of them in his turn contributed what he could to a discussion on the function and method of an orator.

83 "Some of them were for maintaining, as did your authority Mnesarchus himself, that those whom we called orators were nothing but a sort of artisans with ready and practised tongues, whereas no one was an orator save the wise man only, and that eloquence itself, being, as it was, the science of speaking well, was one type of virtue, and he who possessed a single virtue possessed all of them, and the virtues were of the same rank and equal one with another, from which it followed that the man of eloquence had every virtue and was a wise man. But this was a thorny and dry sort of language, and entirely out of harmony
84 with anything we thought. Charmadas, however, would speak far more copiously upon the same topics, not that he intended thereby to reveal his own opinion,—it being an accepted tradition of the Academy always and against all comers to be of the opposition in debate—just then, however, he was pointing out that those who were styled rhetoricians and propounded rules of eloquence, had no clear comprehension of anything, and that no man could attain skill in speaking unless he had studied the discoveries of the philosophers.

85 "Certain Athenians, accomplished speakers and experienced in politics and at the Bar, argued on the other side, among them too being that Menedemus, who was lately in Rome as my guest; and when he asserted that there was a special sort of wisdom, which had to do with investigating the principles of founding and governing political communities, this roused up a man of quick temper and full to overflowing of learning of every kind and a really incredible diversity and multiplicity of facts. For he proceeded to inform us that every part of this same wisdom had to be sought from philosophy, nor were those institutions in a State which dealt with the immortal gods, the training of youth, justice, endurance, self-control, or moderation in all things, or the other principles without which States could not exist or at any rate be well-conditioned, to
86 be met with anywhere in the paltry treatises of rhetoricians. Whereas, if those teachers of rhetoric embraced within their art so vast a multitude of the noblest themes, how was it, he inquired, that their books were stuffed full of maxims relating to prefaces, perorations and similar trumpery—for so did he describe them—while concerning the organization of States, or the drafting of laws, or on the topics of fair-dealing, justice, loyalty, or the subduing of the passions or the
87 building of human character, not a syllable was to be found in their pages? But as for their actual rules he would scoff at them by showing that not only were their authors devoid of that wisdom which they arrogated to themselves, but they were ignorant even of the true principles and methods of eloquence. For he was of opinion that the main object of the orator was that he should both appear himself, to those before whom he was pleading, to be such a man as he would desire to seem (an end to be attained by a reputable mode of life, as to which those teachers of rhetoric had left no hint among their instructions), and that

the hearts of his hearers should be touched in such fashion as the orator would have them touched (another purpose only to be achieved by a speaker who had investigated all the ways wherein, and all the allurements and kind of diction whereby, the judgement of men might be inclined to this side or to that); but according to him such knowledge lay thrust away and buried deep in the very heart of philosophy, and those rhetoricians had not so much as tasted it with the tip of the tongue. These assertions Menedemus would strive to disprove by quoting instances rather than by arguments, for, while reciting from his ready recollection many magnificent passages from the speeches of Demosthenes, he would demonstrate how that orator, when by his eloquence he was compelling the passions of the judges or of the people to take any direction he chose, knew well enough by what means to attain results which Charmadas would say that no one could compass without the aid of philosophy.

"To this Charmadas replied that he did not deny to Demosthenes the possession of consummate wisdom and the highest power of eloquence, but whether Demosthenes owed this ability to natural talent or, as was generally agreed, had been a devoted disciple of Plato, the present question was not what Demosthenes could do, but what those rhetoricians were teaching. More than once too he was carried so far away by his discourse as to argue that there was no such thing as an art of eloquence; and after showing this by arguments—because, as he said, we were born with an aptitude alike for coaxing and unctuously stealing into favour with those from whom a boon had to be sought, and for daunting our antagonists by threats, for setting forth how a deed was done, and establishing our own charges and disproving the allegations of the other side, and for making, in the closing words of a speech, some use of protest and lamentation (in which operations he declared that every resource of the orator was brought into play), and because habit and practice sharpened the edge of discernment and quickened the fluency of delivery, then he would also support his case by an abundance of instances. For in the first place (he would say) not a single writer on rhetoric—it looked as if of set purpose—had been even moderately eloquent, and he searched all the way back to the days of one Corax and a certain Tisias who, he stated, were acknowledged to have been the founders and first practitioners of this art, while on the other hand he would cite a countless host of very eloquent men who had never learned these rules or been at all anxious to make their acquaintance; and among these—whether in jest or because he thought so and had even so heard—he went on to mention me in the list, as one who had never studied those matters and yet (according to him) had some ability in oratory. To one of these points of his—that I had never learned anything—I readily agreed, but as to the other I considered that he was either making game of me or was even himself mistaken. He said, however, that there was no 'art' which did not consist in the knowledge and clear perception of facts, all tending to a single conclusion and incapable of misleading; but everything with which orators dealt was doubtful and uncertain, since all the talking was done by men who had no real grasp of their subject, and all the listening by hearers who were not to have knowledge conveyed to them, but some short-lived opinion that was either untrue or at least not clear. In a word, he then looked like persuading me that no craft of oratory existed, and that no one could speak with address or copiously unless he had mastered the philosophical teachings of the most learned men. And in these discussions Charmadas was wont to speak with warm admiration of your talents, Crassus, explaining that he found in me a very ready listener, in yourself a most doughty antagonist.

94 "And so, won over by these same views, I actually wrote down in a little pamphlet—which slipped abroad without my knowledge or consent and got into the hands of the public—the statement that I had known sundry accomplished speakers, but no one so far who was eloquent, inasmuch as I held anyone to be an accomplished speaker who could deliver his thought with the necessary point and clearness before an everyday audience, and in accord with what I might call the mental outlook of the average human being, whereas I allowed the possession of eloquence to that man only who was able, in a style more admirable and more splendid, to amplify and adorn any subject he chose, and whose mind and memory encompassed all the sources of everything that concerned oratory. If this is a hard matter for ourselves, because, before we have entered on the required study, we are overwhelmed by the hunt for office and the business of the Bar, none the less let it be accepted as attainable in fact and 95 in the nature of things. For personally, so far as I can form a prediction, and judging from the vast supply of talent which I see existent among our fellow-citizens, I do not despair of its coming to pass that some day some one, keener in study than we are or ever have been, endowed with ampler leisure and earlier opportunity for learning, and exhibiting closer application and more intensive industry, who shall have given himself up to listening, reading and writing, will stand forth as an orator such as we are seeking, who may rightly be called not merely accomplished but actually eloquent; and after all, to my mind either Crassus is such a man already, or, should some one of equal natural ability have heard, read and written more than Crassus, he will only be able to improve to some slight extent upon him."

96 At this point, "We never looked for it," exclaimed Sulpicius, "but it has fallen out, Crassus, just as both I and Cotta earnestly hoped, I mean that you two should slip into this particular conversation. For on our way hither we were thinking that it would be delightful enough if, while you and Antonius were talking about anything else, we might still manage to catch from your discourse something worth remembering; but that you should enter at large upon so real and wellnigh exhaustive a discussion of this whole matter—be it practice, art or 97 natural talent—seemed to us a thing we could hardly hope for. The fact is that I, who from my earliest manhood was aglow with enthusiasm for you both, and a positive devotion to Crassus—seeing that on no occasion did I leave his side—could never get a word out of him respecting the nature and theory of eloquence, although I pleaded in person, besides making frequent trial of him through the agency of Drusus, whereas on this subject you, Antonius,—and what I shall say is true—have never failed me at all in my probings or interrogatories, and have many a time explained to me what rules you were 98 wont to observe in practical oratory. Now then that each of you has opened up a way of reaching these very objects of our quest, and since it was Crassus who

led off in this discussion, grant us the favour of recounting with exactness of detail, your respective opinions upon every branch of oratory. If we do win this boon from you both, I shall be deeply grateful, Crassus, to this school in your Tusculan villa, and shall rank these semi-rural training-quarters of yours far above the illustrious Academy and the Lyceum."

Thereupon the other rejoined, "Nay, Sulpicius, but let us rather ask Antonius, who both has the ability to do what you demand, and, as I understand you to say, has been in the habit of so doing. For as for me, you yourself have just told us how I have invariably run away from all discussions of this sort, and time and again have refused compliance with your desire and indeed your importunity. This I used to do, not from arrogance or churlishness, nor because I was unwilling to gratify your entirely legitimate and admirable keenness—the more so as I had recognized that you were above all other men eminently endowed by nature and adapted for oratory—but in solemn truth it was from want of familiarity with arguments of that kind, and awkwardness in handling those theories set forth in what claims to be an art." *99*

Cotta then observed, "Since we have secured what seemed most difficult— that you, Crassus, should say anything at all about these matters—as for what remains, it will now be our own fault if we let you go without explaining to us all that we have been inquiring about." "Limiting the inquiry, I imagine," answered Crassus, "to those subjects which, as the phrase goes in accepting an inheritance, are within my knowledge and power." "By all means," returned Cotta, "for what is beyond your own power or knowledge, who among us is so shameless as to claim to be within his own?" "In that case," replied Crassus, "provided that I may disclaim powers which I do not possess, and admit ignorance of what I do not know,—put what questions to me you please." "Well then," said Sulpicius, "what we ask you to tell us first is your opinion of the view Antonius advanced just now—whether you hold that there is any such thing as an 'art' of oratory?" "How now?" exclaimed Crassus, "Do you think I am some idle talkative Greekling, who is also perhaps full of learning and erudition, that you propound me a petty question on which to talk as I will? For when was it, think you, that I troubled myself about these matters or reflected upon them, and did not rather always laugh to scorn the effrontery of those persons who, from their chairs in the schools, would call upon any man in the crowded assemblage to propound any question that he might have to put? It is related that Gorgias of Leontini was the author of this practice, who was thought to be undertaking and professing something very magnificent when he advertised himself as ready for any topic whatever on which anyone might have a fancy to hear him. Later, however, they began to do this everywhere, and are doing it to this day, with the result of there being no theme so vast, so unforeseen, or so novel, that they do not claim to be prepared to say about it all that there is to be said. But had I supposed that you, Cotta, or you, Sulpicius, wished to listen to anything of the kind, I would have brought some Greek or other here to amuse you with discussions of that sort; and even now this can easily be managed. For staying with Marcus Piso (a young man, but already given up to this pursuit, possessing talent of the highest order and deeply devoted to myself) there is *100 101 102 103 104*

Staseas the Peripatetic, a man whom I know well enough, and who, as I understand to be agreed among experts, is quite supreme in that department of his."

105 "Staseas! what Staseas? what Peripatetic are you talking to me about?" said Mucius. "It is for you, Crassus, to comply with the wishes of young men, who do not want the everyday chatter of some unpractised Greek, or old sing-songs out of the schools, but something from the wisest and most eloquent man in the world, and one who, not in the pages of pamphlets, but in the most momentous causes, and that too in this seat of imperial power and splendour, holds the first place for judgment and eloquence; they are anxious to learn the opinion of the *106* man whose footsteps they long to follow. Moreover, just as I have always accounted you the ideal orator, even so I have never ascribed to you higher praise for eloquence than for kindliness, which quality it becomes you on the present occasion to exercise to the very utmost, and not to run away from the discussion into which two young men of eminent ability are desirous of your entering."

107 "For my part," answered the other, "I am anxious to humour your friends, and I shall make no difficulty about saying, in my brief fashion, what I think upon each point. And to that first question—since I do not think it dutiful, Scaevola, for me to disregard your claims—I answer, 'I think there is either no art of speaking at all or a very thin one,' all the quarrelling in learned circles *108* being really based upon a dispute about a word. For if, as Antonius just now explained, an art is defined as consisting in things thoroughly examined and clearly apprehended, and which are also outside the control of mere opinion, and within the grasp of exact knowledge, then to me there seems to be no such thing as an art of oratory. For all the kinds of language we ourselves use in public speaking are changeable matter, and adapted to the general understand-*109* ing of the crowd. If however the actual things noticed in the practice and conduct of speaking have been heeded and recorded by men of skill and experience, if they have been defined in terms, illuminated by classification, and distributed under subdivisions—and I see that it has been possible to do this—I do not understand why this should not be regarded as an art, perhaps not in that precise sense of the term, but at any rate according to the other and popular estimate. But whether this be an art, or only something like an art, assuredly it is not to be disdained. . . ."

FROM

Book II

On Ethical and Emotional Proofs

182 "A potent factor in success, then," ⟨said Antonius⟩ "is for the characters, principles, conduct and course of life, both of those who are to plead cases and of their clients, to be approved, and conversely those of their opponents condemned; and for the feelings of the tribunal to be won over, as far as possible, to goodwill towards the advocate and the advocate's client as well. Now feelings are won over by a man's merit, achievements or reputable life, qualifications easier to embellish, if only they are real, than to fabricate where nonexistent. But attributes useful in an advocate are a mild tone, a countenance expressive of modesty, gentle language, and the faculty of seeming to be dealing reluctantly and under compulsion with something you are really anxious to prove. It is very helpful to display the tokens of good-nature, kindness, calmness, loyalty and a disposition that is pleasing and not grasping or covetous, and all the qualities belonging to men who are upright, unassuming and not given to haste, stubbornness, strife or harshness, are powerful in winning goodwill, while the want of them estranges it from such as do not possess them; accordingly the very opposites of these qualities must be ascribed to our opponents. But all this *183* kind of advocacy will be best in those cases wherein the arbitrator's feelings are not likely to be kindled by what I may call the ardent and impassioned onset. For vigorous language is not always wanted, but often such as is calm, gentle, mild: this is the kind that most commends the parties. By 'parties' I mean not only persons impeached, but all whose interests are being determined, for that was how people used the term in the old days. And so to paint their characters in *184* words, as being upright, stainless, conscientious, modest and long-suffering under injustice, has a really wonderful effect; and this topic, whether in opening, or in stating the case, or in winding-up, is so compelling, when agreeably and feelingly handled, as often to be worth more than the merits of the case. Moreover so much is done by good taste and style in speaking, that the speech seems to depict the speaker's character. For by means of particular types of thought and diction, and the employment besides of a delivery that is unruffled and eloquent of good-nature, the speakers are made to appear upright, well-bred and virtuous men.

"But closely associated with this is that dissimilar style of speaking which, *185* in quite another way, excites and urges the feelings of the tribunal towards hatred or love, ill-will or well-wishing, fear or hope, desire or aversion, joy or sorrow, compassion or the wish to punish, or by it they are prompted to whatever emotions are nearly allied and similar to these passions of the soul, and to such as these.

"Another desirable thing for the advocate is that the members of the tribunal, of their own accord, should carry within them to Court some mental emotion that is in harmony with what the advocate's interest will suggest. For, *186* as the saying goes, it is easier to spur the willing horse than to start the lazy one. But if no such emotion be present, or recognizable, he will be like a careful physician who, before he attempts to administer a remedy to his patient, must investigate not only the malady of the man he wishes to cure, but also his habits when in health, and his physical constitution.

"This indeed is the reason why, when setting about a hazardous and important case, in order to explore the feelings of the tribunal, I engage wholeheartedly in a consideration so careful, that I scent out with all possible keenness their thoughts, judgements, anticipations and wishes, and the direction in which they seem likely to be led away most easily by eloquence. If they *187* surrender to me, and as I said before, of their own accord lean towards and are prone to take the course in which I am urging them on, I accept their bounty and set sail for the quarter which promises something of a breeze. If however an arbitrator is neutral and free from predisposition, my task is harder, since everything has to be called forth by my speech, with no help from the listener's character. But so potent is that Eloquence, rightly styled, by an excellent poet, 'soulbending sovereign of all things,' that she can not only support the sinking and bend the upstanding, but, like a good and brave commander, can even make prisoner a resisting antagonist.

188 "These are the details for which Crassus was playfully importuning me just now, when he said that I always handled them ideally, and he praised what he called the brilliant treatment of them in the cases of Manius Aquilius, Gaius Norbanus and sundry others. Now I give you my word, Crassus, that I always tremble when these things are handled by yourself in Court: such is the mental power, such the passion, so profound the indignation, ever manifest in your glance, features, gesture, even in that wagging finger of yours; so mighty is the flow of your most impressive and happy diction, so sound, true and original your sentiments, and so innocent of colouring-matter or paltry dye, that to me you seem to be not merely inflaming the arbitrator, but actually on fire yourself.

189 "Moreover it is impossible for the listener to feel indignation, hatred or ill-will, to be terrified of anything, or reduced to tears of compassion, unless all those emotions, which the advocate would inspire in the arbitrator, are visibly stamped or rather branded on the advocate himself. Now if some feigned indignation had to be depicted, and that same kind of oratory afforded only what was counterfeit and produced by mimicry, some loftier art would perhaps be called for. As things stand, Crassus, I do not know how it may be with yourself or the rest, but in my own case there is no reason why I should lie to men of consummate experience, who are also my best friends: I give you my word that I never tried, by means of a speech, to arouse either indignation or compassion, either ill-will or hatred, in the minds of a tribunal, without being really stirred myself, as I worked upon their minds, by the very feelings to which I was 190 seeking to prompt them. For it is not easy to succeed in making an arbitrator angry with the right party, if you yourself seem to treat the affair with indifference; or in making him hate the right party, unless he first sees you on fire with hatred yourself; nor will he be prompted to compassion, unless you have shown him the tokens of your own grief by word, sentiment, tone of voice, look and even by loud lamentation. For just as there is no substance so ready to take fire, as to be capable of generating flame without the application of a spark, so also there is no mind so ready to absorb an orator's influence, as to be inflammable when the assailing speaker is not himself aglow with passion.

191 "Again, lest haply it should seem a mighty miracle, for a man so often to be roused to wrath, indignation and every inward emotion—and that too about other people's business—the power of those reflections and commonplaces, discussed and handled in a speech, is great enough to dispense with all make-believe and trickery: for the very quality of the diction, employed to stir the feelings of others, stirs the speaker himself even more deeply than any of his

hearers. And, not to have us astonished at this happening in litigation, or before arbitrators, or in the impeachments of our friends, or among a crowd of people, or in political life, or public debate, when not only our talent is under criticism (no great matter, though even this should not be overlooked, when you have claimed a proficiency attained by few), but other and far more important attributes are on trial, I mean our loyalty, sense of duty and carefulness, under whose influence, even when defending complete strangers, we still cannot regard them as strangers, if we would be accounted good men ourselves. However, as I said, not to have this seem a marvel among us, what can be so unreal as poetry, the theatre or stage-plays? And yet, in that sort of things, I myself have often been a spectator when the actor-man's eyes seemed to me to be blazing behind his mask, as he spoke those solemn lines,

> Darest thou part from my brother, or Salamis enter without him,
> Dreading the mien of thy sire not at all?

Never did he utter that word 'mien,' without my beholding an infuriated Telamon maddened by grief for his son. Whenever too he lowered his voice to a plaintive tone, in the passage,

> Aged and childless,
> Didst tear and bereave and didst quench me, forgetting the death of
>   thy brother,
> Forgetting his tiny son, though entrusted to thee as a guardian?

I thought I heard sobs of mourning in his voice. Now if that player, though acting it daily, could never act that scene without emotion, do you really think that Pacuvius, when he wrote it, was in a calm and careless frame of mind? That could never be. For I have often heard that—as they say Democritus and Plato have left on record—no man can be a good poet who is not on fire with passion, and inspired by something very like frenzy.

"Do not suppose then that I myself, though not concerned to portray and reproduce in language the bygone misfortunes and legendary griefs of heroes, and though presenting my own personality and not representing another's, did without profound emotion the things I did when closing that famous case, in which my task was to maintain Manius Aquilius in his civic rights. For here was a man whom I remembered as having been consul, commander-in-chief, honoured by the Senate, and mounting in procession to the Capitol; on seeing him cast down, crippled, sorrowing and brought to the risk of all he held dear, I was myself overcome by compassion before I tried to excite it in others. Assuredly I felt that the Court was deeply affected when I called forward my unhappy old client, in his garb of woe, and when I did those things approved by yourself, Crassus—not by way of technique, as to which I know not what to say, but under stress of deep emotion and indignation—I mean my tearing open his tunic and exposing his scars. While Gaius Marius, from his seat in court, was strongly reinforcing, by his weeping, the pathos of my appeal, and I, repeatedly naming him, was committing his colleague to his care, and calling upon him to speak himself in support of the common interests of commanders-in-chief, all this lamentation, as well as my invocation of every god and man, every citizen and ally, was accompanied by tears and vast indignation on my own part; had my personal indignation been missing from all the talking I did on that occasion, my address, so far from inspiring compassion, would positively have deserved ridicule. And so I am telling you this, Sulpicius, as naturally such a kindly and accomplished teacher would do, in order to help you to be wrathful, indignant and tearful in your speech-making.

197 "But why indeed should I teach this to you, who, in prosecuting my comrade and quaestor, had kindled such a blaze, not by eloquence only, but far more by vehemence, indignation and fiery enthusiasm, that I hardly ventured to draw near and put it out? For all the advantages in that case had been yours: you were citing to the Court the violence, the flight, the stone-throwing and the tribunes' ruthlessness that marked the disastrous and lamentable affair of Caepio; then too it was established that Marcus Aemilius, chief of Senate and chief of State, had been struck by a stone, while it was undeniable that Lucius Cotta and Titus Didius, on trying to veto a resolution, had been forcibly driven from sanctuary.

198 "In the result, while you, only a stripling, were thought to be conducting this public prosecution with consummate distinction, I, a past censor, was thought to be acting not quite honourably in bearing to defend a factious citizen, who moreover had been merciless to a past consul in distress. Citizens of the best repute formed the tribunal; men of respectability crowded the Court; so that I had difficulty in winning a grudging sort of acceptance of my plea that at any rate my client was my old quaestor. In these circumstances how can I say I used any particular technique? What I did I will relate, if you think fit, you will give my line of defence some place or other in your system.

199 "I classified all the types of civil discord, their weaknesses and dangers, and that part of my speech I derived from all the vicissitudes in the history of our own community, winding up with the assertion that civil discords, though always troublesome, had yet sometimes been justifiable and well-nigh unavoidable. Next I discussed the considerations lately recalled by Crassus; how that neither the expulsion of kings from this State, nor the establishment of tribunes of the commons, nor the frequent restriction of the consuls' power by decrees of the commons, nor the bestowal upon the Roman People of the right of appeal, that famous buttress of the State and defence of freedom, could any of them have been effected without aristocratic opposition; and that, if those particular civil discords had been beneficial to our community, the mere fact of a popular movement having been caused must not instantly be counted against Gaius Norbanus for heinous wickedness and indeed a capital offence. That if rightfulness had ever been conceded to an incitement of the Roman People to sedition,—a concession which I was showing to have been frequent—, there had never been a juster cause than this one. After that I altered my course and turned my entire speech into a denunciation of the running-away of Caepio and a lament for the destruction of his army: in this way, besides chafing anew by my words the sores of people mourning for their own folk, I was kindling the feelings of the Roman Knights, who constituted the Court I was addressing, into fresh hatred of Quintus Caepio, from whom they had been estranged already over the composition of the criminal Courts.

"But when I felt I had a firm hold on the Court and on my line of defence, and I had won the goodwill of the public, whose claims I had upheld even when involved with civil discord, and I had turned all hearts on the tribunal in favour of my cause, by reason either of the national disaster, or of yearning grief for kindred, or of private hatred of Caepio, then I began to blend with this impetuous and violent type of oratory that other mild and gentle type, which I have already discussed, pleading that I was fighting for my comrade, who by ancestral tradition should stand in a filial relation to myself, and also (I might say) for my own fair fame and general welfare; no happening could more deeply disgrace my reputation, or cause me more bitter sorrow, than for it to be thought that I, so often the saviour of complete strangers to myself, provided only they were my fellow-citizens, had been unable to aid my own comrade. I begged the Court, should they see me affected by justifiable and loyal grief, to excuse this in consideration of my years, official career and achievements, particularly if, in the course of other trials, they had observed that I always made my petitions on behalf of friends in jeopardy, never for myself. Thus all through that speech for the defence, and indeed the trial itself, it was in the fewest possible words that I glanced over and lightly touched the matters which seemed dependent upon scientific treatment, I mean my discussion of the Statute of Appuleius, and my exposition of the nature of treason. By means of these two modes of speech, the one inflammatory, the other eulogistic, and neither of them much elaborated by rules of art, I so managed the whole of that case as to seem most passionate when reviving hatred of Caepio, and mildest when describing my conduct towards my own connexions. So, Sulpicius, it was rather by working upon, than by informing, the minds of the tribunal, that I beat your prosecution on that occasion."

Here Sulpicius observed, "Upon my word, Antonius, your account of those matters is true, for never did I see anything slip through the fingers in the way that verdict slipped that day through mine. For when (as you told us) I had left you with a conflagration rather than a case to dispose of,—ye Gods!—what an opening you made! How nervous, how irresolute you seemed! How stammering and halting was your delivery! How you clung at the outset to the solitary excuse everyone was making for you—that you were defending your own familiar friend and quaestor! So, in the first place, did you prepare the way towards getting a hearing! Then, just as I was deciding that you had merely succeeded in making people think intimate relationship a possible excuse for your defending a wicked citizen,—lo and behold!—so far unsuspected by other people, but already to my own serious alarm, you began to wriggle imperceptibly into your famous defence, of no factious Norbanus, but of an incensed Roman People, whose wrath, you urged, was not wrongful, but just and well-deserved. After that what point against Caepio did you miss? How you leavened every word with hatred, malice and pathos! And all this not only in your speech for the defence, but also in your handling of Scaurus and the rest of my witnesses, whose evidence you rebutted by no disproof, but by fleeing for refuge to that same

204 national outbreak. When just now you were reminding us of these things, I certainly felt no need of any maxims, for that actual reproduction, in your own words, of your methods of defence is to my mind the most instructive of teaching."

"For all that," answered Antonius, "we will, if you please, go on to set forth the principles we generally adopt in speaking, and the points we chiefly keep in view: for a long career and experience in the most weighty affairs have taught us, by this time, to hold fast to the ways of stirring the feelings of mankind.

205 "My own practice is to begin by reflecting whether the case calls for such treatment; for these rhetorical fireworks should not be used in petty matters, or with men of such temper that our eloquence can achieve nothing in the way of influencing their minds, unless we would be deemed fit objects of ridicule, or even of disgust, as indulging in heroics over trifles, or setting out to uproot the 206 immovable. Now, since the emotions which eloquence has to excite in the minds of the tribunal, or whatever other audience we may be addressing, are most commonly love, hate, wrath, jealousy, compassion, hope, joy, fear or vexation, we observe that love is won if you are thought to be upholding the interests of your audience, or to be working for good men, or at any rate for such as that audience deems good and useful. For this last impression more readily wins love, and the protection of the righteous esteem; and the holding-out of a 207 hope of advantage to come is more effective than the recital of past benefit. You must struggle to reveal the presence, in the cause you are upholding, of some merit or usefulness, and to make it plain that the man, for whom you are to win this love, in no respect consulted his own interests and did nothing at all from personal motives. For men's private gains breed jealousy, while their zeal for others' service is applauded.

208 "And here we must be watchful, not to seem to extol unduly the merits and renown—jealousy's favourite target—of those whom we would have beloved for their good works. Then too, from these same commonplaces, we shall learn as well to instigate hatred of others as to turn it away from ourselves and our clients: and these same general heads are to be employed in kindling and also in assuaging wrath. For, if you glorify the doing of something ruinous or unprofitable to your particular audience, hate is engendered: while, if it be something done against good men in general, or those to whom the particular doer should never have done it, or against the State, no such bitter hate is excited, but a 209 disgust closely resembling ill-will or hate. Fear again is struck from either the perils of individuals or those shared by all: that of private origin goes deeper, but universal fear also is to be traced to a similar source.

"The treatment of hope, joy and vexation is similar to this, and identical in each case, but I rather think that the emotion of jealousy is by far the fiercest of all, and needs as much energy for its repression as for its stimulation. Now people are especially jealous of their equals, or of those once beneath them, when they feel themselves left behind and fret at the others' upward flight; but jealousy of their betters also is often furious, and all the more so if these conduct themselves insufferably, and overstep their rightful claims on the strength of pre-eminent rank or prosperity; if these advantages are to be made fuel for jealousy, it should before all be pointed out that they were not the fruit of merit;

next that they even came by vice and wrongdoing, finally that the man's desserts, though creditable and impressive enough, are still exceeded by his arrogance and disdain. To quench jealousy, on the other hand, it is proper to emphasize the points that those advantages were the fruit of great exertion and great risks, and were not turned to his own profit but to that of other people; and that, as for any renown he himself may seem to have won, though no unfair recompense for his risk, he nevertheless finds no pleasure therein, but casts it aside and disclaims it altogether: and we must by all means make sure (since most people are jealous, and this failing is remarkably general and widespread, while jealousy is attracted by surpassingly brilliant prosperity) that the belief in such prosperity shall be weakened, and that what was supposed to be outstanding prosperity shall be seen to be thoroughly blended with labour and sorrow. Lastly compassion is awakened if the hearer can be brought to apply to his own adversities, whether endured or only apprehended, the lamentations uttered over someone else, or if, in his contemplation of another's case, he many a time goes back to his own experience. Thus, while particular occasions of human distress are deeply felt, if described in moving terms, the dejection and ruin of the righteous are especially lamentable. And, just as that other kind of style, which by bearing witness to the speaker's integrity is to preserve the semblance of a man of worth, should be mild and gentle (as I have repeatedly said already), so this kind, assumed by the speaker in order to transform men's feelings or influence them in any desired way, should be spirited and emotional.

"But these two styles, which we require to be respectively mild and emotional, have something in common, making them hard to keep apart. For from that mildness, which wins us the goodwill of our hearers, some inflow must reach this fiercest of passions, wherewith we inflame the same people, and again, out of this passion some little energy must often be kindled within that mildness: nor is any style better blended than that wherein the harshness of strife is tempered by the personal urbanity of the advocate, while his easy-going mildness is fortified by some admixture of serious strife.

"Now in both styles of speaking, the one demanding passion and strife, and the other adapted to recommendation of the speaker's life and manners, the opening of a speech is unhurried, and none the less its closing should also be lingering and long drawnout. For you must not bound all of a sudden into that emotional style, since it is wholly alien to the merits of the case, and people long to hear first just what is peculiarly within their own cognizance, while, once you have assumed that style, you must not be in a hurry to change it. For you could not awaken compassion, jealousy or wrath at the very instant of your onset, in the way that a proof is seized upon as soon as propounded, and a second and third called for. This is because the hearer's mentality corroborates the proof, and no sooner is it uttered than it is sticking in his memory, whereas that passionate style searches out an arbitrator's emotional side rather than his understanding, and that side can only be reached by diction that is rich, diversified and copious, with animated delivery to match. Thus concise or quiet speakers may inform an arbitrator, but cannot excite him, on which excitement everything depends.

"By this time it is plain that the power to argue both sides of every question is abundantly furnished from the same commonplaces. But your opponents' proof must be countered, either by contradicting the arguments chosen to establish it, or by showing that their desired conclusion is not supported by their premisses and does not follow therefrom; or, if you do not so rebut it, you must adduce on the opposite side some proof of greater or equal cogency. Lastly appeals, whether mild or passionate, and whether for winning favour or stirring the feelings, must be swept aside by exciting the opposite impressions, so that goodwill may be done away with by hate, and compassion by jealousy...."

On Wit

"And so, Caesar, I too beg you, if you think proper, to discus fully this type of jesting, and to state your views, lest haply one branch of oratory should be thought to have been passed over, with your approval, in such company as this, and in a conversation so carefully elaborated." "Assuredly, Crassus," replied Caesar, "seeing that you are collecting a boon companion's 'shot,' I will not run away and so give you any occasion for complaint...."

"As regards laughter there are five matters for consideration: first its nature; second, its source; third, whether willingness to produce it becomes an orator; fourth, the limits of his licence; fifth, the classification of things laughable.

"Now the first of these topics, the essential nature of laughter, the way it is occasioned, where it is seated, and how it comes into being, and bursts out so unexpectedly that, strive as we may, we cannot restrain it, and how at the same instant it takes possession of the lungs, voice, pulse, countenance and eyes,—all this I leave to Democritus: for it does not concern the present conversation, and, even if it did, I should still not be ashamed to show ignorance of something which even its professed expositors do not understand.

"Then the field or province, so to speak, of the laughable (this being our next problem), is restricted to that which may be described as unseemly or ugly; for the chief, if not the only, objects of laughter are those sayings which remark upon and point out something unseemly in no unseemly manner.

"And again, to come to our third topic, it clearly becomes an orator to raise laughter, and this on various grounds; for instance, merriment naturally wins goodwill for its author; and everyone admires acuteness, which is often concentrated in a single word, uttered generally in repelling, though sometimes in delivering an attack; and it shatters or obstructs or makes light of an opponent, or alarms or repulses him; and it shows the orator himself to be a man of finish, accomplishment and taste; and, best of all, it relieves dullness and tones down austerity, and, by a jest or a laugh, often dispels distasteful suggestions not easily weakened by reasonings.

"But the limits within which things laughable are to be handled by the orator, that fourth question we put to ourselves, is one calling for most careful consideration. For neither outstanding wickedness, such as involves crime, nor, on the other hand, outstanding wretchedness is assailed by ridicule, for the public would have the villainous hurt by a weapon rather more formidable than ridicule; while they dislike mockery of the wretched, except perhaps if these bear themselves arrogantly. And you must be especially tender of popular esteem, so that you do not inconsiderately speak ill of the well-beloved.

"Such then is the restraint that, above all else, must be practised in jesting. Thus the things most easily ridiculed are those which call for neither strong disgust nor the deepest sympathy. This is why all laughing-matters are found among those blemishes noticeable in the conduct of people who are neither objects of general esteem nor yet full of misery, and not apparently merely fit to be hurried off to execution for their crimes; and these blemishes, if deftly handled, raise laughter. In ugliness too and in physical blemishes there is good enough matter for jesting, but there as elsewhere the limits of licence are the main question. As to this, not only is there a rule excluding remarks made in bad taste, but also, even though you could say something with highly comical effect, an orator must avoid each of two dangers: he must not let his jesting become buffoonery or mere mimicking. We shall more readily understand examples of each kind when we come to the actual classification of things laughable.

"For there are two types of wit, one employed upon facts, the other upon words. Upon facts, whenever any tale is told, some anecdote for instance, just as you, Crassus, alleged one day, in a speech against Memmius, that Memmius 'had made a mouthful of Largus's arm,' when brawling with him at Tarracina over a lady-love; it was a spicy story, but every word of your own fabrication. You wound up by relating that the letters M.M.L.L.L. were inscribed on every wall in Tarracina, and that some ancient inhabitant answered, when you asked what they meant, 'Mordacious Memmius lacerates Largus's limb.' You see plainly how graceful, choice and well befitting an orator is a jest of this sort, whether you have some truth you can relate,—which for all that may be sprinkled with fibs,—or whether you are only fabricating. Now the beauty of such jesting is, that you state your incidents in such a way, that the character, the manner of speaking and all the facial expressions of the hero of your tale, are so presented that those incidents seem to your audience to take place and to be transacted concurrently with your description of them. Another sort of jest depending on facts, is that which is generally derived from what may be called vulgarized mimicry, as when on another occasion, Crassus was adjuring an adversary in the words, 'By your rank, by your lineage!' What else had the assembly to laugh at in this than that mimicry of facial expression and intonation? But when he went on to say, 'By your statuary,' and lent a touch of action to the word by stretching out his arm, we laughed quite consumedly. To this class belongs Roscius's famous representation of an old man, when he quavers out, 'For you, son Antipho, I'm planting these.' I think I am listening to testy Eld personified. However this particular kind of laughing-matter is all such as to need extreme circumspection in the handling of it. For if the caricature is too extravagant, it becomes the work of buffoons in pantomime, as also does grossness. It behoves the orator to borrow merely a suspicion of mimicry, so that his hearer may imagine more than meets his eye; he must also testify to his own well-bred modesty, by avoiding all unseemly language and offensive gestures.

"These then are the two kinds of the jesting that is founded on facts; and they are appropriate to continuous irony, wherein the characters of individuals are sketched and so portrayed, that either through the relation of some anecdote their real natures are understood, or, by the infusion of a trifle of mimicry, they are found out in some fault sufficiently marked to be laughed at.

244 "As regards words, however, the laughter is awakened by something pointed in a phrase or reflection. But just as, with the former kind, both in narrative and in mimicry, all likeness to buffoons in pantomime is to be avoided, so in this latter case the orator must scrupulously shun all buffoonish raillery. How then shall we distinguish from Crassus, from Catulus, and from the others, your familiar acquaintance Granius, or my own friend Vargula? Upon my word, I have never considered this matter, for all of them are witty, none indeed more so than Granius. The first point to make, I think, is that we should not feel
245 bound to utter a witticism every time an occasion offers. A very small witness once came forward. 'May I examine him?' said Philippus. The president of the Court, who was in a hurry, answered, 'Only if you are short.' 'You will not complain,' returned Philippus, 'for I shall be just as short as that man is.' Quite comical; but there on the tribunal sat Lucius Aurifex, and he was even tinier than the witness: all the laughter was directed against Lucius, and the joke seemed merely buffoonish. And so those shafts which may light upon unintended victims, however featly they may be winged, are none the less essentially those of a buffoon. . . .

247 "Regard then to occasions, control and restraint of our actual raillery, and economy in bon-mots, will distinguish an orator from a buffoon, as also will the fact that we people speak with good reason, not just to be thought funny, but to gain some benefit, while those others are jesting from morning to night, and without any reason at all. Thus, when Aulus Sempronius was on canvassing bent, along with Marcus his brother, and embraced Vargula, what good did it do Vargula to shout 'Boy, drive away these buzzers?' His object was to get a laugh—to my mind the very poorest return for cleverness. The right occasion therefore for speaking out we shall fix by our own wisdom and discretion: would that we had some theory of the use of these qualities! though intuition is the sovereign directress.

248 "Now let us summarize the essential natures of the chief sources of laughter. Let our first distinction, then, be this, that a witty saying has its point sometimes in facts, sometimes in words, though people are most particularly amused whenever laughter is excited by the union of the two. But remember this, that whatever subjects I may touch upon, as being sources of laughing-matters, may equally well, as a rule, be sources of serious thoughts. The only difference is that seriousness is bestowed austerely and upon things of good repute, jesting upon what is a trifle unseemly, or, so to speak, uncouth; for example, we can, in identical terms, praise a careful servant, and make fun of one who is good-for-nothing. There is humour in that old remark of Nero's about a thievish servant, 'that he was the only member of the household against whom nothing was sealed up or locked away,' a description frequently applied to a
249 trusty servant also, and that too word for word. In fact all kinds of remarks are derived from identical sources. For his mother's words to Spurius Carvilius, who

was sadly lame from a wound received on national service, and for that reason shy of walking abroad, 'No no, my Spurius, go out! and let every step you take remind you of your gallantry,' are noble and dignified. But what Glaucia said to Calvinus, who was limping, 'Where is that old saying—Can he be hobbling? Nay, but he is wobbling,' is merely absurd. Yet both observations were derived from what the contemplation of lameness might suggest. Scipio's pun, 'Is there an idler knave than this Naevius?,' was intended for austerity. But there was a spark of humour in the remark of Philippus to a malodorous individual, 'I perceive that you are stinking me out.' Yet both kinds of pun lie in the verbal echo that survives the change in a letter.

"Bons-mots prompted by an equivocation are deemed the very wittiest, though not always concerned with jesting, but often even with what is important. What Publius Licinius Varus said to the great Africanus the elder, when he was adjusting a garland to his head at a banquet, and it tore again and again, was praiseworthy and creditable: 'Don't be astonished,' said he, 'if it does not fit, for it is on a Head of vast capacity.' Yet from the same category comes, 'He is bald enough, seeing that he is bald in diction.' So, to bore you no further, there is no source of laughing-matters from which austere and serious thoughts are not also to be derived.

"There is also this to be noted, that all is not witty that is laughable. For can there be anything so droll as a pantaloon? Yet it is for his face, his grimaces, his mimicry of mannerisms, his intonation, and in fact his general bearing, that he is laughed at. Humorous I am able to call him, but humorous for a low comedian, and not in the sense in which I would have an orator humorous.

"Accordingly this kind of wit, though raising as much laughter as any, is not at all our kind: it caricatures peevishness, fanaticism, mistrust, pomposity and folly, characters which are laughed at for their own sakes, masks which we do not put on, but attack. Another kind, quite comical, consists in mimicry, but this we may employ only by stealth, if at all, and but momentarily, as fuller use of it does not befit the well-bred. A third kind is grimacing, which is beneath our dignity. A fourth is indecency, not only degrading to a public speaker, but hardly sufferable at a gentlemen's dinner-party. When all these modes, then, are withheld from this branch of oratory, the residue of wit depends apparently either on the facts or on the language, in accordance with the distinction I have already drawn. For the joke which still remains witty, in whatever words it is couched, has its germ in the facts; that which loses its pungency, as soon as it is differently worded, owes all its humour to the language."

FROM

ORATOR

69   The man of eloquence whom we seek, following the suggestion of Antonius, will be one who is able to speak in court or in deliberative bodies so as to prove, to please and to sway or persuade. To prove is the first necessity, to please is charm, to sway is victory; for it is the one thing of all that avails most in winning verdicts. For these three functions of the orator there are three styles, the plain style for proof, the middle style for pleasure, the vigorous style for persuasion;
70   and in this last is summed up the entire virtue of the orator. Now the man who controls and combines these three varied styles needs rare judgement and great endowment; for he will decide what is needed at any point, and will be able to speak in any way which the case requires. For after all the foundation of eloquence, as of everything else, is wisdom. In an oration, as in life, nothing is harder than to determine what is appropriate. The Greeks call it *prepon*; let us call it *decorum* or "propriety." Much brilliant work has been done in laying down rules about this; the subject is in fact worth mastering. From ignorance of this mistakes are made not only in life but very frequently in writing, both in poetry
71   and in prose. Moreover the orator must have an eye to propriety not only in thought but in language. For the same style and the same thoughts must not be used in portraying every condition in life, or every rank, position or age, and in fact a similar distinction must be made in respect of place, time and audience. The universal rule, in oratory as in life, is to consider propriety. This depends on the subject under discussion, and on the character of both the speaker and the
72   audience. The philosophers are accustomed to consider this extensive subject under the head of duties—not when they discuss absolute perfection, for that is one and unchanging; the literary critics consider it in connexion with poetry; orators in dealing with every kind of speech, and in every part thereof. How inappropriate it would be to employ general topics and the grand style when discussing cases of stillicide before a single referee, or to use mean and meagre language when referring to the majesty of the Roman people. This would be wrong in every respect; but others err in regard to character—either their own or that of the jury, or of their opponents; and not merely in the statement of facts, but often in the use of words. Although a word has no force apart from the thing, yet the same thing is often either approved or rejected according as it is
73   expressed in one way or another. Moreover, in all cases the question must be, "How far?" For although the limits of propriety differ for each subject, yet in general too much is more offensive than too little. Apelles said that those painters also make this error, who do not know when they have done enough. This is an important topic, Brutus, as you well know, and requires another large volume; but for our present discussion the following will be enough: Since we say "This is appropriate"—a word we use in connexion with everything we do or say, great or small,—since, I repeat, we say "This is appropriate" and "That is not appropriate," and it appears how important propriety is everywhere (and that

it depends upon something else and is wholly another question whether you should say "appropriate" or "right";—for by "right" we indicate the perfect line of duty which every one must follow everywhere, but "propriety" is what is fitting and agreeable to an occasion or person; it is important often in actions as well as in words, in the expression of the face, in gesture and in gait, and impropriety has the opposite effect); the poet avoids impropriety as the greatest fault which he can commit; he errs also if he puts the speech of a good man in the mouth of a villain, or that of a wise man in the mouth of a fool; so also the painter in portraying the sacrifice of Iphigenia, after representing Calchas as sad, Ulysses as still more so, Menelaus as in grief, felt that Agamemnon's head must be veiled, because the supreme sorrow could not be portrayed by his brush; even the actor seeks for propriety; what, then, think you, should the orator do? Since this is so important, let the orator consider what to do in the speech and its diferent divisions: it is certainly obvious that totally different styles must be used, not only in the different parts of the speech, but also that whole speeches must be now in one style, now in another.

It follows that we must seek the type and pattern of each kind—a great and arduous task, as we have often said; but we should have considered what to do when we were embarking; now we must certainly spread our sails to the wind, no matter where it may carry us. First, then, we must delineate the one whom some deem to be the only true "Attic" orator. He is restrained and plain, he follows the ordinary usage, really differing more than is supposed from those who are not eloquent at all. Consequently the audience, even if they are no speakers themselves, are sure they can speak in that fashion. For that plainness of style seems easy to imitate at first thought, but when attempted nothing is more difficult. For although it is not full-blooded, it should nevertheless have some of the sap of life, so that, though it lack great strength, it may still be, so to speak, in sound health. First, then, let us release him from, let us say, the bonds of rhythm. Yes, the orator uses certain rhythms, as you know, and these we shall discuss shortly; they have to be employed with a definite plan, but in a different style of speech; in this style they are to be wholly eschewed. It should be loose but not rambling; so that it may seem to move freely but not to wander without restraint. He should also avoid, so to speak, cementing his words together too smoothly, for the hiatus and clash of vowels has something agreeable about it and shows a not unpleasant carelessness on the part of a man who is paying more attention to thought than to words. But his very freedom from periodic structure and cementing his words together will make it necessary for him to look to the the other requisites. For the short and concise clauses must not be handled carelessly, but there is such a thing even as a careful negligence. Just as some women are said to be handsomer when unadorned—this very lack of ornament becomes them—so this plain style gives pleasure even when unembellished: there is something in both cases which lends greater charm, but without showing itself. Also all noticeable ornament, pearls as it were, will be excluded; not even curling-irons will be used; all cosmetics, artificial white and red, will be rejected; only elegance and neatness will remain. The language will be pure Latin, plain and clear; propriety will always be the chief aim. Only one quality will be lacking, which Theophrastus mentions fourth among the qualities of style—the charm and richness of figurative ornament. He will employ an abundance of apposite maxims dug out from every conceivable hiding place; this will be the dominant feature in this orator. He will be modest in his use of what may be called the orator's stock-in-trade. For we do have after a fashion a stock-in-trade, in the stylistic embellishments, partly in thought and partly in words. The embellishment given by words is twofold, from single words and from words as they are connected together. In the case of "proper" and ordinary words, that individual word wins approval which has the best sound, or best expresses the idea; in the case of variations from the common idiom we approve the metaphor, or a borrowing from some source, or a new formation or the archaic and obsolete (yet even obsolete and archaic words are to be classed as "proper" except that we rarely use them). Words when connected together embellish a style if they produce a certain symmetry which disappears when the words are changed, though the thought remains the same; for the figures of thought which remain even if the words are changed are, to be sure, numerous, but relatively few are noticeable. Consequently the orator of the plain style, provided he is elegant and finished, will not be bold in coining words, and in metaphor will be modest, sparing in the use of archaisms, and somewhat subdued in using the other embellishments of language and of thought. Metaphor he may possibly employ more frequently because it is of the commonest occurrence in the language of townsman and rustic alike. The rustics, for example, say that the vines are "bejewelled," the fields "thirsty," the crops "happy," the grain "luxuriant." Any of these metaphors is bold enough, but there is a similarity to the source from which the word is borrowed, or if a thing has no proper term the borrowing seems to be done in order to make the meaning clear, and not for entertainment. The restrained speaker may use this figure a little more freely than others, but not so boldly as if he were speaking in the grandest style. Consequently impropriety—the nature of which should be plain from what has been said about propriety—appears here too, when a metaphor is far-fetched, and one is used in the plain style which would be appropriate in another. This unaffected orator whom certain people call "Attic," and rightly so, except that he is not the only "Attic"—this orator will also use the symmetry that enlivens a group of words with the embellishments that the Greeks call *schēmata*, figures as it were, of speech. (They apply the same word also to figures of thought.) He will, however, be somewhat sparing in using these. For as in the appointments of a banquet he will avoid extravagant display, and desire to appear thrifty, but also in good taste, and will choose what he is going to use. There are, as a matter of fact, a good many ornaments suited to the frugality of this very orator I am describing. For this shrewd orator must avoid all the figures that I described above, such as clauses of equal length, with similar endings, or identical cadences, and the studied charm produced by the change of a letter, lest the elaborate symmetry and a certain grasping after a pleasant effect be too obvious. Likewise if repetition of words requires some emphasis and a raising of the voice, it will be foreign to this plain style of oratory. Other figures of speech he will be able to use freely, provided only he breaks up and divides the periodic structure and uses the commonest words and the mildest of metaphors. He may also brighten his style with such figures of thought as will not be exceedingly glaring. He will not represent the State as speaking or call the dead from the lower world, nor will he crowd a long series of iterations into a single period. This requires stronger lungs, and is not to be expected of him whom we are describing or demanded from him. For he will be rather subdued in voice as in style. But many of these figures of thought will be appropriate to this plain style, although he will use them somewhat harshly: such is the man we are portraying. His delivery is not that of tragedy nor of the stage; he will employ only slight movements of the body, but will trust a great deal to his expression. This must not be what people call pulling a wry face, but must reveal in a well-bred manner the feeling with which each thought is uttered.

A speech of this kind should also be sprinkled with the salt of pleasantry, which plays a rare great part in speaking. There are two kinds, humour and wit. He will use both; the former in a graceful and charming narrative, the latter in hurling the shafts of ridicule. Of this latter there are several kinds , but now we are discussing another subject. We here merely suggest that the orator should use ridicule with a care not to let it be too frequent lest it become buffoonery; nor ridicule of a smutty nature, lest it be that of low farce; nor pert, lest it be impudent; nor aimed at misfortune, lest it be brutal, nor at crime, lest laughter take the place of loathing: nor should the wit be inappropriate to his own character, to that of the jury, or to the occasion; for all these points come under the head of impropriety. He will also avoid far-fetched jests, and those not made up at the moment but brought from home; for these are generally frigid. He will spare his friends and dignitaries, will avoid rankling insult; he will merely prod his opponents, nor will he do it constantly, nor to all of them nor in every manner. With these exceptions he will use wit and humour in a way in which none of these modern "Attics" do, so far as I know, though this is certainly an outstanding mark of Attic style. For my part, I judge this to be the pattern of the plain orator—plain but great and truly Attic; since whatever is witty and wholesome in speech is peculiar to the Athenian orators. Not all of them, however, are humorous. Lysias is adequate and so is Hyperides; Demades is said to have excelled them all, Demosthenes is considered inferior. Yet it seems to me that none is cleverer than he; still he is not witty so much as humorous; the former requires a bolder talent, the latter a greater art.

The second style is fuller and somewhat more robust than the simple style just described, but plainer than the grandest style which we shall presently discuss. In this style there is perhaps a minimum of vigour, and a maximum of charm. For it is richer than the unadorned style, but plainer than the ornate and opulent style. All the ornaments are appropriate to this type of oration, and it possesses charm to a high degree. There have been many conspicuous examples of this style in Greece, but in my judgement Demetrius of Phalerum led them all. His oratory not only proceeds in calm and peaceful flow, but is lighted up by what might be called the stars of "transferred" words (or metaphor) and borrowed words. By "transferred" I now mean, as often before, words transferred by resemblance from another thing in order to produce a pleasing effect, or because of lack of a "proper" word; by "borrowed" I mean the cases in which there is substituted for a "proper" word another with the same meaning drawn from some other suitable sphere. It is, to be sure, a "transfer" when Ennius says

I am bereft of citadel and town,

but a "transfer" of quite a different kind than when he says

Dread Africa trembled with terrible tumult.

The latter is called "hypallage" by the rhetoricians, because as it were words are exchanged for words; the grammarians call it "metonymy" because nouns are transferred. Aristotle, however, classifies them all under metaphor and includes also the misuse of terms, which they call "catachresis," for example, when we say a "minute" mind instead of "small"; and we misuse related words on occasion either because this gives pleasure or because it is appropriate. When there is a continuous stream of metaphors, a wholly different style of speech is produced; consequently the Greeks call it "allegory." They are right as to the name, but from the point of view of classification Aristotle does better in calling them all metaphors. The Phalerian uses these very frequently, and they are attractive to a degree; and although he has many metaphors, yet the cases of metonymy are more numerous than in any other orator. To the same oratorical style—I am discussing the mean and tempered style—belong all figures of language, and many of thought. This speaker will likewise develop his arguments with breadth and erudition, and use commonplaces without undue emphasis. But why speak at length? It is commonly the philosophic schools which produce such orators: and unless he be brought face to face with the more robust speaker, the orator whom I am describing will find approval on his own merits. It is, as a matter of fact, a brilliant and florid, highly coloured and polished style in which all the charms of language and thought are intertwined. The sophists are the source from which all this has flowed into the forum, but scorned by the simple and rejected by the grand, it found a resting-place in this middle class of which I am speaking.

The orator of the third style is magnificent, opulent, stately and ornate; he undoubtedly has the greatest power. This is the man whose brilliance and fluency have caused admiring nations to let eloquence attain the highest power in the state; I mean the kind of eloquence which rushes along with the roar of a mighty stream, which all look up to and admire, and which they despair of attaining. This eloquence has power to sway men's minds and move them in every possible way. Now it storms the feelings, now it creeps in; it implants new ideas and uproots the old. But there is a great difference between this and the other styles. One who has studied the plain and pointed style so as to be able to speak adroitly and neatly, and has not conceived of anything higher, if he has attained perfection in this style, is a great orator, if not the greatest. He is far from standing on slippery ground, and, when once he gets a foothold, he will never fall. The orator of the middle style, whom I call moderate and tempered, once he has drawn up his forces, will not dread the doubtful and uncertain pitfalls of speaking. Even if not completely successful, as often happens, he will not run a great risk; he has not far to fall. But this orator of ours whom we consider the chief,—grand, impetuous and fiery, if he has natural ability for this alone, or trains himself solely in this, or devotes his energies to this only, and does not temper his abundance with the other two styles, he is much to be despised. For the plain orator is esteemed wise because he speaks clearly and adroitly; the one who employs the middle style is charming; but the copious speaker, if he has nothing else, seems to be scarcely sane. For a man who can say nothing calmly and mildly, who pays no attention to arrangement, precision, clarity or pleasantry—especially when some cases have to be handled entirely in this latter style, and others largely so,—if without first preparing the ears of his audience he begins trying to work them up to a fiery passion, he seems to be a raving madman among the sane, like a drunken reveller in the midst of sober men.

We have him now, Brutus, the man whom we are seeking, but in imagination, not in actual possession. If I had once laid my hands on him, not even he with his mighty eloquence would have persuaded me to let him go. But we have certainly discovered that eloquent orator whom Antonius never saw. Who is he, then? I will describe him briefly, and then expand the description at greater length. He in fact is eloquent who can discuss commonplace matters simply, lofty subjects impressively, and topics ranging between in a tempered style. You will say, "There never was such a man." I grant it; for I am arguing for my ideal, not what I have actually seen, and I return to that Platonic Idea of which I had spoken; though we do not see it, still it is possible to grasp it with the mind. For it is not an eloquent *person* whom I seek, nor anything subject to death and decay, but that absolute quality, the possession of which makes a man eloquent. And this is nothing but abstract eloquence, which we can behold only with the mind's eye. He, then, will be an eloquent speaker—to repeat my former definition—who can discuss trivial matters in a plain style, matters of moderate significance in the tempered style, and weighty affairs in the grand manner.

Horace
65–8 B.C.

Quintus Horatius Flaccus was born in Apulia of an unknown mother and a freedman father who managed to acquire a small farm. The father had ambitions for his son and sent him to school in Rome with the sons of the aristocracy. Horace then studied in Athens for about a year but left to join Brutus' army after the death of Caesar. Upon Brutus' defeat in 42 B.C. by the combined forces of Antony and Octavian (later Augustus, first Roman emperor), Horace returned to Rome to find his father dead and his farm confiscated. He later claimed that his newly discovered poverty had driven him to writing verse.

In Rome Horace met Vergil and Varius, and through them was introduced to Maecenas, an influential statesman and literary patron who gave him the Sabine farm where he retired to devote himself to poetry. Over the years he shifted his allegiance to Augustus and enjoyed the emperor's favor. He was secure enough in his position to decline Augustus' offer of a private secretaryship, and after Vergil's death in 19 B.C., he virtually assumed the position of poet laureate until his own death.

Horace was the only Latin poet of any distinction who also engaged in literary criticism. His satires contain reflections on the most effective means of constructing a satire, and his Epistle to Augustus speculates on the relation of poetry to society at large. Ars Poetica ("The Art of Poetry," c. 19–18 B.C.) is said to be based upon the poetic theories of Neoptolemus of Parium (third century B.C.). It takes the form of a versified epistle addressed to a father and two sons surnamed Piso, and it sets forth precepts on the making of poetry.

Horace emerged as a poet during the Augustan classical movement, during which Roman authors turned away from "decadent" and "Asiatic" Alexandrian poetry and adopted the high seriousness of Greek classical models. Ars Poetica, for instance, is noteworthy for its approving references to Greek literature, which earlier Romans had scorned. Like the majority of Roman literary theorists, Horace is an essentially conservative critic, looking back to the Greeks for his literary standards while allowing for some measure of innovation.

By Horace's time, the formalist criticism begun by Aristotle to describe epic, tragedy, and comedy had blossomed into a whole spectrum *of genres including epic, tragedy, comedy, lyric, pastoral, satire, elegy, and epigram. These fixed literary types had acquired what one source (William K. Wimsatt, Jr. and Cleanth Brooks,* Literary Criticism: A Short History*) describes as "a nearly legislative prestige." Criticism, then, often consisted of formulating rules concerning the* decorum *(a specifically Latin word which itself points toward Rome's conservative literary attitudes) or propriety for the various genres.*

Ars Poetica is divided into three themes following the three formal categories developed by Neoptolemus: poiesis, *or poetic subject matter,* poema, *or the poetic form, and* poeta, *or the poet himself. The critical precepts in these areas are concerned that the poet follow the established form, the* decorum, *rather than adopting what contemporary critics might call a "revisionary" stance with regard to prior poetic form. Much of the work dispenses advice to the aspiring poet—that, for instance, he not rush into publishing his work—which is essentially common-sense.*

Horace has been, from the European Enlightenment to the present day, the patron saint of every Neoclassical literary critic, and of many traditional poets as well. In the seventeenth and eighteenth centuries he was especially influential, when men such as Pope and Boileau admired and imitated him.

Ars Poetica, translated by D. A. Russell, is reprinted by permission of Oxford University Press from D. A. Russell and M. Winterbottom, eds., Ancient Literary Criticism: The Principal Texts in New Translations *(Oxford, 1972). © 1972 by Oxford University Press.*

Ars Poetica

Unity and Consistency

Imagine a painter who wanted to combine a horse's neck with a human head, and then clothe a miscellaneous collection of limbs with various kinds of feathers, so that what started out at the top as a beautiful woman ended in a hideously ugly fish. If you were invited, as friends, to the private view, could you help laughing? Let me tell you, my Piso friends, a book whose different features are made up at random like a sick man's dreams, with no unified form to have a head or a tail, is exactly like that picture.

"Painters and poets have always enjoyed recognized[1] rights to venture on what they will." Yes, we know; indeed, we ask and grant this permission turn and turn about. But it doesn't mean that fierce and gentle can be united, snakes paired with birds or lambs with tigers.

Serious and ambitious designs often have a purple patch or two sewn on to them just to make a good show at a distance—a description of a grove and altar of Diana, the meanderings of a stream running through pleasant meads, the River Rhine, the rainbow: but the trouble is, it's not the place for them.

Maybe you know how to do a picture of a cypress tree? What's the good of that, if the man who is paying for the picture is a desperate ship-wrecked mariner swimming to safety? The job began as a wine-jar: the wheel runs round—why is that a tub that's coming out? In short, let it be what you will, but let it be simple and unified.

Skill Needed to Avoid Faults

Most of us poets—father and worthy sons—are deceived by appearances of correctness. I try to be concise, but I become obscure; my aim is smoothness, but sinews and spirit fail; professions of grandeur end in bombast; the over-cautious who fear the storm creep along the ground. Similarly, the writer who wants to give fantastic variety to his single theme paints a dolphin in his woods and a wild boar in his sea.[2] If art is wanting, the flight from blame leads to faults. The poorest smith near the School of Aemilius will reproduce nails and mimic soft hair in bronze, though he has no luck with the over-all effect of his work, because he won't know how to organize the whole. If I were anxious to put anything together, I would as soon be that man as I would live with a mis-shapen nose when my black eyes and black hair had made me a beauty.

You writers must choose material equal to your powers. Consider long what your shoulders will bear and what they will refuse. The man who chooses his subject with full control will not be abandoned by eloquence or lucidity of arrangement.

As to arrangement: its excellence and charm, unless I'm very wrong, consist in saying at this moment what needs to be said at this moment, and postponing and temporarily omitting a great many things. An author who has undertaken a poem must be choosy—cling to one point and spurn another.[3]

As to words: if you're delicate and cautious in arranging them, you will give distinction to your style if an ingenious combination makes a familiar word new. If it happens to be necessary to denote hidden mysteries by novel symbols, it will fall to you to invent terms the Cethegi in their loin-cloths[4] never heard—and the permission will be granted if you accept it modestly—and, moreover, your new and freshly invented words will receive credit, if sparingly derived from the Greek springs. Is the Roman to give Caecilius and Plautus privileges denied to Virgil and Varius? Why am I unpopular if I can make a few acquisitions, when the tongue of Cato and Ennius so enriched their native langauge and produced such a crop of new names for things?

Fashions in Words

It always has been, and always will be, lawful to produce a word stamped with the current mark. As woods change in leaf as the seasons slide on, and the first leaves fall, so the old generation of words dies out, and the newly born bloom and are strong like young men. We and our works are a debt owed to death. Here a land-locked sea protects fleets from the North wind—a royal achievement; here an old barren marsh where oars were plied feeds neighbouring cities and feels the weight of the plough; here again a river gives up a course that damaged the crops and learns a better way. But whatever they are, all mortal works will die; and still less can the glory and charm of words endure for a long life. Many words which have fallen will be born again, many now in repute will fall if usage[5] decrees: for in her hand is the power and the law and the canon of speech.

Metre and Subject

Histories of kings and generals, dreadful wars: it was Homer who showed in what metre these could be narrated. Lines unequally yoked in pairs formed the setting first for lamentations, then for the expression of a vow fulfilled,[6] though who first sent these tiny "elegies" into the world is a grammarians' quarrel and still *sub judice*. Madness armed Archilochus with its own iambus; that too was the foot that the comic sock and tragic buskin held, because it was suitable for dialogue, able to subdue the shouts of the mob, and intended by nature for a life of action. To the lyre, the Muse granted the celebration of gods and the children of gods, victorious boxers, winning race-horses, young men's love, and generous wine. If I have neither the ability nor the knowledge to keep the duly assigned functions and tones of literature, why am I hailed as a poet? Why do I prefer to be ignorant than learn, out of sheer false shame? A comic subject will not be set out in tragic verse; likewise, the Banquet of Thyestes disdains being told in poetry of the private kind, that borders on the comic stage. Everything must keep the appropriate place to which it was allotted.

Nevertheless, comedy does sometimes raise her voice, and angry Chremes perorates with swelling eloquence. Often too Telephus and Peleus[7] in tragedy lament in prosaic language, when they are both poor exiles and throw away their bombast and words half a yard long, if they are anxious to touch the spectator's heart with their complaint.

Emotion and Character

It is not enough for poetry to be beautiful; it must also be pleasing and lead the hearer's mind wherever it will. The human face smiles in sympathy with smilers and comes to the help of those that weep. If you want me to cry, mourn first yourself; *then* your misfortunes will hurt me, Telephus and Peleus. If your words are given you ineptly, I shall fall asleep or laugh. Sad words suit a mournful countenance, threatening words an angry one; sportive words are for the playful, serious for the grave. For nature first shapes us within for any state of fortune—gives us pleasure or drives us to anger or casts us down to the ground with grievous sorrow and pains us—and then expresses the emotions through the medium of the tongue. If the words are out of tune with the speaker's fortunes, the knights and infantry of Rome will raise a cackle. It will make a lot of difference whether the speaker is a god or a hero, an old man of ripe years or a hot youth, an influential matron or a hard-working nurse, a travelling merchant or the tiller of a green farm, a Colchian or an Assyrian, one nurtured at Thebes or at Argos.

Choice and Handling of Myth

Either follow tradition or invent a consistent story. If as a writer you are representing Achilles with all his honours, let him be active, irascible, implacable, and fierce; let him say "the laws are not for me" and set no limit to the claims that arms can make. Let Medea be proud and indomitable, Ino full of tears, Ixion treacherous, Io never at rest, Orestes full of gloom. On the other hand, if you are putting something untried on the stage and venturing to shape a new character, let it be maintained to the end as it began and be true to itself. It is hard to put generalities in an individual way: you do better to reduce the song of Troy to acts than if you were the first to bring out something unknown and unsaid.[8] The common stock will become your private property if you don't linger on the broad and vulgar round, or anxiously render word for word, a loyal interpreter, or again, in the process of imitation, find yourself in a tight corner from which shame, or the rule of the craft, won't let you move; or, once again, if you avoid a beginning like the cyclic poet—

> Of Priam's fortune will I sing, and war
> well known to fame.

If he opens his mouth as wide as that, how *can* the promiser bring forth anything to match it? The mountains shall be in labour, and there shall be born—a silly mouse. How much better was the way of that poet whose every endeavour is to the point!

> Tell me, O Muse, of him who, after Troy
> had fallen, saw the manners and the towns
> of many men.⁹

His plan is not to turn fire to smoke, but smoke to light, so as to relate magnificent wonders thereafter—Antiphates and the Cyclops, Scylla and Charybdis.¹⁰ *He* doesn't start the Return of Diomedes from the death of Meleager, nor begin the Trojan war from the twin egg; he is always making good speed towards the end of the story, and carries his hearer right into the thick of it as though it were already known. He leaves out anything which he thinks cannot be polished up satisfactorily by treatment, and tells his fables and mixes truth with falsehood in such a way that the middle squares with the beginning and the end with the middle.

Let me tell you what I and the public both want, if you're hoping for an applauding audience that will wait for the curtain and keep its seat until the epilogue-speaker says "Pray clap your hands." You must mark the manners of each time of life, and assign the appropriate part to changing natures and ages. The child, just able to repeat words and planting his steps on the ground with confidence, is eager to play with his contemporaries, gets in and out of a temper without much cause, and changes hour by hour. The beardless youth, his tutor at last out of the way, enjoys his horses and dogs and the grass of the sunny Park. Moulded like wax into vice, he is surly to would-be advisers, slow to provide for necessities, prodigal of money, up in the air, eager, and quick to abandon the objects of his sudden love. Soon interests change: the grown man's mind pursues wealth and influential connections, is enslaved to honour, and avoids doing anything he may soon be trying to change. Many distresses surround the old man. He is acquisitive, and, poor man, daren't put his hand on what he has laid up; he is afraid to use it. He goes about his business timidly and coldly, procrastinating, letting things drag on in hope, lazy yet greedy of his future; he is awkward and grumbling, given to praising the days when he was a boy and to criticizing and finding fault with his juniors. Years as they come bring many blessings with them, and as they go take many away. To save yourself giving a young man an old man's role or a boy a grown man's, remember that your character should always remain faithful to what is associated with his age and suits it.

Some Rules for Dramatists¹¹

Actions may be either performed on the stage or reported when performed. What comes in through the ear is less effective in stirring the mind than what is put before our faithful eyes and told by the spectator to himself. However, you are not to bring on to the stage events which ought to be carried out within; you are to remove many things from sight, and let them be related in due course by the eloquence of an eye-witness. Don't let Medea murder the children before the people's gaze, or wicked Atreus cook human offal in public, or Procne be metamorphosed into a bird or Cadmus into a snake. Anything you show me like that earns my incredulity and disgust.

A play that wants to be in demand and to be revived must not be shorter or longer than five acts.[12]

There should be no god to intervene, unless the problem merits such a champion.

No fourth character should attempt to speak.

The chorus should play an actor's part, and do a man's duty.[13] It should not sing between the acts anything which has no relevance to or cohesion with the plot. It should side with the good and give them friendly counsel, restrain the angry, and approve those who scruple to go astray. It should praise a frugal table's fare, sound justice, law, and times of peace when the town's gates stand open. It should keep secrets entrusted to it, and beg and pray the gods that Fortune may return to the wretched and abandon the proud.

Development of Tragedy

The flute used not to be, as it is now, bound with copper and a rival to the trumpet. It was slight and simple, with few apertures, but serviceable to accompany and aid the chorus and to fill with its music the still not too crowded benches, where a population of no great size gathered in numbers easily counted, honest and decent and modest. But when that same population won wars and began to extend its territory, when longer walls came to embrace the cities, and people indulged themselves on holidays by drinking in the daytime, and nobody blamed them, then rhythm and tunes acquired greater licence. For what taste could the uneducated show, the holiday crowd of countrymen and townsmen, honest folk and rogues, all mixed up together? This is how the musician came to add movement and elaboration to his art, and to trail his robe as he roamed the stage. This is how even the austere lyre gained a stronger voice, while lofty eloquence produced strange utterance and thought that shrewdly grasped practical needs and prophesied the future grew indistinguishable from the oracles of Delphi.

Satyr-Plays[14]

The competitor in tragic poetry, who strove for a worthless goat, next showed the rustic Satyrs, naked. Preserving his seriousness despite his keen wit, he made an attempt at a joke, because the audience, drunk and lawless at the end of the festival, had to be prevented from going away by tricks and pleasing innovations. But the way to recommend your laughing, joking satyrs, the way to turn seriousness to jest, is this: no god or hero you bring on the stage, if he was seen not long ago in royal gold and purple, must lower his language and move into a humble cottage; nor, on the other hand, must his efforts to get off the ground lead him to try to grasp clouds and void. Tragedy does not deserve to blurt out trivial lines, but she will modestly consort a little with the forward satyrs, like a respectable lady dancing because she must on a feast day.

As a Satyr-writer, my Piso friends, I shall not limit my liking to plain and proper terms, nor yet try to be so different from the tone of tragedy that there is no difference between Davus talking or bold Pythias, when she's just tricked

Simon out of a talent,[15] and Silenus, at once guardian and servant of the god he has brought up. I shall make up my poem of known elements, so that anyone may hope to do the same, but he'll sweat and labour to no purpose when he ventures: such is the force of arrangement and combination, such the splendour that commonplace words acquire. Your woodland Fauns, if you take my judgement, should beware of behaving as if they were born at the street corner and were creatures of the Forum—they shouldn't play the gallant in languishing verse or crack dirty and disreputable jokes; possessors of horses or ancestors or property take offence at this sort of thing and don't look kindly on work approved by the fried-peas-and-nuts public, or give it the prize.

The Need for Technical Perfection

A long syllable following a short one makes an iambus.[16] He is a quick foot; this is why he ordered iambic lines to be called trimeters, although he was giving six beats to the line, and was the same in form from first to last. Not all that long ago, wanting to fall rather more slowly and weightily upon our ears, he admitted the stately spondees to family privileges—what a comfortable, easy-going foot he is!—but without being quite so complaisant as to give up the second and fourth positions in the line. Rarely does he appear in Accius' noble trimeters, and his rarity in Ennius' weighty lines as they fly out on the stage damns them with the shocking accusation of hasty and careless craftsmanship—or else sheer ignorance of the trade.

Of course, it's not every critic that notices lines that aren't tuneful, and Roman poets have enjoyed undeserved licence. But does that entitle *me* to make mistakes and scribble away carelessly? Or should I rather expect everyone to see my mistakes, and so play safe and cautious, keeping within the bounds of what I can hope to be pardoned for? In that case, all I've done is to avoid blame; I have not deserved praise.

Greek Models

Study Greek models night and day. Your ancestors praised Plautus' metre and his humour. On both counts their admiration was too indulgent, not to say childish, if it's true that you and I know how to distinguish a witless jest from a subtle one and if we've skill in our fingers and ears to know what sounds are permitted.

Inventiveness of the Greeks in Drama

The hitherto unknown genre of the tragic Muse is said to be Thespis' invention; he is supposed to have carried on a cart verses to be sung and acted by performers whose faces were smeared with wine-lees. After him came Aeschylus, the inventor of the mask and splendid robe; he gave the stage a floor of modest boards, and taught the actors to talk big and give themselves height by their high boots. Next came Old Comedy, much praised, though its liberty degenerated into vice and violence deserving restraint of law; the law was accepted, and the chorus fell silent, its right of shameful insult removed.

Inventiveness of the Romans

Our poets have left nothing unattempted. Not the least part of their glory was won by venturing to abandon the footsteps of the Greeks and celebrate our own affairs; some produced historical plays, some comedies in Roman dress. Latium would have been as famous for literature as for valour and deeds of arms if the poets had not, one and all, been put off by the labour and time of polishing their work. Children of Numa, show your disapproval of any poem which long time and much correction have not disciplined and smoothed ten times over, to satisfy the well-pared nail.

The Poet[17]

Democritus thinks native talent a happier thing than poor, miserable art, and banishes sane poets from his Helicon. That's why so many don't bother to cut their nails or beard, but seek solitude and keep away from the bath. For a man is sure to win the reward and name of poet if he never lets barber Licinus get hold of that head that three Anticyras[18] won't make sound. I'm a fool to purge my bile when spring comes round. I could write as good poetry as any; but nothing is worth that price, and so I'll play the part of the whetstone, that can sharpen the knife though it can't itself cut. In other words, without writing myself, I will teach function and duty—where the poet's resources come from, what nurtures and forms him, what is proper and what not, in what directions excellence and error lead.

Wisdom is the starting-point and source of correct writing. Socratic books will be able to point out to you your material, and once the material is provided the words will follow willingly enough. If a man has learned his duty to his country and his friends, the proper kind of love with which parent, brother, and guest should be cherished, the functions of a senator and a judge, the task of a general sent to the front—then he automatically understands how to give each character its proper attributes. My advice to the skilled imitator will be to keep his eye on the model of life and manners, and draw his speech living from there.

Sometimes a play devoid of charm, weight, and skill, but attractive with its commonplaces and with the characters well drawn, gives the people keener pleasure and keeps them in their seats more effectively than lines empty of substance and harmonious trivialities.

Greek and Roman Attitudes

The Greeks have the gift of genius from the Muse, and the power of well-rounded speech. They covet nothing but praise. Roman boys do long sums and learn to divide their *as* into a hundred parts.[19]

"Young Albinus, subtract one uncia from a quincunx: what's left? . . . You could have told me by now . . ."

"A triens."

"Excellent. You'll be able to look after your affairs. Now add an uncia. What is it now?"

"A semis."

Once this rust and care for cash has tainted the soul, can we hope for poems to be written that deserve preserving with cedar oil and keeping safe in smooth cypress?

Poets aim either to do good or to give pleasure—or, thirdly, to say things which are both pleasing and serviceable for life.

Whatever advice you give, be brief, so that the teachable mind can take in your words quickly and retain them faithfully. Anything superfluous overflows from the full mind.

Whatever you invent for pleasure, let it be near to truth. We don't want a play to ask credence for anything it feels like, or draw a living child from the ogress's belly after lunch. The ranks of elder citizens chase things off the stage if there's no good meat in them, and the high-spirited youngsters won't vote for dry poetry. The man who combines pleasure with usefulness wins every suffrage, delighting the reader and also giving him advice; this is the book that earns money for the Sosii,[20] goes overseas and gives your celebrated writer a long lease of fame.

However, there are some mistakes we are ready to forgive. The string doesn't always give the note that the hand and mind intended: it often returns a high note when you ask for a low. The bow won't always hit what it threatens to hit. But when most features of a poem are brilliant, I shan't be offended by a few blemishes thrown around by carelessness or human negligence. But what then? If a copyist goes on making the same mistake however much he is warned, he is not forgiven; if a lyre-player always gets the same note wrong, people laugh at him; so, in my estimation, if a poet fails to come off a good deal, he's another Choerilus, whom I admire with a smile if he's good two or three times. Why, I'm angry even if good Homer goes to sleep, though a doze is quite legitimate in a long piece of work.

Poetry is like painting. Some attracts you more if you stand near, some if you're further off. One picture likes a dark place, one will need to be seen in the light, because it's not afraid of the critic's sharp judgement. One gives pleasure once, one will please if you look it over ten times.

Dear elder son of Piso, though you father's words are forming you in the right way and you have wisdom of your own besides, take this piece of advice away with you and remember it. In some things, a tolerable mediocrity is properly allowed. A mediocre lawyer or advocate is a long way from the distinction of learned Messalla and doesn't know as much as Aulus Cascellius, but he has his value. But neither men nor gods nor shop-fronts allow a poet to be mediocre. Just as music out of tune or thick ointment or Sardinian honey with your poppy gives offence at a nice dinner, because the meal could go on without them, so poetry, which was created and discovered for the pleasure of the mind, sinks right to the bottom the moment it declines a little from the top. The man who doesn't know how to play keeps away from the sporting gear in the park. The man who's never been taught ball or discus or hoop keeps quiet, so that the packed spectators can't get a free laugh. But the man who doesn't know how to make verses still has a go. Why shouldn't he? He's free, and of free birth, he's assessed at an equestrian property rate, and he's not got a fault in the world.

You will never do or say anything if Minerva is against you: your taste and intelligence guarantee us that. But if you do write something some day, let it find its way to critic Maecius' ears, and your father's, and mine, and be stored up for eight years in your notebooks at home. You will be able to erase what you haven't published; words once uttered forget the way home.

Poetry and Its Social Uses and Value

Orpheus, who was a holy man and the interpreter of the gods, deterred the men of the forests from killing and from disgusting kinds of food. This is why he was said to tame tigers and rabid lions. This too is why Amphion, the founder of the city of Thebes, was said to move rocks where he wished by the sound of the lyre and coaxing prayers.[21] In days of old, wisdom consisted in separating public property from private, the sacred from the secular, in checking promiscuity, in laying down rules for the married, in building cities, in inscribing laws on wooden tablets. And that is how honour and renown came to divine poets and poetry. After them came the great Homer and Tyrtaeus, who sharpened masculine hearts for war by their verses. Oracles were uttered in verse. The path of life was pointed out in verse. Kings' favours were won by the Muses' tunes. Entertainment was found there also, and rest after long labour. So there is no call to be ashamed of the Muse with her skill on the lyre or of Apollo the singer.

Art and Nature

Do good poems come by nature or by art? This is a common question. For my part, I don't see what study can do without a rich vein of talent, nor what good can come of untrained genius. They need each other's help and work together in friendship.[22] A boy who wants to reach the hoped-for goal in the race endures and does a lot, sweats and freezes, refrains from sex and wine. The clarinetist who is playing in honour of Apollo learns his lesson first and stands in awe of his master. But nowadays it's enough to say: "I write marvellous poems. The itch take the hindmost! It's a disgrace for me to be left behind and admit I don't know something that, to be sure, I never learned."

A poet who is rich in land and investments bids his flatterers "come and better themselves"—just like an auctioneer collecting a crowd to buy his wares. But if he's a man who can set out a good dinner properly and go bail for a poor and impecunious client and get him out of a grim legal tangle, I shall be surprised if the lucky fellow knows how to distinguish a false friend from a true. If you have given a man a present, or if you want to, don't then lead him, full of joy, to your verses. He's bound to say "Splendid, beautiful, just right"; he'll grow pale here, he'll drip dew from loving eyes, he'll jump about, he'll beat the ground with his foot. Your mocker is more deeply stirred than your true admirer, just as hired mourners at a funeral say and do almost more than those who genuinely grieve. Kings are said to ply a man with many cups and test him with wine if they are trying to discover if he deserves their friendship. If you write poetry, the fox's hidden feelings will never escape you. If you read anything aloud to Quintilius, he'd say "pray change that, and that." You would say you couldn't do better, though you'd tried two or three times, to no purpose. Then he'd tell you to scratch it out and put the badly turned lines back on the anvil. If you preferred defending your error to amending it, he wasted no more words or trouble on preventing you from loving yourself and your handiwork without competition. A wise and good man will censure flabby lines, reprehend harsh ones, put a black line with a stroke of the pen besides unpolished ones, prune pretentious ornaments, force you to shed light on obscurities, convict you of ambiguity, mark down what must be changed. He'll be an Aristarchus.[23] He won't say, "Why should I offend a friend in trifles?" These trifles lead to serious troubles, if once you are ridiculed and get a bad reception.

The Mad Poet

Men of sense are afraid to touch a mad poet and give him a wide berth. He's like a man suffering from a nasty itch, or the jaundice, or fanaticism, or Diana's wrath. Boys chase him and follow him round incautiously. And if, while he's belching out his lofty lines and wandering round, he happens to fall into a well or a pit, like a fowler intent on his birds, then, however long he shouts "Help! Help! Fellow citizens, help!" there'll be no one to bother to pick him up. And if anyone should trouble to help and let down a rope, my question will be, "How do you know that he didn't throw himself down deliberately? Are you sure he wants to be saved?" And I shall tell the tale of the death of the Sicilian poet. Empedocles wanted to be regarded as an immortal god, and so he jumped, cool as you like, into burning Etna. Let poets have the right and privilege of death. To save a man against his will is the same as killing him. This isn't the only time he's done it. If he's pulled out now, he won't become human or lay aside his love of a notorious end.

It's far from clear *why* he keeps writing poetry. Has the villain pissed on his father's ashes? Or disturbed the grim site of a lightning-strike? Anyway, he's raving, and his harsh readings put learned and unlearned alike to flight, like a bear that's broken the bars of his cage. If he catches anyone, he holds on and kills him with reading. He's a real leech that won't let go of the skin till it's full of blood.

NOTES

1. Or "equal."

2. Note this use of the idea of faults related to particular virtues: cf. "Longinus," p. 327.

3. Bentley and others rearrange so that this sentence is taken differently: "As to words: an author who has undertaken a poem should be delicate and cautious in arranging them, like one and spurn another."

4. i.e. primitive Romans.

5. Or "need."

6. Horace is thinking of inscriptions accompanying dedications to gods.
7. Euripidean characters.
8. i.e. to invent names and circumstances for a general theme is undesirable; if you object that the known myths are hackneyed, the remedy is in the treatment of them in a new way.
9. *Od.* 1. 1ff.
10. The various tales in *Od.* 9–12.
11. Cf. Aristotle, *Poetics*, for many of these precepts.
12. Not Aristotelian; but Menander seems normally to have composed his comedies in five acts, separated by choral interludes.
13. *Poetics*, p. 164.
14. These featured Silenus and satyrs in burlesque episodes of myth; style and metre were those of tragedy, not comedy. The piece was commonly performed as a fourth play after three tragedies. Euripides' *Cyclops* is the only complete extant example. Aristotle believed satyr-plays were at the origin of tragedy (*Poetics*, p. 152); others, as Horace here, that they were a later refinement.
15. Typical New Comedy names: slave, maid or prostitute, old man.
16. Horace's main theme in what preceded was propriety; in the next section it is perfection. He marks the transition by humorously giving some very elementary metrical instruction. Greek trimeters have the basic scheme: $\smile - | \smile - | \smile - | \smile - | \smile - | \smile -$, whereas the corresponding old Latin *senarius* (Ennius, Accius) admits spondees (—) also in the second and fourth feet.
17. From this point, the poem turns to topics concerned with the poet himself: inspiration, moral knowledge, care for posterity, commitment. This main theme continues to the end.
18. Hellebore, proverbially a cure for madness, came from Anticyra.
19. 12 unciae = 1 as; 5 unciae = quincunx; 1/3 as = triens; 1/2 as = semis.
20. Booksellers.
21. Horace allegorizes the myths. For similar *exempla* (no allegory), cf. Aristophanes, *Frogs*, p. 56.
22. Cf. "Longinus," p. 326.
23. The great Alexandrian scholar marked spurious or doubtful lines in Homer with the sign which Horace here attributes to the good critic.

Dionysius of Halicarnassus

first-century B.C.

Although Greek by birth, Dionysius of Halicarnassus was one of the presiding spirits of literary criticism in the Augustan age (27 B.C.–A.D. 14) in Rome, perhaps the most significant era for literary criticism since the time of Aristotle. Little is known of his personal life beyond the fact that he arrived at Rome in 30 B.C., remaining there until his death around the year 7 B.C. Throughout that period he taught and wrote in Rome, influencing the literary tastes of an entire generation. His subject matter was Greek literature, and he himself wrote in Greek. That, however, only enhanced his prestige among educated Romans, who were in the midst of a rapid Hellenization that inspired a widespread desire to study and emulate the ancient literature of Greece. It was, for instance, the same period in which Vergil drew upon Homer to create the national epic of Rome, The Aeneid.

Dionysius considered his Early History of Rome, upon which he labored twenty–two years, his magnum opus, and his literary works, for which he is now best appreciated, appeared during that period as occasional pieces. He was very much involved in the controversy over the "Attic" versus the "Asiatic" mode of oratorical and prose composition. The debate had a number of complex ramifications (including Attic "purity" versus Asiatic "decadence"), but it centered around the issue of whether Romans should emulate a plain or highly ornate form of composition. Dionysius came down squarely on the side of Atticism, and he encouraged the imitation of the classic Greek authors, especially Demosthenes. He did, however, believe that it was the Romans of his own day who best recaptured the spirit of Attic classicism.

On Literary Composition *is probably the most important of his literary works, exhibiting both his theoretical precepts and his considerable strengths in close observation of a text. He is primarily interested in what he calls the "music" of language and analyzes it according to his own categories of melody, rhythm, variety, and appropriateness. Dionysius is most original in his use of close reading which interprets the author in question in the light of Dionysius' critical formulae rather than using the author to merely illustrate the formulae. This brings him much closer to the modern idea of the function of a literary critic than almost any other ancient critic.*

The selection from On Literary Composition, *translated by W. Rhys Roberts, is reprinted by permission of the publisher from Dionysius of Halicarnassus,* On Literary Composition *(London: Macmillan, 1910).*

FROM
On Literary Composition

X
Aims and Methods of Good Composition

Now that I have laid down these broad outlines, the next step will be to state what should be the aims kept in view by the man who wishes to compose well, and by what methods his object can be attained. It seems to me that the two essentials to be aimed at by those who compose in verse and prose are charm and beauty. The ear craves for both of these. It is affected in somewhat the same way as the sense of sight which, when it looks upon molded figures, pictures, carvings, or any other works of human hands, and finds both charm and beauty residing in them, is satisfied and longs for nothing more. And let not anyone be surprised at my assuming that there are two distinct objects in style, and at my separating beauty from charm; nor let him think it strange if I hold that a piece of composition may possess charm but not beauty, or beauty without charm. Such is the verdict of actual experience; I am introducing no novel axiom. The styles of Thucydides and of Antiphon of Rhamnus are surely examples of beautiful composition, if ever there were any, and are beyond all possible cavil from this point of view, but they are not remarkable for their charm. On the other hand, the style of the historian Ctesias of Cnidus, and that of Xenophon the disciple of Socrates, are charming in the highest possible degree, but not as beautiful as they should have been. I am speaking generally, not absolutely; I admit that in the former authors there are instances of charming, in the latter of beautiful arrangement. But the composition of Herodotus has both these qualities; it is at once charming and beautiful.

XI
General Discussion of the Sources of Charm and Beauty in Composition

Among the sources of charm and beauty in style there are, I conceive, four which are paramount and essential—melody, rhythm, variety, and the appropriateness demanded by these three. Under "charm" I class freshness, grace, euphony, sweetness, persuasiveness, and all similar qualities; and under "beauty" grandeur, impressiveness, solemnity, dignity, mellowness, and the like. For these seem to me the most important—the main heads, so to speak, in either case. The aims set before themselves by all serious writers in epic, dramatic, or lyric poetry, or in the so-called "language of prose," are those specified, and I think these are all. There are many excellent authors who have been distinguished in one or both of these qualities. It is not possible at present to adduce examples from the writings of each one of them; I must not waste time over such details; and besides, if it seems incumbent on me to say something about some of them individually, and to quote from them anywhere in support of my views, I shall have a more suitable opportunity for doing so, when I sketch the various types of literary arrangement. For the present, what I have said of them is quite sufficient. So I will now return to the division I made of composition into charming and beautiful, in order that my discourse may "keep to the track," as the saying is.

Well, I said that the ear delighted first of all in melody, then in rhythm, thirdly in variety, and finally in appropriateness as applied to these other qualities. As a witness to the truth of my words I will bring forward experience itself, for it cannot be challenged, confirmed as it is by the general sentiment of mankind. Who is there that is not enthralled by the spell of one melody while he remains unaffected in any such way by another,—that is not captivated by this rhythm while that does but jar upon him? Before now I myself, even in the most popular theatres, thronged by a mixed and uncultured multitude, have seemed to observe that all of us have a sort of natural appreciation for correct melody and good rhythm. I have seen an accomplished harpist, of high repute, hissed by the public because he struck a single false note and so spoilt the melody. I have seen, too, a fluteplayer, who handled his instrument with the practiced skill of a master, suffer the same fate because he blew thickly or, through not compressing his lips, produced a harsh sound or so-called "broken note" as he played. Nevertheless, if the amateur critic were summoned to take up the instrument and himself to render any of the pieces with whose performance by professionals he was just now finding fault, he would be unable to do it. Why so? Because this is an affair of technical skill, in which we are not all partakers; the other of feeling, which is nature's universal gift to man. I have noticed the same thing occur in the case of rhythms. Everybody is vexed and annoyed when a performer strikes an instrument, takes a step, or sings a note, out of time, and so destroys the rhythm.

Again, it must not be supposed that, while melody and rhythm excite pleasure, and we are all enchanted by them, variety and appropriateness have less freshness and grace, or less effect on any of their hearers. No, these too fairly enchant us all when they are really attained, just as their absence jars upon us intensely. This is surely beyond dispute. I may refer, in confirmation, to the case of instrumental music, whether it accompanies singing or dancing; if it attains grace perfectly and throughout, but fails to introduce variety in due season or deviates from what is appropriate, the effect is dull satiety and that disagreeable impression which is made by anything out of harmony with the subject. Nor is my illustration foreign to the matter in hand. The science of public oratory is, after all, a sort of musical science, differing from vocal and instrumental music in degree, not in kind. In oratory, too, the words involve melody, rhythm, variety, and appropriateness; so that, in this case also, the ear delights in the melodies, is fascinated by the rhythms, welcomes the variations, and craves always what is in keeping with the occasion. The distinction between oratory and music is simply one of degree.

Now, the melody of spoken language is measured by a single interval, which is approximately that termed a *fifth*. When the voice rises towards the acute, it does not rise more than three tones and a semitone; and, when it falls towards the grave, it does not fall more than this interval. Further, the entire utterance during one word is not delivered at the same pitch of the voice throughout, but one part of it at the acute pitch, another at the grave, another at both. Of the words that have both pitches, some have the grave fused with the acute on one and the same syllable—those which we call circumflexed; others have both pitches falling on separate syllables, each retaining its own quality. Now in disyllables there is no space intermediate between low pitch and high pitch; while in polysyllabic words, whatever their number of syllables, there is but one syllable that has the acute accent (high pitch) among the many remaining graves ones. On the other hand, instrumental and vocal music uses a great number of intervals, not the fifth only; beginning with the octave, it uses also the fifth, the fourth, the third, the tone, the semitone, and, as some think, even the quarter-tone in a distinctly perceptible way. Music, further, insists that the words should be subordinate to the tune, and not the tune to the words. Among many examples in proof of this, let me especially instance those lyrical lines which Euripides has represented Electra as addressing to the Chorus in the *Orestes* (140–42): "Hush, hush! Light be the tread / Of the sandal; not a sound! / This way, far, far from his bed." In these lines the words *sîga sîga leukón* are sung to one note; and yet each of the three words has both low pitch and high pitch. And the word *arbúles* has its third syllable sung at the same pitch as its middle syllable, although it is impossible for a single word to take two acute accents. The first syllable of *títhete* is sung to a lower note, while the two that follow it are sung to the same high note. The circumflex accent of *ktupeîte* has disappeared, for the two syllables are uttered at one and the same pitch. And the word *apopróbate* does not receive the acute accent on the middle syllable; but the pitch of the third syllable has been transferred to the fourth.

The same thing happens in rhythm. Ordinary prose speech does not violate or interchange the quantities in any noun or verb. It keeps the syllables long or short as it has received them by nature. But the arts of rhythm and music alter them by shortening or lengthening, so that often they pass into their opposites: the time of production is not regulated by the quantity of the syllables, but the quantity of the syllables is regulated by the time.

The difference between music and speech having thus been shown, some other points remain to be mentioned. If the melody of the voice—not the singing voice, I mean, but the ordinary voice—has a pleasant effect upon the ear, it will be called melodious rather than in melody. So also symmetry in the quantities or words, when it preserves a lyrical effect, is rhythmical rather than in rhythm. On the precise bearing of these distinctions I will speak at the proper time. For the present I will pass on to the next question, and try to show how a style of civil oratory can be attained which, simply by means of the composition, charms the ear with its melody of sound, its symmetry of rhythm, its elaborate variety, and its appropriateness to the subject. These are the headings which I have set before myself.

XII
How to Render Composition Charming

It is not in the nature of all the words in a sentence to affect the ear in the same way, any more than all visible objects produce the same impression on the sense of sight, things tasted on that of taste, or any other set of stimuli upon the sense to which they correspond. No, different sounds affect the ear with many different sensations of sweetness, harshness, roughness, smoothness, and so on. The reason is to be found partly in the many different qualities of the letters which make up speech, and partly in the extremely various forms in which syllables are put together. Now since words have these properties, and since it is impossible to change the fundamental nature of any single one of them, we can only mask the uncouthness which is inseparable from some of them, by means of mingling and fusion and juxtaposition—by mingling smooth with rough, soft with hard, cacophonous with melodious, easy to pronounce with hard to pronounce, long with short; and generally by happy combinations of the same kind. Many words of few syllables must not be used in succession (for this jars upon the ear), nor an excessive number of polysyllabic words; and we must avoid the monotony of setting side by side words similarly accented or agreeing in their quantities. We must quickly vary the cases of substantives (since, if continued unduly, they greatly offend the ear); and in order to guard against satiety, we must constantly break up the effect of sameness entailed by placing many nouns, or verbs, or other parts of speech, in close succession. We must not always adhere to the same figures, but change them frequently; we must not reintroduce the same metaphors, but vary them; we must not exceed due measure by beginning or ending with the same words too often.

Still, let no one think that I am proclaiming these as universal rules—that I suppose keeping them will always produce pleasure, or breaking them always produce annoyance. I am not so foolish. I know that pleasure often arises from both sources—from similarity at one time, from dissimilarity at another. In every case we must, I think, keep in view good taste, for this is the best criterion of charm and its opposite. But about good taste no rhetorician or philosopher has, so far, produced a definite treatise. The man who first undertook to write on the subject, Gorgias of Leontini, achieved nothing worth mentioning. The nature of the subject, indeed, is not such that it can fall under any comprehensive and systematic treatment, nor can good taste in general be apprehended by science, but only by personal judgment. Those who have continually trained this latter faculty in many connections are more successful than others in attaining good taste, while those who leave it untrained are rarely successful, and only by a sort of lucky stroke.

To proceed. I think the following rules should be observed in composition by a writer who looks to please the ear. Either he should link to one another melodious, rhythmical, euphonious words, by which the sense of hearing is touched with a feeling of sweetness and softness—those which, to put it broadly, come home to it most; or he should intertwine and interweave those which have no such natural effect with those that can so bewitch the ear that the unattractiveness of the one set is overshadowed by the grace of the other. We may compare the practice of good tacticians when marshalling their armies: they mask the weak portions by means of the strong, and so no part of their force proves useless. In the same way I maintain we ought to relieve monotony by the tasteful introduction of variety, since variety is an element of pleasure in everything we do. And last, and certainly most important of all, the setting which is assigned to the subject matter must be appropriate and becoming to it. And, in my opinion, we ought not to feel shy of using any noun or verb, however hackneyed, unless it carries with it some shameful association; for I venture to assert that no part of speech which signifies a person or a thing will prove so mean, squalid, or otherwise offensive as to have no fitting place in discourse. My advice is that, trusting to the effect of the composition, we should bring out such expressions with a bold and manly confidence, following the example of Homer, in whom the most commonplace words are found, and of Demosthenes and Herodotus and others, whom I will mention a little later so far as is suitable in each case. I think I have now spoken at sufficient length on charm of style. My treatment has been but a brief survey of a wide field, but will furnish the main heads of the study.

XIII
How to Render Composition Beautiful

So far, so good. But, if some one were to ask me in what way, and by attention to what principles, literary structure can be made beautiful, I should reply: In no other way, believe me, and by no other means, than those by which it is made charming, since the same elements contribute to both, namely noble melody, stately rhythm, imposing variety, and the appropriateness which all these need. For as there is a charming diction, so there is another that is noble; as there is a polished rhythm, so also is there another that is dignified; as variety in one passage adds grace, so in another it adds mellowness; and as for appropriateness, it will prove the chief source of beauty, or else the source of nothing at all. I repeat, the study of beauty in composition should follow the same lines throughout as the study of charm. The prime cause, here as before, is to be found in the nature of the letters and the phonetic effect of the syllables, which are the raw material out of which the fabric of words is woven. The time may perhaps now have come for redeeming my promise to discuss these.

Quintilian

c. A.D. 35–c. 96

Marcus Fabius Quintilianus was one of the great teachers of rhetoric in the first century, and the chief Latin critic of the post-Augustan period. He was born in what is now Spain and may have been the son of a rhetorician. Whatever his father's occupation, he sent his son to Rome to be educated. There Quintilian eventually attached himself to the orator Domitius Afer and obtained practical experience in the courts. He became famous as a teacher (Pliny the Younger was one of his pupils) and was appointed a salaried professor of rhetoric by the emperor Vespasian. In contrast to Cicero, whom he venerated, he represents the academic approach to the study of rhetoric. The relationship of the two men resembles that of Plato and Aristotle, since both Aristotle and Quintilian systematize the achievements of their illustrious predecessors. Around A.D. 88 he retired to devote himself to writing.

Institutio Oratoria ("The Institutes of Oratory," c. A.D. 95), his primary surviving work, presents a comprehensive plan for the education of the orator. In it Quintilian attempts a complete description of the process of shaping rhetoric to the purposes of oratory. He expounds the five traditional departments of rhetoric (invention, arrangement, style, memory, delivery) at length and concludes with a description of the ideal orator. Encyclopedic in scope, Institutio Oratoria was considered the definitive work on classical rhetoric throughout the Middle Ages and Renaissance.

Like Cicero and Longinus, Quintilian combines his formal analysis of rhetoric with a strong emphasis on morality and the pedagogical usefulness of the literary arts. He argues that the good orator must also be a good man and therefore considers it imperative to evaluate oratory in ethical terms. This concern informs his negative appraisal of prevailing rhetorical standards—"lascivious ornaments of present-day fashion"—and his desire to return to what he sees as the greatness of Ciceronian rhetoric. Because Institutio Oratoria was written under the aegis of the emperor Domitian, who was engaged at the time in a virtual reign of terror against suspected "enemies," Quintilian's high moral tone has laid him open to charges of hypocrisy.

In his discussion of style, Quintilian confirms the long-standing hostility of moralistic literary criticism toward figurative language. For him, the primary requisite of good style is clarity, and this principle dominates his treatment of figurative language. Clarity, he says, relies upon a single "proper" meaning for the text in question; ambiguity, the possibility of a double meaning, must be avoided. Quintilian basically mistrusts figurative language and attempts to circumscribe it.

Quintilian's judgments became canonical for the late Renaissance and the neoclassical era (the complete text of Institutio Oratoria *was discovered in 1416 and printed in 1470). Pope's tribute to Quintilian reflects his tremendous influence throughout that period:*

> *In grave Quintilian's copious work, we find*
> *The justest rules, and clearest method joined.*
> *Thus useful arms in magazines we place*
> *All ranged in order, and disposed with grace;*
> *But less to please the eye, than arm the hand,*
> *Still fit for use, and ready at command.*
> [An Essay on Criticism, 669–674]

The selection from Institutio Oratoria, *translated by H. E. Butler, is reprinted by permission of Harvard University Press and the Loeb Classical Library.*

Institutio Oratoria

FROM
Book III

Every speech ... consists at once of that which is expressed and that which expresses, that is to say of matter and words. Skill in speaking is perfected by nature, art and practice, to which some add a fourth department, namely imitation, which I however prefer to include under art. There are also three aims which the orator must always have in view; he must instruct, move and charm his hearers. This is a clearer division than that made by those who divide the task of oratory into that which relates to things and that which concerns the emotions, since both of these will not always be present in the subjects which we shall have to treat. For some themes are far from calling for any appeal to the emotions, which, although room cannot always be found for them, produce a most powerful effect wherever they do succeed in forcing their way. The best authorities hold that there are some things in oratory which require proof and others which do not, a view with which I agree. Some on the other hand, as for instance Celsus, think that the orator will not speak on any subject unless there is some question involved in it; but the majority of writers on rhetoric are against him, as is also the threefold division of oratory, unless indeed to praise what is allowed to be honourable and to denounce what is admittedly disgraceful are no part of an orator's duty.

It is, however, universally agreed that all questions must be concerned either with something that is written or something that is not. Those concerned with what is written are questions of law, those which concern what is not written are questions of fact. Hermagoras calls the latter *rational* questions, the former *legal* questions, for so we may translate *logikon* and *nomikon*. Those who hold that every question concerns either things or words, mean much the same....

There are three things on which enquiry is made in every case: we ask *whether a thing is, what it is*, and *of what kind it is*. Nature herself imposes this upon us. For first of all there must be some subject for the question, since we cannot possibly determine *what a thing is*, or *of what kind it is*, until we have first ascertained *whether it is*, and therefore the first question raised is *whether it is*. But even when it is clear that a thing *is*, it is not immediately obvious *what it is*. And when we have decided what it is, there remains the question of its *quality*. These three points once ascertained, there is no further question to ask. These heads cover both *definite* and *indefinite questions*. One or more of them is discussed in every demonstrative, deliberative or forensic theme. These heads again cover all cases in the courts, whether we regard them from the point of view of *rational* or *legal questions*. For no legal problem can be settled save by

6.83 the aid of *definition, quality* and *conjecture*. Those, however, who are engaged in instructing the ignorant will find it useful at first to adopt a slightly less rigid method: the road will not be absolutely straight to begin with, but it will be more open and will provide easier going. I would have them therefore learn above all things that there are four different methods which may be employed in every case, and he who is going to plead should study them as first essentials. For, to begin with the defendant, far the strongest method of self-defence is, if possible, to deny the charge. The second best is when it is possible to reply that the particular act with which you are charged was never committed. The third and most honourable is to maintain that the act was justifiable. If none of these lines of defence are feasible, there remains the last and only hope of safety: if it is impossible either to deny the charge or justify the act, we must evade the charge with the aid of some point of law, making it appear that the action has been

6.84 brought against us illegally. Hence arise those questions of *legal action* or *competence*. For there are some things, which, although not laudable in themselves, are yet permitted by law; witness the passage in the Twelve Tables authorising creditors to divide up a debtor's body amongst themselves, a law which is repudiated by public custom. There are also certain things which although equitable are prohibited by law (witness the restrictions placed on

6.85 testamentary disposition). The accuser likewise has four things which he must keep in mind: he must prove that something was done, that a particular act was done, that it was wrongly done, and that he brings his charge according to law. Thus every cause will turn on the same sorts of questions, though the parts of plaintiff and defendant will sometimes be interchanged: for instance in the case of a claim for a reward, it will be the plaintiff's task to show that what was done was right.

6.86 These four schemes or forms of action which I then called *general bases* fall into two classes as I have shown, namely, the *rational* and the *legal*. The *rational* is the simpler, as it involves nothing more than the consideration of the nature of things. In this connection, therefore, a mere mention of *conjecture*,

6.87 *definition* and *quality* will suffice. *Legal questions* necessarily have a larger number of species, since there are many laws and a variety of forms. In the case of one law we rely on the letter, in others on the spirit. Some laws we force to serve our turn, when we can find no law to support our case, others we compare with one another, and on others we put some novel interpretation. Thus from

6.88 these three *bases* we get three resemblances of *bases*: sometimes simple, sometimes complex, but all having a character of their own, as, for instance, when questions of the *letter of the law* and its *intention* are involved, for these clearly come under *conjecture* or *quality*; or again where the syllogism is involved, for this is specially connected with *quality*; or where contradictory laws are involved, for these are on the same footing as the *letter of the law and*

6.89 *intention*; or yet again in cases of *ambiguity*, which is always resolved by *conjecture. Definition* also belongs to both classes of question, namely those concerned with the consideration of *facts* and those concerned with the *letter of the law*. All these questions, although they come under the three *bases*, yet since, as I have mentioned, they have certain characteristic features of their own, require to be pointed out to learners; and we must allow them to be called *legal bases or questions* or *minor heads,* as long as it is clearly understood that none of them involve any other *questions* than the three I have mentioned. As regards questions of *quantity, number, relation,* and, as some have thought, *comparison,* the case is different. For these have no connexion with the complexities of the law, but are concerned with reason only. Consequently they must always be regarded as coming under *conjecture* or *quality,* as, for instance, when we ask with what purpose, or at what time, or place something was done.

But I will speak of individual questions when I come to handle the rules for *division*. This much is agreed to by all writers, that one *cause* possesses one *basis,* but that as regards secondary questions related to the main issue of the trial, there may frequently be a number in one single cause. I also think there is at times some doubt as to which *basis* should be adopted, when many different lines of defence are brought to meet a single charge; and, just as in regard to the complexion to be given to the statement of the facts of the case, that complexion is said to be the best which the speaker can best maintain, so in the present connexion I may say that the best *basis* to choose is that which will permit the orator to develop a maximum of force. It is for this reason that we find Cicero and Brutus taking up different lines in defence of Milo. Cicero says that Clodius was justifiably killed because he sought to waylay Milo, but that Milo had not designed to kill him; while Brutus, who wrote his speech merely as a rhetorical exercise, also exults that Milo has killed a bad citizen. In complicated causes, however, two or three *bases* may be found, or different *bases:* for instance a man may plead that he did not do one thing, and that he was justified in doing another, or to take another similar class of case, a man may deny two of the charges. The same thing occurs when there is a question about some one thing which is claimed by a number of persons who may all of them rely on the same kind of plea (for instance, on the right of the next of kin), or may put in different claims, one urging that the property was left him by will, another that he is next of kin. Now whenever a different defence has to be made against different claimants, there must be different *bases,* as for example the well-known controversial theme: "Wills that are made in accordance with law shall be valid. When parents die intestate, their children shall be the heirs. A disinherited son shall receive none of his father's property. A bastard, if born before a legitimate son, shall be treated as legitimate, but if born after a legitimate son shall be treated merely as a citizen. It shall be lawful to give a son in adoption. Every son given in adoption shall have the right to re-enter his own family if his natural father has died childless. A father of two legitimate sons gave one in adoption, disinherited the other, and acknowledged a bastard, who was born to him later. Finally after making the disinherited son his heir he died. All three sons lay claim to the property." *Nothus* is the Greek word for a bastard; Latin, as Cato emphasized in one of his speeches, has no word of its own and therefore borrows the foreign term. But I am straying from the point. The son who was made heir by the will finds his way barred by the law "A disinherited son shall receive none of his father's property." The *basis* is one resting on the *letter of the law* and *intention*, and the problem is whether he can inherit by any means at all? can he do so in accordance with the intention of his father? or in virtue of the fact that he was made heir by the will? The problem confronting the bastard is twofold, since he was born after the two legitimate sons and was not born before a legitimate son. The first problem involves a syllogism: are those sons who have been cast out from their own family to be regarded as though they had never been born? The second is concerned with the letter of the law and intention. For it is admitted that he was not born before any legitimate son, but he will defend his claim by appealing to the intention of the law, which he will maintain to imply that the bastard, born when there was no legitimate son in the family, should rank as legitimate. He will dismiss the letter of the law, pointing out that in any case the position of a bastard is not prejudiced by the fact that no legitimate son was born after him, and arguing as follows:—"Suppose that the only son is a bastard, what will his position be? Merely that of a citizen? and yet he was not born after any legitimate son. Or will he rank as a son in all respects? But he was not born before the legitimate sons. As it is impossible to stand by the letter of the law we must stand by its intentions." It need disturb no one that one law should originate two *bases*. The law is twofold, and therefore has the force of two laws. To the son who desires to re-enter the family, the disinherited's first reply is, "Even though you are allowed to re-enter the family, I am still the heir." The *basis* will be the same as in the claim put forward by the disinherited son, since the question at issue is whether a disinherited son can inherit. Both the disinherited and the bastard will object, "You cannot re-enter the family, for our father did not die childless." But in this connexion each will rely on his own particular question. For the disinherited son will say that even a disinherited man does not cease to be a son, and will derive an argument from that very law which denies his claim to the inheritance; namely that it was unnecessary for a disinherited son to be excluded from possession of his father's property if he had ceased to be one of the family; but now, since in virtue of his rights as son he would have been his father's heir if he had died intestate, the law is brought to bar his claim; and yet the law does not deprive him of his position as son, but only of his position as heir. Here the *basis* is *definitive*, as turning on the definition of a son. Again the bastard in his turn will urge that his father did not die childless, employing the same arguments that he had used in putting forward his claim that he ranked as a son; unless indeed he too has recourse to definition, and raises the question whether even bastards are not sons. Thus in one case we shall have either two special *legal bases*, namely the *letter of the law* and *intention*, with the *syllogism* and also *definition,* or those three which are really the only *bases* strictly so called, *conjecture* as regards the *letter of the law and intention, quality* in the *syllogism*, and *definition*, which needs no explanation.

Further every kind of case will contain a *cause*, a *point for the decision of the judge*, and a *central argument*. For nothing can be said which does not contain a reason, something to which the decision of the judge is directed, and finally something which, more than aught else, contains the substance of the matter at issue.

FROM
Book VII

I think that enough has been said on the subject of invention. For I have dealt not merely with the methods by which we many instruct the judge, but also with the means of appealing to his emotions. But just as it is not sufficient for those who are erecting a building merely to collect stone and timber and other building materials, but skilled masons are required to arrange and place them, so in speaking, however abundant the matter may be, it will merely form a confused heap unless arrangement be employed to reduce it to order and to give it connexion and firmness of structure. Nor is it without good reason that arrangement is treated as the second of the five departments of oratory, since without it the first is useless. For the fact that all the limbs of a statue have been cast does not make it a statue: they must be put together; and if you were to interchange some one portion of our bodies or of those of other animals with another, although the body would be in possession of all the same members as before, you would none the less have produced a monster. Again even a slight dislocation will deprive a limb of its previous use and vigour, and disorder in the ranks will impede the movements of an army. Nor can I regard as an error the assertion that order is essential to the existence of nature itself, for without order everything would go to wrack and ruin. Similarly if oratory lack this virtue, it cannot fail to be confused, but will be like a ship drifting without a helmsman, will lack cohesion, will fall into countless repetitions and omissions, and, like a traveller who has lost his way in unfamiliar country, will be guided solely by chance without fixed purpose or the least idea either of starting-point or goal.

The whole of this book, therefore, will be devoted to arrangement, an art the acquisition of which would never have been such a rarity, had it been possible to lay down general rules which would suit all subjects. But since cases in the courts have always presented an infinite variety, and will continue to do so, and since through all the centuries there has never been found one single case which was exactly like any other, the pleader must rely upon his sagacity, keep his eyes open, exercise his powers of invention and judgment and look to himself for advice. On the other hand, I do not deny that there are some points which are capable of demonstration and which accordingly I shall be careful not to pass by.

Division, as I have already stated, means the division of a group of things into its component parts, *partition* is the separation of an individual whole into its elements, *order* the correct disposition of things in such a way that what follows coheres with what precedes, while *arrangement* is the distribution of things and parts to the places which it is expedient that they should occupy. But we must remember that *arrangement* is generally dependent on expediency, and that the same question will not always be discussed first by both parties. An example of what I mean, to quote no others, is provided by Demosthenes and Aeschines, who adopt a different order in the trial of Ctesiphon, since the accuser begins by dealing with the legal question involved, in which he thought he had the advantage, whereas the advocate for the defence treats practically every other topic before coming to the question of law, with a view to preparing the judges for a consideration of the legal aspect of the case. For it will often be expedient for the parties to place different points first; otherwise the pleading would always be determined by the good pleasure of the prosecution. Finally, in a case of mutual accusation, where both parties have to defend themselves before accusing their antagonist, the order of everything must necessarily be different. I shall therefore set forth the method adopted by myself, about which I have never made any mystery: it is the result in part of instruction received from others, in part of my own reasoning.

When engaged in forensic disputes I made it a point to make myself familiar with every circumstance connected with the case. (In the schools, of course, the facts of the case are definite and limited in number and are moreover set out before we begin to declaim: the Greeks call them *themes*, which Cicero translates by *propositions*.) When I had formed a general idea of these circumstances, I proceeded to consider them quite as much from my opponent's point of view as from my own. The first point which I set myself to determine (it is easy enough to state, but is still all-important) was what each party desired to establish and then what means he was likely to adopt to that end. My method was as follows. I considered what the prosecutor would say first: his point must either be admitted or controversial: if admitted, no question could arise in this connexion. I therefore passed to the answer of the defence and considered it from the same standpoint: even there the point was sometimes one that was admitted. It was not until the parties ceased to agree that any question arose. Take for example the following case. "You killed a man." "Yes, I killed him." Agreed, I pass to the defence, which has to produce the motive for the homicide. "It is lawful," he urges, "to kill an adulterer with his paramour." Another admitted point, for there is no doubt about the law. We must look for a third point where the two parties are at variance, "They were not adulterers," say the prosecution; "They were," say the defence. Here then is the question at issue: there is a doubt as to the facts, and it is therefore a question of *conjecture*. Sometimes even the third point may be admitted; it is granted that they were adulterers. "But," says the accuser, "you had no right to kill them, for you were an exile" or "had forfeited your civil rights." The question is now one of law. On the other hand, if when the prosecution says, "You killed them," the defence at once replies, "I did not," the issue is raised without more delay.

If it requires some search to discover where the dispute really begins, we must consider what constitutes the first question. The charge may be simple, as for example "Rabirius killed Saturninus," or complex like the following: "The offence committed by Lucius Varenus falls under the law of assassination: for he procured the murder of Gaius Varenus, the wounding of Gnacus Varenus and also the murder of Salarius." In the latter case there will be a number of propositions, a statement which also applies to civil suits as well. But in a complex case there may be a number of *questions* and *bases:* for instance the accused may deny one fact, justify another and plead technical grounds to show that a third fact is not actionable. In such cases the pleader will have to consider what requires refutation and where that refutation should be placed.

As regards the prosecutor, I do not altogether disagree with Celsus, who, though no doubt in so doing, he is following the practice of Cicero, insists with some vehemence on the view that the first place should be given to some strong argument, but that the strongest should be reserved to the end, while the weaker arguments should be placed in the middle, since the judge has to be moved at the beginning and forcibly impelled to a decision at the end. But with the defence it is different: the strongest arguments as a rule require to be disposed of first, for fear that the judge through having his thoughts fixed on those arguments should regard the defence of other points with disfavour. Sometimes, however, this order is subject to alteration; for example if the minor arguments are obviously false and the refutation of the most serious argument a matter of some difficulty, we should attack it last of all, after discrediting the prosecution by demonstrating the falsity of the former, thereby disposing the judges to believe that all their arguments are equally unreliable. We shall, however, require to preface our remarks by explaining why we postpone dealing with the most serious charge, and by promising that we will deal with it at a later stage: otherwise the fact that we do not dispose of it at once may give the impression that we are afraid of it. Charges brought against the past life of the accused should generally be dealt with first in order that the judge may be well-disposed to listen to our defence on that point on which he has to give his verdict. But Cicero in the *pro Vareno* postpones his treatment of such charges to the conclusion, being guided not by the general rule, but by the special circumstances of the case.

When the accusation is simple, we must consider whether to give a single answer to the charge or several. In the former case, we must decide whether the question is one of fact or of law: if it is one of fact, we must deny the fact or justify it: if, on the other hand, it is a question of law, we must decide on what special point the dispute arises and whether the question turns on the letter or the intention of the law. We shall do this by considering what the law is which gives rise to the dispute, that is to say under what law the court has been constituted. In scholastic themes, for example, the laws are sometimes stated merely with a view to connecting the arguments of the cases. Take the following case: "A father who recognises a son whom he has exposed in infancy, shall only take him back after paying for his keep. A disobedient son may be disinherited. A man who took back a son whom he had exposed orders him to marry a wealthy neighbour. The son desires to marry the daughter of the poor man who brought him up." The law about children who have been exposed affords scope for emotional treatment, while the decision of the court turns on the law of disinheritance. On the other hand, a question may turn on more laws than one, as in cases of *antinomia* or contradictory laws. It is by consideration of such points as these that we shall be able to determine the point of law out of which the dispute arises.

As an example of complex defence I may quote the *pro Rabirio:* "If he had killed him, he would have been justified in so doing: but he did not kill him." But when we advance a number of points in answer to a single proposition, we must first of all consider everything that can be said on the subject, and then decide which out of these points it is expedient to select and where to put them

1.17 forward. My views on this subject are not identical with those which I admitted a little while ago on the subject of *propositions* and on that of *arguments* in the section which I devoted to *proofs*, to the effect that we may sometimes begin with the strongest. For when we are defending, there should always be an increase of force in the treatment of questions and we should proceed from the weaker to the stronger, whether the points we raise are of the same or of a

1.18 different character. Questions of law will often arise from one ground of dispute after another, whereas questions of fact are always concerned with one point; but the order to be followed is the same in both cases. We must, however, deal first with points that differ in character. In such cases the weakest should always be handled first, for the reason that there are occasions when after discussing a question we make a concession or present of it to our opponents:

1.19 for we cannot pass on to others without dropping those which come first. This should be done in such a way as to give the impression not that we regard the points as desperate, but that we have deliberately dropped them because we can prove our case without them. Suppose that the agent for a certain person claims the interest on a loan as due under an inheritance. The question may here arise

1.20 whether such a claim can be made by an agent. Assume that, after discussing the question, we drop it or that the argument is refuted. We then raise the question whether the person in whose name the action is brought has the right to employ an agent. Let us yield this point also. The case will still admit of our raising the question whether the person in whose name the suit is brought is

1.21 heir to the person to whom the interest was due and again whether he is sole heir. Grant these points also and we can still raise the question whether the sum is due at all? On the other hand, no one will be so insane as to drop what he considers his strongest point and pass to others of minor importance. The following case from a scholastic theme is of a similar character. "You may not disinherit your adopted son. And if you may disinherit him *qua* adopted son, you may not disinherit one who is so brave. And if you may disinherit one who is so brave, you may not disinherit him because he has not obeyed your every command; and if he was bound to obey you in all else, you may not disinherit him on the ground of his choice of a reward; and even if the choice of a reward may give just ground for disinheriting, that is not true of such a choice as he

1.22 actually made." Such is the nature of dissimilarity where points of law are concerned. Where, however, the question is one of fact, there may be several points all tending to the same result, of which some may be dropped as not essential to the main issue, as for instance if a man accused of theft should say to his accuser, "Prove that you had the property, prove that you lost it, prove that it was stolen, prove that it was stolen by me." The first three can be dropped, but not the last.

1.23 I used also to employ the following method. I went back from the ultimate *species* (which generally contains the vital point of the case) to the first general question or descended from the *genus* to the ultimate *species*, applying this

1.24 method even to deliberative themes. For example, Numa is deliberating whether to accept the crown offered him by the Romans. First he considers the general question, "Ought I to be a king?" Then, "Ought I to be king in a foreign state? Ought I to be king at Rome? Are the Romans likely to put up with such a king as myself?" So too in controversial themes. Suppose a brave man to choose another man's wife as his reward. The ultimate *species* is found in the question whether he is allowed to choose another man's wife. The *general* question is whether he should be given whatever he chooses. Next come questions such as whether he can choose his reward from the property of private individuals, whether he can choose a bride as his reward, and if so, whether he can choose one who is already married. But in our search for such questions we follow an order quite different from that which we employ in actual speaking. For that which as a rule occurs to us first, is just that which ought to come last in our speech: as for instance the conclusion, "You have no right to choose another man's wife." Consequently undue haste will spoil our division of the subject. We must not therefore be content with the thoughts that first offer themselves, but should press our inquiry further till we reach conclusions such as that he ought not even to choose a widow: a further advance is made when we reach the conclusion that he should choose nothing that is private property, or last of all we may go back to the question next in order to the general question, and conclude that he should choose nothing inequitable. Consequently after surveying our opponent's proposition, an easy task, we should consider, if possible, what it is most natural to answer first. And, if we imagine the case as being actually pleaded and ourselves as under the necessity of making a reply, that answer will probably suggest itself. On the other hand, if this is impossible, we should put aside whatever first occurs to us and reason with ourselves as follows: "What if this were not the case?" We must then repeat the process a second and a third time and so on, until nothing is left for consideration. Thus we shall examine even minor points, by our treatment of which we may perhaps make the judge all the better disposed to us when we come to the main issue. The rule that we should descend from the *common* to the *particular* is much the same, since what is *common* is usually *general*. For example, "He killed a tyrant" is *common*, while "A tyrant was killed by his son, by a woman or by his wife" are all *particular*.

I used also to note down separately whatever was admitted both by my opponent and myself, provided it suited my purpose, and not merely to press any admissions that he might make, but to multiply them by partition, as for example in the following controversial theme:—"A general, who had stood against his father as a candidate and defeated him, was captured: the envoys who went to ransom him met his father returning from the enemy. He said to the envoys, 'You are too late.' They searched the father and found gold in his pockets. They pursued their journey and found the general crucified. He cried to them, 'Beware of the traitor.' The father is accused." What points are admitted by both parties? "We were told that there had been treason and told it by the general." We try to find the traitor. "You admit that you went to the enemy, that you did so by stealth, that you returned unscathed, that you brought back gold and had it concealed about your person." For an act of the accused may sometimes be stated in such a way as to tell heavily against him, and if our statement makes a real impression on the mind of the judge, it may serve to close his ears to all that is urged by the defence. For as a general rule it is of advantage to the accuser to mass his facts together and to the defence to separate them.

I used also, with reference to the whole material of the case, to do what I have already mentioned as being done with arguments, namely, after first setting forth all the facts without exception, I then disposed of all of them with the one exception of the fact which I wished to be believed. For example, in *1.32* charges of collusion it may be argued as follows. "The means for securing the acquittal of an accused person are strictly limited. His innocence may be established, some superior authority may intervene, force or bribery may be employed, his guilt may be difficult to prove, or there may be collusion between the advocates. You admit that he was guilty; no superior authority intervened, no violence was used and you make no complaint that the jury was bribed, while *1.33* there was no difficulty about proving his guilt. What conclusion is left to us save that there was collusion?" If I could not dispose of all the points against me, I disposed of the majority. "It is acknowledged that a man was killed: but he was not killed in a solitary place, such as might lead me to suspect that he was the victim of robbers; he was not killed for the sake of plunder, for nothing was taken from him; he was not killed in the hope of inheriting his property, for he *1.34* was poor: the motive must therefore have been hatred, since you are his enemy." The task not merely of division, but of invention as well, is rendered materially easier by this method of examining all possible arguments and arriving at the best by a process of elimination. Milo is accused of killing Clodius. Either he did or did not do the deed. The best policy would be to deny the fact, but that is impossible. It is admitted then that he killed him. The act must then have been either right or wrong. We urge that it was right. If so, the act must have either been deliberate or under compulsion of necessity, for it is *1.35* impossible to plead ignorance. The intention is doubtful, but as it is generally supposed to have existed, some attempt must be made to defend it and to show that it was for the good of the state. On the other hand, if we plead necessity, we shall argue that the fight was accidental and unpremeditated. One of the two parties then must have lain in wait for the other. Which was it? Clodius without doubt. Do you see how inevitably we are led to the right method of defence by *1.36* the logical necessity of the facts? We may carry the process further: either he wished to kill Clodius, who lay in wait for him, or he did not. The safer course is to argue that he did not wish to kill him. It was then the slaves of Milo who did the deed without Milo's orders or knowledge. But this line of defence shows a *1.37* lack of courage and lessens the weight of our argument that Clodius was rightly killed. We shall therefore add the words, "As every man would have wished his slaves to do under similar circumstances." This method is all the more useful from the fact that often we can find nothing to say that really pleases us and yet have got to say something. Let us therefore consider every possible point; for thus we shall discover what is the best line for us to pursue, or at any rate what is least bad. Sometimes, as I have already said in the appropriate context, we may make good use of the statement of our opponent, since occasionally it is equally to the purpose of both parties.

FROM
Book VIII

What the Greeks call *phrasis*, we in Latin call *elocutio* or style. Style is revealed both in individual words and in groups of words. As regards the former, we must see that they are Latin, clear, elegant and well-adapted to produce the desired effect. As regards the latter, they must be correct, aptly placed and adorned with suitable figures. I have already, in the portions of the first book dealing with the subject of grammar, said all that is necessary on the way to acquire idiomatic and correct speech. But there my remarks were restricted to the prevention of positive faults, and it is well that I should now point out that our words should have nothing provincial or foreign about them. For you will find that there are a number of writers by no means deficient in style whose language is precious rather than idiomatic. As an illustration of my meaning I would remind you of the story of the old woman at Athens, who, when Theophrastrus, a man of no mean eloquence, used one solitary word in an affected way, immediately said that he was a foreigner, and on being asked how she detected it, replied that his language was too Attic for Athens. Again Asinius Pollio held that Livy, for all his astounding eloquence, showed traces of the idiom of Padua. Therefore, if possible, our voice and all our words should be such as to reveal the native of this city, so that our speech may seem to be of genuine Roman origin, and not merely to have been presented with Roman citizenship.

Clearness results above all from *propriety* in the use of words. But *propriety* is capable of more than one interpretation. In its primary sense it means calling things by their right names, and is consequently sometimes to be avoided, for our language must not be obscene, unseemly or mean. Language may be described as mean when it is beneath the dignity of the subject or the rank of the speaker. Some orators fall into serious error in their eagerness to avoid this fault, and are afraid of all words that are in ordinary use, even although they may be absolutely necessary for their purpose. There was, for example, the man who in the course of a speech spoke of "Iberian grass," a meaningless phrase intelligible only to himself. Cassius Severus, however, by the way of deriding his affectation, explained that he meant Spanish broom. Nor do I see why a certain distinguished orator thought "fishes conserved in brine" a more elegant phrase than the word which he avoided. But while there is no special merit in the form of *propriety* which consists in calling things by their real names, it is a fault to fly to the opposite extreme. This fault we call *impropriety*, while the Greeks call it *akuron*. As examples I may cite the Virgilian, "Never could I have hoped for such great woe," or the phrase, which I noted had been corrected by Cicero in a speech of Dolabella's, "To bring death," or again, phrases of a kind that win praise from some of our contemporaries, such as, "His words fell from the cross." On the other hand, everything that lacks appropriateness will not necessarily suffer from the fault of positive *impropriety*, because there are, in the first place, many things which have no

2.5 proper term either in Greek or Latin. For example, the verb *iaculari* is specially used in the sense of "to throw a javelin," whereas there is no special verb appropriated to the throwing of a ball or a stake. So, too, while *lapidare* has the obvious meaning of "to stone," there is no special word to describe the throwing
2.6 of clods or potsherds. Hence abuse or *catachresis* of words becomes necessary, while metaphor, also, which is the supreme ornament of oratory, applies words to things with which they have strictly no connexion. Consequently *propriety* turns not on the actual term, but on the meaning of the term, and must be tested
2.7 by the touchstone of the understanding, not of the ear. The second sense in which the word *propriety* is used occurs when there are a number of things all called by the same name: in this case the original term from which the others are derived is styled the *proper* term. For example, the word *vertex* means a whirl of water, or of anything else that is whirled in a like manner: then, owing to the fashion of coiling the hair, it comes to mean the top of the head, while finally, from this sense it derives the meaning of the highest point of a
2.8 mountain. All these things may correctly be called *vertices*, but the *proper* use of the term is the first. So, too, *solea* and *turdus* are employed as names of fish, to mention no other cases. The third kind of *propriety* is found in the case where a thing which serves a number of purposes has a special name in some one particular context; for example, the proper term for a funeral *song* is *naenia*, and for the general's *lent augurale*. Again, a term which is common to a number of things may be applied in a *proper* or special sense to some one of them. Thus we use *urbs* in the special sense of Rome, *venales* in the special sense of newly-purchased slaves, and *Corinthia* in the special sense of bronzes, although there are other cities besides Rome, and many other things which may be styled *venales* besides slaves, and gold and silver are found at Corinth as well as
2.9 bronze. But the use of such terms implies no special excellence in an orator. There is, however, a form of *propriety* of speech which deserves the highest praise, that is to say, the employment of words with the maximum of significance, as, for instance, when Cato said that "Caesar was thoroughly sober when he undertook the task of overthrowing the constitution," or as Virgil spoke of a
2.10 "thin-drawn strain," and Horace of the "shrill pipe," and "dread Hannibal." Some also include under this head that form of *propriety* which is derived from characteristic epithets, such as in the Virgilian phrases, "sweet unfermented wine," or "with white teeth." But of this sort of propriety I shall have to speak
2.11 elsewhere. *Propriety* is also made to include the appropriate use of words in metaphor, while at times the salient characteristic of an individual comes to be attached to him as a *proper* name: thus Fabius was called "Cunctator," the Delayer, on account of the most remarkable of his many military virtues. Some perhaps, may think that words which mean more than they actually say deserve mention in connexion with clearness, since they assist the understanding. I, however, prefer to place *emphasis* among the ornaments of oratory, since it does not make a thing intelligible, but merely more intelligible.
2.12 Obscurity, on the other hand, results from the employment of obsolete words, as, for instance, if an author should search the records of the priests, the earliest treaties and the works of long-forgotten writers with the deliberate

design of collecting words that no man living understands. For there are persons who seek to gain a reputation for erudition by such means as this, in order that they may be regarded as the sole depositories of certain forms of knowledge. Obscurity may also be produced by the use of words which are more familiar in certain districts than in others, or which are of a technical character, such as the wind called "Atabalus," or a "sack-ship," or *in malo cosanum*. Such expressions should be avoided if we are pleading before a judge who is ignorant of their meaning, or, if used, should be explained, as may have to be done in the case of what are called homonyms. For example, the word *taurus* may be unintelligible unless we make it clear whether we are speaking of a bull, or a mountain, or a constellation, or the name of a man, or the root of a tree.

2.13

A greater source of obscurity is, however, to be found in the construction and combination of words, and the ways in which this may occur are still more numerous. Therefore, a sentence should never be so long that it is impossible to follow its drift, now should its conclusion be unduly postponed by transposition or an excessive use of *hyperbaton*. Still worse is the result when the order of the words is confused as in the line

2.14

> In the midmost sea
> Rocks are there by Italians altars called.

Again, parenthesis, so often employed by orators and historians, and consisting in the insertion of one sentence in the midst of another, may seriously hinder the understanding of a passage, unless the insertion is short. For example, in the passage where Virgil describes a colt, the words

2.15

> Nor fears he empty noises,

are followed by a number of remarks of a totally different form, and it is only four lines later that the poet returns to the point and says,

> Then, if the sound of arms be heard afar,
> How to stand still he knows not.

Above all, ambiguity must be avoided, and by ambiguity I mean not merely the kind of which I have already spoken, where the sense is uncertain, as in the clause *Chremetem audivi percussisse Demean*, but also that form of ambiguity which, although it does not actually result in obscuring the sense, falls into the same verbal error as if a man should say *visum a se hominem librum scribentem* (that he had seen a man writing a book). For although it is clear that the book was being written by the man, the sentence is badly put together, and its author has made it as ambiguous as he could.

2.16

Again, some writers introduce a whole host of useless words; for, in their eagerness to avoid ordinary methods of expression, and allured by false ideals of beauty they wrap up everything in a multitude of words simply and solely because they are unwilling to make a direct and simple statement of the facts: and then they link up and involve one of these long-winded clauses with others like it, and extend their periods to a length beyond the compass of mortal breath. Some even expend an infinity of toil to acquire this vice, which, by the way, is

2.17

2.18

nothing new: for I learn from the pages of Livy that there was one, a teacher, who instructed his pupils to make all they said obscure, using the Greek word *skotison* ("darken it"). It was this same habit that gave rise to the famous words of praise, "So much the better: even I could not understand you." Others are consumed with a passion for brevity and omit words which are actually necessary to the sense, regarding it as a matter of complete indifference whether their meaning is intelligible to others, so long as they know what they mean themselves. For my own part, I regard as useless words which make such a demand upon the ingenuity of the hearer. Others, again, succeed in committing the same fault by a perverse misuse of figures. Worst of all are the phrases which the Greeks call *adianoēta*, expressions which, though their meaning is obvious enough on the surface, have a secret meaning, as for example in the phrase *cum ductus est caecus secundum viam stare,* or where the man, who is supposed in the scholastic theme to have torn his own limbs with his teeth, is said to have *lain upon himself.* Such expressions are regarded as ingenious, daring and eloquent, simply because of their ambiguity, and quite a number of persons have become infected by the belief that a passage which requires a commentator must for that very reason be a masterpiece of elegance. Nay, there is even a class of hearer who find a special pleasure in such passages; for the fact that they can provide an answer to the riddle fills them with an ecstasy of self-congratulation, as if they had not merely heard the phrase, but invented it.

For my own part, I regard clearness as the first essential of a good style: there must be propriety in our words, their order must be straightforward, the conclusion of the period must not be long postponed, there must be nothing lacking and nothing superfluous. Thus our language will be approved by the learned and clear to the uneducated. I am speaking solely of clearness in style, as I have already dealt with clearness in the presentation of facts in the rules I laid down for the *statement of the case.* But the general method is the same in both. For if what we say is not less nor more than is required, and is clear and systematically arranged, the whole matter will be plain and obvious even to a not too attentive audience. For we must never forget that the attention of the judge is not always so keen that he will dispel obscurities without assistance, and bring the light of his intelligence to bear on the dark places of our speech. On the contrary, he will have many other thoughts to distract him unless what we say is so clear that our words will thrust themselves into his mind even when he is not giving us his attention, just as the sunlight forces itself upon the eyes. Therefore our aim must be not to put him in a position to understand our argument, but to force him to understand it. Consequently we shall frequently repeat anything which we think the judge has failed to take in as he should. We shall say, for example, "I fear that this portion of our case has been somewhat obscurely stated: the fault is mine, and I will therefore re-state it in plainer and simpler language"; for the pretended admission of a fault on our part creates an excellent impression. . . .

I will now proceed to the next subject for discussion, which is, as I have said, that of *tropes,* or *modes,* as the most distinguished Roman rhetoricians call them. Rules for their use are given by the teachers of literature as well. But I

INSTITUTIO ORATORIA

postponed the discussion of the subject when I was dealing with literary education, because it seemed to me that the theme would have greater importance if handled in connexion with the ornaments of oratory, and that it ought to be reserved for treatment on a larger scale.

By a *trope* is meant the artistic alteration of a word or phrase from its proper meaning to another. This is a subject which has given rise to interminable disputes among the teachers of literature, who have quarrelled no less violently with the philosophers than among themselves over the problem of the *genera* and *species* into which *tropes* may be divided, their number and their correct classification. I propose to disregard such quibbles as in no wise concern the training of an orator, and to proceed to discuss those *tropes* which are most necessary and meet with most general acceptance, contenting myself merely with noting the fact that some *tropes* are employed to help out our meaning and others to adorn our style, that some arise from words used *properly* and others from words used *metaphorically*, and that the changes involved concern not merely individual words, but also our thoughts and the structure of our sentences. In view of these facts I regard those writers as mistaken who have held that *tropes* necessarily involved the substitution of word for word. And I do not ignore the fact that as a rule the *tropes* employed to express our meaning involve ornament as well, though the converse is not the case, since there are some which are intended solely for the purpose of embellishment.

Let us begin, then, with the commonest and by far the most beautiful of *tropes*, namely, *metaphor*, the Greek term for our *translatio*. It is not merely so natural a turn of speech that it is often employed unconsciously or by uneducated persons, but it is in itself so attractive and elegant that however distinguished the language in which it is embedded it shines forth with a light that is all its own. For if it be correctly and appropriately applied, it is quite impossible for its effect to be commonplace, mean or unpleasing. It adds to the copiousness of language by the interchange of words and by borrowing, and finally succeeds in accomplishing the supremely difficult task of providing a name for everything. A noun or a verb is transferred from the place to which it properly belongs to another where there is either no *literal* term or the *transferred* is better than the *literal*. We do this either because it is necessary or to make our meaning clearer or, as I have already said, to produce a decorative effect. When it secures none of these results, our metaphor will be out of place. As an example of a necessary metaphor I may quote the following usages in vogue with peasants when they call a vinebud *gemma,* a gem (what other term is there which they could use?), or speak of the *crops being thirsty* or the *fruit suffering*. For the same reason we speak of a *hard* or *rough* man, there being no *literal* term for these temperaments. On the other hand, when we say that a man is *kindled to anger* or *on fire with greed* or that he has *fallen into error*, we do so to enhance our meaning. For none of these things can be more literally described in its own words than in those which we import from elsewhere. But it is a purely ornamental metaphor when we speak of *brilliance of style, splendour of birth, tempestuous public assemblies, thunderbolts of eloquence*, to which I may add the phrase employed by Cicero in his defence of Milo where he speaks

6.8 of Clodius as the *fountain,* and in another place as *the fertile field and material* of his client's *glory*. It is even possible to express facts of a somewhat unseemly character by a judicious use of metaphor, as in the following passage:

> This do they lest too much indulgence make
> The field of generation slothful grow
> And choke its idle furrows.

6.9 On the whole *metaphor* is a shorter form of *simile*, while there is this further difference, that in the latter we compare some object to the thing which we wish to describe, whereas in the former this object is actually substituted for the thing. It is a comparison when I say that a man did something *like a lion*, it is a metaphor when I say of him, *He is a lion*. Metaphors fall into four classes. In the first we substitute one living thing for another, as in the passage where the poet, speaking of a charioteer, says,

> The steersman then
> With mighty effort wrenched his charger round.

6.10 or when Livy says that Scipio was continually *barked at* by Cato. Secondly, inanimate things may be substituted for inanimate, as in the Virgilian:

> And gave his fleet the rein,

or inanimate may be substituted for animate, as in

> Did the Argive bulwark fall by sword or fate?

or animate for inanimate, as in the following lines:

> The shepherd sits unknowing on the height
> Listening the roar from some far mountain brow.

6.11 But, above all, effects of extraordinary sublimity are produced when the theme is exalted by a bold and almost hazardous metaphor and inanimate objects are given life and action, as in the phrase

> Araxes' flood that scorns a bridge,

6.12 or in the passage of Cicero, already quoted, where he cries, "What was that sword of yours doing, Tubero, the sword you drew on the field of Pharsalus? Against whose body did you aim its point? What meant those arms you bore?" Sometimes the effect is doubled, as in Virgil's.

> And with venom arm the steel.

6.13 For both "to arm the steel" and "to arm with venom" are metaphors. These four kinds of metaphor are further subdivided into a number of *species*, such as transference from rational beings to rational and from irrational to irrational and the reverse, in which the method is the same, and finally from the whole to its parts and from the parts to the whole. But I am not now teaching boys: my readers are old enough to discover the *species* for themselves when once they have been given the *genus*.

While a temperate and timely use of metaphor is a real adornment to style, on the other hand, its frequent use serves merely to obscure our language and weary our audience, while if we introduce them in one continuous series, our language will become allegorical and enigmatic. There are also certain metaphors which fail from meanness, such as that of which I spoke above:

> There is a rocky wart upon the mountain's brow.

or they may even be coarse. For it does not follow that because Cicero was perfectly jusified in talking of "the sink of the state," when he desired to indicate the foulness of certain men, we can approve the following passage from an ancient orator: "you have lanced the boils of the state." Indeed Cicero himself has demonstrated in the most admirable manner how important it is to avoid grossness in metaphor, such as is revealed by the following examples, which he quotes:—"The state was gelded by the death of Africanus," or "Glaucia, the excrement of the senate-house." He also points out that a metaphor must not be too great for its subject or, as is more frequently the case, too little, and that it must not be inappropriate. Anyone who realises that these are faults, will be able to detect instances of them only too frequently. But excess in the use of metaphor is also a fault, more especially if they are of the same species. Metaphors may also be harsh, that is, far-fetched, as in phrases like "the snows of the head" or "Jove with white snow the wintry Alps bespewed." The worst errors of all, however, originate in the fact that some authors regard it as permissible to use even in prose any metaphors that are allowed to poets, in spite of the fact that the latter aim solely at pleasing their readers and are compelled in many cases to employ metaphor by sheer metrical necessity. For my own part I should not regard a phrase like "the shepherd of the people" as admissible in pleading, although it has the authority of Homer, nor would I venture to say that winged creatures "swim through the air," despite the fact that this metaphor has been most effectively employed by Virgil to describe the flight of bees and of Daedalus. For metaphor should always either occupy a place already vacant, or if it fills the room of something else, should be more impressive than that which it displaces.

What I have said above applies perhaps with even greater force to *synecdochè*. For while *metaphor* is designed to move the feelings, give special distinction to things and place them vividly before the eye, *synecdochè* has the power to give variety to our language by making us realise many things from one, the whole from a part, the *genus* from a *species*, things which follow from things which have preceded; or, on the other hand, the whole procedure may be reversed. It may, however, be more freely employed by poets than by orators. For while in prose it is perfectly correct to use *mucro*, the point, for the whole sword, and *tectum*, roof, for a whole house, we may not employ *puppis*, stern, to describe a ship, nor *abies*, fir, to describe planks; and again, though *ferrum*, the steel, may be used to indicate a sword, *quadrupes* cannot be used in the sense of horse. It is where numbers are concerned that *synecdochè* can be most freely employed in prose. For example, Livy frequently says, "The Roman won the day," when he means that the *Romans* were victorious; on the other hand,

6.21 Cicero in a letter to Brutus says, "We have imposed on the people and are regarded as orators," when he is speaking of himself alone. This form of *trope* is not only a rhetorical ornament, but is frequently employed in everyday speech. Some also apply the term *synecdochè* when something is assumed which has not actually been expressed, since one word is then discovered from other words, as in the sentence,

> The Arcadians to the gates began to rush;

6.22 when such omission creates a blemish, it is called an *ellipse*. For my own part, I prefer to regard this as a figure, and shall therefore discuss it under that head. Again, one thing may be suggested by another, as in the line,

> Behold, the steers
> Bring back the plough suspended from the yoke,

from which we infer the approach of night. I am not sure whether this is permissible to an orator except in arguments, when it serves as an indication of some fact. However, this has nothing to do with the question of style.

6.23 It is but a short step from *synecdochè* to *metonymy*, which consists in the substitution of one name for another, and, as Cicero tells us, is called *hypallage* by the rhetoricians. These devices are employed to indicate an invention by substituting the name of the inventor, or a possession by substituting the name of the possessor. Virgil, for example, writes:

> Ceres by water spoiled,

and Horace:

> Neptune admitted to the land
> Protects the fleets from blasts of Aquilo.

6.24 If, however, the process is reversed, the effect is harsh. But it is important to enquire to what extent *tropes* of this kind should be employed by the orator. For though we often hear "Vulcan" used for fire and to say *vario Marte pugnatum est* for "they fought with varying success" is elegant and idiomatic, while *Venus* is a more decent expression than *coitus,* it would be too bold for the severe style demanded in the courts to speak of *Liber* and *Ceres* when we mean bread and wine. Again, while usage permits us to substitute that which contains for that which is contained, as in phrases such as "civilised cities," or "a cup was drunk 6.25 to the lees," or "a happy age," the converse procedure would rarely be ventured on by any save a poet: take, for example, the phrase:

> Ucalegon burns next.

It is, however, perhaps more permissible to describe what is possessed by reference to its possessor, as, for example, to say of a man whose estate is being 6.26 squandered, "the man is being eaten up." Of this form there are innumerable species. For example, we say "sixty thousand men were slain by Hannibal at Cannae," and speak of "Virgil" when we mean "Virgil's poems"; again, we say that supplies have "come," when they have been "brought," that a "sacrilege," and not a "sacrilegious man" has been detected, and that a man possesses a knowledge of "arms," not of "the art of arms." The type which indicates cause by effect is common both in poets and orators. As examples from poetry I may quote: 6.27

> Pale death with equal foot knocks at the poor man's door

and

> There pale diseases dwell and sad old age;

while the orator will speak of "headlong anger," "cheerful youth" or "slothful case."

The following type of *trope* has also some kinship with *synecdochè*. For when I speak of a man's "looks" instead of his "look," I use the plural for the singular, but my aim is not to enable one thing to be inferred from many (for the sense is clear enough), but I merely vary the form of the word. Again, when I call a "gilded roof" a "golden roof," I diverge a little from the truth, because gilding forms only a part of the roof. But to follow out these points is a task involving too much minute detail even for a work whose aim is not the training of an orator. 6.28

Antonomasia, which substitutes someting else for a proper name, is very common in poets: it may be done in two ways: by the substitution of an epithet as equivalent to the name which it replaces, such as "Tydides," "Pelides," or by indicating the most striking characteristics of an individual, as in the phrase "Father of gods and king of men...." 6.29

FROM

Book IX

In my last book I spoke of *tropes*. I now come to *figures*, called *schēmata* in Greek, a topic which is naturally and closely connected with the preceding. For many authors have considered *figures* identical with *tropes*, because whether it be that the latter derive their name from having a certain form or from the fact that they effect alterations in language (a view which has also led to their being styled *motions*), it must be admitted that both these features are found in *figures* as well. Their employment is also the same. For they add force and charm to our matter. There are some again who call *tropes, figures*, Artorius Proculus among them. Further the resemblance between the two is so close that it is not easy to distinguish between them. For although certain kinds differ, while retaining a general resemblance (since both involve a departure from the simple and straightforward method of expression coupled with a certain rhetorical excellence), on the other hand some are distinguished by the narrowest possible dividing line: for example, while *irony* belongs to *figures of thought* just as much as to *tropes, periphrasis, hyperbaton* and *onomatopoea* have been ranked by distinguished authors as *figures of speech* rather than *tropes*. 1.1 1.2 1.3

1.4 It is therefore all the more necessary to point out the distinction between the two. The name of *trope* is applied to the transference of expressions from their natural and principal signification to another, with a view to the embellishment of style or, as the majority of grammarians define it, the transference of words and phrases from the place which is strictly theirs to another to which they do not properly belong. A *figure,* on the other hand, as is clear from the name itself, is the term employed when we give our language a conformation
1.5 other than the obvious and ordinary. Therefore the substitution of one word for another is placed among *tropes,* as for example in the case of *metaphor, metonymy, antonomasia, metalepsis, synechdochè, catachresis, allegory* and, as a rule, *hyperbole,* which may, of course, be concerned either with words or things. *Onomatopoeia* is the creation of a word and therefore involves substitu-
1.6 tion for the words which we should use but for such creation. Again although *periphrasis* often includes the actual word whose place it supplies, it still uses a number of words in place of one. The *epithet* as a rule involves an element of *antonomasia* and consequently becomes a *trope* on account of this affinity. *Hyperbaton* is a change of order and for this reason we may exclude it from *tropes.* None the less it transfers a word or part of a word from its own place to
1.7 another. None of these can be called *figures.* For a *figure* does not necessarily involve any alteration either of the order or the strict sense of words. As regards *irony,* I shall show elsewhere how in some of its forms it is a *trope,* in others a *figure.* For I admit that the name is common to both and am aware of the complicated and minute discussions to which it has given rise. They, however, have no bearing on my present task. For it makes no difference by which name either is called, so long as its stylistic value is apparent, since the meaning of
1.8 things is not altered by a change of name. For just as men remain the same, even though they adopt a new name, so these artifices will produce exactly the same effect, whether they are styled *tropes* or *figures,* since their values lie not in their names, but in their effect. Similarly it makes no difference whether we call a *basis* conjectural or negative, or concerned with fact or substance,
1.9 provided always that we know that the subject of enquiry is the same. It is best therefore in dealing with these topics to adopt the generally accepted terms and to understand the actual thing, by whatever name it is called. But we must note the fact that *trope* and *figure* are often combined in the expression of the same thought, since figures are introduced just as much by the metaphorical as by the literal use of words.

1.10 There is, however, a considerable difference of opinion among authors as to the meaning of the name, the number of *genera* and the nature and number of the *species* into which figures may be divided. The first point for consideration is, therefore, what is meant by a *figure.* For the term is used in two senses. In the first it is applied to any form in which thought is expressed, just as it is to
1.11 bodies which, whatever their composition, must have some shape. In the second and special sense, in which it is called a *schema,* it means a rational change in meaning or language from the ordinary and simple form, that is to say, a change analogous to that involved by sitting, lying down on something or looking back.

Consequently when a student tends to continuous or at any rate excessive use of the same cases, tenses, rhythms or even feet, we are in the habit of instructing him to vary his *figures* with a view to the avoidance of monotony. In so doing we speak as if every kind of language possessed a *figure:* for example *cursitare* and *lectitare* are said to have the same figure, that is to say, they are identical in formation. Therefore in the first and common sense of the word everything is expressed by *figures*. If we are content with this view, there is good reason for the opinion expressed by Apollodorus (if we may trust the statement of Caccilius on this point) to the effect that he found the rules laid down in this connexion quite incomprehensible. If, on the other hand, the name is to be applied to certain attitudes, or I might say gestures of language, we must interpret *schema* in the sense of that which is poetically or rhetorically altered from the simple and obvious method of expression. It will then be true to distinguish between the style which is devoid of figures (or *aschēmatistos*) and that which is adorned with figures (or *eschēmatismenē*). But Zoilus narrowed down the definition, since he restricted the term *schema* to cases when the speaker pretends to say something other than that which he actually does say. I know that this view meets with common acceptance: it is, in fact, for this reason that we speak of *figured* controversial themes, of which I shall shortly speak. We shall then take a *figure* to mean a form of expression to which a new aspect is given by art.

Some writers have held that there is only one kind of *figure*, altogether they differ as regards the reasons which lead them to adopt this view. For some of them, on the ground that a change of words causes a corresponding change in the sense, assert that all *figures* are concerned with words, while others hold that *figures* are concerned solely with the sense, on the ground that words are adapted to things. Both these views are obviously quibbling. For the same things are often put in different ways and the sense remains unaltered though the words are changed, while a *figure of thought* may include several *figures of speech*. For the former lies in the conception, the latter in the expression of our thought. The two are frequently combined, however, as in the following passage: "Now, Dolabella, [I have no pity] either for you or for your children": for the device by which he turns from the judges to Dolabella is a *figure of thought*, while *iam iam* ("now") and *liberum* ("your children") are *figures of speech*.

It is, however, to the best of my knowledge, generally agreed by the majority of authors that there are two classes of *figure,* namely *figures of thought*, that is of the mind, feeling or conceptions, since all these terms are used, and *figures of speech*, that is of words, diction, expression, language or style: the name by which they are known varies, but mere terminology is a matter of indifference. Cornelius Celsus, however, to *figures of thought* and *speech* would add those produced by "glosses"; but he has merely been led astray by an excessive passion for novelty. For who can suppose that so learned a man was ignorant of the fact that "glosses" and "reflexions" both come under the heading of thought? We may therefore conclude that, like language itself, figures are necessarily concerned with thought and with words.

1.19 As, however, in the natural course of things we conceive ideas before we express them, I must take *figures of thought* first. Their utility is at once great and manifold, and is revealed with the utmost clearness in every product of oratory. For although it may seem that proof is infinitesimally affected by the *figures* employed, none the less those same *figures* lend credibility to our

1.20 arguments and steal their way secretly into the minds of the judges. For just as in sword-play it is easy to see, parry, and ward off direct blows and simple and straightforward thrusts, while side-strokes and feints are less easy to observe and the task of the skilful swordsman is to give the impression that his design is quite other than it actually is, even so the oratory in which there is no guile fights by sheer weight and impetus alone; on the other hand, the fighter who feints and varies his assault is able to attack flank or back as he will, to lure his opponent's weapons from their guard and to outwit him by a slight inclination of

1.21 the body. Further, there is no more effective method of exciting the emotions than an apt use of figures. For if the expression of brow, eyes and hands has a powerful effect in stirring the passions, how much more effective must be the aspect of our style itself when composed to produce the result at which we aim? But, above all, *figures* serve to commend what we say to those that hear us, whether we seek to win approval for our character as pleaders, or to win favour for the cause which we plead, to relieve monotony by variation of our language, or to indicate our meaning in the safest or most seemly way.

1.22 But before I proceed to demonstrate what *figures* best suit the different circumstances, I must point out that their number is far from being as great as some authorities make out. For I am not in the least disturbed by the various

1.23 names which the Greeks more especially are so fond of inventing. First of all, then, I must repudiate the views of those who hold that there are as many types of *figure* as there are kinds of emotion, on the ground, not that emotions are not qualities of the mind, but that a figure, in its strict, not its general sense, is not simply the expression of anything you choose to select. Consequently the expression in words of anger, grief, pity, fear, confidence or contempt is not a

1.24 *figure,* any more than persuasion, threats, entreaty or excuse. But superficial observers are deceived by the fact that they find *figures* in all passages dealing with such themes, and select examples of them from speeches; whereas in reality there is no department of oratory which does not admit such *figures*. But it is one thing to admit a *figure* and another to be a *figure;* I am not going to be frightened out of repeating the term with some frequency in my attempt to

1.25 make the facts clear. My opponents will, I know, direct my attention to special figures employed in expressing anger, in entreating for mercy, or appealing to pity, but it does not follow that expressions of anger, appeals to pity or entreaties for mercy are in themselves *figures*. Cicero, it is true, includes all ornaments of oratory under this head, and in so doing adopts, as it seems to me, a middle course. For he does not hold that all forms of expression are to be regarded as *figures,* nor, on the other hand, would he restrict the term merely to those expressions whose form varies from ordinary use. But he regards as figurative all those expressions which are especially striking and most effective in stirring the emotions of the audience.

FROM
Book XII

The orator then, whom I am concerned to form, shall be the orator as defined by Marcus Cato, "a good man, skilled in speaking." But above all he must possess the quality which Cato places first and which is in the very nature of things the greatest and most important, that is, he must be a good man. This is essential not merely on account of the fact that, if the powers of eloquence serve only to lend arms to crime, there can be nothing more pernicious than eloquence to public and private welfare alike, while I myself, who have laboured to the best of my ability to contribute something of value to oratory, shall have rendered the worst of services to mankind, if I forge these weapons not for a soldier, but for a robber. But why speak of myself? Nature herself will have proved not a mother, but a stepmother with regard to what we deem her greatest gift to man, the gift that distinguishes us from other living things, if she devised the power of speech to be the accomplice of crime, the foe to innocence and the enemy of truth. For it had been better for men to be born dumb and devoid of reason than to turn the gifts of providence to their mutual destruction. But this conviction of mine goes further. For I do not merely assert that the ideal orator should be a good man, but I affirm that no man can be an orator unless he is a good man. For it is impossible to regard those men as gifted with intelligence who on being offered the choice between the two paths of virtue and of vice choose the latter, nor can we allow them prudence, when by the unforseen issue of their own actions they render themselves liable not merely to the heaviest penalties of the laws, but to the inevitable torment of an evil conscience. But if the view that a bad man is necessarily a fool is not merely held by philosophers, but is the universal belief of ordinary men, the fool will most assuredly never become an orator. To this must be added the fact that the mind will not find leisure even for the study of the noblest of tasks, unless it first be free from vice. The reasons for this are, first, that vileness and virtue cannot jointly inhabit in the selfsame heart and that it is as impossible for one and the same mind to harbour good and evil thoughts as it is for one man to be at once both good and evil: and secondly, that if the intelligence is to be concentrated on such a vast subject as eloquence it must be free from all other distractions, among which must be included even those preoccupations which are free from blame. For it is only when it is free and self-possessed, with nothing to divert it or lure it elsewhere, that it will fix its attention solely on that goal, the attainment of which is the object of its preparations. If on the other hand inordinate care for the development of our estates, excess of anxiety over household affairs, passionate devotion to hunting or the sacrifice of whole days to the shows of the theatre, rob our studies of much of the time that is their due (for every moment that is given to other things involves a loss of time for study), what, think you, will be the results of desire, avarice, and envy, which waken such violent thoughts within our souls that they disturb our very slumbers and our dreams? There is nothing so preoccupied, so distracted, so rent and torn by so many and

1.8 such varied passions as an evil mind. For when it cherishes some dark design, it is tormented with hope, care and anguish of spirit, and even when it has accomplished its criminal purpose, it is racked by anxiety, remorse and the fear of all manner of punishments. Amid such passions as these what room is there for literature or any virtuous pursuit? You might as well look for fruit in land that is choked with thorns and brambles. Well then, I ask you, is not simplicity of life essential if we are to be able to endure the toil entailed by study? What can we hope to get from lust or luxury? Is not the desire to win praise one of the strongest stimulants to a passion for literature? But does that mean that we are to suppose that praise is an object of concern to bad men? Surely every one of my readers must by now have realised that oratory is in the main concerned with the treatment of what is just and honourable? Can a bad and unjust man

1.9 speak on such themes as the dignity of the subject demands? Nay, even if we exclude the most important aspects of the question now before us, and make the impossible concession that the best and worst of men may have the same talent, industry and learning, we are still confronted by the question as to which of the two is entitled to be called the better orator. The answer is surely clear enough: it will be he who is the better man. Consequently, the bad man and the perfect

1.10 orator can never be identical. For nothing is perfect, if there exists something else that is better. However, as I do not wish to appear to adopt the practice dear to the Socratics of framing answers to my own questions, let me assume the existence of a man so obstinately blind to the truth as to venture to maintain that a bad man equipped with the same talents, industry and learning will be not a whit inferior to the good man as an orator; and let me show that he too is mad.

1.11 There is one point at any rate which no one will question, namely, that the aim of every speech is to convince the judge that the case which it puts forward is true and honourable. Well then, which will do this best, the good man or the bad? The good man will without doubt more often say what is true and

1.12 honourable. But even supposing that his duty should, as I shall show may sometimes happen, lead him to make statements which are false, his words are still certain to carry greater weight with his audience. On the other hand bad men, in their contempt for public opinion and their ignorance of what is right, sometimes drop their mask unawares, and are impudent in the statement of

1.13 their case and shameless in their assertions. Further, in their attempt to achieve the impossible they display an unseemly persistency and unavailing energy. For in lawsuits no less than in the ordinary paths of life, they cherish depraved expectations. But it often happens that even when they tell the truth they fail to win belief, and the mere fact that such a man is its advocate is regarded as an indication of the badness of the case.

1.14 I must now proceed to deal with the objections which common opinion is practically unaminous in bringing against this view. Was not Demosthenes an orator? And yet we are told that he was a bad man. Was not Cicero an orator? And yet there are many who have found fault with his character as well. What am I to answer? My reply will be highly unpopular and I must first attempt to

1.15 conciliate my audience. I do not consider that Demosthenes deserves the serious reflexions that have been made upon his character to such an extent that I am bound to believe all the charges amassed against him by his enemies; for my reading tells me that his public policy was of the noblest and his end most glorious. Again, I cannot see that the aims of Cicero were in any portion of his career other than such as may become an excellent citizen. As evidence I would cite the fact that his behaviour as consul was magnificent and his administration of his province a model of integrity, while he refused to become one of the twenty commissioners, and in the grievous civil wars which afflicted his generation beyond all others, neither hope nor fear ever deterred him from giving his support to the better party, that is to say, to the interests of the common weal. Some, it is true, regard him as lacking in courage. The best answer to these critics is to be found in his own words, to the effect that he was timid not in confronting peril, but in anticipating it. And this he proved also by the manner of his death, in meeting which he displayed a singular fortitude. But even if these two men lacked the perfection of virtue, I will reply to those who ask if they were orators, in the manner in which the Stoics would reply, if asked whether Zeno, Cleanthes or Chrysippus himself were wise men. I shall say that they were great men deserving our veneration, but that they did not attain to that which is the highest perfection of man's nature. For did not Pythagoras desire that he should not be called a wise man, like the sages who preceded him, but rather a student of wisdom? But for my own part, conforming to the language of every day, I have said time and again, and shall continue to say, that Cicero was a perfect orator, just as in ordinary speech we call our friends good and sensible men, although neither of these titles can really be given to any save to him that has attained to perfect wisdom. But if I am called upon to speak strictly and in accordance with the most rigid laws of truth, I shall proclaim that I seek to find that same perfect orator whom Cicero also sought to discover. For while I admit that he stood on the loftiest pinnacle of eloquence, and can discover scarcely a single deficiency in him, although I might perhaps discover certain superfluities which I think he would have pruned away (for the general view of the learned is that he possessed many virtues and a few faults, and he himself states that he has succeeded in suppressing much of his youthful exuberance), none the less, in view of the fact that, although he had by no means a low opinion of himself, he never claimed to be the perfect sage, and, had he been granted longer life and less troubled conditions for the composition of his works, would doubtless have spoken better still, I shall not lay myself open to the charge of ungenerous criticism, if I say that I believe that he failed actually to achieve that perfection to the attainment of which none have approached more nearly, and indeed had I felt otherwise in this connexion, I might have defended my point with greater boldness and freedom. Marcus Antonius declared that he had seen no man who was genuinely eloquent (and to be eloquent is a far less achievement than to be an orator), while Cicero himself has failed to find his orator in actual life and merely imagines and strives to depict the ideal. Shall I then be afraid to say that in the eternity of time that is yet to be, something more perfect may be found than has yet existed? I say nothing of those critics who will not allow sufficient credit even for eloquence to Cicero and Demosthenes, although Cicero himself does not regard Demosthenes as flawless, but asserts that he sometimes nods, while even Cicero fails to satisfy Brutus and Calvus (at any rate they criticised his style to his face), or to win the complete approval of either of the Asinii, who in various passages attack the faults of his oratory in language which is positively hostile.

1.23 However, let us fly in the face of nature and assume that a bad man has been discovered who is endowed with the highest eloquence. I shall none the less deny that he is an orator. For I should not allow that every man who has shown himself ready with his hands was necessarily a brave man, because true 1.24 courage cannot be conceived of without the accompaniment of virtue. Surely the advocate who is called to defend the accused requires to be a man of honour, honour which greed cannot corrupt, influence seduce, or fear dismay. Shall we then dignify the traitor, the deserter, the turncoat with the sacred name of orator? But if the quality which is usually termed goodness is to be found even in quite ordinary advocates, why should not the orator, who has not yet existed, but 1.25 may still be born, be no less perfect in character than in excellence of speech? It is no hack-advocate, no hireling pleader, nor yet, to use no harsher term, a serviceable attorney of the class generally known as *causidici*, that I am seeking to form, but rather a man who to extraordinary natural gifts has added a thorough mastery of all the fairest branches of knowledge, a man sent by heaven to be the blessings of mankind, one to whom all history can find no parallel, 1.26 uniquely perfect in every detail and utterly noble alike in thought and speech. How small a portion of all these abilities will be required for the defence of the innocent, the repression of crime or the support of truth against falsehood in suits involving questions of money? It is true that our supreme orator will bear his part in such tasks, but his powers will be displayed with brighter splendour in greater matters than these, when he is called upon to direct the counsels of 1.27 the senate and guide the people from the paths of error to better things. Was not this the man conceived by Virgil and described as quelling a riot when torches and stones have begun to fly:

> Then, if before their eyes some statesman grave
> Stand forth, with virtue and high service crowned,
> Straight are they dumb and stand intent to hear.

Here then we have one who is before all else a good man, and it is only after this that the poet adds that he is skilled in speaking:

> His words their minds control, their passions soothe.

1.28 Again, will not this same man, whom we are striving to form, if in time of war he be called upon to inspire his soldiers with courage for the fray, draw for his eloquence on the innermost precepts of philosophy? For how can men who stand upon the verge of battle banish all the crowding fears of hardship, pain and death from their minds, unless those fears be replaced by the sense of the duty that they owe their country, by courage and the lively image of a soldier's 1.29 honour? And assuredly the man who will best inspire such feelings in others is he who has first inspired them in himself. For however we strive to conceal it, insincerity will always betray itself, and there was never in any man so great eloquence as would not begin to stumble and hesitate so soon as his words ran counter to his inmost thoughts. Now a bad man cannot help speaking things other than he feels. On the other hand, the good will never be at a loss for honourable words or fail to find matter full of virtue for utterance, since among his virtues practical wisdom will be one. And even though his imagination lacks artifice to lend it charm, its own nature will be ornament enough, for if honour dictate the words, we shall find eloquence there as well. Therefore, let those that are young, or rather let all of us, whatever our age, since it is never too late to resolve to follow what is right, strive with all our hearts and devote all our efforts to the pursuit of virtue and eloquence; and perchance it may be granted to us to attain to the perfection that we seek. For since nature does not forbid the attainment of either, why should not someone succeed in attaining both together? And why should not each of us hope to be that happy man? But if our powers are inadequate to such achievement, we shall still be the better for the double effort in proportion to the distance which we have advanced toward either goal. At any rate let us banish from our hearts the delusion that eloquence, the fairest of all things, can be combined with vice. The power of speaking is even to be accounted an evil when it is found in evil men; for it makes its possessors yet worse than they were before.

I think I hear certain persons (for there will always be some who had rather be eloquent than good) asking, "Why then is there so much art in connexion with eloquence? Why have you talked so much of 'glosses,' the methods of defence to be employed in difficult cases, and sometimes even of actual confession of guilt, unless it is the case that the power and force of speech at times triumphs over truth itself? For a good man will only plead good cases, and those might safely be left to truth to support without the aid of learning." Now, though my reply to these critics will in the first place be a defence of my own work, it will also explain what I consider to be the duty of a good man on occasions when circumstances have caused him to undertake the defence of the guilty. For it is by no means useless to consider how at times we should speak in defence of falsehood or even of injustice, if only for this reason, that such an investigation will enable us to detect and defeat them with the greater ease, just as the physician who has a thorough knowledge of all that can injure the health will be all the more skilful in the prescription of remedies. For the Academicians, although they will argue on either side of a question, do not thereby commit themselves to taking one of these two views as their guide in life to the exclusion of the other, while the famous Carneades, who is said to have spoken at Rome in the presence of Cato the Censor, and to have argued against justice with no less vigour than he had argued for justice on the preceding day, was not himself an unjust man. But the nature of virtue is revealed by vice, its opposite, justice becomes yet more manifest from the contemplation of injustice, and there are many other things that are proved by their contraries. Consequently the schemes of his adversaries should be no less well known to the orator than those of the enemy to a commander in the field. But it is even true, although at first sight it seems hard to believe, that there may be sound reason why at times a good man who is appearing for the defence should attempt to conceal the truth from the judge. If any of my readers is surprised at my making such a statement (although this opinion is not of my own invention, but is derived from those whom antiquity regarded as the greatest teachers of wisdom), I would have him reflect that there are many things which are made honourable or the reverse not

1.37 by the nature of the facts, but by the causes from which they spring. For if to slay a man is often a virtue and to put one's own children to death is at times the noblest of deeds, and if it is permissible in the public interest to do deeds yet more horrible to relate than these, we should assuredly take into consideration not solely and simply what is the nature of the case which the good man

1.38 undertakes to defend, but what is his reason and what his purpose in so doing. And first of all everyone must allow, what even the sternest of the Stoics admit, that the good man will sometimes tell a lie, and further that he will sometimes do so for comparatively trivial reasons; for example we tell countless lies to sick children for their good and make many promises to them which we do not

1.39 intend to perform. And there is clearly far more justification for lying when it is a question of diverting an assassin from his victim or deceiving an enemy to save our country. Consequently a practice which is at times reprehensible even in slaves, may on other occasions be praiseworthy even in wise man. If this be granted, I can see that there will be many possible emergencies such as to justify an orator in undertaking cases of a kind which, in the absence of any

1.40 honourable reason, he would have refused to touch. In saying this I do not mean that we should be ready under any circumstances to defend our father, brother or friend when in peril (since I hold that we should be guided by stricter rules in such matters), although such contingencies may well cause us no little perplexity, when we have to decide between the rival claims of justice and natural affection. But let us put the problem beyond all question of doubt. Suppose a man to have plotted against a tyrant and to be accused of having done so. Which of the two will the orator, as defined by us, desire to save? And if he undertakes the defence of the accused, will he not employ falsehood with no less readiness

1.41 than the advocate who is defending a bad case before a jury? Again, suppose that the judge is likely to condemn acts which were rightly done, unless we can convince him that they were never done. Is not this another case where the orator will not shrink even from lies, if so he may save one who is not merely innocent, but a praiseworthy citizen? Again, suppose that we realise that certain acts are just in themselves, though prejudicial to the state under existing circumstances. Shall we not then employ methods of speaking which, despite

1.42 the excellence of their intention, bear a close resemblance to fraud. Further, no one will hesitate for a moment to hold the view that it is in the interests of the commonwealth that guilty persons should be acquitted rather than punished, if it be possible thereby to convert them to a better state of mind, a possibility which is generally conceded. If then it is clear to an orator that a man who is guilty of the offences laid to his charge will become a good man, will he not

1.43 strive to secure his acquittal? Imagine for example that a skilful commander, without whose aid the state cannot hope to crush its enemies, is labouring under a charge which is obviously true: will not the common interest irresistibly summon our orator to defend him? We know at any rate that Fabricius publicly voted for and secured the election to the consulate of Cornelius Rufinus, despite the fact that he was a bad citizen and his personal enemy, merely because he knew that he was a capable general and the state was threatened with war. And when certain persons expressed their surprise at his conduct, he replied that he had rather be robbed by a fellow-citizen than be sold as a slave by the enemy. Well then, had Fabricius been an orator, would he not have defended Rufinus against a charge of peculation, even though his guilt were as clear as day? I might produce many other similar examples, but one of them taken at random is enough. For my purpose is not to assert that such tasks will often be incumbent on the orator whom I desire to form, but merely to show that, in the event of his being compelled to take such action, it will not invalidate our definition of an orator as a "good man, skilled in speaking." And it is necessary also both to teach and learn how to establish difficult cases by proof. For often even the best cases have a resemblance to bad, and the charges which tell heavily against an innocent person frequently have a strong resemblance to the truth. Consequently, the same methods of defence have to be employed that would be used if he were guilty. Further, there are countless elements which are common to both good cases and bad, such as oral and documentary evidence, suspicions and opinions, all of which have to be established or disposed of in the same way, whether they be true or merely resemble the truth. Therefore, while maintaining his integrity of purpose, the orator will modify his pleading to suit the circumstances.

Since then the orator is a good man, and such goodness cannot be conceived as existing apart from virtue, virtue, despite the fact that it is in part derived from certain natural impulses, will require to be perfected by instruction. The orator must above all things devote his attention to the formation of moral character and must acquire a complete knowledge of all that is just and honourable. For without this knowledge no one can be either a good man or skilled in speaking, unless indeed we agree with those who regard morality as intuitive and as owing nothing to instruction: indeed they go so far as to acknowledge that handicrafts, not excluding even those which are most despised among them, can only be acquired by the result of teaching, whereas virtue, which of all gifts to man is that which makes him most near akin to the immortal gods, comes to him without search or effort, as a natural concomitant of birth. But can the man who does not know what abstinence is, claim to be truly abstinent? or brave, if he has never purged his soul of the fears of pain, death and superstition? or just, if he has never, in language approaching that of philosophy, discussed the nature of virtue and justice, or of the laws that have been given to mankind by nature or established among individual peoples and nations? What a contempt it argues for such themes to regard them as being so easy of comprehension! However, I pass this by; for I am sure that no one with the least smattering of literary culture will have the slightest hesitation in agreeing with me. I will proceed to my next point, that no one will achieve sufficient skill even in speaking, unless he makes a thorough study of all the workings of nature and forms his character on the precepts of philosophy and

2.5 the dictates of reason. For it is with good cause that Lucius Crassus, in the third book of the *de Oratore*, affirms that all that is said concerning equity, justice, truth and the good, and their opposites, forms part of the studies of an orator, and that the philosophers, when they exert their powers of speaking to defend these virtues, are using the weapons of rhetoric, not their own. But he also confesses that the knowledge of these subjects must be sought from the philosophers for the reason that, in his opinion, philosophy has more effective 2.6 possession of them. And it is for the same reason that Cicero in several of his books and letters proclaims that eloquence has its fountain-head in the most secret springs of wisdom, and that consequently for a considerable time the instructors of morals and of eloquence were identical. Accordingly this exhortation of mine must not be taken to mean that I wish the orator to be a philosopher, since there is no other way of life that is further removed from the 2.7 duties of a statesman and the tasks of an orator. For what philosopher has ever been a frequent speaker in the courts or won renown in public assemblies? Nay, what philosopher has ever taken a prominent part in the government of the state, which forms the most frequent theme of their instructions? None the less I desire that he, whose character I am seeking to mould, should be a "wise man" in the Roman sense, that is, one who reveals himself as a true statesman, not in 2.8 the discussions of the study, but in the actual practice and experience of life. But inasmuch as the study of philosophy has been deserted by those who have turned to the pursuit of eloquence, and since philosophy no longer moves in its true sphere of action and in the broad daylight of the forum, but has retired first to porches and gymnasia and finally to the gatherings of the schools, all that is essential for an orator, and yet is not taught by the professors of eloquence, must undoubtedly be sought from those persons in whose possession it has remained. The authors who have discoursed on the nature of virtue must be read through 2.9 and through, that the life of the orator may be wedded to the knowledge of things human and divine. But how much greater and fairer would such subjects appear if those who taught them were also those who could give them most eloquent expression! O that the day may dawn when the perfect orator of our heart's desire shall claim for his own possession that science that has lost the affection of mankind through the arrogance of its claims and the vices of some that have brought disgrace upon its virtues, and shall restore it to its place in the 2.10 domain of eloquence, as though he had been victorious in a trial for the restoration of stolen goods! And since philosophy falls into three divisions, physics, ethics and dialectic, which, I ask you, of these departments is not closely connected with the task of the orator?

Let us reverse the order just given and deal first with the third department which is entirely concerned with words. If it be true that to know the properties of each word, to clear away ambiguities, to unravel perplexities, to distinguish between truth and falsehood, to prove or to refute as may be desired, all form part of the functions of an orator, who is there that can doubt the truth of my 2.11 contention? I grant that we shall not have to employ dialectic with such minute attention to detail when we are pleading in the courts as when we are engaged in philosophical debate, since the orator's duty is not merely to instruct, but also to move and delight his audience; and to succeed in doing this he needs a strength, impetuosity and grace as well. For oratory is like a river: the current is stronger when it flows within deep banks and with a mighty flood, than when the waters are shallow and broken by the pebbles that bar their way. And just as the trainers of the wrestling school do not impart the various *throws* to their pupils that those who have learnt them may make use of all of them in actual wrestling matches (for weight and strength and wind count for more than these), but that they may have a store from which to draw one or two of such tricks, as occasion may offer; even so the science of dialectic, or if you prefer it of disputation, while it is often useful in definition, inference, differentiation, resolution of ambiguity, distinction and classification, as also in luring on or entangling our opponents, yet if it claim to assume the entire direction of the struggles of the forum, will merely stand in the way of arts superior to itself and by its very subtlety will exhaust the strength that has been pared down to suit its limitations. As a result you will find that certain persons who show astonishing skill in philosophical debate, as soon as they quit the sphere of their quibbles, are as helpless in any case that demands more serious pleading as those small animals which, though nimble enough in a confined space, are easily captured in an open field.

Proceeding to moral philosophy or ethics, we may note that it at any rate is entirely suited to the orator. For vast as is the variety of cases (since in them, as I have pointed out in previous books, we seek to discover certain points by conjecture, reach our conclusions in others by means of definition, dispose of others on legal grounds or by raising the question of competence, while the other points are established by syllogism and others involve contradictions or are diversely interpreted owing to some ambiguity of language), there is scarcely a single one which does not at some point or another involve the discussion of equity and virtue, while there are also, as everyone knows, not a few which turn entirely on questions of quality. Again in deliberative assemblies how can we advise a policy without raising the question of what is honourable? Nay, even the third department of oratory, which is concerned with the tasks of praise and denunciation, must without a doubt deal with questions of right and wrong. For the orator will assuredly have much to say on such topics as justice, fortitude, abstinence, self-control and piety. But the good man, who has come to the knowledge of these things not by mere hearsay, as though they were just words and names for his tongue to employ, but has grasped the meaning of virtue and acquired a true feeling for it, will never be perplexed when he has to think out a problem, but will speak out truly what he knows. Since, however, *general* questions are always more important than special (for the particular is contained in the universal, while the universal is never to be regarded as something superimposed on the particular), everyone will readily admit that the studies of which we are speaking are pre-eminently concerned with general questions. Further, since there are numerous points which require to be determined by appropriate and concise definitions (hence the *definitive basis* of cases), it is surely desirable that the orator should be instructed in such things by those who have devoted special attention to the subject. Again, does not every question of law turn either on the precise meaning of words, the discussion of equity, or conjecture as to the intention—subjects which in part encroach on the domain of dialectic and in part on that of ethics? Consequently all oratory involves a natural admixture of all these philosophic elements—at least, that is to say, all oratory that is worthy of the name. For mere garrulity that is ignorant of all such learning must needs go astray, since its guides are either non-existent or false.

2.20

Physics on the other hand is far richer than the other branches of philosophy, if viewed from the standpoint of providing exercise in speaking, in proportion as a loftier inspiration is required to speak of things divine than of things human; and further it includes within its scope the whole of ethics, which as we have shown are essential to the very existence of oratory. For, if the world is governed by providence, it will certainly be the duty of all good men to bear their part in the administration of the state. If the origin of our souls be divine, we must win our way towards virtue and abjure the service of the lusts of our earthly body. Are not these themes which the orator will frequently be called upon to handle? Again there are questions concerned with auguries and oracles or any other religious topic (all of them subjects that have often given rise to the most important debates in the senate) on which the orator will have to discourse, if he is also to be the statesman we would have him be. And finally, how can we conceive of any real eloquence at all proceeding from a man who is ignorant of all that is best in the world? If our reason did not make these facts obvious, we should still be led by historical examples to believe their truth. For Pericles, whose eloquence, despite the fact that it has left no visible record for posterity, was none the less, if we may believe the historians and that free-speaking tribe, the old comic poets, endowed with almost incredible force, is known to have been a pupil of the physicist Anaxagoras, while Demosthenes, greatest of all the orators of Greece, sat at the feet of Plato. As for Cicero, he has often proclaimed the fact that he owed less to the schools of rhetoric than to the walks of Academe: nor would he ever have developed such amazing fertility of talent, had he bounded his genius by the limits of the forum and not by the frontiers of nature herself.

2.21

2.22

2.23

But this leads me to another question as to which school of philosophy is like to prove of most service to oratory, although there are only a few that can be said to contend for this honour. For in the first place Epicurus banishes us from his presence without more ado, since he bids all his followers to fly from learning in the swiftest ship that they can find. Nor would Aristippus, who regards the highest good as consisting in physical pleasure, be likely to exhort us to the toils entailed by our study. And what part can Pyrrho have in the work that is before us? For he will have doubts as to whether there exist judges to address, accused to defend, or a senate where he can be called upon to speak his opinion. Some authorities hold that the Academy will be the most useful school, on the ground that its habit of disputing on both sides of a question approaches most nearly to the actual practice of the courts. And by way of proof they add the fact that this school has produced speakers highly renowned for their eloquence. The Peripatetics also make it their boast that they have a form of study which is near akin to oratory. For it was with them in the main that originated

2.24

2.25

the practice of declaiming on general questions by way of exercise. The Stoics, though driven to admit that generally speaking, their teachers have been deficient both in fullness and charm of eloquence, still contend that no men can prove more acutely or draw conclusions with greater subtlety than themselves. But all these arguments take place within their own circle, for, as though they were tied by some solemn oath or held fast in the bonds of some superstitious belief, they consider that it is a crime to abandon a conviction once formed. On the other hand, there is no need for an orator to swear allegiance to any one philosophic code. For he has a greater and nobler aim, to which he directs all his efforts with as much zeal as if he were a candidate for office, since he is to be made perfect not only in the glory of a virtuous life, but in that of eloquence as well. He will consequently select as his models of eloquence all the greatest masters of oratory, and will choose the noblest precepts and the most direct road to virtue as the means for the formation of an upright character. He will neglect no form of exercise, but will devote special attention to those which are of the highest and fairest nature. For what subject can be found more fully adapted to a rich and weighty eloquence than the topics of virtue, politics, providence, the origin of the soul and friendship? The themes which tend to elevate mind and language alike are questions such as what things are truly good, what means there are of assuaging fear, restraining the passions and lifting us and the soul that came from heaven clear of the delusions of the common herd.

But it is desirable that we should not restrict our study to the precepts of philosophy alone. It is still more important that we should know and ponder continually all the noblest sayings and deeds that have been handed down to us from ancient times. And assuredly we shall nowhere find a larger or more remarkable store of these than in the records of our own country. Who will teach courage, justice, loyalty, self-control, simplicity, and contempt of grief and pain better than men like Fabricius, Curius, Regulus, Decius, Mucius and countless others? For if the Greeks bear away the palm for moral precepts, Rome can produce more striking examples of moral performance, which is a far greater thing. But the man who does not believe that it is enough to fix his eyes merely on his own age and his own transitory life, but regards the space allotted for an honourable life and the course in which glory's race is run as conditioned solely by the memory of posterity, will not rest content with a mere knowledge of the events of history. No, it is from the thought of posterity that he must inspire his soul with justice and derive that freedom of spirit which it is his duty to display when he pleads in the courts or gives counsel in the senate. No man will ever be the consummate orator of whom we are in quest unless he has both the knowledge and the courage to speak in accordance with the promptings of honour.

Our orator will also require a knowledge of civil law and of the custom and religion of the state in whose life he is to bear his part. For how will he be able to advise either in public or in private, if he is ignorant of all the main elements that go to make the state? How can he truthfully call himself an advocate if he has to go to others to acquire that knowledge which is all-important in the courts? He will be little better than if he were a reciter of the poets. For he will be a mere

transmitter of the instructions that others have given him, it will be on the authority of others that he propounds what he asks the judge to believe, and he whose duty it is to succour the litigant will himself be in need of succour. It is true that at times this may be effected with but little inconvenience, if what he advances for the edification of the judge has been taught him and composed in the seclusion of his study and learnt by heart there like other elements of the case. But what will he do, when he is confronted by unexpected problems such as frequently arise in the actual course of pleading? Will he not disgrace himself
3.3 by looking round and asking the junior counsel who sit on the benches behind him for advice? Can he hope to get a thorough grasp of such information at the very moment when he is required to produce it in his speech? Can he make his assertions with confidence or speak with native simplicity as though his arguments were his own? Grant that he may do so in his actual speech. But what will he do in a debate, when he has continually to meet fresh points raised by his opponent and is given no time to learn up his case? What will he do, if he has no legal expert to advise him or if his prompter through insufficient knowledge of the subject provides him with information that is false? It is the most serious drawback of such ignorance, that he will always believe that his
3.4 adviser knows what he is talking about. I am not ignorant of the generally prevailing custom, nor have I forgotten those who sit by our store-chests and provide weapons for the pleader: I know too that the Greeks did likewise: hence the name of *pragmaticas* which was bestowed on such persons. But I am speaking of an orator, who owes it as a duty to his case to serve it not merely by
3.5 the loudness of his voice, but by all other means that may be of assistance to it. Consequently I do not wish my orator to be helpless, if it so chance that he puts in an appearance for the preliminary proceedings to which the hour before the commencement of the trial is allotted, or to be unskilful in the preparation and production of evidence. For who, sooner than himself, should prepare the points which he wishes to be brought out when he is pleading? You might as well suppose that the qualifications of a successful general consist merely in courage and energy in the field of battle and skill in meeting all the demands of actual conflict, while suffering him to be ignorant of the methods of levying troops, mustering and equipping his forces, arranging for supplies or selecting a suitable position for his camp, despite the fact that preparation for war is an
3.6 essential preliminary for its successful conduct. And yet such a general would bear a very close resemblance to the advocate who leaves much of the detail that is necessary for success to the care of others, more especially in view of the fact that this, the most necessary element in the management of a case, is not as difficult as it may perhaps seem to outside observers. For every point of law, which is certain, is based either on written law or accepted custom: if, on the other hand, the point is doubtful, it must be examined in the light of equity.
3.7 Laws which are either written or founded on accepted custom present no difficulty, since they call merely for knowledge and make no demand on the imagination. On the other hand, the points explained in the rulings of the legal experts turn either on the interpretation of words or on the distinction between right and wrong. To understand the meaning of each word is either common to

all sensible men or the special possession of the orator, while the demands of equity are known to every good man. Now I regard the orator above all as being a man of virtue and good sense, who will not be seriously troubled, after having devoted himself to the study of that which is excellent by nature, if some legal expert disagrees with him; for even they are allowed to disagree among themselves. But if he further wishes to know the views of everyone, he will require to read, and reading is the least laborious of all the tasks that fall to the student's lot. Moreover, if the class of legal experts is as a rule drawn from those who, in despair of making successful pleaders, have taken refuge with the law, how easy it must be for an orator to know what those succeed in learning, who by their own confession are incapable of becoming orators! But Marcus Cato was at once a great orator and an expert lawyer, while Scaevola and Servius Sulpicius were universally allowed to be eloquent as well. And Cicero not merely possessed a sufficient supply of legal knowledge to serve his needs when pleading, but actually began to write on the subject, so that it is clear that an orator has not merely time to learn, but even to teach the law.

Let no one, however, regard the advice I have given as to the attention due to the development of character and the study of the law as being impugned by the fact that we are familiar with many who, because they were weary of the toil entailed on those who seek to scale the heights of eloquence, have betaken themselves to the study of law as a refuge for their indolence. Some of these transfer their attention to the praetor's edicts or the civil law, and have preferred to become specialists in *formulae*, or legalists, as Cicero calls them, on the pretext of choosing a more useful branch of study, whereas their real motive was its comparative easiness. Others are the victims of a more arrogant form of sloth; they assume a stern air and let their beards grow, and, as though despising the precepts of oratory, sit for a while in the schools of the philosophers, that, by an assumption of a severe mien before the public gaze and by an affected contempt of others they may assert their moral superiority, while leading a life of debauchery at home. For philosophy may be counterfeited, but eloquence never.

"Longinus"
c. first-century A.D.

"Longinus" is the name commonly assigned to the author of On the Sublime because of its mistaken association with Cassius Longinus, a rhetorician and philosopher of the third century A.D. Though the identity of the author is still a matter of debate, modern scholarship places the work in the first century A.D. on the strength of internal evidence. "Longinus" begins by taking issue with the theories of Caecilius of Calacte, a first-century Sicilian rhetorician, and concludes with a discussion of the relationship between the decline of the art of oratory and the change from republic to monarchy—a subject widely addressed by first-century writers but politically irrelevant at a later date. It is worth noting that "Longinus" was perhaps the first pagan author to cite the Old Testament (see p. 331 for his approving reference to the opening verses of Genesis); some scholars have even speculated that he was a Jew.

Whatever its source, On the Sublime is one of the masterworks of literary criticism. "Longinus" sets out to isolate the quality that informs great poetry. He calls it hupsos, or "sublimity," that which "contains much food for reflection, is difficult or rather impossible to resist, and makes a strong and ineffaceable impression on the memory." Thus, he locates the measure of the literary work in the emotional response it elicits from the reader—a decisive break with Aristotelian poetics and the tradition of rhetorical criticism. "I should myself," Longinus writes, "have no hesitation in saying that there is nothing so productive of grandeur as noble emotion in the right place. It inspires and possesses our words with a kind of madness and divine spirit." The sublime, then, is not a category of mimesis; it represents, contra Aristotle, an effort to define poetry in terms that transcend the boundaries of nature.

The manuscript of On the Sublime has come down to us in damaged form, and there are several gaps in the text. The treatise was apparently not influential in its own time (it is not mentioned in other classical sources), but it had a powerful impact on European literary criticism from the eighteenth century onward. With Aristotle's Poetics, it stands as one of the great statements of literary criticism in antiquity.

On the Sublime, *translated by D. A. Russell, is reprinted by permission of University Press from D. A. Russell and M. Winterbottom, eds.,* Ancient Literary Criticism: The Principal Texts in New Translations *(Oxford, 1972). © 1972 by Oxford University Press.*

ON SUBLIMITY

PREFACE

My dear Postumius Terentianus,

You will recall that when we were reading together Caecilius' monograph *On Sublimity*, we felt that it was inadequate to its high subject, and failed to touch the essential points. Nor indeed did it appear to offer the reader much practical help, though this ought to be a writer's principal object. Two things are required of any textbook: first, that it should explain what its subject is; second, and more important, that it should explain how and by what methods we can achieve it. Caecilius tries at immense length to explain to us what sort of thing "the sublime" is, as though we did not know; but he has somehow passed over as unnecessary the question how we can develop our nature to some degree of greatness. However, we ought perhaps not so much to blame our author for what he has left out as to commend him for his originality and enthusiasm.

You have urged me to set down a few notes on sublimity for your own use. Let us then consider whether there is anything in my observations which may be thought useful to public men. You must help me, my friend, by giving your honest opinion in detail, as both your natural candour and your friendship with me require. It was well said that what man has in common with the gods is "doing good and telling the truth."

Your education dispenses me from any long preliminary definition. Sublimity is a kind of eminence or excellence of discourse. It is the source of the distinction of the very greatest poets and prose writers and the means by which they have given eternal life to their own fame. For grandeur produces ecstasy rather than persuasion in the hearer; and the combination of wonder and astonishment always proves superior to the merely persuasive and pleasant. This is because persuasion is on the whole something we can control, whereas amazement and wonder exert invincible power and force and get the better of every hearer. Experience in invention and ability to order and arrange material cannot be detected in single passages; we begin to appreciate them only when we see the whole context. Sublimity, on the other hand, produced at the right moment, tears everything up like a whirlwind, and exhibits the orator's whole power at a single blow.

Your own experience will lead you to these and similar considerations. The question from which I must begin is whether there is in fact an art of sublimity or profundity.[1] Some people think it is a complete mistake to reduce things like this to technical rules. Greatness, the argument runs, is a natural product, and does not come by teaching. The only art is to be born like that. They believe moreover that natural products are very much weakened by being reduced to the bare bones of a textbook.

In my view, these arguments can be refuted by considering three points:

(i) Though nature is on the whole a law unto herself in matters of emotion and elevation, she is not a random force and does not work altogether without method.

(ii) She is herself in every instance a first and primary element of creation, but it is method that is competent to provide and contribute quantities and appropriate occasions for everything, as well as perfect correctness in training and application.

(iii) Grandeur is particularly dangerous when left on its own, unaccompanied by knowledge, unsteadied, unballasted, abandoned to mere impulse and ignorant temerity. It often needs the curb as well as the spur.

What Demosthenes[2] said of life in general is true also of literature: good fortune is the greatest of blessings, but good counsel comes next, and the lack of it destroys the other also. In literature, nature occupies the place of good fortune, and art that of good counsel. Most important of all, the very fact that some things in literature depend on nature alone can itself be learned only from art.

If the critic of students of this subject will bear these points in mind, he will, I believe, come to realize that the examination of the question before us is by no means useless or superfluous.

[Lacuna equivalent to about two of these printed pages.]

FAULTS INCIDENT TO THE EFFORT TO ACHIEVE SUBLIMITY

3.1

> ... restrain the oven's mighty glow.
> For if I see but one beside his hearth,
> I'll thrust in just one tentacle of storm,
> and fire his roof and turn it all to cinders.
> I've not yet sung my proper song.[3]

This is not tragedy; it is a parody of the tragic manner—tentacles, vomiting to heaven, making Boreas a flute-player, and so on. The result is not impressiveness but turbid diction and confused imagery. If you examine the details closely, they gradually sink from the terrifying to the contemptible.

Now if untimely turgidity is unpardonable in tragedy, a genre which is naturally magniloquent and tolerant of bombast, it will scarcely be appropriate in writing which has to do with real life. Hence the ridicule attaching to Gorgias of Leontini's "Xerxes, the Persians' Zeus" and "their living tombs, the vultures," or to various things in Callisthenes, where he has not so much risen to heights as been carried off his feet. Clitarchus is an even more striking example; he is an inflated writer, and, as Sophocles has it,

> blows at his tiny flute, the mouth-band off[1]

Amphicrates, Hegesias, Matris—they are all the same. They often fancy themselves possessed when they are merely playing the fool.

Turgidity is a particularly hard fault to avoid, for it is one to which all who aim at greatness naturally incline, because they seek to escape the charge of weakness and aridity. They act on the principle that "to slip from a great prize is yet a noble fault." In literature as in the body, puffy and false tumours are bad, and may well bring us to the opposite result from that which we expected. As the saying goes, there is nothing so dry as a man with dropsy.

While turgidity is an endeavour to go above the sublime, puerility[5] is the sheer opposite of greatness; it is a thoroughly low, mean, and ignoble vice. What do I mean by "puerility"? A pedantic thought, so over-worked that it ends in frigidity. Writers slip into it through aiming at originality, artifice, and (above all) charm, and then coming to grief on the rocks of tawdriness and affection.

A third kind of fault—what Theodorus called "the pseudo-bacchanalian"—corresponds to these in the field of emotion. It consists of untimely or meaningless emotion where none is in place, or immoderate emotion where moderate is in place. Some people often get carried away, like drunkards, into emotions unconnected with the subject, which are simply their own pedantic invention. The audience feels nothing, so that they inevitably make an exhibition of themselves, parading their ectasies before an audience which does not share them.

But I reserve the subject of emotion for another place,[6] returning meanwhile to the second fault of those I mentioned: frigidity. This is a constant feature in Timaeus, who is in many ways a competent writer, not without the capacity for greatness on occasion, learned and original, but as unconscious of his own faults as he is censorious of others', and often falling into the grossest childishness through his passion for always starting exotic ideas. I will give one or two examples; Caecilius has already cited most of those available.

4.1

In praise of Alexander the Great, Timaeus writes: "He conquered all Asia in fewer years than it took Isocrates to write the *Panegyricus* to advocate the Persian war." What a splendid comparison this is—the Macedonian king and the sophist! On the same principle, the Lacedaemonians were very much less brave than Isocrates: it took them thirty years to capture Messene,[7] whereas he took only ten to write the *Panegyricus*!

Listen also to Timaeus' comment on the Athenians captured in Sicily. "They were punished for their impiety to Hermes and mutilation of his statues, and the main agent of their punishment was one who had a family connection with their victim, Hermocrates the son of Hermon.[8] I cannot help wondering, my dear Terentianus, why he does not also write about the Tyrant Dionysius, "Because he was impious towards Zeus and Heracles, Dion and Heraclides robbed him of his throne."[9]

But why speak of Timaeus, when those heroes of letters, Xenophon and Plato, for all that they were trained in Socrates' school, forget themselves sometimes for the sake of similar petty pleasures? Thus Xenophon writes in *The Constitution of the Lacedaemonians:* "You could hear their voice less than the voice of stone statues, you could distract their eyes less than the eyes of bronze images; you would think them more bashful than the very maidens in the eyes.[10] It would have been more in keeping with Amphicrates' manner than

Xenophon's to speak of the pupils of our eyes as bashful maidens. And what an absurd misconception to think of everybody's pupils as bashful! The shamelessness of a person, we are told, appears nowhere so plainly as in the eyes. Remember the words Achilles uses to revile Agamemnon's violent temper: "Drunken sot, with a dog's *eyes*!"[11] Timaeus, unable to keep his hands off stolen property, as it were, has not left the monopoly of this frigid conceit to Xenophon. He uses it in connection with Agathocles, who eloped with his cousin from the unveiling ceremony of her marriage to another: "Who would have done this, if he had not had harlots in his eyes for pupils (*koras*)?"[12]

And what of Plato, the otherwise divine Plato? He wants to express the idea of writing-tablets. "They shall write," he says, "and deposit in the temples memorials of cypress."[13] Again: "As for walls, Megillus, I should concur with Sparta in letting walls sleep in the earth and not get up."[14] Herodotus' description[15] of beautiful women as "pains on the eyes" is the same sort of thing, though it is to some extent excused by the fact that the speakers are barbarians and drunk—not that it is a good thing to make an exhibition of the triviality of one's mind to posterity, even through the mouths of characters like these.

5.1 All such lapses from dignity arise in literature through a single cause: that desire for novelty of thought which is all the rage today. Evils often come from the same source as blessings; and so, since beauty of style, sublimity, and charm all conduce to successful writing, they are also causes and principles not only of success but of failure. Variation, hyperbole, and the use of plural for singular are like this too; I shall explain below the dangers which they involve.[16]

SOME MARKS OF TRUE SUBLIMITY

6.1 At this stage, the question we must put to ourselves for discussion is how to avoid the faults which are so much tied up with sublimity. The answer, my friend, is: by first of all achieving a genuine understanding and appreciation of true sublimity. This is difficult; literary judgement comes only as the final product of long experience. However, for the purposes of instruction, I think we can say that an understanding of all this can be acquired. I approach the problem in this way:

7.1 In ordinary life, nothing is truly great which it is great to despise; wealth, honour, reputation, absolute power—anything in short which has a lot of external trappings—can never seem supremely good to the wise man because it is no small good to despise them. People who could have these advantages if they chose but disdain them out of magnanimity are admired much more than those who actually possess them.[17] It is much the same with elevation in poetry and literature generally. We have to ask ourselves whether any particular example does not give a show of grandeur which, for all its accidental trappings, will, when dissected, prove vain and hollow, the kind of thing which it does a man more honour to despise than to admire. It is our nature to be elevated and exalted by true sublimity. Filled with joy and pride, we come to believe we have created what we have only heard. When a man of sense and literary experience hears something many times over, and it fails to dispose his mind to greatness or to leave him with more to reflect upon than was contained in the mere words, but comes instead to seem valueless on repeated inspection, this is not true sublimity; it endures only for the moment of hearing. Real sublimity contains much food for reflection, is difficult or rather impossible to resist, and makes a strong and ineffaceable impression on the memory. In a word, reckon those things which please everybody all the time as genuinely and finely sublime. When people of different trainings, ways of life, tastes, ages, and manners all agree about something, the judgement and assent of so many distinct voices lends strength and irrefutability to the conviction that their admiration is rightly directed.

THE FIVE SOURCES OF SUBLIMITY

There are, one may say, five most productive sources of sublimity (Competence in speaking is assumed as a common foundation for all five; nothing is possible without it.)

(i) The first and most important is the power to conceive great thoughts; I defined this in my work on Xenophon.

(ii) The second is strong and inspired emotion. (These two sources are for the most part natural; the remaining three involve art.)

(iii) Certain kinds of figures. (These may be divided into figures of thought and figures of speech.)

(iv) Noble diction. This has as subdivisions choice of words and the use of metaphorical and artificial language.[18]

(v) Finally, to round off the whole list, dignified and elevated word-arrangement.

Let us now examine the points which come under each of these heads.

I must first observe, however, that Caecilius has omitted some of the five—emotion, for example. Now if he thought that sublimity and emotion were one and the same thing and always existed and developed together, he was wrong. Some emotions, such as pity, grief, and fear, are found divorced from sublimity and with a low effect. Conversely, sublimity often occurs apart from emotion. Of the innumerable examples of this I select Homer's bold account of the Aloadae:

> Ossa upon Olympus they sought to heap; and on Ossa
> Pelion with its shaking forest, to make a path to heaven—

and the even more impressive sequel—

> and they would have finished their work...[19]

In orators, encomia and ceremonial or exhibition pieces always involve grandeur and sublimity, though they are generally devoid of emotion. Hence those orators who are best at conveying emotion are least good at encomia, and conversely the experts at encomia are not conveyers of emotion. On the other hand, if Caecilius thought that emotion had no contribution to make to sublimity and therefore thought it not worth mentioning, he was again completely wrong. I should myself have no hesitation in saying that there is nothing so productive of grandeur as noble emotion in the right place. It inspires and possesses our words with a kind of madness and divine spirit.

(i) Greatness of Thought

9.1 The first source, natural greatness, is the most important. Even if it is a matter of endowment rather than acquisition, we must, so far as is possible, develop our minds in the direction of greatness and make them always pregnant with noble thoughts. You ask how this can be done. I wrote elsewhere something like this: "Sublimity is the echo of a noble mind." This is why a mere idea, without verbal expression, is sometimes admired for its nobility—just as Ajax's silence in the Vision of the Dead is grand and indeed more sublime than any words could have been.[20] First then we must state where sublimity comes from: the orator must not have low or ignoble thoughts. Those whose thoughts and habits are trivial and servile all their lives cannot possibly produce anything admirable or worthy of eternity. Words will be great if thoughts are weighty. This is why splendid remarks come naturally to the proud; the man who, when Parmenio said, "I should have been content". . .[21]

[Lacuna equivalent to about six pages.]

Successful and unsuccessful ways of representing supernatural beings and of exciting awe. . . . the interval between earth and heaven. One might say that this is the measure not so much of Strife as of Homer.[22]

Contrast the line about Darkness in Hesiod—if the *Shield* is by Hesiod:

> Mucus dripped from her nostrils.[23]

This gives a repulsive picture, not one to excite awe. But how does Homer magnify the divine power?

> As far as a man can peer through the mist,
> sitting on watch, looking over the wine-dark sea,
> so long is the stride of the gods' thundering horses.[24]

He uses a cosmic distance to measure their speed. This enormously impressive image would make anybody say, and with reason, that, if the horses of the gods took two strides like that, they would find there was not enough room in the world.

The imaginative pictures in the Battle of the Gods are also very remarkable:

> And the great heavens and Olympus trumpeted around them.
> Aïdoneus, lord of the dead, was frightened in his depths;
> and in fright he jumped from his throne, and shouted,
> for fear the earth-shaker Poseidon might break through
> the ground,
> the gods and men might see
> the foul and terrible halls, which even the gods detest.[25]

Do you see how the earth is torn from its foundations, Tartarus laid bare, and the whole universe overthrown and broken up, so that all things—Heaven and Hell, things mortal and things immortal—share the warfare and the perils of that ancient battle? But, terrifying as all this is, it is blasphemous and indecent unless it is interpreted allegorically; in relating the gods' wounds, quarrels, revenges, tears, imprisonments, and manifold misfortunes, Homer, or so it seems to me, has done his best to make the men of the Trojan war gods, and the gods men. If men are unhappy, there is always death as a harbour in trouble; what he has done for his gods is to make them immortal indeed, but immortally miserable.

Much better than the Battle of the Gods are the passages which represent divinity as genuinely unsoiled and great and pure. The lines about Poseidon, much discussed by my predecessors, exemplify this:

> The high hills and the forest trembled,
> and the peaks and the city of Troy and the Achaean ships
> under the immortal feet of Poseidon as he went his way.
> He drove over the waves, and the sea-monsters gambolled around him,
> coming up everywhere out of the deep; they recognized their king.
> The sea parted in joy; and the horses flew onward.[26]

Similarly, the lawgiver of the Jews, no ordinary man—for he understood and expressed God's power in accordance with its worth—writes at the beginning of his *Laws*: "God said"—now what?—"'Let there be light,' and there was light; 'Let there be earth,' and there was earth."[27]

Perhaps it will not be out of place, my friend, if I add a further Homeric example—from the human sphere this time—so that we can see how the poet is accustomed to enter into the greatness of his heroes. Darkness falls suddenly. Thickest night blinds the Greek army. Ajax is bewildered. "O Father Zeus!," he cries,

> Deliver the sons of the Achaeans out of the mist,
> make the sky clear, and let us see;
> in the light—kill us.[28]

The feeling here is genuinely Ajax's. He does not pray for life—that would be a request unworthy of a hero—but having no good use for his courage in the disabling darkness, and so angered at his inactivity in the battle, he prays for light, and quickly: he will at all costs find a shroud worthy of his valour, though Zeus be arrayed against him.

Comparison between the Iliad and the Odyssey. In this passage, the gale of battle blows hard in Homer; he

> Rages like Ares, spear-brandishing, or the deadly fire
> raging in the mountains, in the thickets of the deep wood.
> Foam shows at his mouth.[29]

In the *Odyssey*, on the other hand—and there are many reasons for adding this to our inquiry—he demonstrates that when a great mind begins to decline, a love of story-telling characterizes its old age. We can tell that the *Odyssey* was his second work from various considerations, in particular from his insertion of the residue of the Trojan troubles in the poem in the form of episodes, and from the way in which he pays tribute of lamentation and pity to the heroes, treating them as persons long known. The *Odyssey* is simply an epilogue to the *Iliad*:

> There lies warlike Ajax, there Achilles,
> there Patroclus, the gods' peer as a counsellor,
> and there my own dear son.[30]

For the same reason, I maintain, he made the whole body of the *Iliad*, which was written at the height of his powers, dramatic and exciting, whereas most of the *Odyssey* consists of narrative, which is a characteristic of old age. Homer in the *Odyssey* may be compared to the setting sun: the size remains without the force. He no longer sustains the tension as it was in the tale of Troy, nor that consistent level of elevation which never admitted any falling off. The outpouring of passions crowding one on another has gone; so has the versatility, the realism, the abundance of imagery taken from the life. We see greatness on the ebb. It is as though the Ocean were withdrawing into itself and flowing quietly in its own bed. Homer is lost in the realm of the fabulous and incredible. In saying this, I have not forgotten the storms in the *Odyssey,* the story of Cyclops, and a few other episodes; I am speaking of old age—but it is the old age of a Homer. The point about all these stories is that the mythical element in them predominates over the realistic.

I digressed into this topic, as I said, to illustrate how easy it is for great genius to be perverted in decline into nonsense. I mean things like the story of the wineskin, the tale of the men kept as pigs in Circe's palace ("howling piglets," Zoilus called them), the feeding of Zeus by the doves (as though he were a chick in the nest), the ten days on the raft without food, and the improbabilities of the murder of the suitors.[31] What can we say of all this but that it really is "the dreaming of a Zeus"?[32]

There is also a second reason for discussing the *Odyssey*. I want you to understand that the decline of emotional power in great writers and poets turns to a capacity for depicting manners. The realistic description of Odysseus' household forms a kind of comedy of manners.

10.1   *Selection and organization of material.* Now have we any other means of making our writing sublime? Every topic naturally includes certain elements which are inherent in its raw material. It follows that sublimity will be achieved if we consistently select the most important of these inherent features and learn to organize them as a unity by combining one with another. The first of these procedures attracts the reader by the selection of details, the second by the density of those selected.

Consider Sappho's treatment of the feelings involved in the madness of being in love. She uses the attendant circumstances and draws on real life at every point. And in what does she show her quality? In her skill in selecting the outstanding details and making a unity of them:

> To me he seems a peer of the gods, the man who sits facing you and hears your sweet voice
> and lovely laughter; it flutters my heart in my breast. When I see you only for a moment, I cannot speak;
> my tongue is broken, a subtle fire runs under my skin; my eyes cannot see, my ears hum;
> cold sweat pours off me; shivering grips me all over; I am paler than grass; I seem near to dying;
> but all must be endured . . .[33]

Do you not admire the way in which she brings everything together—mind and body, hearing and tongue, eyes and skin? She seems to have lost them all, and to be looking for them as though they were external to her. She is cold and hot, mad and sane, frightened and near death, all by turns. The result is that we see in her not a single emotion, but a complex of emotions. Lovers experience all this; Sappho's excellence, as I have said, lies in her adoption and combination of the most striking details.

A similar point can be made about the descriptions of storms in Homer, who always picks out the most terrifying aspects. The author of the *Arimaspea* on the other hand expects these lines to excite terror:

> This too is a great wonder to us in our hearts:
> there are men living on water, far from land, on the deep sea:
> miserable they are, for hard is their lot;
> they give their eyes to the stars, their lives to the sea;
> often they raise their hands in prayer to the gods,
> as their bowels heave in pain.[34]

Anyone can see that this is more polished than awe-inspiring. Now compare it with Homer (I select one example out of many):

> He fell upon them as upon a swift ship falls a wave,
> huge, wind-reared by the clouds. The ship
> is curtained in foam, a hideous blast of wind
> roars in the sail. The sailors shudder in terror:
> they are carried away from under death, but only just.[35]

Aratus[36] tried to transfer the same thought:

> A little plank wards off Hades.

But this is smooth and unimpressive, not frightening. Morevover, by saying "a plank wards off Hades," he has got rid of the danger. The plank *does* keep death away. Homer, on the other hand, does not banish the cause of fear at a stroke; he gives a vivid picture of men, one might almost say, facing death many times with every wave that comes. Notice also the forced combination of naturally uncompoundable prepositions: *hupek*, "from under." Homer has tortured the words to correspond with the emotion of the moment, and expressed the emotion magnificently by thus crushing words together. He has in effect stamped the special character of the danger on the diction: "they are carried away from under death."

Compare Archilochus on the shipwreck, and Demosthenes on the arrival of the news ("It was evening . . .").[37]

In short, one might say that these writers have taken only the very best pieces, polished them up and fitted them together. They have inserted nothing inflated, undignified, or pedantic. Such things ruin the whole effect, because they produce, as it were, gaps or crevices, and so spoil the impressive thoughts which have been built into a structure whose cohesion depends upon their mutual relations.[38]

11.1 *Amplification.* The quality called "amplification" is connected with those we have been considering. It is found when the facts or the issues at stake allow many starts and pauses in each section. You wheel up one impressive unit after another to give a series of increasing importance. There are innumerable varieties of amplification: it may be produced by commonplaces, by exaggeration or intensification of facts or arguments, or by a build-up of action or emotion. The orator should realize, however, that none of these will have its full effect without sublimity. Passages expressing pity or disparagement are no doubt an exception; but in any other instance of amplification, if you take away the sublime element, you take the soul away from the body. Without the strengthening influence of the sublimity, the effective element in the whole loses all its vigour and solidity.

What is the difference between this precept and the point made above about the inclusion of vital details and their combination in a unity? What in general is the difference between amplification and sublimity? I must define my position briefly on these points, in order to make myself clear.

12.1 I do not feel satisfied with the definition given by the rhetoricians: "amplification is expression which adds grandeur to its subject." This might just as well be a definition of sublimity or emotion or tropes. All these add grandeur of some kind. The difference lies, in my opinion, in the fact that sublimity depends on elevation, whereas amplification involves extension; sublimity exists often in a single thought, amplification cannot exist without a certain quantity and superfluity. To give a general definition, amplification is an aggregation of all the details and topics which constitute a situation, strengthening the argument by dwelling on it; it differs from proof in that the latter demonstrates the point made . . .

[Lacuna equivalent to about two pages.]

A comparison between Plato and Demosthenes, with a word on Cicero. . . . spreads out richly in many directions into an open sea of grandeur. Accordingly, Demosthenes, the more emotional of the two, displays in abundance the fire and heat of passion while Plato, consistently magnificent, solemn, and grand, is much less intense—without of course becoming in the least frigid. These seem to me, my dear Terentianus—if a Greek is allowed an opinion—to be also the differences between the grandeur of Cicero and the grandeur of Demosthenes. Demosthenes has an abrupt sublimity; Cicero spreads himself. Demosthenes burns and ravages; he has violence, rapidity, strength, and force, and shows them in everything; he can be compared to a thunderbolt or a flash of lightning. Cicero, on the other hand, is like a spreading conflagration. He ranges everywhere and rolls majestically on. His huge fires endure; they are renewed in various forms from time to time and repeatedly fed with fresh fuel.—But this is a comparison which your countrymen can make better than I.

Anyway, the place for the intense, Demosthenic kind of sublimity is in indignant exaggeration, in violent emotion, and in general wherever the hearer has to be struck with amazement. The place for expansiveness is where he has to be deluged with words. This treatment is appropriate in *loci communes*, epilogues, digressions, all descriptive and exhibition pieces, historical or scientific topics, and many other departments.

To return to Plato, and the way in which he combines the "soundless flow"[39] of his smooth style with grandeur. A passage of the *Republic*[40] you have read makes the manner quite clear: "Men without experience of wisdom and virtue but always occupied with feasting and that kind of thing naturally go downhill and wander through life on a low plane of existence. They never look upwards to the truth and never rise, they never taste certain or pure pleasure. Like cattle, they always look down, bowed earthwards and tablewards; they feed and they breed, and their greediness in these directions makes them kick and butt till they kill one another with iron horns and hooves, because they can never be satisfied."

13.1

Imitation of earlier writers as a means to sublimity. Plato, if we will read him with attention, illustrates yet another road to sublimity, besides those we have discussed. This is the way of imitation and emulation of great writers of the past. Here too, my friend, is an aim to which we must hold fast. Many are possessed by a spirit not their own. It is like what we are told of the Pythia at Delphi: she is in contact with the tripod near the cleft in the ground which (so they say) exhales a divine vapour, and she is thereupon made pregnant by the supernatural power and forthwith prophesies as one inspired. Similarly, the genius of the ancients acts as a kind of oracular cavern, and effluences flow from it into the minds of their imitators. Even those previously not much inclined to prophesy become inspired and share the enthusiasm which comes from the greatness of others. Was Herodotus the only "most Homeric" writer? Surely Stesichorus and Archilochus earned the name before him. So, more than any, did Plato, who diverted to himself countless rills from the Homeric spring. (If Ammonius had not selected and written up detailed examples of this, I might have had to prove the point myself.) In all this process there is no plagiarism. It resembles rather the reproduction of good character in statues and works of art.[41] Plato could not have put such a brilliant finish on his philosophical doctrines or so often risen to poetical subjects and poetical language, if he had not tried, and tried whole-heartedly, to compete for the prize against Homer, like a young aspirant challenging an admired master. To break a lance in this way may well have been a brash and contentious thing to do, but the competition proved anything but valueless. As Hesiod says, "this strife is good for men."[42] Truly it is a noble contest and prize of honour, and one well worth winning, in which to be defeated by one's elders is itself no disgrace.

We can apply this to ourselves. When we are working on something which

14.1

needs loftiness of expression and greatness of thought, it is good to imagine how Homer would have said the same thing, or how Plato or Demosthenes or (in history) Thucydides would have invested it with sublimity. These great figures, presented to us as objects of emulation and, as it were, shining before our gaze, will somehow elevate our minds to the greatness of which we form a mental image. They will be even more effective if we ask ourselves "How would Homer or Demosthenes have reacted to what I am saying, if he had been here? What would his feelings have been?" It makes it a great occasion if you imagine such a jury or audience for your own speech, and pretend that you are answering for what you write before judges and witnesses of such heroic stature. Even more stimulating is the further thought: "How will posterity take what I am writing?" If a man is afraid of saying anything which will outlast his own life and age, the conceptions of his mind are bound to be incomplete and abortive; they will miscarry and never be brought to birth whole and perfect for the day of posthumous fame.

15.1 *Visualization (phantasia).* Another thing which is extremely productive of grandeur, magnificence and urgency, my young friend, is visualization (*phantasia*). I use this word for what some people call image-production. The term *phantasia* is used generally for anything which in any way suggests a thought productive of speech;[43] but the word has also come into fashion for the situation in which enthusiasm and emotion make the speaker *see* what he is saying and bring it *visually* before his audience. It will not escape you that rhetorical visualization has a different intention from that of the poets: in poetry the aim is astonishment, in oratory it is clarity. Both, however, seek emotion and excitement.

> Mother, I beg you, do not drive them at me,
> the women with the blood in their eyes and the snakes—
> they are here, they are here, jumping right up to me.[44]

Or again:

> O! O! She'll kill me. Where shall I escape?[45]

The poet himself saw the Erinyes, and has as good as made his audience see what he imagines.

Now Euripides devotes most pains to producing a tragic effect with two emotions, madness and love. In these he is supremely successful. At the same time, he does not lack the courage to attempt other types of visualization. Though not formed by nature for grandeur, he often forces himself to be tragic. When the moment for greatness comes, he (in Homer's words)

> whips flank and buttocks with his tail
> and drives himself to fight.[46]

For example, here is Helios handing the reins to Phaethon:[47]

> "Drive on, but do not enter Libyan air—
> it has no moisture in it, and will let
> your wheel fall through—"

and again:

> "Steer towards the seven Pleiads."
> The boy listened so far, then seized the reins,
> whipped up the winged team, and let them go.
> To heaven's expanse they flew.
> His father rode behind on Sirius,
> giving the boy advice: "That's your way, there:
> turn here–turn here."

May one not say that the writer's soul has mounted the chariot, has taken wing with the horses and shares the danger? Had it not been up among those heavenly bodies and moved in their courses, he could never have visualized such things.

Compare, too, his Cassandra:

> Ye Trojans, lovers of horses...[48]

Aeschylus, of course, ventures on the most heroic visualizations; he is like his own Seven against Thebes—

> Seven men of war, commanders of companies,
> killing a bull into a black-bound shield,
> dipping their hands in the bull's blood,
> took oath by Ares, by Enyo, by bloodthirsty Terror—

in a joint pledge of death in which they showed themselves no mercy. At the same time, he does sometimes leave his thoughts unworked, tangled and hard. The ambitious Euripides does not shirk even these risks. For example, there is in Aeschylus a remarkable description of the palace of Lycurgus in its divine seizure at the moment of Dionysus' epiphany:

> the palace was possessed, the house went bacchanal.

Euripides expresses the same thought less harshly:

> the whole mountain went bacchanal with them.[49]

There is another magnificent visualization in Sophocles' account of Oedipus dying and giving himself burial to the accompaniment of a sign from heaven,[50] and in the appearance of Achilles over his tomb at the departure of the Greek fleet.[51] Simonides has perhaps described this scene more vividly than anyone else; but it is impossible to quote everything.

The poetical examples, as I said, have a quality of exaggeration which belongs to fable and goes far beyond credibility. In an orator's visualizations, on the other hand, it is the element of fact and truth which makes for success; when the content of the passage is poetical and fabulous and does not shrink from any impossibility, the result is a shocking and outrageous abnormality. This is what happens with the shock orators of our own day; like tragic actors, these fine fellows *see* the Erinyes, and are incapable of understanding that when Orestes says

> Let me go; you are one of my Erinyes,
> you are hugging me tight, to throw me into Hell,[52]

he visualizes all this *because he is mad*.

What then is the effect of rhetorical visualization? There is much it can do to bring urgency and passion into our words; but it is when it is closely involved with factual arguments that it enslaves the hearer as well as persuading him. "Suppose you heard a shout this very moment outside the court, and someone said that the prison had been broken open and the prisoners had escaped—no one, young or old, would be so casual as not to give what help he could. And if someone then came forward and said 'This is the man who let them out,' our friend would never get a hearing; it would be the end of him."[53] There is a similar instance in Hyperides' defence of himself when he was on trial for the proposal to liberate the slaves which he put forward after the defeat.[54] "It was not the proposer," he said, "who drew up this decree: it was the battle of Chaeronea." Here the orator uses a visualization actually in the moment of making his factual argument, with the result that his thought has taken him beyond the limits of mere persuasiveness. Now our natural instinct is, in all such cases, to attend to the stronger influence, so that we are diverted from the demonstration to the astonishment caused by the visualization, which by its very brilliance conceals the factual aspect. This is a natural reaction: when two things are joined together, the stronger attracts to itself the force of the weaker.

This will suffice for an account of sublimity of thought produced by greatness of mind, imitation, or visualization.

(iii) Figures[55]

16.1 *An example to illustrate the right use of figures: the "oath" in "On the Crown."* The next topic is that of figures. Properly handled, figures constitute, as I said, no small part of sublimity. It would be a vast, or rather infinite, labour to enumerate them all; what I shall do is to expound a few of those which generate sublimity, simply in order to confirm my point.

Here is Demosthenes putting forward a demonstrative argument on behalf of his policy.[56] What would have been the natural way to put it? "You have not done wrong, you who fought for the liberty of Greece; you have examples to prove this close at home: the men of Marathon, of Salamis, of Plataea did not do wrong." But instead of this he was suddenly inspired to give voice to the oath by the heroes of Greece: "By those who risked their lives at Marathon, you have not done wrong!" Observe what he effects by this single figure of conjuration, or "apostrophe" as I call it here. He deifies his audience's ancestors, suggesting that it is right to take an oath by men who fell so bravely, as though they were gods. He inspires the judges with the temper of those who risked their lives. He transforms his demonstration into an extraordinary piece of sublimity and passion, and into the convincingness of this unusual and amazing oath. At the same time he injects into his hearers' minds a healing specific, so as to lighten their hearts by these paeans of praise and make them as proud of the battle with Philip as of the triumphs of Marathon and Salamis. In short, the figure enables him to run away with his audience.

Now the origin of this oath is said to be in the lines of Eupolis:

> By Marathon, by *my* battle,
> no one shall grieve me and escape rejoicing.[57]

But the greatness depends not on the mere form of the oath, but on place, manner, occasion, and purpose. In Eupolis, there is nothing but the oath; he is speaking to the Athenians while their fortunes are still high and they need no comfort; and instead of immortalizing the men in order to engender in the audience a proper estimation of their valour, he wanders away from the actual people who risked their lives to an inanimate object, namely the battle. In Demosthenes, on the other hand, the oath is addressed to a defeated nation, to make them no longer think of Chaeronea as a disaster. It embraces, as I said, a demonstration that they "did no wrong," an illustrative example, a confirmation, an encomium, and an exhortation. Moreover, because he was faced with the possible objection "your policies brought us to defeat—and yet you swear by victories!" he brings his thought back under control and makes it safe and unanswerable, showing that sobriety is needed even under the influence of inspiration: "By those who *risked their lives* at Marathon, and *fought in the ships* at Salamis and Artemisium, and *formed the line* at Plataea!" He never says *conquered;* throughout he withholds the word for the final issue, because it was a happy issue, and the opposite to that of Chaeronea. From the same motives he forestalls his audience by adding immediately: "all of whom were buried at the city's expense, Aeschines—all, not only the successful."

The relation between figures and sublimity. At this point, my friend, I feel I ought not to pass over an observation of my own. It shall be very brief: figures are natural allies of sublimity and themselves profit wonderfully from the alliance. I will explain how this happens.

17.1

Playing tricks by means of figures is a peculiarly suspect procedure. It raises the suspicion of a trap, a deep design, a fallacy. It is to be avoided in addressing a judge who has power to decide, and expecially in addressing tyrants, kings, governors, and anybody in a high place. Such a person immediately becomes angry if he is led astray like a foolish child by some skilful orator's figures. He takes the fallacy as indicating contempt for himself. He becomes like a wild animal. Even if he controls his temper, he is now completely conditioned against being convinced by what is said. A figure is therefore generally thought to be best when the fact that it is a figure is concealed.

Thus sublimity and emotion are a defence and a marvellous aid against the suspicion which the use of figures engenders. The artifice of the trick is lost to sight in the surrounding brilliance of beauty and grandeur, and it escapes all suspicion. "By the men of Marathon . . ." is proof enough. For how did Demosthenes conceal the figure in that passage? By sheer brilliance, of course. As fainter lights disappear when the sunshine surrounds them, so the sophisms of rhetoric are dimmed when they are enveloped in encircling grandeur. Something like this happens in painting: when light and shadow are juxtaposed in colours on the same plane, the light seems more prominent to the eye, and both stands out and actually appears much nearer. Similarly, in literature, emotional and sublime features seem closer to the mind's eye, both because of a certain natural kinship[58] and because of their brilliance. Consequently, they always show up above the figures, and overshadow and eclipse their artifice.

18.1 *Rhetorical questions.* What are we to say of inquiries and questions? Should we not say that they increase the realism and vigour of the writing by the actual form of the figure?[59]

"Or—tell me—do you want to go round asking one another 'Is there any news?'? What could be hotter news than that a Macedonian is conquering Greece? 'Is Philip dead?' 'No, but he's ill.' What difference does it make to you? If anything happens to him, you will soon create another Philip."[60]

Again: "Let us sail to Macedonia. 'Where shall we anchor?' says someone. The war itself will find out Philip's weak spots.[61] Put in the straightforward form, this would have been quite insignificant; as it is, the impassioned rapidity of question and answer and the device of self-objection have made the remark, in virtue of its figurative form, not only more sublime but more credible. For emotion carries us away more easily when it seems to be generated by the occasion rather than deliberately assumed by the speaker, and the self-directed question and its answer represent precisely this momentary quality of emotion. Just as people who are unexpectedly plied with questions become annoyed and reply to the point with vigour and exact truth, so the figure of question and answer arrests the hearer and cheats him into believing that all the points made were raised and are being put into words on the spur of the moment.

Again—this sentence in Herodotus is believed to be a particularly fine example of sublimity[62]...

[Lacuna equivalent to about two pages.]

Asyndeton. ... the words tumble out without connection, in a kind of stream, almost getting ahead of the speaker: "Engaging their shields, they pushed, fought, slew, died" (Xenophon).[63]

> We went as you told us, noble Odysseus, up the woods,
> we saw a beautiful palace built in the glades,

says Homer's Eurylochus.[64]

Disconnected and yet hurried phrases convey the impression of an agitation which both obstructs the reader and drives him on. Such is the effect of Homer's asyndeta.

20.1 *Asyndeton combined with anaphora.* The conjunction of several figures in one phrase also has a very stirring effect. Two or three may be joined together in a kind of team, jointly contributing strength, persuasiveness, charm. An example is the passage in *Against Midias*,[65] where asyndeton is combined with anaphora and vivid description. "The aggressor would do many things—some of which his victim would not even be able to tell anyone else—with gesture, with look, with voice." Then, to save the sentence from monotony and a stationary effect—for this goes with inertia, whereas disorder goes with emotion, which is a disturbance and movement of the mind—he leaps immediately to fresh instances of asyndeton and epanaphora: "With gesture, with look, with voice, when he insults, when he acts as an enemy, when he slaps the fellow, when he slaps him on the ears..." The orator is doing here exactly what the bully does—hitting the jury in the mind with blow after blow. Then he comes down with a fresh onslaught, like a sudden squall: "... when he slaps the fellow, when he slaps him on the ears. That rouses a man, that makes him lose control, when he is not used to being insulted. No one could bring out the horror of such a moment by a mere report." Here Demosthenes keeps up the natural effect of epanaphora and asyndeton by frequent variation. His order becomes disorderly, his disorder in turn acquires a certain order.

Polysyndeton. Now add the conjunctions, as Isocrates' school does. "Again, one must not omit this point, that the aggressor would do many things, first with gesture, then with look, and finally with voice." As you proceed with these insertions, it will become clear that the urgent and harsh character of the emotion loses its sting and becomes a spent fire as soon as you level it down to smoothness by the conjunctions. If you tie a runner's arms to his side, you take away his speed; likewise, emotion frets at being impeded by conjunctions and other additions, because it loses the free abandon of its movement and the sense of being, as it were, catapulted out.

Hyperbaton. Hyperbaton belongs to the same general class. It is an arrangement of words or thoughts which differs from the normal sequence...[66] It is a very real mark of urgent emotion. People who in real life feel anger, fear, or indignation, or are distracted by jealousy or some other emotion (it is impossible to say how many emotions there are; they are without number), often put one thing forward and then rush off to another, irrationally inserting some remark, and then hark back again to their first point. They seem to be blown this way and that by their excitement, as if by a veering wind. They inflict innumerable variations on the expression, the thought, and the natural sequence. Thus hyperbaton is a means by which, in the best authors, imitation approaches the effect of nature. Art is perfect when it looks like nature, nature is felicitous when it embraces concealed art. Consider the words of Dionysius of Phocaea in Herodotus:[67] "Now, for our affairs are on the razor's edge, men of Ionia, whether we are to be free or slaves—and worse than slaves, runaways—so if you will bear hardships now, you will suffer temporarily but be able to overcome your enemies." The natural order of thought would have been: "Men of Ionia, now is the time for you to bear hardships, for our affairs are on the razor's edge." The speaker has displaced "men of Ionia"; he begins with the cause of fear, as though the alarm was so pressing that he did not even have time to address the audience by name. He has also diverted the order of thought. Before saying that they must suffer hardship themselves (that is the gist of his exhortation), he first gives the reason why it is necessary, by saying "our affairs are on the razor's edge." The result is that he seems to be giving not a premeditated speech but one forced on him by the circumstances.

It is even more characteristic of Thucydides to show ingenuity in separating by transpositions even things which are by nature completely unified and indivisible.

Demosthenes is less wilful in this than Thucydides, but no one uses this kind of effect more lavishly. His transpositions produce not only a great sense of urgency but the appearance of extemporization, as he drags his hearers with him into the hazards of his long hyperbata. He often holds in suspense the meaning which he set out to convey and, introducing one extraneous item after another in an alien and unusual place before getting to the main point, throws the hearer into a panic lest the sentence collapse altogether, and forces him in his excitement to share the speaker's peril, before, at long last and beyond all expectation, appositely paying off at the end the long due conclusion; the very audacity and hazardousness of the hyperbata add to the astounding effect. There are so many examples that I forbear to give any.

23.1 *Changes of case, tense, person, number gender; plural for singular and singular for plural.* What is called polyptoton, like accumulation, variation, and climax, is, as you know, extremely effective and contributes both to ornament and to sublimity and emotion of every kind.[68]

How do variations in case, tense, person, number, and gender diversify and stimulate the style? My answer to this is that, as regards variations of number, the lesser effect (though a real one) is produced by instances in which singular forms are seen on reflection to be plural in sense:

> The innumerable host
> were scattered over the sandy beach, and shouted.

More worthy of note are the examples in which plurals give a more grandiose effect, and court success by the sense of multitude expressed by the grammatical number. An example comes in Sophocles, where Oedipus says:

> Weddings, weddings
> you bred me and again released my seed,
> made fathers, brothers, children, blood of the kin,
> brides, wives, mothers—all
> the deeds most horrid ever seen in men.[69]

All this is about Oedipus on the one hand and Jocasta on the other, but the expansion of the number to the plural forms pluralizes the misfortunes also.
Another example is:

> Hectors and Sarpedons came forth.[70]

Another is the Platonic passage about the Athenians, which I have quoted elsewhere:[71] "No Pelopses or Cadmuses or Aegyptuses or Danauses or other barbarians by birth have settled among us; we are pure Greeks, with no barbarian blood," and so on. Such an agglomeration of names in crowds naturally makes the facts sound more impressive. But the practice is only to be followed when the subject admits amplification, abundance, hyperbole, or emotion—one or more of these. Only a sophist has bells on his harness wherever he goes.

24.1 The contrary device—the contraction of plurals into singulars—also sometimes produces a sublime effect. "The whole Peloponnese was divided."[72] "When Phrynichus produced *The Capture of Miletus* the theatre burst into tears" ("theatre" for "spectators").[73] To compress the separate individuals into the corresponding unity produces a more solid effect.

The cause of the effect is the same in both cases. Where the nouns are singular, it is a mark of unexpected emotion to pluralize them.[74] Where they are plural, to unite the plurality under one well-sounding word is again surprising because of the opposite transformation of the facts.

Vivid present tense. To represent past events as present is to turn a narrative into a thing of immediate urgency. "A man who has fallen under Cyrus' horse and is being trampled strikes the horse in the belly with his sword. The horse, convulsed, shakes Cyrus off. He falls" (Xenophon).[75] This is common in Thucydides.

Imaginary second person. Urgency may also be conveyed by the replacement of one grammatical person by another. It often gives the hearer the sense of being in the midst of the danger himself.

> You would say they were tireless, never wearied in war,
> so eagerly they fought (Homer).[76]

> May you never be drenched in the sea in that month! (Aratus).[77]

> You will sail upstream from Elephantine, and then you will come to a smooth plain. After crossing this, you will embark on another boat and sail for two days. Then you will come to a great city called Meroe (Herodotus).[78]

Do you see, my friend, how he grips your mind and takes it on tour through all these places, making hearing as good as seeing? All such forms of expression, being directed to an actual person, bring the hearer into the presence of real events.

Moreover, if you speak as though to an individual and not to a large company, you will affect him more and make him more attentive and excited, because the personal address stimulates:

> You could not tell with whom Tydides stood.[79]

Lapses into direct speech. Sometimes a writer, in the course of a narrative in the third person, makes a sudden change and speaks in the person of his character. This kind of thing is an outburst of emotion.

> Hector shouted aloud to the Trojans
> to rush for the ships, and leave the spoils of the dead.
> "If I see anyone away from the ships of his own accord,
> I will have him killed on the spot."[80]

Here the poet has given the narrative to himself, as appropriate to him, and then suddenly and without warning has put the abrupt threat in the mouth of the angry prince. It would have been flat if he had added "Hector said." As it is, the change of construction is so sudden that it has outstripped its creator.

Hence the use of this figure is appropriate when the urgency of the moment gives the writer no chance to delay, but forces on him an immediate change from one person to another. "Ceyx was distressed at this, and ordered the children to depart. 'For I am unable to help you. Go therefore to some other country, so as to save yourselves without harming me'" (Hecataeus).[81]

Somewhat different is the method by which Demosthenes in *Against*

Aristogiton[82] makes variation of person produce the effect of strong emotion and rapid change of tone: "Will none of you be found to feel bile or anger at the violence of this shameless monster, who—you vile wretch, your right of free speech is barred not by gates and doors which can be opened, but . . . !" He makes the change before the sense is complete, and in effect divides a single thought between two persons in his passion ("who—you vile wretch . . . !"), as well as turning to Aristogiton and giving the impression of abandoning the course of his argument—with the sole result, so strong is the emotion, of giving it added intensity.

So also Penelope:

> Herald, why have the proud suitors sent you here?
> Is it to tell Odysseus' maidservants
> to stop their work and get dinner for them?
> After their wooing, may they never meet again!
> May this be their last dinner here—
> you who gather together so often and waste wealth,
> who never listened to your fathers when you were children
> and they told you what kind of man Odysseus was![83]

28.1 *Periphrasis.* No one, I fancy, would question the fact that periphrasis is a means to sublimity. As in music the melody is made sweeter by what is called the accompaniment, so periphrasis is often heard in concert with the plain words and enhances them with a new resonance. This is especially true if it contains nothing bombastic or tasteless but only what is pleasantly blended. There is a sufficient example in Plato, at the beginning of the Funeral Speech:[84] "These men have received their due, and having received it they go on their fated journey, escorted publicly by their country and privately each by his own kindred." Plato here calls death a "fated journey" and the bestowal of regular funeral rites a public escort by the country. This surely adds no inconsiderable impressiveness to the thought. He has lyricized the bare prose, enveloping it in the harmony of the beautiful periphrasis.

"You believe labour to be the guide to a pleasant life; you have gathered into your souls the noblest and most heroic of possessions: you enjoy being praised more than anything else in the world" (Xenophon).[85] In this passage "you make labour the guide to a pleasant life" is put for "you are willing to labour." This and the other expansions invest the praise with a certain grandeur of conception.

Another example is the inimitable sentence of Herodotus: "The goddess inflicted a feminine disease on the Scythians who plundered the temple."[86]

29.1 Periphrasis, however, is a particularly dangerous device if it is not used with moderation. It soon comes to be heavy and dull, smelling of empty phrases and coarseness of fibre. This is why Plato—who is fond of the figure and sometimes uses it unseasonably—is ridiculed for the sentence in the *Laws*[87] which runs: "Neither silvern wealth nor golden should be permitted to establish itself in the city." If he had wanted to prohibit cattle, says the critic, he would have talked of "ovine and bovine" wealth.

Conclusion of the section on figures. So much, my dear Terentianus, by way of digression on the theory of the use of those figures which conduce to sublimity. They all make style more emotional and excited, and emotion is as essential a part of sublimity as characterization is of charm.[88]

(iv) Diction

Thought and expression are of course very much involved with each other. We have therefore next to consider whether any topics still remain in the field of diction. The choice of correct and magnificent words is a source of immense power to entice and charm the hearer. This is something which all orators and other writers cultivate intensely. It makes grandeur, beauty, old-world charm, weight, force, strength, and a kind of lustre bloom upon our words as upon beautiful statues; it gives things life and makes them speak. But I suspect there is no need for me to make this point; you know it well. It is indeed true that beautiful words are the light that illuminates thought.

Magniloquence, however, is not always serviceable: to dress up trivial material in grand and solemn language is like putting a huge tragic mask on a little child. In poetry and history, however . . .

[Lacuna equivalent to about four pages.]

Use of everyday words. . . . and productive, as is Anacreon's "I no longer turn my mind to the Thracian filly."[89] Similarly, Theopompus' much-admired phrase seems to me to be particularly expressive because of the aptness of the analogy, though Caecilius manages to find fault with it: "Philip was excellent at stomaching facts." An idiomatic phrase is sometimes much more vivid than an ornament of speech, for it is immediately recognized from everyday experience, and the familiar is inevitably easier to credit. "To stomach facts" is thus used vividly of a man who endures unpleasantness and squalor patiently, and indeed with pleasure, for the sake of gain. There are similar things in Herodotus: "Cleomenes in his madness cut his own flesh into little pieces with a knife till he had sliced himself to death," "Pythes continued fighting on the ship until he was cut into joints."[90] These phrases come within an inch of being vulgar, but they are so expressive that they avoid vulgarity.

Metaphors. As regards number of metaphors, Caecilius seems to agree with the propounders of the rule that not more than two or at most three may be used of the same subject. Here too Demosthenes is our canon. The right occasions are when emotions come flooding in and bring the multiplication of metaphors with them as a necessary accompaniment. "Vile flatterers, mutilators of their countries, who have given away liberty as a drinking present, first to Philip and now to Alexander, measuring happiness by the belly and the basest impulses, overthrowing liberty and freedom from despotism, which Greeks of old regarded as the canons and standards of the good."[91] In this passage the orator's anger against traitors obscures the multiplicity of his metaphors.

This is why Aristotle and Theophrastus say that there are ways of softening bold metaphors—namely by saying "as if," "as it were," "if I may put it so," or "if we may venture on a bold expression." Apology, they say, is a remedy for audacity. I accept this doctrine, but I would add—and I said the same about figures—that strong and appropriate emotions and genuine sublimity are a specific palliative for multiplied or daring metaphors, because their nature is to sweep and drive all these other things along with the surging tide of their movement. Indeed it might be truer to say that they *demand* the hazardous. They never allow the hearer leisure to count the metaphors, because he too shares the speaker's enthusiasm.

At the same time, nothing gives distinction to commonplaces and descriptions so well as a continuous series of tropes. This is the medium in which the description of man's bodily tabernacle is worked out so elaborately in Xenophon and yet more superlatively by Plato.[92] Thus Plato calls the head the "citadel" of the body; the neck is an "isthmus" constructed between the head and the chest; the vertebrae, he says, are fixed underneath "like pivots." Pleasure is a "lure of evil" for mankind; the tongue is a "taste-meter." The heart is a "knot of veins" and "fountain of the blood that moves impetuously round," allocated to the "guard-room." The word he uses for the various passages of the canals is "alleys." "Against the throbbing of the heart," he continues, "in the expectation of danger and in the excitation of anger, when it gets hot, they contrived a means of succour, implanting in us the lungs, soft, bloodless, and with cavities, a sort of cushion, so that when anger boils up in the heart, the latter's throbbing is against a yielding obstacle, so that it comes to no harm." Again: he calls the seat of the desires "the women's quarters," and the seat of anger "the men's quarters." The spleen is for him "a napkin for the inner parts, which therefore grows big and festering through being filled with secretions." "And thereafter," he says again, "they buried the whole under a canopy of flesh," putting the flesh on "as a protection against dangers from without, like felting." Blood he called "fodder of the flesh." For the purpose of nutrition, he says also, "they irrigated the body, cutting channels as in gardens, so that the streams of the veins might flow as it were from an incoming stream, making the body an aqueduct." Finally: when the end is at hand, the soul's "ship's cables" are "loosed," and she herself "set free."

The passage contains countless similar examples; but these are enough to make my point, namely that tropes are naturally grand, that metaphors conduce to sublimity, and that passages involving emotion and description are the most suitable field for them. At the same time, it is plain without my saying it that the use of tropes, like all other good things in literature, always tempts one to go too far. This is what people ridicule most in Plato, who is often carried away by a sort of literary madness into crude, harsh metaphors or allegorical fustian. "It is not easy to understand that a city ought to be mixed like a bowl of wine, wherein the wine seethes madness, but when chastened by another, sober god, and achieving a proper communion with him, produces a good and moderate drink."[93] To call water "a sober god," says the critic, and mixture "chastening," is the language of a poet who is far from sober himself.

Digression: Genius versus mediocrity. Faults of this kind formed the subject of Caecilius' attack in his book on Lysias, in which he had the audacity to declare Lysias in all respects superior to Plato. He has in fact given way without discrimination to two emotions: loving Lysias more deeply than he loves himself, he yet hates Plato with an even greater intensity. His motive, however, is desire to score a point, and his assumptions are not, as he believed, generally accepted. In preferring Lysias to Plato he thinks he is preferring a faultless and pure writer to one who makes many mistakes. But the facts are far from supporting his view.

Let us consider a really pure and correct writer. We have then to ask ourselves in general terms whether grandeur attended by some faults of execution is to be preferred, in prose or poetry, to a modest success of impeccable soundness. We must also ask whether the greater *number* of good qualities or the greater good qualities ought properly to win the literary prizes. These questions are relevant to a discussion of sublimity, and urgently require an answer. 33.1

I am certain in the first place that great geniuses are least "pure." Exactness in every detail involves a risk of meanness; with grandeur, as with great wealth, there ought to be something overlooked. It may also be inevitable that low or mediocre abilities should maintain themselves generally at a correct and safe level, simply because they take no risks and do not aim at the heights, whereas greatness, just because it is greatness, incurs danger.

I am aware also of a second point. All human affairs are, in the nature of things, better known on their worse side; the memory of mistakes is ineffaceable, that of goodness is soon gone. I have myself cited not a few mistakes in Homer and other great writers, not because I take pleasure in their slips, but because I consider them not so much voluntary mistakes as oversights let fall at random through inattention and with the negligence of genius. I do, however, think that the greater good qualities, even if not consistently maintained, are always more likely to win the prize—if for no other reason, because of the greatness of spirit they reveal. Apollonius makes no mistakes in the *Argonautica*; Theocritus is very felicitous in the *Pastorals*, apart from a few passages not connected with the theme; but would you rather be Homer or Apollonius? Is the Eratosthenes of that flawless little poem *Erigone* a greater poet than Archilochus, with his abundant, uncontrolled flood, that bursting forth of the divine spirit which is so hard to bring under the rule of law? Take lyric poetry: would you rather be Bacchylides or Pindar? Take tragedy: would you rather be Ion of Chios or Sophocles? Ion and Bacchylides are impeccable, uniformly beautiful writers in the polished manner; but it is Pindar and Sophocles who sometimes set the world on fire with their vehemence, for all that their flame often goes out without reason and they collapse dismally. Indeed, no one in his senses would reckon all Ion's works put together as the equivalent of the one play *Oedipus*.

If good points were totted up, not judged by their real value, Hyperides would in every way surpass Demosthenes. He is more versatile,[94] and has more good qualities. He is second-best at everything, like a pentathlon competitor; always beaten by the others for first place, he remains the best of the nonspecialists. In fact, he reproduces all the good features of Demosthenes, except his word-arrangement, and also has for good measure the excellences and graces of Lysias. He knows how to talk simply where appropriate; he does not deliver himself of everything in the same tone, like Demosthenes. His expres- 34.1

sion of character has sweetness and delicacy. Urbanity, sophisticated sarcasm, good breeding, skill in handling irony, humour neither rude nor tasteless but flavoured with true Attic salt, an ingenuity in attack with a strong comic element and a sharp sting to its apt fun—all this produces inimitable charm. He has moreover great talents for exciting pity, and a remarkable facility for narrating myths with copiousness and developing general topics with fluency. For example, while his account of Leto is in his more poetic manner, his Funeral Speech is an unrivalled example of the epideictic style.[95] Demosthenes, by contrast, has no sense of character. He lacks fluency, smoothness, and capacity for the epideictic manner; in fact he is practically without all the qualities I have been describing. When he forces himself to be funny or witty, he makes people laugh at him rather than with him. When he wants to come near to being charming, he is furthest removed from it. If he had tried to write the little speech on Phryne or that on Athenogenes,[96] he would have been an even better advertisement for Hyperides. Yet Hyperides' beauties, though numerous, are without grandeur: "inert in the heart of a sober man," they leave the hearer at peace. Nobody feels frightened reading Hyperides.

But when Demosthenes begins to speak, he concentrates in himself excellences finished to the highest perfection of his sublime genius—the intensity of lofty speech, living emotions, abundance, acuteness, speed where speed is vital, all his unapproachable vehemence and power. He concentrates it all in himself—they are divine gifts, it is almost blasphemous to call them human—and so outpoints all his rivals, compensating with the beauties he has even for those which he lacks. The crash of his thunder, the brilliance of his lightning make all other orators, of all ages, insignificant. It would be easier to open your eyes to an approaching thunderbolt than to face up to his unremitting emotional blows.

35.1 To return to Plato and Lysias, there is, as I said, a further difference between them. Lysias is much inferior not only in the importance of the good qualities concerned but in their number; and at the same time he exceeds Plato in the number of his failings even more than he falls short in his good qualities.

What then was the vision which inspired those divine writers who disdained exactness of detail and aimed at the greatest prizes in literature? Above all else, it was the understanding that nature made man to be no humble or lowly creature, but brought him into life and into the universe as into a great festival, to be both a spectator and an enthusiastic contestant in its competitions. She implanted in our minds from the start an irresistible desire for anything which is great and, in relation to ourselves, supernatural.

The universe therefore is not wide enough for the range of human speculation and intellect. Our thoughts often travel beyond the boundaries of our surroundings. If anyone wants to know what we were born for, let him look round at life and contemplate the splendour, grandeur, and beauty in which it everywhere abounds. It is a natural inclination that leads us to admire not the little streams, however pellucid and however useful, but the Nile, the Danube, the Rhine, and above all the Ocean. Nor do we feel so much awe before the little flame we kindle, because it keeps its light clear and pure, as before the fires of heaven, though they are often obscured. We do not think our flame more worthy of admiration than the craters of Etna, whose eruptions bring up rocks and whole hills out of the depths, and sometimes pour forth rivers of the earth-born, spontaneous fire. A single comment fits all these examples: the useful and necessary are readily available to man, it is the unusual that always excites our wonder.

So when we come to great geniuses in literature—where, by contrast, grandeur is not divorced from service and utility—we have to conclude that such men, for all their faults, tower far above mortal stature. Other literary qualities prove their users to be human; sublimity raises us towards the spiritual greatness of god. Freedom from error does indeed save us from blame, but it is only greatness that wins admiration. Need I add that every one of those great men redeems all his mistakes many times over by a single sublime stroke? Finally, if you picked out and put together all the mistakes in Homer, Demosthenes, Plato, and all the other really great men, the total would be found to be a minute fraction of the successes which those heroic figures have to their credit. Posterity and human experience—judges whose sanity envy cannot question—place the crown of victory on their heads. They keep their prize irrevocably, and will do so

36.1

> so long as waters flow and tall trees flourish.[97]

It has been remarked that "the failed Colossus is no better than the Doryphorus of Polyclitus."[98] There are many ways of answering this. We may say that accuracy is admired in art and grandeur in nature, and it is *by nature* that man is endowed with the power of speech; or again that statues are expected to represent the human form, whereas, as I said, something higher than human is sought in literature.

At this point I have a suggestion to make which takes us back to the beginning of the book. Impeccability is generally a product of art; erratic excellence comes from natural greatness; therefore, art must always come to the aid of nature, and the combination of the two may well be perfection.

It seemed necessary to settle this point for the sake of our inquiry; but everyone is at liberty to enjoy what he takes pleasure in.

Similes. We must now return to the main argument. Next to metaphors come comparisons and similes. The only difference is . . .

37.1

[Lacuna equivalent to about two pages.]

Hyperbole. . . . such expressions as: "Unless you've got your brains in your heels and are walking on them."[99] The important thing to know is how far to push a given hyperbole; it sometimes destroys it to go too far; too much tension results in relaxation, and may indeed end in the contrary of the intended effect. Thus Isocrates' zeal for amplifying everything made him do a childish thing. The argument of his *Panegyricus* is that Athens surpasses Sparta in services to the Greek race. Right at the beginning we find the following:[100] "Secondly, the power of speech is such that it can make great things lowly, give grandeur to the trivial, say what is old in a new fashion, and lend an appearance of antiquity to recent events." Is Isocrates then about to reverse the positions of Athens and

38.1

Sparta? The encomium on the power of speech is equivalent to an introduction recommending the reader not to believe what he is told! I suspect that what we said of the best figures is true of the best hyperboles: they are those which avoid being seen for what they are. The desired effect is achieved when they are connected with some impressive circumstance and with moments of high emotion. Thucydides' account of those killed in Sicily is an example: "The Syracusans came down and massacred them, especially those in the river. The water was stained; but despite the blood and the dirt, men continued to drink it, and many still fought for it."[101] It is the intense emotion of the moment which makes it credible that dirt and blood should still be fought for as drink. Herodotus has something similar about Thermopylae: "Meanwhile though they defended themselves with swords (those who still had them), and with hands and mouths, the barbarians buried them with their missiles."[102] What is meant by fighting armed men with mouths or being buried with missiles? Still, it is credible; for we form the impression that the hyperbole is a reasonable product of the situation, not that the situation has been chosen for the sake of the hyperbole. As I keep saying, acts and emotions which approach ecstasy provide a justification for, and an antidote to, any linguistic audacity. This is why comic hyperboles, for all their incredibility, are convincing because we laugh at them so much: "He had a farm, but it didn't stretch as far as a Laconic letter." Laughter is emotion in amusement (*hēdonē*).

There are hyperboles which belittle as well as those which exaggerate. Intensification is the factor common to the two species, vilification being in a sense an amplification of lowness.

(v) Word-Arrangement or Composition[103]

39.1   There remains the fifth of the factors contributing to sublimity which we originally enumerated. This was a certain kind of composition or word-arrangement. Having set out my conclusions on this subject fully in two books, I shall here add only so much as is essential for our present subject.

Effect of rhythm. Harmony is a natural instrument not only of conviction and pleasure but also to a remarkable degree of grandeur and emotion. The *aulos*[104] fills the audience with certain emotions and makes them somehow beside themselves and possessed. It sets a rhythm, it makes the hearer move to the rhythm and assimilate himself to the tune, "untouched by the Muses though he be."[105] The notes of the lyre, though they have no meaning, also, as you know, often cast a wonderful spell of harmony with their varied sounds and blended and mingled notes. Yet all these are but spurious images and imitations of persuasion, not the genuine activities proper to human nature of which I spoke.[106] Composition, on the other hand, is a harmony of words, man's natural instrument, penetrating not only the ears but the very soul. It arouses all kinds of conceptions of words and thoughts and objects, beauty and melody—all things native and natural to mankind. The combination and variety of its sounds convey the speaker's emotions to the minds of those around him and make the hearers share them. It fits his great thoughts into a coherent structure by the way in which it builds up patterns of words. Shall we not then believe that by all these methods it bewitches us and elevates to grandeur, dignity, and sublimity both every thought which comes within its compass and ourselves as well, holding as it does complete domination over our minds? It is absurd to question facts so generally agreed. Experience is proof enough.

The idea which Demosthenes used in speaking of the decree[107] is reputed very sublime, and is indeed splendid. "This decree made the danger which then surrounded the city pass away like a cloud (*touto to psēphisma ton tote tē polei peristanta kindūnon parelthein epoiēsen hōsper nephos*)." But the effect depends as much on the harmony as on the thought. The whole passage is based on dactylic rhythms, and these are very noble and grand. (This is why they form the heroic, the noblest metre we know.) . . .

[A short phrase missing.]

. . . but make any change you like in the order:

touto to psēphisma hōsper nephos epoiēse ton tote kindūnon parelthein,

or cut off a syllable:

epoiēse parelthein hōs nephos.

You will immediately see how the harmony echoes the sublimity. The phrase *hōsper nephos* rests on its long first unit (– –) which measures four shorts; the removal of a syllable (*hōs nephos*) at once curtails and mutilates the grand effect.

Now lengthen the phrase:

parelthein epoiēsen hōsperei nephos.

It stills means the same, but the effect is different, because the sheer sublimity is broken up and undone by the breaking up of the run of long syllables at the end.

Effect of period structure. I come now to a principle of particular importance for lending grandeur to our words. The beauty of the body depends on the way in which the limbs are joined together, each one when severed from the others having nothing remarkable about it, but the whole together forming a perfect unity. Similarly great thoughts which lack connection are themselves wasted and waste the total sublime effect, whereas if they co-operate to form a unity and are linked by the bonds of harmony, they come to life and speak just by virtue of the periodic structure. It is indeed generally true that, in periods, grandeur results from the total contribution of many elements.

I have shown elsewhere[108] that many poets and other writers who are not naturally sublime, and may indeed be quite unqualified for grandeur, and who use in general common and everyday words which carry with them no special effect, nevertheless acquire magnificence and splendour, and avoid being thought low or mean, solely by the way in which they arrange and fit together their words. Philistus, Aristophanes sometimes, Euripides generally, are among the many examples. Thus Heracles says after the killing of the children:

> I'm full of troubles, there's no room for more.[109]

This is a very ordinary remark, but it has become sublime, as the situation demands.[110] If you re-arrange it, it will become apparent that it is in the composition, not in the sense, that Euripides' greatness appears.

Dirce is being pulled about by the bull:

> And where it could, it writhed and twisted round,
> dragging at everything, rock, woman, oak,
> juggling with them all.[111]

The conception is fine in itself, but it has been improved by the fact that the word-harmony is not hurried and does not run smoothly; the words are propped up by one another and rest on the intervals between them; set wide apart like that, they give the impression of solid strength.

FEATURES DESTRUCTIVE OF SUBLIMITY

41.1 *Bad and affected rhythm.* Nothing is so damaging to sublime effect as effeminate and agitated rhythm, pyrrhics ($\smile\smile$), trochees ($-\smile$ or $\smile\smile\smile$) and dichorei ($-\smile-\smile$); they turn into a regular jig. All the rhythmical elements immediately appear artificial and cheap, being constantly repeated in a monotonous fashion without the slightest emotional effect. Worst of all, just as songs distract an audience from the action[112] and compel attention for themselves, so the rhythmical parts of speech produce on the hearer the effect not of speech but of rhythm, so that they foresee the coming endings and sometimes themselves beat time for the speaker and anticipate him in giving the step, just as in a dance.

The "chopped up" style. Phrases too closely knit[113] are also devoid of grandeur, as are those which are chopped up into short elements consisting of short syllables, bolted together, as it were, and rough at the joins.

42.1 *Excessive brevity.* Exxcessively cramped expression also does damage to sublimity. It cripples grandeur to compress it into too short a space. I do not mean proper compression, but cutting up into tiny pieces. Cramping mutilates sense; brevity gives directness. Conversely with fully extended expressions: anything developed at unseasonable length falls dead.[114]

Undignified vocabulary. Lowness of diction also destroys grandeur.

43.1 The description of the storm in Herodotus is magnificent in conception, but includes expressions which are below the dignity of the subject.[115] "The sea seethed" is one instance: the cacophony does much to dissipate the sublime effect. "The wind slacked" is another example; yet another is the "unpleasant end" which awaited those who were thrown against the wreckage. "Slack" is an undignified, colloquial word; "unpleasant" is inappropriate to such an experience.

Similarly, Theopompus first gives a magnificent setting to the descent of the Persian king on Egypt, and then ruins it all with a few words:[116]

> What city or nation in Asia did not send its embassy to the King? What thing of beauty or value, product of the earth or work of art, was not brought him as a gift? There were many precious coverlets and cloaks, purple, embroidered, and white; there were many gold tents fitted out with all necessities; there were many robes and beds of great price. There were silver vessels and worked gold, drinking cups and bowls, some studded with jewels, some elaborately and preciously wrought. Countless myriads of arms were there, Greek and barbarian. There were multitudes of pack animals and victims fattened for slaughter, many bushels of condiments, many bags and sacks and pots of onions and every other necessity. There was so much salt meat of every kind that travellers approaching from a distance mistook the huge heaps for cliffs of hills thrusting up from the plain.

He passes from the sublime to the mean; the development of the scene should have been the other way round. By mixing up the bags and the condiments and the sacks in the splendid account of the whole expedition, he conjures up the vision of a kitchen. Suppose one actually had these beautiful objects before one's eyes, and then dumped some bags and sacks in the middle of the gold and jewelled bowls, and silver vessels, the gold tents, and the drinking-cups—the effect would be disgusting. It is the same with style: if you insert words like this when they are not wanted, they make a blot on the context. It was open to Theopompus to give a general description of the "hills" which he says were raised, and, having made this change,[117] to proceed to the rest of the preparations, mentioning camels and multitudes of beasts of burden carrying everything needed for luxury and pleasure of the table, or speaking of "heaps of all kinds of seeds and everything that makes for fine cuisine and dainty living." If he had wanted at all costs to make the king self-supporting,[118] he could have talked of "all the refinements of *maîtres-d'hôtel* and chefs."

It is wrong to descend, in a sublime passage, to the filthy and contemptible, unless we are absolutely compelled to do so. We ought to use words worthy of things. We ought to imitate nature, who, in creating man, did not set our private parts or the excretions of our body in the face, but concealed them as well as she could, and, as Xenophon says,[119] made the channels of these organs as remote as possible, so as not to spoil the beauty of the creature as a whole.

CONCLUSION

There is no urgent need to enumerate in detail features which produce a low effect. We have explained what makes style noble and sublime; the opposite qualities will obviously make it low and undignified.

APPENDIX: CAUSES OF THE DECLINE OF LITERATURE[120]

44.1   I shall not hesitate to add for your instruction, my dear Terentianus, one further topic, so as to clear up a question put to me the other day by one of the philosophers.

"I wonder," he said, "and so no doubt do many others, why it is that in our age there are minds which are strikingly persuasive and practical, shrewd, versatile, and well-endowed with the ability to write agreeably, but no sublime or really great minds, except perhaps here and there. There is a universal dearth of literature.

"Are we to believe," he went on, "the common explanation that democracy nurtures greatness, and great writers flourished with democracy and died with it? Freedom, the argument goes, nourishes and encourages the thoughts of the great, as well as exciting their enthusiasm for rivalry with one another and their ambition for the prize. In addition the availability of political reward sharpens and polishes up orators' talents by giving them exercise; they shine forth, free in a free world. We of the present day, on the other hand," he continued, "seem to have learned in infancy to live under justified slavery, swathed round from our first tender thoughts in the same habits and customs, never allowed to taste that fair and fecund spring of literature, freedom. We end up as flatterers in the grand manner."

He went on to say how the same argument explained why, unlike other capacities, that of the orator could never belong to a slave.

"The inability to speak freely and the consciousness of being a prisoner at once assert themselves, battered into him as they have been by the blows of habit. As Homer says,[121] 'The day of slavery takes half one's manhood away.' I don't know if it's true, but I understand that the cages in which dwarfs or Pygmies are kept not only prevent the growth of the prisoners but cripple them because of the fastening which constricts the body. One might describe all slavery, even the most justified,[122] as a cage for the soul, a universal prison."

"My good friend," I replied, "it is easy to find fault with the present situation; indeed it is a human characteristic to do so. But I wonder whether what destroys great minds is not the peace of the world, but the unlimited war which lays hold on our desires, and all the passions which beset and ravage our modern life. Avarice, the insatiable disease from which we all suffer, and love of pleasure—these are our two slave-masters; or perhaps one should say that they sink our ship of life with all hands. Avarice is a mean disease; love of pleasure is base through and through. I cannot see how we can honour, or rather deify, unlimited wealth as we do without admitting into our souls the evils which attach to it. When wealth is measureless and uncontrolled, extravagance comes with it, sticking close beside it, and, as they say, keeping step. The moment wealth opens the way into cities and houses, extravagance also enters and dwells therein. These evils then become chronic in people's lives, and, as the philosophers say,[123] nest and breed. They are soon busy producing offspring:

greed, pride, and luxury are their all-too-legitimate children. If these offspring of wealth are allowed to mature, they breed in turn those inexorable tyrants of the soul, insolence, lawlessness, and shamelessness. It is an inevitable process. Men will no longer open their eyes or give thought to their reputation with posterity. The ruin of their lives is gradually consummated in a cycle of such vices. Greatness of mind wanes, fades, and loses its attraction when men spend their admiration on their mortal parts and neglect to develop the immortal. One who has been bribed to give a judgement will no longer be a free and sound judge of rightness and nobility. The corrupt man inevitably thinks his own side's claim just and fair. Yet nowadays bribery is the arbiter of the life and fortunes of every one of us—not to mention chasing after other people's deaths and conspiring about wills. We are all so enslaved by avarice that we buy the power of making profit out of everything at the price of our souls. Amid such pestilential corruption of human life, how can we expect that there should be left to us any free, uncorrupt judge of great things of permanent value? How can we hope not to lose our case to the corrupt practices of the love of gain?

"Perhaps people like us are better as subjects than given our freedom. Greed would flood the world in woe, if it were really released and let out of the cage, to prey on its neighbours."

Idleness, I went on to say, was the bane of present-day minds. We all live with it. Our whole regime of effort and relaxation[124] is devoted to praise and pleasure, not to the useful results that deserve emulation and honour.

"Best to let these things be,"[125] and proceed to our next subject. This was emotion, to which we promised to devote a separate treatise. It occupies, as I said, a very important place among the constituents of literature in general, and sublimity in particular . . .

[A few words missing at the end.]

NOTES

1. This is to translate *bathous*. The simple, eighteenth-century emendation *pathous* means "emotion." The English word "bathos" seems to have acquired its meaning from a misunderstanding of this passage; see Pope's *Peri Bathous or on the Art of Sinking* (1728).

2. *Orations* 23. 113.

3. Aesch. fr. 281 Nauck. The speaker is Boreas, the North Wind, who is enraged with King Erechtheus of Athens because he will not give him his daughter Orithyia. As the passage is incomplete, the point of some of the critical comment is lost.

4. Fr. 701 Nauck.

5. The context shows what is meant: the shallow pedantry of the immature.

6. Presumably in the lost passage on p. 330, or perhaps in the separate work mentioned at the end of the treatise, above.

7. In the eighth century B.C. Our other sources make this war last twenty years; we do not know the source of the variant (assuming the text to be correct).

8. The disastrous Athenian expedition against Syracuse (415–413 B.C.) had been preceded by a mysterious incident at Athens, in which the "Hermae" in the city were mutilated one night.

9. Dionysius II, expelled in 356. The name Dion is etymologically connected with Zeus (accusative *Dia*, genitive *Dios*).

10. The word *korē* means both "girl" and "pupil"; Xenophon replaces it by *parthenos*, which means unambiguously "maiden."

11. *Il*. 1. 225.—The text of this sentence in "Longinus" is uncertain, but the general sense beyond doubt.

12. Agathocles was ruler of Syracuse from 317 to 287. The "unveiling ceremony" was normally held on the third day after the marriage.

13. *Laws* 741c.

14. *Laws* 778d.

15. 5. 18.

16. See p. 342f., p. 349f.

17. Compare Aristotle's "magnanimous man": *Nic. Eth*. 4. 3.

18. Or "and coined words."

19. *Od*. 11. 315–17.

20. *Od*. 11. 563. Note that this is not an example, but a simile illustrating the point that ideas in themselves can be grand.

21. Parmenio said to Alexander that if he were Alexander he would be content, and would not go on fighting. "So would I, if I were Parmenio," replied Alexander.

22. The reference is to *Il*. 4. 440ff., where Strife is described as having her head in the sky and walking on the earth. "Longinus" means that Homer too is a colossus of cosmic dimensions.

23. *Shield of Heracles* 267.

24. *Il*. 5. 770–72.

25. See *Il*. 21. 388 and 20. 61ff.

26. See *Il*. 13. 18ff., and 20. 60.

27. Controversy about the genuineness of this reference to Genesis 1 has raged since the eighteenth century. For the influence of the reference on literary taste, see S. H. Monk, *The Sublime*, 33.

28. *Il*. 17. 645ff.

29. From *Il*. 15. 605ff.

30. Spoken by Nestor, *Od*. 3. 109ff.

31. For these various stories, see *Od*. 10. 17ff., 10. 237ff., 12. 447ff., 22. 79ff.

32. Sense uncertain. Possibly the text is corrupt. "A sick man's dream" has been suggested: cf. Horace, *Ars Poetica*, p. 265.

33. See D. L. Page, *Sappho and Alcaeus*, Oxford, 1955, chap. 2, for this poem (=Sappho, fragment 31). Eighteenth-century translation by Ambrose Phillips, *Spectator* 229, with criticism by Addison; Romantic translation by W. Headlam, *Oxford Book of Greek Verse in Translation*, no. 141; recent version by Richmond Lattimore, *Greek Lyrics*, 2nd edn., Chicago, 1960, p. 39.

34. From a lost poem attributed to Aristeas of Proconnesus, a prophet of Apollo said to have travelled in Siberia in the seventh century B.C. The lines perhaps express the surprised comment of innocent continentals, deep in Asia, on the tales they have heard about ships and seagoing.

35. *Od*. 15. 624ff.

36. *Phaenomena* 299.

37. The example from Archilochus cannot be certainly identified. That from Demosthenes (*On the Crown* 169) describes the alarm at Athens when news arrived of

Philip's occupation of Elatea (339 B.C.): "It was evening when somebody brought the *prutaneis* the news that Elatea was captured. Some of them got up in the middle of dinner and began to drive the traders from the stalls in the *agora* and burn the wicker hurdles. Others sent for the generals and gave instructions to the trumpeter. The town was full of uproar."

38. Text uncertain in detail; general sense clear.
39. *Theaetetus* 144b.
40. *Rep.* 9. 586a (adapted).
41. Text uncertain: perhaps "the reproduction of beauty of form..."
42. *Works and Days* 24: healthy rivalry contrasted with the strife that produces war.
43. A Stoic definition.
44. Eurip. *Or.* 255–57. Orestes sees the Furies.
45. Eurip. *Iph. Taur.* 291. Again Orestes and the Furies.
46. *Il.* 20. 170.
47. Fr. 779 Nauck. Euripides' lost *Phaethon* told the story of Phaethon's marriage and how his mother Clymene revealed to him that Helios was his father; he then begs to be allowed to drive the sun's chariot, and disaster follows. The passages quoted are probably from a messenger's speech recounting Phaethon's fall.
48. Fr. 935 Nauck, perhaps from the *Alexandros*. As the context is lost, we do not know the point. Compare n. 37 for a similar abridged quotation, where "Longinus" assumes his readers to know the context.
49. Aesch. fr. 58 Nauck; Eurip. *Bacchae* 726. Euripides makes the idea easier by adding the notion that the mountain *shared* the ecstasy of the bacchanals themselves.
50. Closing scene of *Oedipus Coloneus*.
51. Probably in the lost *Polyxena*. It is possible that something is lost between this sentence and the reference to Simonides.
52. Eurip. *Or.* 264–5.
53. Demosthenes 24. 208.
54. i.e. after Philip's victory at Chaeronea (338 B.C.). The speech is not extant.
55. The second "source," emotion, does not appear in its expected place: see n. 6.
56. The passage discussed is in 18. 208. Cf. Hermogenes, p. 411.
57. From the lost comedy *Demoi*. Eupolis parodies Eurip. *Medea* 395ff.
58. See p. 348.
59. Notice that these remarks are themselves cast as rhetorical questions.
60. Dem. 4. 10.
61. Ibid. 44.
62. Perhaps Herod. 7. 21.
63. *Hellenica* 4. 3. 19.
64. *Od.* 10. 251–52.
65. Dem. 21. 72.
66. Probably a few words are missing here.
67. 6. 11.
68. "Polyptoton" is the occurrence of the same word in various inflexions. It is not certain whether "Longinus" thinks of accumulation (*athroismos*), variation (*metabolē*), and climax as species of it or as distinct. For what the ancient rhetoricians called "climax," compare Romans 5:3, 8; 29–30.
69. *Oed. Tyr.* 1403ff.
70. A line of an unknown tragedy.
71. *Menexenus* 245d. Not quoted in any other extant part of this book.
72. Dem. 18. 18.
73. Herod. 6. 21.

74. Or "it is a mark of emotion to pluralize them unexpectedly."
75. *Cyropaedia* 7. 1. 37.
76. *Il.* 15. 697.
77. *Phaenomena* 287.
78. 2. 29.
79. *Il.* 5. 85.
80. *Il.* 15. 346.
81. Fr. 30 Jacoby.
82. 25. 27 (a spurious speech).
83. *Od.* 4. 681ff.
84. *Menexenus* 236d.
85. *Cyropaedia* 1. 5. 12.
86. 1. 105.
87. 801b.
88. "*Pathos*" (emotion) characterizes truly "sublime" writing; "*ēthos*" (realistic depiction of manners or humours) belongs rather to lower, more human, and even comic, genres: cf. the *Iliad-Odyssey* contrast, p. 332. "*Hēdonē*" (pleasure, charm) is the typical aim and effect of this second kind of literature. In terms of the "three styles," it consorts with the "smooth" style as pathos and sublimity do with the lofty style.
89. Fr. 96 Bergk. "Filly" is a probable, but not certain, supplement. The text here is uncertain. Perhaps: ". . . But not Anacreon's 'I turn my mind . . .'"
90. 6. 75; 7. 181.
91. Dem. 18. 296
92. Xenophon, *Memorabilia* 1. 4. 5ff.; Plato *Timaeus* 65c–85e ("Longinus" picks various details out of this long passage, and runs them together).
93. *Laws* 773c–d.
94. Or perhaps "fluent."
95. The speech (*Deliacus*) in which the myth of Leto was told is lost; the Funeral Speech is extant (*Oration* 2).
96. The first is lost; the second is *Oration* 3 (5).
97. "Epigram on the tomb of Midas," ascribed to Homer: see Plato *Phaedrus* 264d.
98. It is not certain whether "Longinus" means the Colossus of Rhodes or some other large statue. For the Doryphorus, famous for its proportions, see, e.g., G. M. A. Richter, *Handbook of Greek Art*, Phaidon, 1959, 110.
99. Dem. 7. 45—a speech generally thought to be spurious.
100. *Panegyricus* 6.
101. 7. 84.
102. 7. 225.
103. Cf. in general Dionysius.
104. Oboe or clarinet rather than flute, though the word is often so translated.
105. Eurip. fr. 663 Nauck.
106. Presumably in the works referred to in 39. 1.
107. The decree making provision for war after Philip's occupation of Elatea.
108. Presumably in the two books on "composition."
109. Eurip. *Herc. Fur.* 1245.
110. Or "in accordance with its structure."
111. From Euripides' lost *Antiope* (fr. 221 Nauck). The Greek contains the words *perix helixas* and *petran drun*, and these are the effects to which the comment refers.
112. Of a play, presumably.
113. Obscure: is this the same as the "chopped up" manner or a separate fault?

114. Again an obscure section, partly because "Longinus" seems to intend it as an example of "brevity."

115. 7. 188, 191; 8. 13.

116. The passage is also quoted by Athenaeus (2, 67f). "Longinus" probably got it (like many of his quotations) from a collection of excerpts rather than from the original.

117. Translation doubtful. Perhaps "and then make a change of arrangement and proceed . . ."

118. Text suspect.

119. *Memorabilia* 1. 4. 6.

120. It has been suggested that this chapter is out of place, and belongs after the discussion of visualization, on p. 338. This is impossible to prove, but it is an ingenious solution to the problem of the book's arrangement.

121. *Od.* 17. 322–23.

122. I translate as though the adjective *dikaios* meant the same as it does just above; but perhaps "justly exercised," i.e. humane.

123. Cf. Plato *Rep.* 9. 573e.

124. Or "all our effort and all that we undertake."

125. Eurip. *El.* 379.

Plutarch
c. 46–c. 120

Plutarch is famous primarily for his Lives, *a series of paired biographies of the noble Greeks and Romans. Born in Greece, he studied at Athens, showing particular enthusiasm for ethics, and was associated with the Academy. He visited Rome often and held citizenship there as well as in Athens. A devotee of the Delphic oracle, he became a priest for life around* A.D. *95 and was prominent in the revival of interest in the oracle during the reign of the emperor Trajan (98–117).*

Plutarch's literary criticism displays the same moralistic tendencies evident in his biographical writings. He is concerned with literature's moral effect on readers, and he advocates interpretation as a corrective to potentially harmful passages. Where interpretation fails, he believes that the offending passages should be deleted or emended. At the same time, he mixes his mistrust of poetry's ill effects with a genuine appreciation for its grace "and the sweet attractions of the style." Poetry, for Plutarch, is like a wine that must be taken in moderation.

As a critic, Plutarch stands in a long line of Platonists who attempt to temper Plato's rejection of poetry by showing that poetry can be tamed and domesticated for purposes of moral instruction.

Plutarch's Moralia, *a collection of more than sixty essays on a great diversity of topics ("On Eating Flesh," "Whether Land or Sea Animals Are More Intelligent," "Whether the Athenians Were More Famous in War or in Wisdom"), is the main source for his views on literature. Known to the Byzantines, it was not rediscovered in the West until the sixteenth century. From then until the nineteenth century, Plutarch was one of the most widely read and quoted classical authors in Europe. His essay "How the Young Man Should Study Poetry" was particularly influential during the Renaissance.*

"How the Young Man Should Study Poetry," translated by Frank Cole Babbitt, is reprinted from Plutarch's Moralia *by permission of Harvard University Press and the Loeb Classical Library.*

FROM

Moralia

HOW THE YOUNG MAN SHOULD STUDY POETRY

If, my dear Marcus Sedatus, it is true, as the poet Philoxenus used to say, that 1. of meats those that are not meat, and of fish those that are not fish, have the best flavour, let us leave the expounding of this matter to those persons of whom Cato said that their palates are more sensitive than their minds. And so of philosophical discourses it is clear to us that those seemingly not at all philosophical, or even serious, are found more enjoyable by the very young, who present themselves at such lectures as willing and submissive hearers. For in perusing not only Aesop's *Fables*, and *Tales from the Poets*, but even the *Abaris* of Heracleides, the *Lycon* of Ariston, and philosophic doctrines about the soul when these are combined with tales from mythology, they get inspiration as well as pleasure. Wherefore we ought not only to keep the young decorous in the pleasures of eating and drinking, but, even more, in connexion with what they hear and read, by using in moderation, as a relish, that which gives pleasure, we should accustom them to seek what is useful and salutary therein. For close-shut gates do not preserve a city from capture if it admit the enemy through one; nor does continence in the other pleasures of sense save a young man, if he unwittingly abandon himself to that which comes through hearing. On the contrary, inasmuch as this form of pleasure engages more closely the man that is naturally given to thought and reason, so much the more, if neglected, does it injure and corrupt him that receives it. Since, then, it is neither possible, perhaps, nor profitable to debar from poetry a boy as old as my Soclarus and your Cleander now are, let us keep a very close watch over them, in the firm belief that they require oversight in their reading even more than in the streets. Accordingly, I have made up my mind to commit to writing and to send to you some thoughts on poetry which it occurred to me recently to express. I beg that you will take them and peruse them, and if they seem to you to be no worse than the things called amethysts which some persons on convivial occasions hang upon their persons or take beforehand, then impart them to Cleander, and thus forestall his natural disposition, which, because it is slow in nothing, but impetuous and lively in everything, is more subject to such influences.

Bad may be found in the head of the cuttle-fish; good there is also,

because it is very pleasant to eat but it makes one's sleep full of bad dreams and subject to strange and disturbing fancies, as they say. Similarly also in the art of poetry there is much that is pleasant and nourishing for the mind of a youth, but quite as much that is disturbing and misleading, unless in the hearing of it he have proper oversight. For it may be said, as it seems, not only of the land of the Egyptians but also of poetry, that it yields

> Drugs, and some are good when mixed and others baneful
> ⟨Homer⟩

to those who cultivate it.

> Hidden therein are love and desire and winning converse,
> Suasion that steals away the mind of the very wisest.
> ⟨Homer⟩

For the element of deception in it does not gain any hold on utterly witless and foolish persons. This is the ground of Simonides' answer to the man who said to him, "Why are the Thessalians the only people whom you do not deceive?" His answer was, "Oh, they are too ignorant to be deceived by me"; and Gorgias called tragedy a deception wherein he who deceives is more honest than he who does not deceive, and he who is deceived is wiser than he who is not deceived. Shall we then stop the ears of the young, as those of the Ithacans were stopped, with a hard and unyielding wax, and force them to put to sea in the Epicurean boat, and avoid poetry and steer their course clear of it; or rather shall we set them against some upright standard of reason and there bind them fast, guiding and guarding their judgement, that it may not be carried away from the course by pleasure towards that which will do them hurt?

> No, not even Lycurgus, the mighty son of Dryas
> ⟨Homer⟩

had sound sense, because, when many became drunk and violent, he went about uprooting the grapevines instead of bringing the springs of water nearer, and thus chastening the "frenzied god," as Plato says, "through correction by another, a sober, god." For the tempering of wine with water removes its harmfulness without depriving it at the same time of its usefulness. So let us not root up or destroy the Muses' vine of poetry, but where the mythical and dramatic part grows all riotous and luxuriant, through pleasure unalloyed, which gives it boldness and obstinacy in seeking acclaim, let us take it in hand and prune it and pinch it back. But where with its grace it approaches a true kind of culture, and the sweet allurement of its language is not fruitless or vacuous, there let us introduce philosophy and blend it with poetry. For as the mandragora, when it grows beside the vine and imparts its influence to the wine, makes this weigh less heavily on those who drink it, so poetry, by taking up its themes from philosophy and blending them with fable, renders the task of learning light and agreeable for the young. Wherefore poetry should not be avoided by those who are intending to pursue philosophy, but they should use poetry as an introductory exercise in philosophy, by training themselves habitually to seek the profitable in what gives pleasure, and to find satisfaction therein; and if there be nothing profitable, to combat such poetry and be dissatisfied with it. For this is the beginning of education,

> If one begin each task in proper way
> So is it likely will the ending be,

as Sophocles says.

2. First of all, then, the young man should be introduced into poetry with nothing in his mind so well imprinted, or so ready at hand, as the saying, "Many the lies the poets tell," some intentionally and some unintentionally; intentionally, because for the purpose of giving pleasure and gratification to the ear (and this is what most people look for in poetry) they feel that the truth is too stern in comparison with fiction. For the truth, because it is what actually happens, does not deviate from its course, even though the end be unpleasant; whereas fiction, being a verbal fabrication, very readily follows a roundabout route, and turns aside from the painful to what is more pleasant. For not metre nor figure of speech nor loftiness of diction nor aptness of metaphor nor unity of composition has so much allurement and charm, as a clever interweaving of fabulous narrative. But, just as in pictures, colour is more stimulating than line-drawing because it is life-like, and creates an illusion, so in poetry falsehood combined with plausibility is more striking, and gives more satisfaction, than the work which is elaborate in metre and diction, but devoid of myth and fiction. This explains why Socrates, being induced by some dreams to take up poetry, since he was not himself a plausible or naturally clever workman in falsehood, inasmuch as he had been the champion of truth all his life, put into verse the fables of Aesop, assuming that there can be no poetic composition which has no addition of falsehood. It is true that we know of sacrifices without dancing or flute, but we do not know of any poetic composition without fable or without falsehood. The verses of Empedocles and of Parmenides, the *Antidotes against Poisons* of Nicander, and the maxims of Theognis, are merely compositions which have borrowed from poetic art its metre and lofty style as a vehicle in order to avoid plodding along in prose. Whenever, therefore, in the poems of a man of note and repute some strange and disconcerting statement either about gods or lesser deities or about virtue is made by the author, he who accepts the statement as true is carried off his feet, and has his opinions perverted; whereas he who always remembers and keeps clearly in mind the sorcery of the poetic art in dealing with falsehood, who is able on every such occasion to say to it,

"Device more subtly cunning than the lynx,

why knit your brows when jesting, why pretend to instruct when practising deception?" will not suffer any dire effects or even acquire any base beliefs, but he will check himself when he feels afraid of Poseidon and is in terror lest the god rend the earth asunder and lay bare the nether world; he will check himself when he is feeling wroth at Apollo in behalf of the foremost of the Achaeans,

> Whose praises he himself did sing, himself
> Was present at the feast, these words he spoke
> Himself, and yet himself brought death to him;

he will cease to shed tears over the dead Achilles and over Agamemnon in the nether world, as they stretch out their impotent and feeble arms in their desire to be alive; and if, perchance, he is beginning to be disturbed by their suffering and overcome by the enchantment, he will not hesitate to say to himself,

> Hasten eager to the light, and all you saw here
> Lay to heart that you may tell your wife hereafter.

Certainly Homer has put this gracefully in reference to the visit to the shades, indicating that it is fit stuff for a woman's ear because of the element of fable in it.

Such things as this are what the poets fabricate intentionally, but more numerous are the things which they do not fabricate, but think and believe in their own hearts, and then impart to us in their false colouring. Take for example what Homer has said relating to Zeus:

> In the scales he placed two fates of Death so grievous,
> One of Achilles and the other of horse-taming Hector;
> Grasping the middle he poised it, and Hector's fated day descended.
> Down to Hades he went, and Phoebus Apollo forsook him.

Now Aeschylus has fitted a whole tragedy to this story, giving it the title of *The Weighing of Souls*, and has placed beside the scales of Zeus on the one side Thetis, and on the other Dawn, entreating for their sons who are fighting. But it is patent to everybody that this is a mythical fabrication which has been created to please or astound the hearer. But in the lines

> Zeus, appointed to decide the outcome of men's fighting

and

> A fault doth God create in men
> Whene'er he wills to crush a house in woe,

we have at last statements in accord with their opinion and belief, as they thus publish to us and try to make us share their delusion and ignorance regarding the gods. Then again the monstrous tales of visits to the shades, and the descriptions, which in awful language create spectres and pictures of blazing rivers and hideous places and grim punishments, do not blind very many people to the fact that fable and falsehood in plenty have been mingled with them like poison in nourishing food. And not Homer nor Pindar nor Sophocles really believed that these things are so when they wrote:

> From there the slow-moving rivers of dusky night
> Belch forth a darkness immeasurable,

and

> On past Ocean's streams they went and the headland of Leucas,

and

> The narrow throat of Hades and the refluent depths.

However, take the case of those who, bewailing and fearing death as something piteous, or want of burial as something terrible, have given utterance to sentiments like these:

> Go not hence and leave me behind unwept, unburied,
> ⟨Homer⟩

and

> Forth from his body went his soul on wing to Hades,
> Mourning its fate and leaving its vigour and manhood,
> ⟨Homer⟩

and

> Destroy me not untimely; for 'tis sweet
> To see the light. Compel me not to gaze
> Upon the regions underneath the earth.
> ⟨Euripides⟩

These are the voices of persons affected by emotion and prepossessed by opinions and delusions. For this reason such sentiments take a more powerful hold on us and disturb us the more, inasmuch as we become infected by their emotions and by the weakness from whence they proceed. Against these influences, then, once more let us equip the young from the very outset to keep ever sounding in their ears the maxim, that the art of poetry is not greatly concerned with the truth, and that the truth about these matters, even for those who have made it their sole business to search out and understand the verities, is exceedingly hard to track down and hard to get hold of, as they themselves admit; and let these words of Empedocles be constantly in mind:

> Thus no eye of man hath seen nor ear hath heard this,
> Nor can it be comprehended by the mind,

and the words of Xenophanes:

> Never yet was born a man nor ever shall be
> Knowing the truth about the gods and what I say of all things,

and by all means the words of Socrates, in Plato, when he solemnly disavows all acquaintance with these subjects. For young people then will give less heed to the poets, as having some knowledge of these matters, when they see that such questions stagger the philosophers.

3. We shall steady the young man still more if, at his first entrance into poetry, we give a general description of the poetic art as an imitative art and faculty analogous to painting. And let him not merely be acquainted with the oft-repeated saying that "poetry is articulate painting, and painting is inarticulate poetry," but let us teach him in addition that when we see a lizard or an ape or the face of Thersites in a picture, we are pleased with it and admire it, not as a beautiful thing, but as a likeness. For by its essential nature the ugly cannot become beautiful; but the imitation, be it concerned with what is base or with what is good, if only it attain to the likeness, is commended. If, on the other hand, it produces a beautiful picture of an ugly body, it fails to give what propriety and probability require. Some painters even depict unnatural acts, as Timomachus painted a picture of Medea slaying her children, and Theon of Orestes slaying his mother, and Parrhasius of the feigned madness of Odysseus, and Chaerephanes of the lewd commerce of women with men. In these matters it is especially necessary that the young man should be trained by being taught

that what we commend is not the action which is the subject of the imitation, but the art, in case the subject in hand has been properly imitated. Since, then, poetry also often gives an imitative recital of base deeds, or of wicked experiences and characters, the young man must not accept as true what is admired and successful therein, nor approve it as beautiful, but should simply commend it as fitting and proper to the character in hand. For just as when we hear the squealing of a pig, the creaking of a windlass, the whistling of the winds, and the booming of the sea, we are uneasy and annoyed; but if anybody gives a plausible imitation of these, as Parmeno imitated a pig, and Theodorus a windlass, we are pleased; and just as we avoid a diseased and ulcerous person as an unpleasant sight, but take delight in seeing Aristophon's Philoctetes and Silanion's Jocasta, who are represented on the stage as pining away or dying; so too the young man, as he reads what Thersites the buffoon, or Sisyphus the seducer of women, or Batrachus the bawd, is represented as saying or doing, must be taught to commend the faculty and art which imitates these things, but to repudiate and condemn the disposition and the actions which it imitates. For it is not the same thing at all to imitate something beautiful and something beautifully, since "beautifully" means "fittingly and properly" and ugly things are "fitting and proper" for the ugly. Witness the boots made for the crippled feet of Damonidas, who prayed once, when he had lost them, that the man who had stolen them might have feet which they would fit; they were sorry boots, it is true, but they fitted their owner. Consider the following lines:

> If one must needs do wrong, far best it were
> To do it for a kingdom's sake, ⟨Euripides⟩

and

> Achieve the just man's good repute, but deeds
> That fit the knave; therein shall be your gain,

and

> A talent dowry! Shall I not accept?
> Can I still live if I should overlook
> A talent? Shall I ever sleep again
> If I should give it up? In Hell shall I
> Not suffer for impiety to gold?

These, it is true, are wicked and fallacious sentiments, but fitting respectively for Eteocles, Ixion, and an old usurer. If then we remind our sons that authors write them, not because they commend or approve them, but with the idea of investing mean and unnatural characters and persons with unnatural and mean sentiments, they could not be harmed by the opinions of poets; nay, on the contrary, the suspicion felt against the person in question discredits both his actions and words, as being mean because spoken or done by a mean man. Of such sort is the account of Paris in his wife's arms after his cowardly escape from battle. For since the poet ⟨Homer⟩ represents no other save this licentious

MORALIA

and adulterous man as dallying with a woman in the daytime, it is clear that he classes such sensuality as a shame and reproach.

4. In these passages, close attention must be given to see whether the poet himself gives any hints against the sentiments expressed to indicate that they are distasteful to himself; just as Menander in the prologue of his *Thaïs* has written:

> Oh, sing to me, my muse, of such a girl,
> One bold and fair, and of persuasive tongue,
> Unjust, exclusive, and demanding much,
> In love with none, but always feigning love.

But Homer has best employed this method; for he in advance discredits the mean and calls our attention to the good in what is said. His favourable introductions are after this manner:

> Then at once he spoke; his words were gentle and winning

and

> He would stand by his side, and speak soft words to restrain him.

But in discrediting in advance, he all but protests and proclaims that we are not to follow or heed the sentiments expressed, as being unjustifiable and mean. For example, when he is on the point of narrating Agamemnon's harsh treatment of the priest, he says in advance,

> Yet Agamemnon, Atreus' son, at heart did not like it;
> Harshly he sent him away;

that is to say, savagely and wilfully and contrary to what he should have done; and in Achilles' mouth he puts the bold words,

> Drunken sot, with eyes of a dog and the wild deer's courage,

but he intimates his own judgement in saying,

> Then once more with vehement words did the son of Peleus
> Speak to the son of Atreus, nor ceased as yet from his anger;

hence it is likely that nothing spoken with anger and severity can be good. In like manner also, he comments upon actions:

> Thus he spoke, and Hector divine he treated unseemly,
> Stretching him prone in the dust by the bier of the son of Menoetius.

He also employs his closing lines to good purpose, as though adding a sort of verdict of his own to what is done or said. Of the adultery of Ares, he represents the gods as saying,

> Evil deeds do not succeed: the swift by the slow is taken,

and on the occasion of Hector's great arrogance and boasting he says,

> Thus he spoke in boast; queen Hera's wrath was kindled

and regarding Pandarus's archery,

> Thus Athena spoke, and the mind of the fool she persuaded.

Now these declarations and opinions contained in the words of the text may be discovered by anybody who will pay attention, but from the actions themselves the poets supply other lessons: as, for example, Euripides is reported to have said to those who railed at his Ixion as an impious and detestable character, "But I did not remove him from the stage until I had him fastened to the wheel." In Homer this form of instruction is given silently, but it leaves room for a reconsideration, which is helpful in the case of those stories which have been most discredited. By forcibly distorting these stories through what used to be termed "deeper meanings," but are nowadays called "allegorical interpretations," some persons say that the Sun is represented as giving information about Aphrodite in the arms of Ares, because the conjunction of the planet Mars with Venus portends births conceived in adultery, and when the sun returns in his course and discovers these, they cannot be kept secret. And Hera's beautifying of herself for Zeus's eyes, and the charms connected with the girdle, such persons will have it, are a sort of purification of the air as it draws near the fiery element;—as though the poet himself did not afford the right solutions. For, in the account of Aphrodite, he teaches those who will pay attention that vulgar music, coarse songs, and stories treating of vile themes, create licentious characters, unmanly lives, and men that love luxury, soft living, intimacy with women, and

> Changes of clothes, warm baths, and the genial bed of enjoyment.

This too is the reason why he has represented Odysseus as bidding the harper

> Come now, change the theme and sing how the horse was builded,

thus admirably indicating the duty of musicians and poets to take the subjects of their compositions from the lives of those who are discreet and sensible. And in his account of Hera, he has shown excellently well how the favour that women win by philters and enchantments and the attendant deceit in their relations with their husbands, not only is transitory and soon sated and unsure, but changes also to anger and enmity, so soon as the pleasurable excitement has faded away. Such, in fact, are Zeus's angry threats as he speaks to Hera in this wise:

> So you may see if aught you gain from the love and caresses
> Won by your coming afar from the gods to deceive me.

For the description and portrayal of mean actions, if it also represents as it should the disgrace and injury resulting to the doers thereof, benefits instead of injuring the hearer. Philosophers, at any rate, for admonition and instruction, use examples taken from known facts; but the poets accomplish the same result by inventing actions of their own imagination, and by recounting mythical tales.

Thus it was Melanthius who said, whether in jest or in earnest, that the Athenian State was perpetually preserved by the quarrelling and disorder among its public speakers; for they were not all inclined to crowd to the same side of the boat, and so, in the disagreement of the politicians, there was ever some counterpoise to the harmful. And so the mutual contrarieties of the poets, restoring our belief to its proper balance, forbid any strong turning of the scale toward the harmful. When therefore a comparison of passages makes their contradictions evident, we must advocate the better side, as in the following examples:

> Oft do the gods, my child, cause men to fail,
> ⟨Euripides⟩

as compared with

> You've named the simplest way; just blame the gods;
> ⟨Euripides⟩

and again

> You may rejoice in wealth, but these may not,
> ⟨Euripides⟩

as compared with

> 'Tis loutish to be rich, and know naught else;
> ⟨Euripides⟩

and

> What need to sacrifice when you must die?

as compared with

> 'Tis better thus; God's worship is not toil.

For such passages as these admit of solutions which are obvious, if, as has been said, we direct the young, by the use of criticism, toward the better side. But whenever anything said by such authors sounds preposterous, and no solution is found close at hand, we must nullify its effect by something said by them elsewhere to the opposite effect, and we should not be offended or angry at the poet, but with the words, which are spoken in character and with humorous intent. As an obvious illustration, if you wish, over against Homer's accounts of the gods being cast forth by one another, their being wounded by men, their disagreements, and their displays of ill-temper, you may set the line:

> Surely you know how to think of a saying better than this one,

and indeed elsewhere you do think of better things and say more seemly things, such as these:

> Gods at their ease ever living,

and

> There the blessed gods pass all their days in enjoyment,

and

> Thus the gods have spun the fate of unhappy mortals
> Ever to live in distress, but themselves are free from all trouble.

These, then, are sound opinions about gods, and true, but those other accounts have been fabricated to excite men's astonishment. Again, when Euripides says,

> By many forms of artifice the gods
> Defeat our plans, for they are stronger far,

it is not bad to subjoin,

> If gods do aught that's base, they are no gods,

which is a better saying of his. And when Pindar very bitterly and exasperatingly has said,

> Do what you will, so you vanquish your foe,

"Yet," we may reply, "you yourself say that

> Most bitter the end
> Must surely await
> Sweet joys that are gained
> By a means unfair."

And when Sophocles has said,

> Sweet is the pelf though gained by falsity.

"Indeed," we may say, "but we have heard from you that

> False words unfruitful prove when harvested."

And over against those statements about wealth:

> Clever is wealth at finding ways to reach
> Both hallowed and unhallowed ground, and where
> A poor man, though he even gain access,
> Could not withal attain his heart's desire.
> An ugly body, hapless with its tongue,
> Wealth makes both wise and comely to behold.

he will set many of Sophocles' words, among which are the following:

> E'en without wealth a man may be esteemed,

and

> To beg doth not degrade a noble mind,

and

> In the blessings of plenty
> What enjoyment is there,
> If blest wealth owe its increase
> To base-brooding care?

And Menander certainly exalted the love of pleasure, with a suggestion of boastfulness too, in these glowing lines that refer to love:

> All things that live and see the self-same sun
> That we behold, to pleasure are enslaved.

But at another time he turns us about and draws us towards the good, and uproots the boldness of licentiousness, by saying:

> A shameful life, though pleasant, is disgrace.

The latter sentiment is quite opposed to the former, and it is better and more useful. Such comparison and consideration of opposing sentiments will result in one of two ways: it will either guide the youth over toward the better side, or else cause his belief to revolt from the worse.

In case the authors themselves do not offer solutions of their unjustifiable sayings, it is not a bad idea to put on the other side declarations of other writers of repute, and, as in a balance, make the scales incline toward the better side. For example, if Alexis stirs some people when he says,

> The man of sense must gather pleasure's fruits,
> And three there are which have the potency
> Truly to be of import for this life—
> To eat and drink and have one's way in love,
> All else must be declared accessory,

we must recall to their minds that Socrates used to say just the opposite—that "base men live to eat and drink, and good men eat and drink to live." And he who wrote

> Not useless 'gainst the knave is knavery,

thus bidding us, in a way, to make ourselves like knaves, may be confronted with the saying of Diogenes; for, being asked how one might defend himself against his adversary, he said, "By proving honourable and upright himself." We should use Diogenes against Sophocles, too; for Sophocles has filled hosts of men with despondency by writing these lines about the mysteries:

> Thrice blest are they
> Who having seen these mystic rites shall pass
> To Hades' house; for them alone is life
> Beyond; for others all is evil there.

But Diogenes, hearing some such sentiment as this, said, "What! Do you mean to say that Pataecion, the robber, will have a better portion after death than

Epaminondas, just because he is initiate?" And when Timotheus, in a song in the theatre, spoke of Artemis as

> Ecstatic Bacchic frantic fanatic,

Cinesias at once shouted back, "May you have a daughter like that!" Neat too is Bion's retort to Theognis, who said:

> Any man that is subject to poverty never is able
> Either to speak or to act; nay, but his tongue is tied.

"How is it, then," said Bion, "that you, who are poor, can talk much nonsense, and weary us with this rubbish?"

5. We must not neglect, either, the means for rectifying a statement which are afforded by the words that lie near, or by the context; but just as physicians, in spite of the fact that the blister-fly is deadly, think that its feet and wings are helpful to counteract its potent effect, so in poetry if a noun or adjective or a verb by its position next to another word blunts the point which the passage, in its worse interpretation, would have, we should seize upon it and add explanation, as some do in the case of the following:

> Thus, at the last, can honour be paid by miserable mortals
> Cutting the hair from their heads while the tears stream down their faces,

and

> Thus, then, the gods have spun the fate of unhappy mortals
> Ever to live in distress.

For he (Homer) did not say that absolutely and to all mankind a grievous life has been allotted by the gods, but to the silly and foolish, whom, since they are wretched and pitiable on account of wickedness, he is wont to call by the name of "unhappy" and "miserable."

6. Another method, again, which transfers from the worse to the better sense suspicious passages in poetry, is that which works through the normal usage of words, in which it were better to have the young man trained than in what are called "glosses." It is indeed learned, and not unpleasing, to know that "rhigedanos" means "dying miserably" (for the Macedonians call death "danos"), that the Aeolians call a victory won by patience and perseverance an "outlasting," that the Dryopians call the divinities "popoi." But it is necessary and useful, if we are to be helped and not harmed by poetry, to know how the poets employ the names of the gods, and again the names of bad and of good things, and what they mean when they speak of Fortune or of Fate, and whether these belong to the class of words which in their writings are used in one sense only or in several senses, as the case is with many other words. For, to illustrate (with examples from Homer), they apply the term "house" sometimes to a dwelling house, as

> Into the lofty house,

and sometimes to property, as

> My house is being devoured;

and the term "living" they apply sometimes to life, as

> But dark-haired Poseidon
> Thwarted his spear, nor would let him end his foeman's living,

and sometimes to possessions, as

> And others are eating my living;

and the expression "be distraught" is used sometimes instead of "be chagrined" and "be at one's wits' end":

> Thus he spoke, and she departed distraught and sore troubled

and at other times, instead of "to be arrogant" and "be delighted," as

> Are you now distraught since you vanquished Irus, the vagrant?

and by "huddle" they mean either "be in motion," as Euripides says:

> A monster huddling from th' Atlantic's surge,

or "sit down" and "be seated," as Sophocles says:

> What means your huddling in these places here
> With suppliant garlands on the boughs ye bear?

It is a graceful accomplishment also to adapt the usage of the words to fit the matter in hand, as the grammarians teach us to do, taking a word for one signification at one time, and at another time for another, as for example,

> Better commend a small ship, but put your goods on a big one. (Hesiod)

For by "commend" is meant "recommend," and the very expression of "recommend" to another is used nowadays instead of deprecating for one's self, as in everyday speech we say, "It's very kind," and "Very welcome," when we do not want a thing and do not accept it. In this way also some persons will have it that it must be "commendable Persephone" because she is deprecated.

Let us then observe closely this distinction and discrimination of words in greater and more serious matters, and let us begin with the gods, in teaching the young that when the poets employ the names of the gods, sometimes they apprehend in their conception the gods themselves, and at other times they give the same appellation to certain faculties of which the gods are the givers and authors. To take an obvious example, it is clear that Archilochus, when he says in his prayer,

> Hear my prayer, O Lord Hephaestus, and propitious
> Lend thy aid, and bestow what thy mercy bestows,

is calling on the god himself; but when, lamenting his sister's husband who was lost at sea and received no formal burial, he says that he could have borne the calamity with greater moderation,

> If upon his head and his body so fair,
> All in garments clean, Hephaestus had done his office,

it is fire that he called by this name and not the god. And again when Euripides said in an oath,

> By Zeus amidst the stars and Ares murderous,

he named the gods themselves; but when Sophocles says,

> Blind and unseeing Ares, worthy dames,
> With snout like that of swine upturns all ills,

the name is to be understood as meaning war; just as again it suggests weapons of bronze in the passage where Homer says,

> Dark red blood of these men by the fair-flowing river Scamander
> Keen-edged Ares has shed.

Since, then, many words are used in this way, it is necessary to know and to remember that under the name Zeus also (or Zēn) the poets address sometimes the god, sometimes Fortune, and oftentimes Fate. For when they say,

> Father Zeus, enthroned on Ida, most glorious and mighty,
> Grant to Ajax victory, ⟨Homer⟩

and

> O Zeus! who boasts to be more wise than thou?

they mean the god himself; but when they apply the name of Zeus to the causes of all that happens, and say,

> Many valiant souls it sent to the realm of Hades,
> Goodly men, and their bodies gave to the dogs as ravin
> And to birds a feast—the design of Zeus in fulfilment,
> ⟨Homer⟩

they mean Fate. For the poet does not imagine that it is the god who contrives evils for mankind, but by the name he rightly implies the compelling force of circumstances, that States and armies and leaders, if they show self-control, are destined to succeed and to prevail over their enemies, but if they fall into passions and errors, if they disagree and quarrel among themselves, as these heroes did, then are they destined to act discreditably and to become disorganized and to come to a bad end, as Sophocles says:

> For fated is it that from evil plans
> An evil recompense shall mortals reap;

and certainly Hesiod in representing Prometheus as exhorting Epimetheus

> Never to welcome
> Any gifts from Zeus of Olympus, but always return them,

employs the name of Zeus as a synonym for the power of Fortune. For he has given the name of "gifts of Zeus" to the blessings of Fortune, such as wealth, marriage, office, and, in a word, all outward things, the possession of which is unprofitable to those who cannot make good use of them. Wherefore he thinks that Epimetheus, who is a worthless man and a fool, ought to be on his guard against any piece of good fortune, and be fearful of it, as he is likely to be injured and corrupted by it. And again when the poet says,

> Never dare to reproach any man for accursed and woeful
> Poverty, gift of the blessed gods whose life is for ever,

he now speaks of what happens by chance as god-given, with the suggestion that it is not meet to impugn those who are poor through misfortune, but to reproach the penury that is accompanied by laziness, soft living, and extravagance, since then it is disgraceful and reprehensible. For at a time when men did not as yet use the name "Fortune," but knew the force of causation as it traverses its irregular and indeterminate course, so strong, so impossible for human reason to guard against, they tried to express this by the names of the gods, exactly as we are wont to call deeds and characters, and in fact even words and men, "divine" and "godlike." In this manner, then, a corrective is to be found for most of the seemingly unjustifiable statements regarding Zeus, among which are the following:

> Fixed on Zeus' floor two massive urns stand ever,
> Filled with happy lives the one, the other with sorrows,
> ⟨Homer⟩

and

> Cronos' son, enthroned on high, hath made naught of our pledges,
> but for both our hosts with evil thought is planning,   ⟨Homer⟩

and

> Then rolled forth the beginning of trouble
> Both on Trojans and Greeks through designs of Zeus the almighty.
> ⟨Homer⟩

These are to be interpreted as referring to Fortune or Fate, in which guise are denoted those phases of causation which baffle our logic, and are, in a word, beyond us. But wherever there is appropriateness, reason, and probability in the use of the name, let us believe that there the god himself is meant, as in the following:

> But he ranged to and fro 'gainst the lines of the rest of the fighters;
> Only with Ajax, Telamon's son, he avoided a conflict,
> Seeing that Zeus was wroth if he fight with a man far better,
> ⟨Homer⟩

and

> For Zeus takes thought for mortals' greatest weal;
> The little things he leaves to other gods.

Particular attention must be paid to the other words also, when their signification is shifted about and changed by the poets according to various circumstances. An example is the word "virtue." For inasmuch as virtue not only renders men sensible, honest, and upright in actions and words, but also often enough secures for them repute and influence, the poets, following this notion, make good repute and influence to be virtue, giving them this name in exactly the same way that the products of the olive and the chestnut are called "olives" and "chestnuts," the same names as the trees that bear them. So then when poets say,

> Sweat the gods have set before the attainment of virtue,
> ⟨Hesiod⟩

and

> Then the Greeks by their virtue broke the line of their foemen,
> ⟨Homer⟩

and

> If to die be our fate,
> Thus to die is our right
> Merging our lives into virtue,
> ⟨Euripides⟩

let our young man at once feel that these sayings relate to the best and godliest estate to which we can attain, which we think of as correctness of reasoning, the height of good sense, and a disposition of soul in full agreement therewith. But when at another time, in his reading, he finds this line,

> Zeus makes virtue in men both to increase and diminish,
> ⟨Homer⟩

or this,

> Virtue and glory are attendant on riches,
> ⟨Hesiod⟩

let him not "sit" astounded and "amazed" at the rich, as though they were able to purchase virtue without ado for money, nor let him believe either that the increase or diminution of his own wisdom rests with Fortune, but let him consider that the poet has employed "virtue" instead of repute, or influence, or good fortune, or the like. For assuredly by "evil" the poets sometimes signify badness in its strict sense, and wickedness of soul, as when Hesiod says,

> Evil may always be had by all mankind in abundance,

and sometimes some other affliction or misfortune, as when Homer says,

> Since full soon do mortals who live in evil grow aged.

And so too anybody would be sadly deceived, should he imagine that the poets give to "happiness" the sense which the philosophers give to it, namely, that of complete possession or attainment of good, or the perfection of a life gliding smoothly along in accord with nature, and that the poets do not oftentimes by a perversion of the word call the rich man happy and blessed, and call influence or repute happiness. Now Homer has used the words correctly:

> No delight have I in ruling these possessions,

and so has Menander:

> A great estate have I, and rich am called
> By all, but I am called by no man blest.

But Euripides works much disturbance and confusion when he says,

> May I ne'er have a painful happy life,

and

> Why do you honour show to tyranny,
> Happy iniquity?

unless, as has been said, one follows the figurative and perverted use of the words. This, then, is enough on this subject.

7. There is a fact, however, which we must recall to the minds of the young not once merely, but over and over again, by pointing out to them that while poetry, inasmuch as it has an imitative basis, employs embellishment and glitter in dealing with the actions and characters that form its groundwork, yet it does not forsake the semblance of truth, since imitation depends upon plausibility for its allurement. This is the reason why the imitation that does not show an utter disregard of the truth brings out, along with the actions, indications of both vice and virtue commingled; as is the case with that of Homer, which emphatically says good-bye to the Stoics, who will have it that nothing base can attach to virtue, and nothing good to vice, but that the ignorant man is quite wrong in all things, while, on the other hand, the man of culture is right in everything. These are the doctrines that we hear in the schools; but in the actions and in the life of most men, according to Euripides,

> The good and bad cannot be kept apart
> But there is some commingling.

But when poetic art is divorced from the truth, then chiefly it employs variety and diversity. For it is the sudden changes that give to its stories the elements of the emotional, the surprising, and the unexpected, and these are attended by very great astonishment and enjoyment; but sameness is unemotional and prosaic. Therefore poets do not represent the same people as always victorious or prosperous or successful in everything; no, not even the gods, when they project themselves into human activities, are represented in the poets' usage as free from emotion or fault, that the perturbing and exciting element in the poetry shall nowhere become idle and dull, for want of danger and struggle.

8. Now since this is so, let the young man, when we set him to reading poems, not be prepossessed with any such opinions about those good and great names, as, for instance, that the men were wise and honest, consummate kings, and standards of all virtue and uprightness. For he will be greatly injured if he approves everything, and is in a state of wonderment over it, but resents nothing, refusing even to listen or accept the opinion of him who, on the contrary, censures persons that do and say such things as these ⟨in Homer⟩:

> This I would, O Zeus, Athena, and Apollo,
> That not one escape death of all the Trojans living
> And of the Greeks; but that you and I elude destruction,
> So that we alone may raze Troy's sacred bulwarks,

and

> Saddest of all the sad sounds that I heard was the cry of Cassandra,
> Priam's daughter, whom Clytemnestra craftily planning
> Slew o'er my body,

and

> That I seduce the girl and ensure her hate for my father.
> So I obeyed her and did it,

and

> Father Zeus, none other of the gods is more baleful.

Let the young man, then, not get into the habit of commending anything like this, nor let him be plausible and adroit in making excuses or in contriving some specious quibbles to explain base actions, but rather let him cherish the belief that poetry is an imitation of character and lives, and of men who are not perfect or spotless or unassailable in all respects, but pervaded by emotions, false opinions, and sundry forms of ignorance, who yet through inborn goodness frequently change their ways for the better. For if the young man is so trained, and his understanding so framed, that he feels elation and a sympathetic enthusiasm over noble words and deeds, and an aversion and repugnance for the mean, such training will render his perusal of poetry harmless. But the man who admires everything, and accommodates himself to everything, whose judgement, because of his preconceived opinion, is enthralled by the heroic names, will, like those who copy Plato's stoop or Aristotle's lisp, unwittingly become inclined to conform to much that is base. One ought not timorously, or as though under the spell of religious dread in a holy place, to shiver with awe at everything, and fall prostrate, but should rather acquire the habit of exclaiming with confidence "wrong" and "improper" no less than "right" and "proper." For example, Achilles summons an assembly of the soldiers, who are suffering from an illness, since he is most impatient of all over the slow progress of the war because of his conspicuous position and reputation on the field; moreover, because he has some knowledge of medicine, and perceives now after the ninth day, on which these maladies naturally reach their crisis, that the disease is out of the ordinary and not the result of familiar causes, he does not harangue the multitude when he rises to speak, but makes himself an adviser to the king:

> Son of Atreus, now, as I think, are we destined to wander
> Back to seek our homes again.

Rightly, moderately, and properly is this put. But after the seer has said that he fears the wrath of the most powerful of the Greeks, Achilles no longer speaks rightly and moderately, when he swears that nobody shall lay hands on the seer while he himself is alive,

> No, not though you name Agamemnon,

thus making plain his slight regard and his contempt for the leader. A moment later his irritation becomes more acute, and his impulse is to draw his sword with intent to do murder; not rightly, either for honour or for expediency. Again, later, repenting,

> Back he thrust his massive blade once more to its scabbard
> Nor ignored Athena's words,

this time rightly and honourably, because, although he could not altogether eradicate his anger, yet before doing anything irreparable he put it aside and checked it by making it obedient to his reason. Then again, although Agamemnon is ridiculous in his actions and words at the Assembly, yet in the incidents touching Chryseïs he is more dignified and kingly. For whereas Achilles, as Briseïs was being led away,

> Burst into tears and withdrawing apart sat aloof from his comrades,

Agamemnon, as he in person put aboard the ship, and gave up and sent away, the woman of whom, a moment before, he has said that he cared more for her than for his wedded wife, committed no amorous or disgraceful act. Then again, Phoenix, cursed by his father on account of the concubine, says:

> True in my heart I had purposed to slay him with keen-pointed dagger,
> Save that one of the deathless gods put an end to my anger,
> Bringing to mind the people's talk and men's many reproaches,
> Lest I be known among the Greeks as my father's slayer.

Now Aristarchus removed these lines from the text through fear, but they are right in view of the occasion, since Phoenix is trying to teach Achilles what sort of a thing anger is, and how many wild deeds men are ready to do from temper, if they do not use reason or hearken to those who try to soothe them. So also the poet introduces Meleager angry at his fellow-citizens, and later mollified, and he rightly finds fault with his emotions, but, on the other hand, his refusal to yield, his resistance, his mastery over them, and his change of heart the poet commends as good and expedient.

Now in these cases the difference is manifest; but in cases where Homer's judgement is not made clear, a distinction is to be drawn by directing the young man's attention in some such manner as the following: If, on the one hand, Nausicaa, after merely looking at a strange man, Odysseus, and experiencing Calypso's emotions toward him, being, as she was, a wanton child and at the age for marriage, utters such foolish words as these to her maid-servants,

> How I wish that a man like this might be called my husband,
> Living here with us, and be contented to tarry,

then are her boldness and lack of restraint to be blamed. But if, on the other hand, she sees into the character of the man from his words, and marvels at his conversation, so full of good sense, and then prays that she may be the consort of such a person rather than of some sailor man or dancing man of her own townsmen, then it is quite right to admire her. And again, when Penelope enters into conversation with the suitors, not holding herself aloof, and they favour her with gifts of garments and other apparel, Odysseus is pleased

> Since she had coaxed all these gifts from them, and had cozened their senses.

If, on the one hand, he rejoices at the receipt of the presents and the profit, then in his prostitution of his wife he outdoes Poliager, who is satirized in the comedy as

> Poliager blest
> Who keeps a Cyprian goat to yield him wealth.

But if, on the other hand, he thinks that he shall have them more in his power, while they are confident because of their hopes and blind to the future, then his pleasure and confidence has a reasonable justification. Similarly, in the enumeration of his possessions which the Phaeacians had put ashore with him before they sailed away, if on the one hand, upon finding himself in such solitude and in such uncertainty and ambiguity regarding his surroundings, he really fears about his possessions,

> Lest the men on the ship had sailed away with something,

then it is quite right to pity or indeed even to loathe his avarice. But if, on the other hand, he, as some say, being of two minds whether he were in Ithaca, thinks that the safety of his possessions is a demonstration of the rectitude of the Phaeacians (for otherwise they would not have carried him for nothing, put him ashore in a strange land, and left him there, at the same time keeping their hands off his possessions), then he makes use of no mean proof, and it is quite right to praise his forethought. But some critics find fault also with the very act of putting him ashore, if this really was done while he was asleep, and assert that the Etruscans still preserve a tradition that Odysseus was naturally sleepy, and that for this reason most people found him difficult to converse with. Yet if his sleep was not real, but if, being ashamed to send away the Phaeacians without gifts and entertainment, and at the same time unable to elude his enemies if the Phaeacians were in company with him, he provided himself with a cloak for his embarrassment in feigning himself asleep, then they find this acceptable.

By indicating these things to the young, we shall not allow them to acquire any leaning toward such characters as are mean, but rather an emulation of the better, and a preference for them, if we unhesitatingly award censure to the one class and commendation to the other. It is particularly necessary to do this with tragedies in which plausible and artful words are framed to accompany disreputable and knavish actions. For the statement of Sophocles is not altogether true when he says:

> From unfair deed fair word cannot proceed.

For, as a fact, he is wont to provide for mean characters and unnatural actions alluring words and humane reasons. And you observe also that his companion-at-arms in the dramatic art ⟨Euripides⟩ has represented Phaedra as preferring the charge against Theseus that it was because of his derelictions that she fell in love with Hippolytus. Of such sort, too, are the frank lines, aimed against Hecuba, which in the *Trojan Women* he gives to Helen, who there expresses her feeling that Hecuba ought rather to be the one to suffer punishment because she brought into the world the man who was the cause of Helen's infidelity. Let the young man not form the habit of regarding any one of these things as witty and adroit, and let him not smile indulgently, either, at such displays of verbal ingenuity, but let him loathe the words of licentiousness even more than its deeds.

9. Now in all cases it is useful also to seek after the cause of each thing that is said. Cato, for example, used, even as a child, to do whatever the attendant in charge of him ordered, yet he also demanded to know the ground and reason for the order. And so the poets are not to be obeyed as though they were our keepers or law-givers, unless their subject matter be reasonable; and this it will be if it be good, but if it be vile, it will be seen to be vacuous and vain. But most people are sharp in demanding the reasons for trivial things like the following, and insist on knowing in what sense they are intended:

> Never ought the ladle atop of the bowl to be rested
> While the bout is on, ⟨Hesiod⟩

and

> Whoso from his car can reach the car of another
> Let him thrust with his spear. ⟨Homer⟩

But in far weightier matters they take things on faith without testing them at all, such, for example, as these:

> A man, though bold, is made a slave whene'er
> He learns his mother's or his sire's disgrace,
> ⟨Euripides⟩

and

> Who prospers not must be of humble mind.
> ⟨Euripides⟩

And yet these sentiments affect our characters and disorder our lives, by engendering in us mean judgements and ignoble opinions, unless from habit we can say in answer to each of them, "Why must the man who has 'not prospered be of humble mind,' and why must he not rather rise up against Fortune, and make himself exalted and not humbled? And why, though I be the son of a bad and foolish father, yet if I myself am good and sensible, is it unbecoming for me to take pride in my good qualities, and why should I be dejected and humble on account of my father's crassness?" For he who thus meets and resists, and refuses to entrust himself broadside on to every breath of doctrine, as to a wind, but believes in the correctness of the saying that "a fool is wont to be agog at every word that's said" ⟨Heracleitus⟩ will thrust aside a good deal of what is not true or profitable therein. This, then, will take away all danger of harm from the perusal of poetry.

10. But, just as amid the luxuriant foliage and branches of a vine the fruit is often hidden and unnoticed from being in the shadow, so also amid the poetic diction and the tales that hang clustered about, much that is helpful and profitable escapes a young man. This, however, ought not to happen to him, nor should he allow his attention to be diverted from the facts, but he should cling especially close to those that lead toward virtue and have the power to mould character. In which regard it may not be a bad thing to treat this topic briefly, touching summarily the principal points, but leaving any extended and constructive treatment, and long list of examples, to those who write more for display. In the first place, then, as the young man takes note of good and bad characters and personages, let him pay attention to the lines and the actions which the poet assigns to them as respectively befitting. For example, Achilles says to Agamemnon, although he speaks with anger:

> Never a prize like yours is mine whene'er the Achaeans
> Capture and sack some goodly and populous town of the Trojans.

But Thersites in reviling the same man says:

> Full of bronze are your quarters, and many, too, are the women,
> Chosen from all the captives for you, and these we Achaeans
> Give to you first of all whenever we capture a city.

And on another occasion Achilles says,

> If perchance Zeus ever
> Grants to us that we plunder Troy, the well-walled city,

but Thersites,

> One that I or another Achaean may bring in as captive.

At another time, in the Inspection, when Agamemnon upbraided Diomede, the latter made no answer,

> Showing respect for the stern rebuke of a king so respected.

But Sthenelus, a man of no account, says:

> Son of Atreus, speak not to deceive, knowing how to speak clearly;
> We can avow ourselves to be better far than our fathers.

A difference of this sort then, if not overlooked, will teach the young man to regard modesty and moderation as a mark of refinement, but to be on his guard against boasting and self-assertion as a mark of meanness. It is useful to note also the behaviour of Agamemnon in this case; for Sthenelus he passed by without a word, but Odysseus he did not disregard, but made answer and addressed him,

> When he saw he was wroth, and tried to retract his saying.

For to defend one's actions to everybody smacks of servility, not of dignity, while to despise everybody is arrogant and foolish. And most excellently does Diomede in the battle hold his peace, although upbraided by the king, but after the battle he uses plain speech to him:

> First let me say that you 'mid the Danaans slighted my prowess.

It is well, too, not to miss a difference that exists between a man of sense and a seer who courts popularity. For example, Calchas had no regard to the occasion, and made nothing of accusing the king before the multitude, alleging that he had brought the pestilence upon them; but Nestor, though anxious to put in a word for the reconciliation with Achilles, yet, in order that he may not seem to discredit Agamemnon with the multitude as having made a mistake and indulged in anger, says,

> Give a feast for the elders; 'tis fitting and not unbefitting;
> Then, when many are gathered, whoever shall offer best counsel
> Him you will follow,

and after the dinner he sends forth the envoys. For this was the way to amend an error; the other was arraignment and foul abuse.

Moreover, the difference between the two peoples should be observed, their behaviour being as follows: the Trojans advance with shouting and confidence, but the Achaeans

> Silently, fearing their captains.

For to fear one's commanders when at close quarters with the enemy is a sign of bravery and of obedience to authority as well. Wherefore Plato tries to establish the habit of fearing blame and disgrace more than toils and dangers, and Cato used to say that he liked people that blushed better than those that blanched.

There is also in the promises of the heroes a special character. For Dolon promises:

> Straight to the midst of their host shall I go till I come to the vessel
> Which Agamemnon commands.

Diomede, however, promises nothing, but says that he should be less frightened if he were sent in company with another man. Prudence, then, is characteristic of a Greek and of a man of refinement, while presumption is barbaric and cheap: the one should be emulated and the other detested. And it is not unprofitable to consider how the Trojans and Hector were affected, at the time when Ajax was about to engage with him in single combat. Once when a boxer at the Isthmian games was struck in the face, and a clamour arose, Aeschylus said, "What a thing is training. The onlookers cry out; it is the man who is struck who says nothing." In like manner, when the poet says that when Ajax appeared resplendent in his armour, the Greeks rejoiced at seeing him, whereas

> Dreadful trembling seized on the limbs of every Trojan;
> Even Hector himself felt his heart beat quick in his bosom,

who could fail to admire the difference? For the heart of the man who is facing the danger only throbs, as though indeed he were simply going to wrestle or run a race, while the onlookers tremble and shiver in their whole bodies through loyalty and fear for their king. Here, too, one should carefully consider the difference between the very valiant man and the craven. For Thersites

> Hateful was most of all to Achilles as well as Odysseus,

while Ajax was always friendly to Achilles, and says to Hector regarding him—

> Now alone from one man alone shall you learn quite clearly
> What sort of men with us are the Danaans' chieftains
> Even after the smiter of men, lion-hearted Achilles.

This is the compliment paid to Achilles, but these succeeding lines in behalf of all are put in such a way as to be useful:

> Yet are we of such sort as are ready to face you,
> Yea, and many of us,

thereby declaring himself not the only man or the best, but only one among many equally capable of offering defence.

This is enough on the subject of differences, unless perhaps we desire to add, that of the Trojans many were taken alive, but none of the Achaeans; and that of the Trojans some fell down at the feet of the enemy, as did Adrastus, the sons of Antimachus, Lycaon, and Hector himself begging Achilles for burial, but of the Achaeans none, because of their conviction that it is a trait of barbarian peoples to make supplication and to fall at the enemy's feet in combat, but of Greeks to conquer or to die fighting.

11. Now just as in pasturage the bee seeks the flower, the goat the tender shoot, the swine the root, and other animals the seed and the fruit, so in the reading of poetry one person culls the flowers of the story, another rivets his attention upon the beauty of the diction and the arrangement of the words, as Aristophanes says of Euripides,

> I use the rounded neatness of his speech;

but as for those who are concerned with what is said as being useful for character (and it is to these that our present discourse is directed), let us remind them how strange it is if the lover of fables does not fail to observe the novel and unusual points in the story, and the student of language does not allow faultless and elegant forms of expression to escape him, whereas he that affects what is honourable and good, who takes up poetry not for amusement but for education, should give but a slack and careless hearing to utterances that look toward manliness or sobriety or uprightness, such, for example, as the following:

> Son of Tydeus, what has made us forget our swift prowess?
> Hither, stand, my friend, by me. Disgrace will befall us
> If yon Hector, gleaming-helmed, shall capture our vessels.

For to observe that the most wise and prudent man, when he is in danger of being destroyed and lost, together with the whole host, fears shame and disapprobation, but not death, will make the young man keenly alive to the moral virtues. And by the line,

> Glad was Athena because of the man that was prudent and honest,

the poet ⟨Homer⟩ permits us to draw a similar conclusion in that he represents the goddess as taking delight, not in some rich man or in one who is physically handsome or strong, but in one who is wise and honest. And again when she says that she does not overlook Odysseus, much less desert him,

> Since he is courteous and clever of mind and prudent,

her words indicate that the only one of our attributes that is dear to the gods and divine is a virtuous mind, if it be true that it is the nature of like to delight in like.

Since it seems to be, and really is, a great thing to master one's anger, and since a greater thing is the exercise of precaution and forethought so as not to become involved in anger or to be made captive by it, we must make a point of indicating to our young readers such matters as this: that Achilles, being not tolerant or mild in temper, bids Priam in these words to be quiet and not to exasperate him:

> Anger me now no more, old man (to ransom your Hector
> I myself am disposed; from Zeus has come such a message),
> Lest, old man, even here 'neath my roof I leave you not scatheless
> Suppliant though you are, and sin against Zeus's commandments,

and having washed and shrouded the body of Hector, he places it with his own hands on the wagon before its disfigurement was seen by the father,

> Lest with heart so distressed he fail to master his anger,
> Seeing his son, and Achilles' heart be stirred with resentment,
> So that he slay him there, and sin against Zeus's commandments.

For it is mark of a wondrous foresight for a man whose hold on his temper is uncertain, who is naturally rough and quick-tempered, not to be blind to his own weakness, but to exercise caution, and to be on his guard against possible grounds for anger, and to forestall them by reason long beforehand, so that he may not even inadvertently become involved in such emotions. After the same manner should he that is fond of wine be on his guard against drunkenness, and he that is amorous against love. So did Agesilaus, who would not submit to being kissed by the handsome boy who approached him, so did Cyrus, who durst not even to look at Pantheia; but the uneducated, on the contrary, gather fuel to kindle their passions, casting themselves headlong into those wherein they are weakest and least sure of themselves. Yet Odysseus not only restrains himself when enraged, but perceiving from some words of Telemachus that he too is angry and filled with hatred of the wicked, labours to mitigate his feelings and prepares him well beforehand to keep quiet and restrain himself, bidding him,

> Even if they within my own house shall dishonour me sorely,
> Let your heart within you endure all the wrongs that I suffer:
> Though through the house they should drag me out by the feet to the open,
> Yea, or with missiles smite me, still you must patient behold it.

For just as drivers do not curb their horses during the race, but before the race, so with those persons who are quick-tempered and hard to hold back when dangers threaten, we first gain control over them by reasoning, and make them ready beforehand, and then lead them into the strife.

While it is also necessary not to pass over the words carelessly, yet one should eschew the puerility of Cleanthes; for there are times when he uses a mock seriousness in pretending to interpret ⟨Homer's⟩ words.

> Father Zeus, enthroned on Ida,

and

> Zeus, lord of Dodona,

bidding us in the latter case to read the last two words as one (taking the word "lord" as the preposition "up") as though the vapour exhaled from the earth were "updonative" because of its being rendered up! And Chrysippus also is often quite petty, although he does not indulge in jesting, but wrests the words ingeniously, yet without carrying conviction, as when he would force ⟨Homer's⟩ phrase "wide-seeing" son of Cronos to signify "clever in conversation," that is to say, with a widespread power of speech.

It is better, however, to turn these matters over to the grammarians, and to hold fast rather to those in which is to be found both usefulness and probability, such as

> Nor does my heart so bid me, for I have learned to be valiant,

and

> For towards all he understood the way to be gentle.

For by declaring that bravery is a thing to be learned, and by expressing the belief that friendly and gracious intercourse with others proceeds from understanding, and is in keeping with reason, the poet ⟨Homer⟩ urges us not to neglect our own selves, but to learn what is good, and to give heed to our teachers, intimating that both boorishness and cowardice are but ignorance and defects of learning. With this agrees very well what he says regarding Zeus and Poseidon:

> Both, indeed, were of one descent and of the same birthplace,
> Yet was Zeus the earlier born and his knowledge was wider.

For he declares understanding to be a most divine and kingly thing, to which he ascribes the very great superiority of Zeus, inasmuch as he believes that all the other virtues follow upon this one.

At the same time, the young man must get the habit of perusing with a mind wide awake such sayings as these ⟨in Homer⟩:

> Falsehood he will not utter because he is very prudent,

and

> What an act is this, Antilochus, prudent aforetime!
> You have put my skill to disgrace and hindered my horses,

and

> Glaucus, what cause has a man like you for words so disdainful?
> Truly I thought, my friend, that in sense you excelled all the others.

the implication being that men of sense do not lie or contend unfairly in games, or make unwarranted accusations against other people. And from the poet's saying that Pandarus was persuaded because of his want of sense to bring to naught the sworn agreement, he clearly shows his opinion that the man of sense would not do wrong. It is also possible to give similar intimations in regard to self-control, by directing the young man's attention to statements like these ⟨in Homer⟩:

> Mad for him was Proetus' royal wife Anteia
> Lusting to make him her lover in secret, but could not persuade him,
> Since the wise Bellerophon thought more of virtue.

and

> She at the first would not consent to a deed so unseemly,
> Royal Clytemnestra, since her thoughts were for virtue.

In these lines the poet attributes to understanding the cause of self-control; and in his exhortations to battle he says on the several occasions:

> Shame, men of Lycia, whither now flee ye? Now be ye valiant,

and

> But let all your minds be imbued with
> Shame and resentment, for now, as you see, great strife has arisen,

and thereby he appears to represent the men of self-control as brave because of their being ashamed of disgrace, and as able to overcome pleasures and to undergo dangerous adventures. Timotheus also adopted this point of view, when in his *Persians* he urged the Greeks, not infelicitously, to have

> Respect for shame that helps the brave in war;

and Aeschylus sets it down as a point of good sense not to be puffed up with fame, nor to be excited and elated by popular praise, when he writes of Amphiaraüs,

> His wish is not to seem, but be, the best,
> Reaping the deep-sown furrow of his mind
> In which all goodly counsels have their root.

For to take pride in oneself and in one's state of mind when it is altogether good, marks the man of good sense; and since everything may be referred to understanding, it follows that every form of virtue is added unto him from reason and instruction.

12. Now the bee, in accordance with nature's laws, discovers amid the most pungent flowers and the roughest thorns the smoothest and most palatable honey; so children, if they be rightly nurtured amid poetry, will in some way or other learn to draw some wholesome and profitable doctrine even from passages that are suspect of what is base and improper. For example, Agamemnon is suspected of having, for a bribe, released from service in the army the rich man who made him a present of the mare Aetha,

> Gift so he fare not with him to Troy where the wind never ceaseth,
> But enjoy himself at home; for wealth in abundance
> Zeus had bestowed upon him. ⟨Homer⟩

But, as Aristotle observes, he did quite right in preferring a good mare to a man of that type. For a coward, and a weakling, made dissolute by wealth and soft living, is not, I swear, worth a dog or even an ass. Again, it appears most shameful in Thetis when she incites her son to pleasures and reminds him of love. But even there we must contrast Achilles' mastery of himself, that although he is in love with Briseïs, who has come back to him, and although he knows that the end of his life is near, yet he does not make haste to enjoy love's pleasures, nor, like most men, mourn for his friend by inactivity and omission of his duties, but as he refrains from such pleasures because of his grief, so he bestirs himself in the business of his command. Again, Archilochus cannot be commended, because while grieving over his sister's husband, who was lost at sea, he is minded to fight against his grief by means of wine and amusement; he has, however, alleged a cause that has some appearance of reason,

> By my tears I shall not cure it, nor worse make it
> By pursuing joys, yea, and festivities.

For if he thought that he should not make matters "worse by pursuing joys, yea, and festivities," how shall our present condition be any the worse if we engage in the study of philosophy or take part in public life, if we go out to the

MORALIA

market-place or down to the Academy, or if we pursue our farming? Wherefore the corrected versions which Cleanthes and Antisthenes employed are themselves not without value. Antisthenes, observing that the Athenians had raised an uproar in the theatre at the line,

> What's shameful if its doer think not so?
> ⟨Euripides⟩

at once interpolated,

> A shame's a shame, though one think so or no

and Cleanthes, taking the lines about riches,

> Give to your friends, and when your body's ill
> Save it by spending, ⟨Euripides⟩

rewrote them in this manner,

> To harlots give, and when your body's ill
> Waste it by spending.

And Zeno in amending the lines of Sophocles,

> Whoever comes to traffic with a king
> To him is slave however free he come,

rewrote it thus:

> Is not a slave if only free he come,

by the word "free" as he now uses it designating the man who is fearless, high-minded, and unhumbled. What, then, is to hinder us also from encouraging the young to take the better course by means of similar rejoinders, dealing with the citations something like this:

> Most enviable is the lot of him
> The shaft of whose desire hits what he would.

"Not so," will be our retort, "but

> The shaft of whose desire hits what is good,"

For to gain and achieve one's wish, if what one wishes is not right, is pitiable and unenviable. Again,

> Not for good and no ill came thy life from thy sire,
> Agamemnon, but joy
> Thou shalt find interwoven with grief.
> ⟨Euripides⟩

"No, indeed," we shall say, "but you must find joy and not grief if your lot be but moderate, since

> Not for good and no ill came thy life from thy sire,
> Agamemnon;"

and:

> Alas, from God this evil comes to men,
> When, knowing what is good, one does it not.
> ⟨Euripides⟩

"No, rather is it bestial," we reply, "and irrational and pitiable that a man who knows the better should be led astray by the worse as a result of a weak will and soft living."

And again:

> 'Tis character persuades, and not the speech.

"No, rather it is both character and speech, or character by means of speech, just as a horseman uses a bridle, or a helmsman uses a rudder, since virtue has no instrument so humane or so akin to itself as speech." And:

> To women more than men is he inclined?
> Where there is beauty, either suits him best.

But it were better to say

> "Where there is virtue, either suits him best,

of a truth, and there is no difference in his inclination; but the man who is influenced by pleasure or outward beauty to shift his course hither and thither is incompetent and inconstant." Again:

> God's doings make the wise to feel afraid.

"Not so by any means, but

> God's doings make the wise to feel assured,

but they do make the silly and foolish and ungrateful to feel afraid, because such persons suspect and fear the power which is the cause and beginning of every good thing, as though it did harm." Such then is the system of amendment.

13. Chrysippus has rightly indicated how the poet's statements can be given a wider application, saying that what is serviceable should be taken over and made to apply to like situations. For when Hesiod says,

> Nor would even an ox disappear were there not a bad neighbour,

he says the same thing also about a dog and about an ass and about all things which in a similar way can "disappear." And again when Euripides says,

> What man who recks not death can be a slave?

we must understand that he makes the same statement also about trouble and disease. For, as physicians who have learnt the efficacy of a drug adapted to one malady take it over and use it for every similar malady, so also when a statement has a general and universal value, we ought not to suffer it to be fixed upon one matter alone, but we ought to apply it to all the like, and inure the young men to see its general value, and quickly to carry over what is appropriate, and by many examples to give themselves training and practice in keen appreciation; so that when Menander says,

> Blest is the man who has both wealth and sense,

they may think of the statement as holding good also about repute and leadership and facility in speaking; and so also that when they hear the rebuke which was administered by Odysseus to Achilles as he sat among the maidens in Scyrus,

> Dost thou, to dim the glory of thy race,
> Card wool, son of the noblest man in Greece?

they may imagine it to be addressed also to the profligate and the avaricious and the heedless and the ill-bred, as, for example,

> Dost drink, son of the noblest man in Greece,

or gamble, or follow quail-fighting, or petty trading, or the exacting of usury, without a thought of what is magnanimous or worthy of your noble parentage?

> Speak not of Wealth. I can't admire a god
> Whose ready favour basest men secure.
> ⟨Euripides⟩

Therefore speak not of repute, either, or of personal beauty, or the general's cloak, or the priestly crown, to all which we see the worst of men attaining.

> For ugly is the brood of cowardice,

and the same we may also aver of licentiousness, superstition, envy, and all the other pestilent disorders. Most excellently has Homer said

> Paris, poor wretch, excelling in looks,

and

> Hector, excelling in looks

(for he declares the man deserving of censure and reproach who is endowed with no good quality better than personal comeliness), and this we must make to apply to similar cases, thereby curtailing the pride of those who plume themselves on things of no worth, and teaching the young to regard as a disgrace and reproach such phrases as "excelling in wealth" and "excelling in dinners" and "excelling in children" or "oxen," and in fact even the use of the word "excelling" in such a connexion. For we ought to aim at the pre-eminence which comes from noble qualities, and we should strive to be first in matters of first importance, and to be great in the greatest: but the repute which comes from small and petty things is disreputable and paltry.

This illustration at once reminds us to consider carefully instances of censure and commendation, particularly in Homer's poems. For he gives us expressly to understand that bodily and adventitious characteristics are unworthy of serious attention. For, to begin with, in their greetings and salutations, they do not call one another handsome or rich or strong, but they employ such fair words as these—

> Heaven-sprung son of Laertes, Odysseus of many devices,

and

> Hector, son of Priam, peer of Zeus in counsel,

and

> Son of Peleus, Achilles, great glory to the Achaeans,

and

> Noble son of Menoetius, in whom my soul finds pleasure.

In the second place they reproach without touching at all upon bodily characteristics, but they direct their censure to faults:

> Drunken sot, with eyes of a dog and the wild deer's courage,

and

> Ajax, excelling at wrangling, ill advised,

and

> Why, Idomeneus do you brag so soon? Unfitting
> Is it for you to be braggart,

and

> Ajax, blundering boaster,

and finally Thersites is reproached by Odysseus, not as lame or bald or hunchbacked, but as indiscreet in his language, while on the other hand the mother of Hephaestus affectionately drew an epithet from his lameness when she addressed him thus:

> Up with you, club-foot, my child!

Thus Homer ridicules those who feel ashamed of lameness or blindness, in that he does not regard as blameworthy that which is not shameful, or as shameful that which is brought about, not through our own acts, but by fortune.

Plainly, then, two great advantages accrue to those who accustom themselves carefully to peruse works of poetry: the first is conducive to moderation, that we do not odiously and foolishly reproach anybody with his fortune; while the second is conducive to magnanimity, that when we ourselves have met with chances and changes we be not humiliated or even disturbed, but bear gently with scoffings and revilings and ridicule, having especially before us the words of Philemon:

> There's naught more pleasing or in better taste
> Than having strength to bear when men revile

But if anybody is plainly in need of reprehension, we should reprehend his faults and his giving way to emotion, after the fashion in which Adrastus of the tragedy, when Alcmaeon said to him,

> You are the kin of her who slew her spouse,

replied

> And you have murdered her who gave you birth.

For just as those who scourge the clothes do not touch the body, so those who scoff at misfortune or low birth, do but vainly and foolishly assail externals, never touching the soul or even such matters as really need correction and stinging reproof.

14. Moreover, just as in what we have said above we felt that by setting against cheap and harmful poems the sayings and maxims of statesmen and men of repute, we were inducing a revolt and revulsion of faith from such poetry, so whenever we find any edifying sentiment neatly expressed in the poets we ought to foster and amplify it by means of proofs and testimonies from the philosophers, at the same time crediting these with the discovery. For this is right and useful, and our faith gains an added strength and dignity whenever the doctrines of Pythagoras and of Plato are in agreement with what is spoken on the stage or sung to the lyre or studied at school, and when the precepts of Chilon and of Bias lead to the same conclusions as our children's readings in poetry. Hence it is a duty to make a point of indicating that ⟨Homer's⟩ lines

> You, my child, have not the gift of arms in battle,
> Your concern must be for loving arms in wedlock,

and

> Seeing that Zeus is wroth if you fight with a man far better,

do not differ from "Know thyself," but have the same purport as this; and ⟨Hesiod's⟩ lines,

> Fools! They know not how much more than all a half is,

and

> Evil counsel is the worst for him who gives it

are identical with the doctrines of Plato in the *Gorgias* and the *Republic* upon the principle that "to do wrong is worse than to be wronged" and "to do evil is more injurious than to suffer evil." And on the words of Aeschylus,

> Fear not; great stress of pain is not for long,

we ought to remark that this is the oft repeated and much admired statement originating with Epicurus, namely "that great pains shortly spend their force, and long continued pains have no magnitude." Of these two ideas Aeschylus has perspicuously stated the one and the other is a corollary thereto; for if great and intense pain is not lasting, then that which does not last is not great or hard to endure. Take these lines of Thespis:

> You see that Zeus is first of gods in this,
> Not using lies or boast or silly laugh;
> With pleasure he alone is unconcerned.

What difference is there between this and the statement, "for the Divine Being sits throned afar from pleasure and pain," as Plato has put it? Consider what is said by Bacchylides:

> I shall assert that virtue hath the highest fame,
> But wealth with even wretched men is intimate,

and again by Euripides to much the same effect:

> There's naught that I hold
> In a higher esteem
> Than a virtuous life;
> 'Twill ever be joined
> With those that are good.

and

> Why seek vain possessions? Do ye think
> Virtue by wealth to compass?
> Wretched amid your comforts shall ye sit.

Is not this a proof of what the philosophers say regarding wealth and external advantages, that without virtue they are useless and unprofitable for their owners?

This method of conjoining and reconciling such sentiments with the doctrines of philosophers brings the poet's work out of the realm of myth and impersonation, and, moreover, invests with seriousness its helpful sayings. Besides, it opens and stimulates in advance the mind of the youth by the sayings in philosophy. For he comes to it thus not altogether without a foretaste of it, nor without having heard of it, nor indiscriminately stuffed with what he has heard always from his mother and nurse, and, I dare say, from his father and his tutor as well, who all beatify and worship the rich, who shudder at death and pain, who regard virtue without money and repute as quite undesirable and a thing of naught. But when they hear the precepts of the philosophers, which go counter to such opinions, at first astonishment and confusion and amazement take hold of them, since they cannot accept or tolerate any such teaching, unless, just as if they were now to look upon the sun after having been in utter darkness, they have been made accustomed, in a reflected light, as it were, in which the dazzling rays of truth are softened by combining truth with fable, to face facts of this sort without being distressed, and not to try to get away from them. For if they have previously heard or read in poetry such thoughts as these:

> To mourn the babe for th' ills to which he comes;
> But him that's dead, and from his labours rests,
> To bear from home with joy and cheering words,
> ⟨Euripides⟩

and

> What needs have mortals save two things alone,
> Demeter's grain and draught from water-jar?
> ⟨Euripides⟩

and

> O Tyranny, beloved of barbarous folk,

and

> And mortal men's felicity
> Is gained by such of them as feel least grief,

they are less confused and disquieted upon hearing at the lectures of the philosophers that "Death is nothing to us," and "The wealth allowed by Nature is definitely limited," and "Happiness and blessedness do not consist in vast possessions or exalted occupations or offices or authority, but on impassivity, calmness, and a disposition of the soul that sets its limitations to accord with Nature" ⟨Epicurean principles⟩.

Wherefore, both because of these considerations and because of those already adduced, the young man has need of good pilotage in the matter of reading, to the end that, forestalled with schooling rather than prejudice, in a spirit of friendship and goodwill and familiarity, he may be convoyed by poetry into the realm of philosophy.

Hermogenes

c. first-century A.D.

Hermogenes was born in Tarsus around 160, near the beginning of the reign of Marcus Aurelius. An oratorical prodigy in his youth, he later taught in Rome and wrote numerous rhetorical treatises, of which On Types of Style is the most important. In it, he sets out to improve upon what he considers the "muddled and diffident way" in which his predecessors have dealt with the various stylistic qualities. Accordingly, he constructs a highly elaborate typology intended to isolate the qualities in themselves, independent of their use (or misuse) by a particular writer. Like Dionysius of Halicarnassus, Hermogenes regards Demosthenes as the model of rhetorical composition, "the author whose style possesses most variety and the most striking combination of all the 'types.'"

Hermogenes' work was quite influential in the schools of the Byzantine empire, though he has not been widely read in the history of Western literature. Many modern commentators consider his contribution to the theory of rhetoric rigid and sterile, but this is a judgment that may be too severe.

On Types of Style, *translated by D. A. Russell, is reprinted by permission of Oxford University Press from D. A. Russell and M. Winterbottom, eds.,* Ancient Literary Criticism: The Principal Texts in New Translations *(Oxford, 1972). © 1972 by Oxford University Press.*

FROM
On Types

General Concepts

Perhaps the most necessary subject for the orator to understand is that of the "types" (*ideai*) of style: what are their characteristics and how are they produced? Without this knowledge, one cannot know how to judge excellence and craftsmanship, or the lack of them, in other writers, ancient or modern; and if one wishes oneself to be a craftsman in words, fine and noble words such as the ancients used, then this branch of study is indispensable—unless one is prepared to deviate widely from standards of good workmanship. Imitation (*mimēsis*) and emulation (*zēlos*) of the ancients cannot in my opinion be successful, however well-endowed the writer, if they depend simply on experience and some sort of irrational knack. Indeed, natural advantages rushing towards random objectives without science or principle may well lead to greater disasters;[1] whereas with a knowledge and understanding of this subject even a student of moderate ability will not fail. Of course it is better to have natural advantages on one's side also: the success will be the greater. But failing this, let us achieve what can be achieved by the process of learning and teaching, which depends on nothing outside our control. Indeed, the less well endowed may well overtake the more favoured, just by dint of exercise and practice on the right lines.

The study of "types," then, is important and necessary to the future writer and the future critic, and even more so to one who would be both. No wonder therefore if we find it a difficult subject, not capable of simple treatment. Nothing good is easily obtained; and it would surprise me if there is anything better for man, who is a *logical* creature, than fine and good *logoi* and all the types of them.[2]

Before I proceed to actual instruction on the various topics involved, I must make one preliminary point. We are not here concerned with the "type" peculiar to Plato or Demosthenes or any individual writer; that will be discussed later. For the moment, the question before us is to consider each quality in itself, and explain what sort of thing solemnity (*semnotēs*) is, and how it is produced, and similarly with asperity, simplicity, and the rest. However, the reason why we need this subject is for the study of individual famous writers. Consequently, if we put before ourselves the author whose style possesses most variety and the most striking combination of all the "types," we shall find that in discussing him we have discussed them all. If we can explain the general and the particular features of such a writer, their origin, composition, nature and essence, we shall have given an accurate account of every type of style. We shall have explained how they may be combined, and how, as a result of combinations of the same types, the whole style (*logos*) can become poetical or unpoetical, panegyrical, deliberative, forensic, or what you will.

Now the man who, more than anyone else, handled language in this way and diversified his writing continuously is, in my opinion, Demosthenes. Thus in considering him and what may be found in his work, we shall also be considering all the "types" of style. I would beg the reader not to criticize this approach or this critical judgement until he has heard all that I am going to say. I suspect that if attention is given to what follows I shall earn admiration, especially for distinctness, rather than criticism.

The main point is this. Demosthenes' mastery of political oratory is such that, if one considers him with some sophistication, it is not very difficult to see how he is always combining styles, not separating his deliberative manner rigorously from the forensic or panegyrical, nor indeed abandoning any of these styles when concentrating on one of them. What is very difficult indeed is to discover the stylistic elements which he uses to form his own style as he does—the elements which, in combination with one another, compose all manners, including the panegyrical. Nor is it less difficult to express these plainly when one has actually uncovered them. To my knowledge, no one has yet dealt with them with exactness; those who have touched on the subject have done so in a muddled and diffident way, so that their accounts are thoroughly confused. For instance, those who have some repute as exponents of Demosthenes, because they have investigated him in detail, to the limit of their ability, without however troubling much about general principles—solemnity, simplicity, the other "types" in themselves—may indeed prove instructive on Demosthenes or the parts of Demosthenes they claim to discuss, but do nothing to inform us about style and "types" of writing in general, in metre, poetry or prose.

Difficult as it is to discover these things and expound them distinctly, avoiding our predecessors' failures, the attempt must nevertheless be made by the method I have proposed. If we can enumerate and describe the elements and first principles of Demosthenic style, and say how they are produced and combined, and what effect various kinds of combination have, we may find that we have given an account of style in general. To quote the great orator himself, "this is a large undertaking, but the execution will answer for itself here and now; let whoso wishes be my judge."[3]

The factors which make up the style of Demosthenes, considered as a unity, are the following: clarity (*saphēneia*), grandeur (*megethos*), beauty (*kallos*), rapidity (*gorgotēs*), "character" (*ēthos*), sincerity (*alētheia*), and vehemence (*deinotēs*). By "as a unity," I mean that all these are interwoven and interpenetrating: that is what Demosthenes' style is like. Of these "types," some stand by themselves and exist separately, others have subordinate "types" under them, which help to produce them; others again have one or more parts in common. In general terms, some are genera consisting of species, some overlap other "types" in respect of some specific difference, though distinct in all other ways, while others remain on their own and need no additional help. What I mean will become clearer as we proceed to discuss each "type" separately.

We must first state the elements of which all speech is made up, and without which no kind of speech can exist. This will make it easier to follow when we have before us the subordinate qualities we have mentioned, and have to explain their genesis.

All speech has a thought or thoughts, an approach (*methodos*) corresponding to the thought, and diction appropriate to these. Diction has its own charactersitics; it involves figures, cola, word-arrangement, pauses, and rhythm. Rhythm is the product of the two preceding, since to arrange the parts of speech in a particular way and to bring speech to a pause in a particular way will produce rhythm of a particular kind.

This may be obscure, and so I will clarify it by an example. Suppose we aim to produce sweetness. The thoughts appropriate to sweetness are those connected with myth or the like, and certain others, which we will discuss in the section on sweetness. The "approaches" consist in handling the subject as the main theme and in narrative fashion, not allusively or in any other manner. The appropriate diction is that which makes much use of adjectives, has a sharp flavour, and is poetical without being elevated or diffuse by nature. Any diction associated with purity of style will also do. Within the sphere of diction, the figures to be recommended are generally those involving straightforward expression without interruptions. The cola should be commatic in scale or not much bigger. The arrangement of words should be relaxed because of the character of the diction, but not wholly without coherence, since sweetness must achieve some of its pleasurable effect by means of rhythm; its metrical basis should be anapaestic or dactylic. A full discussion of rhythm and word-arrangement would involve syllables and letters, since these, together with clausulae, are the elements of rhythm, as will become clear later. The clausula appropriate to sweetness, corresponding to this word-arrangement, is the firmly-based kind. Rhythm, like shape, follows arrangement and clausulae of a certain kind, although it is separate from all of them—just as when stones or timbers of a certain kind are put together to make a house or a ship in a certain way and with certain limits set to the operation, the shape of the house or ship is thereby determined, though it is actually something distinct from the manner of putting together and from the limit set to the operation.

All kinds of style, then, are to be seen under the following heads, and depend on the following factors: thought, approach (*methodos*), diction, figure, colon, word-arrangement, clausula, rhythm. I am aware that these need further clarification, and I do not think, as some do, that they might be clarified by proposing examples. They do indeed need exemplification, but I do not agree that clarity would follow if we were to exemplify them now. Indeed, the discussion would be greatly prolonged by the addition here of examples of these various points, and greater confusion would probably result. It has not been my purpose here to talk about "sweetness"—we shall discuss it in greater detail later—except so far as to show how any one type of writing may be produced in its pure state. I hope, as I said, that we may thereby be better equipped to study the rest of the subject. I return to the main point.

This being so, and every "type" being produced in these ways, it is difficult or impossible to find in any ancient writer a specimen of style belonging to one type in all respects—theme, approach, diction, and the rest. What gives every writer his particular character is the predominance in him of qualities appropriate to a given type. I exclude Demosthenes. Unlike the rest, he has not got an abnormal preponderance of any one type, though there is one part or species of one type that he does employ more than others—abundance (*peribolē*). (The discussion of grandeur and abundance which is to follow is the place to explain in detail his practice in this respect.) But the preponderance is confined to one fraction of a single type: all the others he uses in their due place, according due weight to each. Elevated and brilliant thoughts are scaled down by special approaches or figures or by some other means; the delicate or trivial is similarly roused to life and given new stature. In fact he mixes every quality on the same principles with elements not peculiar or particularly appropriate to it, and by thus diversifying his style makes everything fit together and form a unity in which all the various types interpenetrate. So all beauties merge in the one supremely beautiful style, the Demosthenic.

Strictly speaking, then, a single style cannot be found in any ancient writer. No doubt it is in principle a fault to construct one's style in a single form without variety. But—to recapitulate—different authors exceed the norm in different features and this is how their styles come to be characterized in one way or another. By "exceeding the norm" I do not mean that they use a large number of the factors that make up a type (approach, figures, word-order, pause, etc.), although this might have some significance, but rather that they make special use of the most vital factors in each type. This is what most helps to produce the type, and "exceed the norm" means "use the most important factors" in it. It sometimes happens that an author who employs every other means, and indeed "exceeds the norm" in them, but falls short in these, actually fails to achieve the stylistic effort to which the means he *has* used are appropriate.

We must turn now to the effect of the factors that, as we said, contribute to types of style.

First, and always most important, is the thought. Second comes the diction, third the figure—the figure of diction I mean, because the figure of thought, in other words the approach, is my fourth factor, though this position in the list does not correspond to its value in "vehemence" (*deinotēs*), when it may be said, as will be explained, to hold the first place. Word-arrangement and clausula may be placed last, though sometimes they are not least in importance, especially in poetry. One of them without the other can indeed make little or no contribution to style, but together, and combined with rhythm, they can do much. In fact, the musicians may raise the point that they ought to be put before thought. Rhythm, they will tell us, by itself, and without articulate speech, is more effective than any type of style. Appropriate rhythms produce pleasure in the mind more than any panegyrical speech, pain more than any rhetorical appeal to pity, anger more than any violent and vehement talk, and so on. We will not quarrel with the musicians for teasing us about all these points; let rhythm come first or last or in the middle, just as anyone likes. What I hope to show is the nature of the rhythms appropriate to each quality, limiting myself to the extent to which it is possible to apply rhythm to prose without making a song out of it. If rhythm is as important in this situation as it is in music generally, let it come first: if not, it shall come in its proper place. My own view is that rhythm does sometimes contribute much to the quality of style, but not as much as they say. . . .

Dignity, Grandeur, Solemnity

The discussion of grandeur (*megethos*) naturally follows that of clarity, because clarity must be accompanied by a certain grandeur, "bulk" (*onkos*), and dignity, since the commonplace (*to euteles*) is next door to great clarity, and this is the opposite of grandeur. Demosthenes, I am convinced, recognized this. Since it is an absolute necessity for the style of the practical orator to be clear, he consistently used the elements that produce clarity, but as this involved a danger of his style declining into a rather workaday manner, he combined them with elements that produce grandeur, and was especially strong in the quality of "abundance" (*peribolē*) . . .

The qualities that produce grandeur, "bulk," and dignity are therefore the following: solemnity, abundance, asperity, brilliance, florescence (*akmē*), vehemence—though this last, as will be seen when we come to discuss it, is not very different from asperity. Of these, solemnity and abundance exist on their own, whereas all the others are combined (or not combined) with others in some respect, having some areas in common and some distinct. I shall therefore discuss solemnity now, and the rest later. Abundance does indeed, as I said before, exist on its own, but I postpone the treatment of it because Demosthenes excels in it and the reason why he employs it to achieve "bulk" cannot be understood until we have learned about asperity, brilliance, florescence, and vehemence.

First, then, solemnity. Its opposite, I suggest, is simplicity (*apheleia*), which we shall discuss in the section on 'character' (*ēthos*).

Solemn thoughts include in the first place things said of the gods *qua* gods. Things like

> The son of Kronos spoke, and clasped his wife in his arms[4]

are not spoken of gods *qua* gods: they are far removed from solemnity of thought, and partake more of the nature of charm (*hēdonē*) and sweetness. They are expressions of human emotion—in general terms, they are poetical, and pleasure is the main aim of poetry. An example of something said of gods *qua* gods is: "He was good, and no good being has any envy of anything," or: "God wanted all things to be good and nothing bad, so far as possible," or again: "God took all that was visible, when it was not at rest but moving in disharmony and disorder, and reduced it from disorder to order, thinking this in every way better."[5] Many such thoughts can be found in Plato (these are from the *Timaeus*); they are not to be found in the orators, for Hyperides' *Deliacus*[6] is more poetical and mythical—I need not here explain why. There are however in Demosthenes, and here and there in the other orators, thoughts of a second or third order of solemnity. The first order, as I said, comprises thoughts about gods *qua* gods; the second are thoughts about truly divine things—e.g. an inquiry into the nature and causes of the seasons, the nature and revolution of the universe, movements of earth or sea, thunderbolts, and so on. Now if these subjects are handled only with respect to causes, they have power only to make the writing *solemn*, not to give it practical value as oratory. For where is the practical oratory in the passage of Herodotus about "the sun, driven away in the winter season,"[7] or in Plato's "The circular path of the universe, including all the kinds in its ambit, compresses them in every direction, and allows no empty space; in consequence, fire passes through everything, next comes air, the second most subtle, and so on with the others . . ."?[8] Or again, where is the relevance to practical oratory of inquiries into earthquakes, the flood and ebb of water, the impact of thunderbolts, or any such matters? Considered in this way, such thoughts make the context solemn without being in a practical sense oratorical. They form therefore the *second* class of "solemn" thoughts.

If however one handles such topics not with a view to inquiry into causes but as a description (*ekphrasis*), the result will be both solemn and practical. There is an example in Aristides' speech against Callixenus,[9] who had advised against granting burial to the ten generals, when they had been executed as a result of a single vote. Aristides on their behalf described the storm. "It was a bolt from heaven that prevented them, Callixenus, beyond description and beyond bearing. The battle had scarce begun when the sea swelled, and a brisk Hellespontine gale got up . . ."

The third group of thoughts conducive to solemnity comprises matters which are by nature divine, but are commonly seen in human affairs—e.g. the immortality of the soul, justice, temperance, or the like, or some discussion of life in general or the definition of law or nature. For instance: "Law is an invention and gift of the gods," or "Law is common, ordered, the same for all; nature is without order, peculiar to the individual," or "The end of all men's life is death, even though a man should keep himself shut up at home . . . ," or "All human life is governed by nature and laws."[10] In brief, all universal and general statements possess in some measure solemnity of thought, especially if the universality is consistently maintained. If you add a special detail, the effect is changed: "A bad thing, men of Athens, a bad thing is an informer, a thoroughly malicious, fault-finding creature; but this little fellow was *born* a trickster."[11] The addition of the detail has changed the effect; a combination of the universal and the particular produces the style of practical oratory and of abundance, but not necessarily that of solemnity.

The fourth type of solemn effect is produced by thought concerned with matters entirely human, but great and glorious: the battles of Marathon or Plataea or Salamis, Athos and the Hellespont, and so forth. The additon of a *fabulous* solemnity accompanied by charm, as in Herodotus (e.g. the Iacchus story)[12] makes a further difference.

So much for the thoughts appropriate to solemnity: the appropriate approaches (*methodoi*) are forms of exposition involving direct statement without hesitiation. (i) When we aim at consistent solemnity we must speak exactly and with dignity, as though we are certain, and not with any hesitation. "Be they gods or heroes"[13] is solemn in thought, but the expression of doubt gives it more of the character of practical oratory and persuasion. (ii) The allegorical approach, if consistently maintained, also produces solemnity: "The great leader in heaven, Zeus, rides his winged chariot..."[14] This happens, however, only when the writer does not choose everyday, commonplace matter for his allegory; if he does, the result is not solemnity but writing characterized by another kind of thought, the commonplace. (iii) Another feature of the solemn approach is the use of suggestive hints to indicate darkly, in the manner of the mysteries and initiations, something within the sphere of solemn thoughts. By appearing to know, but to be unable to reveal, we give an impression of grandeur and solemnity: e.g. "verily being" or "he was good..." in Plato.[15] Plato in fact in one passage expands this approach: "To discover this is difficult, to reveal it to all on discovery, impossible." Such approaches are valuable in amplifying solemnity when the thoughts concerned are by nature solemn; hints like this however do not produce solemnity in subjects of practical concern—they have a different effect.

From the thoughts and approaches of solemnity we pass to the diction. This includes, first, all broad sounds which make us open our mouths wide, so as to give a pompous impression, and, as it were, force us into a manner which some speakers deliberately cultivate. This applies especially to words containing many long *a*'s or *o*'s. Thus Plato tells us how some people call *oiōnistikē* (augury) *ōōnistikē* "to make it more solemn."[16] Similarly with *a*. Theocritus represents a man as angry with women who speak Doric and use the *a* continually in their broad accent.[17] Long *o* and *a* particularly elevate and enlarge words if they occur in the closing syllables: ... *hēgemōn en ouranō Zeus* ("... leader in heaven, Zeus").

A second class of solemn words is made up of those containing a short *o* by itself, ending in a long syllable, as in *Orontēs*. We must add also words which contain a number of long syllables or diphthongs, and those which end in such sounds, except the diphthong *ei*. Recurrent *i*, however, does not make for solemnity, since it contracts the mouth instead of opening it, and produces a rictus.

Thirdly: tropical expressions are solemn and grand, but their use involves considerable risks. Moderate tropes do indeed give the desired effect: "putting forward good hopes"[18] instead of "hoping for good" is an example, because—you see this?—the expression is so moderate that the trope is not even noticed. Any excess, however, produces asperity: for example "the cities were sick."[19] This expression needed explanation—"the politicians accepted bribes..." is simply explanation of "sick."

Further excess makes for even greater harshness: "hamstrung," "sold himself," "robbery with violence to Greece."[20] To go further still in the same direction produces coarseness and indeed vulgarity. One could not find an example of this, indeed, in Demosthenes—there aren't any—but our friends the bogus sophists would yield many. They call vultures (whose attentions they deserve themselves) "living tombs,"[21] and use many other such frigid expressions. Tragedy, which contains many instances of such things, and poets like Pindar who have a tragic style, are their downfall. There may well be things to say in defence of the use of language in this way by these writers—Pindar and the tragedians, I mean—but it does not belong to the present occasion, and must be postponed. For writers who use crassitudes like this in oratory, I find no excuse.

Fourthly: nouns and nominal diction also produce solemnity. By "nominal diction," I mean diction involving a conversion from verb to noun, and the use of participles, pronouns, etc. In the solemn manner one should use as few verbs as possible. Thucydides always aims at this; he has done it most noticeably in the description of the revolution at Corcyra.[22] Apart from the verb "was considered," everything is nouns or in nominal form: "irrational daring was considered loyal courage, cautious delay specious cowardice, discretion a cloak for unmanliness," etc. (I am not here concerned with the element of harshness or asperity in the passage.) Similar is a passage of Demosthenes,[23] on the effect of which he comments himself: "words, he said, do not strengthen associations": then comes the comment—"a very solemn way of putting the point."

So much for diction: the figures appropriate to solemnity are those which also give purity: i.e. directness and the like. "Confirmations" (*epikriseis*), whether to be regarded as thoughts or figures, are solemn: "But to pay them in speech what honour remains is enjoined by the law, and is our duty";[24] "They were willing to give themselves up to danger for the sake of honour and glory, and their decision was honourable and right."[25] All this sort of thing is solemn and dignified. "Confirmations" combined with expressions of doubt, on the other hand, are characterful (*ēthikai*) but not solemn: "I am no lover of invective, but I am bound to say . . ." Any touch of doubt or hesitation lends an individual character to a passage. A speaker who wishes to give his words dignity and solemnity needs to be dogmatic: "Philip had no way of putting an end to, or getting out of, his war with us." If you say "I imagine Philip had . . ." you produce an effect of "character" (*ēthos*). On the other hand, to attribute something of what you are going to say to your own opinion *is* dignified and solemn: "What I want to say is this . . .";[26] "Agamemnon seems to me to have been the most powerful ruler of the time . . ."[27]

"Apostrophe" and "hypostrophe" are not appropriate to the solemn manner or to the pure: indeed, they undermine and destroy them, because they break the piece up by interruptions and upset the free run, making it more ordinary and oratorical. Compare the effect of the phrase "whether they dwell in a great city or a small" placed in the middle of the sentence "the whole life of men is governed by nature and by laws."[28] To arrange the clauses in the order I have just given them would produce a different effect from that given by dividing the sentence by hypostrophe and writing "the whole life of men, whether they dwell in a great city or a small, is governed by nature and laws." This last is rapid, as well as being oratorical, and solemn; the other would be solemn and homogeneous in a pure manner. This therefore is the treatment to be adopted if the speech is to remain solemn throughout; otherwise, we should prefer the other.

As to cola: "solemn" cola are the "pure" cola—i.e. the shorter ones. They should be as it were aphorisms. "Every soul is undying, for the ever-moving is undying."²⁹ "Law is the invention and gift of the gods, and the decision of intelligent men."³⁰ There may however be longer cola for some necessary reason in a context of solemnity.

As to word-arrangement: the "solemn" types are those which are not fussy about vowel-clashes, but are broadly speaking dactylic, anapaestic, or paeonic, sometimes iambic, and especially spondaic. Forms based on the epitrite thus suit the solemn manner, while trochaic and ionic rhythms do not . . .

[We omit some examples.]

Clausulae in the "solemn" manner again follow the same principles as those in the "pure." The sentence must rest on one of the feet appropriate to solemnity, and with no catalexis, so that the "basis" does not become trochaic, or the rhythm turn hurried instead of steady. It will be steady if it ends in a noun or nominal expression at least three syllables long:

*eis toutonī ton agōna.*³¹

Alternatively, there may be a majority of long syllables at the clausula, so that a double spondee or any epitrite other than the fourth forms the "basis":

*hapās ho tōn anthrōpōn bios phusei kai nomois dioikeitai.*³²

The rhythm has a particularly solemn base if the clausula has last, or next to last, a broad sound which forces the mouth open—a point I made above in connection with solemn *diction*.

The nature of the rhythm should be clear from the above. Note however that if the general rhythmical character is epitritic or dactylic or the like, but the clausula fails to terminate in such a way that what follows (?) has the kind of feet appropriate to solemnity, the rhythm is not solemn. This principle is true of all "types." If a composition is formed of feet of a certain nature, which are supposed to produce a certain type, but the clausulae are not formed of complete feet of the same kind, but the feet are broken up, the rhythm is changed and becomes appropriate to a different manner from that associated with the feet of which the whole context was composed. . . .

"Character," Simplicity

"Character" (*ēthos*) in speech is produced by moderation (*epieikeia*) and simplicity, and also by the genuineness and sincerity apparent in it. Weightiness also is involved in writing in character, though it is not an essential part of it, as simplicity, moderation, genuineness, and sincerity all are. Nor indeed can it be seen on its own—it needs with it simplicity or moderation or some other characterful quality. This will be clearer after a discussion of the several qualities.

The thoughts of simplicity are in general those of purity. Thoughts common to mankind, reaching, or believed to reach, everyman, with nothing deep or sophisticated about them, are obviously simple and pure. "Think me a villain, but let him go"³³ is an example. It is generally agreed, too, that pure thoughts will necessarily be simple, and vice versa. Simple in a more special sense are the characters who are unaffected and childish—not to say silly—to some degree.

For example, it gives this effect to go over events or tell a story that is unnecessary and that no one has asked for. There is much in Anacreon of this kind, and in Theocritus' pastorals, and in many other writers: for example,

> I'm serenading Amaryllis, while my goats graze on the mountain,[34]

and the context. Now as the examples we gave under "purity" were of a more oratorical and contentious kind ("think me a villain, but let him go" is perhaps of this sort also), and as we gave no instances of pure and simple thoughts in other kinds of prose writing, something more must be said now. I make no separation of "pure" thoughts as a category distinct from "simple," nor of "simple" as distinct from "pure." What I mean is that of these "pure and simple" thoughts, some suit oratory better than others, and some do not suit it at all. These last are the thoughts that are strictly peculiar to simplicity, as I said, though at the same time perfectly "pure." They are, for example, the thoughts of infants, men of infantile mind, women, countrymen, and generally speaking simple, guileless folk of any kind. "How lovely grandpa is, mother!" "They are bad men," said Cyrus of the Assyrians, "and they ride bad horses."[35] See how simple the thought is! Or again:

> Sweet is the murmuring, goatherd, and yonder pine . . .[36]

—and indeed most, if not all, bucolic poetry. There are similar passages in Anacreon, while in Menander one could find innumerable such things, spoken by women or young men in love or cooks or similar characters. And in general, because the characters of all such personages (gluttons, countrymen, etc.) fall under the head of "character," all or most of them must come under simplicity: they are what are strictly called "character" elements. It should be noted also that "pure" thoughts in this sense, which are also simple, are essential and useful if one is reporting what in the narrow sense is called a "character" personage; otherwise they have no relevance to oratorical writing.

"Simple" also are thoughts that appear to border on the vulgar. These are found when one speaks about vulgar or ordinary matters. For example, in the speech against Stephanus for false witness, we have the phrase "showered the nuts over him," and again "strip the rose-garden." In the Appeal against Eubulides, we find the speaker saying that his mother used to sell ribbons in the market.[37] This sort of thing is common in private speeches, even commoner in Lysias. In public speeches it is rare, and is introduced with some degree of apology: for example the phrase "riots without his mask"[38] is raised above the level of utter vulgarity by the addition of the spontaneous "the appalling Kyrebion" and "in the processions." Again: " . . . how your mother made use of the daily weddings in the hut by the Hero of the Splints, and brought you up as a lovely statue or a supreme third-part actor."[39] This is of the same general type, even if it is introduced with vehemence, for the subject is vulgar; but it earns its defence with the phrase "daily weddings," the vehemence, the irony, and so on. Again: the phrase "squashing the brown snakes" and the whole passage down to "and all the names the old women called you" is of this kind, but it is justified by the fact that Demosthenes deprecates what is said himself, because these were words used by old women.[40] There is another passage which some people have—perhaps rightly—obelized and deleted because of its extreme vulgarity. It is the one that begins: "She wandered around all the summer, crying baked beans . . ." This might be suitable in a private speech, but could not possibly do in a public speech, or one with that level of dignity, or in regard to a person or event of that kind. Similar is the passage, obelized by some, in the speech against Neaera: "ply her profession through three openings." This is very vulgar, even if it is vigorous.[41]

"Simple" also are thoughts occurring in arguments drawn from irrational animals. "The ox strikes with his horn, the horse with his hoof, the dog with his mouth, the boar with his tusk."[42] A very similar effect is given by arguments from plants, though these have even more simplicity of sentiment in them, being close to "sweetness" and thus common in the poets. In the poets indeed these features may possess grandeur, and this is not surprising: for one thing, they do not use examples of this kind in quantity, as we do in prose, but take just one, and this does not make the whole context simple; and secondly, poets are naturally concerned with the grand as well as the pleasant, and therefore elevate their subject by diction or figures even if in its own nature it is simple and pleasant.

More about "sweetness" anon. The foregoing example gains in simplicity by having a number of distinct parts. Now this multiplication of parts is a matter not of the thought appropriate to simplicity but of the method or approach. In the expression "Except for harvesters and others working for hire,"[43] if one were to remove the indefiniteness and dwell on the details, one would make the passage "simple": for example "except for harvesters and diggers and binders and shepherds and herdsmen." This dwelling on details would produce great simplicity.

Simple and character-revealing in thought is also the appeal to an oath rather than to facts. "I call on all the gods and goddesses of the land of Attica, and on Apollo of Delphi." "First, men of Athens, I pray to all gods and goddesses."[44] There are countless such examples in Demosthenes and all these oaths are "in character" (*ēthika*) and simple. So also if one binds the audience or one's opponent by an oath; this is not a debating move, like "For the sake of Zeus and the gods, do not accept . . ."[45] and the like, but a matter of convincing character and persuasiveness. On the other hand, if one were to process (*methodeuein*) a debating proof or something else in such a way that it falls into the figure of an oath, this is something different, and not simple or "in character." For it is then no longer an oath, but a processed form of something else. Retaining its original force, it acquires additional qualities through the process adopted. "No, by those of our ancestors who risked their lives at Marathon . . ."[46] This is a notable example and proof of the fact that it was the city's habit to fight and take risks for the liberty of Greece, so "processed" as to fall into an oath; the result is thus splendour and grandeur, not simplicity and character. . . .

The Purely "Panegyric" Mode and Its Exponents

It is not very easy to say anything about the purely "panegyric,"[47] except that all the elements which produce the finest, Platonic panegyric can, by their isolated predominance, produce a kind of panegyric mode: viz. solemnity by itself, simplicity, sweetness, purity, care, all the qualities mentioned above. Those ancient writers who have the highest reputation for panegyric evidently wrote in this manner. They form my present subject.

But first, some remarks by way of necessary preface. The best panegyric must possess grandeur with charm, ornament, and clarity, as well as realistic representation of character and all the other things discussed in our section on the panegyrrical style. Not only poetry and prose in general (*logographia*) possess these qualities. History has them in abundance. Historians must therefore definitely be placed among the panegyrists. They do indeed belong here, for their aims are grandeur and pleasure and all the other usual objects, even if they do not attain them in the same way as Plato. They must therefore be discussed here. First, however, we must proceed to writers distinguished in panegyric in the school of Plato, especially as some practised history as well as other sorts of prose-writing—for example, Xenophon, with whom I begin.

Xenophon is a particularly simple writer. He is stronger on this side than in the other aspects of the panegyric manner. He makes ample use of the pleasures of simplicity, rather more sparing use of the sweetness resulting, for example, from myths and the like. For example, in his pleasant account of dogs, he produces his effect by intensification of simplicity, not by anything naturally peculiar to sweetness.[48] On the other hand, the character and emotion in the story of Abradates and Panthea[49] acquire their great pleasurableness from the mythical fiction: similarly with Tigranes and his wife Armenia.[50] Such sweetnesses, as I said, he uses sparingly; but he does use them. He often touches grandeur in thought, but brings it down to earth and forces it into a simple mould by his methods, diction, and everything related to diction. Xenophon is as pure and distinct as any writer there is; he likes tartness and sharpness—qualities we discussed in connection with sweetness and simplicity. He shows great care and study, within the limits of a simple, unaffected style. Indeed, his simplicity is much simpler than Plato's, because it arises in the subject-matter, not only in the diction and accompanying qualities. Each wrote a *Symposium*: Xenophon does not refuse to describe—and with charm—entrances of dancing-girls, dance-figures, kisses, and so on. Plato "leaves all that to the women,"[51] to use his own phrase, and guides the simplicity of the subject in a more solemn direction. Xenophon maintains similar characteristics in his historical works. "They wore garlands of straw"; "they talked to the slaves as though they were deaf and dumb"; "they had to bend over the bowl and drink like cattle."[52] The charm of such passages is due to their surpassing simplicity, which Plato does not match. Xenophon also excels in the representation of persons, when he is concerned with simple, unaffected, tender, and pleasing characters, for instance the boy Cyrus. There is nothing like this in Plato, except what is to do with young boys—Theaetetus or some similar character—but this is not to be compared with the boy Cyrus, the lady Armenia, or the like. It is also a peculiarity of Xenophon to use at intervals poetical expressions which are by nature sharply distinguished from the rest of his diction—for example *porsunein* for "to provide."

Aeschines (the Socratic) may well come next after Xenophon. He too is an outstanding example of the simple writer, but he uses the pure and distinct manner even more than the simple. He is thus more delicate in diction than Xenophon, with (once again) a fair number of more solemn thoughts and a moderate use of the charms of fable and the fabulous. You might say he excels Xenophon in delicacy as much as Xenophon's simplicity excels that of Plato. He is much purer, and more careful than Xenophon, yet still within the limits of the simple manner.

Nicostratus,[53] who deserves or demands mention next, is as simple as any of these, but more delicate and pure. His style is exceptionally slight (*huperischnon*), with no grandeur except in the thought. He likes fables and their charms—indeed, he has invented many fables himself, and not only Aesopic ones but such as could be the subject of plays. He is extremely careful in arrangement, but without violating his simplicity . . .

I come next to the distinguished historians. The Olympic, Panathenaic, and indeed Panegyric speeches of Isocrates and Lysias—despite their title!—are clearly something different. They possess a certain panegyric element, such as a deliberative or forensic speech might admit, but even if they did belong to this category because (in particular) of Isocrates' artistry in word-order, what has been said of them in the discussion of deliberative and forensic orators still suffices. We must now discuss the historians other than Xenophon, whose style we have already considered.

The most panegryrical of the historical panegyrists, then, is Herodotus. This is because he abounds in charm as well as purity and distinctness. His thoughts are almost all mythical, his language is throughout poetical. He often displays grandeur of thought, but it is his care and the richness of his artistry that ensures the double achievement of grandeur and charm. Most of his rhythms in word-arrangements and clausulae are dactylic, anapaestic, spondaic, and in general solemn. His representations of character and emotion are among the finest and most poetical there are; this indeed is how he achieves so much grandeur, notably in Book 7 in the conversation of Xerxes with Artabanus and the latter's reply on human destiny.[54]

In approaching Thucydides, I have one preliminary point to make clear. That I mention him after Herodotus and the others carries no implication that I regard him as their inferior in literary skill and capacity. I should certainly not put Herodotus after Nicostratus or Aeschines, nor indeed after Xenophon, in terms of power and skill—especially as we are discussing the panegyric mode. I have simply followed the order dictated by the sequence of the discussion of this style, placing the historians in a separate category from the other panegyrists. I then placed Herodotus first among the historians, because he is more panegyrical and more charming not only than Thucydides but than any other practitioner in this manner. Of Thucydides indeed, it might be doubted into which category he falls; he is as much forensic and deliberative as panegyrical, in his thought and the elaboration with which he introduces every point. Let him however occupy his proper place, by genre and by his superiority to some and (it may be) inferiority to others in literary capacity. I shall merely describe him as he is.

Thucydides aims at grandeur, and he does in a sense achieve it—but not the grandeur that I think he wanted. He aims, I fancy, at solemnity, the proper quality of panegyrical grandeur, but he obviously goes too far in the direction of roughness, harshness, and hence obscurity. This is true especially of his diction, but also of his word-arrangement. He takes great trouble over artistic adornment, but here too aims at sublimity and great grandeur, with the result that he overshoots the mark in hyperbole and novel word-order—whence comes harshness, and then obscurity. He is extremely dignified, and his thought possesses a remarkable combination of the oratorical and the solemn. Nothing even in his historical narrative goes unelaborated.

In his "methods" or approaches, he is quite different. He introduces even his elaborations with some notable piece of grandeur or the like, and thus is almost wholly without sweetness. Where this does occur, it is conspicuously alien to the style: for instance "Tereus who took Procne the daughter of Pandion from Athens as his wife" etc.[55] Were there no such instances, one would have cause for surprise that his writing does sometimes achieve charm; virtually no other individual style, that chooses and perfects some particular manner, can appear pure without making at any rate some contact with all the other possible manners. As a historian, Thucydides employs representation (*mimēsis*) in his speeches and in some dialogues,[56] but he has the same characeristics here—indeed, they are even more marked. In his actual narrative he is less harsh and rough with many pure and distinct passages, far surpassing (in this and in much else) his teacher Antiphon.

Hecataeus of Miletus, from whom Herodotus learned much, is pure and lucid, and sometimes shows considerable charm. His pure, unmixed Ionic, without the variety of that of Herodotus, makes him less poetical in diction. Nor is he as studied or as ornamental in diction; his charms thus are far inferior to Herodotus', despite the fact that almost his whole subject is myth and narrative of that character. On the other hand, not only is his subject capable of giving rise to any kind of style, but his diction, and the features associated with diction—figures, cola, word-order, rhythm, clausulae—are well adapted to produce charm and sweetness like that of Herodotus, and indeed any other of the various kinds of writing. Hecataeus' inferiority, it seems, is thus due to his failure to take sufficient care about accuracy and ornament of diction.

It seemed unnecessary here to discuss Theopompus, Ephorus, Hellanicus, Philistus, and their like. For one thing, it is easy to characterize them on the basis of the theory of types, and of our discussion of individual authors. Secondly, their styles have, to the best of my knowledge, never been thought worthy of imitation or rivalry by Greeks, as have those of Thucydides, Herodotus, Hecataeus, Xenophon, and some others.

NOTES

1. Cf. "Longinus," p. 326.
2. The point depends on the range of meaning of *logos*, which includes both "word" and "reason": cf. "Longinus," p. 349.
3. Dem. 4. 15.
4. *Il.* 14. 346.
5. *Timaeus* 29e, 30a.
6. Cf. "Longinus," p. 348.
7. 2. 24.
8. *Timaeus* 58a.
9. An example from a second-century sophistic *suasoria*. This speech of Aristides is lost: see A. Boulanger, *Aelius Aristide*, Paris, 1923, 157, n. 1.
10. [Dem.] 25. 15–16; Dem. 18. 97.
11. Dem. 18. 242.
12. Herod. 8. 65.
13. Dem. 23. 70.
14. *Phaedrus* 246e.
15. *Timaeus* 28c, 29e, for these passages.
16. *Phaedrus* 244d.
17. Theocritus 15. 87ff.: the two women are talking in a crowd in a street in Alexandria.
18. Dem. 18. 97.
19. Dem. 18. 45.
20. Dem. 3. 31; 19. 6; 9. 22.
21. Gorgias: cf. "Longinus," p. 326.
22. Thuc. 3. 82.
23. 18. 35.
24. Plato, *Menexenus* 236d.
25. Dem. 18. 97.
26. Dem. 9. 20.
27. Thuc. 1. 9.
28. [Dem.] 25. 15.
29. Plato, *Phaedrus* 245c.
30. [Dem.] 25. 16.
31. Dem. 18. 1 ("to this contest").
32. [Dem.] 25. 15, quoted more than once already: "the whole life of man is governed by nature and by laws."
33. Dem. 19. 8.
34. Theocr. 3. 1.
35. Xenophon, *Cyropaedia* 1. 3. 2; 1. 4. 19.
36. Theocr. 1. 1.
37. Dem. 45. 74; 57. 31, 35.
38. Dem. 19. 287.
39. Dem. 18. 129.
40. 18. 260.
41. These passages are not in our Demosthenes MSS.: the obelizers have prevailed.
42. Xen. *Cyropaedia* 2. 3. 9.
43. Dem. 18. 51.

44. Dem. 18. 141, 1.
45. Dem. 19. 78.
46. Dem. 18. 208; cf. "Longinus," p. 338.
47. An extended sense of this term. Of the three branches of oratory—forensic, deliberative, epideictic or panegyric—the last can be regarded as in a sense covering also all non-oratorical prose; thus Hermogenes is able to regard Plato as the great "panegyrist," and history also as a species of "panegyric." The term here does not mean only "encomiastic."
48. *Cynegeticus*.
49. *Cyropaedia* 5. 1, 6. 1, 6. 4, 7. 3.
50. *Cyropaedia* 3. 1. 36.
51. Plato, *Symp.* 176e.
52. *Anabasis* 4. 5. 32.
53. A sophist and philosopher of the second century A.D. None of his works survive. The novel *Lucius or the Ass* has been attributed to him without solid reason (C. A. Behr, *Aelius Aristides*, Amsterdam, 1968, 13, n. 34).
54. 7. 46ff.
55. Thuc. 2. 29.
56. Notably the Melian Dialogue in Book 5.

Plotinus
205–c. 270

Plotinus is frequently considered the most powerful philosophic mind between Aristotle and Aquinas. His Neoplatonism was deeply influential throughout the Middle Ages although he was not a Christian. Porphyry, his student and friend, writes in his biography of the philosopher, "Plotinus . . . seemed ashamed of being in the body. So deeply rooted was this feeling that he could never be induced to tell of his ancestry, his parentage, or his birthplace." This reticence, while certainly true to the principles of his own Neoplatonism, makes it difficult to construct an accurate picture of his life. He wrote nothing until he was fifty, and even then only a series of essays intended primarily for circulation among his students. After his death, Porphyry collected and arranged these into six books of nine chapters each (hence the title Enneads, *which means "groups of nine").*

We do know that Plotinus was born in Egypt in 205 and that Greek was almost certainly his native tongue. He did not turn to the study of philosophy until he was twenty-eight, and then he studied at Alexandria for eleven years with Ammonius Saccas, a philosopher of whom even less is known than of Plotinus. In 242–43 he joined the emperor Gordian's unsuccessful expedition against Persia, hoping to learn something about Eastern thought. By the age of forty he had settled in Rome to teach philosophy. There he became the center of an influential group of intellectuals.

The Neoplatonic system Plotinus constructed follows Platonism in its metaphysical hierarchy, which favors unity over multiplicity, spirit over matter. "The One" occupies the highest place in this hierarchy. It is Being and the Good and the Beautiful, but it is past the power of the human mind and can only be conceived negatively. This "One" is a creative force that "overflows" through World-mind (nous), World-soul (psuche), and Nature (phusis) until it comes to Matter, which is the last and lowest emanation of creative power. That which does not participate in this creative emanation can have none of the attributes of Being, Beauty, or Goodness.

Plotinus significantly departs from Plato in his evaluation of art. Like Plato, he bases his aesthetics upon an Ideal Form, which is a unified essence of the Beautiful. But unlike Plato, who denigrates all art as merely a copy of copies, Plotinus rehabilitates art in metaphysical philosophy. He distinguishes two varieties of art. One is simply the imitation of imitation, a copy of mere Matter, while the other is a higher imitation which directly copies the emanations of "the One." About the former Plotinus is as harsh as Plato. He chooses to allegorize the myth of Narcissus as a cautionary tale of someone who fell for a beauty that was material rather than Ideal. "For if anyone follow what is like a beautiful shape playing over water—is there not a myth telling in symbol of such a dupe, how he sank into the depths of the current and was swept away to nothingness?" The other type of imitation does not imitate the particular material thing. Rather, it shapes from its inward vision of "the One." He writes:

> *Still the arts are not to be slighted on the ground that they create by imitation of natural objects; for, to begin with, these natural objects are themselves imitations; then, we must recognize that they (the arts) give no bare reproduction of the thing seen but go back to the Ideas from which nature derives, and furthermore, that much of their work is all their own; they are molders of beauty and add where nature is lacking. Thus Pheidias wrought the Zeus upon no model among things of sense but by apprehending what form Zeus must take if he chose to become manifest to sight.*

It is this revision of Plato's estimate of art which directly inspired many later defenses of poetry: the later Neoplatonists, St. Augustine, even the Schlegels in Germany and Coleridge and Shelley in England.

Plotinus spent his last years teaching and writing. In 269–70 he retired to Campania at the approach of death. According to Porphyry, a friend arrived at Plotinus' deathbed in his final hours: "Plotinus said, 'I have been a long time waiting for you; I am striving to give back the Divine in myself to the Divine in the All.' As he spoke a snake crept under the bed on which he lay and slipped away into a hole in the wall: at the same moment Plotinus died."

The selection from The Enneads, *translated by Stephen MacKenna, is reprinted by permission of Faber & Faber Ltd. from Stephen Mac-Kenna, trans.,* Plotinus: The Enneads.

FROM
The Enneads

Beauty

Beauty addresses itself chiefly to sight; but there is a beauty for the hearing (1.) too, as in certain combinations of words and in all kinds of music, for melodies and cadences are beautiful; and minds that lift themselves above the realm of sense to a higher order are aware of beauty in the conduct of life, in actions, in character, in the pursuits of the intellect; and there is the beauty of the virtues. What loftier beauty there may be, yet, our argument will bring to light.

What, then, is it that gives comeliness to material forms and draws the ear to the sweetness perceived in sounds, and what is the secret of the beauty there is in all that derives from soul?

Is there some one principle from which all take their grace, or is there a beauty peculiar to the embodied and another for the bodiless? Finally, one or many, what would such a principle be?

Consider that some things, material shapes for instance, are gracious not by anything inherent but by something communicated, while others are lovely of themselves, as, for example, virtue.

The same bodies appear sometimes beautiful, sometimes not; so that there is a good deal between being body and being beautiful.

What, then, is this something that shows itself in certain material forms? This is the natural beginning of our inquiry.

What is it that attracts the eyes of those to whom a beautiful object is presented, and calls them, lures them, towards it, and fills them with joy at the sight? If we possess ourselves of this, we have at once a standpoint for the wider survey.

Almost everyone declares that the symmetry of parts towards each other and towards a whole, with, besides, a certain charm of color, constitutes the beauty recognized by the eye, that in visible things, as indeed in all else, universally, the beautiful thing is essentially symmetrical, patterned.

But think what this means.

Only a compound can be beautiful, never anything devoid of parts; and only a whole; the several parts will have beauty, not in themselves, but only as working together to give a comely total. Yet beauty in an aggregate demands beauty in details: it cannot be constructed out of ugliness; its law must run throughout.

All the loveliness of color and even the light of the sun, being devoid of parts and so not beautiful by symmetry, must be ruled out of the realm of beauty. And how comes gold to be a beautiful thing? And lightning by night, and the stars, why are these so fair?

In sounds also the simple must be proscribed, though often in a whole noble composition each several tone is delicious in itself.

Again since the one face, constant in symmetry, appears sometimes fair and sometimes not, can we doubt that beauty is something more than symmetry, that symmetry itself owes its beauty to a remoter principle?

Turn to what is attractive in methods of life or in the expression of thought; are we to call in symmetry here? What symmetry is to be found in noble conduct, or excellent laws, in any form of mental pursuit?

What symmetry can there be in points of abstract thought?

The symmetry of being accordant with each other? But there may be accordance or entire identity where there is nothing but ugliness: the proposition that honesty is merely a generous artlessness chimes in the most perfect harmony with the proposition that morality means weakness of will; the accordance is complete.

Then again, all the virtues are a beauty of the soul, a beauty authentic beyond any of these others; but how does symmetry enter here? The soul, it is true, is not a simple unity, but still its virtue cannot have the symmetry of size or of number: what standard of measurement could preside over the compromise or the coalescence of the soul's faculties or purposes?

Finally, how by this theory would there be beauty in the intellectual-principle, essentially the solitary?

(2.) Let us, then, go back to the source, and indicate at once the principle that bestows beauty on material things.

Undoubtedly this principle exists; it is something that is perceived at the first glance, something which the soul names as from an ancient knowledge and, recognizing, welcomes it, enters into unison with it.

But let the soul fall in with the ugly and at once it shrinks within itself, denies the thing, turns away from it, not accordant, resenting it.

Our interpretation is that the soul—by the very truth of its nature, by its affiliation to the noblest existents in the hierarchy of being—when it sees anything of that kin, or any trace of that kinship, thrills with an immediate delight, takes its own to itself, and thus stirs anew to the sense of its nature and of all its affinity.

But, is there any such likeness between the loveliness of this world and the splendors in the supreme? Such a likeness in the particulars would make the two orders alike: but what is there in common between beauty here and beauty there?

We hold that all the loveliness of this world comes by communion in ideal-form.

All shapelessness whose kind admits of pattern and form, as long as it remains outside of reason and idea, is ugly by that very isolation from the divine reason-principle. And this is the absolute ugly: an ugly thing is something that has not been entirely mastered by pattern, that is by reason, the matter not yielding at all points and in all respects to ideal-form.

But where the ideal-form has entered, it has grouped and coordinated what from a diversity of parts was to become a unity: it has rallied confusion into co-operation: it has made the sum one harmonious coherence: for the idea is a unity and what it molds must come to unity as far as multiplicity may.

And on what has thus been compacted to unity, beauty enthrones itself, giving itself to the parts as to the sum: when it lights on some natural unity, a thing of like parts, then it gives itself to that whole. Thus, for an illustration, there is the beauty, conferred by craftsmanship, of all a house with all its parts, and the beauty which some natural quality may give to a single stone.

This, then, is how the material thing becomes beautiful—by communicating in the reason-principle that flows from the divine.

(3.) And the soul includes a faculty peculiarly addressed to beauty—one incomparably sure in the appreciation of its own, when soul entire is enlisted to support its judgment.

Or perhaps the faculty acts immediately, afirming the beautiful where it finds something accordant with the ideal-form within itself, using this idea as a canon of accuracy in its decision.

But what accordance is there between the material and that which antedates all matter?

On what principle does the architect, when he finds the house standing before him correspondent with his inner ideal of a house, pronounce it beautiful? Is it not that the house before him, the stones apart, is the inner idea stamped upon the mass of exterior matter, the indivisible exhibited in diversity?

So with the perceptive faculty: discerning in certain objects the ideal-form which has bound and controlled shapeless matter, opposed in nature to idea, seeing further stamped upon the common shapes some shape excellent above the common, it gathers into unity what still remains fragmentary, catches it up and carries it within, no longer a thing of parts, and presents it to the inner ideal-principle as something concordant and congenial, a natural friend: the joy here is like that of a good man who discerns in a youth the early signs of a virtue consonant with the achieved perfection within his own soul.

The beauty of color is also the outcome of a unification: it derives from shape, from the conquest of the darkness inherent in matter by the pouring-in of light, the unembodied, which is a rational-principle and an ideal-form.

Hence it is that fire itself is splendid beyond all material bodies, holding the rank of ideal-principle to the other elements, making ever upwards, the subtlest and sprightliest of all bodies, as very near to the unembodied; itself alone admitting no other, all the others penetrated by it: for they take warmth but this is never cold; it has color primally; they receive the form of color from it: hence the splendor of its light, the splendor that belongs to the idea. And all that has resisted and is but uncertainly held by its light remains outside of beauty, as not having absorbed the plenitude of the form of color.

And harmonies unheard in sound create the harmonies we hear and wake the soul to the consciousness of beauty, showing it the one essence in another kind: for the measures of our sensible music are not arbitrary but are determined by the principle whose labor is to dominate matter and bring pattern into being.

Thus far of the beauties of the realm of sense, images and shadow-pictures, fugitives that have entered into matter—to adorn, and to ravish, where they are seen.

(4.) But there are earlier and loftier beauties than these. In the sense-bound life we are no longer granted to know them, but the soul, taking no help from the organs, sees and proclaims them. To the vision of these we must mount, leaving sense to its own low place.

As it is not for those to speak of the graceful forms of the material world who have never seen them or known their grace—men born blind, let us suppose—in the same way those must be silent upon the beauty of noble conduct and of learning and all that order who have never cared for such things, nor may those tell of the splendor of virtue who have never known the face of justice and of moral-wisdom beautiful beyond the beauty of evening and of dawn.

Such vision is for those only who see with the soul's sight—and at the vision, they will rejoice, and awe will fall upon them and a trouble deeper than all the rest could ever stir, for now they are moving in the realm of truth.

This is the spirit that beauty must ever induce, wonderment and a delicious trouble, longing and love and a trembling that is all delight. For the unseen all this may be felt as for the seen; and this the souls feel for it, every soul in some degree, but those the more deeply that are the more truly apt to this higher love—just as all take delight in the beauty of the body but all are not stung as sharply, and those only that feel the keener wound are known as lovers.

(5.) These lovers, then, lovers of the beauty outside of sense, must be made to declare themselves.

What do you feel in presence of the grace you discern in actions, in manners, in sound morality, in all the works and fruits of virtue, in the beauty of souls? When you see that you yourselves are beautiful within, what do you feel? What is this Dionysiac exultation that thrills through your being, this straining upwards of all your soul, this longing to break away from the body and live sunken within the veritable self?

These are no other than the emotions of souls under the spell of love.

On the Intellectual Beauty

(1.) It is a principle with us that one who has attained to the vision of the intellectual cosmos and grasped the beauty of the authentic intellect will be able also to come to understand the father and transcendent of that divine being. It concerns us, then, to try to see and say, for ourselves and as far as such matters may be told, how the beauty of the divine intellect and of the intellectual cosmos may be revealed to contemplation.

Let us go to the realm of magnitudes:—suppose two blocks of stone lying side by side: one is unpatterned, quite untouched by art; the other has been minutely wrought by the craftsman's hands into some statue of god or man, a Grace or a Muse, or if a human being, not a portrait but a creation in which the sculptor's art has concentrated all loveliness.

Now it must be seen that the stone thus brought under the artist's hand to the beauty of form is beautiful not as stone—for so the crude block would be as pleasant—but in virtue of the form or idea introduced by the art. This form is not in the material; it is in the designer before ever it enters the stone; and the artificer holds it not by his equipment of eyes and hands but by his participation in his art. The beauty, therefore, exists in a far higher state in the art; for it does not come over integrally into the work; that original beauty is not transferred; what comes over is a derivative and a minor: and even that shows itself upon the statue not integrally and with entire realization of intention but only in so far as it has subdued the resistance of the material.

Art, then, creating in the image of its own nature and content, and working by the idea or reason-principle of the beautiful object it is to produce, must itself be beautiful in a far higher and purer degree since it is the seat and source of that beauty, indwelling in the art, which must naturally be more complete than any comeliness of the external. In the degree in which the beauty is diffused by entering into matter, it is so much the weaker than that concentrated in unity; everything that reaches outwards is the less for it, strength less strong, heat less hot, every power less potent, and so beauty less beautiful.

Then again every prime cause must be, within itself, more powerful than its effect can be: the musical does not derive from an unmusical source but from music; and so the art exhibited in the material work derives from an art yet higher.

Still the arts are not to be slighted on the ground that they create by imitation of natural objects; for, to begin with, these natural objects are themselves imitations; then, we must recognize that they give no bare reproduction of the thing seen but go back to the reason-principles from which nature itself derives, and, furthermore, that much of their work is all their own; they are holders of beauty and add where nature is lacking. Thus Pheidias wrought the Zeus upon no model among things of sense but by apprehending what form Zeus must take if he chose to become manifest to sight.

(2.) But let us leave the arts and consider those works produced by nature and admitted to be naturally beautiful which the creations of art are charged with imitating, all reasoning life and unreasoning things alike, but especially the consummate among them, where the molder and maker has subdued the material and given the form he desired. Now what is the beauty here? It has nothing to do with the blood or the menstrual process: either there is also a color and form apart from all this or there is nothing unless sheer ugliness or (at best) a bare recipient as it were the mere matter of beauty.

Whence shone forth the beauty of Helen, battle-sought; or of all those women like in loveliness to Aphrodite; or of Aphrodite herself; or of any human being that has been perfect in beauty; or of any of these gods manifest to sight, or unseen but carrying what would be beauty if we saw?

In all these is it not the form-idea, something of that realm but communicated to the produced from within the producer, just as in works of art, we held, it is communicated from the arts to their creations? Now we can surely not believe that, while the made thing and the reason-principle thus impressed upon matter are beautiful, yet the principle not so alloyed but resting still with the creator—the idea primal and immaterial—is not beauty.

If material extension were in itself the ground of beauty, then the creating principle, being without extension, could not be beautiful: but beauty cannot be made to depend upon magnitude since, whether in a large object or a small, the one idea equally moves and forms the mind by its inherent power. A further indication is that as long as the object remains outside us we know nothing of it; it affects us by entry; but only as an ideal-form can it enter through the eyes which are not of scope to take an extended mass: we are, no doubt, simultaneously possessed of the magnitude which, however, we take in not as mass but an elaboration upon the presented form.

Then again the principle producing the beauty must be, itself, ugly, neutral, or beautiful: ugly, it could not produce the opposite; neutral, why should its product be the one rather than the other? The nature, then, which creates things so lovely must be itself of a far earlier beauty; we, undisciplined in discernment of the inward, knowing nothing of it, run after the outer, never understanding that it is the inner which stirs us; we are in the case of one who sees his own reflection but not realizing whence it comes goes in pursuit of it.

Euanthius and Donatus

fourth-century A.D.

Euanthius' On Drama *and Donatus'* On Comedy *represented for the Middle Ages the primary sources of information concerning the historical development of the classic drama. The two essays are grouped together both because of the similarity of subject matter and because both essays were attributed to Donatus throughout the Middle Ages.*

Very little is known about Euanthius, the fourth-century grammarian (the Middle Ages followed Quintilian's definition of grammar as "the science of correct speaking and the reading of poets"). He was the author of a commentary on Terence, of which On Drama *is the only section which remains. Tiberius Claudius Donatus, on the other hand, was the best-known grammarian of the Middle Ages. His two* artes *(works concerning the form and function of language), the* Ars Minor *and the* Ars Major *were standard textbooks throughout the Middle Ages. The term "donet," meaning a Latin grammar, became a common noun in Middle English. In addition, he composed commentaries on Vergil and Terence which heavily influenced medieval understanding of those authors. Both Euanthius and Donatus were important links between Roman antiquity and the Middle Ages, ensuring a continuation of the classical tradition throughout the Middle Ages.*

Both essays provide the standard etymologies of tragedy and comedy, drawing upon Horace's Ars Poetica. *Tragedy arose from Bacchic festivals and comedy from festivals to Apollo. In Euanthius'* On Drama, *Terence emerges from the history as the foremost Latin comic poet. His essay is perhaps most important because in distinguishing between tragedy and comedy he makes no reference to staging. Thus, later medieval writers could think of tragedy and comedy as poems to be recited rather than plays to be acted, and we thus have the "tragedies" narrated by Chaucer's Monk and Dante's defense of the "comic" nature of* The Divine Comedy *in the* Letter to Can Grande della Scala.

On Drama *and* On Comedy, *translated by O. B. Hardison, Jr., are reprinted by permission of the publisher from Alex Preminger et al., eds.,* Classical and Medieval Literary Criticism: Translations and Interpretations *(New York: Frederick Ungar Publishing Co., 1974).*

ON DRAMA

Tragedy and comedy began in religious ceremonies which the ancients held to give thanks for a good harvest.

The sort of song which the sacred chorus offered to Father Bacchus when the altars had been kindled and the sacrificial goat brought in was called tragedy. This is from *apo tou tragou kai tes oides*—that is, from "goat," an enemy of vineyards, and from "song." There is a full reference to this in Vergil's *Georgics* [2. 380ff.], either because the poet of this sort of song was given a goat, or because a goatskin full of new wine was the usual reward to the singers; or else because the players used to smear their faces with wine-lees prior to the introduction of masks by Aeschylus. "Wine-lees" in Greek is *truges*. And the word "tragedy" was invented for these reasons.

But while the Athenians were not yet confined to the city and Apollo was called "Nomius" [shepherd] and "Aguieus" [guardian]—that is, guardian of shepherds and villages—they erected altars for divine worship around the hamlets, farms, villages, and crossroads of Attica and solemnly chanted a festival song to him. It was called comedy *apo ton komon kai tes oides*—the name composed, as I think, from "villages" [*komai*] and "song" [*oide*]. Or else it was composed *apo tou komazein kai aidein*—going to a revel singing. This is not unlikely since the comic chorus was drunk or engaged in love making on the sacred day.

And once the historical sequence has been established, it is clear that tragedy appeared first. For man moved little by little from barbarism and brutality to a civilized condition. Later towns were founded and life became more mild and easier. Thus the matter of tragedy was discovered long before the matter of comedy.

Thespis is thought to be the inventor of tragedy by those who study ancient history. And Eupolis, along with Cratinus and Aristophanes, is thought to be the father of old comedy. But Homer, who is, as it were, the copious fountainhead of all poetry, provided exemplars for these sorts of poetry and established almost a law for their composition. We know that he wrote the *Iliad* in the form of a tragedy and that the *Odyssey* has the form of a comedy. In the beginning such poems were crude and not all polished and graceful as they later became. And after Homer's excellent and copious work they were regularized in their structure and parts by clever imitators.

Now that we have discussed the early history of the two forms in order to determine their origin, let us proceed to necessary matters. But, keeping within the limits of the title of this work, we will defer those subjects that are proper to tragedy for a later time, and will talk of the sorts of drama that Terence imitated.

Old comedy, like tragedy, was once simply a song, as we previously observed. The chorus sang it to a flute accompaniment while grouped around the smoking altar. At times the chorus walked, at times stood still, and at times it danced in circles. Then one character was taken from the group who spoke to the group, each taking alternate turns—that is, . . . [lacuna; perhaps the Greek word *amoibaios*, "alternately"]—and with a different melody. Then there appeared a second and a third character; and at length, as the number of characters was increased by various authors, masks and *pallia* [robes] began to be used, and boots and the comic sock and the other adornments and costumes used by the actors. Eventually, each type of character came to have his own costume. Finally, as there were actors who played in the first part, the second, the third, the fourth, and the fifth, the whole drama was divided into five acts.

While comedy was still, as it were, in its cradle and had hardly begun, it was called *archaia komoidia* and *ep'onomatos*, because it was "old" [*archaia*] in comparison to what has been discovered more recently. And *ep'onomatos* [by name] because the fable has, as it were, the historical validity of a true story, and real citizens are named and freely described.

The early poets, unlike the moderns, did not write fictional plots but wrote openly about things which citizens had done, often using real names. This was very beneficial to the morals of the society since every citizen avoided immorality in order not to become a public spectacle and a disgrace to his family. But as the poets came to use their pens with greater license and began to pillory good men right and left just for the fun of it, they were silenced by a law forbidding anyone from writing a poem slandering another person.

From this situation a new type of drama, satyr play, originated. "Satyr play" derived its name from satyrs, who are, as we know, supernatural beings always involved in games and wanton sports, although some wrongly think the word has a different derivation. Satyr play took the form of a poem which, through the device of crude and, as it were, rustic jesting, attacked the vices of citizens without mentioning specific names. This species of comedy was damaging to many poets since they were suspected by powerful citizens of making their deeds worse than they really were, and of disgracing the upper class by their manner of writing. Lucilius began composing this kind of poem in a new way, and he wrote "poesy"—that is, a single poem in several books.

Forced by the abuses already mentioned to give up satyr play, poets invented another kind of poem—*nea komoidia*—that is, "new comedy." This kind of poem was concerned with more typical situations and in general terms with men who live a middle-class life. It gave the spectator less bitterness and more pleasure, being close-knit in plot, true to life in characterization, useful in its sentiments, delightful for its wit, and apt in its prosody. Just as those earlier works were celebrated for their authors, so new comedy is the work of many earlier and later writers, and especially Menander and Terence.

Although a great deal can be said about these matters, it will be enough to instruct the reader, to summarize what the writings of the ancients say about the comic art. Old comedy consisted in the beginning of the chorus. Little by little it expanded, by increasing the number of characters, into five acts. Eventually, as the chorus was reduced and thinned out, it came about that in new comedy the chorus is not only not brought onstage, but there is not even a place left for it. As times became more leisurely, the audience grew more sophisticated and as the play changed from the acted part to the singing the spectators began to grow restless and leave. The poets learned from this and reduced the choral part, leaving almost no place for it. Menander left out the chorus for this reason and not for another, as some other writers think. Eventually the poets did not leave any place at all for the chorus. The Latin comic poets wrote in this way, and this is why it is difficult to decide where the divisions of the five acts occur in the plays.

Moreover the Greeks do not have prologues, which we Latins customarily include. Like the Greeks, all the Latin writers but Terence have *theoi apo mechanes*—that is, "gods from a machine"—to narrate stories. Besides, the other comic writers do not readily admit *protatika prosopa*—that is, characters drawn from outside the plot—while Terence often uses them since the plot becomes clearer through introducing them.

The ancient poets were rather careless in meter, demanding only an iamb in the second and fourth place. But they are outdone by Terence, who, by relaxing the meter, reduced it as far as possible to the nature of prose.

As for the laws of characterization in respect to moral habits, age, station in life, and type roles, no one was more diligent than Terence. He alone dared—since verisimilitude is required in fiction—to defy the comic prescriptions, and at times to introduce prostitutes who were not evil. There is both a reason given for their goodness and the fact itself gives a certain pleasure.

Terence did these things most artistically, and it is especially admirable that he kept within the bounds of comedy and tempered the emotional element so that he did not slide over into tragedy. This effect, along with others, was seldom achieved, we observe, by Plautus and Afranius and Appius and the many other comic poets. Among the other virtues, it is also admirable that Terence's plays are so well controlled in style that they neither swell up to tragic elevation nor degenerate into the baseness of mime.

Add that Terence never brings in abstruse material or things that have to be glossed by antiquaries, as Plautus often does, and that Plautus is more obscure than Terence in many places. Add that Terence is careful about plot and style; that he always avoided or was very circumspect about topics that could give offense; and that he joined the beginning, middle, and end so carefully that nothing seems extraneous and everything appears to be composed from the same material and to have a single body.

It is also admirable that he never brings four characters together in such a way that their differences are unclear. And further, that he never has a character address the audience directly, as though outside the comedy, which is a frequent vice of Plautus. It also seems laudable, among other things, that he chose to make his story more full by means of double plots. Except for *Hecyra*, which deals with the love of Pamphilus alone, the other five comedies have two young couples.

It is clear that after new comedy the Latins developed many kinds of drama. For example, the *togata*, based on Roman events and stories; the *praetextata*, from the dignity of its noble characters taken from Roman history; the *Atellana*, from the town of Campania where this kind of drama was first acted; the

Rinthonica, from the name of the author; the *tabernaria* from the lowness of the plot and style, and the *mime* from constant imitation of base subject matter and wanton characters.

Of the many differences between tragedy and comedy, the foremost are these: In comedy the fortunes of men are middle-class, the dangers are slight, and the ends of the actions are happy; but in tragedy everything is the opposite—the characters are great men, the fears are intense, and the ends disastrous. In comedy the beginning is troubled, the end tranquil; in tragedy events follow the reverse order. And in tragedy the kind of life is shown that is to be shunned; while in comedy the kind is shown that is to be sought after. Finally, in comedy the story is always fictitious; while tragedy often has a basis in historical truth.

Latin dramas were first written by Livius Andronicus. The form was so new that he was both the author of his dramas and acted in them.

Comedies are either "active" or "quiet" or "mixed." The "active" are more turbulent, the "quite" are more tranquil, and the "mixed" have elements of both.

Comedy is divided into four parts: prologue, protasis, epitasis, and catastrophe. The prologue is a kind of preface to the drama. In this part and this part only it is permissible to say something extrinsic to the argument, addressed to the audience and for the benefit of the poet or the drama or an actor. The protasis is the first act and the beginning of the drama. The epitasis is the development and enlargement of the conflict and, as it were, the knot of all the error. The catastrophe is the resolution of the course of events so that there is a happy ending which is made evident to all by the recognition of past events.

On Comedy

Comedy is a form of drama dealing with the various qualities and conditions of civil and private persons. Through it one learns what is useful in life and what, on the contrary, is to be avoided. The Greeks define it as follows: "Comedy deals with the acts of private persons in a story that lacks serious danger." Comedy, says Cicero, is "an imitation of life, a mirror of character, and an image of truth."

Comedy received its name from an ancient custom. In early times this kind of song was sung "in the villages" [*apo tes komes*]—as is the case with the "crossroads festivals" [*compitalia*] in Italy. A term was added for the spoken part with which the audience was entertained during the changing of the events. That is, they were held by the acting out of the lives of men who live "in the villages" because of the middle state of their fortunes, not in royal palaces like the characters of tragedy. And comedy, because it is written to imitate life and character with verisimilitude, employs gesture and speech.

No-one knows who invented comedy among the Greeks. The Roman inventor is known. Livius Andronicus was the first Roman to write comedy, tragedy, and *fabula togata*. He said comedy is "a mirror of daily life" and the observation is just. When we gaze into a mirror we readily see the features of truth by means of the reflection. Likewise, by reading comedy we readily discover the image of life and custom.

The original concept came in from foreign cities and with foreign customs. When the Athenians, the guardians of Attic propriety, wanted to rebuke anyone for an immoral life, they used to gather together from all sides, happily and eagerly, at the villages and crossroads. There they used to describe the vices of individuals publicly and with proper names. Comedy was named from this custom.

At first they sang their songs in grassy meadows. And there was no lack of prizes to incite the wits of the more learned to writing. And gifts were offered to the actors to encourage them freely to use pleasing modulations of voice to gain sweet commendation. A goat [*tragos*] was given to them as a reward, because the animal was considered an enemy of vineyards. From this custom the name "tragedy" arose. Many authorities, however, prefer the idea that "tragedy" was derived from *amurca*—that is, oil-lees—which has a watery quality, the word being suggested by "trygodia" [from Greek *truges*, "lees"].

Since these revels were performed at ceremonies in honor of Father Bacchus, the writers of tragedy and comedy began to worship and venerate the spirit of this god as though he were present. This is the probable explanation of the matter: these primitive songs were written for the purpose of setting forth and celebrating the fame and glorious deeds of Bacchus.

Little by little the reputation of this art form grew. Thespis first brought it to the attention of all. Aeschylus wrote next, following the example of his predecessor. On these matters, Horace writes in the *Ars Poetica:*

> Thespis is said to have invented tragedy, a type unknown previously, and to have carried his plays around in carts, to be performed by actors whose faces were smeared with wine-lees. After him came Aeschylus, who introduced the tragic mask and robe. He designed a stage built of small planks and taught the players to speak in a grand manner and wear the tragic buskin. Then came old comedy, which won popular praise, but the freedom it employed degenerated into excess and violence that had to be restrained by law. Prevented from attacking people's characters, the chorus lapsed into shamed silence. The Latin poets have left no style untried. Nor do those poets deserve the least honor who dared to forsake the track laid out by the Greeks and celebrate the deeds of their own country, whether in the tragedy *praetexta* or the *togata* form of comedy. [*Ars Poetica*, 274–88]

Drama is a general term. Its two chief parts are tragedy and comedy. Tragedy, if it concerns Roman subjects, is called *praetexta*. Comedy has many species. It is *palliata* or *togata* or *tabernaria* or *Atellana* or *mime* or *Rinthonica* or *planipedia*.

Planipedia is named from the baseness of the subject matter and the lowness of the actors, who do not act on a stage or platform in the boot or sock, but act "in bare feet"—or else because the subject matter does not include things appropriate for people living in houses with towers and large halls, but only things appropriate for those in low and humble places.

They say that Cincius Faliscus was the first to use masks in comedy, and in tragedy, Minucius Prothymus.

The titles of all comedies are taken from four areas: name, place, deed, and result. Names as exemplified in the *Phormio, Hecyra, Cruculio,* and *Epidicus*. Places in the *Andria, Leucadia,* and *Brundisina*. Deeds in the *Eunuchus, Asinaria,* and *Captivi*. Result in the *Commorientes, Crimen,* and *Heautontimorumenos*.

There are three forms of comedy. *Palliata* uses Greek dress; *togata* exhibits the sort of people who wear a Roman toga—many people call this form *tabernaria*—; and the *Atellana* which is based on wit and jests that have no value except their antiquity.

Comedies are divided into four parts: prologue, protasis, epitasis, and catastrophe. Prologue is the first speech, so called from Greek *protos logos* ["first word" or "first speech"] preceding the complication of the plot proper [*ho pro tou dramatos logos*]. There are four types. There is the *sustatikos*—the "commendatory"—where the poet or the story is praised. Then the *epitimetikos*—the "relative" prologue—where the poet either curses some rival or praises the audience. Then the *dramatikos*—"relating to the story"—which explains the argument of the drama. And there is the *miktos*—"mixed"—which includes all these things.

There is this difference according to some between a *prologue* and a *prologium:* a *prologue* is where the poet is vindicated or the story praised. A *prologium,* however, says something about the story.

Protasis is the first action of the drama, where part of the story is explained, part held back to arouse suspense among the audience. *Epitasis* is the complication of the story, by excellence of which its elements are intertwined. *Catastrophe* is the unravelling of the story, through which the outcome is demonstrated.

In most dramas the title came before the name of the author; in several the authors were named before the dramas. In ancient times there was a diversity of practice. For when men first presented dramas to the public, the titles were announced before the poet to prevent his being discouraged because of hostility. But when the poets had gained reputations as a result of presenting many dramas, then their names came first so that the name might draw attention to the drama.

It is clear that plays were presented at various kinds of games. There are four kinds of games which the officials provide for the public: the Megalenses, dedicated to the major gods, whom the Greeks call *megaloi* ["great"]; the *Funebres,* devised to draw the attention of the people while funeral ceremonies in honor of some noble person were performed; the *Plebei,* held for the benefit of the people; and the *Apollinares,* in honor of Apollo.

Usually, two altars were placed on the stage. The right one was sacred to Bacchus. The left was sacred to the god whose games are being celebrated. Thus Terence says in the *Andria:* "Take some consecrated boughs from the altar" [4.3.724].

They always have Ulysses wear a *pilleus* [cap] either because he once feigned madness so that he would not be recognized and forced to go to war, or because of his singular wisdom which often made him a protection and aid to his companions. He had a special talent for deception. Many commentators note that the inhabitants of Ithaca wore the *pilleus,* as do the Locrians. The costumes of Achilles and Neoptolemus include diadems although neither hero ever possessed the royal sceptre. Proof of this is the fact that they never joined the other Greek youths in the sacred oath to wage war on the Trojans, nor were they ever under the command of Agamemnon.

Old men in comedy wear a white costume, because white is associated with old age. Youths wear a varicolored costume. Slaves in comedy are clothed in a short garment in token of their age-old poverty, or so that their actions will be unencumbered. Parasites come on with a *pallium* [cloak] wrapped around them. The successful man has a white garment; the unlucky man wears an old one; the rich man a purple one; the poor man a Phoenician [reddish-purple] robe. A soldier wears a short purple cloak. A girl wears a foreign costume. A pimp wears a cloak of various colors; a prostitute wears a yellow one symbolizing greed.

Syrmata [robes with a long train] are named from the fact that they are dragged along the ground—this garment was invented by the luxurious Ionians. When worn by characters in mourning they symbolize carelessness resulting from self-neglect. Embroidered *aulaea* [curtains] are also spread out in front of the stage. This ornate decoration was taken from Attalus' palace in Pergamum all the way to Rome. Later, a *siparium* [comic drop-curtain] was used instead of *aulaea*. There was also a mimer's curtain used to block off the audience's view while the scene was being changed.

The actors spoke their lines in iambic dialogue, but the songs had melodies invented not by the poet but by a skillful musician. And a single song did not have a single melody. Rather, the melodies were often varied, and this is indicated by three numbers used to mark the comedies. These different numbers indicate the varying melodies of the song. The name of the musician who composed the melodies was placed at the beginning of the drama following the names of the author and principal actor.

Songs of this kind were played on flutes. When they were heard many of the spectators could tell what drama the players were going to present, even before the title was announced. The songs were played by matched flutes for the right and left hand, and by unmatched flutes. The flutes for the right hand played grave music and foreshadowed the serious kind of comedy. Those for the left hand foreshadowed the sportive kind of comedy by their high pitch. And when the drama called for flute playing for both right and left hands, both seriousness and sport were foreshadowed.

St. Augustine
354–430

St. Augustine has been called "a great sinner who became a great saint," although his Confessions probably exaggerates the extent of his depravity. His influence in the development of early Christianity was immense, because of his ability to synthesize the new religion with ancient learning. He became the standard for Christian intellectual inquiry in the centuries following his death.

Augustine was born to a Christian mother and a pagan father in what is now part of Algeria. In preparation for a career in public life, his father sent him to study in Carthage. He recalled reading the Scriptures during the course of his studies, but considered them simple-minded in comparison to the polished rhetoric of Cicero. In Carthage he had a mistress and a son, Adeodatus, both of whom he seems to have treated well throughout his life. During that same period, at the age of eighteen, he became associated with the Manichees, a proscribed sect which had been founded by Manes (or Mani) before his crucifixion in Persia in 277. The sect had gained both notoriety and popularity throughout much of the Mediterranean world. Its followers believed in a universe inhabited by forces of light and darkness engaged in constant struggle, and considered the flesh abhorrent. Augustine, however, grew increasingly dissatisfied with the Manichean doctrine, and began to read the Neoplatonists. In 384, though not yet a Christian, he journeyed to Milan in order to attend the sermons of St. Ambrose. Two years later he converted to Christianity.

In 396 Augustine was consecrated assistant Bishop of Hippo to Valerius, who died a year later, leaving Augustine as Bishop. In 396-7 he completed his Confessions, inaugurating a torrent of intellectual activity. He wrote 118 treatises as an apologist for Christianity, many of them directly attacking the Manicheans. The sack of Rome by Alaric and the Goths in 410 prompted Augustine to write City of God in response to the claims that Christianity and the loss of faith in pagan gods led to the fall of the city. The book became the first great statement of a coherent Christian political and philosophical system. In 428 the Vandals invaded North Africa, and Augustine died during the fourth month of their seige at Hippo, in August 430.

On Christian Doctrine is the work in which Augustine deals with the problem of a specifically Christian hermeneutics. It was begun around 396, and in 427 he revised and added to the text. The historical situation which informs the work is one in which Christianity had begun the process of supplanting pagan culture, creating the problem for Christian theorists of how to utilize pagan culture to Christian ends. Augustine called pagan literature "Egyptian gold," indicating his belief in the utility of such texts. The phrase alludes to the exodus from Egypt, in which the Hebrews were allowed to carry away the gold of their pagan masters as they fled. Augustine's defense of allegorical interpretation, originally developed by Philo of Alexandria, the Jewish Hellenistic philosopher, allowed Christian intellectuals to "circulate" the "gold" by re-interpreting the classic texts in order to appropriate them to a Christian meaning. The allegorical method, says Augustine, enables the interpreter to apprehend the "invisible things of God," or the spiritual meaning, within "the things which are made," which are the pagan texts themselves. This mode of interpretation ushers in a whole tradition of exegesis in which very obscure, "hidden" interpretations are often plucked from the text. The whole tradition of "Christianizing" the work of Vergil is just one example. It is Augustine who points out just how much is at stake for the Christian interpreter. "But following certain traces he may come to the hidden sense without any error, or at least he will not fall into the absurdity of wicked meanings."

Closely related to his work upon allegorical interpretation is his development of a theory of language which has deeply influenced Western ideas of how the process of signification works. In Augustine's system the individual word or phrase is of value only as it points outside itself toward a "signified" meaning. "Sign" is associated with the material and the temporal while the "signified" becomes the spiritual and atemporal (something like the realm of unchanging Ideas), inserting a Christian Platonism into the theory of language.

Augustine is really the father of Christian philosophy and learning. Both his Christian hermeneutics and theory of language provided the framework for humanistic studies throughout the Middle Ages and have remained the basis for much Christian thinking up to our own time.

The selection from On Christian Doctrine, *translated by D. W. Robertson, is reprinted by permission of Bobbs-Merrill Educational Publishing.*

ON CHRISTIAN DOCTRINE

Book II

I

1. Just as I began, when I was writing about things, by warning that no one should consider them except as they are, without reference to what they signify beyond themselves, now when I am discussing signs I wish it understood that no one should consider them for what they are but rather for their value as signs which signify something else. A sign is a thing which causes us to think of something beyond the impression the thing itself makes upon the senses. Thus if we see a track, we think of the animal that made the track; if we see smoke, we know that there is a fire which causes it; if we hear the voice of a living being, we attend to the emotion it expresses; and when a trumpet sounds, a soldier should know whether it is necessary to advance or to retreat, or whether the battle demands some other response.

2. Among signs, some are natural and others are conventional. Those are natural which, without any desire or intention of signifying, make us aware of something beyond themselves, like smoke which signifies fire. It does this without any will to signify, for even when smoke appears alone, observation and memory of experience with things bring a recognition of an underlying fire. The track of a passing animal belongs to this class, and the face of one who is wrathful or sad signifies his emotion even when he does not wish to show that he is wrathful or sad, just as other emotions are signified by the expression even when we do not deliberately set out to show them. But it is not proposed here to discuss signs of this type. Since the class formed a division of my subject, I could not disregard it completely, and this notice of it will suffice.

II

3. Conventional signs are those which living creatures show to one another for the purpose of conveying, in so far as they are able, the motion of their spirits or something which they have sensed or understood. Nor is there any other reason for signifying, or for giving signs, except for bringing forth and transferring to another mind the action of the mind in the person who makes the sign. We propose to consider and to discuss this class of signs in so far as men are concerned with it, for even signs given by God and contained in the Holy Scriptures are of this type also, since they were presented to us by the men who wrote them. Animals also have signs which they use among themselves, by means of which they indicate their appetites. For a cock who finds food makes a sign with his voice to the hen so that she runs to him. And the dove calls his mate with a cry or is called by her in turn, and there are many similar examples which may be adduced. Whether these signs, or the expression or cry of a man

in pain, express the motion of the spirit without intention of signifying or are truly shown as signs is not in question here and does not pertain to our discussion, and we remove this division of the subject from this work as superfluous.

III

4. Among the signs by means of which men express their meanings to one another, some pertain to the sense of sight, more to the sense of hearing, and very few to the other senses. For when we nod, we give a sign only to the sight of the person whom we wish by that sign to make a participant in our will. Some signify many things through the motions of their hands, and actors give signs to those who understand with the motions of all their members as if narrating things to their eyes. And banners and military standards visibly indicate the will of the captains. And all of these things are like so many visible words. More signs, as I have said, pertain to the ears, and most of these consist of words. But the trumpet, the flute, and the harp make sounds which are not only pleasing but also significant, although as compared with the number of verbal signs the number of signs of this kind are few. For words have come to be predominant among men for signifying whatever the mind conceives if they wish to communicate it to anyone. However, Our Lord gave a sign with the odor of the ointment with which His feet were anointed;[1] and the taste of the sacrament of His body and blood signified what He wished;[2] and when the woman was healed by touching the hem of His garment,[3] something was signified. Nevertheless, a multitude of innumerable signs by means of which men express their thoughts is made up of words. And I could express the meaning of all signs of the type here touched upon in words, but I would not be able at all to make the meanings of words clear by these signs.

IV

5. But because vibrations in the air soon pass away and remain no longer than they sound, signs of words have been constructed by means of letters. Thus words are shown to the eyes, not in themselves but through certain signs which stand for them. These signs could not be common to all peoples because of the sin of human dissension which arises when one people seizes the leadership for itself. A sign of this pride is that tower erected in the heavens where impious men deserved that not only their minds but also their voices should be dissonant.[4]

V

6. Thus it happened that even the Sacred Scripture, by which so many maladies of the human will are cured, was set forth in one language, but so that it could be spread conveniently through all the world it was scattered far and wide in the various languages of translators that it might be known for the salvation of peoples who desired to find in it nothing more than the thoughts and desires of those who wrote it and through these the will of God, according to which we believe those writers spoke.

VI

7. But many and varied obscurities and ambiguities deceive those who read casually, understanding one thing instead of another; indeed, in certain places they do not find anything to interpret erroneously, so obscurely are certain sayings covered with a most dense mist. I do not doubt that this situation was provided by God to conquer pride by work and to combat disdain in our minds, to which those things which are easily discovered seem frequently to become worthless. For example, it may be said that there are holy and perfect men with whose lives and customs as an exemplar the Church of Christ is able to destroy all sorts of superstitions in those who come to it and to incorporate them into itself, men of good faith, true servants of God, who, putting aside the burden of the world, come to the holy laver of baptism and, ascending thence, conceive through the Holy Spirit and produce the fruit of a twofold love of God and their neighbor. But why is it, I ask, that if anyone says this he delights his hearers less than if he had said the same thing in expounding that place in the Canticle of Canticles where it is said of the Church, as she is being praised as a beautiful women, "Thy teeth are as flocks of sheep, that are shorn, which come up from the washing, all with twins, and there is none barren among them"?[5] Does one learn anything else besides that which he learns when he hears the same thought expressed in plain words without this similitude? Nevertheless, in a strange way, I contemplate the saints more pleasantly when I envisage them as the teeth of the Church cutting off men from their errors and transferring them to her body after their hardness has been softened as if by being bitten and chewed. I recognize them most pleasantly as shorn sheep having put aside the burdens of the world like so much fleece, and as ascending from the washing, which is baptism, all to create twins, which are the two precepts of love, and I see no one of them sterile of this holy fruit.

8. But why it seems sweeter to me than if no such similitude were offered in the divine books, since the thing perceived is the same, is difficult to say and is a problem for another discussion. For the present, however, no one doubts that things are perceived more readily through similitudes and that what is sought with difficulty is discovered with more pleasure. Those who do not find what they seek directly stated labor in hunger; those who do not seek because they have what they wish at once frequently become indolent in disdain. In either of these situations indifference is an evil. Thus the Holy Spirit has magnificently and wholesomely modulated the Holy Scriptures so that the more open places present themselves to hunger and the more obscure places may deter a disdainful attitude. Hardly anything may be found in these obscure places which is not found plainly said elsewhere.

VII

9. Before all it is necessary that we be turned by the fear of God toward a recognition of his will,[6] so that we may know what He commands that we desire and what He commands that we avoid. Of necessity this fear will lead us to thought of our mortality and of our future death and will affix all our proud motions, as if they were fleshly members fastened with nails, to the wood of the

cross. Then it is necessary that we become meek through piety so that we do not contradict Divine Scripture, either when it is understood and is seen to attack some of our vices, or when it is not understood and we feel as though we are wiser than it is and better able to give precepts. But we should rather think and believe that which is written to be better and more true than anything which we could think of by ourselves, even when it is obscure.

10. After these two steps of fear and piety the third step of knowledge confronts us, which I now propose to treat. In this every student of the Divine Scriptures must exercise himself, having found nothing else in them except, first, that God is to be loved for Himself, and his neighbor for the sake of God; second, that he is to love God with all his heart, with all his soul, and with all his mind; and third, that he should love his neighbor as himself, that is, so that all love for our neighbor should, like all love for ourselves, be referred to God. Concerning these two precepts we have written in the previous book, where we discussed things. Then it follows that the student first will discover in the Scriptures that he has been enmeshed in the love of this world, or of temporal things, a love far remote from the kind of love of God and of our neighbor which Scripture itself prescribes. Then, indeed, that fear which arises from the thought of God's judgment, and that piety which can do nothing except believe in and accede to the authority of the sacred books, will force him to lament his own situation. For this knowledge of a good hope thrusts a man not into boasting but into lamentation. This attitude causes him to ask with constant prayers for the consolation of divine assistance lest he fall into despair, and he thus enters the fourth step of fortitude, in which he hungers and thirsts for justice. And by means of this affection of the spirit he will extract himself from all mortal joy in transitory things, and as he turns aside from this joy, he will turn toward the love of eternal things, specifically toward that immutable unity which is the Trinity.

11. When, in so far as he is able, he has seen this Trinity glowing in the distance, and has discovered that because of his weakness he cannot sustain the sight of that light, he purges his mind, which is rising up and protesting in the appetite for inferior things, of its contaminations, so that he comes to the fifth step, the counsel of mercy. Here he eagerly exercises the love of his neighbor and perfects himself in it; and now, filled with hope and fortified in strength, when he arrives at the love of his enemy he ascends to the sixth step, where he cleanses that eye through which God may be seen, in so far as he can be seen by those who die to the world as much as they are able. For they are able to see only in so far as they are dead to this world; in so far as they live in it, they do not see. And now although the light of the Trinity begins to appear more certainly, and not only more tolerably but also more joyfully, it is still said to appear "through a glass in a dark manner"[7] for "we walk more by faith than by sight"[8] when we make our pilgrimage in this world, although "our community is in heaven."[9] On this step he so cleanses the eye of his heart that he neither prefers his neighbor to the Truth nor compares him with it, nor does he do this with himself because he does not so treat him whom he loves as himself. Therefore this holy one will be of such simple and clean heart that he will not turn away from the Truth

either in a desire to please men or for the sake of avoiding any kind of adversities to himself which arise in this life. Such a son ascends to wisdom, which is the seventh and last step, where he enjoys peace and tranquillity. "For the fear of the Lord is the begining of wisdom." From fear to wisdom the way extends through these steps.

VIII

12. But let us turn our attention to the third step which I have decided to treat as the Lord may direct my discourse. He will be the most expert investigator of the Holy Scriptures who has first read all of them and has some knowledge of them, at least through reading them if not through understanding them. That is, he should read those that are said to be canonical. For he may read the others more securely when he has been instructed in the truth of the faith so that they may not preoccupy a weak mind nor, deceiving it with vain lies and fantasies, prejudice it with something contrary to sane understanding. In the matter of canonical Scriptures he should follow the authority of the greater number of catholic Churches, among which are those which have deserved to have apostolic seats and to receive epistles. He will observe this rule concerning canonical Scriptures, that he will prefer those accepted by all catholic Churches to those which some do not accept; among those which are not accepted by all, he should prefer those which are accepted by the largest number of important Churches to those held by a few minor Churches of less authority. If he discovers that some are maintained by the larger number of Churches, others by the Churches of weightiest authority, although this condition is not likely, he should hold them to be of equal value.

13. The whole canon of the Scriptures on which we say that this consideration of the step of knowledge should depend is contained in the following books: the five books of Moses, that is, Genesis, Exodus, Leviticus, Numbers, and Deuteronomy; one book of Josue, one of Judges, one short book called Ruth which seems rather to pertain to the beginning of Kings; then the four books of Kings and two of Paralipomenon, not in sequence, but as if side by side and running at the same time. These are made up of history and are arranged according to the sequence of time and the order of things; there are others arranged in a different order which neither follow this order nor are connected among themselves, like Job, Tobias, Esther, Judith, two books of Machabees, and two books of Esdras. The last two seem to follow the ordered history after the end of Kings or Paralipomenon. Then there are the Prophets, among which are one book of the Psalms of David, and three books of Solomon: Proverbs, the Canticle of Canticles, and Ecclesiastes. For those two books, one of which is called Wisdom and the other Ecclesiasticus, are said to be Solomon's through a certain similitude, since it is consistently said that they were written by Jesus son of Sirach. Nevertheless, since they have merited being received as authoritative, they are to be numbered among the prophetic books. The remainder are those books called Prophets in a strict sense, containing twelve single books of Prophets joined together. Since they have never been separated, they are

thought of as one. The names of the Prophets are Osee, Joel, Amos, Abdias, Jonas, Micheas, Nahum, Habacuc, Sophonias, Aggeus, Zacharias, and Malachias. Then there are four books of four major Prophets: Isaias, Jeremias, Daniel, Ezechiel. The authority of the Old Testament ends with these forty-four books. The New Testament contains the four evangelical books, according to Matthew, Mark, Luke, and John; the fourteen epistles of Paul the Apostle, to the Romans, two to the Corinthians, to the Galatians, to the Ephesians, to the Philippians, two to the Thessalonians, to the Colossians, two to Timothy, to Titus, to Philemon, to the Hebrews; two Epistles of Peter, three of John, one of Jude, and one of James; a book of the Acts of the Apostles, and a book of the Apocalypse of John.

IX

14. In all of these books those fearing God and made meek in piety seek the will of God. And the first rule of this undertaking and labor is, as we have said, to know these books even if they are not understood, at least to read them or to memorize them, or to make them not altogether unfamiliar to us. Then those things which are put openly in them either as precepts for living or as rules for believing are to be studied more diligently and more intelligently, for the more one learns about these things the more capable of understanding he becomes. Among those things which are said openly in Scripture are to be found all those teachings which involve faith, the mores of living, and that hope and charity which we have discussed in the previous book. Then, having become familiar with the language of the Divine Scriptures, we should turn to those obscure things which must be opened up and explained so that we may take examples from those things that are manifest to illuminate those things which are obscure, bringing principles which are certain to bear on our doubts concerning those things which are uncertain. In this undertaking memory is of great value, for if it fails rules will not be of any use.

X

15. There are two reasons why things written are not understood: they are obscured either by unknown or by ambiguous signs. For signs are either literal or figurative. They are called literal when they are used to designate those things on account of which they were instituted; thus we say *bos* [ox] when we mean an animal of a herd because all men using the Latin language call it by that name just as we do. Figurative signs occur when that thing which we designate by a literal sign is used to signify something else; thus we say "ox" and by that syllable understand the animal which is ordinarily designated by that word, but again by that animal we understand an evangelist, as is signified in the Scripture, according to the interpretation of the Apostle, when it says, "Thou shalt not muzzle the ox that treadeth out the corn."[10]

XI

16. Against unknown literal signs the sovereign remedy is a knowledge of languages. And Latin-speaking men, whom we have here undertaken to instruct, need two others for a knowledge of the Divine Scriptures, Hebrew and Greek, so that they may turn back to earlier exemplars if the infinite variety of Latin translations gives rise to any doubts. Again, in these books we frequently find untranslated Hebrew words, like *amen, alleluia, racha, hosanna,* and so on, of which some, although they could be translated, have been preserved from antiquity on account of their holier authority, like *amen* and *alleluia;* others, like the other two mentioned above, are said not to be translatable into another language. For there are some words in some languages which cannot be translated into other languages. And this is especially true of interjections which signify the motion of the spirit rather than any part of a rational concept. And these two belong to this class: *racha* is said to be an expression of indignation and *hosanna* an expression of delight. But a knowledge of these two languages is not necessary for these few things, which are easy to know and to discover, but, as we have said, it is necessary on account of the variety of translations. We can enumerate those who have translated the Scriptures from Hebrew into Greek, but those who have translated them into Latin are innumerable. In the early times of the faith when anyone found a Greek codex, and he thought that he had some facility in both languages, he attempted to translate it.

XII

17. This situation would rather help than impede understanding if readers would only avoid negligence. For an inspection of various translations frequently makes obscure passages clear. For example, one translator renders a passage in the prophet Isaias: "Despise not the family of thy seed"; but another says: "Despise not thy own flesh."[11] Either confirms the other, for one may be explained by means of the other. Thus the "flesh" may be taken literally, so that one may find himself admonished that no one should despise his own body, and the "family of the seed" may be taken figuratively so that it is understood to mean "Christians" born spiritually from the seed of the Word which produced us. But a collation of the translations makes it probable that the meaning is a literal precept that we should not despise those of our own blood, since when we compare "family of the seed" with "flesh," blood relations come especially to mind. Whence, I think, comes the statement of the Apostle, who said, "If, by any means, I may provoke to emulation them who are my flesh, and may save some of them,"[12] that is, so that, emulating those who had believed, they also might believe. He calls the Jews his "flesh" because of blood relationship. Again, a text of the prophet Isaias reads: "If you will not believe, you shall not understand," and in another translation: "If you will not believe, you shall not continue."[13] Which of these is to be followed is uncertain unless the text is read in the original language. But both of them nevertheless contain something of great value for the discerning reader. It is difficult for translators to become so

disparate that they do not show a similarity in one area of meaning. Thus, although understanding lies in the sight of the Eternal, faith nourishes as children are nourished with milk in the cradles of temporal things. Now "we walk by faith and not by sight."[14] Unless we walk by faith, we shall not be able to come to that sight which does not fail but continues through a cleansed understanding uniting us with Truth. On account of this principle one said, "If you will not believe, you shall not continue," and the other said, "If you will not believe, you shall not understand."

18. Many translators are deceived by ambiguity in the original language which they do not understand, so that they transfer the meaning to something completely alien to the writer's intention. Thus some codices have "their feet are sharp to shed blood," for the word *oxús* in Greek means both "sharp" and "swift." But he sees the meaning who translates "their feet swift to shed blood";[15] the other, drawn in another direction by an ambiguous sign, erred. And such translations are not obscure; they are false, and when this is the situation the codices are to be emended rather than interpreted. The same situation arises when some, because *móschos* in Greek means "calf," do not know that *moscheúmata* means "transplantings," and have translated it "calves." This error appears in so many texts that one hardly finds anything else written, although the sense is very clear and is supported by the succeeding words. For the expression "bastard slips shall not take deep root"[16] makes better sense than to speak of "calves," which walk on the earth and do not take root in it. The rest of the context, moreover, supports this translation.

XIII

19. Since the meaning which many interpreters, according to their ability and judgment, seek to convey is not apparent unless we consult the language being translated, and since many translators err from the sense of the original authors unless they are very learned, we must either seek a knowledge of those languages from which Scripture is translated into Latin or we must consult the translations of those who translate word for word, not because they suffice but because by means of them we may test the truth or falsity of those who have sought to translate meanings as well as words. For often not only single words but whole locutions are translated because they cannot be expressed in Latin if one wishes to adhere to the ancient and customary idiom of the Latin language. These unidiomatic expressions do not impede the understanding, but they offend those who take more delight in things when the signs for them are governed by a certain correctness. For what is called a solecism is nothing else than an arrangement of words which does not conform to the law followed by those who have spoken before us with some authority. Whether one says "among men" by saying *inter homines* or by saying *inter hominibus* does not affect the person considering things rather than signs. In the same way, what else is a barbarism except a word pronounced with letters or sounds different from those which those who spoke Latin before us were accustomed to use? Whether *ignoscere* [to forgive] is spoken with a long or short third syllable makes little difference to a man asking God to forgive his sins, in whatever way

he can pronounce the word. What then is integrity of expression except the preservation of the customs of others, confirmed by the authority of ancient speakers?

20. The more men are offended by these things, the weaker they are. And they are weaker in that they wish to seem learned, not in the knowledge of things, by which we are truly instructed, but in the knowledge of signs, in which it is very difficult not to be proud. For even the knowledge of things frequently raises the neck unless it is disciplined by the yoke of the Lord. It does not impede the understanding of the reader to find written: "What is the land in which these dwell upon it, whether it is good or evil, and what are the cities in which these dwell in them?"[17] I consider this to be the idiom of an alien tongue rather than the expression of a more profound meaning. There is also the expression that we cannot now take away from the chant of the people: "but upon him shall my sanctification flourish."[18] Nothing is detracted from the meaning, although the more learned hearer may wish to correct it so that *florebit* is spoken instead of *floriet*, and nothing impedes the correction but the custom of the chanters. These things may easily be disregarded if one does not wish to pay attention to that which does not detract from a sound understanding. Then there is the expression of the Apostle; "The foolishness of God is wiser than men; and the weakness of God is stronger than men."[19] If anyone wished to keep the Greek idiom and say "The foolishness of God is wiser of men, and the weakness of God is stronger of men," the labor of the vigilant reader would lead him to the true meaning, but a somewhat slower reader might either not understand it or misunderstand it. For not only is such a phrase incorrect in the Latin language, it also obscures the truth in ambiguity. Thus the foolishness of men or the weakness of men might seem wiser or stronger than God's. And even *sapientius est hominibus* [wiser than men] does not lack ambiguity, although it contains no solecism. Without the illumination of the idea being conveyed it is not clear whether *hominibus* is ablative or dative. It would be better to say *sapientius est quam homines* and *fortius est quam homines*, which express the ideas "wiser than men" and "stronger than men" without any possible ambiguity.

XIV

21. We shall speak later of ambiguous signs; now we are discussing unknown signs, of which there are two forms, in so far as they apply to words. For either an unknown word or an unknown expression may impede the reader. If these come from foreign languages we must consult one who speaks those languages, or learn them ourselves if we have leisure and ability, or make a comparison of various translations. If we do not know certain words or expressions in our own language, we become familiar with them by reading and hearing them. Nothing is better commended to the memory than those types of words and expressions which we do not know, so that when one more learned appears who may be questioned, or when a passage appears in reading where the preceding or following context makes their meaning clear, we may easily with the aid of the memory refer to them and learn them. Such is the force of

habit even in learning that those who are nourished and educated in the Holy Scriptures wonder more at other expressions and think them poorer Latin than those used in the Scriptures, even though these do not appear in the writings of the Latin authors. In this matter of learning a comparison and weighing of various translations is also useful. But falsity should be rejected. For those who desire to know the Sacred Scriptures should exercise their ingenuity principally that texts not emended should give way to those emended, at least among those which come from one source of translation.

XV

22. Among these translations the *Itala* is to be preferred, for it adheres to the words and is at the same time perspicacious regarding meaning.[20] And in emending Latin translations, Greek translations are to be consulted, of which the Septuagint carries most authority in so far as the Old Testament is concerned. In all the more learned churches it is now said that this translation was so inspired by the Holy Spirit that many men spoke as if with the mouth of one. It is said and attested by many of not unworthy faith that, although the translators were separated in various cells while they worked, nothing was to be found in any version that was not found in the same words and with the same order of words in all of the others. Who would compare any other authority with this, or, much less, prefer another? But even if they conferred and arrived at a single opinion on the basis of common judgment and consent, it is not right or proper for any man, no matter how learned, to seek to emend the consensus of so many older and more learned men. Therefore, even though something is found in Hebrew versions different from what they have set down, I think we should cede to the divine dispensation by which they worked to the end that the books which the Jewish nation refused to transmit to other peoples, either out of envy or for religious reasons, might be revealed so early, by the authority and power of King Ptolemy, to the nations which in the future were to believe in Our Lord. It may be that the Holy Spirit judged that they should translate in a manner befitting the people whom they addressed and that they should speak as if with one voice. Yet, as I have said before, a comparison with those translators who adhered most closely to the words of the original is not without use in explaining their meaning. Latin translations of the Old Testament, as I set out to say, are to be emended on the authority of the Greeks, and especially on the authority of those who, although there were seventy, are said to have spoken as if with one voice. Moreover, if the books of the New Testament are confusing in the variety of their Latin translations, they should certainly give place to the Greek versions, especially to those which are found among more learned and diligent Churches.

XVI

23. Among figurative signs, if any impede the reader, he should study them partly with reference to a knowledge of languages and partly with reference to a knowledge of things. Thus the pool of Siloe, where the Lord commanded the

man whose eyes he had anointed with clay made of spittle to wash, has some value as a similitude and undoubtedly suggests some mystery [e.g., baptism], but the name Siloe in an unknown language, if it had not been interpreted for us by the Evangelist,[21] would have concealed a very important perception. In the same way many Hebrew names which are not explained by the authors of those books undoubtedly have considerable importance in clarifying the enigmas of the Scriptures, if someone were able to interpret them. Some men, expert in that language, have rendered no small benefit to posterity by having explained all of those words taken from the Scriptures without reference to place and have translated Adam, Eve, Abraham, Moses, and names of places like Jerusalem, Sion, Jericho, Sinai, Lebanon, Jordan, or whatever other names in that language are unknown to us; and since these things have been made known, many figurative expressions in the Scriptures have become clear.

24. An ignorance of things makes figurative expressions obscure when we are ignorant of the natures of animals, or stones, or plants, or other things which are often used in the Scriptures for purposes of constructing similitudes. Thus the well-known fact that a serpent exposes its whole body in order to protect its head from those attacking it illustrates the sense of the Lord's admonition that we be wise like serpents.[22] That is, for the sake of our head, which is Christ, we should offer our bodies to persecutors lest the Christian faith be in a manner killed in us, and in an effort to save our bodies we deny God. It is also said that the serpent, having forced its way through narrow openings, sheds its skin and renews its vigor. How well this conforms to our imitation of the wisdom of the serpent when we shed the "old man," as the Apostle says, and put on the "new";[23] and we shed it in narrow places, for the Lord directs us, "Enter ye in at the narrow gate."[24] Just as a knowledge of the nature of serpents illuminates the many similitudes which Scripture frequently makes with that animal, an ignorance of many other animals which are also used for comparisons is a great impediment to understanding. The same thing is true of stones, or of herbs or of other things that take root. For a knowledge of the carbuncle which shines in the darkness also illuminates many obscure places in books where it is used for similitudes, and an ignorance of beryl or of diamonds frequently closes the doors of understanding. In the same way it is not easy to grasp that the twig of olive which the dove brought when it returned to the ark[25] signifies perpetual peace unless we know that the soft surface of oil is not readily corrupted by an alien liquid and that the olive tree is perennially in leaf. Moreover, there are many who because of an ignorance of hyssop—being unaware of its power either to purify the lungs or, as it is said, to penetrate its roots to the rocks in spite of the fact that it is a small and humble plant—are not able at all to understand why it is said, "Thou shalt spinkle me with hyssop, and I shall be cleansed."[26]

25. An ignorance of numbers also causes many things expressed figuratively and mystically in the Scriptures to be misunderstood. Certainly, a gifted and frank person cannot avoid wondering about the significance of the fact that Moses, Elias, and the Lord Himself all fasted for forty days.[27] The knot, as it were, of this figurative action cannot be untied without a knowledge and consideration of this number. For it contains four tens, to indicate the knowl-

edge of all things involved in times. The day and the year both run their courses in a quaternion: the day in hours of morning, noon, evening, and night; the year in the months of spring, summer, autumn, and winter. But while we live in these times we should abstain and fast from temporal delight because of the eternity in which we wish to live, for in the very courses of time the doctrine in accordance with which we condemn temporal things and desire the eternal is suggested. Again, the number ten signifies a knowledge of the Creator and the creature; for the trinity is the Creator and the septenary indicates the creature by reason of his life and body. For with reference to life there are three, whence we should love God with all our hearts, with all our souls, and with all our minds; and with reference to the body there are very obviously four elements of which it is made. Thus when the number ten is suggested to us with reference to time, or, that is, when it is multiplied by four, we are admonished to live chastely and continently without temporal delight, or, that is, to fast for forty days. This the Law, represented in the person of Moses; the Prophets, whose person is acted by Elias; and the Lord Himself all admonish. He, as if bearing the testimony of the Law and the Prophets, appeared between these two on the Mount to His three watching and amazed disciples.[28] Then it may be asked how the number fifty, which is very sacred in our religion because of the feast of Pentecost, proceeds from forty; or how, when it is tripled because of the three times—before the Law, during the Law, and under Grace—or because of the name of the Father, the Son, and the Holy Spirit, and the number of the most high Trinity is added, it refers to the mystery of the most pure Church and arrives at the number of the hundred and fifty-three fish which the net caught "on the right side" after the Resurrection of the Lord.[29] In the same way many other numbers and patterns of numbers are placed by way of similitudes in the sacred books as secrets which are often closed to readers because of ignorance of numbers.

26. An ignorance of some things concerning music also halts and impedes the reader. A certain writer has well explained some figures of things on the basis of the difference between the psaltery and the harp. It may be inquired not unreasonably among the learned whether the psalterium of ten strings follows any musical law which demands strings of that number, or, if no such law exists, whether that number should be considered more sacred either on account of the Ten Commandments (if a question is raised about that number, we can apply it to the Creator and the creature), or whether it is used because of the explanation of the number ten we have used above. And the number mentioned in the Gospel in connection with the building of the temple, forty-six years,[30] somehow has a musical sound, and, when it is applied to the structure of Our Lord's body, it causes some heretics to confess the Son of God to be clothed not falsely but with a true and human body.[31] And we find both number and music given an honorable position in many places in the Sacred Scriptures.

XVII

27. We must not listen to the superstition of the pagans who professed that the nine Muses are the daughters of Jove and Memory. They were refuted by Varro,

than whom among the pagans I know of no one more eager and learned in such matters. He says that a certain city, the name of which I have forgotten, contracted with three sculptors for triple statues of the Muses to be placed as an offering in the temple of Apollo with the stipulation that only the group of the artist who wrought most beautifully would be purchased. It so happened that the work of the sculptors was of equal beauty and that the city was pleased with all nine figures so that all were bought and dedicated in the temple. He says that later the poet Hesiod named all nine of them. Thus Jupiter did not beget the nine Muses, but three artists made triple statues. Moreover, that city did not hit on the number three because someone had seen three Muses in a dream, or because so many had appeared to anyone's eyes, but because it is easy to see that all sound which furnishes material for songs is of a threefold nature. It is either produced by the voice, like the sound made by those who sing from the throat without instrumental accompaniment, by the breath, like the sound made by trumpets and flutes, or by striking, like the sound produced by harps, drums, or other percussion instruments.

XVIII

28. But whether Varro's account is to be accepted or not, we should not avoid music because of the superstition of the profane if we can find anything in it useful for understanding the Holy Scriptures, although we should not turn to their theatrical frivolities to discover whether anything valuable for spiritual purposes is to be gathered from their harps and other instruments. But we should not think that we ought not to learn literature because Mercury is said to be its inventor, nor that because the pagans dedicated temples to Justice and Virtue and adored in stones what should be performed in the heart, we should therefore avoid justice and virtue. Rather, every good and true Christian should understand that wherever he may find truth, it is his Lord's. And confessing and acknowledging this truth also in the sacred writings, he will repudiate superstitious imaginings and will deplore and guard against men who "when they knew God . . . have not glorified him as God, or given thanks; but became vain in their thoughts, and their foolish heart was darkened. For professing themselves to be wise, they became fools. And they changed the glory of the incorruptible God into the likeness of the image of a corruptible man, and of birds, and of four-footed beasts, and of creeping things."[32]

XIX

29. But in order that we may explain this whole matter, which is very important, more thoroughly, I should add that there are two kinds of doctrine which are of force in the mores of the pagans. One of these concerns things which men have themselves instituted; the other concerns those things which they have seen to be firmly established or divinely ordained. That which concerns the institutions of men is partly superstitious and partly not superstitious.

XX

30. Among superstitious things is whatever has been instituted by men concerning the making and worshiping of idols, or concerning the worshiping of any creature or any part of any creature as though it were God. Of the same type are things instituted concerning consultations and pacts involving prognostications with demons who have been placated or contracted with. These are the endeavors of the magic arts, which the poets are accustomed to mention rather than to teach. To the same class belong, although they show a more presumptuous vanity, the books of haruspicy and augury. Here also belong those amulets and remedies which medical science also condemns, whether these involve enchantments, or certain secret signs called "characters," or the hanging, tying, or in any way wearing of certain things, not for the purpose of healing the body, but because of certain significations, either occult or manifest. These are given the mild name of "physics" so that they may seem not to be involved with superstitions but to be helpful to nature. Of this type are the rings hung in the top of each ear, or the little rings of ostrich bones on the fingers, or the practice of telling a person with hiccups to hold his left thumb in his right hand.

31. To these may be added a thousand vacuous observances to follow if a limb trembles or if a stone, dog, or child comes between friends walking arm in arm. The custom of kicking a stone, as if it were a destroyer of friendship, is less obnoxious than that of hitting an innocent child with the fist if he runs between two people walking together. And it is fitting that sometimes children are avenged by dogs; for some persons are so superstitious that they even dare to hit a dog that has come between them, and not without paying for it. For sometimes the dog quickly sends him who strikes him from a vain remedy to a true physician. Other similar practices are the following: to step on the threshold when you leave your house by the front door, to go back to bed if anyone sneezes while you are putting on your shoes, to return to the house if you stumble going out, or, when your clothes are torn by mice, to dread more the omen of a future evil than the actual damage. Whence that elegant saying of Cato, who, when consulted by a man whose shoes had been gnawed by mice, observed that there was nothing strange about the fact, but that it would have been strange indeed if the shoes had gnawed the mice.

XXI

32. Nor are those to be excluded from this sort of pernicious superstition who are called *genethliaci* because they are concerned with birthdays, or, commonly, *mathematici* [judicial astrologers]. Although these men may seek out and even find the exact position of the stars at the time someone is born, yet when they seek to predict on that basis either our actions or the outcome of our actions they err greatly and sell unlearned men into a miserable servitude. For a man who is free when he goes to such an astrologer gives his money that he may leave him as the servant either of Mars or of Venus, or rather of all the stars to which those who first erred in this way and passed their error on to posterity

gave names of beasts because of resemblances, or names of men in an effort to honor those men. That they did so was not strange, for even in more modern and recent times the Romans wished to give to the star we call Lucifer the honor and the name of Caesar. Perhaps they might have succeeded and established a tradition if his ancestor Venus had not already occupied the estate of that name; nor could she according to any law pass on to her descendants what she had never possessed nor sought to possess in life. But where a place was vacant and not held in honor of someone who had died earlier, the usual practice in such matters was adhered to. Thus we call the quintile and sextile months July and August, so named in honor of Julius Caesar and Augustus Caesar, and anyone who wishes may understand that in the same way the stars once moved in the sky without the names we now give them. When certain men died whose memory was honored either because of the power of kings or the pleasure of human vanity, their names were given to the stars and they themselves were thought to be thus raised to the heavens after death. But whatever they may be called by men, the stars are those which God created and arranged as He wished, and their motion, in accordance with which times vary and are distinguished, is certain.[33] It is easy to notice this motion, however it may be, at the time a person is born according to the rules discovered and written down by those whom Scripture condemns, saying: "For if they were able to know so much as to make a judgment of the world, how did they not more easily find out the Lord thereof?"[34]

XXII

33. To desire to predict at birth, on the basis of such observations, the habits, actions, and fortunes of men is a great error and a great madness. Among those who know something about this vain knowledge, the superstition may be altogether refuted. For they observe the configurations of the stars which they call constellations at the time of birth of the one concerning whom these wretched men are consulted by those even more wretched. But it may happen that twins emerge from the uterus in such rapid succession that no one can observe the interval of time between them and note it in the numbers of the constellations. Whence it follows that some twins have the same constellation. But they do not have the same fortunes with respect to what they do or what they suffer. Instead, they are frequently different, so that while one lives very happily, the other lives very unhappily. Thus we know that Esau and Jacob were born twins in such a way that Jacob, who was born last, was found holding with his hand the foot of his brother who went before.[35] Certainly, the day and hour of birth for these two could not be otherwise noted except in such a way that the constellation for both should be the same. Yet what a difference there was in the manners, deeds, labors, and fortunes of these two men the Scripture, now accessible to all men, testifies.

34. Nor is it pertinent to say that the least moment and the smallest portion of time which separates the births of twins is of great importance in nature and in the very rapid course of the heavenly bodies. Even when it is conceded that it

matters a great deal, it cannot be discovered by the astrologer in the constellations by which he professes to foretell destinies. Therefore he does not find any difference in constellations since he must observe the same ones whether he is consulted concerning Jacob or concerning his brother. It is of no help to him if there is a difference of time in the heavens which he rashly and negligently blames when there is no difference in the chart which he fruitlessly and solicitously examines. Thus those beliefs in certain signs of things instituted by human presumption are to be classed with those which result from certain pacts and contracts with demons.

XXIII

35. For it is brought about as if by a certain secret judgment of God that men who desire evil things are subjected to illusion and deception as a reward for their desires, being mocked and deceived by those lying angels to whom, according to the most beautiful ordering of things, the lowest part of this world is subject by the law of Divine Providence. By these illusions and deceptions it happens that many things concerning the past and future determined by these superstitious and pernicious methods of divination actually happen as they are so determined; many things happen for the diviners in accordance with their divinations, so that, enmeshed in them, they are made more curious and entangle themselves more and more in the multiple snares of a most pernicious error. This kind of fornication of the spirit is happily not passed over in silence by the Holy Scripture, nor has it frightened the soul away in such a way that it avoids these things because falsehoods are spoken by those who profess them; but rather, "if they speak to you," it says, "and it comes to pass, do not believe them."[36] If the image of the dead Samuel predicted truths to King Saul,[37] those sacrileges by which that image was called up are no less to be condemned. Again, in the Acts of the Apostles, although the woman with the Pythonical spirit gave true testimony of the apostles of the Lord, the Apostle Paul nevertheless did not spare that spirit but cleansed the woman by denouncing and driving out the demon.[38]

36. Therefore all arts pertaining to this kind of trifling or noxious superstition constituted on the basis of a pestiferous association of men and demons as if through a pact of faithless and deceitful friendship should be completely repudiated and avoided by the Christian, "not that the idol is anything," as the Apostle says, but because "the things which the heathens sacrifice, they sacrifice to devils, and not to God. And I would not that you should be made partakers with devils."[39] For what the Apostle says concerning idols and the sacrifices that are made in their honor should be understood concerning all imaginary signs which lead to the cult of idols or to the worship of a creature or its parts as God, or pertain to the concern for remedies and other observations which are not as it were publicly and divinely constituted for the love of God and of our neighbor but rather debauch the hearts of the wretched through their love for temporal things. With reference to all teachings of this kind, therefore, the society of demons is to be feared and avoided, since they seek to do nothing

under their leader the Devil but to block and cut off our return homeward. Just as human and deceptive conjectures have been established by men concerning the stars which God created and ordered, many similar speculations have been made concerning things that are born or things having their being through the administration of Divine Providence and have been set down as if according to rule to account for unusual occurrences like the foaling of a mule or the striking of lightning.

XXIV

37. All such omens are valid only in so far as through previously established imaginings, as if these were a common language, they are agreed upon with demons. Moreover, they all imply a pestiferous curiosity, an excruciating solicitude, and a mortal slavery. They were not noticed because of any innate validity, but they were made to have a validity through being noticed and pointed out. And thus they seem different to different people in accordance with their thoughts and presumptions. Those spirits who wish to deceive procure for each one those effects as they discern them by means of which he may be ensnared by his own suspicions and customary habits of thought. To use an analogy, one figure of a letter X set down in the form of a cross mark means one thing among the Latins, another among the Greeks, not because of its nature, but because of agreement and consent to its significance. And thus he who knows both languages does not use that sign with the same signification when he wishes to convey something in writing to a Greek that he implies when he writes to a man who speaks Latin. And the single sign *beta* means a letter among the Greeks but a vegetable among the Latins. When I say *lege,* a Greek understands one thing by these two syllables, a Latin understands another. Therefore just as all of these significations move men's minds in accordance with the consent of their societies, and because this consent varies, they move them differently, nor do men agree upon them because of an innate value, but they have a value because they are agreed upon, in the same way those signs which form the basis for a pernicious alliance with demons are of value only in accordance with the observations of the individual. This fact is very obvious in the rites of the augurs who arrange not to see birds nor to hear their cries before or after their observations because what they see or hear is significant only if the observer consents to consider it so.

XXV

38. When these things have been cut off and eradicated from the Christian mind, then those practices are to be examined which are not superstitious, that is, which are not based upon agreements with demons but upon agreements among men themselves. For all practices which have value among men because men agree among themselves that they are valuable are human institutions; and of these some are superfluous and extravagant, others useful and necessary. Thus if those signs which the actors make in their dances had a natural meaning and not a meaning dependent on the institution and consent of men,

the public crier in early times would not have had to explain to the Carthaginian populace what the dancer wished to convey during the pantomime. Many old men still remember the custom, as we have heard them say. And they are to be believed, for even now if anyone unacquainted with such trifles goes to the theater and no one else explains to him what these motions signify, he watches the performance in vain. It is true that everyone seeks a certain verisimilitude in making signs so that these signs, in so far as is possible, may resemble the things that they signify. But since one thing may resemble another in a great variety of ways, signs are not valid among men except by common consent.

39. Where pictures or statues are concerned, or other similar imitative works, especially when executed by skilled artists, no one errs when he sees the likeness, so that he recognizes what things are represented. And all things of this class are to be counted among the superfluous institutions of men except when it is important to know concerning one of them why, where, when, and by whose authority it was made. Then there are thousands of imagined fables and falsehoods by whose lies men are delighted, which are human institutions. And nothing is more typical of men among those things which they have from themselves than what is deceitful and lying. But the useful and necessary institutions established by men with men include whatever they have agreed upon concerning differences of dress and the adornment of the person useful for distinguishing sex or rank, and innumerable kinds of signs without which human society could not or could not easily function, including weights and measures, differences of value and impression in coinage appropriate to specific states and peoples, and other things of this kind. If these had not been purely human institutions they would not vary among different peoples nor in single nations according to the will of their leaders.

40. But all this part of human institutions helpful to the necessary conduct of life is not to be shunned by the Christian; rather, as such institutions are needed, they are to be given sufficient notice and remembered.

XXVI

Human institutions are imperfect reflections of natural institutions or are similar to them. Those which pertain to association with demons, as we have said, should be completely repudiated and disdained; those which men have established among themselves are to be adopted in so far as they are not extravagant and superfluous, and especially the forms of letters without which we cannot read, and a sufficient variety of languages, which we have discussed above. Of the same class are the characters of the type used by those who are now called shorthand writers. These are useful; they neither are learned in an illicit way, nor do they enmesh anyone in superstition, nor enervate through extravagance, if they occupy us only so far that they do not interfere with more important things to which we should devote our attention.

XXVII

41. At the same time we must must consider as human institutions those things which men did not establish but which have been fruitful subjects of investigation as they appear either in the course of time or by divine institution. Of these, some pertain to the corporal senses, others to reason. Those which pertain to the corporal senses we either believe when they are explained to us, experience when they are demonstrated to us, or infer when we have experienced them.

XXVIII

42. Thus whatever evidence we have of past times in that which is called history helps us a great deal in the understanding of the sacred books, even if we learn it outside of the Church as a part of our childhood education. For we are required to know many things in accordance with the Olympiads and the names of the consuls; and an ignorance of the consulship at the time Our Lord was born and of that at the time of His Passion has caused some to err in such a way that they thought the Lord suffered His Passion at the age of forty-six, since the Jews said that so many years were required for the building of the temple, which is a figure for the body of Our Lord.[40] Now we know that He was baptized, on the authority of the Gospel,[41] at about the age of thirty, and it is possible to estimate on the basis of His actions as they are described in this text how much longer He lived. Nevertheless, lest any shadow of doubt should arise from any other source, it can be determined more clearly and certainly on the basis of a comparison of pagan history with that of the gospel. Then it will be seen that it was not vainly said that the temple was built in forty-six years, for since the number could not refer to the age of Our Lord, it may refer to a more secret instruction concerning the human body, which the only Son of God, through whom all things are made, did not disdain to put on for our benefit.

43. With reference to the usefulness of history, if I may omit the Greeks, what a question our Ambrose solved after the calumnies of the readers and admirers of Plato, who dared to say that all the lessons of Our Lord Jesus Christ, which they were forced to admire and to teach, were learned from the writings of Plato, since it cannot be denied that Plato lived long before the advent of the Lord! Did not the famous bishop, when he had considered the history of the pagans and found that Plato had traveled in Egypt during the time of Jeremias, show that Plato had probably been introduced to our literature by Jeremias so that he was able to teach or to write doctrines that are justly commended? Pythagoras himself did not live before the literature of the Hebrew nation, in which the cult of one God took its origin and from which Our Lord came "according to the flesh,"[42] was written. And from the disciples of Pythagoras these men claim that Plato learned theology. Thus from a consideration of times it becomes more credible that the Platonists took from our literature whatever they said that is good and truthful than that Our Lord Jesus Christ learned from them. To believe the latter view is the utmost madness.

44. Although human institutions of the past are described in historical narration, history itself is not to be classed as a human institution; for those things which are past and cannot be revoked belong to the order of time, whose creator and administrator is God. It is one thing to describe what has been done, another to describe what should be done. History narrates what has been done faithfully and usefully; but books of haruspicy and all similar books seek to show what should be done or observed with the audacity of the author, not with the faith of a guide.

XXIX

45. There is also a type of narrative resembling description which points out to the ignorant facts about the present rather than about the past. To this class belong things that have been written about the location of places, or the nature of animals, trees, plants, stones, or other objects. We have spoken of these writings above where we taught that they are valuable for the solution of enigmas in the Scriptures, not that they should be considered as signs for superstitious remedies or machinations. For we distinguish that type from the legitimate and open type to be discussed here. For it is one thing to say, "If you drink the juice of this herb, your stomach will not hurt," and quite another to say, "If you hang this herb around your neck, your stomach will not hurt." The first course is recommended as a healthful remedy; the second is to be condemned as a superstitious sign. Even though there are no incantations, invocations, or "characters" involved, the question often remains as to whether the thing which is to be tied or in any way attached to heal the body is valid because of the force of nature, in which case it is to be used freely, or is valid because of some signifying convention, in which case the Christian should avoid it the more cautiously the more it seems to be efficacious in doing good. For where the cause for the efficacy of a thing is hidden, the intention for which it is used is to be considered in so far as it concerns the healing or tempering of bodies either in medicine or in agriculture.

46. The stars, of which Scripture mentions only a very few, are known through description rather than narration. Although the course of the moon, which is relevant to the celebration of the anniversary of the Passion of Our Lord, is known to many, there are only a few who know well the rising or setting or other movements of the rest of the stars without error. Knowledge of this kind in itself, although it is not allied with any superstition, is of very little use in the treatment of the Divine Scriptures and even impedes it through fruitless study; and since it is associated with the most pernicious error of vain prediction it is more appropriate and virtuous to condemn it. It contains beyond a description of present circumstances an element akin to historical narration, since on the basis of the present position and motion of the stars it is possible to trace their past courses according to rule. It also includes predictions concerning the future made according to rule which are not superstitious and portentous but certain and fixed by calculation. We do not seek to learn from these any applications to our deeds and fates in the manner of the ravings of the astrologers but only information that pertains to the stars themselves. For just as he who computes

the phases of the moon, when he has observed its condition today, can determine its condition at a given period of years in the past or in the future, so in the same way those who are competent can make assertions about any of the other stars. I have stated my opinion about knowledge of this kind in so far as its usefulness is concerned.

XXX

47. Among other arts some are concerned with the manufacture of a product which is the result of the labor of the artificer, like a house, a bench, a dish, or something else of this kind. Others exhibit a kind of assistance to the work of God, like medicine, agriculture, and navigation. Still others have all their effect in their proper actions, like dancing, running, and wrestling. In all of these arts experience with the past makes possible inferences concerning the future, for no artificer in any of them performs operations except in so far as he bases his expectations of the future on past experience. A knowledge of these arts is to be acquired casually and superficially in the ordinary course of life unless a particular office demands a more profound knowledge, a possibility with which we are not here concerned. We do not need to know how to perform these arts but only how to judge them in such a way that we are not ignorant of what the Scripture implies when it employs figurative locutions based on them.[43]

XXXI

48. There remain those institutions which do not pertain to the corporal senses but to the reason, where the sciences of disputation and number hold sway. The science of disputation is of great value for understanding and solving all sorts of questions that appear in sacred literature. However, in this connection the love of controversy is to be avoided, as well as a certain puerile ostentation in deceiving an adversary. There are, moreover, many false conclusions of the reasoning process called sophisms, and frequently they so imitate true conclusions that they mislead not only those who are slow but also the ingenious when they do not pay close attention. For example, a man holding a discussion with another submits the proposition: "What I am, you are not." The other, because it is true in part, or because the speaker is deceitful and he is simple, agrees. Then the first adds, "I am a man." When this too is agreed upon, he concludes, saying, "Therefore you are not a man." As I see it, the Scripture condemns this kind of captious conclusion in that place where it is said, "He that speaketh sophistically is hateful."[44] At times a discourse which is not captious, but which is more abundant than is consistent with gravity, being inflated with verbal ornament, is also called sophistical.

49. There are also valid processes of reasoning having false conclusions which follow from the error of the disputant. An error of this kind may be led to its conclusions by a good and learned man so that the disputant, being ashamed of them, relinquishes his error. For if he maintains it, he will also be forced to maintain conclusions which he himself condemns. For example, the Apostle did not infer the truth when he said "then Christ is not risen," or when he said "then

is our preaching vain, and your faith also vain."[45] He added other things altogether false, since Christ has risen and the preaching of those who announced this fact was not vain, nor was the faith of those who believed it. But these false conclusions most truly follow from the premise of those who said that "there is no resurrection of the dead."[46] When these false conclusions, which would be true if the dead did not arise, are repudiated, the resurrection of the dead follows as a consequent. Since correct inferences may be made concerning false as well as true propositions, it is easy to learn the nature of valid inference even in schools which are outside of the Church. But the truth of propositions is a matter to be discovered in the sacred books of the Church.

XXXII

50. However, the truth of valid inference was not instituted by men; rather it was observed by men and set down that they might learn or teach it. For it is perpetually instituted by God in the reasonable order of things. Thus the person who narrates the order of events in time does not compose that order himself; and he who shows the location of places or the natures of animals, plants, or minerals does not discuss things instituted by men; and he who describes the stars or their motions does not describe anything instituted by himself or by other men. In the same way, he who says, "When a consequent is false, it is necessary that the antecedent upon which it is based be false also," speaks very truly; but he does not arrange matters so that they are this way. Rather, he simply points out an existing truth. This rule is the basis for what we have quoted from the Apostle Paul. Those whose error the Apostle wished to refute had set forth the antecedent that there is no resurrection of the dead. But the consequent follows from this antecedent that there is no resurrection of the dead that "then Christ is not risen," but this consequent is false. For Christ arose, so that the antecedent is false that there is no resurrection of the dead. It follows that there is a resurrection of the dead. This may be put briefly as follows: "If there is no resurrection of the dead, neither was Christ resurrected. But Christ was resurrected. Therefore there is a resurrection of the dead." The principle that if the consequent is false the antecedent must also be false was not instituted by men, but discovered. And this rule applies to the validity of inferences, not to the truth of propositions.

XXXIII

51. When the argument about resurrection is presented in this way, both the rules of inference and the meaning of the conclusion are true. Valid inferences may be made from false premises in this way. Suppose someone to have conceded, "If a snail is an animal, it has a voice." When this has been conceded and it has been shown that a snail has no voice, the antecedent is invalidated since the consequent appears that a snail is not an animal. This consequent is false, but the inference from the false antecedent is correct. Thus the truth of a proposition is inherent in itself, but the truth of a consequent depends on the opinion or agreement of the disputant. Thus, as we said above, a

false premise should be led to its valid inferences so that he whose error we wish to correct will abandon it when he sees that the consequences to which it leads are to be rejected. Now it is easy to understand that just as valid consequents may be derived from false antecedents, so also true antecedents may be led to false consequents. Suppose someone should say, "If he is just, he is good," and that this proposition is granted. Then let him add, "But he is not just," and let this also be accepted. He may conclude, "He is therefore not good." Although all of these things may be true, the conclusion is not valid according to rule. For the invalidation of the antecedent does not necessarily invalidate the consequent in the way that the invalidation of the consequent also invalidates the antecedent. Altough it is true when we say, "If he is an orator, he is a man," it does not follow that we may infer "He is not a man" if we add to the first antecedent the assertion, "He is not an orator."

XXXIV

52. In this way it is one thing to know the rules of valid inference, another thing to know the truth of propositions. Concerning inferences, one learns what is consequent, what is inconsequent, and what is incompatible. It is logical that "If one is an orator, he is a man"; it is illogical that "If one is a man, he is an orator"; and the parts of "If one is a man, he is a quadruped" are incompatible. In these instances, the inferences themselves are judged. Concerning the truth of propositions, however, the rules of inference are not relevant and the propositions are to be considered in themselves. But when true and certain propositions are joined by valid inferences to propositions we are not sure about, the latter, also, necessarily become certain. There are those who boast when they have learned the rules of valid inference as if they had learned the truth of propositions. And on the other hand, there are some who know many true propositions but think ill of themselves because they do not know the rules of inference. But he who knows that there is a resurrection of the dead is better than another who knows that it follows from the proposition that there is no resurrection of the dead that "then Christ is not risen."

XXXV

53. In the same way the science of definition, division, and partition, although it may be applied to falsehoods, is neither false in itself nor instituted by men; rather it was discovered in the order of things. Although poets have used it in their fables, and false philosophers in the expression of their erroneous opinions, and even heretics or false Christians have been accustomed to use it, there is nevertheless nothing false in the fact that in definition, division, and partition anything is to be used which is pertinent to the subject and nothing is to be used which is not pertinent. This is true even though that which is defined or distributed into its various parts is not true. For falsehood itself may be defined, when we say that a signification attributed to a thing is false when the thing itself does not justify that signification, or define the false in some other way. And this definition is true even though the false may not be true. We may

also divide this subject, saying that there are two kinds of falsehood, one of which involves things that are not possible, and the other of which involves things that are possible but nevertheless do not exist. For he who says that seven and three are eleven says something that cannot be at all; but he who says that it rained, let us say, on January 1, even though it did not rain on that day, describes something that might be true. Thus the definition and division of the false may be very true, but the false itself cannot be true in any way.

XXXVI

54. There are, moreover, certain precepts for a more copious discourse which make up what are called the rules of eloquence, and these are very true, even though they may be used to make falsehoods persuasive. Since they can be used in connection with true principles as well as with false, they are not themselves culpable, but the perversity of ill using them is culpable. Men did not themselves institute the fact that an expression of charity conciliates an audience, or the fact that it is easy to understand a brief and open account of events, or that the variety of a discourse keeps the auditors attentive and without fatigue. There are other similar principles which may be employed either in false or in true causes, but which are themselves true in so far as they cause things to be known or to be believed, or move men's minds either to seek or to avoid something. And these are rather discovered than instituted.

XXXVII

55. But when these precepts are learned they are to be applied more in expressing those things which are understood than in the pursuit of understanding. However, a knowledge of inference, definition, and division aids the understanding a great deal, provided that men do not make the mistake of thinking that they have learned the truth of the blessed life when they have learned them. Moreover, it frequently happens that men more easily learn the things themselves on account of which these principles are learned than the very knotty and spiny precepts of these disciplines. It is as if one should wish to give rules for walking and admonishes that the rear foot is not to be raised until the first foot is put down, and then goes on to describe in detail how the hinges of the joints and knees are to be moved. He speaks truly, nor is it possible to walk in any other way. Yet men more easily do these things when they walk than pay attention to them while they are doing them or understand them when they are described. But those who cannot walk care about the rules much less, since they cannot try them by experience. In the same way an ingenious person more easily discerns a false conclusion than he learns the rules governing it. And a stupid person who does not discern it is much less apt to understand the rules. And in all of these things the semblances of truth more frequently delight us than prove themselves helpful to us in disputing or judging. They may make men's discernment more alert, but they may also make men malign and proud so that they love to deceive with specious arguments and questions or to think themselves great because they have learned these things and therefore place themselves above good and innocent people.

XXXVIII

56. It is perfectly clear to the most stupid person that the science of numbers was not instituted by men, but rather investigated and discovered. Virgil did not wish to have the first syllable of *Italia* short, as the ancients pronounced it, and it was made long.[47] But no one could in this fashion because of his personal desire arrange matters so that three threes are not nine, or do not geometrically produce a square figure, or are not the triple of the ternary, or are not one and a half times six, or are evenly divisible by two when odd numbers cannot be so divided. Whether they are considered in themselves or applied to the laws of figures, or of sound, or of some other motion, numbers have immutable rules not instituted by men but discovered through the sagacity of the more ingenious.

57. But whoever delights in these things in such a way that he boasts among the unlearned, and does not seek to learn the source of the truths which he has somehow perceived and to know whence those things are not only true but immutable which he has seen to be immutable, and thus, arising from corporal appearances to the human mind, when he finds this to be mutable since it is now learned and now unlearned, does not come to understand that it is placed between immutable things above it and other mutable things below it, and so does not turn all his knowledge toward the praise and love of one God from whom he knows that everything is derived—this man may seem to be learned. But he is in no way wise.

XXXIX

58. Thus is seems to me that studious and intelligent youths who fear God and seek the blessed life might be helpfully admonished that they should not pursue those studies which are taught outside of the Church of Christ as though they might lead to the blessed life. Rather they should soberly and diligently weigh them. And if they find some which are instituted by men which vary because of the diverse wills of those who founded them and because of the base notions of those in error, and especially if they imply a society with demons through certain significations made as if through pacts or agreements, these are to be repudiated and detested. They should also avoid superfluous and extravagant institutions of men. But they should not neglect those human institutions helpful to social intercourse in the necessary pursuits of life. Among other teachings to be found among the pagans, aside from the history of things both past and present, teachings which concern the corporal senses, including the experience and theory of the useful mechanical arts, and the sciences of disputation and of numbers, I consider nothing to be useful. And in all of these, the maxim is to be observed, "Nothing in excess." And this is especially true with reference to those arts pertaining to the corporal senses, since they are limited by times and places.

59. Just as certain scholars have interpreted separately all the Hebrew, Syrian, Egyptian, and other foreign names and words that appear in the Holy Scriptures without interpretation, and just as Eusebius has written a history because of questions in the divine books which demand its use, so that it is not

necessary for Christians to engage in much labor for a few things, in the same way I think it might be possible, if any capable person could be persuaded to undertake the task for the sake of his brethren, to collect in order and write down singly explanations of whatever unfamiliar geographical locations, animals, herbs and trees, stones, and metals are mentioned in the Scripture. The same thing could be done with numbers so that the rationale only of those numbers which are mentioned in the Holy Scripture is explained. I have discovered that some of this material, or, indeed, almost all of it, contrary to my expectation, has already been explained and written down by good and learned Christians, but either because of common negligence or envious disregard it remains hidden. Whether the same sort of thing could be done with the science of disputation I do not know, but I suspect that it would not be possible because that knowledge is interwoven throughout the text of Scripture like so many nerves. Moreover, it is of more use to the reader in solving and explaining ambiguities, which we shall discuss later, than in clarifying unknown signs, which we are discussing now.

XL

60. If those who are called philosophers, especially the Platonists, have said things which are indeed true and are well accommodated to our faith, they should not be feared; rather, what they have said should be taken from them as from unjust possessors and converted to our use.[48] Just as the Egyptians had not only idols and grave burdens which the people of Israel detested and avoided, so also they had vases and ornaments of gold and silver and clothing which the Israelites took with them secretly when they fled, as if to put them to a better use. They did not do this on their own authority but at God's commandment, while the Egyptians unwittingly supplied them with things which they themselves did not use well.[49] In the same way all the teachings of the pagans contain not only simulated and superstitious imaginings and grave burdens of unnecessary labor, which each one of us leaving the society of pagans under the leadership of Christ ought to abominate and avoid, but also liberal disciplines more suited to the uses of truth, and some most useful precepts concerning morals. Even some truths concerning the worship of one God are discovered among them. These are, as it were, their gold and silver, which they did not institute themselves but dug up from certain mines of divine Providence, which is everywhere infused, and perversely and injuriously abused in the worship of demons. When the Christian separates himself in spirit from their miserable society, he should take this treasure with him for the just use of teaching the gospel. And their clothing, which is made up of those human institutions which are accommodated to human society and necessary to the conduct of life, should be seized and held to be converted to Christian uses.

61. For what else have many of our good faithful done? May we not see with how much gold and silver and clothing bundled up the most sweet teacher and most blessed martyr Cyprian fled from Egypt? Or how much Lactantius took with him? Or how much Victorinus, Optatus, Hilary carried with them, not to speak of those still living? Or how much innumerable Greeks have taken? This

was done first by that most faithful servant of God, Moses, of whom it is written that he "was instructed in all the wisdom of the Egyptians."[50] The superstitious custom of the pagans would never have accommodated all of these men with disciplines which they might find useful, especially in those times when through objections to the yoke of Christ the pagans were persecuting Christians, if it had been suspected that the knowledge would prove useful in the worship of one God, through which the vain cult of idols is abolished. But they gave their gold, silver, and clothing to the people of God fleeing from Egypt not knowing that they yielded those things which they gave "unto the obedience of Christ."[51] That which was done in Exodus was undoubtedly a figure that it might typify these things. I say this without prejudice to any other equal or better understanding.

XLI

62. When the student of Holy Scripture, having been instructed in this way, begins to approach his text, he should always bear in mind the apostolic saying, "Knowledge puffs up; but charity edifies."[52] Thus he will feel that, although he has fled rich from Egypt, he cannot be saved unless he has observed the Pasch. "For Christ our pasch is sacrificed,"[53] and the sacrifice of Christ emphasizes for us nothing more than that which He said as if to those whom He saw laboring under Pharaoh: "Come to me, all you that labour, and are burdened, and I will refresh you. Take up my yoke upon you, and learn of me, because I am meek, and humble of heart: and you shall find rest to your souls. For my yoke is sweet and my burden light."[54] To whom is it thus light except to those of meek and humble heart whom knowledge does not inflate but charity edifies? Students should remember, therefore, concerning those who once celebrated the Pasch with appearances of shadows, that when they were commanded to mark the door-posts with the blood of the lamb, they were to be marked with hyssop.[55] This is a meek and humble herb, and yet nothing is stronger or more penetrating than its roots. Thus "rooted and founded in charity," we "may be able to comprehend, with all the saints, what is the breadth, and length, and height, and depth,"[56] which things make up the Cross of Our Lord. Its breadth is said to be in the transverse beam upon which the hands are stretched; its length extends from the ground to the crossbar, and on it the whole body from the hands down is affixed; its height reaches from the crossbar to the top where the head is placed; and its depth is that part which is hidden beneath the earth. In the Sign of the Cross the whole action of the Christian is described: to perform good deeds in Christ, to cling to Him with perseverance, to hope for celestial things, to refrain from profaning the sacraments. Having been cleansed by this action, we shall be able "to know also the charity of Christ, which surpasseth all knowledge," through which He is equal with the Father, by whom all things are made, so that we "may be filled unto all the fullness of God."[57] There is also in hyssop a cleansing power, lest, inflated by the knowledge of wealth taken from the Egyptians, the swollen lung should breathe forth in pride: "Thou shalt sprinkle me with hyssop, and I shall be cleansed: thou shalt wash me, and I shall be made whiter than snow. To my hearing thou shalt give joy and

gladness." And then the Psalmist adds as a consequence that he may show hyssop to signify a cleansing from pride, "and the bones that have been humbled shall rejoice."[58]

XLII

63. To the extent that the wealth of gold and silver and clothing which that people took with them from Egypt was less than that they afterwards acquired at Jerusalem, especially during the reign of King Solomon,[59] the knowledge collected from the books of the pagans, although some of it is useful, is also little as compared with that derived from the Holy Scriptures. For whatever a man has learned elsewhere is censured there if it is harmful; if it is useful, it is found there. And although anyone may find everything which he has usefully learned elsewhere there, he will also find very abundantly things which are found nowhere else at all except as they are taught with the wonderful nobility and remarkable humility of the Holy Scriptures. Therefore, when the reader has been prepared by this instruction so that he is not impeded by unknown signs, with a meek and humble heart, subjected easily to Christ with a burden that is light, established, rooted, and built up in charity so that knowledge cannot puff him up, let him turn next to the examination and consideration of ambiguous signs in the Scriptures, concerning which I shall essay to set forth in the third book what the Lord has granted to me.

NOTES

1. John 12:3–8.
2. Matt. 26:28; Luke 22:19–20.
3. Matt. 9:20–22.
4. Cf. Gen. 11:1–9.
5. Cant. [Song of Sol.] 4:2.
6. Cf. Ps. 110:10 [111:10]; Prov. 1:7; 9:10; Ecclus. 1:16.
7. 1 Cor. 13:12.
8. 2 Cor. 5:7.
9. Phil. 3:20.
10. Deut. 25:4. For the apostolic interpretation, see 1 Cor. 9:9; 1 Tim. 5:18.
11. Isa. 58:7 (Ancient and Vulgate versions).
12. Rom. 11:14.
13. Isa. 7:9 (Ancient and Vulgate versions).
14. 2 Cor. 5:7.
15. Rom. 3:15 (from Prov. 1:16).
16. Wisd. 4:3.
17. Cf. Num. 13:20.
18. Ps. 131:18 [132:18], with *floriet* instead of *efflorebit* as in the Vulgate.
19. 1 Cor. 1:25.
20. For a discussion of St. Augustine's preferences among Scriptural texts, see Maurice Pontet, *L'exégèse de Saint Augustin prédicateur* (Paris, 1946), pp. 220 ff.

21. John 9:7.
22. Matt. 10:16.
23. Eph. 4:22–25; Col. 3:9–10.
24. Matt. 7:13.
25. Gen. 8:11.
26. Ps. 50:9 [51:7].
27. Exod. 24:18; 3 Kings [1 Kings] 19:8; Matt. 4:2.
28. Matt. 17:3.
29. John 21:6–11.
30. John 2:20.
31. Cf. 2. 28. 42. The number 46 was taken as a sign of Christ's human body, since A D A M may be thought of as 1 plus 4 plus 1 plus 40.
32. Rom. 1:21–23
33. Cf. Gen. 1:14.
34. Wisd. 13:9.
35. Gen. 25:26.
36. Cf. Deut. 13:1–3.
37. 1 Kings [1 Sam.] 28:15–19.
38. Acts 16:16–18.
39. 1 Cor. 10:19–20.
40. Cf. John 2:20–21.
41. Luke 3:23.
42. Rom. 9:5.
43. It should be emphasized that throughout this discussion St. Augustine is concerned primarily with the education of the Christian exegete.
44. Ecclus. 37:23.
45. 1 Cor. 15:13, 14.
46. 1 Cor. 15:12.
47. Virg. *Aen.* 1. 2, *et passim.*
48. For Augustine's influence on the preservation of the Platonic tradition, see R. Klibansky, *The Continuity of the Platonic Tradition during the Middle Ages* (London, 1939).
49. Exod. 3:22; 11:2; 12:35.
50. Acts 7:22.
51. 2 Cor. 10:5.
52. 1 Cor. 8:1.
53. 1 Cor. 5:7.
54. Matt. 11:28–30.
55. Exod. 12:22.
56. Eph. 3:17–18.
57. Eph. 3:19.
58. Ps. 50:9–10 [51:7–8].
59. Kings [1 Kings] 10:14–17.

Proclus
410–485

Proclus, who lived in the fifth century A.D., is the last in the line of major Greek philosophers of antiquity. He was the author of numerous commentaries on Plato, and two systematic manuals, Elements of Theology *and* Elements of Physics. *In addition, he completed works on religious symbolism which are lost to us.*

As a young man, Proclus intended to become a lawyer, but he experienced a "conversion" to philosophy. He then trained to become the "Platonic successor"—the administrator of the Athenian School of Neoplatonism. He lived the life of a vegetarian and semiascetic. Proclus was himself anti-Christian, although, ironically, he was a tremendous influence upon pseudo-Dionysius the Areopagite and his Platonist negative theology, which in turn has been a permanent influence upon the Eastern Orthodox Church.

Proclus is the first to apply Neoplatonic theory directly to literary theory. In so doing, he stood Plato's negative evaluation of poetry on its head. Proclus advanced the theory that poetry is really a more profound philosophy. For him, the poet was a seer and the imagination reached higher than reason.

Proclus utilized the Neoplatonic division of the soul into three parts—intellect (mens) allied to the divine, reason allied to human life, and fancy (phantasia) or the capturing of images—and mirrored the division with three kinds of poetry. One he called the "rage for beauty" which he related to the divine. Didactic poetry taught prudence and the other human virtues. The lowest form of poetry, he said, was mere imitation. In essence, then, he accepted Plato's low opinion of much if not most art as imitation, but at the same time he insisted that an art existed which transcended reason and was akin to religious experience.

In writing about the Republic, Proclus closely examines Plato's various statements about art and reveals the ambiguity in their view of the subject. He attempts to demonstrate that Plato himself can be re-interpreted in accord with the Neoplatonic rehabilitation of art.

The legacy of Proclus and other followers of Plotinus was the insertion of a strong mystical tendency in medieval interpretation, in contradistinction to the formalist tradition transmitted to the medieval writers by Cicero, Horace, and Donatus. In addition, they stimulated *the critical theory of humanists throughout the Renaissance and the Enlightenment.*

On the More Difficult Questions in the "Republic": The Nature of Poetic Art, *translated by Kevin Kerrane (revising Thomas Taylor's translation), is reprinted by permission of the publisher from Alex Preminger et al., eds.,* Classical and Medieval Literary Criticism: Translations and Interpretations *(New York: Frederick Ungar Publishing Co., 1974).*

The Nature Of Poetic Art

There are three lives in the soul. The best and most perfect is through the faculty which allies and conjoins it with the gods, so that the soul lives a life united to them through the highest similitude. The soul, no longer existing in itself, but deriving life from a divine source infusing the mind, is filled with ineffable impressions of the divine, and connects like with like—its own light with that of the gods, and that which is most uniform in its own essence and life with that which is above all essence and life. The second life of the soul is through a faculty of middle dignity and power: the soul, not divinely inspired, realizes its own individuality by ordaining intellect and science as the principle of its energy, evolving the multitude of its reasons. It surveys the various mutations of forms, unites through abstraction the intellect and its object, and expresses in images an intellectual and intelligible essence. The third life of the soul is that which accords with its inferior faculties: the soul, expressing itself through them, employs phantasies and irrational senses, and is filled entirely with things of a subordinate nature.

Just as there are these three forms of life in souls, so poetry, as it proceeds from the various faculties, is diversified into the first, middle, and last modes of being. The first kind of poetry has the highest existence: it is full of divine goods, and it establishes the soul in the causes themselves of things, according to a certain ineffable union, leading that which is filled into sameness with its replenishing source. The soul subjects itself to spiritual illumination, and the divine is impelled to a communication of light—thus, according to the Oracle, "perfecting works, by mingling the rivers of incorruptible fire." This kind of poetry produces one divine bond, a union of participation, in which that which is subordinate partakes of that which is more excellent, so that the divine energy infuses all. The inferior nature withdraws, and conceals itself in that which is superior. This, then, in short, is an apparent madness better than temperance, and is distinguished by a divine quality. And as every different kind of poetry subsists according to a different hyparxis, or summit of divine essence, so this first kind of poetry, proceeding from divine inspiration, fills the soul with symmetry, and hence adorns even its least energies with measures and rhythms. And just as we define prophetic fury as according with truth, and the amatory inclinations as according with beauty, so in like manner we define the poetic mania as according with divine symmetry.

The second kind of poetry, which is subordinate to this first and divinely inspired species, and which has a middle existence in the soul, derives its being from a scientific and intellectual faculty. Hence this kind of poetry embodies the essence of things, strives to contemplate beautiful works and reasonings, and leads everything toward a measured and rhythmical interpretation. For you will find many works of good poets to be of this kind, rivaling the wisdom of great men—full of admonitions, the best counsels, and intellectual harmony. This kind of poetry teaches prudence and every other virtue to those of a naturally good disposition, and it explores and reflects on the periods of the soul, its eternal reasons, and various powers.

The third species of poetry, subordinate to these, is mingled with opinions and phantasies. It is composed by means of imitation; it is said to be—and is nothing other than—imitative poetry. Sometimes it uses likeness-making alone, and sometimes it relies on a likeness that is only apparent, not real. It strongly intensifies very moderate passions, astonishing the hearers; using appropriate names and words, mutations of harmonies and varieties of rhythms, it changes the dispositions of souls. It indicates the nature of things not as they are, but as they appear to the many, being a certain adumbration, and not an accurate knowledge of things. It also establishes as its goal the delight of the hearers, and looks particularly to the passive part of the soul, which is naturally adapted to rejoice or be afflicted. But of this species of poetry, as we have said elsewhere, one division is *assimilative,* in which the imitation is accurate, while the other is *phantastic,* affording only apparent imitation.

Such, then, in short are the species of poetry. It now remains to show that these are also mentioned by Plato, and to treat other matters compatible with his teachings about each. First we shall discuss those wonderful conceptions of divine poetry which may be collected by anyone who reads Plato attentively. And once these are clear, I think it will be easy to understand the other two species of poetry.

In the *Phaedrus* Plato calls divine poetry "a possession from the Muses, and a mania" [244–45], and says that it is imparted from above to a tender and solitary soul. Its employment excites and inspires with Bacchic fury, in odes and other poetic forms, and its purpose is to instruct posterity in celebrating the infinite deeds of the ancients.

From these words it is perfectly evident that Plato identifies the original and first-operating cause of poetry as the gift of the Muses. For just as the Muses fill with harmony and rhythmical motion all the other divine creations, both the apparent and the unapparent, so in like manner they produce a vestige of divinity in those souls they take possession of, and this illuminates inspired poetry. I think that Plato calls such an illumination a *possession* and a *mania* because the whole energy of the illuminating power is divine, and because that which is illuminated gives itself up to this energy and, abandoning its own habits, yields to the force of that which is divine and uniform. He calls it a possession because the whole illuminated soul surrenders itself to the present effect of the illuminating deity. Plato calls it a mania because such a soul abandons its own proper energies for those of the illuminating powers.

In the second place, Plato describes the characteristics of the soul possessed by the Muses, and says that it ought to be tender and solitary. A soul hard and resisting, and disobedient to divine illumination, would oppose the energy of divinely inspired possession, because it would exist in itself rather than through the illuminating power, and it would be incapable of appreciating the gifts of this power. And a soul given over to various opinions, and filled with thoughts alien to a divine nature, would obscure the process of inspiration by mingling itself and its energies with those derived from the Muses. The soul which is to be possessed by the Muses must therefore be tender and solitary—so that it may be properly receptive to divinity and harmonize with it, and it should be unreceptive to and unmingled with other things.

In the third place, Plato mentions the common occurrence of such an aptitude in combination with possession and mania from the Muses. For to excite and inspire with Bacchic fury is the province both of that which illuminates and that which is illuminated, and the two processes become one: the divine force moving from above, and the soul surrendering itself to this motion. Excitation is a purified energy of the soul, lifting it from the world of matter and time and into divinity. Bacchic fury is a divinely inspired motion and, as it were, an unwearied dance upward toward the divine, giving perfection to the possessed. But again, a correct disposition of the soul is as necessary as the divine power, so that the possessed will not incline to that which is worse, but will easily be moved to a more excellent nature.

In the fourth place, Plato adds that the purpose of this divine poetry is to instruct posterity in celebrating the infinite deeds of the ancients. This implies that human affairs become more perfect and splendid when they are presented by a divinely inspired poet, and that such poetry produces true learning in its hearers. It does not aim primarily at the training of the young, but is directed more toward those already schooled in civic virtue, who still need a greater spiritual understanding of divine matters. More than any other kind of poetry, this species instructs the hearers, once its divine nature becomes manifest to them. Hence Plato very properly prefers this poetry, which subsists from the Muses in tender and solitary souls, to every other human art: "For the poet who approaches the poetic gates without such a mania will be imperfect, and his poetry, so far as it is dictated by prudence, will vanish before that which is the outcome of fury" [*Phaedrus* 245]. Thus does Socrates in the *Phaedrus* instruct us in the peculiarities of divine poetry—which differs both from divine prophecy and from prudent, calculated art—and he attributes to the gods its first unfolding into light.

Socrates' comments in the *Ion*, when he is discoursing with the rhapsodist about this species of poetry, confirm these views. Here Socrates states clearly that the poetry of Homer is divine, and that it is a source of enthusiastic energy to those conversant with it. For when the rhapsodist says that he can speak copiously on the poems of Homer, but not at all on the writings of other poets, Socrates explains this by saying: "It is not from technical skill that you speak well concerning Homer, but because you are moved by a divine power" [533d]. And the truth of this is indeed perfectly evident. For those who do something by means of art are able to produce the same effect in all similar situations. But those who work by means of divine inspiration on something truly harmonious cannot regularly produce the same effect when working with other, similar things. The rhapsodist receives divine inspiration when reciting Homer, but not when reciting other poets. Socrates then instructs us by using the stone commonly called Herculean as a clear analogy to perfect possession by the Muses: "This stone, then, not only draws to itself iron rings, but imparts to them a power to attract similar things, so as to enable them to draw other rings, and form a chain of rings, or pieces of iron, each hanging from the other" [533d–e].

Let us now consider Socrates' continued remarks on divine poetry. "Thus then," he says, "the Muse makes men divine; and, from these men thus inspired, others catch the sacred power to form a chain of divine enthusiasts" [533e]. Here, in the first place, he speaks of the divine cause in the singular number, calling it the Muse and not, as in the *Phaedrus*, a possession from the Muses. Socrates refers to the divine cause as a single mania affecting a whole multitude, in order to attribute all enthusiastic power to one spiritual substance, the primary principle of poetry. For poetry subsists uniformly and mysteriously in the first mover, but secondarily and indirectly in poets moved by that spiritual power, and still more indirectly in the rhapsodists, who are led back to the first cause through the agency of the poets. By thus extending the principle of divine inspiration as far as the rhapsodists, Socrates celebrates the fecundity of the first moving power. At the same time he clearly states that poets themselves participate in inspiration: the poets' ability through their poems to excite others to a divinely inspired state indicates that a divine nature is conspicuously present in their souls. Consequently, Socrates adds this comment: "The best epic poets, and all who similarly excel in composing any kind of verse to be recited, do not frame their admirable poems from the rules of art; but, possessed by the Muse, they write from divine inspiration. Nor is it otherwise with the best lyric poets, and all other fine writers of verse to be sung" [533e]. And again, afterwards, he says: "For a poet is a thing light and volatile, and sacred, nor is he able to write poetry till he becomes divine, and has no longer the command of his intellect" [534b]. And lastly, Socrates adds: "Hence it is that the poets indeed say many fine things, whatever their subject, just as you do concerning Homer; but not doing it through any rules of art, each of them succeeds through a divine calling in that species of poetry to which he is uniquely impelled by the Muse" [534c].

In all these citations, it is evident that Plato traces divine poetry to a divine cause, which he calls a Muse. In this he emulates Homer, who at one time refers to a multitude of Muses and at another to the union of the Muses in a single principle—as when he says "O Muses, sing" and "Sing me the man, O Muse." Midway between this divine cause of enthusiasm and the last echoes of inspiration in the responses of the rhapsodists, Plato locates poetic mania. Moving and being moved, filled from on high and transferring to others the illumination thus derived, the poetic mania joins together even the last participants in a communion with the divine substance.

With these things we may also bring into accord what the Athenian Guest says about poetry in the third book of the *Laws*, and what Timaeus says about poets. The Athenian Guest says that "poetry is divinely inspired," and that "it composes sacred hymns, and, with certain Graces and Muses, relates many things that have been truly transacted" [682]. Timaeus exhorts us to follow poets inspired by Apollo, in that they are "the sons of gods, knowing their fathers' concerns, even though their assertions are not probable and are unaccompanied by demonstrations." From all this it is easy to understand what Plato thought about divine poetry, and how he characterized inspired poets as special messengers of divine powers, eminently acquainted with the affairs of their fathers. When, therefore, Plato takes notice of mythical fictions, and corrects the more serious part of the writings of the poets—such as those dealing with bonds, castrations, loves, sexual connections, tears, and laughter among the gods—we must say that he also especially testifies that these things are properly presented as allegorical, concealing the idea as under veils. For whoever thinks that poets are particularly worthy of belief in affairs respecting the gods, even though they speak through inspiration rather than logical demonstration, must certainly admire the divine fables through which they deliver the truth concerning the nature of the gods. Whoever calls poetry divine cannot also ascribe to it an impious and exaggerated treatment of the divine. And whoever shows that the assertions of poets are attended with certain Graces and Muses must certainly judge an inelegant, unharmonious, and ungraceful phantasy to be very remote from the theory of poetic inspiration. Thus, when Plato in his *Republic* establishes by law that poetry and allegorical fables are not adapted to the ears of the young, he is very far from despising poetry itself; he merely protects the juvenile mind, which is inexperienced in hearing such things, from fiction of this sort. For, as he says in the *Second Alcibiades,* "The whole of poetry is naturally enigmatical, and is not obvious to the understanding of everyone" [147]. And hence in the *Republic* he clearly says that "youth is not able to distinguish what is allegory and what is not" [2. 377]. We must say, therefore, that Plato entirely approves of inspired poetry, which he calls divine, and thinks it proper that those who compose it should be venerated in silence. This concludes our examination of the first kind of poetry, which subsists, from a divine origin, in tender and solitary souls.

Now let us contemplate that species of poetry which has a scientific knowledge of things, and which proceeds according to intellect and prudence. It reveals to men many spiritual essences, and brings to light many probable tenets in practical philosophy. It investigates the most beautiful symmetry in human behavior, and examines the disposition to vice. And it adorns all of these things with proper measures and rhythms.

The Athenian Guest in the *Laws* says that the poetry of Theognis is of this kind, which he praises beyond that of Tyrtaeus, because Theognis is a teacher of the whole of virtue, including the whole of political life. Theognis teaches a fidelity which receives its completion from all the virtues, expelling from politics that most pernicious vice sedition, and changing the lives of those who are persuaded. On the other hand, Tyrtaeus merely praises the habit of fortitude by itself, preaching it to those who neglect other virtues. But it will be better to listen to Plato's own words: "We also have the poet Theognis as a witness in our favor, who was a citizen of Megara in Sicily. For he says, 'Who keeps his faith amid seditious cries/Is worth his weight in silver and in gold.' We say therefore that such a person will conduct himself better in the most difficult kind of war, much in the same degree as justice, temperance, and prudence, when united with fortitude, are better than fortitude alone. For no one can be both faithful and effective in civil strife without the whole of virtue" [*Laws* 1. 630]. Here, therefore, Plato recognizes Theognis as partaking of political science, and all the virtues.

In the *Second Alcibiades* Plato, defining the most right and healthy mode of prayer, attributes it to a certain wise poet: "To me, Alcibiades, it seems probable that some wise man or other, happening to be connected with certain persons void of understanding, and observing them to pursue and pray for things for which it were better for them to be without, but which appeared to them good, composed for their use a common prayer in words like these—'King Jupiter, grant us what is good, whether or not it is the subject of our prayers, and avert from us what is evil, even if we should pray for it'" [142–43]. For only the scientific man, in whom a divine nature is adapted to the middle faculties of man, knows how to distinguish between good and evil in daily life. And on this account Socrates calls the poet who composed the prayer a wise man: through science alone, rather than through divine inspiration or right opinion, the poet formed a judgment on the natures and habits of those who prayed, and he reserved to the gods that which falls under their beneficent power. For it was the work of wisdom and science, and not of anything casual, to have converted those people through prayer to the one kingly providence of Jupiter, to have attributed the existence of good to the power of divinity, to have prevented the generation of true evils by calling upon the benevolence of a more excellent nature, and in short to have asserted that these things were unknown to those who prayed and were instead within the province of the divinity. Very properly, therefore, we say that such poetry is wise and scientific. For the poetry which is able to adapt truths to the middle faculties of man must itself exist by means of perfect science.

In the third place, let us now speak about imitative poetry, which, as we have already said, sometimes makes accurate likenesses of things, and at other times expresses things according to mere appearance. In the *Laws* the Athenian Guest clearly explains to us the assimilative part of this poetry, but in the *Republic* Socrates describes its phantastic part. And in the *Sophist* the Eleatean Guest apprises us of how the assimilative and phantastic species of imitation differ from each other:

> GUEST: For I seem to perceive two species of imitation—one being the art of making likenesses, which is executed when someone produces an imitation by copying an original model in all proportions (length, breadth, and depth) and colors.
>
> THEAETETUS: Do not all imitators try to do this?
>
> GUEST: Not those who perform or paint any great work. For if sculptors, for example, were to follow the exact proportions of their models, then the upper parts, which we see from farther off, would appear smaller than they should be, and the lower parts would seem too large.

THEAETETUS: Entirely so. And thus artists forego accuracy in their imitations; they do not produce in images truly beautiful proportions, but only those which appear to be so. [235]

Very properly, I think, does the Eleatean Guest at the end of the dialogue, wishing to bind the sophist by the definitive method, distinguish between assimilative imitation (in which the image is a true likeness of the model) and phantastic imitation (in which the likeness is only apparent).

In the second book of the *Laws* the Athenian Guest speaks only of assimilative poetry, and he discusses music which, rather than making pleasure its end, aims at a true imitation of its model. On the other hand, Socrates in the *Republic* deals with phantastic poetry. And having shown that a poet of this kind is third from the truth and merely derivative, Socrates compares such poetry to a picture which represents not the works of nature but of artificers—and these not as they truly are, but only as they appear to be. Thus Socrates clearly shows that the phantastic species of poetry aims only at delighting the audience. Of the two kinds of imitative poetry, the phantastic is inferior to the assimilative for this very reason: whereas assimilative poetry is concerned with accuracy of imitation, phantastic poetry is concerned merely with how the power of the phantasy can produce pleasure in the audience.

Such, then, are the species of poetry which Plato thought worthwhile to distinguish—one as better than science, another as scientific, a third as conversant with, and a fourth as falling off from, right opinion.

Having clarified these matters, let us now return to the poetry of Homer and contemplate every poetic habit that shines in it, especially those concerned with truth and beauty. When Homer is filled with enthusiastic energy, is possessed by the Muses, and communicates mystical ideas about the gods themselves, then he operates according to the first and divinely inspired principle of poetry. When he speaks of the life of the soul, the diversities in its nature, and its relation to civic virtue, then he especially speaks scientifically. When he presents forms of imitation truly similar to specific things and persons, then he employs assimilative imitation. And, finally, when Homer directs his attention not to the truth of things, but only as they appear to the multitude, and thus seduces the souls of his hearers, then he produces phantastic poetry.

I wish now to illustrate these poetic habits in Homer, beginning with phantastic imitation. He sometimes describes the rising and setting of the sun, not by accurately recounting in his verses each of these as it actually happens, but merely as it appears to us from a distance. These and all similar examples may be called the phantastic part of his poetry. But when Homer imitates heroes as warring or consulting or speaking according to the forms of real life—some as prudent, others as brave, and others as ambitious—then I would call this assimilative poetry. The scientific habit of poetry is manifested, I believe, when Homer unfolds and teaches the workings of the soul, based on his knowledge of the various faculties within it or of the relation between an image and the soul's use of it, or when he deals with the order of the elements within the universe (earth, water, fire, air), or other similar matters. And I would say that Homer is filled with enthusiastic energy, and is possessed by the Muses, when he devises fables that teach us about such mysteries as the demiurge, the triadic emanation of the one, the bonds of Vulcan, or the relation between the paternal ideas of Jupiter and the fertile divinity of Juno.

In addition, Homer's portrayal of Demodocus the bard [*Odyssey*, Book 8] attributes to him an energy originating from the gods. Ulysses says that Demodocus was impelled by a god when he began his song, that he was divinely inspired, that the Muse loved him, and that God is the leader of the Muses: "The Muse, Jove's daughter, or Apollo, taught/Thee aptly thus the fate of Greece to sing,/And all the Grecians, hardy deeds and toils" [488–90]. It is a standard interpretation that Homer intended to represent himself in the character of Demodocus, and their personal calamities are indeed similar. There seems to be a direct reference to the fabled blindness of Homer in the statement that the gods "With clouds of darkness quenched his visual ray,/But gave him power to raise the lofty lay" [62–64]. Homer thus clearly contends that Demodocus says what he says by means of divine inspiration.

It is well that we have mentioned Demodocus and his inspired song, for it seems to me that the musicians Homer thought worthy of mentioning illustrate the various poetic habits discussed above. Demodocus, as we have said, was inspired, both in narrating divine and human concerns, and is said to have received his songs from the gods. On the other hand, the Ithacan bard Phemius is characterized merely according to a scientific knowledge of divine and human affairs. In Book 1 of the *Odyssey* Penelope addresses him: "Alluring arts thou knowest, and what of old/Of gods and heroes sacred bards have told" [337–39]. A third bard is the lyrist of Clytemnestra, who seems to have been an imitative poet, employing right opinion. He performed melodies of temperance for Clytemnestra's benefit, and as long as he remained with her she perpetrated no unholy deed: the disciplining effect of his song converted her irrational tendencies into temperate behavior. A fourth musician, Thamyris, may be taken to represent the phantastic species of poetry. It is said that his song made the Muses indignant, so that they caused it to cease, for he practiced a music much more diversified and sensuous, and calculated to please the vulgar. By preferring a more varied music than the simpler mode adapted to the Muses, Thamyris is said to have fallen into contention with them, and to have lost the benevolence of the goddesses. The anger of the Muses does not refer to any passion in them, but indicates that Thamyris was unsuited to participate with them: his kind of song is phantastic and most remote from truth, calling forth the passions of the soul, and possessing no value with respect to imitation, right opinion, or science.

We may therefore behold all the kinds of poetry in Homer, but particularly the enthusiastic which, as we have said, principally characterizes him. Nor are we alone in this opinion: as we observed earlier, Plato himself in many places calls Homer a divine poet, the most divine of poets, and a proper imitator in the best sense. But imitative and phantastic poetry has a very obscure place in Homer's work, since he uses it merely in order to gain the credibility of the vulgar multitude, and only when it is totally unavoidable. If a man entered a well regulated city and beheld intoxication employed there for a certain useful purpose, he might decide to imitate not the prudence or whole order in the city, but intoxication itself alone. In such a case the city is hardly to be blamed for his conduct, which is due rather to the peculiar imbecility of his judgment. And in like manner, I think, the tragic poets, who emulate the phantastic species of Homer's poetry, should refer the principle of their error not to Homer, but to their own weakness. Homer may therefore be called the leader of tragedy, insofar as tragic poets emulate him in other respects and distribute the different parts of his poetry—imitating phantastically what he asserts assimilatively, and adapting to the ears of the vulgar what he composes scientifically. But Homer is not only the teacher of tragedy (for he is this merely by means of the phantastic element of his poetry), but he is also the teacher of all that is imitative in Plato, and of the whole theory of that philosopher.

It seems to me that the reason Plato wrote so severely against Homer, and against the whole species of imitative poetry, was the corruption of the times in which he lived. Philosophy was then despised, some calling it useless and others condemning it entirely. By contrast, poetry was then held in immoderate admiration. Its imitative power was the subject of emulation, and it was considered as adequate by itself for purposes of discipline. And poets, because they imitated everything, persuaded themselves that they knew all things, as is evident from what Socrates says in the *Republic*. Hence Plato, indignant at the prevalence of such an opinion, shows that poetry and imitation wander far from the truth imparted by philosophy, the savior of souls. In the same benevolent spirit in which he criticizes the sophists and popular orators for their inability to contribute anything to virtue, Plato also criticizes the poets—particularly the composers of tragedy, and those imitators who devise works to charm the audience without promoting virtue, enchanting the multitude without instructing them. And Plato considers that Homer deserves a similar criticism, insofar as he is the leader of this species of poetry and the model for the tragedians' emulation. It was necessary for Plato to do this in order to recall the men of his age from their total admiration of poetry, because their immoderate attachment to it led to a neglect of true discipline. And so with a view to the instruction of the multitude, to correct an absurd phantasy, and to exhort men to a philosophic life, Plato reproves the tragedians (who were then thought of as public teachers) for directing their attention to nothing rational. At the same time, Plato gives up his reverence for Homer and, ranking him in the same class with tragic poets, blames him as an imitator.

It should not seem strange for Plato to call the same poet both divine and third from the truth. For insofar as Homer is possessed by the Muses, he is divine; but insofar as he is an imitator, he is third from the truth.

Fulgentius
c. sixth-century A.D.

Little is known of the life of Fabius Planciades Fulgentius save that he was a native of Africa and a Christian, probably a cleric, who was deeply interested in pagan literature, especially its esoteric meanings. He wrote The Exposition of the Content of Vergil According to the Principles of Moral Philosophy *around 500* A.D., *and was the author of two other works: the* Three Books of Mythology, *which presents allegorical interpretations of the most important pagan myths, and a brief allegorical exegesis of the* Thebiad *of Statius, a Latin epic which borrows heavily from Vergil.*

Fulgentius' Exposition *is the last in a series of Vergil commentaries which include the work of Servius, Macrobius, and Donatus. Unlike his predecessors, however, who approached Vergil primarily from the standpoint of rhetorical criticism, Fulgentius' intention is to demonstrate that Vergil concealed a consistent system of ethics in the* Aeneid. *He utilizes the allegorical criticism which had by then gained prestige, especially among Christians, and which had its origin in the works of Philo of Alexandria. The* Exposition *is the earliest sustained allegorical reading of a Latin poetic classic that has survived. Fulgentius turns the story of Aeneas' travels into the exemplary life of Everyman, and heavily allegorizes each aspect of the narrative. Thus, the shipwreck of the Trojans which begins the* Aeneid *becomes in his allegory the metaphysical truth of the birth of the soul into a tempestuous and painful life. Fulgentius insists that poetry contains an esoteric wisdom, that the poet is an inspired prophet, and that poetic truth is a kind of revelation. The wisdom of Vergil is so profound that no mere mortal can hope to understand it without divine assistance. For Fulgentius, that assistance comes in the form of the ghost of Vergil himself, anticipating Dante's use of Vergil as a divine prophet in* The Divine Comedy.

Fulgentius' Latin is labored and involuted, probably as a result of trying to write according to the formulas of Asiatic (as against Attic) style. No direct borrowings from other writers can be discerned, but the method reflects traces of the influence of Alexandrians such as Philo Judaeus, Clement, and Origen, all of whom believed that the divine logos *manifested itself in all cultures. Perhaps more directly, it mirrors Proclus' Neoplatonic valorization of poetry as an inspired truth.*

The Exposition of the Content of Vergil According to the Principles of Moral Philosophy, *translated by O. B. Hardison, Jr., is reprinted by permission of the publisher from Alex Preminger et al., eds.,* Classical and Medieval Literary Criticism: Translations and Interpretations *(New York: Frederick Ungar Publishing Co., 1974).*

ON VERGIL

[To Calcidius the Grammarian]

O most holy of Deacons, because of my age I thought complete silence proper. Not only did my mind cease to recall what it had learned, but it was becoming forgetful that it lived at all. But because I am subject to the New Law of charity, and the rule of love makes refusal impossible, I have touched on the hidden natural lore of Vergil, avoiding those things which are more dangerous than praiseworthy. Woe to me, I say, should I know and possess anything improper.

Therefore I have omitted the *Eclogues* and *Georgics* in which are interwoven concepts so profound that in those books Vergil has included the inner secrets of almost every art. In the first, second, and third eclogue he has given in philosophic terms the characteristics of the three kinds of life [contemplative, active, voluptuary]. In the fourth he treated the art of prophecy. In the fifth, priestly matters. In the sixth, with his exquisite meters, the art of music, and in part of this eclogue he explained physiology according to the Stoic view. In the seventh he touched on botany. In the eighth he described the art of music and also magic, and at the end, omens, which he continued to discuss in the ninth. In the eighth he says:

> Lo, while I hesitate to carry it away,
> The ash itself has spontaneously
> Enveloped the altar with flickering flames,
> May the omen be good!
> Something has been determined; and the dog Hylax barks at the
>   gate.   [2. 105–7]

In the ninth he says: "I remember this was forecast by the oaks struck by heaven" [not *Eclogue* 9 but 1. 17]; and again, "Wolves beheld Moeris first" [9. 54].

The first *Georgic* is astrological throughout and toward the end deals with omens. The second deals with physiognomy and medicine. The third deals entirely with augury. And he also touches on this subject in the sixth book of the *Aeneid*, where he says: "Plucking the topmost hairs between the horns,/[The priestess] lays them on the fire as first offerings" [245–46]. The fourth is wholly concerned with music, and has interpretative comments on the art of music at the end.

I have, then, omitted teachings exceeding the limits of the times so that he who seeks reputation will not end by fracturing his skull. Be content, my Lord, with the modest posy that I have picked for you from the flowery gardens of the Hesperides. For, if you seek golden apples, you must play Eurystheus[1] to some other stronger man, who, like Hercules, is willing to risk his life. You will be able peacefully to take many ideas from this posy which will gratify your wishes.

Now, laying aside the rancid bitterness of the Hellebore of Chrysippus, I will say something pleasing to the Muses:

> O Maids of Helicon—and I do not call
> On Calliope alone—assist me.
> Give your blessing to my mind.
> I undertake a more difficult task.
> A single Muse will not suffice.
> Run, Pierian Maidens, you are my greatest care.
> Strike the Arcadian lyre with an ivory plectrum.

I think this little invocation will satisfy the Vergilian Muses.

Send me now the Mantuan Bard in person, so that I can lead his fugitive meanings into the light. And behold—he comes toward me well filled with a draught of the spring of Mt. Helicon. He is a proper image of a Bard with his tablets raised in order to treat his topic, and with a fixed frown murmurs some mysterious truth that wells up from within him.

I said: "If you please, put aside your frowning expressions, o most famous of Italian poets. Sweeten the bitter sauce of your difficult ideas with the condiment of sweet honey. For I do not search your words for what Pythagoras says about harmonic numbers, or Heraclitus fire, or Plato ideas, or Hermes the stars, or Chrysippus numbers,[2] or Aristotle entelechies.[3] Nor am I interested in what Dardanus says about powers, or Battiades about daemons, or Campester about spirits of the underworld and ghosts. I seek only the easy things taught by grammarians to their childish pupils for monthly fees."

Then, wrinkling his brow, Vergil said: "I thought, little man, that you were too foolish for me to load my heavier burdens on your heart. You are more dense than a dirt clod and will sleep through anything weighty."

I said: "Save that sort of knowledge, I pray, for your Romans for whom it is honorable and harmless. It will be enough for me to touch the lowest hem of your robe."

He said: "As far as your coarse intelligence and the timidity of your age permit you to learn, I will dip out just a few drops from the fountain of my swelling genius and explain these matters to you. This small measure will prevent you from becoming so drunk that you get sick. Now make the seats of your ears vacant so that my words can enter."

And then, settling into the posture of an orator, with two fingers erect in the form of an "I" and the third pressing the thumb, he began: "In all my works I treated subjects relating to natural philosophy. And in the twelve books of the *Aeneid* I revealed fully the condition of man's life. And I began the exordium with 'Arms and the man I sing'—referring to virtue[4] by 'arms' and wisdom by 'man.' For perfection consists of virtue of body and wisdom of mind."

I said: "If I am not mistaken about your meaning, most excellent bard, Holy Scripture sang Christ the Redeemer of our world as virtue and wisdom because God assumed the condition of a perfect man."[5]

He said: "You know what true Majesty has taught you. Meanwhile, I can only relate what I think. Now it is proper according to logic to speak of the person first and then the things relating to the person so that substance comes first and then the accidents—as it were, to mention 'man' first and then 'arms,' since virtue is inherent in the man. But because I wrote according to the forms of praise,[6] I mentioned the merit of the man before the man himself. Thus we come to the person with his merit already recognized. This, in fact, is how things are commonly done in letter-writing, where we first write 'Most excellent' and then the name of the man addressed.

"But to understand more readily that I have written in the form of praise, notice the wording of the lines that follow. I say 'an outcast through fate' and 'by the power of the gods' to show that Fortune was to blame for the flight of Aeneas, not lack of virtue. He exposed himself to danger because of the gods, not through lack of wisdom. This accords with the ancient maxim of Plato, 'The spirit of man is his god.'[7] If it is worthy, God will be kindly. And Carneades in the *Telesias* says, 'All Fortune resides in the intelligence of the wise man.'[8]

"Moreover, I wanted to mention 'virtue' first then 'wisdom' because, although wisdom rules virtue, wisdom flourishes in a virtuous soul. A lack of virtue is a weakness in wisdom because when wisdom intends to do something, if the virtue to accomplish it is inadequate, wisdom is cut off in its effects and languishes.

"Now about beginning with 'arms'—I knew that the word 'man,' if placed first, would indicate the sex of the individual, not his honor. There are many men, but not all of them are praiseworthy. Therefore, I placed first the word suggesting the 'virtue' for which the man is praiseworthy. In this I followed Homer, who says, 'The wrath, O goddess, sing of Achilles' [*Iliad* 1. 1]—mentioning the wrath of the man before the man himself. Moreover, Homer symbolizes virtue in the figure of Minerva, and he writes: 'She caught the hair of Achilles' [*Iliad* 1. 197]."

I said: "You did not speak badly in this. Divine Wisdom, far surpassing your understanding, began in like manner, saying, 'Blessed is the man who walks not in the counsel of the ungodly' [Ps. 1:1]. Note that the most perfect teacher of the righteous life, the Prophet David, placed the reward for virtuous living—'blessedness'—before the sweat of the struggle."

He said: "I rejoice, little fellow, at these added sentiments, because, although I did not know the full truth concerning the nature of the righteous life, still, truth sprinkled its sparks in my darkened mind with a kind of blind favor.

"Now, as I began to say, 'virtue' is related to substance, and 'wisdom' is what controls substance. As Sallust said, 'All our strength is in our soul and body' [*On Cataline's Conspiracy*, 1. 2].

"To satisfy your mind more fully, there are three phases in human life: first possession, second control of what you possess, and third graceful adorning of what you control. Note that these three phases are included in my first line; that is, 'arms,' 'man,' and 'first.' 'Arms'—that is, virtue—refers to a natural characteristic. 'Man'—that is, wisdom—to a mental characteristic. And 'first'—that is, foremost—to judgment. Thus the order is: to possess, to control, and to adorn.

"Thus through an historical allegory I have shown the whole condition of human life, which involves first nature, second learning, and third success. Be careful to understand these phases. As I said before, first comes inner capacity which is a gift of nature and permits man to improve—for you cannot educate a creature that is not born with the ability to be educated. Second comes learning which enhances nature as it improves. This is like gold, for gold is malleable and beautiful by nature, but it is brought to perfection by the hammer of the workman. Like gold, the mind is born capable of expansion. It improves because it was born, and success comes along to adorn what improves.

"These phases of life should be followed by the young children to whom my poem is taught. Every worthy person is born capable of education. The person is educated so that this natural capacity will not be wasted. He is adorned with success so that the gift of learning will not be useless. Plato, explaining the triple order of human life, said: 'Each good is either inborn, or learned, or imposed.'[9] It is born through nature, learned through study, and imposed through experience.

"Now, having completed the preliminaries, I proceed to the beginning of the story. But to make sure that I am not explaining my story to untutored ears, tell me the content of the first book. Then, if all is well, I will explain the book to you."

I said: "If the memory of past studies does not fail me, first Juno asks Aeolus to cause shipwreck of the Trojans. Aeneas escapes with seven ships. He reaches the shore of Libya. He sees his mother but does not recognize her. He and Achates are enveloped in a cloud. Then his soul is stirred by pictures. After dinner he is soothed by the music of a lyre. You now have a brief summary of the contents of the first book. Now I wish to know what you meant by them."

He said: "The shipwreck symbolizes the perils of birth in which the mothers suffers birth-pangs, and the infant endures the danger of being born. All human beings necessarily share in this. And to make this meaning very plain, the shipwreck is caused by Juno, the goddess of childbirth. And she sends Aeolus: Aeolus in Greek is *eonolus* [aion + oloos]—that is, 'the destructiveness of time.'[10] As Homer says, 'The destructive wrath that brought woes innumerable on the Achaeans' [*Iliad* 1. 2]. And note what is promised to Aeolus: Deiopea, Juno's nymph, as his bride. *Demos* in Greek means 'public'; *iopa* is 'eyes' or 'vision.' To those being born the temporal world is dangerous. But an unclouded vision of perfection is promised by the goddess of birth to Aeolus. Next Aeneas escapes with seven ships. This is symbolic, for seven is the harmonic number of birth. I will briefly explain the reason for this if you like."

I said: "I discuss this sufficiently in the book that I recently wrote about medicine. There I commented on the whole arithmetic significance of seven and nine, and I would be wordy if I put in one book what I included in another. Anyone who wants to learn about such matters can read my book on physiology. Now I await what remains."

He said: "As I began to say, as soon as Aeneas reaches land, he sees his mother Venus but does not recognize her. This symbolizes infancy because those recently born can see their mothers from the moment of birth but do not immediately recognize and respond to them. Next Aeneas is enveloped in a cloud and recognizes his companions but cannot speak to them. Note how plainly I have depicted the characteristics of the very young children. They have the ability to recognize people but not to speak. And I placed Achates with Aeneas at the beginning. Achates is his arms bearer after the shipwreck, and he is also enveloped in the cloud. Achates is Greek *aconetos* [achos + ethos]; that is, 'the habit of sorrow.' Humanity is doomed to hardship from infancy, as Euripides says in the tragedy of *Iphigenia:*

> Nothing can be described that is so terrible—
> Be it physical pain or heaven-sent affliction—
> That man's nature could not bear it.[11]

That is: there is nothing so terrible and no experience so dire that human nature has not endured it. There is no armor against sorrow except tears. Infants console and call attention to themselves by crying. Although we are scarcely able to laugh by the fifth month, tears flow freely on the very threshold of life.

"That Aeneas vainly feasts his soul on a picture clearly symbolizes childish thought. An infant can see but he cannot understand what he sees—just as pictures can be looked at but lack rational meaning.

"Then Aeneas is taken to dinner and soothed by the sound of the lyre. Little children characteristically seek nothing more than to be pleased by sweet music and filled with food. And note the name of the lyre-player. Iopas in Greek is *siopas* [siope]—that is, the silence of a child. Infants are always soothed by the sweet words and songs of nurses; and to symbolize this I described Iopas with long hair like that of a woman [cf. *Aeneid* 1. 740]. And also, Aeneas sees Cupid [1. 715–17]. Youth is always wanting or desiring something. And therefore I wrote the verse that comes in the second book after the lyre playing is over: 'Who could refrain from tears' [2. 8].

"In the second and third books Aeneas is diverted by tales of the sort that usually amuse talkative young children. At the end of the third book [613ff.] Aeneas sees the Cyclops after Achaemenides describes them. *Achos* [achos] means sorrow in Greek; *ciclos* [kuklos] means 'circle.' Also, *pes* [pais] means 'boy.' The sense is that the child, when released from fear of his guardians, does not yet have rational knowledge of grief and gives himself over to the wandering of wild youth. The Cyclops is described as having a single eye in his forehead because the wandering of wild youth is not directed by a full or a rational vision, and the whole of youth rests on Cyclopean vanity. The single eye in the head of the Cyclops symbolizes that he cannot see and understand anything but vanity. The wise Ulysses put out the eye: that is, vainglory is blinded by the flame of reason. And I called him Polyphemus—that is, *apolunta femen* [apoleipo + pheme], which means 'loss of reputation' in Latin. For a blind later life follows youth's pride and indifference to reputation.

"To make the sequence perfectly obvious, Aeneas next buries his father. As the child grows up he rejects the force of paternal authority. He buries his father at the port of Drepanum [3. 707]. *Drepanos* is *drimpedos*, and *drimos* [drimos] means 'keen' and *pes* [pais] 'boy.' This symbolizes the fact that immaturity rejects parental discipline.

"And now that the soul of Aeneas is free of his father's authority, in the fourth book he goes hunting and is aroused by the fire of love. Driven on by a storm and mist—symbolizing a disturbed mind—he commits adultery. And when he has dallied for a long time, he gives up his immoral love at the urging of Mercury. Mercury is the god of reason. This symbolizies that at the prompting of reason the more mature person breaks the bonds of lust. And indeed, the object of passion [i.e. Dido] dies when it has been rejected. Totally consumed, it wastes away to ashes. When lust is expelled from the youthful heart by reason, it flickers out and is buried in the ashes of oblivion.

"In the fifth book Aeneas is aroused by the memory of his father and engages in the sports of young men. This symbolizes that when one reaches the age of prudence, he follows examples provided by his father's memory and exercises his body in manly activities.

"Note that they engage in boxing. That is, Entellus and Dares [5. 362ff.] practice a manly sport. *Entellin* [entello] in Greek means 'command' and *derin* [dero] 'cudgel'—which masters often do when teaching.

"Then the ships are burned [5. 641]. They are the dangerous instruments that lure a youth onto the stormy seas of vanity where he is constantly buffeted by tempests, as it were, of dangerous impulses. By the excellent fire of reason all these are destroyed, and, as knowledge is added to intelligence, they all vanish like dreams in the ashes of oblivion. And Beroë—that is, 'the order of truth'—makes the fire.

"In the sixth book Aeneas comes to the temple of Apollo and descends into the underworld. Apollo is the god of learning and he is a friend of the Muses. Now the shipwreck and dangers of youth are over, and Palinurus has been lost. Palinurus is *planonorus* [plane + horao]—that is, 'wandering vision.' Therefore in Book 4 [363] I wrote concerning amorous glances, 'her silent glances *wander* over the whole man'; and also in the *Eclogues,* 'the *wandering* footsteps of a bull' [5. 58].

"Having put these things behind him, Aeneas now comes to the temple of Apollo—that is, learning from studies. And there he ponders the course of his future life and seeks out the path to the underworld. This symbolizes that whenever anyone considers the future he must penetrate the hidden and secret mysteries of knowledge. And Aeneas must bury Misenus first [6. 227]. *Misio* [misos] in Greek means 'spite' and *enos* [ainos] 'praise.' Unless you reject ostentatious and vain praise you will never reach the secrets of wisdom. The appetite for vain praise never seeks truth but thinks that false things flatteringly attributed to the self are truly possessed. Also there is the contest between Misenus and Triton with his horn and shell [6. 171–76]. Note how precise the symbolism. The bubble of vain praise is pubbed up by a windy voice and Triton destroys it. Triton is *tetrimemenon* [?tetinmenos] in Greek, which we Latins call 'contrition.' Contrition always deflates vain praise. And for this reason Tritonia is called the goddess of wisdom: contrition always makes a man wise."

I said: "Having better knowledge on this subject, I approve your sentiment. Our divine and life-giving teaching tells us that God does not despise a humble and contrite heart [Ps. 50:19]. And this is true and manifest wisdom."

He said: "To make my story fully and explicitly clear, I wrote that Carineus

[Corynaeus; 6. 227] cremated the body of Misenus in a fire. *Carin* [charis] in Greek means 'favor'; and we call *eon* [aion] 'time.' This symbolizes that through the favor of time the ashes of vainglory are inevitably buried.

"But no one learns about hidden knowledge until he has plucked the golden bough; that is, the study of philosophy and letters. I intended the golden bough to symbolize knowledge, recalling that my mother dreamed she gave birth to a branch,[12] and because Apollo is painted holding a branch. Moreover, the bough is said to be '*apo tes rapsodias*,' that is, 'from writings' by Dionysius [?Thrax] in his book on Greek expressions. And I called the bough 'golden' because I wanted to symbolize the splendor of eloquence, recalling the saying of Plato that when Diogenes the Cynic attempted to steal Plato's estate, he found nothing there except a golden tongue. Tiberianus recounts this in his book *On the God of Socrates*.[13]

"I referred to ten golden apples in the *Eclogues*: that is, the polished eloquence of the ten eclogues. Hercules took golden apples from the Hesperides. And the Hesperian maidens are said to be Aegle, Hespera, Medusa, and Arethusa, which in Latin are study, understanding, memory, and eloquence. First comes study, second understanding, third memorization of what you understand, and then adorning in eloquent language what you retain. In a similar way virtue seeks to grasp the golden prize of learning."

I said: "Most learned man, you are surely speaking the truth. Just now I recalled a passage in Scripture which speaks of a golden tongue and virtuous skills stolen from iniquity,[14] just as eloquence may be recovered from the gentiles. But pray go on to what remains."

He said: "As I previously remarked, having taken up the golden bough, that is, learning, Aeneas enters the lower regions and investigates the secrets of knowledge. In the outer chamber of Hades he sees sorrow, disease, wars, discord, old age, and poverty. This symbolizes that when all things in the mind and heart of man are considered, when learning has been mastered and the darkness dispelled by higher knowledge, one sees that old age and its cousin death are empty dreams, and war the child of greed, and disease the offspring of disorder and intemperance, and quarrels the consequence of drunkenness, and hunger the handmaid of laziness and sloth.

"So Aeneas descends into Hades and there he witnesses the punishments meted out to evil men and the rewards of good ones and sees the sad confusion of lovers.

"Charon the ferryman carries him and he crosses Acheron. This river symbolizes the boiling emotions of youthful activity. It is call 'muddy' because youths do not have mature and clear ideas. *Acheron* [akairos] is Greek for 'without time.' Charon is *ceron* [kairos] which means 'time.' Therefore he is said to be the son of Polidegmon. *Polidegmon* [polus + deigma] is Greek for 'much knowledge.' This symbolizes that when one has reached the age of much knowledge he moves past time—muddied waters and the dregs of his own bad habits.

"He drugs three-headed Cerberus with a morsel dipped in honey [6. 420]. I [that is, here, Fulgentius] have already explained in my *Mythologies* that the

Tricerberus story is an allegory of quarreling and legal wrangles. Petronius says of Euscios, 'Cerberus was a trial lawyer.'[15] For men learn quarreling slander and use eloquence in other people's affairs simply for money, when true learning should be used for improvement—as is seen even today among lawyers. The bitterness of altercation, treated with the honey of wisdom, regains its sweet taste.

"Now that Aeneas has been admitted to the secrets of wisdom, he looks on the shades of heroic men. That is, he considers the achievements and monuments of virtue. And he sees the punishment of Deiphobus. Deiphobus is Greek for either *Dimofobus* [deima + phobos] or *demofobus* [demios + phobos]—that is 'fear of terror' or 'fear of the people.' Whatever kind of fear is intended, it is properly depicted with hands cut off and blinded and without ears [6. 495–97]. The reason is that fear never perceives what it sees or knows what it hears or, lacking hands to feel, recognizes what it does. And Deiphobus was killed by Menelaus when sleeping. Menelaus is *menelau* [mene + laos], that is 'valor of the people,' for this valor always overcomes slothful fear.

"Then Aeneas sees Dido, now an empty shadow of love and lust. But to the wise man the memory of lust, even though it has been deadened by indifference, brings penitent tears.

"We have now reached the place where I say:

> In front stands the huge gate and pillars
> Of solid adamant, so that no human power
> Not even the sons of heaven, can uproot them in war.
> There stands the iron tower soaring high.
>
> [6. 552–55]

Note how obvious I have made this image of pride and vanity. I put adamantine columns on the tower because this kind of rock is indestructible. The Greek [*adoneo*] means, in fact, 'untouched'—for neither fear of the gods nor human virtue nor fear of a bad reputation can control pride. 'An iron tower soaring high' signifies high and unbending arrogance. And who sustains this arrogance but Tisiphone, meaning 'raging voice' [?*tisis* + *phone*]. When I said 'The Hydra still more cruel with fifty black and gaping throats' [6. 576], I symbolized nothing less than that the swelling vanity in the heart of proud men is worse than the hot air of boasting coming from their mouths. When I said 'Tartarus itself yawns open twice as far' [6. 577–78], this symbolizes the final punishment of pride. The punishment for pride is to be thrown down. The more arrogant a proud man is, the more anguish he will endure when his arrogance collapses. Whoever is raised up by pride will therefore be doubly struck down. On this subject, recall the epigram of Porphyrius:

> Fortune aids you Quintus (by my soul)
> And takes your sneering face all over town.
> By heaven it's true: You are some stinking hole:
> The bigger you get, the more men stare you down.[16]

"Next Aeneas sees the giants [6. 580] and Ixion [6. 601] and Salmoneus

[6. 585] all damned to punishment for pride, and Tantalus also [6. 602]. Tantalus is Greek *teantelon* [?te + anta + ethelo]; that is, 'greedy to see,' for avarice is reluctant to use a thing and is fed merely by looking at it.

"But here the judge Rhadamanthus of Cnossos appears [6. 566–77]. Rhadamanthus is Greek *tarematadamonta* [ta rema + ta damonta]—that is, 'ruling the word'—and *gnoso* [gnosis] means 'understand.' That is, he who knows how to control the force of words punishes and denounces pride. Next, Aeneas is frightened by loud noise. That is, the honest man flees the call of pride and fears the punishment meted out to evil men. Then, fixing the golden bough on the sacred doorposts, he enters Elysium. This symbolizes that when the labor of learning is over, one celebrates a perfected memory. Learning is fixed in the memory forever, like the golden bough on the sacred doorposts.

"Aeneas enters the Elysian Fields. *Elisis* [eleusis] is Greek for 'freeing'—that is, after the fear of teachers, life becomes like a holiday. And Proserpine is queen of the Underworld. That is, memory is the queen of knowledge. Extending [*proserpens*] itself, it reigns forever in the liberated mind. The golden bough of learning is dedicated to memory. Concerning memory, Cicero used to say that it was the store-house of knowledge [*de Oratore* 1. 5. 18].

"In the Elysian Fields Aeneas first sees Musaeus [6. 66]—as it were, 'the gift of the Muses'—exalted above all the rest. Musaeus introduces him to his father Anchises and shows him the river Lethe. He is shown his father to emphasize the need to retain a grave character. He is shown Lethe to bring out the need to forget the levity of youth. And note the name Anchises. Anchises is Greek *ano scenon*—that is, 'living in one's homeland.' There is one God, Father and King of all, dwelling alone on high, who is discovered whenever knowledge points the way. Note what Anchises teaches his son:

> In the beginning an indwelling spirit
> Infused the heavens and the earth
> And the watery plains and the shining orb
> Of the moon and the stars of Titan
> [6. 724–25]

You can see that the creator must be God and that Anchises teaches about the hidden mysteries of nature, and describes the souls returning again and again from life, and reveals the future."

I said: "O truest of Italian bards, how could you have obscured your brilliant genius in the darkness of such a stupid line of defense? When you were writing allegorically in the *Eclogues*, you once said: 'Now a virgin returns and the reign of Saturn returns. / Now a new race is promised by high heaven' [4. 6]. But here, snoring out some sort of Academic tripe while your wit is drowsing, you say: 'Heavenly souls go up to heaven / And then return again to sluggish bodies' [6. 720]. Why did you put blackberries among so many sweet apples and obscure the torch of your brilliant genius?"

Smiling he said: "If I had not mixed something Epicurean in with so many Stoic truths, I would not have been a pagan. No people except you Christians on whom the sun of truth has shone can know all of the truth. But I did not come here to explain your Scripture and argue about what I should have known, but to explain those things that I did know. Now listen to what remains.

"In the seventh book Caieta the nurse is buried [7. 2]—that is, the heavy burden of fear of one's teachers. Caieta means 'forcer of youth.' Among the ancients *caiatio* meant 'the yielding of children.' Thus Plautus in his comedy *Cistolaria* wrote, 'Are you afraid your doxy will not *yield* herself to your arms?' And I made it very plain that Caieta symbolizes discipline when I said, 'Dying you gave eternal fame, O Caieta' [7. 2]. Although the discipline of learning is eventually removed, it passes on the eternal seed of memory.

"Therefore, having buried school matters, Aeneas arrives at his much-desired Ausonia—that is, 'increase of good' toward which the desire of wise men eagerly hastens. *Ausonia* is from *apo tu ausenin* [apo toi auxanein]—that is, 'of increase.' Another explanation is that even at this age the body continues to grow.

"Next he seeks Lavinia as his wife—that is, 'the path of hard work.' About this time of life, everyone chooses labors which increase his worldly advantages. And Lavinia is called the daughter of Latinus, a descendent of Caunus [i.e., Faunus; 7. 47]. *Latinus* is from *latitando* [lying in wait] because hard work lies in wait in many different places. *Latona* is from *luna* [moon] because at one time she conceals her upper parts, at another her lower parts and then, at another, is entirely concealed. *Caunus* is *camnonus* [kamno + nous]—that is, mental labor. And Caunus is married to the nymph Marica—that is, *merica* [merimna] or 'counsel.' As Homer says, 'His heart within his shaggy breast was divided in *counsel*' [*Il.* 1. 189].

"In Book 8 Aeneas seeks Evander as an ally. *Evandros* [eo + andros] in Greek is 'good man.' This symbolizes that the perfected individual seeks the companionship of good men. From Evander he hears of the excellence of goodness—that is, the glory of Hercules [8. 193ff.] and how he slew Cacus, a name [i.e., kakos] that means 'evil' among the Latins. Then he puts on the armor of Vulcan [8. 612ff.]; that is, the protection of the alert intelligence against all the temptations of evil. *Vulcan* is *bulencauton* [boule + kautes], or, as we say, 'ardent wisdom.' All the virtues of the Romans are displayed on this armor because all happiness is either provided by or foreseen through the careful protection of wisdom. To act well is the harbinger of future good, and he who acts well insures good for himself. Thus wisdom both produces good things and can look forward to them.

"In Book 9, assisted by the arms of Vulcan, Aeneas fights Turnus. *Turnus* is *turosnus* [thouros + nous] in Greek—that is, 'raging mind.' The arms of wisdom and intelligence always oppose rage. As Homer says, '[Athena] spoke and led the raging Ares from battle' [*Il.* 5. 35].

"Next Aeneas kills Mezentius, the belittler of the gods [10. 907–8]. God ordains all things and commands them to be good. But when the spirit which inhabits the body despises the good it fails in its proper duty and neglects goodness to its own harm. The wise man sallies out to slay wrongdoers and slays Mezentius and his son Lausus [10. 815–16].

"This symbolizes the wise man's conquest of his own soul. And who is said to be the friend of Turnus? Messapus—that is, *misonepos* [misos + epos], which is 'threatening speech' in Latin. As Euripides says in his tragedy of *Iphigenia*, 'Nothing can be described that is so terrible...' [*Orestes* 1].

"Then Juturna is forced to desist from war [12. 875]. She was driving the chariot of her brother. Juturna symbolizes calamity because calamity always [*diuturne*] threatens. Calamity is the sister of rage. And the chariot of Turnus which she uses to drive him away and save him from death is also calamity because it can cause rage to go on without end.

"First Turnus had Metiscus as his driver. *Metiscos* [methusko] is Greek for 'intoxicated.' Intoxication first produces rage. Then calamity arrives to prolong rage. But while Juturna is said to be eternal, Turnus is mortal. Rage can cease in a short time, but calamity continues forever. And Juturna drives the chariot everywhere—that is, she continues for a long time. The wheels symbolize time. Fortune is said to have a wheel, symbolizing the mutability of time."

The end.

Farewell, my Lord. Read cautiously these thorny outgrowths of my heart.

Here ends the exposition of the content of Vergil according to moral philosophy by the distinguished Fabius Planciadis Fulgentius.

NOTES

1. He imposed the twelve labors on Hercules.
2. A reference to the theory of the Greek Stoic philosophers about the number of human souls (which remains constant).
3. States of completion or perfection; actuality as contrasted with potentiality.
4. *Virtus.* Alternately, "courage." Here and below, the term "virtue" has been chosen because it fits best in later contexts. The formula anticipates the medieval prescription for the epic virtues of *fortitudo* and *sapientia* (fortitude and wisdom).
5. 1 Cor. 7:24.
6. *Materiam laudis,* that is, the formulas of epideictic rhetoric, the rhetorical formulas of praise and blame.
7. Cf. *Corpus Hermeticorum*, ed. A. D. Nock (Paris, 1945), 12. 1.
8. Work unknown.
9. Not by Plato. Helm cites Tertullian, *On Modesty* 1.
10. Here and below the Greek readings in brackets are conjecture. Fulgentius does not explain his often bizarre etymologies.
11. The quotation is from *Orestes* 1–3. The error in ascription probably derives from an anthology of quotations used by Fulgentius.
12. The story is told by Donatus in his *Life of Vergil.*
13. A book *On the God of Socrates* was written by Apuleius. The reference by Fulgentius is unclear.
14. Cf. Ezek. 7:20.
15. Reference unclear.
16. *Epigrams,* ed. Kluge (Leipzig, 1926), p. 37.

Dante Alighieri
1265–1321

Dante Alighieri was born in 1265, the same year that his native city of Florence founded the first democracy in modern European history. He came from a family of urban nobility which boasted several important figures in the foundation and development of Florence. In later years, however, his family had declined in importance, and Dante in his poetry prefers to hearken back to his more distant and illustrious ancestors. His family was a member of the Guelf party in Florence, which sided with the Pope in opposing the interference of the Holy Roman Emperor in Italian affairs. The Guelfs had recently triumphed over the Ghibellines, who sided with the Emperor for the control of Florence.

Dante probably went to a grammar school run by the Franciscan friars, whose religious fervor and dislike for Church politics must have influenced the boy. In general, little is known about Dante's education, save that he credits Brunetto Latini in the Inferno as being his greatest teacher (at the same time, he gains a pupil's revenge by—sadly—placing Latini among the tortures of Hell). It seems probable that he largely conducted his own education. In any case, by the age of eighteen he had sufficient confidence in himself to submit a sonnet to the famous poet Guido Cavalcanti, who approved his talents.

Dante claims to have met and fallen in love with the famous Beatrice at the tender age of nine. She plays an important role in his poetry as the representative of heavenly love, although (or perhaps because) they only met once again, nine years later, when Dante considered himself privileged to receive her salute. After her death in 1290, Dante composed the Vita Nuova in her honor.

He married Gemma Donati—who had been chosen for him by his father when he was twelve—sometime before 1294. At about the same time, Dante became passionately involved in Florentine politics, avidly participating in the new democracy. He held a number of offices in the communal government, rising to the position of Prior of the Guilds, the highest office in the city, for the summer of 1300.

It was during this period that the politics of the city was polarized between the Whites, who opposed the attempts of Pope Boniface VIII to bring Florence under his control, and the Blacks, who supported the

Pope. In 1301, the Pope invited a foreign army, under Charles of Valois, to enter Italy. Dante, at this point, became one of the most outspoken critics of Boniface. He was sent to Rome along with two other envoys in order to avert warfare. Boniface, however, kept Dante in Rome while Charles and the Blacks consolidated power in Florence. Dante returned to Florence to find that he had been banished, and he spent the rest of his life in exile, refusing to accept the conditions set for his return. It is to his exile, however, that we owe his greatest work, the Commedia.

In the years from 1310 to 1313, Dante placed all of his political hopes upon Emperor Henry VII in his attempts to unify Italy, but the movement failed at the gates of Florence. The poet spent the last years of his life in Ravenna at the house of Guido Novella da Polenta, together with his daughter and one of his sons. According to tradition, he finished the last canto of his Paradiso shortly before his death on September 21, 1321. Boccaccio recounts a legend that the poet's spirit returned in order to show his son the hiding place of the manuscript.

Two of Dante's major treatises on literary theory, the Convivio and De Vulgari Eloquentia, date from the first years of his exile, 1304–6. Both are incomplete. De Vulgari Eloquentia takes some material from the mass of medieval literature dealing with the art of poetry, but it is really quite original as a philosophical analysis of language. It is the first empirical survey of a modern European language, Italian, and in that respect it is properly the work of the early Renaissance. Dante is aware of his own daring, stating that "our purpose is to investigate matters in which we are supported by the authority of none." Such a statement is extraordinary for the Middle Ages, an era in which thinkers relied almost exclusively upon authority for verification of ideas.

Dante is the first great poet of the vernacular in Western Europe, and so his survey of the Italian language is particularly important. The vernacular is inherently variable: "since man is a most unstable and changeable animal, no human language can be lasting and continuous, but must needs vary like other properties of ours, as for instance our manners and our dress." This understanding stands in opposition to that of an original, Adamic language with a single form which could be understood universally. Language plays a tremendous cultural role because it is a major (perhaps the major) unifying element in human society. Dante maintains that, as languages multiply, men become more and more isolated from one another; it is a movement away from divinely-ordained unity. His concern, then, as a poet of the variable vernacular, is to discover what he calls the underlying "form of speech," instilled by God in the first soul, which provides a grammar beneath the *varying forms of the vernacular. Dante himself defines the qualities which he would require of this "form of speech":*

> *We declare the illustrious, cardinal, courtly, and curial vernacular language in Italy to be that which belongs to all the towns in Italy but does not appear to belong to any one of them, and by which all the municipal dialects of the Italians are measured, weighed, and compared.*

In many ways, this would resemble a Platonic or "Ideal" form of the Italian language. This ideal form corresponds to Dante's dream of a unified Italy, something that he hints at when he insists that it must be "courtly." By explicitly linking poetic culture to society at large Dante makes a major contribution to the first stirrings of the Renaissance revival of humanism.

Dante's Letter to Can Grande, *which was probably written between 1316 and 1319, elucidates the allegorical structure of his* Divine Comedy: *it is a "practical" version of the medieval tradition of allegorical reading, and helps bridge the abyss between Biblical commentary and the criticism of secular literature.*

The selections from De Vulgari Eloquentia *are taken from A. G. Ferrers Howell and Philip H. Wicksteed,* A Translation of the Latin Works of Dante Alighieri *(London: Dent, 1904). The selections from* Letter to Can Grande Della Scala, *translated by Allan H. Gilbert, are reprinted with his permission from Allan H. Gilbert, ed.,* Literary Criticism: Plato to Dryden *(Detroit: Wayne State University Press, 1962).*

FROM
De Vulgari Eloquentia

Book I

I

Since we do not find that any one before us has treated of the science of the vernacular language, while in fact we see that this language is highly necessary for all, inasmuch as not only men, but even women and children, strive, in so far as nature allows them, to acquire it; and since it is our wish to enlighten to some little extent the discernment of those who walk through the streets like blind men, generally fancying that those things which are [really] in front of them are behind them, we will endeavor, the Word aiding us from heaven, to be of service to the the vernacular speech; not only drawing the water of our own wit for such a drink, but mixing with it the best of what we have taken or compiled from others, so that we may thence be able to give draughts of the sweetest hydromel.[1] But because the business of every science is not to prove but to explain its subject, in order that men may know what that is with which the science is concerned, we say (to come quickly to the point) that what we call the vernacular speech is that to which children are accustomed by those who are about them when they first begin to distinguish words; or to put it more shortly, we say that the vernacular speech is that which we acquire without any rule, by imitating our nurses. There further springs from this another secondary speech, which the Romans called grammar. And this secondary speech the Greeks also have, as well as others, but not all. Few, however, acquire the use of this speech, because we can only be guided and instructed in it by the expenditure of much time, and by assiduous study. Of these two kinds of speech also, the vernacular is the nobler, as well because it was the first employed by the human race, as because the whole world makes use of it, though it has been divided into forms differing in pronunciation and vocabulary. It is also the nobler as being natural to us, whereas the other is rather of an artificial kind; and it is of this our nobler speech that we intend to treat.

II

This [then] is our true first speech. I do not, however, say "our" as implying that any other kind of speech exists beside man's; for to man alone of all existing beings was speech given, because for him alone was it necessary. Speech was not necessary for the angels or for the lower animals, but would have been given to them in vain, which nature, as we know, shrinks from doing. For if we clearly consider what our intention is when we speak, we shall find that it is nothing else but to unfold to others the thoughts of our own mind. Since, then, the angels have, for the purpose of manifesting their glorious thoughts, a most ready and indeed ineffable sufficiency of intellect, by which one of them is known in all respects to another, either of himself, or at least by means of that most brilliant mirror in which all of them are represented in the fulness of their beauty, and into which they all most eagerly gaze, they do not seem to have required the outward indications of speech. And if an objection be raised concerning the spirits who fell, it may be answered in two ways. First we may say that inasmuch as we are treating of those things which are necessary for well-being, we ought to pass over the fallen angels, because they perversely refused to wait for the divine care.[2] Or secondly (and better), that the devils themselves only need, in order to disclose their perfidy to one another, to know, each of another, that he exists, and what is his power: which they certainly do know, for they had knowledge of one another before their fall.

The lower animals also, being guided by natural instinct alone, did not need to be provided with the power of speech, for all those of the same species have the same actions and passions; and so they are enabled by their own actions and passions to know those of others. But among those of different species not only was speech unnecessary, but it would have been altogether harmful, since there would have been no friendly intercourse between them.

And if it be objected concerning the serpent speaking to the first woman, or concerning Balaam's ass, that they spoke, we reply that the angel in the latter, and the devil in the former, wrought in such a manner that the animals themselves set their organs in motion in such wise that the voice thence sounded clear like genuine speech; not that the sound uttered was to the ass anything but braying, or to the serpent anything but hissing.

But if any one should argue in opposition, from what Ovid says in the fifth book of the *Metamorphoses*[3] about magpies speaking, we reply that he says this figuratively, meaning something else. And if any one should rejoin that even up to the present time magpies and other birds speak, we say that it is false, because such action is not speaking, but a kind of imitation of the sound of our voice, or in other words, we say that they try to imitate us in so far as we utter sounds, but not in so far as we speak. If accordingly any one were to say expressly "Pica" [magpie], and "Pica" were answered back, this would be but a copy or imitation of the sound made by him who had first said the word.

And so it is evident that speech has been given to man alone. But let us briefly endeavor to explain why this was necessary for him.

III

Since, then, man is not moved by natural instinct but by reason, and reason itself differs in individuals in respect of discernment, judgment, and choice, so that each one of us appears almost to rejoice in his own species, we are of opinion that no one has knowledge of another by means of his own actions or passions, as a brute beast; nor does it happen that one man can enter into another by spiritual insight, like an angel, since the human spirit is held back by the grossness and opacity of its mortal body. It was therefore necessary that the human race should have some sign, at once rational and sensible, for the intercommunication of its thoughts, because the sign, having to receive something from the reason of one and to convey it to the reason of another, had to be rational; and since nothing can be conveyed from one reason to another except through a medium of sense, it had to be sensible; for, were it only rational, it could not pass [from the reason of one to that of another]; and were it only sensible it would neither have been able to take from the reason of one nor to deposit in that of another.

Now this sign is that noble subject itself of which we are speaking; for in so far as it is sound, it is sensible, but in so far as it appears to carry some meaning according to the pleasure [of the speaker] it is rational.

IV

Speech was given to man alone, as is plain from what has been said above. And now I think we ought also to investigate to whom of mankind speech was first given, and what was the first thing he said, and to whom, where, and when he said it; and also in what language this first speech came forth. Now, according to what we read in the beginning of Genesis, where the most sacred Scripture is treating of the origin of the world, we find that a woman spoke before all others, I mean that most presumptuous Eve, when in answer to the inquiry of the devil she said, "We eat of the fruit of the trees which are in Paradise, but of the fruit of the tree which is in the midst of Paradise God has commanded us not to eat, nor to touch it, lest peradventure we die." But though we find it written that the woman spoke first, it is, however, reasonable for us to suppose that the man spoke first; and it is unseemly to think that so excellent an act of the human race proceeded even earlier from woman than from man. We therefore reasonably believe that speech was given to Adam first by him who had just formed him.

Now I have no doubt that it is obvious to a man of sound mind that the first thing the voice of the first speaker uttered was the equivalent of God, namely *El*, whether in the way of a question or in the way of an answer. It seems absurd and repugnant to reason that anything should have been named by man before God, since man had been made by him and for him. For as, since the transgression of the human race, every one begins his first attempt at speech with a cry of woe, it is reasonable that he who existed before that transgression should begin with joy; and since there is no joy without God, but all joy is in God, and God himself is wholly joy, it follows that the first speaker said first and before anything else "God." Here also this question arises from our saying above that man spoke first by the way of answer: If an answer, was it addressed to God? For if so it would seem that God had already spoken, which appears to make against what has been said above. To which we reply that he might well have made answer when God questioned him; but it does not follow from this that God uttered what we call speech. For who doubts that whatsoever is can be bent according to the will of God? For by him all things were made, by him they are preserved, and by him also they are governed. Therefore since the air is made to undergo such great disturbances by the ordinance of that lower nature which is the minister and workmanship of God, that it causes the thunder to peal, the lightning to flash, the water to drop, and scatters the snow and hurls down the hail, shall it not be moved to utter certain words rendered distinct by him who has distinguished greater things? Why not? Wherefore we consider that these observations are a sufficient answer to this difficulty, and to some others.

V

Thinking then (not without reason drawn as well from the foregoing considerations as from those which follow) that the first man directed his speech first of all to the Lord himself, we may reasonably say that this first speaker at once, after having been inspired by the vivifying power, spoke without hesitation. For in man we believe it to be more characteristic of humanity to be heard than to hear, provided he be heard and hear as a man. If, therefore, that workman and origin and lover of perfection by his breath made the first of us complete in all perfection, it appears to us reasonable that this most noble of animals did not begin to hear before he began to be heard. But if any one raises the objection that there was no need for him to speak, as he was, so far, the only human being, whilst God discerns all our secret thoughts without any words of ours, even before we do ourselves, we say with that reverence which we ought to use in judging anything respecting the eternal will, that though God knew, nay, even fore-knew (which is the same thing in respect of God) the thought of the first man who spoke, without any words being said, still he wished that the man should also speak, in order that, in the unfolding of so great a gift, he himself who had freely bestowed it might glory. And therefore it is to be believed that it is by God's appointment that we rejoice in the well-ordered play of our emotions.

Hence also we can fully determine the place where our first speech was uttered; for if man was inspired with life outside Paradise, he first spoke outside; but if within, we have proved that the place of his first speech was within.

VI

Since human affairs are carried on in very many different languages, so that many men are not understood by many with words any better than without words, it is appropriate for us to make investigation concerning that language which that man who had no mother, who was never suckled, who never saw either childhood or youth, is believed to have spoken. In this as in much else Pietramala is a most populous city, and the native place of the majority of the children of Adam. For whoever is so offensively unreasonable as to suppose that the place of his birth is the most delightful under the sun, also rates his own vernacular (that is, his mother-tongue) above all others, and consequently believes that it actually was that of Adam. But we, to whom the world is our native country, just as the sea is to the fish, though we drank of Arno before our teeth appeared, and though we love Florence so dearly that for the love we bore her we are wrongfully suffering exile—we rest the shoulders of our judgment on reason rather than on feeling. And although as regards our own pleasure or sensuous comfort there exists no more agreeable place in the world than Florence, still, when we turn over the volumes both of poets and other writers in which the world is generally and particularly described, and take account within ourselves of the various situations of the places of the world and their arrangement with respect to the two poles and to the equator, our deliberate and firm opinion is that there are many countries and cities both nobler and more delightful than Tuscany and Florence of which we are a native and a citizen, and also that a great many nations and races use a speech both more agreeable and more serviceable than the Italians do. Returning therefore to our subject, we say that a certain form of speech was created by God together with the first soul. And I say "a form," both in respect of words and sentences and of the utterance of sentences; and this form every tongue of speaking men would use, if it had not been dissipated by the fault of man's presumption, as shall be shown further on.

In this form of speech Adam spoke; in this form of speech all his descendants spoke until the building of the Tower of Babel, which is by interpretation the tower of confusion; and this form of speech was inherited by the sons of Heber, who after him were called Hebrews. With them alone did it remain after the confusion, in order that our Redeemer (who was, as to his humanity, to spring from them) might use, not the language of confusion, but of grace. Therefore Hebrew was the language which the lips of the first speaker formed.

VII

It is, alas! with feelings of shame that we now recall the ignominy of the human race. But since it is impossible for us to avoid passing through it, we will hasten through it, though the blush of shame rises to our cheeks and our mind recoils. O thou our human nature, ever prone to sin! O thou, full of iniquity from the first and ever afterwards without cessation! Did it suffice for thy correction that, deprived of light through thy first transgression, thou wast banished from thy delightful native land? Did it suffice, did it suffice that through the universal lust and cruelty of thy family, one house alone excepted, whatsoever was subject to thee had perished in the Flood, and that the animals of earth and air had already been punished for what thou hadst committed? Certainly this should have been enough! But as men are wont to say in the proverb, "Thou shalt not ride on horseback before the third time," thou, wretched one, didst choose rather to come to a wretched steed.

See, reader, how man, either forgetting or despising his former discipline, and turning aside his eyes from the marks of the stripes which had remained, for the third time provoked the lash by his stupid and presumptuous pride! For incorrigible man, persuaded by the giant, presumed in his heart to surpass by his own skill not only nature, but even the very power that works in nature, who is God; and he began to build a tower in Sennear, which was afterwards called Babel, that is, confusion, by which he hoped to ascend to heaven; purposing in his ignorance, not to equal, but to surpass his Maker. O boundless clemency of the heavenly power! Who among fathers would bear so many insults from a son? But he arose, and, with a scourge which was not hostile but paternal and had been wont at other times to smite, he chastised his rebellious son with correction at once merciful and memorable. For almost the whole human race had come together to the work of wickedness. Some were giving orders, some were acting as architects, some were building the walls, some were adjusting the masonry with rules, some were laying on the mortar with trowels, some were quarrying stone, some were engaged in bringing it by sea, some by land; and different companies were engaged in different other occupations, when they were struck by such confusion from heaven, that all those who were attending to the work, using one and the same language, left off the work on being estranged by many different languages and never again came together in the same intercourse. For the same language remained to those alone who were engaged together in the same kind of work; for instance, one language remained to all the architects, another to those rolling down blocks of stone, another to those preparing the stone; and so it happened to each group of workers. And the human race was accordingly then divided into as many different languages as there were different branches of the work; and the higher the branch of work the men were engaged in, the ruder and more barbarous was the language they afterwards spoke.

But those to whom the hallowed language remained were neither present, nor countenanced the work; but utterly hating it, they mocked the folly of those engaged in it. But these, a small minority, were of the seed of Shem (as I conjecture), who was the third son of Noah; and from them sprang the people of Israel, who made use of the most ancient language until their dispersion.

VIII

On account of the confusion of tongues related above we have no slight reason for thinking that men were at that time first scattered through all the climates of the world, and the habitable regions and corners of those climates. And as the original root of the human race was planted in the regions of the East, and our race also spread out from there on both sides by a manifold diffusion of shoots, and finally reached the boundaries of the West, it was then perhaps that rational throats first drank of the rivers of the whole of Europe, or at least of some of them. But whether these men then first arrived as strangers, or whether they came back to Europe as natives, they brought a threefold language with them, and of those who brought it some allotted to themselves the southern, others the northern part of Europe, while the third body, whom we now call Greeks, seized partly on Europe and partly on Asia.

Afterwards, from one and the same idiom received at the avenging confusion, various vernaculars drew their origin, as we shall show farther on. For one idiom alone prevailed in all the country which from the mouths of the Danube, or marshes of Mæotis to the western boundary of England, is bounded by the frontiers of Italy and France and by the ocean; though afterwards through the Slavs, Hungarians, Teutons, Saxons, English, and many other nations it was drawn off into various vernaculars, this alone remaining to almost all of them as a sign of their common origin, that nearly all the above-named answer in affirmation *io*.

Starting from this idiom, that is to say eastward from the Hungarian frontier, another language prevailed over all the territory in that direction comprised in Europe, and even extended beyond. But a third idiom prevailed in all that part of Europe which remains from the other two, though it now appears in a threefold form. For of those who speak it, some say in affirmation *oc*,[4] others *oïl*, and others *sì*, namely the Spaniards, the French, and the Italians. Now the proof that the vernaculars of these nations proceed from one and the same idiom is obvious, because we see that they call many things by the same names, as *Deum, celum, amorem, mare, terram, vivit, moritur, amat,* and almost all other things. Now those of them who say *oc* inhabit the western part of the South of Europe, beginning from the frontier of the Genoese; while those who say *sì* inhabit the country east of the said frontier, namely that which extends as far as that promontory of Italy where the Gulf of the Adriatic Sea begins, and Sicily. But those who say *oïl* lie in some sort to the north of these last; for they have the Germans on their east and north; on the west they are enclosed by the English sea, and bounded by the mountains of Aragon; they are also shut off on the south by the inhabitants of Provence, and the precipices of the Apennines.

IX

We must now put whatever reason we possess to the proof, since it is our purpose to investigate matters in which we are supported by the authority of none, namely, the change which has passed over a language which was originally of one and the same form. [And] because it is safer as well as quicker to travel by known paths, let us proceed with that language alone which belongs to us, neglecting the others. For that which we find in one appears by analogy to exist in the others also.

The language, then, which we are proceeding to treat of is threefold, as has been mentioned above; for some of those who speak it say *oc*, others *sì*, and others *oïl*. And that this language was uniform at the beginning of the confusion (which must first be proved) appears from the fact that we agree in many words, as eloquent writers show, which agreement is repugnant to that confusion which expiated the crime [committed] in the building of Babel.

The writers of all three forms of the language agree, then, in many words, especially in the word *Amor*. Giraut de Borneil says: "*Sim sentis fezelz amics / per ver encusera Amor.*"[5] The King of Navarre: "*De fine amor si vient sen et bonté.*"[6] Messer Guido Guinizelli: "*Nè fa amor prima che gentil core / nè gentil cor prima che amor natura.*"[7] Let us now inquire why it is that this language has varied into three chief forms, and why each of these variations varies in itself; why, for instance, the speech of the right side of Italy varies from that of the left (for the Paduans speak in one way and the Pisans in another); and also why those who live nearer together still vary in their speech, as the Milanese and Veronese, the Romans and the Florentines, and even those who have the same national designation, as the Neapolitans and the people of Gaeta, those of

Ravenna and those of Faenza, and what is stranger still, the inhabitants of the same city, like the Bolognese of the Borgo S. Felice and the Bolognese of the Strada Maggiore. One and the same reason will explain why all these differences and varieties of speech occur.

We say, therefore, that no effect as such goes beyond its cause, because nothing can bring about that which itself is not. Since therefore every language of ours, except that created by God with the first man, has been restored at our pleasure after the confusion, which was nothing else but forgetfulness of the former language, and since man is a most unstable and changeable animal, no human language can be lasting and continuous, but must needs vary like other properties of ours, as for instance our manners and our dress, according to distance of time and place. And so far am I from thinking that there is room for doubt as to the truth of our remark that speech varies "according to difference of time," that we are of opinion that this is rather to be held as certain. For, if we consider our other actions, we seem to differ much more from our fellow-countrymen in very distant times than from our contemporaries very remote in place. Wherefore we boldly affirm that if the ancient Pavians were to rise from the dead they would talk in a language varying or differing from that of the modern Pavians. Nor should what we are saying appear more wonderful than to observe that a young man is grown up whom we have not seen growing. For the motion of those things which move gradually is not considered by us at all; and the longer the time required for perceiving the variation of a thing, the more stable we suppose that thing to be. Let us not therefore be surprised if the opinions of men who are but little removed from the brutes suppose that the citizens of the same town have always carried on their intercourse with an unchangeable speech, because the change in the speech of the same town comes about gradually, not without a very long succession of time, whilst the life of man is in its nature extremely short.

If, therefore, the speech of the same people varies (as has been said) successively in course of time, and cannot in any wise stand still, the speech of people living apart and removed from one another must needs vary in different ways; just as manners and dress vary in different ways, since they are not rendered stable either by nature or by intercourse, but arise according to men's inclinations and local fitness. Hence were set in motion the inventors of the art of grammar, which is nothing else but a kind of unchangeable identity of speech in different times and places. This, having been settled by the common consent of many peoples, seems exposed to the arbitrary will of none in particular, and consequently cannot be variable. They therefore invented grammar in order that we might not, on account of the variation of speech fluctuating at the will of individuals, either fail altogether in attaining, or at least attain but a partial knowledge of the opinions and exploits of the ancients, or of those whom difference of place causes to differ from us.

X

Our language being now spoken under three forms (as has been said above), we feel, when comparing it with itself, according to the three forms that it has assumed, such great hesitation and timidity in placing [its different forms] in the balances, that we dare not, in our comparison, give the preference to any one of them, except in so far as we find that the founders of grammar have taken *sic* as the adverb of affirmation, which seems to confer a kind of precedence on the Italians, who say *sì*. For each of the three divisions [of our language] defends its pretensions by copious evidence. That of *oïl*, then, alleges on its behalf that because of its being an easier and pleasanter vernacular language, whatever has been translated into or composed in vernacular prose belongs to it, namely, the compilations of the exploits of the Trojans and Romans, the exquisite legends of King Arthur, and very many other works of history and learning. Another, namely that of *oc*, claims that eloquent speakers of the vernacular first employed it for poetry, as being a more finished and sweeter language, for instance Peter of Auvergne and other ancient writers. The third also, which is the language of the Italians, claims pre-eminence on the strength of two privileges: first, that the sweetest and most subtle poets who have written in the vernacular are its intimate friends and belong to its household, like Cino of Pistoia and his friend[8]; second, that it seems to lean more on grammar, which is common: and this appears a very weighty argument to those who examine the matter in a rational way.

We, however, decline to give judgment in this case, and confining our treatise to the vernacular Italian, let us endeavor to enumerate the variations it has received into itself, and also to compare these with one another. In the first place, then, we say that Italy has a twofold division into right and left. But, if any should ask what is the dividing line, we answer shortly that it is the ridge of the Apennines, which like the ridge of a tiled roof discharges its droppings in different directions on either side, and pours its waters down to either shore alternately through long gutter-tiles, as Lucan describes in his second book. Now the right side has the Tyrrhenian Sea as its basin, while the waters on the left fall into the Adriatic. The districts on the right are Apulia (but not the whole of it), the Duchy [of Spoleto], Tuscany, and the March of Genoa. Those on the left are part of Apulia, the March of Ancona, Romagna, Lombardy, and the March of Treviso with Venetia. Friuli and Istria cannot but belong to the left of Italy, and the islands of the Tyrrhenian Sea, namely Sicily and Sardinia, must belong to, or be associated with the right of Italy. Now in each of these two sides, and those districts which follow them, the languages of the inhabitants vary, as for instance the language of the Sicilians as compared with that of the Apulians, of the Apulians with that of the Romans, of the Romans with that of the Spoletans, of these with that of the Tuscans, of the Tuscans with that of the Genoese, of the Genoese with that of the Sardinians; also of the Calabrians with that of the people of Ancona, of these with that of the people of Romagna, of the people of Romagna with that of the Lombards, of the Lombards with that of the Trevisans and Venetians, and of these last with that of the Aquileians, and of them with that of the Istrians; and we do not think that any Italian will disagree with us in this statement. Whence it appears that Italy alone is diversified by fourteen dialects at least, all of which again vary in themselves: as for instance in Tuscany the Sienese differ in speech from the Aretines; in Lombardy the Ferrarese from the Placentines; in the same city also we observe some variation, as we remarked above in the last chapter. Wherefore if we would calculate the primary, secondary, and subordinate variations of the vulgar tongue of Italy, we should find that in this tiny corner of the world the varieties of speech not only come up to a thousand but even exceed that figure.

XI

As the Italian vernacular has so very many discordant varieties, let us hunt after a more fitting and an illustrious Italian language; and in order that we may be able to have a practicable path for our chase, let us first cast the tangled bushes and brambles out of the wood. Therefore, as the Romans think that they ought to have precedence over all the rest, let us in this process of uprooting or clearing away give them (not undeservedly) precedence, declaring that we will have nothing to do with them in any scheme of a vernacular language. We say, then, that the vulgar tongue of the Romans, or rather their hideous jargon, is the ugliest of all the Italian dialects; nor is this surprising, since in the depravity of their manners and customs also they appear to stink worse than all the rest. For they say *"Mezzure, quinto dici?"*[9] After them, let us get rid of the inhabitants of the March of Ancona, who say, *"Chignamente scate sciate?"*[10] with whom we reject the Spolentans also. Nor must we forget that a great many canzoni have been written in contempt of these three peoples, among which we have noticed one correctly and perfectly constructed, which a certain Florentine named Castra had composed. It began: *"Una fermana scopai da Cascióli / Cita cita sen gia'n grande aina."*[11] And after these let us weed out the people of Milan and Bergamo with their neighbors, in reproach of whom we recollect that some one has sung: *"Enti l'ora del vesper, / Ciò fu del mes d' ochiover."*[12] After them let us sift out the Aquileians and Istrians, who belch forth with cruelly harsh accents, *Ces fastu?"*[13] And with these we cast out all the mountainous and rural dialects, as those of Casentino and Prato, which by the extravagance of their accent always seem discordant to the citizens dwelling in the midst of the towns. Let us also cast out the Sardinians, who are not Italians, but are, it seems, to be associated with them; since they alone seem to be without any vulgar tongue of their own, imitating Latin as apes do men: for they say, *"Domus nova"*[14] and *"dominus meus."*[15]

XII

Having sifted, so to speak, the Italian vernaculars, let us, comparing together those left in our sieve, briefly choose out the one most honorable and conferring most honor. And first let us examine the genius of the Sicilian, for the Sicilian vernacular appears to arrogate to itself a greater renown than the others, both because whatever poetry the Italians write is called Sicilian, and because we find that very many natives of Sicily have written weighty poetry, as in the canzoni, *"Ancor che l'aigua per lo focho lassi,"*[16] and *"Amor che lungiamente m'ài menato."*[17] But this fame of the land of Trinacria[18] appears, if we rightly examine the mark to which it tends, only to have survived by way of a reproach to the princes of Italy, who, not in a heroic but in a plebeian manner, follow pride. But those illustrious heroes Frederick Cæsar[19] and his happy-born son Manfred, displaying the nobility and righteousness of their character, as long as fortune remained favorable, followed what is human, disdaining what is bestial; wherefore those who were of noble heart and endowed with graces strove to attach themselves to the majesty of such great princes; so that in their time, whatever the best Italians attempted first appeared at the court of these mighty sovereigns. And from the fact that the royal throne was Sicily it came to pass that whatever our predecessors wrote in the vulgar tongue was called Sicilian; and this name we also retain, nor will our successors be able to change it. Racha, racha![20] what is the sound now uttered by the trumpet of the latest Frederick?[21] What is that uttered by the bell of Charles II? What is that uttered by the horns of the powerful Marquises John and Azzo? What is that uttered by the flutes of the other magnates? What but "Come, ye murderers; come, ye traitors; come, ye followers of avarice."

But it is better to return to our subject than to speak in vain: and we declare that if we take the Sicilian dialect, that namely spoken by the common people, out of whose mouths it appears our judgment should be drawn, it is in nowise worthy of preference, because it is not uttered without drawling, as for instance here: *"Tragemi d'este focara, se t'este a boluntate."*[22] If, however, we choose to take the language as it flows from the mouths of the highest Sicilians, as it may be examined in the canzoni quoted before, it differs in nothing from that language which is the most worthy of praise, as we show further on.

The Apulians also, because of their own harshness of speech, or else because of their nearness to their neighbors who are the Romans and the people of the March [of Ancona], make use of shameful barbarisms, for they say, *"Volzera che chiangesse lo quatraro."*[23]

But though the natives of Apulia commonly speak in a hideous manner, some of them have been distinguished by their use of polished language, inserting more *curial* words into their canzoni, as clearly appears from an examination of their works, for instance, *"Madonna, dir vi voglio,"*[24] and *"Per fino amore vo sì letamente."*[25]

Wherefore it should become clear to those who mark what has been said above, that neither the Sicilian nor the Apulian dialect is that vulgar tongue which is the most beautiful in Italy, for we have shown that eloquent natives of those parts have diverged from their own dialect.

XIII

Next let us come to the Tuscans, who, infatuated through their frenzy, seem to arrogate to themselves the title of the illustrious vernacular; and in this matter not only the minds of the common people are crazed, but we find that many distinguished men have embraced the delusion; for instance Guittone of Arezzo, who never aimed at the curial vernacular, Bonagiunta of Lucca, Gallo of Pisa, Mino Mocato of Siena, and Brunetto of Florence, whose works, if there be leisure to examine them, will be found to be not curial but merely municipal. And since the Tuscans exceed the rest in this frenzied intoxication, it seems right and profitable to deal with the dialects of the Tuscan towns one by one, and to take off somewhat of their vain glory. The Florentines open their mouths and say, "*Manichiamo introque—Noi non facciano atro*";[26] the Pisans, "*Bene andonno li fanti De Fiorensa per Pisa*";[27] the people of Lucca, "*Fo voto a Dio che in gassarra eie lo comuno de Lucca*";[28] the Sienes, "*Onche renegata avesse io Siena!*"[29] "*Ch'ee chesto?*"[30] the Aretines, "*Vo tu venire ovelle?*"[31] (We do not intend to deal with Perugia, Orvieto, and Città Castellana at all, because of their close connection with the Romans and Spoletans.) But obtuse as almost all the Tuscans are in their degraded dialect, we notice that some have recognized wherein the excellence of the vernacular consists, namely, Guido, Lapo, and another, all Florentines, and Cino of Pistoja, whom we now undeservedly put last, having been not undeservedly driven to do so. Therefore if we examine the Tuscan dialects reflecting how the writers commended above have deviated from their own dialect, it does not remain doubtful that the vernacular we are in search of is different from that which the people of Tuscany attain to.

But if any one thinks that what we say of the Tuscans may not also be said of the Genoese, let him but bear this in mind, that if the Genoese were through forgetfulness to lose the letter z, they would have either to be dumb altogether, or to discover some new kind of speech, for z forms the greatest part of their dialect, and this letter is not uttered without great harshness.

XIV

Let us now cross the leaf-clad shoulders of the Apennines, and hunt inquiringly, as we are wont, over the left side of Italy, beginning from the east.

Entering Romagna, then, we remark that we have found in Italy two alternating types of dialect with certain opposite characteristics in which they respectively agree. One of these, on account of the softness of its words and pronunciation, seems so feminine that it causes a man, even when speaking like a man, to be believed to be a woman. This type of dialect prevails among all the people of Romagna, and especially those of Forli, whose city, though the newest, seems to be the centre of all the province. These people say *deuscì* in affirmation, and use "*Oclo meo*"[32] and "*Corada mea*"[33] as terms of endearment. We have heard that some of them have diverged in poetry from their own dialect, namely the Faentines Thomas and Ugolino Bucciola.

There is also, as we have said, another type of dialect, so bristling and shaggy in its words and accents that, owing to its rough harshness, it not only distorts a woman's speech, but makes one doubt whether she is not a man. This type of dialect prevails among all those who say *magara*,[34] namely the Brescians, Veronese, and Vicentines, as well as the Paduans, with their ugly syncopations of all the participles in *tus* and denominatives in *tas*, as *mercò* and *bontè*. With these we also class the Trevisans, who, like the Brescians and their neighbors, pronounce *f* for consonantal *u*, cutting off the final syllable of the word, as *nof* for *novem*,[35] *vif* for *vivo*, which we disapprove as a gross barbarism.

Nor do the Venetians also deem themselves worthy of possessing that vernacular language which we have been searching for; and if any of them, trusting in error, should cherish any delusion on this point, let him remember whether he has ever said *"Per le plage de Dio tu non veràs."*[36]

Among all these we have noticed one man striving to depart from his mother-tongue, and to apply himself to the *curial* vernacular language, namely Ildebrandino of Padua.

Wherefore, on all the dialects mentioned in the present chapter coming up for judgment, our decision is that neither that of Romagna nor its opposite (as we have mentioned), nor that of Venice is that illustrious vernacular which we are seeking.

XV

Let us now endeavor to clear the way by tracking out what remains of the Italian wood.

We say, then, that perhaps those are not far wrong who assert that the people of Bologna use a more beautiful speech [than the others], since they receive into their own dialect something borrowed from their neighbors of Imola, Ferrara, and Modena, just as we conjecture that all borrow from their neighbors, as Sordello showed with respect to his own Mantua, which is adjacent to Cremona, Brescia, and Verona; and he who was so distinguished by his eloquence, not only in poetry but in every other form of utterance forsook his native vulgar tongue. Accordingly the above-mentioned citizens [of Bologna] get from those of Imola their smoothness and softness [of speech], and from those of Ferrara and Modena a spice of sharpness characteristic of the Lombards. This we believe has remained with the natives of that district as a relic of the admixture of the immigrant Longobards with them: and this is the reason why we find that there has been no poet among the people of Ferrara, Modena, or Reggio; for from being accustomed to their own sharpness they cannot adopt the courtly vulgar tongue without a kind of roughness; and this we must consider to be much more the case with the people of Parma, who say *monto* instead of *multo*. If, therefore, the people of Bologna borrow from both these kinds of dialect, as has been said, it seems reasonable that their speech should by this mixture of opposites remain tempered to a praiseworthy sweetness; and this we without hesitation judge to be the case. Therefore if those who place the people of Bologna first in the matter of the vernacular merely have regard in their comparison to the municipal dialects of the Italians, we are disposed to agree with them; but if they consider that the dialect of Bologna is, taken absolutely, worthy of preference, we disagree with them altogether; for this dialect is not that language which we term courtly and illustrious, since if it had been so, the greatest Guido Guinizelli, Guido Ghisilieri, Fabruzzo, and Onesto, and other poets of Bologna would never have departed from their own dialect; and these were illustrious writers, competent judges of dialects. The greatest Guido wrote: *"Madonna lo fermo core"*;[37] Fabruzzo, *"Lo meo lontano gire"*;[38] Onesto, *"Più non attendo il tuo secorso, Amore"*;[39] and these words are altogether different from the dialect of the citizens of Bologna.

And since we consider that no one feels any doubt as to the remaining towns at the extremities of Italy (and if any one does, we do not deem him worthy of any answer from us), little remains to be mentioned in our discussion. Wherefore being eager to put down our sieve so that we may quickly see what is left in it, we say that the towns of Trent and Turin, as well as Alessandria, are situated so near the frontiers of Italy that they cannot possess pure languages, so that even if their vernaculars were as lovely as they are hideous, we should still say that they were not truly Italian, because of their foreign ingredients. Wherefore if we are hunting for an illustrious Italian language, what we are hunting for cannot be found in them.

XVI

After having scoured the heights and pastures of Italy, without having found that panther which we are in pursuit of, in order that we may be able to find her, let us now track her out in a more rational manner, so that we may with skillful efforts completely enclose within our toils her who is fragrant everywhere but nowhere apparent.

Resuming, then, our hunting-spears, we say that in every kind of things there must be one thing by which all the things of that kind may be compared and weighed, and which we may take as the measure of all the others; just as in numbers all are measured by unity and are said to be more or fewer according as they are distant from or near to unity; so also in colors all are measured by white, for they are said to be more or less visible according as they approach or recede from it. And what we say of the predicaments which indicate quantity and quality, we think may also be said of any of the predicaments and even of substance; namely, that everything considered as belonging to a kind becomes measurable by that which is simplest in that kind. Wherefore in our actions, however many the species into which they are divided may be, we have to discover this standard by which they may be measured. Thus, in what concerns our actions as human beings simply, we have virtue, understanding it generally; for according to it we judge a man to be good or bad; in what concerns our actions as citizens, we have the law, according to which a citizen is said to be good or bad; in what concerns our actions as Italians, we have certain very simple standards of manners, customs, and language, by which our actions as Italians are weighed and measured. Now the supreme standards of those activities which are generically Italian are not peculiar to any one town in Italy, but are common to all; and among these can now be discerned that vernacular language which we were hunting for above, whose fragrance is in every town, but whose lair is in none. It may, however, be more perceptible in one than in another, just as the simplest of substances, which is God, is more perceptible in a man than in a brute, in an animal than in a plant, in a plant than in a mineral, in a mineral than in an element, in fire than in earth. And the simplest quantity, which is unity, is more perceptible in an odd than in an even number; and the simplest color, which is white, is more perceptible in orange than in green.

Having therefore found what we were searching for, we declare the illustrious, cardinal, courtly, and curial vernacular language in Italy to be that which belongs to all the towns in Italy but does not apear to belong to any one of them, and by which all the municipal dialects of the Italians are measured, weighed, and compared.

XVII

We must now set forth why it is that we call this language we have found by the epithets illustrious, cardinal, courtly, and curial; and by doing this we disclose the nature of the language itself more clearly. First, then, let us lay bare what we mean by the epithet illustrious, and why we call the language illustrious. Now we understand by this term "illustrious" something which shines forth illuminating and illuminated. And in this way we call men illustrious either because, being illuminated by power, they illuminate others by justice and charity; or else because, having been excellently trained, they in turn give excellent training, like Seneca and Numa Pompilius. And the vernacular of which we are speaking has both been exalted by training and power, and also exalts its followers by honor and glory.

Now it appears to have been exalted by training, inasmuch as from amid so many rude Italian words, involved constructions, faulty expressions, and rustic accents we see that it has been chosen out in such a degree of excellence, clearness, completeness, and polish as is displayed by Cino of Pistoja and his friend in their canzoni.

And that it has been exalted by power is plain; for what is of greater power than that which can sway the hearts of men, so as to make an unwilling man willing, and a willing man unwilling, just as this language has done and is doing?

Now that it exalts by honor is evident. Do not they of its household surpass in renown kings, marquises, counts, and all other magnates? This has no need at all of proof.

But how glorious it makes its familiar friends we ourselves know, who for the sweetness of this glory cast [even] our exile behind our back. Wherefore we ought deservedly to proclaim this language illustrious.

XVIII

Nor it is without reason that we adorn this illustrious vernacular language with a second epithet, that is, that we call it cardinal: for as the whole door follows its hinge, so that whither the hinge turns the door also may turn, whether it be moved inward or outward, in like manner also the whole herd of municipal dialects turns and returns, moves and pauses according as this illustrious language does, which really seems to be the father of the family. Does it not daily root out the thorny bushes from the Italian wood? Does in not daily insert grafts or plant young trees? What else have its foresters to do but to take away and bring in, as has been said? Wherefore it surely deserves to be adorned with so great a name as this.

Now the reason why we call it "courtly" is that if we Italians had a court it would be spoken at court. For if a court is a common home of all the realm and an august ruler of all parts of the realm, it is fitting that whatever is of such a character as to be common to all [parts] without being peculiar to any, should frequent this court and dwell there; nor is any other abode worthy of so great an inmate. Such in fact seems to be that vernacular language of which we are speaking; and hence it is that those who frequent all royal palaces always speak the illustrious vernacular. Hence also it is that our illustrious language wanders about like a wayfarer, and is welcomed in humble shelters, seeing we have no court.

This language is also deservedly to be styled "curial," because "curiality" is nothing else but the justly balanced rule of things which have to be done; and because the scales required for this kind of balancing are only wont to be found in the most excellent courts of justice, it follows that whatever in our actions has been well balanced is called curial. Wherefore since this illustrious language has been weighed in the balances of the most excellent court of justice of the Italians, it deserves to be called curial. But it seems mere trifling to say that it has been weighed in the balances of the most excellent court of justice of the Italians, because we have no [Imperial] court of justice. To this the answer is easy. For though there is no court of justice of Italy in the sense of a single [supreme] court, like the court of the king of Germany, still the members of such a court are not wanting. And just as the members of the German court are united under one prince, so the members of ours have been united by the gracious light of reason. Wherefore, though we have no prince, it would be false to assert that the Italians have no [such] court of justice, because we have a court, though in the body it is scattered.

XIX

Now we declare that this vernacular language, which we have shown to be illustrious, cardinal, courtly, and curial, is that which is called the Italian vernacular. For just as a vernacular can be found peculiar to Cremona, so can one be found peculiar to Lombardy; and just as one can be found peculiar to Lombardy, [so] can one be found peculiar to the whole of the left side of Italy. And just as all these can be found, so also can that which belongs to the whole of Italy. And just as the first is called Cremonese, the second Lombard, and the third Semi-Italian, so that which belongs to the whole of Italy is called the Italian vernacular language. For this has been used by the illustrious writers who have written poetry in the vernacular throughout Italy, as Sicilians, Apulians, Tuscans, natives of Romagna, and men of both the Marches. And because our intention is, as we promised in the beginning of this work, to give instruction concerning the vernacular speech, we will begin with this illustrious Italian as being the most excellent, and treat in the books immediately following of those whom we think worthy to use it; and for what, and how, and also where, when, and to whom, it ought to be used. And after making all this clear, we will make it our business to throw light on the lower vernaculars, gradually coming down to that which belongs to a single family.

Book II

I

Urging on once more the nimbleness of our wit, which is returning to the pen of useful work, we declare in the first place that the illustrious Italian vernacular is equally fit for use in prose and in verse. But because prose writers rather get this language from poets, and because poetry seems to remain a pattern to prose writers, and not the converse, which things appear to confer a certain supremacy, let us first disentangle this language as to its use in meter, treating of it in the order we set forth at the end of the first book.

Let us then first inquire whether all those who write verse in the vernacular should use this illustrious language; and so far as a superficial consideration of the matter goes, it would seem that they should, because every one who writes verse ought to adorn his verse as far as he is able. Wherefore, since nothing affords so great an adornment as the illustrious vernacular does, it would seem that every writer of verse ought to employ it. Besides, if that which is best in its kind be mixed with things inferior to itself, it not only appears not to detract anything from them but even to improve them. Wherefore if any writer of verse, even though his verse be rude in matter, mixes the illustrious vernacular with his rudeness of matter, he not only appears to do well, but to be actually obliged to take this course. Those who can do little need help much more than those who can do much, and thus it appears that all writers of verse are at liberty to use this illustrious language. But this is quite false, because not even poets of the highest order ought always to assume it, as will appear from a consideration of what is discussed farther on. This illustrious language, then, just like our behavior in other matters and our dress, demands men of like quality to its own; for munificence demands men of great resources, and the purple, men of noble character, and in the same way this illustrious language seeks for men who excel in genius and knowledge, and despises others, as will appear from what is said below. For everything which is suited to us is so either in respect of the genus, or of the species, or of the individual, as sensation, laughter, war; but this illustrious language is not suited to us in respect of our genus, for then it would also be suited to the brutes; nor in respect of our species, for then it would be suited to all men; and as to this there is no question; for no one will say that this language is suited to dwellers in the mountains dealing with rustic concerns: therefore it is suited in respect of the individual. But nothing is suited to an individual except on account of his particular worth, as for instance commerce, war, and government. Wherefore if things are suitable according to worth, that is the worthy (and some men may be worthy, others worthier and others worthiest), it is plain that good things will be suited to the worthy, better things to the worthier, and the best things to the worthiest. And since language is as necessary an instrument of our thought as a horse is of a knight, and since the best horses are suited to the best knights, as has been said, the best language will be suited to the best thoughts. But the best thoughts cannot exist except where knowledge and genius are found; therefore the best language is only suitable in those in whom knowledge and genius are found; and so the best language is not suited to all who write verse, since a great many write without knowledge and genius; and consequently neither is the best vernacular [suited to all who write verse]. Wherefore, if it is not suited to all, all ought not to use it, because no one ought to act in an unsuitable manner. And as to the statement that every one ought to adorn his verse as far as he can, we declare that it is true; but we should not describe an ox with trappings or a swine with a belt as adorned, nay rather we laugh at them as disfigured; for adornment is the addition of some suitable thing.

As to the statement that superior things mixed with inferior effect an improvement [in the latter], we say that it is true if the blending is complete, for instance when we mix gold and silver together; but if it is not, the inferior things appear worse, for instance when beautiful women are mixed with ugly ones. Wherefore, since the theme of those who write verse always persists as an ingredient distinct from the words, it will not, unless of the highest quality, appear better when associated with the best vernacular, but worse; like an ugly woman if dressed out in gold or silk.

II

After having proved that not all those who write verse, but only those of the highest excellence, ought to use the illustrious vernacular, we must in the next place establish whether every subject ought to be handled in it, or not; and if not, we must set out by themselves those subjects that are worthy of it. And in reference to this we must first find out what we understand by that which we call *worthy*. We say that a thing which has worthiness is worthy, just as we say that a thing which has nobility is noble; and if when that which confers the habit is known, that on which the habit is conferred is [also] known, as such, then if we know what worthiness is, we shall know also what *worthy* is. Now worthiness is an effect or end of deserts; so that when any one has deserved well we say that he has arrived at worthiness of good; but when he has deserved ill, at worthiness of evil. Thus we say that a soldier who has fought well has arrived at worthiness of victory; one who has ruled well, at worthiness of a kingdom; also that a liar has arrived at worthiness of shame, and a robber at worthiness of death.

But inasmuch as [further] comparisons are made among those who deserve well, and also among those who deserve ill, so that some deserve well, some better, and some best; some badly, some worse, and some worst; while such comparisons are only made with respect to the end of deserts, which (as has been mentioned before) we call *worthiness*, it is plain that worthinesses are compared together according as they are greater or less, so that some are great, some greater, and some greatest; and, consequently, it is obvious that one thing is worthy, another worthier, and another worthiest. And whereas there can be no such comparison of worthinesses with regard to the same object [of desert] but [only] with regard to different objects, so that we call *worthier* that which is worthy of greater objects, and *worthiest* that which is worthy of the greatest, because no thing can be more worthy [than another] in virtue of the same qualification, it is evident that the best things are worthy of the best [objects of desert], according to the requirement of the things. Whence it follows that, since the language we call illustrious is the best of all the other forms of the vernacular, the best subjects alone are worthy of being handled in it, and these we call the *worthiest* of those subjects which can be handled; and now let us hunt out what they are. And, in order to make this clear, it must be observed that, as man has been endowed with a threefold life, namely, vegetable, animal, and rational, he journeys along a threefold road; for in so far as he is vegetable he seeks for what is useful, wherein he is of like nature with plants; in so far as he is animal he seeks for that which is pleasurable, wherein he is of like nature with the brutes; in so far as he is rational he seeks for what is right—and in this he stands alone, or is a partaker of the nature of the angels. It is by these three kinds of life that we appear to carry out whatever we do; and because in each one of them some things are greater, some greatest, within the range of their kind, it follows that those which are greatest appear the ones which ought to be treated of supremely, and consequently, in the greatest vernacular.

But we must discuss what things are greatest; and first in respect of what is useful. Now in this matter, if we carefully consider the object of all those who are in search of what is useful, we shall find that it is nothing else but safety. Secondly, in respect of what is pleasurable; and here we say that that is most pleasurable which gives pleasure by the most exquisite object of appetite, and this is love. Thirdly, in respect of what is right; and here no one doubts that virtue has the first place. Wherefore these three things, namely, safety, love, and virtue, appear to be those capital matters which ought to be treated of supremely, I mean the things which are most important in respect of them, as prowess in arms, the fire of love, and the direction of the will. And if we duly consider, we shall find that the illustrious writers have written poetry in the vulgar tongue on these subjects exclusively; namely, Bertran de Born on Arms, Arnaut Daniel on Love, Giraut de Borneil on Righteousness, Cino of Pistoja on Love, his friend on Righteousness. For Bertan says: 'Non posc mudar c'un cantar non exparja."[40] Arnaut: "*L'aura amara fals bruols brancuz clairir.*"[41] Giraut: "*Per solaz reveillar/que s'es trop endormitz.*"[42] Cino: "*Digno sono eo de morte.*"[43] His friend: "*Doglia mi reca nello core ardire.*"[44] I do not find, however, that any Italian has as yet written poetry on the subject of Arms.

Having then arrived at this point, we know what are the proper subjects to be sung in the highest vernacular language.

III

But now let us endeavor carefully to examine how those matters which are worthy of so excellent a vernacular language are to be restricted. As we wish, then, to set forth the form by which these matters are worthy to be bound, we say that it must first be borne in mind that those who have written poetry in the vernacular have uttered their poems in many different forms, some in that of canzoni, some in that of ballate, some in that of sonnets, some in other illegitimate and irregular forms, as will be shown farther on. Now we consider that of these forms that of canzoni is the most excellent; and therefore, if the most excellent things are worthy of the most excellent, as has been proved above, those subjects which are worthy of the most excellent vernacular are worthy of the most excellent form, and consequently ought to be handled in canzoni. Now we may discover by several reasons that the form of canzoni is such as has been said. The first reason is that though whatever we write in verse is a canzone, the canzoni [technically so called] have alone acquired this name; and this has never happened apart from ancient provision.

Moreover, whatever produces by itself the effect for which it was made, appears nobler than that which requires external assistance. But canzoni produce by themselves the whole effect they ought to produce; which ballate do not, for they require the assistance of the performers for whom they are written; it therefore follows that canzoni are to be deemed nobler than ballate, and therefore that their form is the noblest of any, for no one doubts that ballate excel sonnets in nobility of form.

Besides, those things appear to be nobler which bring more honor to their author; but canzoni bring more [honor] to their authors than ballate; therefore they are nobler [than these], and consequently their form is the noblest of any.

Furthermore, the noblest things are the most fondly preserved; but among poems canzoni are the most fondly preserved, as is evident to those who look into books; therefore canzoni are the noblest [poems], and consequently their form is the noblest.

Also, in works of art, that is noblest which embraces the whole art. Since, therefore, poems are works of art, and the whole of the art is embraced in canzoni alone, canzoni are the noblest poems, and so their form is the noblest of any. Now, that the whole of the art of poetic song is embraced in canzoni is proved by the fact that whatever is found to belong to the art is found in them; but the converse is not true. But the proof of what we are saying is at once apparent; for all that has flowed from the tops of the heads of illustrious poets down to their lips is found in canzoni alone. Wherefore, in reference to the subject before us, it is clear that the matters which are worthy of the highest vulgar tongue ought to be handled in canzoni.

IV

Having then labored by a process of disentangling [to show] what persons and things are worthy of the courtly vernacular, as well as the form of verse which we deem worthy of such honor that it alone is fitted for the highest vernacular, before going off to other topics, let us explain the form of the canzone, which many appear to adopt rather at haphazard than with art; and let us unlock the workshop of the art of that form which has hitherto been adopted in a casual way, omitting the form of ballate and sonnets, because we intend to explain this in the fourth book of this work, when we shall treat of the middle vernacular language.

Reviewing, therefore, what has been said, we remember that we have frequently called those who write verse in the vernacular poets; and this we have doubtless ventured to say with good reason, because they are in fact poets, if we take a right view of poetry, which is nothing else but a rhetorical composition set to music. But these poets differ from the great poets, that is, the regular ones, for the language of the great poets was regulated by art, whereas these, as has been said, write at haphazard. It therefore happens that the more closely we copy the great poets, the more correct is the poetry we write; whence it behooves us, by devoting some trouble to the work of teaching, to emulate their poetic teaching.

Before all things therefore we say that each one ought to adjust the weight of the subject to his own shoulders, so that their strength may not be too heavily taxed, and he be forced to tumble into the mud. This is the advice our master Horace gives us when he says in the beginning of his "Art of Poetry" ["Ye who write] take up a subject [suited to your strength"].

Next we ought to possess a discernment as to those things which suggest themselves to us as fit to be uttered, so as to decide whether they ought to be sung in the way of tragedy, comedy, or elegy. By tragedy we bring in (*sic*) the higher style, by comedy the lower style, by elegy we understand the style of the wretched. If our subject appears fit to be sung in the tragic style, we must then assume the illustrious vernacular language, and consequently we must bind up a canzone. If, however, it appears fit to be sung in the comic style, sometimes the middle and sometimes the lowly vernacular should be used; and the discernment to be exercised in this case we reserve for treatment in the fourth book. But if our subject appears fit to be sung in the elegiac style, we must adopt the lowly vernacular alone.

But let us omit the other styles and now, as is fitting, let us treat of the tragic style. We appear then to make use of the tragic style when the stateliness of the lines as well as the loftiness of the construction and the excellence of the words agree with the weight of the subject. And because, if we remember rightly, it has already been proved that the highest things are worthy of the highest, and because the style which we call tragic appears to be the highest style, those things which we have distinguished as being worthy of the highest song are to be sung in that style alone, namely, Safety, Love, and Virtue, and those other things, our conceptions of which arise from these; provided that they be not degraded by any accident.

Let every one therefore beware and discern what we say; and when he purposes to sing of these three subjects simply, or of those things which directly and simply follow after them, let him first drink of Helicon, and then, after adjusting the strings, boldly take up his *plectrum*[45] and begin to ply it. But it is in the exercise of the needful caution and discernment that the real difficulty lies; for this can never be attained to without strenuous efforts of genius, constant practice in the art, and the habit of the sciences. And it is those [so equipped] whom the poet in the sixth book of the *Æneid* describes as beloved of God, raised by glowing virtue to the sky, and sons of the Gods, though he is speaking figuratively. And therefore let those who, innocent of art and science, and trusting to genius alone, rush forward to sing of the highest subjects in the highest style, confess their folly and cease from such presumption; and if in their natural sluggishness they are but geese, let them abstain from imitating the eagle soaring to the stars.

V

We seem to have said enough, or at least as much as our work requires, about the weight of the subjects. Wherefore let us hasten on to the stateliness of the lines, in respect of which it is to be observed that our predecessors made use of different lines in their canzoni, as the moderns also do; but we do not find that any one has hitherto used a line of more than eleven or less than three syllables. And though the Italian poets have used the lines of three and of eleven syllables and all the intermediate ones, those of five, seven, and eleven syllables are more frequently used [than the others], and next to them, that of three syllables in preference to the others. But of all these the line of eleven syllables seems the stateliest, as well by reason of the length of time it occupies as of its capacity in regard to subject, construction, and words: and the beauty of all these things is more multiplied in this line [than in the others], as is plainly apparent; for wherever things that weigh are multiplied so also is weight. And all the teachers seem to have given heed to this, beginning their illustrious canzoni with a line of eleven syllables, as Giraut de Borneil: *"Ara auzirez encabalitz cantars."*[46]

And though this line appears to be of ten syllables, it is in reality of eleven, for the last two consonants do not belong to the preceding syllable. And though they have no vowel belonging to them, still they do not lose the force of a syllable; and the proof of this is that the rhyme is in this instance completed by one vowel, which could not be the case except by virtue of another understood there. The king of Navarre writes: *"De fine Amor si vient sen et bonté,"*[47] where, if the accent and its cause be considered the line will be found to have eleven syllables. Guido Guinizelli writes: *"Al cor gentil repara sempre Amore."*[48] The Judge [Guido] delle Colonne of Messina: *"Amor che lungiamente m' ài menato."*[49] Rinaldo d'Aquino: *"Per fino amore vo sì letamente."*[50] Cino of Pistoja: *"Non spero che già mai per mia salute."*[51] His friend: *"Amor che movi tua vertù da cielo."*[52] And though this line which has been mentioned appears, as is worthy, the most celebrated of all, yet, if it be associated in some slight degree with the line of seven syllables (provided only it retain its supremacy), it seems to rise still more clearly and loftily in its stateliness. But this must be left for further explanation.

We say also that the line of seven syllables follows next after that which is greatest in celebrity. After this we place the line of five, and then that of three syllables. But the line of nine syllables, because it appeared to consist of the line of three taken three times, was either never held in honor or fell into disuse on account of its being disliked. As for the lines of an even number of syllables, we use them but rarely, because of their rudeness; for they retain the nature of their numbers, which are subject to the odd numbers as matter to form. And so, summing up what has been said, the line of eleven syllables appears to be the stateliest line, and this is what we were in search of. But now it remains for us to investigate concerning exalted constructions and pre-eminent words; and at length, after having got ready our sticks and ropes, we will teach how we ought to bind together the promised faggot, that is the canzone.

VI

Inasmuch as our intention has reference to the illustrious vernacular, which is the noblest of all, and we have distinguished the things which are worthy of being sung in it, which are the three noblest subjects, as has been established above, and have chosen the form of canzoni for them, as being the highest form of any, and have also (in order that we may be able more perfectly to give thorough instruction in this form) already settled certain points, namely the style and the line, let us now deal with the construction.

Now it must be observed that we call construction a regulated arrangement of words, as "Aristotle philosophised in Alexander's time." for here there are five words arranged by rule, and they form one construction. Now in reference to this we must first bear in mind that one construction is congruous, while another is incongruous; and inasmuch as, if we recollect the beginning of our distinction, we are only pursuing the highest things, the incongruous construction finds no place in our pursuit, because it has not even proved deserving of a lower degree of goodness. Let therefore illiterate persons be ashamed—I say, let them be ashamed of being henceforth so bold as to burst forth into canzoni, for we laugh at them as at a blind man making distinctions between colors.

It is, then, it seems, the congruous construction after which we are following. But here we come to a distinction of not less difficulty before we can reach that construction which we are in search of, the construction, I mean, which is most full of refinement. For there are a great many degrees of constructions; namely, [first] the insipid, which is that of uncultivated people; as, "Peter is very fond of Mistress Bertha." [Then] there is that which has flavor but nothing else, which belongs to rigid scholars or masters; as, "I, greater in pity than all, am sorry for all those who, languishing in exile, only revisit their native land in their dreams." There is also that which has flavor and grace, which belongs to some who have taken a shallow draught of rhetoric; as, "The praiseworthy discernment of the Marquis of Este and his munificence prepared for all makes him beloved." Then there is that which has flavor and grace and also elevation, which belongs to illustrious writers; as, "Having cast the greatest part of the flowers out of thy bosom, O Florence, the second Totila went fruitlessly to Trinacria." This degree of construction we call the most excellent, and this is the one we are seeking for, since, as has been said, we are in pursuit of the highest things. Of this alone are illustrious canzoni found to be made up as [that by] Giraut de Borneil,

> *Si per mon Sobre-totz no fos.*[53]

[that by] Folquet of Marseilles,

> *Tan m' abellis l'amoros pensamens.*[54]

[that by] Arnaut Daniel,

> *Sols sui qui sai lo sobraffan quem sortz.*[55]

> [that by] Aimeric de Belenoi,
> *Nuls hom non pot complir addreciamen.*[56]
> [that by] Aimeric de Pegulhan,
> *Si com l'arbres que per sobrecarcar.*[57]
> [that by] the King of Navarre,
> *Ire d'amor qui en mon cor repaire.*[58]
> [that by] Guido Guinizelli,
> *Tegno de folle 'mpresa a lo ver dire.*[59]
> [that by] Guido Cavalcanti,
> *Poi che di doglia cor conven ch'io porti.*[60]
> [that by] Cino of Pistoja,
> *Avegna che io aggia più per tempo.*[61]
> [that by] his friend,
> *Amor che nella mente mi ragiona.*[62]

Nor, reader, must you be surprised at our calling to memory so many poets; for we cannot point out that construction which we call the highest except by examples of this kind. And it would possibly be very useful in order to the full acquirement of this construction if we had surveyed the regular poets, I mean Virgil, Ovid in his *Metamorphoses*, Statius, and Lucan, as well as other writers who have employed the most lofty prose, as Titus Livius, Pliny, Frontinus, Paulus Orosius, and many others whom friendly solitude invites us to consult. Let, then, those followers of ignorance hold their peace who praise up Guittone of Arezzo and some others who have never got out of the habit of being plebeian in words and in construction.

VII

The next division of our progress now demands that an explanation be given as to those words which are of such grandeur as to be worthy of being admitted into that style to which we have awarded the first place. We declare therefore to begin with that the exercise of discernment as to words involves by no means the smallest labor of our reason, since we see that a great many sorts of them can be found. For some words are *childish*, some *feminine*, and some *manly;* and of these last some are *sylvan*, others *urban;* and of those we call urban we feel that some are *combed-out* and *glossy*, some *shaggy* and *rumpled*. Now among these urban words the combed-out and the shaggy are those which we call *grand;* whilst we call the glossy and the rumpled those whose sound tends to superfluity, just as among great works some are works of magnanimity, others of smoke; and as to these last, although when superficially looked at there may be thought to be a kind of ascent, to sound reason no ascent, but rather a headlong fall down giddy precipices will be manifest, because the marked-out path of virtue is departed from. Therefore look carefully, Reader, consider how much it behooves thee to use the sieve in selecting noble words; for if thou hast regard to the illustrious vulgar tongue which (as has been said above) poets ought to use when writing in the tragic style in the vernacular (and these are the persons whom we intend to fashion), thou wilt take care that the noblest words alone are left in thy sieve. And among the number of these thou wilt not be able in any wise to place childish words, because of their simplicity, as *mamma* and *babbo*, *mate* and *pate;* nor feminine words, because of their softness, as *dolciada* and *placevole;* nor sylvan words, because of their roughness, as *greggia* and *cetra;* nor the glossy nor the rumpled urban words, as *femina* and *corpo*. Therefore thou wilt see that only the combed-out and the shaggy urban words will be left to thee, which are the noblest, and members of the illustrious vulgar tongue. Now we call those words *combed-out* which have three, or as nearly as possible three syllables; which are without aspirate, without acute or circumflex accent, without the double letters *z* or *x*, without double liquids, or a liquid placed immediately after a mute, and which, having been planned (so to say), leave the speaker with a certain sweetness, like *amore, donna, disio, vertute, donare, letitia, salute, securitate, defesa*.

We call *shaggy* all words besides these which appear either necessary or ornamental to the illustrious vulgar tongue. We call *necessary* those which we cannot avoid, as certain monosyllables like *sì, no me, te, se, a, e, i, o, u,* the interjections, and many more. We describe as *ornamental* all polysyllables which when mixed with combed-out words produce a fair harmony of structure, though they may have the roughness of aspirate, accent, double letters, liquids, and length; *as terra, honore, speranza, gravitate, alleviato, impossibilità, impossibilitate, benaventuratissimo, inanimatissimamente, disaventuratissimamente, sovramagnificentissimamente,* which last has eleven syllables. A word might yet be found with more syllables still; but as it would exceed the capacity of all our lines it does not appear to fall into the present discussion; such is the word *honorificabilitudinitate*, which runs in the vernacular to twelve syllables, and in grammar to thirteen, in two oblique cases.

In what way shaggy words of this kind are to be harmonised in the lines with combed-out words, we leave to be taught farther on. And what has been said [here] on the pre-eminent nature of the words to be used may suffice for every one of inborn discernment.

VIII

Having prepared the sticks and cords for our faggot, the time is now come to bind it up. But inasmuch as knowledge of every work should precede performance, just as there must be a mark to aim at, before we let fly an arrow or javelin, let us first and principally see what that faggot is which we intend to bind up. That faggot, then (if we bear well in mind all that has been said before), is the canzone. Wherefore let us see what a canzone is, and what we mean when we speak of a canzone. Now canzone, according to the true meaning of the name, is the action or passion itself of singing, just as *lectio*[63] is the passion or action of reading. But let us examine what has been said, I mean whether a canzone is so called as being an action or as being a passion. In reference to this we must bear in mind that a canzone may be taken in two ways. In the first way, as its author's composition, and thus it is an action; and it is in this way that Virgil says in the first book of the *Æneid*, "I sing of arms and the man." In another way, when, after having been composed it is uttered either by the author or by some one else, whether with or without modulation of sound; and thus it is a passion. For in the first case it is acted, but in the second it appears to act on some one else; and so in the first case it appears to be the action of some one, and in the second it also appears to be the passion of some one. And because it is acted on before it acts, it appears rather, nay, altogether, to get its name from its being acted and being the act of some one than from its acting on others. Now the proof of this is, that we never say "This is Peter's canzone," meaning that he utters it, but meaning that he has composed it.

Moreover, we must discuss the question whether we call a canzone the composition of the words which are set to music, or the music itself; and, with regard to this, we say that no music [alone] is ever called a canzone, but a sound, or tone, or note, or melody. For no trumpeter, or organist, or lute-player calls his melody a canzone, except in so far as it has been wedded to some canzone; but those who write the words for music call their words canzoni. And such words, even when written down on paper without any one to utter them, we call canzoni; and therefore a canzone appears to be nothing else but the completed action of one writing words to be set to music. Wherefore we shall call canzoni not only the canzoni of which we are now treating, but also ballate and sonnets, and all words of whatever kind written for music, both in the vulgar tongue and in Latin. But, inasmuch as we are only discussing works in the vulgar tongue, setting aside those in Latin, we say that of poems in the vulgar tongue there is one supreme which we call canzone by super-excellence. Now the supremacy of the canzone has been proved in the third chapter of this book. And since the term which has been defined appears to be common to many things, let us take up again the common term which has been defined, and distinguished by means of certain differences that thing which alone we are in search of. We declare therefore that the canzone as so called by super-excellence which we are in search of is a joining together in the tragic style of equal stanzas without a *ripresa*,[64] referring to one subject, as we have shown in our composition "*Donne che avete intellecto d'amore.*"[65] Now the reason why we call it "a joining together in the tragic style" is because when such a composition is made in the comic style we call it diminutively *cantilena*, of which we intend to treat in the fourth book of this work. And thus it appears what a canzone is, both as it is taken generally, and as we call it in a super-excellent sense. It also appears sufficiently plain what we mean when we speak of a canzone, and consequently what that faggot is which we are endeavoring to bind up.

IX

Inasmuch as the canzone is a joining together of stanzas, as has been said, we must necessarily be ignorant of the canzone if we do not know what a stanza is, for knowledge of the thing defined results from knowledge of the things defining; and it therefore follows that we must treat of the stanza, in order, that is, that we may discover what it is, and what we mean to understand by it. And in reference to this matter we must observe that this word has been invented solely with respect to the art [of the canzone]; namely, in order that that in which the whole art of the canzone is contained should be called stanza, that is a *room* able to hold, or a receptacle for the whole art. For just as the canzone embosoms the whole theme, so the stanza embosoms the whole art; nor is it lawful for the subsequent stanzas to call in any additional scrap of the art, but only to clothe themselves with the art of the first stanza; from which it is plain that the stanza of which we are speaking will be the delimitation or putting together of all those things which the canzone takes from the art; and if we explain them, the description we are in search of will become clear. The whole art, therefore, of the canzone appears to depend on three things: first, on the division of the musical setting; second, on the arrangement of the parts; third, on the number of the lines and syllables. But we make no mention of rhyme, because it does not concern the peculiar art of the canzone, for it is allowable in any stanza to introduce new rhymes and to repeat the same at pleasure, but this would by no means be allowed if rhyme belonged to the peculiar art of the canzone, as has been said. Anything, however, relating to rhyme which the art, as such, is concerned to observe will be comprised under the heading "Arrangement of the Parts."

Wherefore we may thus collect the defining terms from what has been said, and declare that a stanza is a structure of lines and syllables limited by reference to a certain musical setting, and to the arrangement [of its parts].

X

If we know that man is a rational animal, and that an animal consists of a sensible soul and a body, but are ignorant concerning what this soul is or concerning the body itself, we cannot have a perfect knowledge of man, because the perfect knowledge of every single thing extends to its ultimate elements, as the master of the wise[66] testifies in the beginning of the *Physics*. Therefore in order to have that knowledge of the canzone which we are panting for, let us now compendiously examine the things which define its defining term;[67] and first let us inquire concerning the musical setting, next concerning the arrangement [of the parts], and afterwards concerning the lines and syllables.

We say, therefore, that every stanza is set for the reception of a certain ode; but they appear to differ in the modes [in which this is done]; for some proceed throughout to one continuous ode, that is, without the repetition of any musical phrase, and without any diesis: and we understand by diesis a transition from one ode to another. (This when speaking to the common people we call *volta*). And this kind of stanza was used by Arnaut Daniel in almost all his canzoni, and we have followed him in ours beginning, "*Al poco giorno e al gran cerchio d'ombra.*"[68]

But there are some stanzas, which admit of a diesis: and there can be no diesis in our sense of the word unless a repetition of one ode be made either before the diesis, or after, or both. If the repetition be made before [the diesis] we say that the stanza has feet; and it ought to have two, though sometimes there are three; very rarely, however. If the repetition be made after the diesis, then we say that the stanza has verses. If no repetition be made before [the diesis] we say that the stanza has a *Fronte;* if none be made after, we say that it has a *Sirma* or Coda. See, therefore, Reader, how much license has been given to poets who write canzoni, and consider on what account custom has claimed so wide a choice; and if reason shall have guided thee by a straight path, thou wilt see that this license of which we are speaking has been granted by worthiness of authority alone.

Hence it may become sufficiently plain how the art of the canzone depends on the division of the musical setting; and therefore let us go on to the arrangement [of the parts].

XI

It appears to us that what we call the arrangement [of the parts of the stanza] is the most important section of what belongs to the art [of the canzone], for this depends on the division of the musical setting, the putting together of the lines, and the relation of the rhymes; wherefore it seems to require to be most diligently treated of.

We therefore begin by saying that the *fronte* with the verses, and the feet with the coda or *sirma,* and also the feet with the verses, may be differently arranged in the stanza. For sometimes the *fronte* exceeds or may exceed the verses in syllables and in lines; and we say "may exceed' because we have never yet met with this arrangement. Sometimes [the *fronte*] may exceed [the verses] in lines, and be exceeded by them in syllables; as, if the *fronte* had five lines, and each verse had two lines, while the lines of the *fronte* were of seven syllables and those of the verses of eleven syllables. Sometimes the verses exceed the *fronte* in syllables and in lines, as in our canzone *"Traggemi de la mente Amor la stiva."*[69] Here the *fronte* was composed of four lines, three of eleven syllables and one of seven syllables; for it could not be divided into feet, since an equality of lines and syllables is required in the feet with respect to one another, and also in the verses with respect to one another. And what we say of the *fronte* we might also say of the verses; for the verses might exceed the *fronte* in lines and be exceeded by it in syllables; for instance, if each verse had three lines of seven syllables and the *fronte* were made up of five lines, two of eleven syllables and three of seven syllables.

And sometimes the feet exceed the coda in lines and syllables as in our canzone, *"Amore che movi tua vertù da cielo."*[70] Sometimes the feet are exceeded by the *sirma* both in lines and syllables, as in our canzone, *"Donna pietosa e di novella etate."*[71] And just as we have said that the *fronte,* [though] exceeded [by the verses] in syllables may exceed them in lines, and conversely, so we say of the *sirma* [in relation to the feet].

The feet likewise may exceed the verses in number, and be exceeded by them; for there may be in a stanza three feet and two verses, or three verses and two feet; nor are we limited by that number so as not to be able to combine more feet as well as verses in like manner.

And just as we have spoken of the victory of lines and syllables in comparing the other parts of the stanza together, we now also say the same as regards the feet and verses [compared together]: for these can be conquered and conquer in the same way.

Nor must we omit to mention that we take feet in a sense contrary to that of the regular poets, because they said that a line consisted of feet, but we say that a foot consists of lines, as appears plainly enough.

Nor must we also omit to state again that the feet necessarily receive from one another an equality of lines and syllables, and their arrangement, for otherwise the repetition of the melodic section could not take place. And we declare that the same rule is to be observed in the verses.

XII

There is also, as has been said above, a certain arrangement which we ought to consider in putting the lines together; and therefore let us deal with this, repeating what we have said above respecting the lines.

In our practice three lines especially appear to have the prerogative of frequent use, namely, the line of eleven syllables, that of seven syllables, and that of five syllables, and we have shown that the line of three syllables follows them, in preference to the others. Of these, when we are attempting poetry in the tragic style, the line of eleven syllables deserves, on account of a certain excellence, the privilege of predominance in the structure [of the stanza]. For there is a certain stanza which rejoices in being made up of lines of eleven syllables alone, as this one of Guido of Florence: *"Donna me prega, perch' io voglio dire."*[72] And we also say: *"Donne ch' avete intellecto d'amore."*[73] The Spaniards have also used this line, and I mean by Spaniards those who have written poetry in the vernacular of *oc*. Aimeric de Belenoi [has written] *"Nuls hom non pot complir adrechamen."*[74]

There is a stanza where a single line of seven syllables is woven in, and this cannot be except where there is a *fronte* or a coda, since (as has been said) in the feet and verses an equality of lines and syllables is observed. Wherefore also neither can there be an odd number of lines where there is no *fronte* or no coda, but where these occur, or one of them alone, we may freely use an even or an odd number of lines. And just as there is a certain stanza formed containing a single line of seven syllables, so it appears that a stanza may be woven together with two, three, four, or five such lines, provided only that in the tragic style the lines of eleven syllables predominate in number, and one such line begin. We do indeed find that some writers have begun with a line of seven syllables in the tragic style, namely, Guido dei Ghisilieri and Fabruzzo, both of Bologna, as thus: *"Di fermo sofferire,"*[75] and, *"Donna, lo fermo core,"*[76] and, *"Lo meo lontano gire,"* and some others also. But if we go carefully into the sense of these writers, their tragedy will not appear to have proceeded without a certain faint shadow of elegy.

With regard to the line of five syllables also, we are not so liberal in our concessions; in a great poem it is sufficient for a single line of five syllables to be inserted in the whole stanza, or two at most in the feet: and I say "in the feet," because of the requirements of the musical setting in the feet and verses.

But it by no means appears that the line of three syllables existing on its own account should be adopted in the tragic style; and I say, "existing on its own account," because it often appears to have been adopted by way of a certain echoing of rhymes, as may be discovered in that canzone of Guido of Florence, *"Donna me prega,"* and in the following of ours: *"Poscia ch' Amor del tutto m' ha lasciato."*[77] And there the line of three syllables does not appear at all on its own account, but only as a part of a line of eleven syllables, answering like an echo to the rhyme of the line before.

This further point also must be specially attended to with regard to the arrangement of the lines, [namely] that if a line of seven syllables be inserted in the first foot, it must take up the same position in the second that it receives in the first. For instance, if a foot of three lines has the first and last of eleven syllables, and the middle one—that is the second—of seven syllables, so the second foot must have the second line of seven syllables and the first and last of eleven syllables, otherwise the repetition of the melodic section, with reference to which the feet are constructed, as has been said, could not take place; and consequently there could be no feet.

And what we have said of the feet we say of the verses also; for we see that the feet and the verses differ in nothing but position, the former term being used before the diesis of the stanza, and the latter after it.

And we declare also that what has been said of the foot of three lines is to be observed in all other feet. And what we have said of one line of seven syllables we also say of more than one, and of the line of five syllables, and of every other line.

Hence, Reader, you are sufficiently able to choose how your stanza is to be arranged as regards the arrangement which it appears should be considered with reference to the lines.

XIII

Let us apply ourselves to the relation of the rhymes, not [however] in any way treating of rhyme in itself; for we put off the special treatment of them (*sic*) till afterwards, when we shall deal with poems in the middle vulgar tongue.

At the beginning of this chapter it seems advisable to exclude certain things: one is the unrhymed stanza, in which no attention is given to arrangement of rhymes; and Arnaut Daniel very often made use of this kind of stanza, as here: *"Sim fos Amors de joi donar"*;[78] and we say: *"Al poco giorno."* Another is the stanza all of whose lines give the same rhyme; and here it is plainly unnecessary to seek for any arrangement [of rhymes].

And so it remains for us only to dwell upon the mixed rhymes. And first it must be remarked that in this matter almost all writers take the fullest license; and this is what is chiefly relied on for the sweetness of the whole harmony. There are, then, some poets who sometimes do not make all the endings of the lines rhyme in the same stanza, but repeat the same endings, or make rhymes to them, in the other stanzas: as Gotto of Mantua, who recited to us many good canzoni of his own. He always wove into his stanza one line unaccompanied by a rhyme, which he called the key. And as one such line is allowable, so also are two and perhaps more.

There are also some other poets, and almost all the authors of canzoni, who never leave any line unaccompanied in the stanza without answering it by the consonance of one or more rhymes.

Some poets also make the rhymes of the lines following the diesis different from the rhymes of the lines preceding it; while some do not do this, but bring back the endings of the former [part of the] stanza, and weave them into the lines of the latter part. But this occurs oftenest in the ending of the first line of the latter part of the stanza, which very many poets make to rhyme with the ending of the last line of the former part; and this appears to be nothing else but a kind of beautiful linking together of the whole stanza.

Also with regard to the arrangement of the rhymes, according as they are in the *fronte* or coda, every wished-for license should, it seems, be conceded; but still the endings of the last lines are most beautifully disposed if they fall with a rhyme into silence.

But in the feet we must be careful; and [here] we find that a particular arrangement has been observed; and, making a distinction, we say that a foot is completed with either an even or odd number of lines, and in both cases there may be rhymed and unrhymed endings. In [the foot of] an even number of lines, no one feels any doubt [as to this]; but in the other, if any one is doubtful let him remember what was said in the next preceding chapter about the line of three syllables, when, as forming part of a line of eleven syllables, it answers like an echo. And if there happens to be an unrhymed ending in one of the feet, it must by all means be answered by a rhyme in the other. But if all the endings in one of the feet are rhymed, it is allowable in the other either to repeat the endings, or to put new ones, either wholly, or in part, at pleasure, provided, however, that the order of the preceding endings be observed in its entirety; for instance, if in a first foot of three lines, the extreme endings, that is, the first and last, rhyme together, so the extreme endings of the second foot must rhyme together; and according as the middle line in the first foot sees itself accompanied or unaccompanied by a rhyme, so let it rise up again in the second; and the same rule is to be observed with regard to the other kinds of feet. In the verses also we almost always obey this law; and we say "almost," because on account of the above-mentioned linking together [of the two parts of the stanza], and combination of the final endings, it sometimes happens that the order now stated is upset.

Moreover, it seems suitable for us to add to this chapter what things are to be avoided with regard to the rhymes, because we do not intend to deal any further in this book with the learning relating to rhyme. There are, then, three things, which with regard to the placing of rhymes it is unbecoming for a courtly poet to use, namely, [first], excessive repetition of the same rhyme, unless perchance something new and before unattempted in the art claim this for itself; just like the day of incipient knighthood, which disdains to let the period of initiation pass without any special distinction. And this we have striven to accomplish in the canzone, *"Amor, tu vedi ben che questa donna."*[79]

The second of the things to be avoided is that useless equivocation which always seems to detract somewhat from the theme; and the third is roughness of rhymes, unless it be mingled with smoothness; for from a mixture of smooth and rough rhymes the tragedy itself gains in brilliancy.

And let this suffice concerning the art [of the canzone] so far as it relates to the arrangement [of the parts of the stanza].

XIV

Having sufficiently treated of two things belonging to the art in the canzone, it now appears that we ought to treat of the third, namely, the number of the lines and syllables. And in the first place we must make some observations with regard to the stanza as a whole; then we will make some observations as to its parts.

It concerns us therefore first to make a distinction between those subjects which fall to be sung of, because some stanzas seem to desire prolixity, and others do not. For whereas we sing of all the subjects we are speaking of either with reference to something favorable or else to something unfavorable, so that it happens that we sing sometimes persuasively, sometimes dissuasively, sometimes in congratulation, sometimes in irony, sometimes in praise, sometimes in contempt, let those words whose tendency is unfavorable always hasten to the end, and the others gradually advance to the end with a becoming prolixity. . . .

NOTES

1. A liquor consisting of honey diluted in water; when fermented, it becomes mead.
2. I.e., "They anticipated the divine solicitude for their well-being." The expression "divine care" appears to be used as meaning "the time appointed by God's providence."
3. 295–99.
4. *Oc*-Lat. *hoc* (this); *oïl* results from the combination of affirmative *hoc* with *ille* (he). The speakers of the language of *oc* are not inaptly called Spaniards, since a dialect of the language we now call Provençal prevailed over the whole of Aragon and Catalonia.
5. "If a faithful friend heard me, I would make accusation against love."
6. "From pure love proceeds wisdom and goodness."
7. "Before the gentle heart, in nature's scheme / Love was not, nor the gentle heart ere love" (Rossetti's tr.). These are the third and fourth lines of the first stanza of the canzone whose first line is quoted in 2.5.
8. Dante.
9. "Sir, what are you saying?"
10. Meaning uncertain.
11. "I met a peasant girl (?) from Cascioli; she was slinking off in a great hurry."
12. "At the hour of evening, in the month of October."
13. "What are you doing?"
14. "New house."
15. "My lord."

16. "Even though through fire water forsakes [its great coldness]."
17. "O love, who long has led me." This line and the preceding one are the opening lines of two canzoni by Guido delle Colonne, a judge and notary of Messina (fl. 1257–88). "Weighty poetry" refers to the dignity of its subject matter.
18. Ancient name of Sicily.
19. Frederick II, crowned emperor in 1220.
20. An expression of contempt taken from Matthias 5:22.
21. I.e., Frederick II, king of Sicily from 1296-1337.
22. "Draw me from these fires, if it is thy will." The third line of a poem in the form of a dialogue between a lover and his mistress.
23. Meaning uncertain.
24. "Lady, I will tell you (how love has seized me)." The first line of a canzone by Jacopo da Lentino (fl. first half of 13th century).
25. "For pure love I go so joyfully." The first line of a canzone by Rinaldo d'Aquino, a contemporary of Jacopo.
26. "Let us eat meantime—we do nothing else."
27. "Truly the soldiers of Florence are going through Pisa."
28. "Thank God the commonwealth of Lucca is in a happy state"(?).
29. "Would that I had never forsworn Siena!"
30. "What is this?"
31. "Will you come somewhere?"
32. "My eye."
33. "My heart."
34. "Would it were so."
35. *Novem* is the Latin for "nine" (Ital. *nove*).
36. "By God's wounds thou shalt not come."
37. "Lady, the steadfast heart."
38. "My going afar."
39. "No more do I await thy succor, Love."
40. "I cannot choose but utter a song."
41. "The bitter blast strips bare the leafy woods."
42. "For the awakening of gallantry which is too fast asleep."
43. "Worthy am I of death."
44. "Grief furnishes my heart with daring."
45. A small stick or quill for striking the strings of the lyre.
46. "Now you shall hear perfect songs."
47. See n. 6.
48. "To the gentle heart love ever flies for shelter."
49. See n. 17.
50. See n. 25.
51. "I have no hope that ever for my well-being."
52. "Love who wieldest thy virtue from heaven" (Rossetti's tr.).
53. "Were it not for my all-excelling one."
54. "So pleasing is to me the amorous thought."
55. "I alone am he who knows the excessive grief which rises [in my heart]."
56. "No man can properly fulfill [what he has in his heart]."
57. "Even as the tree which through being overladen."
58. "Sorrow of love which in my heart abides."
59. "To say the truth, I hold his conduct foolish [who yields himself to one too powerful]."

60. "Since I must needs bear a heart of woe."
61. "Albeit my prayers have not so long delayed" (Rossetti's tr.).
62. "Love that discourses to me in my mind."
63. The Latin *lectio* is retained since there is no word in English which expresses at once the "action" and "passion" of reading.
64. The words "without *ripresa*" *(sine responsorio)* are added to distinguish the canzone from the ballata. The *ripresa* was the opening portion of the ballata, and was repeated at its close.
65. "Ladies that have understanding of love." This is the first line of the first canzone in Dante's *Vita Nuova*.
66. Aristotle.
67. The stanza.
68. "To the short day and the great sweep of shadow."
69. "Love drags the plough-pole of my mind."
70. See n. 52.
71. "A very pitiful lady, very young" (Rossetti's tr.). The second canzone of the *Vita Nuova*.
72. "A lady prays me, therefore I will speak." The opening line of Guido Cavalcante's celebrated canzone on the nature of love.
73. See n. 65.
74. See n. 56.
75. "Of steadfast endurance."
76. See n. 37, n. 38.
77. "Now that love has entirely forsaken me."
78. "If love were as bountiful in bestowing joy upon me [as I am towards her in purity and sincerity of affection]."
79. "Love, you can well see that this woman."

FROM
Letter to Can Grande

6. Wishing to say something by way of introduction to the part [i.e. the *Paradise*] of the entire *Comedy* already mentioned, I have decided first to say something on the work as a whole, that the approach to the part may be easier and more adequate. There are six things to be inquired about at the beginning of any work of instruction, to wit the subject, the author, the form, the end, the title of the work, and the genus of its philosophy. There are three of these in which the part I have determined to address to you varies from the whole, to wit the subject, the form, and the title. In the others it does not vary, as appears to him who looks at it; hence, in respect to the consideration of the whole the three are to be separately inquired into. When this has been done, the way to the introduction of the part will lie open. Then we shall examine the other three not merely with respect to the whole, but also with respect to the part in question.

7. For the clarity of what is to be said, one must realize that the meaning of this work is not simple, but is rather to be called polysemous, that is, having many meanings. The first meaning is the one obtained through the letter; the second is the one obtained through the things signified by the letter. The first is called literal, the second allegorical or moral or anagogical. In order that this manner of treatment may appear more clearly, it may be applied to the following verses: "When Israel went out of Egypt, the house of Jacob from a people of strange language, Judah was his sanctuary and Israel his dominion."[1] For if we look to the letter alone, the departure of the children of Israel from Egypt in the time of Moses is indicated to us; if to the allegory, our redemption accomplished by Christ is indicated to us; if to the moral sense, the conversion of the soul from the woe and misery of sin to a state of grace is indicated to us; if to the anagogical sense, the departure of the consecrated soul from the slavery of this corruption to the liberty of eternal glory is indicated. And though these mystic senses may be called by various names, they can all generally be spoken of as allegorical, since they are diverse from the literal or historical. For allegory is derived from *alleon* in Greek, which in Latin appears as *alienum*, or diverse.[2]

8. When these things have been observed, it is evident that the subject with which the alternative senses are concerned ought to be double. So one must look at the subject of this work as it is accepted according to the letter; then at the subject as it is understood allegorically. The subject of the whole work, then, taken merely in its literal sense, is simply the state of the souls after death, for from that subject comes the course of the whole work and with that it is occupied. But if the whole work is taken allegorically, the subject is man as by reason of meriting and demeriting through the freedom of the will he is liable to the rewarding and the punishing of justice.

9. The form is double: the form of the treatise, and the form of treatment. The form of the treatise is triple, according to a triple division. The first division is that by which the whole work is divided into three *cantiche*. The second is

that by which each *cantica* is divided into cantos. The third that by which each canto is divided into verses. The form or mode of treating is poetic, fictitious, descriptive, digressive, transumptive, and withal definitive, divisive, probative, improbative, and with the positing of examples.

10. The title of the book is: "Here begins the *Comedy* of Dante Alighieri, a Florentine by nation but not by habits." For the explanation of this it must be known that comedy gets its name from *comos*, a village, and *oda*, a song; therefore comedy is as it were a villagers' song. And comedy is a certain genus of poetic imitation differing from all others. It differs from tragedy in its matter in this respect, that tragedy in the beginning is good to look upon and quiet, in its end or exit is fetid and horrible; for this reason it gets its name from *tragos*, which is goat, and *oda*, as though to say *goatish song*, that is, fetid in the manner of a goat; this is made plain by the example of Seneca in his tragedies.[3] Comedy, however, at the beginning deals with the harsh aspect of some affair, but its matter terminates prosperously, as is shown by the example of Terence in his comedies.[4] Hence certain authors in their salutations are in the habit of saying, instead of the usual greeting, "a tragic beginning and a comic end." Likewise the two differ in their mode of speaking: tragedy speaks in an elevated and sublime fashion, but comedy in a lowly and humble way, according to the prescription of Horace in his *Art of Poetry* where he grants that sometimes comic actors may speak like tragedians, and conversely:

> At times, however, even Comedy exalts her voice, and an angry Chremes rants and raves; often, too, in a tragedy Telephus or Peleus utters his sorrow in the language of prose (93–6).[5]

From this it is clear why the present work is called *Comedy*. For if we consider the material, at the beginning it is horrible and fetid, since it begins with Hell, but at the end it is attractive and pleasing, since it ends with Heaven. As to mode of expression, its mode is lowly and humble, since it is the speech of the masses in which even womenfolk converse. . . .

11. In what I am going to say I can make plain in what way the subject of the part now in question is to be assigned. For if the subject of the whole work taken literally is the state of the souls after death, with no restrictions but taken simply, manifestly the subject of this part is the same, but with a restriction, namely it is the state of sainted souls after death. And if the subject of the whole work taken allegorically is man as by reason of meriting and demeriting through the freedom of the will he is liable to the rewarding and punishing of justice, it is manifest that the subject of this part is limited to man as by reason of meriting he is subject to the rewarding of justice. . . .

15. The end of the whole and the part can be multiplex, that is, near at hand and remote; but omitting all subtle investigation, one may say briefly that the end of the whole and the part is to remove those living in this life from a state of misery and to lead them to a state of happiness.

16. The genus of philosophy under which the work proceeds in the whole and in part is moral activity or ethics, for the whole and the part are devised not

for the sake of speculation but of possible action. For if in any place or passage the method of discussion is that of speculative thought, it is not for the sake of speculative thought but for the sake of practical activity, since, as the Philosopher says in the second of the *Metaphysics*, "practical men now and then speculate on something or other."

17. Having said these things by way of premise, we draw near to the exposition of the letter as a sort of offering of the first fruits; as to this it should be understood beforehand that the exposition of the letter is nothing other than the manifestation of the form of the work. This part or third *cantica* which is called *Paradise* is then divided chiefly into two parts, to wit a prologue and a part giving the main development. . . .

18. Concerning the first part it should be known that though in ordinary speech it can be called the exordium, in accurate speech it should be called nothing other than the prologue, as the Philosopher seems to hint in the third book of the *Rhetoric*, where he says that the "proemium is the beginning in rhetorical speech as is the prologue in poetry and the prelude in music on the pipes." It is also to be observed beforehand that this prefatory matter, which commonly is called the exordium, is handled in one way by the poets and otherwise by the orators. For the orators have agreed to prefix some words to prepare the spirit of the auditor; but the poets not merely do this, but after it they utter a certain invocation. And this is proper for them, since they have great need of an inovcation, because something contrary to the way of life common among men is to be sought from the superior beings, as a sort of divine gift. Hence the present prologue is divided into two parts, since in the first what is to be said is introduced, and in the second Apollo is to be invoked. . . .

33. On the part giving the main development, which in the division was set over against the prologue, nothing will be said at present either by way of dividing or explaining, except this, that everywhere the procedure will be that of ascending from heaven to heaven, and something will be said on the blessed souls found in each orb, and that true beatitude consists in perceiving the beginning of truth, as is made clear by John when he says: "This is life eternal, that they might know thee, the true God, etc."; likewise by Boethius in the third of the *Consolation:* "To see thee is the end." Thence it is that, to show the glory of blessedness in those souls, from them, as from those who see all the truth, many things are asked that have great utility and delight.[6] And when the beginning or the first thing, to wit God, has been found, there is nothing beyond that can be sought for, since he is Alpha and Omega, that is, the beginning and the end, as the Vision of John relates; hence the treatment is ended in God himself, who is blessed world without end.[7]

NOTES

1. Ps. 114:1–2.

2. *Allegory* is now said to be derived from the Greek *allegoria,* from *allos* and *agoreuo.* Dante did not know Greek. The Latin *alius,* from which comes *alienum,* "alien," is related to *allos.*

3. There has been an attempt to prove by parallel passages that Dante had read Seneca's dramas. It still seems possible, however, that, if he had seen them at all, he had seen only excerpts.

4. There is no proof that Dante had read any of the works of Terence.

5. ⟨See pp. 266–67.⟩

6. For example, in *Paradise* 13, Dante learns from St. Thomas Aquinas the relation of the wisdom of Adam, Solomon, and Christ. This and other theological passages have often been objected to by critics of the *Comedy* as over learned; the question has even been raised whether they are genuinely poetry. Benedetto Croce finds some poetical justification for them (*The Poetry of Dante* [New York, 1922], pp. 224–30). Dante obviously felt that they were of the essence of poetry, fulfilling the demand of Horace for profit and delight in *Art of Poetry* 333 (see p. 272), to which Dante alludes in the sentence now under consideration. Horace's work was known to Dante (*De Vulgari Eloquentia* 2. 4, p. 517).

7. *Paradise* 33. 49–145.

BIBLIOGRAPHY

GENERAL

ABRAMS, M. H. *The Mirror and the Lamp: Romantic Theory and the Critical Tradition.* New York: Oxford University Press, 1953.

Allen, Judson B. *The Friar as Critic: Literary Attitudes in the Later Middle Ages.* Nashville: Vanderbilt University Press, 1971.

Arendt, Hannah. *Between Past and Future: Eight Exercises in Political Thought.* New York: Viking Press, 1961.

Atkins, J. W. H. *Literary Criticism in Antiquity,* 2 vols. Cambridge: At the University Press, 1934.

Auerbach, Erich. "Figura." In *Scenes from the Drama of European Literature.* New York: Meridian Books, 1959.

———. *Literary Language and Its Public in Latin Antiquity and the Middle Ages.* Translated by Ralph Manheim. New York: Pantheon Books, 1965.

Baldwin, Charles S. *Ancient Rhetoric and Poetic.* New York: Macmillan Co., 1924.

———. *Medieval Rhetoric and Poetic.* New York: Macmillan Co., 1928.

Beardsley, Monroe C. *Aesthetics from Classical Greece to the Present.* New York: Macmillan Co., 1966.

Bonner, S. F. *Education in Ancient Rome.* London: Methuen, 1977.

———. *Roman Declamation in the Late Republic and Early Empire.* Liverpool: University Press of Liverpool, 1949.

Bruyne, Edgar de. *The Esthetics of the Middle Ages.* Translated by Eileen B. Hennessey. New York: Frederick Ungar Publishing Co., 1969.

Burckhardt, Jakob. *History of Greek Culture.* Translated by Palmer Hilty. New York: Frederick Ungar Publishing Co., 1963.

Burke, Kenneth. *Counterstatement.* New York: Harcourt, Brace and Co., 1931.

———. *A Rhetoric of Motives.* New York: Prentice-Hall, 1950.

———. "Rhetoric—Old and New." *Journal of General Education* 5 (1951): 202–9.

Caplan, Harry, et al., eds. *Of Eloquence: Studies in Ancient and Medieval Rhetoric.* Ithaca: Cornell University Press, 1966.

Chadwick, Henry. *Early Christian Thought and the Classical Tradition: Studies in Justin, Clement, and Origen.* New York: Oxford University Press, 1966.

Clark, D. L. *Rhetoric in Graeco-Roman Education.* New York: Columbia University Press, 1957.

Clark, M. L. *Rhetoric at Rome.* London: Cohen and West, 1953.

Crane, R. S., ed. *Critics and Criticism: Ancient and Modern.* Chicago: University of Chicago Press, 1952.

Curtius, Ernst Robert. *European Literature and the Latin Middle Ages.* Translated by Eileen B. Hennessey. New York: Pantheon Books, 1953.

D'Alton, J. F. *Roman Literary Theory and Criticism: A Study in Tendencies.* London: Longmans, Green, 1931.

Dodds, E. R. *The Greeks and the Irrational.* Berkeley: University of California Press, 1951.

Fletcher, Angus. *Allegory: The Theory of a Symbolic Mode*. Ithaca: Cornell University Press, 1964.
Fränkel, Hermann. *Early Greek Poetry and Philosophy*. Translated by Moses Hadas and James Willis. New York: Harcourt Brace Jovanovich, 1975.
Fry, Paul. *The Reach of Criticism: Method and Perception in Literary Theory*. New Haven: Yale University Press, 1983.
Gomme, A. W. *The Greek Attitude to Poetry and History*. Berkeley: University of California Press, 1954.
Grube, G. M. A. *The Greek and Roman Critics*. Toronto: University of Toronto Press, 1965.
Guthrie, W. K. C. *A History of Greek Philosophy*. Cambridge: Cambridge University Press, 1978.
Harriott, Rosemary. *Poetry and Criticism Before Plato*. London: Methuen, 1969.
Haskins, Charles H. *The Renaissance of the Twelfth Century*. New York: Meridian Books, 1957.
Heidegger, Martin. *Early Greek Thinking*. Translated by David Farrell Krell and Frank A. Capuzzi. New York: Harper and Row, 1975.
Hine, Daryl. *Introduction to Theocritus: Idylls and Epigrams*. New York: Atheneum Publishers, 1982.
Jaeger, Werner. *Paideia*. Translated by Gilbert Highet. 3 vols. Oxford: Oxford University Press, 1939–44.
Kennedy, George A. *The Art of Persuasion in Greece*. Princeton: Princeton University Press, 1963.
———. *The Art of Rhetoric in the Roman World: 300 B.C.—A.D. 300*. Princeton: Princeton University Press, 1972.
———. *Classical Rhetoric and Its Christian and Secular Tradition from Ancient to Modern Times*. Chapel Hill: University of North Carolina Press, 1980.
Kitto, H. D. F. *Poiesis*. Berkeley: University of California Press, 1966.
Klibansky, Raymond. *The Continuity of the Platonic Tradition During the Middle Ages*. London: Warburg Institute, 1939.
Krieger, Murray. *Theory of Criticism: A Tradition and Its System*. Baltimore: Johns Hopkins University Press, 1976.
Lee, E. N.; Mourelatos, A. D. P.; and Rorty, R. M., eds. *Exegesis and Argument: Studies in Greek Philosophy Presented to Gregory Vlastos*. Atlantic Highlands, N.J.: Humanities Press, 1973.
Liebeschütz, Hans. *Medieval Humanism in the Life and Writings of John of Salisbury*. London: Warburg Institute, 1950.
McCall, M. H. *Ancient Rhetorical Theories of Simile and Comparison*. Cambridge: Harvard University Press, 1969.
McKeon, Richard. "Rhetoric in the Middle Ages." In *Critics and Criticism: Ancient and Modern*, edited by R. S. Crane, pp. 260–96. Chicago: University of Chicago Press, 1952.
Nietzsche, Friedrich. *"The Birth of Tragedy" and "The Case of Wagner."* Translated by Walter Kaufmann. New York: Vintage Books, 1967.
———. "Homer's Contest." In *The Portable Nietzsche*. Translated by Walter Kaufmann. New York: Viking Press, 1954.
Paetow, Louis J. *The Arts Course at Medieval Universities, with Special Reference to Grammar and Rhetoric*. Urbana: University of Illinois Press, 1910.

Parsons, Edward A. *The Alexandrian Library*. New York: Elsevier, 1952.
Pfeiffer, Rudolf. *History of Classical Scholarship from the Beginnings to the End of the Hellenistic Age*. Oxford: Oxford University Press, 1968.
Pollitt, J. J. *The Ancient View of Greek Art*. New Haven: Yale University Press, 1974.
Quain, E. A. "The Medieval *Accessus ad Auctores*." *Traditio* 3 (1945): 215–64.
Roberts, W. Rhys. *Greek Rhetorical and Literary Criticism*. New York: Longmans, Green, 1928.
Robertson, D. W. *A Preface to Chaucer: Studies in Medieval Perspectives*. Princeton: Princeton University Press, 1962.
Rorty, Richard. *Philosophy and the Mirror of Nature*. Princeton: Princeton University Press, 1979.
Russell, D. A. *Criticism in Antiquity*. London: Duckworth and Co., 1981.
Saintsbury, George. *A History of Criticism and Literary Taste in Europe*. 3 vols. Edinburgh and London: Blackwood, 1900–04.
Sikes, E. E. *The Greek View of Poetry*. London: Methuen, 1931.
Snell, Bruno. *The Discovery of the Mind: The Greek Origins of European Thought*. Translated by T. G. Rosenmeyer. Cambridge: Harvard University Press, 1953.
———. *Poetry and Society: The Role of Poetry in Ancient Greece*. Bloomington: Indiana University Press, 1961.
Tate, J. "The Beginnings of Greek Allegory." *Classical Review* 31 (1927): 214–15.
———. "On the History of Allegorism." *Classical Quarterly* 28 (1934): 105–14.
Trimpi, Wesley. *Muses of One Mind: The Literary Analysis of Experience and Its Continuity*. Princeton: Princeton University Press, 1983.
Tuve, Rosemond. *Allegorical Imagery: Some Medieval Books and Their Posterity*. Princeton: Princeton University Press, 1964.
Van Hook, La Rue. *The Metaphorical Terminology of Greek Rhetoric and Literary Criticism*. Chicago: University of Chicago Press, 1905.
Verdenius, W. J. "The Principles of Greek Literary Criticism." *Mnemosyne* 36 (1983): 14–58.
Warry, J. G. *Greek Aesthetic Theory: A Study of Callistic and Aesthetic Concepts in the Works of Plato and Aristotle*. New York: Barnes and Noble, 1962.
Webster, T. B. L. "Greek Theories of Art and Literature down to 400 B.C." *Classical Quarterly* 33 (1939).
Williams, Gordon. *Change and Decline: Roman Literature in the Early Empire*. Berkeley: University of California Press, 1978.
Wimsatt, W. K., and Brooks, Cleanth. *Literary Criticism: A Short History*. New York: Alfred A. Knopf, 1967.

GORGIAS

Coulter, J. A. "The Relation of the *Apology* of Socrates to Gorgias' *Defense of Palamedes* and Plato's Critique of Gorgianic Rhetoric." *Harvard Studies in Classical Philology* 68 (1964): 269–303.
Kerferd, G. B. *The Sophistic Movement*. Cambridge: Cambridge University Press, 1981.
Kirk, G. S., and Raven, J. E. *The Presocratic Philosophers*. Cambridge: Cambridge University Press, 1957.

Segal, Charles P. "Gorgias and the Psychology of the Logos." *Harvard Studies in Classical Philology* 66 (1962): 99–155.
Untersteiner, Mario. *The Sophists*. Translated by Kathleen Freeman. Oxford: Blackwell, 1954.
Verdenius, W. J. "Gorgias' Doctrine of Deception." In *The Sophists and Their Legacy*, edited by G. B. Kerferd. Proceedings of the Fourth International Colloquium of Ancient Philosophy. Wiesbaden: Steiner, 1981.

ARISTOPHANES

Cornford, Francis M. *The Origin of Attic Comedy*. Edited by Theodore H. Gaster. Garden City, N.Y.: Anchor Books, 1961.
Dover, K. J. *Aristophanic Comedy*. Berkeley: University of California Press, 1972.
Gomme, A. W. "Aristophanes and Politics." In *More Essays in Greek History and Literature*, pp. 70–91. Oxford: Blackwell, 1962.
Littlefield, David J., comp. *Twentieth Century Interpretations of "The Frogs."* Englewood Cliffs, N.J.: Prentice-Hall, 1968.
Murray, Gilbert. *Aristophanes: A Study*. New York: Oxford University Press, 1933.
Strauss, Leo. *Socrates and Aristophanes*. New York: Basic Books, 1966.
Whitman, Cedric. *Aristophanes and the Comic Hero*. Cambridge: Harvard University Press, 1964.

PLATO

Black, E. "Plato's View of Rhetoric." *Quarterly Journal of Speech* 44 (1958): 361–74.
Brumbaugh, Robert S. "A New Interpretation of Plato's *Republic*." *Journal of Philosophy* 64 (1967).
Carter, Robert E. "Plato and Inspiration." *Journal of the History of Philosophy* 5 (1967): 661–70.
Coulter, J. A. "The Relation of the *Apology* of Socrates to Gorgias' *Defense of Palamedes* and Plato's Critique of Gorgianic Rhetoric." *Harvard Studies in Classical Philology* 68 (1964): 269–303.
Derrida, Jacques. "Plato's Pharmacy." In *Dissemination*. Translated by Barbara Johnson. Chicago: University of Chicago Press, 1981.
Findlay, J. N. *Plato and Platonism: An Introduction*. New York: Times Books, 1978.
Friedlander, Paul. *Plato: An Introduction*. Translated by Hans Meyerhoff. Princeton: Princeton University Press, 1958.
Gadamer, Hans-Georg. *Dialogue and Dialectic: Eight Hermeneutical Studies on Plato*. Translated by P. Christopher Smith. New Haven: Yale University Press, 1980.
Gallop, D. "Image and Reality in Plato's *Republic*." *Archiv fur Geschichte der Philosophie* 47 (1965): 113–31.
Gilbert, Allen H. "Plato's *Ion*, Comic and Serious." In *Studies in Honor of De W. T. Starnes*, edited by Thomas P. Harrison et al., pp. 259–84. Austin: University of Texas Press, 1967.
Gould, Thomas R. "Plato's Hostility to Art." *Arion* 3 (1964): 70–91.

Greene, W. Chase. "Plato's View of Poetry." *Harvard Studies in Classical Philology* 29 (1918): 1–76.
Grube, G. M. A. *Plato's Thought*. Indianapolis: Hackett Publishing Co., 1980.
Havelock, Eric A. *Preface to Plato*. Cambridge: Harvard University Press, 1963.
Jaspers, Karl. *Plato and Augustine*. New York: Harcourt, Brace and World, 1962.
Lodge, Rupert C. *Plato's Theory of Art*. London: Routledge and Kegan Paul, 1953.
Maguire, Joseph P. "Beauty and the Fine Arts in Plato: Some *Aporiai*." *Harvard Studies in Classical Philology* 70 (1965): 171–93.
Moss, Leonard. "Plato and the *Poetics*." *Philosophical Quarterly* 50 (1971): 533–42.
Ringbom, Sixten. "Plato on Images." *Theoria* 31 (1965): 86–109.
Schnakel, Peter J. "Plato's *Phaedrus* and Rhetoric." *Southern Speech Journal* 32 (1966): 124–32.
Tate, J. "Plato and 'Imitation.'" *Classical Quarterly* 26 (1932): 161–69.
Verdenius, W. J. *Mimesis: Plato's Doctrine of Artistic Imitation and Its Meaning to Us*. Leiden: Brill, 1949.

ARISTOTLE

Burke, Kenneth. "On *Catharsis*, or Resolution, with a Postscript." *Kenyon Review* 21 (1959): 337–75.
Butcher, S. H. *Aristotle's Theory of Poetry and Fine Art*. New York: Dover Publications, 1951.
Chroust, Anton-Hermann. "Aristotle's Earliest 'Course of Lectures on Rhetoric.'" *L'Antiquité Classique* 33 (1964): 58–72.
Cooper, Lane. *Aristotelian Papers*. Ithaca: Cornell University Press, 1939.
———. *The "Poetics" of Aristotle: Its Meaning and Influence*. Ithaca: Cornell University Press, 1927.
———. *The "Rhetoric" of Aristotle*. Englewood Cliffs, N.J.: Prentice-Hall, 1960.
Dawe, R. D. "Some Reflections on *Ate* and *Hamartia*." *Harvard Studies in Classical Philology* 72 (1967): 89–123.
Draper, John W. "Aristotelian Mimesis in Eighteenth Century England." *PMLA* 36 (1921): 372–400.
Fergusson, Francis, ed. *Aristotle's "Poetics."* New York: Hill and Wang, 1961.
Golden, Leon. "Catharsis." *Transactions of the American Philological Association* 93 (1962): 51–60.
———. "Is Tragedy the 'Imitation of a Serious Action'?" *Greek, Roman and Byzantine Studies* 6 (1965): 283–89.
———. "*Mimesis* and *Katharsis*." *Classical Philology* 64 (1969): 145–53.
Goldstein, Harvey D. "*Mimesis* and *Catharsis* Reexamined." *Journal of Aesthetics and Art Criticism* 24 (1966): 567–77.
Gomme, A. W. "Aristotle and the Tragic Character." In *More Essays in Greek History and Literature*, pp. 194–214. Oxford: Blackwell, 1962.
Grube, G. M. A. *Aristotle on Poetry and Style*. New York: Library of Liberal Arts, 1958.
Hauser, Gerard A. "The Example in Aristotle's *Rhetoric*: Bifurcation or Contradiction?" *Philosophy and Rhetoric* 1 (Spring 1968): 78–90.
House, Humphry. *Aristotle's "Poetics": A Course of Eight Lectures*. Revised by C. Hardie. London: R. Hart Davis, 1956.

Jaeger, Werner. *Aristotle: Fundamentals of the History of His Development.* Oxford: Oxford University Press, 1948.
Jones, John. *On Aristotle and Greek Tragedy.* London: Oxford University Press, 1962.
Lucas, D. W. *Aristotle: "Poetics."* Oxford: Oxford University Press, 1968.
McKeon, Richard. "Aristotle's Conception of Language and the Arts of Language." In *Critics and Criticism: Ancient and Modern*, edited by R. S. Crane, pp. 176–231. Chicago: University of Chicago Press, 1952.
Murray, Gilbert, "An Essay in the Theory of Poetry." *Yale Review* 10 (1921): 482–99.
Olson, Edler, ed. *Aristotle's "Poetics" and English Literature: A Collection of Critical Essays.* Chicago: University of Chicago Press, 1965.
Pottle, Frederick. "Catharsis." *Yale Review* 40 (1950–51): 621–41.
Solmsen, Friedrich. "The Origins and Methods of Aristotle's *Poetics.*" *Classical Quarterly* 29 (1935): 192–201.
———. "The Aristotelian Tradition in Ancient Rhetoric." *American Journal of Philology* 62 (1941): 35–50, 169–90.
Stinton, T. C. W. "*Hamartia* in Aristotle and Greek Tragedy." *Classical Quarterly* 25 (1975): 221–54.
Van Straaten, M., and De Vries, G. J. "Some Notes on the *Rhetoric* of Aristotle," *Mnemosyne* 17 (1964): 140–47.
Wimsatt, W. K. "Aristotle and Oedipus or Else." In *Hateful Contraries: Studies in Literature and Criticism.* Lexington: University of Kentucky Press, 1966.

DEMETRIUS

Grube, G. M. A. *A Greek Critic: Demetrius on Style.* Toronto: University of Toronto Press, 1961.
Schenkeveld, Dirk M. *Studies in Demetrius on Style.* Amsterdam: Hakkert, 1964.

CICERO

Ferguson, J.; Thompson, L. A.; Hands, A. R.; and Laidlaw, W. A. *Studies in Cicero.* Rome: Centro di Studi Ciceroniani Editore, 1962.
Fiske, George C. *Cicero's "De Oratore" and Horace's "Ars Poetica."* University of Wisconsin Studies in Language and Literature #7. Madison: University of Wisconsin Press, 1920.
Grube, G. M. A. "Educational, Rhetorical, and Literary Theory in Cicero." *The Phoenix* 16 (1962): 234–57.
Grute, Harold. "Cicero's Attitude to the Greeks." *Greece and Rome* 9 (1962): 142–59.
Hubbell, Harry M. "Cicero on Styles of Oratory." *Yale Classical Studies* 19 (1966): 171–86.
Laughton, Eric. "Cicero and the Greek Orator." *American Journal of Philology* 82 (1961): 27–49.
Murphy, James J. "Cicero's Rhetoric in the Middle Ages." *Quarterly Journal of Speech* 53 (1967): 334–41.
Ramage, Edwin S. "*Urbanitas:* Cicero and Quintilian, a Contrast in Attitudes." *American Journal of Philology* 84 (1963): 390–414.

Sattler, William M. "Some Platonic Influences on the Rhetorical Works of Cicero." *Quarterly Journal of Speech* 35 (1949): 164–69.
Schick, Thomas. "Cicero and the Pathetical Appeal in Oratory." *Classical Bulletin* 42 (1965): 17–18.
Shurr, William. "Cicero and English Prose Style." *Classical Bulletin* 37 (1961): 49–50.
Sprott, S. E. "Cicero's Theory of Prose Style." Philological Quarterly 34 (1955): 1–17.

HORACE

Brink, Charles O. *Horace on Poetry.* 2 vols. Cambridge: At the University Press, 1963.
Commager, Steele. *The Odes of Horace.* New Haven: Yale University Press, 1962.
Fiske, George C. *Cicero's "De Oratore" and Horace's "Ars Poetica."* University of Wisconsin Studies in Language and Literature #7. Madison: University of Wisconsin Press, 1920.
———. *Lucilius and Horace: A Study in the Classical Theory of Imitation.* University of Wisconsin Studies in Language and Literature #7. Madison: University of Wisconsin Press, 1920.
Fraenkel, Eduard. *Horace.* Oxford: Oxford University Press, 1957.
Frank, Tenney. "Horace on Contemporary Poetry." *Classical Journal* 13 (1917–18): 550–64.
———. "Horace's Definition of Poetry." *Classical Journal* 31 (1935–36): 167–74.
Greenberg, Nathan A. "The Use of *Poiema* and *Poiesis.*" *Harvard Studies in Classical Philology* 65 (1961): 1–65.
Hack, Roy K. "The Doctrine of Literary Forms." *Harvard Studies in Classical Philology* 27 (1916): 1–65.
Haight, Elizabeth H. "Horace on Art: *ut pictura poiesis.*" *Classical Journal* 47 (1952): 157–62.
Herrick, Marvin T. *The Fusion of Horatian and Aristotelian Literary Criticism, 1531–1555.* University of Illinois Studies in Language and Literature, vol. 32, no. 1. Urbana: University of Illinois Press, 1946.
La Drière, Craig. "Horace and the Theory of Imitation." *American Journal of Philology* 60 (1939): 288–300.

DIONYSIUS OF HALICARNASSUS

Bonner, S. F. *The Literary Treatises of Dionysius of Halicarnassus.* Cambridge: At the University Press, 1939.

QUINTILIAN

Coleman, Robert. "Two Linguistic Topics in Quintilian." *Classical Quarterly* 13 (1963): 1–18.
Kennedy, George A. *Quintilian.* New York: Twayne Publishers, 1969.
Ramage, Edwin S. "*Urbanitas:* Cicero and Quintilian, a Contrast in Attitudes." *American Journal of Philology* 84 (1963): 390–414.
Rayment, Charles Sanford. "How Realistic Are Quintilian's Themes?" *Classical Bulletin* 27 (1952): 43–45.

LONGINUS

Grube, G. M. A. "Notes on the *Peri Hupsous.*" *American Journal of Philology* 78 (1957): 355–74.

Henn, T. R. *Longinus in English Criticism*. Cambridge: At the University Press, 1934.

Hertz, Neil. "The Notion of Blockage in the Literature of the Sublime." In *Psychoanalysis and the Question of the Text*, edited by Geoffrey Hartman. Selected Papers from the English Institute, 1976–77. Baltimore: Johns Hopkins University Press, 1978.

———. "A Reading of Longinus." *Critical Inquiry* 9 (March 1983): 579–96.

Monk, Samuel H. *The Sublime: A Study of Critical Theories in Eighteenth Century England*. Ann Arbor: University of Michigan Press, 1960.

Olson, Elder. "The Argument of Longinus' *On The Sublime*." In *Critics and Criticism: Ancient and Modern*, edited by R. S. Crane. Chicago: University of Chicago Press, 1952.

Russell, D. A. "Longinus Revisited." *Mnemosyne* 34 (1981): 72–86.

Segal, Charles P. "*Hupsos* and the Problem of Cultural Decline." *Harvard Studies in Classical Philology* 64 (1959).

Tate, Allen. "Longinus and the 'New Criticism.'" In *The Man of Letters in the Modern World*. New York: Meridian Books, 1955.

PLUTARCH

Betz, Hans Dieter, ed. *Plutarch's Theological Writings and Early Christian Literature*. Leiden: Brill, 1975.

Gianakaris, C. J. *Plutarch*. New York: Twayne Publishers, 1970.

Howard, Martha Walling. *The Influence of Plutarch in the Major European Literatures of the Eighteenth Century*. Chapel Hill: University of North Carolina Press, 1970.

Jones, Roger Miller. *The Platonism of Plutarch*. New York: Garland Publishing, 1980.

Russell, D. A. *Plutarch*. London: Duckworth, 1973.

HERMOGENES

Nadeau, Ray. "Hermogenes *On Stasis:* A Translation with an Introduction and Notes." *Speech Monographs* 31 (1964): 361–424.

PLOTINUS

Brehier, Emile. *The Philosophy of Plotinus*. Translated by Joseph Thomas. Chicago: University of Chicago Press, 1958.

Inge, William Ralph. *The Philosophy of Plotinus*. 2 vols. London: Longmans, Green, 1948.

Pistorius, Phillipus Villiers. *Plotinus and Neoplatonism*. Cambridge: Bowes and Bowes, 1952.

Wallis, R. T. *Neoplatonism*. New York: Scribners, 1972.

EUANTHIUS AND DONATUS

Hardison, O. B., Jr. Introduction and commentary, in *Classical and Medieval Literary Criticism: Translations and Interpretations*, edited by Alex Preminger et al., pp. 263–309. New York: Frederick Ungar Publishing Co., 1974.

ST. AUGUSTINE

Burke, Kenneth. *The Rhetoric of Religion: Studies in Logology.* Boston: Beacon Press, 1961.
Ferguson, Margaret W. "St. Augustine's Region of Unlikeness: The Crossing of Exile and Unlikeness." *The Georgia Review* 29 (Winter 1975): 842–64.
Gilson, Etienne. *The Christian Philosophy of St. Augustine.* Translated by L. E. M. Lynch. New York: Random House, 1960.
Jackson, B. Darrell. "The Theory of Signs in St. Augustine's De Doctrina Christiania." In *Augustine: A Collection of Critical Essays*, edited by R. A. Marcus, pp. 92–147. Garden City, N.Y.: Anchor Books, 1972.
Jaspers, Karl. *Plato and Augustine.* New York: Harcourt, Brace and World, 1962.
Markus, R. A. "St. Augustine on Signs." In *Augustine: A Collection of Critical Essays*, edited by R. A. Marcus, pp. 61–91. Garden City, N.Y.: Anchor Books, 1972.
Meagher, Robert E. *An Introduction to Augustine.* New York: New York University Press, 1978.
Murphy, James J. "St. Augustine and the Christianization of Rhetoric." *Western Speech* 28 (1964): 206–11.
———. "St. Augustine and the Debate about a Christian Rhetoric." *Quarterly Journal of Speech* 46 (1960): 400–410.
O'Connell, Robert J. *Art and the Christian Intelligence in St. Augustine.* Cambridge: Harvard University Press, 1978.

PROCLUS

Rosán, Laurance. *The Philosophy of Proclus: The Final Phase of Ancient Thought.* New York: Cosmos Press, 1949.
Sheppard, Anne D. R. *Studies in the Fifth and Sixth Essays of Proclus' Commentary on the "Republic."* Göttingen: Vandenhoeck und Ruprecht, 1980.

FULGENTIUS

Whitbread, Leslie, trans. *Fulgentius the Mythographer.* Columbus: Ohio State University Press, 1972.

DANTE

Anderson, William. *Dante the Maker.* London and Boston: Routledge and Kegan Paul, 1980.
Auerbach, Erich. *Dante: Poet of the Secular World.* Translated by Ralph Manheim. Chicago: University of Chicago Press, 1961.

Bergin, Thomas G. *Dante*. New York: Orion Press, 1965.
Burckhardt, Jakob. *The Civilization of the Renaissance in Italy*. New York: Harper and Row, 1958.
Eliot, T. S. *Dante*. London: Faber and Faber, 1929.
Hollander, Robert. "Dante *Theologus-Poeta*." *Studies in Dante*. Ravenna: Longo Editore, 1979.
Maritain, Jacques. *Art and Scholasticism*. Translated by J. F. Scanlan. London: Sheed and Ward, 1930.
Mazzeo, Joseph Anthony. *Medieval Cultural Tradition in Dante's Comedy*. Westport, Conn.: Greenwood Press, 1977.